W9-BBT-445

Masked

Also by Alfred Habegger

Gender, Fantasy, and Realism in American Literature
Henry James and the "Woman Business"
The Father: A Life of Henry James, Sr.
My Wars Are Laid Away in Books: The Life of Emily Dickinson

Masked

The Life of Anna Leonowens,
Schoolmistress at the Court of Siam

Alfred Habegger

THE UNIVERSITY OF WISCONSIN PRESS

The University of Wisconsin Press
1930 Monroe Street, 3rd Floor
Madison, Wisconsin 53711-2059
uwpress.wisc.edu

3 Henrietta Street
London WC2E 8LU, England
eurospanbookstore.com

Printed in the United States of America

Library of Congress Cataloging-in-Publication Data

Habegger, Alfred, author.
Masked : the life of Anna Leonowens, schoolmistress at the court of Siam /
Alfred Habegger.
pages   cm — (Wisconsin studies in autobiography)
Includes bibliographical references and index.
ISBN 978-0-299-29830-2 (cloth : alk. paper) — ISBN 978-0-299-29833-3 (e-book)
1. Leonowens, Anna Harriette, 1831–1915. 2. Mongkut, King of Siam, 1804–1868.
3. Teachers—Thailand—Biography. 4. Governesses—Thailand—Biography.
5. Thailand—Social life and customs—19th century. 6. Women authors—
19th century—Biography. 7. Racially mixed women—India—Biography.
I. Title. II. Series: Wisconsin studies in autobiography.
DS578.32.L44H33   2014
959.3′034092—dc23
[B]
2013038597

Thou shalt not bear false witness against thy neighbour.

—Exodus 20:16, King James Version

En verité le mentir est un maudit vice. . . . Et depuis qu'on a donné ce faux train à la langue, c'est merveille combien il est impossible de l'en retirer. (Lying is an accursed vice. . . . Once let the tongue acquire the habit of lying and it is astonishing how impossible it is to make it give it up.)

—Montaigne, "Essay on Lying" (translation by M. A. Screech)

Only those who are sincere in every thought of their hearts are worth any thing. I am growing daily more convinced that it is the best thing in life—perfect & transparent sincerity in every thought, word & deed. But oh, how hard it is to be frank in our present complex civilization!

—From a letter of Anna Leonowens to her daughter

Contents

List of Illustrations	ix
Note on Transliteration	xi
Introduction: America's Anna	3

BEFORE BANGKOK: 1739–1862

1	Descent from the Gentry	17
2	A Hard School	32
3	The Unnamed Stepfather	49
4	Travel and Study with the Badgers	60
5	Beloved Wife of Thomas Leonowens	72
6	Selina's Death and Keesah's Last Long Look	95
7	An Accidental Life in Perth, Western Australia	105
8	The Convict Hiring Depot at Lynton	119
9	Widowed in the Straits Settlements	130

BANGKOK: 1862–1867

10	King Mongkut of Siam	147
11	The English School Mastress Comes to Bangkok	164
12	Anna and the Siamese Understanding of Human Sexuality	199

13 A Teacher Strained at Every Point   215

14 The Death of Fa Ying   228

15 The Slave Chained to the Ground   235

16 A Troubled Crusader   250

17 Getting in Deeper: Son Klin in the Dungeon   263

18 Anna and Tuptim   271

19 Leaving Bangkok   287

AFTER BANGKOK: 1867–1915

20 The English Governess Comes to America   309

21 Success and Decline   330

AFTERLIFE: 1944 TO THE PRESENT

22 Raised from the Dead by Margaret Landon   359

23 Anna in Hollywood and on Broadway   382

Acknowledgments   409

Abbreviations   414

Appendix 1: Family Chart for Anna Leonowens   416

Appendix 2: Family Chart for Anna's Spouse,
             Thomas Leonowens   418

Appendix 3: Anna as Plagiarist   420

Notes   425

Selected Bibliography   517

Index   533

Illustrations

Fred Arthur Neale's "Native Map of Siam"   217

following page 180

Anna Leonowens's mother's father's father, Reverend Cradock Glascott

Anna's nephew, Reverend Thomas Arthur Savage, principal of Cathedral
   High School, Bombay

Eliza Sara Millard Pratt, Anna's niece and the mother of Boris Karloff

Anna Leonowens, ca. 1870

Anna's son, Louis T. Leonowens

Anna's daughter, Avis Leonowens Fyshe

Thomas Leonowens's signature on a petition in Western Australia

Earliest known photo of the jail and other structures at the convict hiring
   depot at Lynton, Western Australia

Tan Kim Ching (Chen Jinzhong), Singapore businessman and agent of
   King Mongkut

Mongkut, king of Siam, 1865

"Please come & ride on our Eliphunt": Letter from King Mongkut to
   David Olyphant King

Mary Mattoon

Reverend Stephen Mattoon

Reverend Dan Beach Bradley

Reverend Samuel Jones Smith

Sisuriyawong, the *kalahom* (minister of the south and the military)

Gabriel Aubaret, French naval officer and consul

Louis Leonowens, Prince Chulalongkorn, and others, ca. 1865

Prince Chulalongkorn and his two full brothers

Prince Chulalongkorn

A royal child and his crouching attendant

Conclusion of Anna's letter to Dan Beach Bradley, 17 May 1870

Anna in old age

Margaret and Kenneth Landon

Note on Transliteration

This book retains the usual English spelling of Thai names and other words often seen in the West, such as *Mongkut, Chulalongkorn, chao* ("lord"). With other words, two of the rules observed in transliterating require comment.

Unlike English, in which "t" and "p" are aspirated (formed with an expulsion of air), Thai has both an aspirated and non-aspirated form of each consonant. I spell the aspirated form "th" and "ph," as in *thaat* ("slave") or *phanung* (the traditional lower garment in old Siam). The "h" should not be pronounced. It stands for the puff of breath that is absent from non-aspirated "t" and "p." In Thailand, Westerners who utter these non-aspirated forms with too much force are sometimes said to have a "hard mouth."

By the same token, Thai can strike English speakers as a "soft-spoken" tongue. Consonants are less emphatic at the ends of words, and vowels have tones and may be long or short, thus playing a more exacting role in the differentiation of sound. I have made no attempt to indicate tones, but I represent long vowels by doubling the letter, as in *puu* ("person") or *saalaa* ("pavilion").

Masked

Introduction

America's Anna

IN THE MID-TWENTIETH CENTURY the English-speaking world was captivated by a story about a brave Victorian widow who sailed to Siam to instruct the many children of that nation's polygamous monarch. The story told of her encounter with a hermetic Eastern culture, her difficult relations with the testy and half-barbaric despot who employs her, and her sterling influence on the crown prince, who, thanks to her teaching, democratizes the nation after ascending the throne. The message—hugely appealing in post–World War II America—was that this is how the world can be saved.

This story originated with the woman herself, Anna Leonowens, who arrived in the United States in 1867. Regarded as a proper English lady whose complexion had been darkened in the tropics, she attracted considerable interest for her startling firsthand accounts of Siamese slavery and concubinage and soon became a popular author and lecturer. She became even more famous in 1944, thirty years after her death, when a novice writer named Margaret Landon made her the heroine of a fictionalized biography, *Anna and the King of Siam*. A best seller, the book was turned into a successful motion picture of the same title, with Irene Dunne as the intrepid lady teacher and young Rex Harrison as the king of Siam. But it was in 1951, when Rodgers and Hammerstein molded the story into the Broadway musical *The King and I*, with Gertrude Lawrence and an unknown named Yul Brynner, that Anna became a powerful Western myth. The 1956 screen adaptation starring Deborah Kerr and the now-famous Brynner was seen by everyone.

3

Behind all these versions lay an assumption that, if the story was enhanced and embroidered, it was still basically historical. Anna was a true
English governess, she was genuinely responsible for terminating Siamese
slavery, and the lesson was that the West's democratic principles could take
hold anywhere, without the ugliness of colonial rule and the machinery of
empire. All that is required, the story claims, is the ideal individual Westerner: bold, upright, intelligent, determined, and of genteel birth.

The actual Anna Leonowens had the first, third, and fourth of those
qualities but not the second and fifth. Aspiring and full of contradictions,
disciplined, idealistic, and mendacious to the bone, she would always be
opaque to others, even her grandchildren, who never realized that she had
been born in India. Starting with her two books about her time in Bangkok
and coming down to the present, all extended treatments of her life in print,
film, or the theater have subsided into one or another soft global fantasy.

For Leonowens herself, candor was never an option. Not only did she
face great odds, but a kind of high-minded fraudulence was built into her
from the start. To make sense of her remarkable life, a biographer has to do
two things: find the traces of what she covered up in her worldwide odyssey,
and pay attention to the remarkable fit between her powerful lies and the
New World's innocent and ignorant dreams.

When Leonowens left Siam in 1867, she had worked five and a half years
for King Mongkut (the name by which he is known in the West). Her life at
court had been rich and empowering, lifting her to a new social level, but it
had also brought severe personal trouble: a series of threatening illnesses, a
deepening outrage at Thai law and custom, and a suspicion of the king that
verged on the delusional. "No friend of mine knew," she would write in *The
English Governess at the Siamese Court*, "how hard it was for me to bear up,
in the utter loneliness and forlornness of my life, under the load of cares and
provocations and fears that gradually accumulated upon me."

The cares and fears were far from over as she booked passage in Singapore for the West. A widow with two children to bring up, she was painfully
anxious about her future, not knowing how she would earn her livelihood
or where in the world she would earn it. Even her identity was at risk,
for although she would term herself an English governess, she had been a
schoolmistress instead of a governess, had never been to England, and had

no family relations there. If worse came to worst, she might have to return to her old job in Bangkok, a prospect she dreaded.

Thanks to three American friends she had known in Singapore and Bangkok, she ended up in New York State, where, instead of looking for work as a teacher, she spent much of her first year desperately writing. Her plan: to scratch together a book about her life in Siam that would appeal to New World readers.

What Americans knew about the faraway land pretty much came down to Chang and Eng, the conjoined "Siamese" twins who had won fame as a traveling freak show. A few excellent and comprehensive accounts of Siam had appeared in France and England, but in the States there had been very little, nothing but magazine essays and segments of travelogues. For Leonowens—ambitious, hardworking, and with inside knowledge of the royal harem—the opportunity was obvious. Here was a niche that she alone could fill, if only she could devise a general account of Siam keyed to her life at court.

The book was still unfinished and without a publisher when circumstances forced her to leave the friend's house where she had been living and begin earning her keep. An appeal was launched on her behalf by an expert Quaker activist with top-drawer connections, and within a month Leonowens found herself in a heady and very personal conversation with the woman who would open doors for her.

Her name was Laura Winthrop Johnson. A descendant of John Winthrop, the first governor of Massachusetts Bay Colony, she was one of several New Englanders living in West New Brighton, a patrician neighborhood on Staten Island's North Shore. Johnson and her friends had enlightened views, powerful allies in distant cities, and large homes and grounds a short ferry ride from downtown New York City. The men wrote, lectured, and edited newspapers, and the women were idealistic and generous and civic-minded. Strong abolitionists in the years before Secession, they had made painful sacrifices during the Civil War, they were ardent against tyranny, they favored women's rights, and they were mesmerized by the visitor's tales of slaves and concubines in Siam, a nation about which they knew nothing.[1]

---

1. Johnson's brother, Theodore Winthrop, was the first Northern officer killed in action. Other North Shore residents included the parents of Colonel Robert Gould Shaw, who lost his life while leading an African American regiment against a South Carolina fort. The colonel's father, Francis George Shaw, became one of Leonowens's patrons.

About the British Empire's racial and military codes—codes that had produced the visitor and her tanned skin (tanned, it was thought, from exposure to the sun in India, Singapore, and Bangkok)—they knew very little more.

Laura Johnson's conversation with Leonowens convinced her that the newcomer was just the person to open the select kindergarten the North Shore needed. Who better to form their children's speech and manners than a royal governess with a British accent? Together with the wife of a prominent neighbor, Johnson drummed up enough pupils to make the school pay, and then she sat down and wrote a long and enthusiastic letter about the exotic teacher and her wonderful stories to a close friend in Boston, Annie Fields.

Fields was an influential literary hostess who was married to a distinguished and successful publisher. Leonowens would not have realized it at first, but in addition to securing remunerative work she had been given the entrée she needed as an unknown writer. One year after getting off the boat she had found her way to the most respected publicity apparatus in all of North America.

Two years later the book that made her famous, *The English Governess at the Siamese Court*, was issued by Fields and Osgood. Two years more and the firm brought out an exciting sequel, *The Romance of the Harem*. The contemporary appeal of these volumes was summed up by a reviewer in the *New York Times*: "The inner life of the harem was open to her, and she saw and describes such scenes as perhaps no European ever witnessed before." That was the promise—that Leonowens's books would shine the light of day on the most fabled and forbidden of Oriental institutions.

More was on offer, however, than mere sensationalism. The new author's chief claim was that her teaching and personal influence had liberated Siam. Portraying King Mongkut as a half-Westernized Oriental monster, she presented herself as the principled English lady who had boldly stood up to him. When King Chulalongkorn, his son and successor, announced a series of minor reforms and a rumor spread that slavery had been abolished in Siam, Leonowens was quick to take credit: this was the result of her work. What the United States had achieved by means of the bloody Civil War had been put through in remote Southeast Asia by a lone white woman teacher—peacefully.

However, there were two reviewers who took forceful exception to her books. Henry George Kennedy, a graduate of Cambridge University, had served in the British Consulate in Bangkok, where he attained a good command of the Thai language. Samuel Jones Smith, of mixed Indian, Portuguese, and British parentage, had been taken to Siam as a boy and in time became a missionary, journalist, and Thai-language publisher. These two men made it clear—in print, in English, in London and Bangkok—that something was radically amiss in Leonowens's writings. In Smith's view, *The English Governess* was a kind of joke, out of control, "overwrought," open to "severe criticism." Kennedy, writing in the *Athenæum*, the leading Liberal review, compiled a sobering list of the author's mistaken claims and hinted that some of her purported adventures may not have happened.[2] But his shrewd judgments never registered in the States, where the universal reaction, from the *New York Times* to the *Princeton Review*, was ardent and supportive.

A brilliant storyteller and public speaker, Leonowens soon proved a major draw on the lecture circuit. She dressed well, commanded attention, spoke with what sounded to North American ears like the mother country's accent, and in the course of an evening gave her listeners a fascinating personal tour of Siamese society. An object of curiosity herself, she drew up a brief explanatory autobiography for the lecture agency that organized her tours. Designed to be circulated, the statement left audiences in no doubt that she was of respectable British ancestry. "Anna Harriette Leonowens," it began, "was born in Caernarvon in Wales, in the old homestead of an ancient Welsh family named Edwards. The youngest daughter of the house (mother of Mrs. Leonowens) accompanied her husband, Thomas Maxwell Crawford, to India, while their daughter was left in charge of an eminent Welsh lady (Mrs. Wallpole), to be educated in Wales." The sketch detailed a succession of painful events, starting with her father's death in the "Sikh Rebellion" and her widowed mother's marriage to a domestic tyrant. At age fifteen the girl supposedly took passage to India, where she found her hostile stepfather implacably opposed to the British officer she loved and insisted on marrying. Worse followed: the deaths of two children and her husband, the further

2. The attribution to Kennedy, made here for the first time, is based on the *Athenæum*'s house copy, preserved at City University in London. Scribbled diagonally across the two reviews are, respectively, the words "Kennedy" and "Kenedy."

loss of family in the "heart-rending calamities" of the Indian Mutiny, the disappearance of her inheritance, and the "pain and torture" she had endured in Siam.[3] This moving life story served as her lecture billing: it showed she came of good white stock, explained why she had lived in Asia and had to support herself, and promised listeners a novel and touching evening.

Her hold on adult audiences was gripping but short-lived. In 1876, going down-market, she began writing a series of highly colored stories set in Siam and India for a children's magazine. When her daughter married a Scots-Canadian banker, she joined the couple in Halifax, Nova Scotia, making her home with them first in that city and then in Montreal. During her long life in Canada (to which this biography gives little attention) she turned her vast energies to a number of educational and progressive causes, including female suffrage, women's prison reform, First Nations rights, and the single-tax system of Henry George. In 1881 she made a daring journalistic tour of Russia. In 1897, now in her sixties, she accompanied a granddaughter to Germany for musical instruction and, for herself, sat in on Sanskrit classes at the University of Leipzig.

She loved to regale her grandchildren with dramatic tales from her early years, but there would be striking inconsistencies and some odd omissions, most notably the name of her stepfather, a blank she flatly refused to fill in. Finally, complying with her family's persistent requests, she produced a brief narrative summary of her life before Bangkok. This "terse précis," as a granddaughter called it, began as follows: "I believe I was born in Wales, in the old homestead of an ancient Welsh family named Edwards, the youngest daughter of which, my mother, accompanied her husband, Thomas Maxwell Crawford, to India, while I was left in charge of an eminent Welsh lady, Mrs. Walpole, a distant relative of my Father, to be educated in Wales." It was basically the old publicity release devised decades earlier for a Boston lecture agency. Taking it at face value, the children were never to learn their grandmother's true origins or what she had been through.

Her death in 1915 at age eighty-three went largely unnoticed outside of Canada. She would not have lived on as the heroine of a Broadway musical and major Hollywood movies if Margaret Landon, an aspiring writer from

---

3. As the family chart on pages 416–17 shows, none of her Anglo-Indian relatives died in 1857, the year of the rebellion. There was almost no violence in the section of India where they resided, the Bombay Presidency.

the Upper Midwest, had not been fascinated by her books. Landon read them in Siam while serving as missionary wife and schoolmistress, and after returning to the States in the late thirties she set about weaving Leonowens's best stories into a sequential biographical narrative.

It seemed the perfect project. Not only could Landon speak and read Thai, but she was able to get access to her subject's surviving papers; in addition, her husband was an expert on Southeast Asia. But in two respects she was poorly prepared. She had no training as a scholar or historian, and she approached her work with an evangelical missionary's partisan cast of mind. Whenever she ran into an inconsistency resulting from her heroine's doctoring of the record, she explained it away. What she ended up with was an inspiring account of a simple, brave, honest, unassuming woman who (in her publisher's advertisement) "taught King Mongkut's children, wives and concubines the rules of English speech and the principles of human freedom."

Landon's original title, *Anna Leonowens and the King of Siam*, was cut when her editor balked at the unwieldy surname and persuaded her to drop it. In Leonowens's day a stranger who had the temerity to call the imposing woman *Anna* would have been stared down. Even in letters from one friend to another she was almost never *Anna*. Just to *think* of her as *Anna* struck a granddaughter as unseemly. But *Anna* is how she has come to be known, and that is what she will be from now on in this biography. And to be frank, it is a relief not to have to keep repeating *Leonowens*. This unfamiliar surname, owned by no other family in the known universe, was devised by her husband, who had been baptized Thomas Lean Owens.

Landon aside, no one did more to transform the formidable woman into simple, likeable Anna than the artist, Margaret Ayer, who was commissioned to illustrate *Anna and the King of Siam*. Sketches of Anna from her own time have her in dresses that hang straight down. Looking back from the 1940s, however, Ayer made her into an iconic Victorian—a slight, girlish, pug-nosed ingénue whose immense hoopskirts, so out of place in the tropics, are a sign of her refusal to compromise as well as of her gentility.

The book came out on cheap wartime paper in 1944, the penultimate year of World War II. Not only was this a moment when American eyes were on Asia as never before, but the publisher specialized in Asian authors and subjects. The head of the firm, Richard J. Walsh, had recently married Pearl

Buck, author of *The Good Earth*. Both were convinced that America must play a more active role in the Far East. Both belonged to the Asia Society.

The book got a vigorous boost from another advocate for American involvement in Asia, Henry R. Luce, the owner of *Time*. In reviewing *Anna and the King of Siam*, this magazine assured readers that it was true to history and that King Mongkut's reign had been as oppressive as the "Gestapo." As processed by *Time*, which Luce closely supervised, Landon's book was full of implicit lessons. Chief among them: Siam had been a version of Nazi Germany, and Anna was "a more subversive influence than anyone knew."

One year after the war ended, Twentieth Century Fox released a motion picture that skillfully dramatized that influence. Carrying the same title as the book, *Anna and the King of Siam* was a classic studio production with pretty much everything one could ask for: excellent writing, casting, acting. Sets and costumes were so lavish that they reminded reviewers of the generous production standards of the thirties, before wartime austerities. Major liberties were taken with the facts, yet there were countless gestures toward authenticity: bits of spoken Thai, touches of old Siamese fashion and subservient posture, subtle hints that the story can be documented. The historical illusion was overwhelming.

An overwhelmed editorial in America's newspaper of record shows how powerful Anna's story had grown. Soon after it became known that Elizabeth Gray Vining, a writer of juvenile historical fiction, was to be the governess of the future emperor of Japan, the *New York Times* declared:

> The comparison is inevitable between Mrs. Vining and Mrs. Anna Leonowens, whose intelligent labors at the Court of Siam in the Eighteen Sixties . . . were so well and skillfully recounted by Margaret Landon in her novel, "Anna and the King of Siam," and even more widely publicized in the motion picture of the same name. Anna Leonowens' main task, as will be that of Elizabeth Vining, was to instruct the young Crown Prince. Crown Prince Chulalongkorn of Siam was an apt pupil, not only of English but of burning faith in democracy and the dignity of the human being. When he became King one of his first acts was to free the Siamese slaves.

Once again the Anna story had tapped into America's sense of mission and can-do spirit. Sinister forces had been overcome at a huge cost, as in the Civil War, and the public was hungry for a mythic enactment of the power of ordinary decency. The lesson drawn by peacetime America was that oppressed humanity could truly be saved by "faith in democracy and the dignity of the human being." Mrs. Vining would deflect Japan from its authoritarian and militaristic past. Sweeping reform was at hand, accompanied by an inspiring vision of America's global role now that the European empires were starting to crumble. As you watched the movie or read the book, a thrilling vista opened before your eyes. This was the future as revealed by the past. It was almost messianic.

When Rodgers and Hammerstein developed *The King and I*, they kept that liberal optimism, and they relied as well (without admitting it) on the story lines of the Harrison-Dunne film. Their innovation was to replace the illusion of history with the clear outlines of cartoon fantasy. There would be no more boring simulations of Siamese customs, no nice touches of the historic Mongkut. Instead, they encouraged Yul Brynner to come up with his electric physical act—his glaring, strutting embodiment of hyper-masculine charm and brutality. This kind of virility, a new feature in American entertainment, had recently sprung to life in Marlon Brando's surly Stanley Kowalski in *A Streetcar Named Desire* and would soon be showing up everywhere. Brynner's "primitive" "Asiatic" male sexuality was vital, dangerous, immensely exciting, and very much of its time. And it was light-years removed from the historic figure whom Anna had worked for—a thin, elderly man who had labored at Latin, English, and astronomy; had spent twenty-seven years in the Buddhist monkhood before becoming king; and, unlike earlier Siamese kings, had tried to educate and Westernize his wives.

In Thailand (Siam's new name since 1939) Brynner's portrayal of a progressive monarch was felt to be scandalously disrespectful, not only trampling on national history but trashing deep-seated practices of deference and cultivated restraint. To see the fourth king of the Chakri dynasty turned into a tragic buffoon, with his legacy awarded to a superior Englishwoman, was intolerable, and the movie was denied a license: it could not be screened. The artistic team behind *The King and I* had liberal sympathies, yet if one tries to watch the musical with Thai eyes it becomes an act of colonization—an invasion that seizes not land or material products but a people's sense of their past.

The reaction came in 1976, when William Syer Bristowe, an Imperial Chemical Industries executive, brought out a debunking account of Anna. On prewar business trips to Siam, Bristowe had made contact with an aged son of King Mongkut, Prince Damrong Rajanubhab, who had run the Interior Ministry and was now dean of Siamese historians. A powerful establishment voice, Damrong assured Bristowe that Anna had exaggerated her influence at court "in order to make money from her books." This confirmed the Englishman's suspicion of "her historical integrity," but it was only after her resurrection by Landon that he began investigating. He went to the baptism, marriage, and burial registers of British India, preserved in London, and what he found was a revelation. Contrary to her claim that she came from Wales, the daughter of an officer later sent to India, she had been born in an East India Company military cantonment in the Bombay Presidency. Her father was not Captain Crawford but Sergeant Edwards, and the man she married was not an officer but a clerk. At the time of his death he was managing a hotel in Penang. That was three years before Anna went to Siam.

These discoveries left no doubt that her origins were humbler than she had let on. But Bristowe was too bent on discrediting her. A marriage record he turned up gives her mother's maiden name as *Glasscott*. Altering this to *Glasscock*, he unearthed in distant Bengal a gunner of that name whose bride, Anne, had no surname and then declared that this was Anna's grandfather. And since rank-and-file soldiers regularly partnered with native or Eurasian women, it was a short step to the conclusion that Anna's grandmother was at least part Indian. This was a shrewd guess, yet Bristowe's way of trumpeting it was offensive in the extreme: "Thus our Anna, descended from John Glasscock and Anne, may have had what was called 'a touch of the tar-brush' in her veins." The jocular phrase, a remnant of colonial habits of speech, evokes the dismissive smirks a respectable mixed-race girl would have had to endure in nineteenth-century British India.

For the next three decades no one checked Bristowe's sources, yet virtually everyone accepted his inferences. Landon, terribly challenged, confided to one of her children, "This man is my enemy." The new consensus was that Anna had been an army brat who clawed her way up from poverty and squalor. Those who took offense at her treatment of the Siamese could write her off as a lowborn adventuress or imposter. Those not offended could admire the feminist pluck with which she reinvented herself.

The lowborn interpretation has generally found favor in Thailand and to some extent in the United Kingdom, but in the United States the feminist reading has prevailed, most notably in *Anna and the King*, the 1999 movie in which Jodie Foster saves Siam's entire royal line from a palace revolt by means of a preposterous ruse. This, the third and least successful filming of the Anna story, began as a smart globalized remake, with Chow Yun-Fat as King Mongkut, but then reverted to the fine old myth: Anna as the white Western savior of a backward nation.

In 2004 a mostly reliable summary of her life appeared in the *Oxford Dictionary of National Biography*, in which Elizabeth Baigent and Lois K. Yorke conjectured that Anna's mother was "the illegitimate Eurasian daughter of William Vawdrey Glasscott . . . lieutenant in the Bombay army." This seemed to announce the end of fantasy. But four years later, when the first full-length biography appeared, *Bombay Anna* by Susan Morgan, it proved as lightly researched as it was heavily fictionalized, especially in its portrayal of the heroine's girlhood. As imagined by Morgan, Anna had been a "child of poverty and ignorance" who grew up in an era when the Bombay Presidency "was very heaven" for mixed-race children. Freely roaming the streets, this female version of Kipling's Kim got to know the city from the bottom up, learning its castes and tribes, picking up languages, and laying a foundation for the tolerant and brilliantly multifaceted woman she became.

In other words, as late as 2008 Anna Leonowens remained pretty much what she had been after the Civil War and again in the 1940s and 1950s: the blank screen on which a perennial American optimism could happily and innocently project itself.

That Mrs. Wallpole or Walpole? The "eminent Welsh lady" credited with guiding Anna's education in the biographical sketch she drew up for her lecture agent? The truth emerges only if one is lucky enough to stumble on a certain 1841 Indian newspaper. The woman's real name was Yates, she was the temporary matron of the boarding school to which the girl was sent at age nine or ten, and the school was not in England or Wales but Bombay. It was operated by the Bombay Education Society and known as the Central or Byculla school. A strict Protestant charity institution, it took in mixed-race children whose white military fathers were dead or absent and trained them for lives of humble Christian "usefulness." Most of the girls were married off at age fifteen to eligible bachelors in the East India Company's army, with the ablest ones steered toward teaching. Those with outstanding promise might come in for special but discreet encouragement from chaplains, board members, and a ladies' oversight committee. In Anna's case there are indications she was put forward by a chaplain and one of the ladies.

Without the combined repression and support that characterized certain sectors of the British Empire, Anna could not have become the person she was. Subjected from an early age to a benevolent, race-based, colonial regimen, she acquired a correct and dignified manner, a determination to use her talents to better herself, an obscure racial shame, a habit of always rewriting her past, and a rooted melancholy. Tense, conflicted, and with a divided sense of self, she felt she was one with the women of the East, of whom she wrote with unprecedented sympathy, and yet she had to pass as white.

This biography of a heroic fraud draws on extensive new documentary material from five continents. Although I defer to a later page my detailed acknowledgment of the generous help I have been given by so many, I here single out my wife, Nellie, who joined in the travel and research; my son, Simon, who patiently helped me with the Thai-language materials; and my Thai daughter-in-law, Naowarat, who, when she finally had a chance to watch a DVD of *The King and I*, was amazed that Yul Brynner as king would be so undignified as to "wave his arms like a monkey."

BEFORE BANGKOK

1739–1862

1

Descent from the Gentry

IN THE BRIEF AUTOBIOGRAPHY that Anna Leonowens gave an American publicist and decades later handed her grandchildren as the true story of her early years, she traced her origins to royal Caernarfon in northwest Wales. She identified her place of birth as "the old homestead of an ancient Welsh family named Edwards." Edwards, she claimed, had been her mother's maiden name, her father being a Crawford.

Very little of this matched the facts. Edwards was her father's surname rather than her mother's, and she herself was born in India. But the doctored autobiography did not come out of thin air. Like Anna's other inventions, it reflected a strong understanding of her place in the world. In particular, the transfer of her father's name to her mother's "ancient" family hints at a linked pride and shame: a sense of ancestral worth, a belief that this fine inheritance came down through her mother, and a pained conviction that the maternal line had been so badly compromised it could not, must not, be named.

Wales had, in fact, been the home of her mother's forebears, but they didn't arise in the rugged and romantic northwest—"land of elf and Merlin," as Margaret Landon would have it in *Anna and the King of Siam*. Instead, they lived in south Wales in a town on the Bristol Channel—land, one might say, of early industrialization and evangelical zeal. It was in Cardiff that Anna's traceable story begins: in a family whose middle-class standing was solidly based on saddle making, ironworking, and devout Protestant faith.

In 1739, soon after the Wesley brothers had begun the preaching tours that would lead to the emergence of the Methodist Church, John Wesley made his first visit to Cardiff, where he spoke to a gathering in the home of Thomas Glascott, a saddler. Pious and civic-minded, a vestryman and overseer of the poor, Thomas struck Charles Wesley as "one of the excellent of the earth." At his death his earthly wealth would be inventoried at a very respectable £531. His wife, Elizabeth, daughter of a prosperous ironmonger, seems to have been a person of substance and conviction in her own right.

Unlike most eighteenth-century Britons, who tended to see religious passion as something best moderated, Thomas and Elizabeth Glascott not only shared a fervent evangelicalism but were determined to fan the flames. In 1758 they had John Wesley give another talk in their home, and this time their two teenage daughters were "cut to the heart . . . and cried to God with strong cries and tears." As a younger son put it over sixty years later, the Glascott parents "were not ashamed of the faith of Xt [Christ] crucified at a time when true religion met with much contempt and ridicule."

Those defiant words came from Cradock Glascott, the couple's longest-lived child and a great-grandfather of Anna Leonowens. Born in Cardiff in 1742, Cradock was the first in the family to attend Oxford University, where, at Jesus College, he underwent an evangelical conversion of his own. The results: a supportive letter from John Wesley and a resolution to devote his life to proclaiming the Gospel. Since Wesleyan Methodism was still a movement within the Church of England rather than a distinct sect, Cradock took orders and obtained a curacy. But, in the words of an admirer, "his zealous mode of preaching gave offence," and he was removed from his pulpit.

As it happened, a network of independent Calvinist preachers had recently been organized by the astonishing Selina, Countess of Huntingdon. Taking no interest in the leisure she could have enjoyed after unexpectedly coming into her title, Selina put all her resources into what was soon known as the Countess of Huntingdon's Connexion, the one Protestant sect named for a woman. She supported sixty chapels, a Welsh college founded to train ministers, and a corps of itinerant preachers. The young Reverend Cradock Glascott signed on to this vigorous Nonconforming enterprise and quickly became one of the countess's most effective proselytizers. This was hardly a respectable career for an Oxford graduate, yet the young man had the full backing of his father, Thomas, who "rejoice[d] to find that you are faithful in the work that the Lord hath called you to."

For fourteen years, supported by Selina, Cradock traveled and preached in Wales and England. He met with occasional hostility—once a pail of butcher's blood was emptied on him—but for the most part his audiences were peaceable and serious, even enthusiastic. In 1781, according to a report sent to his patroness, he "preached out of doors, to at least two thousand, and in the evening . . . to near the same number." In Nottingham his crowd of listeners was estimated at five thousand. Decades later, when those stirring days were over and Cradock was in his seventies, he noticed some groups of people walking to church. "Ah! this reminds me of good old times," he was remembered as saying, "when multitudes used to be seen coming down over the mountains of Wales, from all directions for miles around to hear the word of God." The man evidently had a taste for challenging adventures, a good stock of fortitude, and a loud speaking voice— three qualities his great-granddaughter would also possess.

When Cradock approached the age of forty, his father died, and he decided to take a wife and lead a more settled life. Leaving the countess's employ (over her protests), he obtained a curacy in the village of Hatherleigh in north Devonshire. In his first sermon, making it quite clear that his tenure would be neither liberal nor relaxed, he announced that he was resolved "to know nothing among you, save Jesus Christ and him crucified." This was the hard core of evangelicalism: everyone has sinned, the only way to get into heaven is to accept Christ's sacrifice, preaching on any other subject is a waste of time. Some parishioners objected, but now the zealous curate seems to have had his bishop's support. For the next half-century, Sunday after Sunday, the people of Hatherleigh would get the basic evangelical message, nothing less, nothing more.

Once, a group of strolling players came to the village to spend the winter. Like other evangelicals, Cradock considered the theater an immoral institution, and he had the troupe evicted. Before departing, the lead actor was persuaded to go to church and listen to the preacher responsible for his expulsion. Afterward the man was heard to say, "Never before in my life have I witnessed such a scene as this! why it appears to me like an affectionate father conversing with his children! is it possible that such a man as this can have it in his heart to hurt a poor player!!!"

It was a shrewd observation: Cradock could be as cold, tight, and narrow as he was congenial and direct. The title of a pamphlet he published in 1776, *The Best Method of Putting an End to the American War*, suggests he had given some thought to Britain's first great colonial crisis, but in fact the text hardly glances at the transatlantic revolt. Instead, the pamphlet (originally a sermon) says again and again that everything boils down to one thing: "The source of every evil is sin. All calamities, public as well as private, flow from it. . . . Without entering into the *political* disputes which attend the *American* war, I may safely affirm that rebellion against God, and the dreadful profaneness of the age are the unhappy causes of it." As the preacher saw it, there was an easy way to settle the American rebellion. Everyone should get religion.

This sermon, written well before the birth of Cradock's children, partly explains why he would fail to establish a connection with his descendants in India. In the midst of a story about a deathbed conversion, he paused to observe, in his one glance at the world of his time, that army officers were notoriously "addicted to very gross and abominable iniquities." His reference, veiled but obvious, was to sex not sanctioned by matrimony—the only sin he singled out for condemnation.

Cradock sired three sons. The first and third followed him to Oxford, took orders, and spent the rest of their lives as village curates. The second, William Vaudrey, chose another path, one that was both like and unlike his father's stirring life on the road: he became an officer in the East India Company's army. Cradock was "very much averse" to this career choice, but he still gave William his parental consent.[1]

Applying to cadet school, the boy stated that he had been given a "Commercial" education that went as far as "the Square & Cube Roots." His spelling of Hatherleigh as "Etherley" hints at how local he was, still taking for granted the West Country drawl.

Cadet school trained young men to be officers in the East India Company's huge private overseas army. It was while serving in that force that William Vaudrey Glascott met the unidentified Indian or mixed-race woman who became his intimate companion and bore him three children, the oldest of whom would be Anna's mother.

1. Only 6 percent of company cadets were sons of clergymen, according to Wilson, *History of British India*, 3:551.

PROBLEMATIC UNIONS

William landed in Bombay (today Mumbai) in 1810. From then on, the contrast between the strict paternal code he brought from Hatherleigh and the relaxed sexual mores of Indian military life must have been insistent and troublesome.

Because the East India Company did not ship single Englishwomen to India, it was taken for granted that soldiers and officers would find solace, as the phrase was, with women of the country. For enlisted men, forced to be in barracks much of the time, a visit to a nearby bazaar and a "brown Indian beauty" was an obvious choice. Among officers, it was customary to find a young and suitable *bibi* and contract some kind of connubial union with her.[2] An 1810 guidebook for English gentlemen planning to enter the East India Company's employ openly recommended the use of native mistresses and concubines . . . in the plural.

The first imperial historians gave little attention to unions between European men and Indian women. It was a later generation of scholars who pointed out how common these unions were and how close, affectionate, and enduring they often proved. When C. J. Hawes investigated the late eighteenth-century wills of British officers, he found that "many partnerships of Indian women with British upper class men were long term—marriages in all but legal name. Many wills suggest ties of affection, loyalty on both sides, and happy companionships. British men often asked their close friends to be executors and to care for their Indian partners, referring to them as 'well beloved,' 'female friend,' and 'worthy friend.'" An Anglo-Indian descendant of such a partnership, Herbert Alick Stark (a name we will meet again), gloried in his ancestry and defiantly maintained that the upper-class Britons who "solaced themselves by taking for their partners in life the women of the land . . . *were in a position to pick the best*."

But this aggressive pride was not the usual attitude. Starting in the late eighteenth century, mixed unions came to be seen as problematic. In 1813, when a certain memsahib refused to invite Eurasian guests, the act of racial exclusion was still so unusual that it caused "a great sensation." Twelve years

---

2. *Bibi* came into English from Urdu and before that Persian, in which it meant "lady." "Brown Indian beauty" comes from a prostitute's photographic advertisement pasted inside a London telephone booth.

later, however, a traveler to Bombay discovered that "connection with native women, though sadly common among the elder officers of the army," had ceased to be "a fashionable vice." Within a generation the nonwhite mistresses of European officers were felt to be "quite unvisitable." As William Dalrymple has shown, British attitudes in India underwent a seismic shift, most notably during the ten years of William Vaudrey Glascott's service. Before his time hybrid unions were more or less accepted, but by 1831, when granddaughter Anna was born, they were frowned on, hidden, even denied.

The consequences for mixed-race children were immense. Stigmatized as "half-castes" by the increasingly race-conscious English, these children were not permitted to travel to England for their education or to enter the better careers and were soon seen as forming a well-defined subclass. And the more their numbers grew, the less recognition they got. In the 1770s half the children baptized at St. John's Calcutta had been illegitimate. By 1830 the fraction was down to one in ten, and yet most soldiers, Hawes points out, "still lived unmarried" with native or mixed-race women. Which is to say, Eurasian children were becoming simultaneously more common, more shunned, and less traceable.

Anna's embarrassment about her family lineage is hardly surprising. In a society bound by rigid rules of propriety, respectability, and social status, there was a keen sense of shame.

The Example of Licentiousness

Anna's grandfather spent his first year in Bombay completing his training. In May 1811 he left cadet school, one of seven young men singled out for their attention to duty and "Gentleman-like good conduct." A close friend, John Sutherland, was awarded the same honors and got the same first assignment, the Fourth Regiment of Native Infantry, stationed at the time in the old port city of Surat. It was a good posting, yet William was sorry to leave Bombay and miss the grand "Chinese fireworks" celebrating the taking of Mauritius from the French.

By late June, when he wrote his father from Surat, William was face to face with a notorious aspect of camp life, how "insufferably dull and tedious" it could be. He was also wrestling with another problem that plagued ensigns: how to make ends meet. But instead of dwelling on these troubles, he made his letter home as upbeat as possible, succeeding so well that Reverend Cradock copied and sent it to his brother John.

This, the only known letter by Anna's grandfather, is a classic report of a young man's tentative first steps in his career. The writer boasted that the commander in chief had promised his "assistance in forwarding me in the world" and that the adjutant general had seen to William's placement in the Fourth Regiment. This outfit, he assured his father, was famous for its sobriety, its officers being "the most gentlemanly & steady of any."

William also wanted his parent to realize how benevolent the army's mission was. "It is beyond belief," he wrote, "what cruelties have been practised by the musselmans & other disorderly casts or sects upon the harmless & peaceable inhabitants, who are now safe under the British protection, & enjoy the same rights as any of his majesty's subjects." In fact, as William's future progeny would find, even the mixed-race children of officers were denied "the same rights" as Englishmen.

The letter was everything an anxious parent could have asked for. To be sure, the boy was exposed, but he continued to receive "consolation from that throne of grace & mercy, whence all true happiness is obtained." Yes, company chaplains were "relaxed," but the boy had come under the influence of the great Henry Martyn, an early missionary and translator of the Bible whose preaching convinced William that "an able & true minister of the Church would reap a great harvest in Bombay."

Only at the end of this reassuring letter did the young man note how boring and long the days were in Surat. But then he at once added, knowing *exactly* what his father was thinking, "You have nothing to fear from the example of licenciousness."

To his brother John, the Reverend Cradock confided that this well-crafted letter had afforded "great satisfaction." But it was the last letter from India that he would copy or even praise. Over the years he detailed his son's postings, promotions, and salary ("£60 pr month . . . his fortune is made"), but nothing more was ever said about the lad's spiritual state or the threat of licentiousness. By 1819 William's letters had become infrequent and uncommunicative. When it was learned that he had been appointed adjutant (a commanding officer's personal staff officer, selected from the most talented young men in a regiment), the news came from a company official. Two letters arrived in 1821, but Cradock copied neither, offering instead a dry and guarded summary: "As he said nothing to the contrary, we may safely conclude, he enjoys the blessings of health. He longs to revisit his native country, but thinks it highly imprudent in present circumstances, as in that case, he would be obliged to resign his adjutantship, a place of trust and emolument, which he now holds together with his commission: but he hopes, if his life is preserved, in the course of three or four years, to embrace once more his dear friends at Hatherleigh." At the time, William's two Indian daughters were nearly old enough to attend school.

To get a somewhat better purchase on his life in India, one turns to the East India Company's voluminous, methodical, and frustratingly impersonal ledgers. They give the impression that William was a dependable and versatile officer who could fill in where needed and that his postings were by and large routine, supporting the army's overall mission. Unlike Sutherland, his Scottish friend from cadet school, he apparently never saw active service, not even during the fierce Mahratta War of 1817–18.

In June 1820 William was shifted to the newly created Twelfth Regiment and for six months helped get it organized. Early December saw him temporarily posted back to the Fourth Regiment and sent to Suvarnadurga, where he served as acting executive engineer during another man's absence. Located in the southern Konkan, the narrow coastal plain running south from Bombay, Suvarnadurga was the site of a captured island fort. Reputed to have "a fine breeze" and to be a good place for an army convalescent hospital, it was probably a comfortable assignment. But the young officer's luck was about to run out.

As part of its campaign to suppress Arab piracy in the Persian Gulf, the Bombay government had recently established a base in the Strait of Hormuz. To man it, the Twelfth Regiment's Second Battalion had been transported in late 1820 to the formidably hot and dry island of Qeshm. Since William had returned to his old regiment, the Fourth, the order did not affect him, and he remained in India. But Qeshm was taking a heavy toll on the health of British and Indian troops, and it wasn't long before the battalion was so short-staffed that the adjutant, Robert Waite, had to take charge of the commissariat. Another officer was needed, and so, filling in again, William sailed to the island to serve as acting adjutant. The date of his appointment was 20 July 1821.

Qeshm was not a soft posting. Thanks to a traveling English envoy who stopped at the base just before William's arrival, we know what awaited him: a garrison in such distress that only three hundred sepoys were fit for duty and only three officers (one of them Waite) were physically able to attend parade. The rest were ill, dying, or dead from what was termed "a severe bilious fever." The envoy had never seen such "ghastly objects" as the men on Qeshm. The sick had no "protection from the scorching heats or parching winds" and "hardly water enough to quench the constant thirst of exhaustion."

For a time William beat the odds. A letter he sent home on 15 October moved his father to report that he was "in good health and spirits." Two weeks later he was dead. The brief announcement in the *Asiatic Journal* reads: "*Oct.* 31. At Kishme, after a short illness, Lieut. Wm. Glascott, Acting Adj. of the 2d bat. 12th regt N.I. [Native Infantry], aged 29." That the base was abandoned a year later made his death all the more pointless.

In the days before steam-powered ships, the telegraph, and the Suez Canal, it could take half a year for news from South Asia to reach England. It wasn't until July 1822 that Cradock, reading the *Asiatic Journal* (to which he subscribed), learned that his son had died. He sent to East India House, Leadenhall Street, London, for confirmation, and when it came he wrote "the commanding officer of his [son's] corps, and to his agents at Bombay, requesting full information respecting his effects, and the particulars of his last illness."

The answer was another half year in coming. As Cradock informed his brother, it took the form of a letter "from a brother officer and very intimate friend of [William's] in India, who gives a very favourable account of his general character, and that he was highly respected among all his acquaintance: It seems he died without a will, but on his death bed appropriated his property—What the amount thereof may be, or how he has disposed of the same, we have not yet learned." And that is the last we hear of William in family letters: a restatement of the father's wish for information about his son's estate in India. Apparently, the brother officer had neglected or declined to specify the value of that estate and the name or names of those to whom it had been orally bequeathed.

Fortunately, an obituary slightly more revealing than the *Asiatic Journal*'s stark death notice was published in the *Bombay Courier*. Here, William was extolled as one "whose professional good qualities, acquirements, and private worth, deservedly insured to him the esteem & regard of his brother officers in the Regiment in which he served ten years; and his loss will be deeply felt by them, and by those friends and acquaintance with whom he associated." What distinguishes this tribute is its glance at private life. The deceased will be missed by civilian "friends and acquaintance" as well as officers.

Friends, a deceptively simple word, has gone through a change in usage over the last two centuries. Today, when we speak of *friends and family*, we are invoking separate and discrete categories. But well into the nineteenth century *friends* not only included close relatives or household members but at times specifically designated them. When Cradock expressed the hope, quoted above, that William would come home to embrace his father and mother, he did not write "parents," though that is what he meant; he wrote "his dear friends at Hatherleigh." Elsewhere, we hear of "a large packet from William, containing letters to his brothers, sister, *& other friends* [my italics]." And as we earlier saw, "worthy friend" could be a term for one's intimate companion. *Friends* was a way of alluding to parents, spouse, siblings, offspring without encroaching on privacy.

William's dear friends in India, as his brother officer surely understood, were now dependent on the estate that William had left. It just wouldn't do to disclose the existence of these unofficial inheritors—*bibi* and children— to the good Reverend Cradock, with his proven interest in money and social position and his long-standing fear that his son would be seduced by the example of licentiousness.

Attaining the age of eighty-eight or eighty-nine, Cradock outlived William by ten years. When he finally died, in August 1831, the bulk of his estate went to his daughter and two clerical sons, all of whom resided in England. Nothing, not even minor legacies, went to descendants in India. Whether he was conscious of their existence is unknown.

Three months after his death a great-granddaughter was born in a cantonment near the city of Ahmadnagar in the Bombay Presidency: the future Anna.

Colonel John Sutherland, Executor and Guardian

Although there are no baptismal records for William's three children, other documents serve to identify them. The oldest, born in 1815, was Mary Ann, named after her aunt in England. The second, Eliza, was born in August 1816. The third, William Frederick Glasscott, was born in 1821 or 1822, possibly after his father's death. A quarter century later this son would signalize the filial connection by changing his middle name to Vaudrey.

One of the few things we know about these orphaned siblings is how much they valued the Glascott family bond. Not only did Mary Ann name her firstborn after sister Eliza and a son after William, but she and her siblings went to considerable trouble to be present at family weddings, regardless of bad roads and slow, animal-drawn conveyances. When Anna got married in Pune in 1849, Uncle William arrived from Bombay, a trip of about four days, and left his name on the register. When she and her husband set off for Australia in 1852, this uncle traveled with them. Given these and other indications of the closeness of the Glascotts, it is all the more striking that Anna chose to strike out on her own, breaking with her family in India and drawing *her* children's names from her husband's side. Anna was proud of her maternal lineage, but mixed with that pride was something too bitter to be acknowledged.

The brutal fact is that the three children sired by Lieutenant Glascott belonged to an ambiguous social category. Since he was an officer his offspring had a claim to British position and privilege, but because they were of mixed race they were debarred from the gentry class. The boy worked for years as a clerk alongside other Eurasians in Bombay's central military office, and the girls married sergeants in the Corps of Engineers. Sergeant engineers were a kind of elite, a respected rank that working-class men of ability could aim for. All the same, the Glascott daughters would have been well aware that, unlike their father, their husbands would never get an officer's commission. The three children were slotted for life in an extremely visible second-class niche. This sharply defined middling status would be a part of Anna's inheritance and a key to her psychology.

Mary Ann's first husband, Thomas Edwards (Anna's father), was a cabinetmaker from London. Born in 1802 or 1803, he enlisted in the Indian army in 1825. A table of recruits shows that he stood five feet five and had brown hair, gray eyes, a "long" face, and a "fresh" complexion. Soon after reaching Bombay, he was transferred from the Infantry to the Corps of Sappers and Miners—that is, the engineers. He died, it is not known how, in July 1831. His widow, pregnant with Anna and with no known means of support, had little choice but to marry again, and quickly, which she did. Born that November, Anna never knew her progenitor. Her stepfather was the only male parent she knew.

The story she told was that her father had been an officer killed in action ("cut to pieces by Sikhs") in about 1840 after leaving Wales for India and that by the terms of his will two men were appointed executor-guardians: the man his widow married and a colonel with the fine-sounding moniker of Rutherford Sutherland.

Though there was no one by that name in India, this claim, like many of Anna's stories, preserves an exact historical trace, one that was so highly treasured that it was never forgotten—*Colonel Sutherland*. His name marks an authentic connection, though not with Anna's father. The real link, jumping a generation, was with her *mother's* father, William Vaudrey Glascott. In October 1821, as the lieutenant lay dying in the boiling Persian Gulf far from *bibi* and children, he dictated his last wishes and appointed John Sutherland, his old comrade from cadet school and the Fourth Regiment, to execute them.

The details are in the musty 1822 casualty returns for the Twelfth Regiment's Second Battalion. According to this record, Lieutenant Glascott's estate was worth 3,189 rupees. This was equivalent to £320, with a modern value of perhaps a hundred times as much—say, $50,000. Under the heading "To whom Bequeathed," we read that this sum was turned over to two executors, "Lieutt Sutherland Nizam Horse & Lieutt R. Waite 2nd Batt 12th Regt N.I." As regards the ultimate beneficiaries—the key point—the entry is silent.

Lieutenant Waite, the second executor, was the man whose reassignment had brought William to Qeshm. A few years older, he seems to have been a hard case. Once, he and some other officers trespassed on a Brahmin's garden in Pune and provoked a riot that ended with two Indians being blown from guns (meaning, they were strapped to a cannon's mouth so that the ball was shot through their bodies). Waite may not have been a particular friend, but there were two good reasons to turn to him: he was one of the few officers still standing, and he was there to hear William's last wishes.

The other executor was the real one. For several years Lieutenant John Sutherland had headed a cavalry unit attached to the Nizam of Hyderabad, a princely state in south-central India. Sutherland had distinguished himself in battle and was proving an able administrator and diplomat. The encomiums heaped on him conjure up the sort of officer generals and governors dream of: brave, resourceful, trustworthy, good-humored. While Glascott was being posted here and there, Sutherland became the companion and protégé of the Resident at Hyderabad, Charles Metcalfe (later Lord). As Metcalfe rose to be the Resident at Delhi and Deputy Governor of all India, Sutherland stayed with him, latterly as private secretary. In Metcalfe's estimation, he was "one of the best Servants who have ever served the state in India. . . . In honorable upright character and chivalrous devotion to duty he has never been surpassed." He made lieutenant colonel in 1838, a year after bringing out a critical survey of British policy toward India's native states.

Sutherland came from a farming family near the Moray Firth, with the second Earl of Duffus a near ancestor. Unlike Glascott, with his commercial squares and cubes, Sutherland had received a liberal education: Latin and French. When the racy travel writer Fanny Parkes dined in his tent, she found him "the life of the party" and felt she had "seldom passed a more agreeable evening." She was also taken by "the gaiety and cheerfulness of marching under [his] flag." The posts he would eventually assume in northwest India—Commissioner of Ajmer and Governor General's Agent in Rajputana—attest to his dashing qualities as well as his solid administrative skill. These assignments were much coveted. As David Gilmour puts it, "The princedoms of Rajputana stirred the normally invisible romanticism of Anglo-India like nowhere else."

The future Commissioner's fine abilities made him the obvious choice to look after his friend's orphaned children, but the clincher was that Sutherland *also* had a non-European "friend." In 1820 he had married a Persian of high birth, Ushrut Hussaini, in the principal mosque of Bharatpur, with Metcalfe as witness. It was a grandson of this union, Herbert Alick Stark, who would boast in the early twentieth century that upper-class Europeans who took a native consort were able *"to pick the best."* The same may be said of Glascott: he too picked the best possible protector for his *bibi* and children.

Further, since both men were in the same battalion in 1815, the year Glascott's unknown companion first gave birth, Sutherland must have been acquainted with her. That was one more guarantee that he could be trusted to keep her from destitution.

Was William's *bibi* Muslim, like Sutherland's Ushrut? If so, and the union was formalized by Islamic rites, there would have been some opprobrium and the potential for a legal challenge—threats Sutherland would have known how to meet.[3] In his own will he identified Ushrut as "the Mother of my Children" rather than "my wife." Although this language can't have pleased his children, as it implied illegitimacy, it insured that his wife could not be disinherited even if English courts refused to recognize her marriage.

Given such ambiguities, it was imperative that William select a sophisticated and well-disposed executor. Waite's job was to take charge of William's effects on Qeshm and hear and relay his last wishes. Sutherland's job, acting through his Bombay agent, was to see that they were carried out year after year. What made this duty all the more critical was that, if William and his "friend" were *not* legally married (after all, the more likely alternative), she would not have qualified for a widow's pension.

Then there was the other delicate duty. When the inevitable letter of inquiry came from the Reverend Cradock Glascott, curate of Hatherleigh, with the obvious questions about his son's estate and inheritors, Sutherland— the "brother officer and very intimate friend"—would have to fend the good man off as kindly and diplomatically as possible.

But here came the hitch: the man who had preached to thousands in the open air and evicted a troupe of actors from Hatherleigh was *not* to be fended off. Cradock had a solid middle-class respect for money, and he seems to have demanded a full legal process. Rather than allow William's estate to be quietly dispersed, Cradock retained the Bombay firm of Shotton and Malcolm, and in July 1824, nearly three years after his son's death, probate was granted by Bombay's Supreme Court. Now it appeared that the estate's true value was eight thousand rupees, more than double the original tally.

Who got the money? Since Cradock is the only interested person named in the letters of administration, he was probably entitled to take all of it. Was an off-the-record provision made for William's family—a humane private compromise? One would like to think so, but then one recalls how intolerant and uncompromising the Reverend Glascott could be, and how

3. Gentry-class unions between Muslims and Christians in India were unusual but not out of bounds. According to William Linnaeus Gardner, who had several wives, "a Moslem lady's marriage with a Christian, by a Cazee [or Cadi, an Islamic religious judge], is as legal in this country as if the ceremony had been performed by the Bishop of Calcutta."

much he detested sexual license in the military, and also that his last will and testament is silent about his Indian descendants.

So William's three children would have to stay in India and be raised in such a way as to minimize their social handicaps. That would require sustained attention and some quiet string pulling. For the Glascotts of Devon, Sutherland was the distant officer who testified to William's character but left the money questions open. For the Glascotts of India, he was the highborn protector who kept a self-respecting mixed-race family from descending into poverty and obloquy.

One of the things Anna got from her mother was the sense of belonging to a high, beset lineage. Looking back, she took pride and comfort in her British origins, which she of course mythologized. Looking forward, she fought off snubs and sneers with her strikingly dignified manner. Some have seen her as a social climber or even an imposter, but such categories are inexact. What they leave out is her sense of herself in history: the feeling of dimly remembered fallen grandeur and the steely determination to reclaim it.

As late as 1962 a granddaughter still remembered Grandmama's solemn but quite mystifying counsel: "*'Unto the third and fourth generation' our descendants would have to suffer for our evil deeds*, we were incessantly warned!" This sibylline head shaking appears to have been Anna's one and only reference to her Glascott past. No one, it seems, had the remotest idea whom she was glancing at so meaningly: the ancestor who had fathered a mixed-race progeny in India and by so doing had left his descendants—left her at least—a legacy of shame, ambition, painful effort, and endless concealment.

A Hard School

A BRITISH FATHER, STEPFATHER, or guardian responsible for raising a Eurasian girl faced some difficult choices. Since a career was not an
option, it was pointless to bring her up for anything but marriage. But what
sort of marriage could she reasonably hope to contract, and what kind
of education would best prepare her for it? Questions like these, which
brought to the surface the pressures and compromises of colonial life, were
formative for the Glascott women. Anna's mother, aunt, and older sister all
settled for the usual answers. Anna did not, a refusal that went to the heart
of what she was and that set the terms for how her life would unfold.

After the death of William Vaudrey Glascott, the guardian of Anna's
mother and aunt had to decide what to do with his female wards. To understand his apparent course of action, we should briefly consider the steps
taken by Captain George Grenville Malet, Third Bombay Light Cavalry.
Malet was in many ways a typical nineteenth-century officer. He loved
to hunt, he had a keen eye for horses and dogs, and he kept an attractive,
well-born Islamic mistress who bore him several children, whom he also
loved. When one of his daughters was nearly eight, he decided that she
should leave her mother's home for boarding school. We know that because
this officer did one thing that wasn't typical: he kept a journal. In it, on 30
April 1840, after returning home and finding "all my people horses & dogs
well," he penned a memorandum: "Sent my dear little girl Mary to school
at Deesa last Tuesday." Disa, as the city is now spelled, was the site of a large
East India Company cantonment with a garrison school.

That sort of thing was good enough for Mary's earlier years, but as the journals show, sooner or later a British officer would want to offer his biracial children something more suitable to their class—meaning, something European. When Malet was granted a two-year sick leave in 1847, he sailed west with his three living Anglo-Indian offspring, Mary included, and placed them with a clergyman and his wife in a village in the north of England. The arrangement was suggested by the chaplain at Disa who had baptized Malet's children; he was an old school friend of the clergyman. When the officer's leave ended, he traveled north to pick up his children, sailed back to India with them, and placed them with Robert Xavier Murphy in Bombay. Murphy was an interpreter and translator at the Supreme Court. He lived in Colaba, a nice part of town. He cost three hundred rupees a month. That was what you did to get your mixed-race progeny started in life if you had the means, connections, and opportunity.

John Sutherland, who amassed considerable wealth in India and was more closely bound to the mother of his children than Malet was to his, did even better. He placed his three Scots-Persian daughters in the care of a "pious and strict" governess on the large farm he had acquired in the Cape Province of South Africa, and he saw that his sons got the same classical foundation he had received, thus enabling them to enter the University of Edinburgh.

These two officers did what they could to maintain their Eurasian offspring in or near the gentry class. Both men would have known what was all too likely to happen to biracial children whose British fathers died or returned to Europe. Numbering in the thousands, such children were thought of as orphans even if their Indian mother was alive. Many became assimilated with their maternal relatives and were henceforth "lost" to Christian nurture. Others joined the raucous street children described by John Williamson Palmer, one of the few Americans who wrote about Indian life in the first half of the nineteenth century. In Palmer's eyes, the abandoned children of British soldiers were the "sturdiest and toughest of Anglo-Indian urchins . . . much given to . . . early coquetry, and early beer, hot curries, loud clothes, bad English, and fast pertness."

That was one of the fates that Sutherland had to fend off from the three Glascott children. Yet once they outgrew the army schools, their options were painfully few. The newly created Martinière Colleges in Bengal were too far away. Protestant missionary schools were out of the question: not only were they conducted in the Gujarati or Marathi language, but most Indian parents did not want their children to associate with Eurasians. Foster guardians like the Murphys, at three hundred rupees a month, were too expensive. Inevitably, Mary Ann and her siblings had to descend a few rungs on the social ladder. Their only choice was to enter the tightly regimented institution that prepared mixed-race orphans for a life of what was called "usefulness."

THE BOMBAY EDUCATION SOCIETY

Established in 1815, the Bombay Education Society was a semi-independent organization created by philanthropic officials, military officers, and merchants with the backing of the Bombay government and Anglican hierarchy. Its reason for being was to sponsor boarding schools for Eurasian military orphans. The three children of Lieutenant Glascott were almost certainly sent to one of these schools, just as Anna and one or both of her maternal cousins were sent a generation later.

The society's income came chiefly from "subscribers," who pledged at a basic level, and "benefactors," who gave additional amounts. Subscribers were allowed to recommend children for admission. No doubt benefactors had further privileges, perhaps involving how their wards were treated. Colonial benevolence was very well organized, with ample allowance for discreet private arrangements.

In each category, subscriber and benefactor, Sutherland was among the society's most generous and dependable supporters. Starting in 1818, as shown by the published annual reports, his yearly contribution was 150 rupees. In 1821, the year William Glascott died, there was a dramatic jump in support, with a "2nd donation" of 100 rupees. For several years, in spite of the fact that he was living outside the Bombay Presidency, Sutherland continued to make this second donation, giving a total of 250 rupees annually. From 1825 to 1833 he gave even more, 270 rupees.

The mission of the Bombay Education Society was to ensure that biracial children whose fathers had died or returned to Britain were raised as Christians and Europeans and given vocational training. Such children, it was feared, were apt "to be supported entirely by the [Indian] mother; and then not only become deeply tainted by a familiar intercourse with domestic profligacy, but are brought up in the lowest superstitions of the Roman Church, or . . . become followers of the impostor Mahomet, or the more degraded and idolatrous votaries of Brahma." To rule out these dire eventualities and the likelihood that poor girls would be corrupted, the society resolved to break their attachment to their homes. Mothers and guardians were required to sign away all control. Girls who entered the society's schools at five or six were held till they were fourteen or fifteen, with home visits strictly limited. After the Ladies' Committee proposed that girls *never* go home, "as it is generally found, after a temporary absence . . . with their friends in this country, that they have learned some bad habit which is injurious to their morals," a rule was adopted that "no Girl shall be allowed to go out from the School, to her Friends even during the Vacations, except her Parents are Married and bear unexceptionable characters."

The regimen one glimpses in the Bombay Education Society's annual reports seems extremely spartan, yet it was not unusual for the times. After rising at five and going to prayers, the girls spent three mornings a week learning to read, write, and cipher. Even more of their time was given to needlework: two mornings a week and each weekday afternoon. The articles of clothing they produced were offered for sale at set prices, the proceeds going to defray the school's expenses. At night, the large schoolroom was converted into a dormitory, with the girls lying "on the floor on carpets."

In the boys' school the control and discipline may have been even more spartan. Once, when the younger boys neglected to bring in their bedding before a rainstorm, they were made to carry their "wet carpets" on their head and march in a circle "almost ankle deep in water and mud." When a new master came out from England, he was shocked to observe "the total depression of spirits, restlessness, and apathy which pervaded the children of this Institution, not only when formed into classes for instruction but when dismissed to their own amusements. During school hours it was with difficulty that I could induce many of them to speak above a whisper." He attributed this behavior both to "the want of amusement and relaxation in play hours" and to the "constant, undue and indiscriminate corporal punishment."

After 1826 the school was situated in the Byculla suburb, three miles north of Bombay's administrative center. Two large buildings were erected, each capable of accommodating two hundred pupils. To ensure that the children were "kept separate from intercourse with the bazars and people without," the grounds were "enclosed by a wall and railing." Incarceration and indoctrination were precisely the point.

Originally, as girls reached adulthood they were placed in domestic service in Bombay's respectable British households. This practice ceased, however, when it was realized that well-trained females had a higher use. Henceforth, as the girls neared their fifteenth birthday they were (in an annual report's carefully weighed diction) "either disposed of by marriage, or with due consideration . . . restored to their friends." If the former, a girl's husband was likely to be an older sergeant or conductor in the employ of the East India Company. Thanks to the Bombay Education Society, the company could count on a steady supply of well-trained girls for the bed and board of its single men.

The earlier a marriageable girl could be disposed of, the sooner a younger one on the waiting list could be admitted. The thing was done with brisk efficiency and little pretense of romance. If you needed a wife, you applied to the headmistress. If she found your qualifications and character in order, you were asked to a select tea party in her room so that you could inspect the "dark beauties" on offer that year. According to one of the rare accounts of this delicate private ceremony, the girls "who desire to enter the matrimonial lists, come forward and signify their wish to join the party. Frequently four or five competitors make their appearance on these occasions in the mistress's room. The gentleman, whilst doing his best to make himself universally agreeable, yet contrives, in the course of the evening, to mark his preference for one particular lady." The man's proposal was expected the next morning. If the object of his rapid affection wasn't drawn to him, she was said to be "at perfect liberty" to decline his offer. But if her answer was yes, a wedding quickly followed, with the school providing a small trousseau and the bride's classmates sewing her outfits.

That account, with its stress on freedom of choice, was written by a man. A more acute treatment of the pressures brought to bear on fourteen-year-old schoolgirls is found in a shrewd book by Emma Roberts, *Scenes and Characteristics of Hindostan*. Roberts was amused by "the straight-forward, business-like manner in which marriages in India are brought about," but she was also sensitive to "the sort of compulsion used to effect the consent" of young brides: "Many young women in India may be considered almost homeless; their parents or friends have no means of providing for them except by a matrimonial establishment; they feel that they are burthens upon families who can ill afford to support them, and they do not consider themselves at liberty to refuse an offer, although the person proposing may not be particularly agreeable to them." Roberts was thinking of girls like the Glascott sisters—"the orphan daughters, legitimate and illegitimate," of Britons residing in India. As Roberts noted, this class of females had grown "exceedingly numerous." That they were "at perfect liberty" seems unlikely.

Anna's mother and aunt were married in 1829 and 1831, respectively. We don't know how their unions were arranged, but statistically they conform to the pattern. Mary Ann Glascott was about fourteen when she married Sergeant Thomas Edwards, who was about twenty-six. Two years later her sister, Eliza, was just short of her fifteenth birthday when she married Corporal Tobias Butler, age twenty-two. Were these matches "agreeable" to the girlish brides? Perhaps. Prior to enlisting, both men had been skilled workmen rather than the usual laborers: Thomas had been a cabinetmaker from London, and Tobias, from St. Cannice Parish in county Kilkenny, Ireland, seems to have been a basket maker (the handwriting is hard to read). Once in India, they were assigned to the much-sought-after Corps of Sappers and Miners, or engineers. Significantly, both men were more youthful than the "grisly bombardier of forty" whom girls often ended up with. On balance, it appears Anna's mother and aunt were in a position to be choosy and that the candidates for their hand had been carefully vetted by a matron or headmistress.

Moreover, the weddings were proper and dignified. When Anna's Aunt Eliza got married, all three witnesses had a connection to the Corps of Engineers. First to sign was Foster P. Thomas, formerly a clerk, now a sergeant engineer, and about to be forwarded to the Native Education Society in Bombay (an unusual promotion). Second came Anna's mother, whose first and second husbands were engineers. Third was Harriet Cloudesley, also married to a sergeant engineer. The picture, admittedly faint, reveals a tight group of girlish wives with husbands in the same fairly select outfit. Did the young women feel they had done well for themselves? Without question, if your spouse was an engineer, you enjoyed more security and respect than if you had married into the infantry or artillery. And whatever the hardships, you had infinitely more privacy than at boarding school.

In time the marriage-market teas came to be seen as a bad old custom from the past. "At variance with the received notions of propriety," sniffed Emma Roberts in 1835. Still, for years to come India's mixed-race women were married off as soon as possible. In a poem earnestly defending the practice, a certain Mrs. Abdy urged readers not to pity the young bride whose girlhood was so soon ended but instead to reflect that "tranquil happiness repays / The early woo'd and won."

When Anna's older sister married in 1845, she was two days short of turning fifteen. Her husband, a sergeant major in the Horse Artillery, was thirty-eight, a lot older than the men her mother and aunt had chosen. Did *she* enjoy the happiness Mrs. Abdy predicted? Perhaps, but it couldn't have been tranquil. By the time she died of peritonitis at age thirty-four, a month after giving birth, she had produced six children.

Anna's decided preference was *not* to join "the early woo'd and won." Striking out on a path taken by none of her female kin, she refused (she later said) to marry the older man selected for her. Her act, a sign of her robustly independent character, was an early step toward her eventual rejection of the family she was born into.

Tough Love

What sort of mother would you be if, like Mary Ann Glascott Edwards, you had grown up in the hard early years of the Bombay Education Society's girls' school?

The few stories Anna told about her mother represented her as a principled and unbending Englishwoman of the gentry class. Her standards were the highest, and she was never anything less than severe and correct. One of Anna's letters to an upper-class American woman speaks of "the stern English rightmindedness in which I have been brought up." Her implication was that, thanks to her upbringing, she found it hard to lie.

In a way she was right, if only because it is fiendishly difficult to devise a credible alternative past. Try as she might to disguise her origins, Anna's stories about her mother had a kind of bedrock sincerity. That is why they reveal not a correct English lady but a toughened survivor of a colonial charity school. Anna's mother was the product of an institution that drilled into children the understanding that they could *never* (as C. J. Hawes nicely put it) "join the ruling race on their own ground and so their upbringing should be spartan and Christian." If you are raised on that premise, you know the world is not your oyster and that your children won't get by without strict training. The great irony is that Anna's "stern English rightmindedness" turns out to be a subordinate's idealization. It was one more way of identifying with the master race.

Once, in her later years, Anna made a grandchild copy for the third time a letter that was not considered neat enough. When the child burst into tears, Anna said, "*My* mother sometimes made me rewrite a letter thirteen times." True or not, the story hints at the lessons Anna was taught by her mother. Learn to do hard things well. Don't expect sympathy if you fail. Everything must be perfect when you present yourself in a letter or in person. Never relax, unless you want to reveal your inadequate beginnings.

Another story has an equally spartan flavor. Anna placed it in Wales, but it must have occurred at some military base—in Disa? Pune?—where she and her sister had the use of riding ponies. One day Anna was thrown by her mount and had to return home on foot. Although it was still daylight, her mother sent her to bed with the words "A little miss who cannot sit her pony had best think it over in bed." This lesson, an extremely important one, was not just about horsemanship and mastery (mastery of a skill taken for granted by the ruling class) but about how to pick oneself up. To keep from being punished like a little miss, Anna should have gotten back in the saddle and kept quiet about her fall. *Big misses know how to cover up*: something to think about while tossing in bed.

A third story, this one even more revealing about Mary Ann's character and circumstances in India, tells how she saved a large cache of rupees from being stolen. The story survives in two versions. The first, sold to *Youth's Companion*, was adapted to the tastes and expectations of a juvenile readership and took obvious liberties with the facts. In this sensationalized account, Anna makes herself an eyewitness and the would-be robber one of the famously sinister Thugs. The narrative marches from treachery to a final scene of justice, with an act of open defiance forming the high point: "His large dark eyes shone upon us out of the gloom. . . . There he stood, confronting that pale English woman, my mother, with a sort of demoniacal grin."

The second version, intended for adults and much more sober, was incorporated into Anna's *Life and Travel in India: Being Recollections of a Journey*

before the Days of Railroads. Here we learn that she was not present, that
there was a band of robbers, and that they were Bhils, a tribal people of
western India who hunted with bow and arrow and lived in wattle-and-
daub huts. Inevitably, there is a degree of embroidery, but the social and
geographical details seem right, and the setup is congruent with the known
facts about Anna's stepfather, a civil engineer.

Briefly, the stepfather had been ordered to survey a new road into
Gujarat, the province at the head of the Gulf of Cambay, north of Bombay.
Since Anna's mother had "a fair knowledge" of the Gujarati language, she
went along in order to assist her husband in "settling disputes about payments of money for work done." They traveled with their servants, a small
guard of sepoys, and a "tumbril" holding the cash to pay the laborers.

The little expedition pitched its tents in the village of Balmere. Anna's
mother and stepfather occupied separate rooms in a double-poled, double-
walled tent. The tumbril was in the mother's room. A small lamp was left
burning.

In the middle of the night, woken by a noise, Mary Ann found herself
confronted by the Bhil robbers. "Woman," one of them said in Gujarati, "we
do not desire to hurt you; we only mean to possess ourselves of what we
need, the money in that cart there."

> To scream for help would imperil her own and her husband's life . . . but
> to permit them quietly to rob the government treasury would be almost as
> fatal, entailing on them endless delay, trouble, and perhaps even unjust suspi-
> cion at head-quarters. The intrepid wife suddenly remembered that the Bhils
> had a superstitious reverence for the person of a woman, and before they had
> time to reach the tumbril she flung herself on her face and hands across their
> path, and said solemnly in Guzerati [Gujarati], "Only by stepping over a
> woman's body can you obtain possession of what is entrusted to the care of
> her husband." There she lay, not daring to utter another word, trembling from
> head to foot.

When she finally lifted her head, she was alone. The candle-lit tumbril was
untouched.

Aside from that "reverence for the person of a woman," which sounds
unlikely, the story does have some history in it. Most Bhil tribes spoke a

dialect of Gujarati, one of western India's major languages. As for the tumbril and the wife's conviction that her husband would be held to account if it was broken into, there was a formal directive that "public treasure be kept only in Tumbrils, or in Chests so weighty, or so secured, as not to be removable otherwise than by the combined means of many persons. . . . [O]fficers neglecting this precaution, will always be held responsible for any losses that may in consequence occur." Further, the story captures an emerging assumption about a British wife's proper role in India, namely, that she was to be a coadjutor of her husband, an imperial helpmate. As Mary A. Procida observes in *Married to the Empire*, because a wife's domestic staff freed her from household duties, she was expected to ride, shoot, settle disputes, and so forth. By putting her command of Gujarati at her husband's service in his dealings with his road crew, Anna's mother was simply doing her job.

The big revelation, however, is her linguistic skill. Anna wanted readers to see her mother as an English lady who had picked up "a fair knowledge" of Gujarati, but the diaries, memoirs, and travelogues of the time show that this language was studied chiefly by missionaries. The tongue the British worked at was Hindustani, a stripped-down language useful for basic communication. If Mary Ann Glascott Edwards Donohoe was fluent in Gujarati, that was because she had learned it in girlhood from *her* mother, Lieutenant Glascott's *bibi*. Like many of Anna's autobiographical stories, this one inadvertently discloses a Eurasian past. Indeed, it makes the same point that India's educated Eurasians were always insisting on: that they were indispensable to British administration precisely because they knew the native languages and cultures and could act as intermediaries. Which is what Mary Ann does so triumphantly in this story.

The other revelation concerns the psychology of Anna's mother as a well-trained product of a spartan regimen. Putting it bluntly, she was a dedicated subordinate, willing to put her life at risk to protect her husband's reputation for probity and reliability and thus his career. Yet she was hardly a passive follower, unable to think and act for herself. She was dutiful, but she was also resolute and self-reliant. Her defiance of the robbers was based on a reasoned calculation, and her bluff paid off.

One of Anna's few treasures from her mother was a locket containing the admonition *Tibi seris tibi metis*. As you sow, so shall you reap. Nicely summing up the tough mentality instilled in Mary Ann, this ancient and widespread motto says that there is justice in life and that what you get is what you deserve. No matter what you have to endure in life, you are the responsible agent.

Such, it seems, was Anna's "half-caste" mother: a stickler for the rules, yet proud and aloof; always the subordinate, yet never doubting that one is mistress of one's fate and must sit one's pony. She must have been a very powerful force in her daughter's life.

ANNA AT BYCULLA

There was a profound social chasm between the well-to-do young ladies who sailed to England for their education and then came back in their teens and the rough-cut girls whose fathers and guardians couldn't afford that sort of refining. Girls of the latter class, according to Roberts's *Scenes and Characteristics of Hindostan*, spoke an English nearly as barbarous as that of Americans and faced a dim outlook in the marriage market. Roberts pitied them.

Desperate to be on the right side of that divide, Anna wanted it understood that she, too, had been educated in Britain and that her arrival in India at the age of fifteen had been a momentous transition. Thus, she began her third book, *Life and Travel in India*, by recalling the pleasant November day when "the steamer from Aden came to anchor in the harbor of Bombay, bringing me among its many passengers. Here I was in this strange land, a young girl fresh from school, now entering upon a life so different." This picture was consistent with her claim that she had been educated at a British boarding school for girls run by a distant relative of her mother, a Mrs. Walpole.

The great incongruity was that, after spending so many years in Walpole's school, Anna had only a single story about its internal operations. Avis Selina Fyshe, the Canadian granddaughter who tried to write Anna's biography, could not explain this uncharacteristic poverty of memory and anecdote.

Although the names of the Bombay Education Society's scholars have not been preserved, two pieces of evidence show that Anna attended the society's girls' school at Byculla in the early 1840s. The first is the printed society reports recording the payment of the monthly school fee by her stepfather. The second is none other than her Walpole story, which reflects a scandal so strange and troubling that it was aired in a Bombay newspaper. The event that Anna placed in Britain can only have taken place at Byculla.

Technically, the fees paid by Anna's stepfather, Patrick Donohoe, went to the Military Asylum, a benefit program run by the Bombay Education Society. At its founding, this program promised British soldiers that if they subscribed in amounts proportioned to their rank, their children would be guaranteed an education. Regimental money flowed in, but then enthusiasm cooled, and the society found itself taking too many orphans on an insecure income. By 1840 most of the new admissions to the Byculla schools were the children of nonsubscribers. The Military Asylum idea wasn't working, and a "vigorous exertion" was made to give the program a sound fiscal basis. Soldiers were urged to sign up, the rules for admission were revised, and monthly assessment rates were reset: eight annas (half a rupee) for sergeants, four annas for married rank and file. These regulations took effect in January 1841. A few months later nine-year-old Anna entered the school as a full-time boarding pupil.

When the new rules were finally published in the society's report for 1843, Donohoe (his name mangled) was listed among the staff sergeants subscribing to the Military Asylum. The next year the name of another family member showed up: Corporal Butler, Anna's uncle by marriage. Evidently, one or both of Tobias and Eliza Butler's daughters (born in 1833 and 1835) were at Byculla. Butler's subscription ended in 1846, but Donohoe's continued into 1847, the year Anna turned sixteen, too old to be in school. In all, her stepfather paid in for at least five years.

Did he subscribe specifically for her? We can't be certain, seeing that his first two children, John and Ellen, born in 1833/34 and 1836, were old enough to enroll. Still, it is clear that Byculla was seen as the fitting educational institution for Lieutenant Glascott's descendants. One or both of Anna's first cousins attended, and so, in all likelihood, did her older sister Eliza and some of her half-siblings. There is no reason to think an exception was made for Anna. The payments made by her uncle and stepfather create a presumption that she, too, was schooled at Byculla.

Ironically, this presumption is confirmed by her own story about Mrs. Walpole's British school. Like her other tales, this amusing account of misguided girlish heroism must have been polished in multiple retellings. But even as the teller enhanced it, she kept a few seemingly fortuitous details—

oddities not required by the drama. It is these bits that come straight out of a troubled period in the history of the Byculla girls' school.

About the time little Anna entered school, the story goes, the older girls became fixated on Mrs. Walpole's habit of always wearing a bonnet tied under her chin with a wide starched band. The girls decided that she must be a man in disguise who took this means of hiding his beard and sneaking in to a roomful of girls. Someone would have to tell *Miss* Walpole of this dreadful thing and get her to "forbid her pseudo-mother to come in and . . . kiss them goodnight." But who would be brave enough to do this?

The tale survives in Avis Selina Fyshe's uncompleted biography. Her version of how the scandalous situation was cleared up nicely conveys the feel of Anna's dramatic storytelling:

> Secret conclaves, thrills, palpitations and faint hearts! Finally this duty was forced upon the newest comer, little Miss Anna Crawford. She lay in her small bed, trembling when the "lights out" moment came, and as Miss Walpole tucked her up, she stammered, "Please, Miss, we don't want your mother to come into our room." "Don't want mother to kiss you good-night?" asked the young woman in amazement, "and pray, why not? She would be deeply grieved to think you did not want her. She loves you all so much."
>
> "Because," in brave but quavering tones, "because your mother is a man!"

Upon which Mrs. Walpole reappears, unties her bonnet, and reveals the "large tufted mole" she had hoped to conceal.

It is a lovely anecdote and a credit to Anna's narrative skill, but, like so many of her stories, its premises seem shaky. If the older girls had been in Mrs. Walpole's school for some time, why would they suddenly become anxious about her bonnet strings and suspect her of being a man? Isn't this suspicion a little strange for a group of British schoolgirls, who would have seen all kinds of bonnets? And who is this *Miss* Walpole, and why does she suddenly appear to be in charge of her mother's boarding school?

The answers are to be found in the Byculla girls' school's escalating difficulties starting in 1840. At the time, a Mrs. Ginger had been headmistress for years. One of two former pupils who rose to be principal, she was a tough and able administrator, though criticized for her severity. She was induced to take on the additional position of matron, which doubled her workload, but she was then replaced as headmistress by a Mrs. Hatteroth, wife of the master of the boys' school and recently arrived from England. Given the low regard for teachers who were "country born," Ginger may well have found her demotion a bitter pill. In March or April 1840 she resigned.

For the next year and a half the school was in such turmoil, with so many staffing changes and flying rumors, that a Bombay newspaper printed an anonymous four-column exposé. While Anna's story can't be confirmed in every detail, it evidently reflects this unstable period of rapid turnovers. The surname of the matron and schoolmistress she remembered was not Walpole but Yates: Mrs. and Miss Yates.

Mrs. Yates took over as matron and housekeeper after Ginger left, but before long Hatteroth submitted *her* "abrupt resignation," and the school was without a headmistress. While awaiting a new one to come out from England, "the Ladies' Committee committed the whole charge of the school to the Matron, Mrs. Yates, permitting her to avail herself of the assistance of her daughter, recently arrived from England, in the department of instruction." Miss C. Yates, the daughter and new teacher, had reached Bombay on 8 May 1841. She was the Miss Walpole who tucked in nine-year-old Anna and the other girls. But she and her mother didn't last long. The school chaplain, the Reverend William Kew Fletcher, objected to them so strongly (the *Gazette* disclosed) that "every trifling thing that transpired in the Girl's school was magnified with slanderous ingenuity into the most hideous form." So Mrs. Yates was sacked "at the shortest notice," and her daughter either resigned or was asked to leave.

The nature of these hideous rumors was not spelled out in the newspaper exposé. The closest we get to them is in the Bombay Education Society's annual report for 1841, which admitted that the girls' school had been passing through a period of "disorder and insubordination." During this time "reports circulated" of such a nature that the school's managers felt compelled to declare them "utterly *unfounded*." The blame was pinned on matron Mrs. Yates (Anna's Mrs. Walpole), who was accused of being too indulgent and leaving her post of duty. However, others were involved, or so one gathers from the new regulations the upheaval prompted. These stipulated that, while the chaplain would retain his pastoral relation to the school, he was in future explicitly excluded from "the internal and domestic arrangement."

It sounds as if Reverend Fletcher had been too intrusive, perhaps entering the girls' dormitory in Mrs. Yates's absence and thus giving rise to exaggerated fears and scandalous talk.

Such were the obscure events behind Anna's story of a group of girls alarmed at the thought of a disguised male intruder. That sort of panic would have been much more in the order of things in Bombay than in Britain. In a culture where women lived in purdah, strictly segregated from men not in their family, girls taken from their mothers' homes to an unfamiliar Christian institution would naturally be anxious about exposure to men. Some of Anna's schoolmates knew very little about these strange English folk, with their bonnets and kissing and the like; some came to school "not knowing a word of English." As matrons came and went and rumors flew, the girls' fears became inflamed.

Anna's story offers a unique glimpse into the school that helped make her. It also tells us something about her girlhood character. That she was delegated by the older pupils to break some very bad news to Miss Yates shows she already possessed a certain eminence—eminence based on both her personal qualities and her obvious social status.

As Hawes shrewdly notes, the "Eurasian social hierarchy reflect[ed] the orders of British society, albeit at a lesser level." Just as the Glascotts in India valued their descent from an English officer, so the Byculla school made distinctions among scholars. High-performing older girls became paid pupil-teachers, and two able alumnae (Ginger one of them) rose to be headmistress. Decades later, without spilling the truth, Anna liked to attribute her success to her early training in elocution. In all likelihood, her talents were recognized by teachers, chaplains, and others, her spoken English was cleansed of the "chee-chee" accent that was thought to characterize Eurasian speech,[1] and she was steered toward teaching.

Was she quietly put forward in ways she never forgot? Her book on India roundly declares that "the English residents in Calcutta, Madras, and Bombay are among the most kind and liberal people in the world . . . privately support[ing] a vast number of charitable institutions." The book mentions Byculla's "fine English school-house for all classes of children" and specifically

1. To some English ears, this accent had a "sing-song, almost Welsh" ring. "Chee-chee" was a highly derogatory term.

acknowledges the "English ladies of high rank, who take turns in visiting it." The reference was to the body that supervised the girls' school, the Ladies' Committee, one of whose members was surnamed Conybeare. Anna's daughter was baptized Avis Annie Leonowens but at some later point was given a far more impressive middle name: Connybeare. Perhaps this was Anna's way of memorializing—discreetly—the gratitude she felt to a kind early benefactress.

But how many ladies really did prove kind, liberal, and encouraging? In 1848 the Bombay Education Society got a new patroness, wife of the recently appointed governor. Lady Falkland was an amateur painter who brought a keen sense of color on her official visits, and in addition she kept a journal from which she distilled a book she titled *Chow-Chow* (a term for a miscellany). In it we see exactly how Anna and her biracial mates looked when they were inspected through a lorgnette. "The girls are certainly singularly plain," wrote the governor's lady, "their complexions being of all kinds of neutral tints and shades of yellow; their hair is cut short; their dress is one of the greatest simplicity." Gratified with the "sound religious and moral training" they were getting, she sniffed at the notion that they could be anything more than a housewife or upper servant: "They receive a very good education; and, *hitherto*, have not been over-educated, merely learning what will be necessary for them when they go forth into the world. In all the various *ologies* which could be of no possible use to them, they are not instructed." Once, a tiny forlorn pupil with "a complexion shading off from bistre into yellow ochre" clung to the legs of a gentleman from England and, "looking up most imploringly into his face, cried out, 'Pa-pa! Pa-pa!'" No one could pull the child away. People got embarrassed. And the lady patroness? She "hastened to escape from a scene which was much too laughable."

This lack of empathy epitomizes the stony institutional benevolence that formed and deformed Anna and set her on a path all her own. Thanks to her mother's discipline, her family's middling social position, her own drive and intelligence, and an occasional leg up from helpful mentors, she smashed the fetters of her charity-school education and managed to pass, at least in North America, as *herself* a well-born British lady. Sadly, the very nature of this gutsy achievement meant she could never show who she was and thus unveil the amazing thing she had pulled off. The best she could do was to brandish traces of her past while continuing to bury it—that story about Mrs. Walpole, for instance.

For someone who grew up as Anna did, the key to success was presentation. You developed a dignified, determined, unassailable front. You were disciplined, you always maintained a high tone. You mastered the art of bluffing, never letting on that you hadn't sat your pony. You rewrote the letter thirteen times, and not just the letter: you rewrote everything—what happened in India, Australia, Singapore, and, most important, Siam. Whenever you looked back, you fixed things up, concealing, arranging, improving, inventing. You added the haughty and official overlay that seemed part of being English, and you did it with a perfectly good conscience, because that was what it took.

3

The Unnamed Stepfather

ONE OF THE CHIEF OBSTACLES in Anna's path was Patrick Donohoe, the stepfather whose Irish Catholic identity was simply not compatible with the genteel origins she was determined to claim. His name alone would have drawn stares in the United States, where a large influx of destitute Irish immigrants had left behind a toxic image of an ignorant, turbulent, priest-ridden underclass. *Paddys* they were called, after the familiar form of *Patrick*. The reason Anna concealed her stepfather's name is obvious.

But her stepfather problem went deeper than ethnic or sectarian prejudice. Donohoe was a working-class man—a tough, skilled, reliable, level-headed sergeant engineer tramping the long road to an upper midlevel social standing. Anna respected his success, mentioning more than once that he attained "a prominent position in the Public Works Department" in Pune, India, but there was something that never stopped rankling: what she called his "domestic tyranny." He had opposed her marriage "with so much rancor that all correspondence between them ceased from that date," and in addition he had taken possession of her mother's ancestral Welsh homestead, leaving Anna no choice but to enter the colonial labor market after being widowed.

The castle in Wales being fictive, we may dismiss the second charge. As for the first, it does appear that Patrick disapproved of Thomas Leonowens and that a break ensued. Yet it is equally clear that Anna's stepfather didn't stand in the way of her marriage. He attended the wedding and, by leaving his signature on the register, *P. Donohoe*, made known his implicit parental consent. What's more, surviving letters reveal that Anna continued to make lengthy stays at the Donohoe home in Pune. All correspondence *can't* have ceased. Her account is incomplete.

What's missing is some acknowledgment of family conflict—conflict that seems to have been too messy and intricate for a public laundering. Between Anna's mother and stepfather there were major differences in class and religion, and between her stepfather and husband lay a gulf so wide it couldn't be bridged. In retrospect, it looks as if Anna's marital choice *had* to produce a family rupture.

Mother's Remarriage

After Sergeant Thomas Edwards died on 31 July 1831, his meager estate, worth 112 rupees, was reserved for "Payment of his Regimental debt." There is no reason to think that any of it went to his pregnant widow and infant daughter.

Three months later, on 6 November 1831, Anna was born. At the time Mary Ann was living in the Honorable Company's cantonment on the outskirts of Admadnagar, a city of fifty thousand that had once been a Mughal administrative center. American missionaries were impressed by the old city's "palaces, mosques, aqueducts & numerous ruins," and travelers from England admired the military camp's vineyards, vegetable gardens, and "general air of comfort." But Mary Ann Edwards's attention would have been elsewhere, as she had two babies on her hands and may have had no means of support.

A soldier's mixed-race widow was eligible for a pension lasting six months, and when it terminated her only option was to remarry. For army wives, as historian Durba Ghosh has observed, "serial monogamy"—one marriage after another—was "a standard feature of cantonment life." Following this pattern, Mary Ann Glascott Edwards chose a second husband who belonged to the same outfit as her first. Chances are, she knew him well enough to feel assured of his reliability. Their wedding took place in January 1832, five months after her bereavement and two months after her delivery. She was a sixteen-year-old widowed mother of two, and she was probably still lactating.

The marriage was a mixed one in three ways. Ethnically, Mary Ann was Anglo-Indian and Patrick was Irish. Socially, she could claim an ambiguous gentry-class origin, whereas he had been a skilled laborer. And religiously, she was Church of England and he was Roman Catholic, having been baptized in St. John's Parish, county Limerick.

Ordinarily, before a Protestant-Catholic union could be solemnized, a number of sticky questions had to be settled. This time one of them at least—whose priest is going to perform the ceremony?—could be finessed. The base happened to be without a regular Anglican chaplain, so it was up to the regimental colonel to tie the knot. But Glascott tradition still held, with the bride's sister, Eliza Butler, arriving from Sirur to sign the register and (one imagines) welcome Donohoe into the family.

Mary Ann's new husband had enlisted in the East India Company army in 1827. A smith, he had an advantage over the unskilled laborers who made up the bulk of recruits, and thus he moved from the Infantry to the Sappers and Miners sometime after his troop ship reached Bombay. By October 1830 he was in the Corps of Engineers. Over the next several years he was posted to Ahmadnagar, Belgaum, and Sirur, rising from private to corporal to sergeant. In 1835, three years after marrying, his name showed up on the Town Major's List, a special category for soldiers in certain support roles. Technically, he was still a sergeant engineer subject to military orders, but for all practical purposes he now belonged to the prestigious Public Works Department—the PWD, as everyone called it. Like other non-commissioned officers, he was in the Subordinate Branch.

The range of skills that Patrick had to master was extensive and demanding. The rules stipulated that "no soldier from the corps of sappers and miners will hereafter be admitted to [the PWD] who shall not be found to possess a sufficient knowledge of English writing and accounts, to enable him to keep and prepare the various books and returns required by existing regulations; and such a knowledge of plan-drawing, as to enable him to frame an estimate, and lay down a building from a plan." Candidates also had to know a native language well enough "to converse in it." Was Patrick up to speed in Gujarati when he helped lay out the road into Gujarat? If not, that could explain why Mary Ann accompanied him as translator (and go-between with robbers).

In 1837 or 1838 the cantonment at Disa, the Northern Provinces' administrative capital, became Patrick's domestic base. Like many engineers in the Subordinate Branch, he and his family may have lived in a tent or partitioned barracks: their home for the next ten years. After 1841 Anna would have been mostly away, having entered the Bombay Education Society's school in Byculla, where half-sister Ellen Donohoe seems to have joined her. Perhaps their return trips on holiday gave Anna the setting for one of her best and most chilling stories, published in a children's magazine decades later.[1]

Thanks to Anna, we know that Patrick helped survey a road to the summit of Mount Abu, a four-thousand-foot peak the army saw as a promising resort for sick or convalescent soldiers. The survey crew ran into many problems but managed to lay out a provisional route by late 1846. For early travelers, the road was a triumph of engineering. One invalid could not imagine "the immensity of labor" it had taken to negotiate the "gulfs, ravines, and steep acclivities."

Patrick's competence brought its due reward. In July 1847 his name headed a list of promotions in the PWD's Subordinate Branch. No longer an overseer, he was now a subconductor and assistant supervisor. If he took pride in his new grade, he would have had reason: the entire Bombay Presidency had only three assistant supervisors.

A social historian of British India notes that "the upper levels" of the PWD ranked high in the social hierarchy. That is exactly what one would guess from Anna's boasts about her stepfather's career, as when, casually inflating his position, she called him "an officer of engineers . . . appointed by the Department of Public Works at Bombay." The hard truth, however, was that no matter how well Patrick did, the class system would see that he never got out of the Subordinate Branch and joined the real officers.

Which brings us to his stepdaughter's early feelings about the family situation in Disa. What exactly did she think of Patrick's tightly delimited success? How did she see this man who sweated so hard to reach a level so far below her glorified British ancestor?

1. In "An Encounter with an Ulwar Sawad," Anna recalls what she and "my little sister" saw while traveling at night by cart, with their parents' cart supposedly following. The girls' cart stops. A giant boa constrictor is lying in the road, its eyes fixed on a monkey holding her infant. The monkey leaps about in terror, frantically resisting the fatal charm, then dashes into the snake's "very jaws." The sound of crunched bones is heard, Hindu servants propitiate the monster, and the girls proceed "on our way to Mount Aboo." Nothing more is said of the parents.

One guesses at the answer from a fateful event in the later years of her family's residence in Disa—the arrival of a paymaster's clerk who lacked Donohoe's practical abilities but was well read and articulate, strongly opinionated, historically informed, and almost a gentleman. Anna fell in love, and within a few years she was engaged to marry a man of a very different stamp from the one her widowed mother had accepted.

HOUSEHOLD STRAINS

Meanwhile, as Patrick's career moved forward and Mary Ann gave birth to more and more children, a crack appeared in the couple's domestic foundations.

The original understanding seems to have been that none of their offspring would be raised Catholic. John, the eldest, born in 1833 or 1834, is known to have worshiped at an Anglican chapel in his teens, and Charlotte and Ellen, the next two children, born in 1835 and 1836, were given Anglican baptisms. Is it surprising that Patrick let his young wife have her way in the matter of religious training? Not if one remembers that she was an officer's daughter who had gone to a Protestant school that considered the "superstitions of the Roman Church" to be on a par with Hindu idolatry. As Anna's stories make clear, Mary Ann could be an extremely proud, stubborn, principled woman.

However, by the 1840s the Roman Church had greater respectability in British India. With perhaps 40 percent of the army's soldiers belonging to the Church, the East India Company had begun appointing Catholic chaplains and contributing to the support of a Catholic seminary in Bombay. A priest was assigned to Disa, and in March 1844, when Anna was twelve, her mother gave birth to a boy who was baptized by "Marulino Antao Roman Catholic Preyt [priest]."[2] There was a repeat performance in October 1847, when Father Ireneus from St. Theresa baptized Charles Patrick Donohoe.

---

2. The name of this priest shows he was Portuguese, which raised another contentious matter. In Bombay and Goa there had been extensive intermarriage between Indians and Portuguese, whose descendants had darker skin than most Europeans. In the eyes of Richard Burton, this population was the most "degraded looking race" in Asia: "The forehead is low and flat, the eyes small, quick, and restless; there is a mixture of sensuality and cunning about the region of the mouth." That this ugly but widespread view rubbed off on Anna is apparent from her statement that "the native Portuguese are darker than the darkest of the better class of Indians, showing a mixed and degenerate

The marriage must have been under a strain. How the couple managed to resolve it is suggested by the baptismal rites for their last two children: Blanche, born in 1853, christened by an Anglican chaplain, and Vaudry Glasscott, born in 1858, baptized by a Catholic priest. Mary Ann got the girl, Patrick the boy, and newborn Vaudry Glasscott Donohoe served as the emblem of compromise: sprinkled by a Roman priest but given the name of his low church grandfather.

Significantly, the earliest known sign of this religious divide dates from March 1844, when twelve-year-old Anna was getting her Protestant indoctrination at Byculla. Decades later, her beliefs would be so eclectic that she didn't care whether her grandchildren went to church or not, but well into her thirties she was not only devout but conspicuously so. At age twenty-one she left the Church of England for the evangelical Methodists, and soon after, in her first attempt to start a school of her own, she advertised that it would instill "the principles of the Reformed Religion." Her earliest known photo has her wearing a cross as large and emphatic as a bishop's pectoral.

So what did Anna think when she returned to Disa on school holidays and found a revolution? With Patrick reasserting his ancestral faith, did she see her mother as a kind of victim? Anna would make it very clear in Bangkok and the States that she could be exceptionally stiff-necked and difficult, not to say absolute. Did the young teenager feel that a war between good and evil had erupted in her home? Was this the period in which she concluded that her stepfather was a domestic tyrant?

Then, in December 1845, when she was fourteen—the age when Eurasian girls were expected to turn their minds to marriage—Her Majesty's Twenty-Eighth Regiment marched into camp bringing a smart young paymaster's clerk named Thomas Leon Owens. Royal regiments spent only a few years in India, where they enjoyed more prestige than the company's commercial regiments, which were there for life. Thomas was to be stationed in Disa for two years—time enough for a mutual attraction to spring up between him and Anna. Several things made him stand out: he was a reader with strong

---

race." Similarly, in Bangkok, where the Portuguese who intermarried with the Siamese were concentrated in the Tâmsèng neighborhood, she would be fixated on signs of degradation—"squalid, dirty streets" and so forth.

opinions on social questions, he was disposed to challenge authority, and he was Anglo-Irish.

He came from Enniscorthy in county Wexford. Presided over by descendants of Protestant colonists from England and Wales, the county smoldered with Catholic anger. When the United Irishmen rose in 1798, local Protestants suffered terrible atrocities, and after the rebels were defeated on Vinegar Hill the counteratrocities were no less vicious. Vinegar Hill looms right over Enniscorthy, a constant reminder.

Throughout Thomas's boyhood his parish church, St. Mary's, Church of Ireland, remained in what was termed a "very ruinous state." It was rebuilt soon after he left town, becoming the stark, high-walled, fortress-like building it is to this day. A church militant, it even has crenellations, as if built for war. If stones could speak, what these might say is that *here* is where the tribe of Thomas will forever defy the tribe of Patrick.[3]

Thomas would take a passionate interest in Europe's religious wars and England's heritage of parliamentary liberty. In a debate on the beheading of Charles I, he called the king a despot and a traitor and praised the Puritans who killed him as "the Holiest & best men of the time." One of the books we know Thomas read was Leopold von Ranke's *History of the Popes*, which tells of the secret strategy by which the Papacy consolidated its temporal power in the Counter-Reformation.[4] The man Anna fell in love with at a time when Patrick was reclaiming his Catholic roots almost looks like a Protestant zealot.

Another way to say that is that Ireland's bitter history had come to Disa to haunt Patrick. But the man had other reasons for frowning on Anna's young romance. For one, her army clerk had poor prospects for gainful employment. For another (as will be seen in chapter 5), he committed an offense in Disa that brought punishment, a temporary reduction from sergeant to

3. When Enniscorthy's Roman Catholic cathedral (by Pugin) was restored in 1994, St. Mary's Parish, in a gesture of reconciliation, turned over its sanctuary for services. Colm Tóibín, who grew up Catholic in the town, has put on record what it felt like to enter the building for the first time and hear mass in the ancestral enemy's plain, rectilinear sanctuary.

4. Proof that Thomas paid attention to this influential work is in the minutes of the Swan River Mechanics' Institute, which record his tardiness in returning library book no. 420. According to the organization's early book catalog, no. 420 was the first of three volumes of *History of the [Popes]* by "Rankes."

private. Did Patrick see Thomas as unreliable or unstable—an unpromising breadwinner? If so, the roving life that Anna shared with him in Australia, Singapore, and Penang would have confirmed the engineer in his opinion.

Still, in spite of everything, he let Anna have her way. She had a powerful will, and on Christmas Day, 1849, her stepfather dutifully entered the little Anglican church at Pune and witnessed her marriage. To that extent he was not an inflexible parent, let alone a despotic one.

But the tensions were still there. The wedding announcement submitted to two Bombay newspapers, probably by Donohoe, put on record some sharp distinctions: "At St. Mary's Church, Poona, by the Reverend J. N. Allen, M.A., on the 25th December, Thomas Leone Owens, to Anne Harriet Edwards, step-daughter of Mr. Donohoe, Assistant Supervisor Public Works." That Anna's husband was plain untitled *Thomas* while her stepfather was *Mr. Donohoe* was in conformity with correct usage, seeing that Thomas had left the army and was now a clerk, and it was also proper to specify his father-in-law's respected occupational grade while remaining silent about his own more humble employment. But what about the odd misspelling of his middle name (in both newspapers) and the overall implication that he was a nobody next to Mr. Donohoe? Anna's feelings can easily be imagined.

If one glances for comparison at the announcement of Patrick's daughter Ellen's marriage, one finds the bridegroom's rank and unit stated and the father-in-law's success given less emphasis. Ellen's husband was in the Sappers and Miners. He would have had more in common with Patrick than Anna's pen-pushing office worker did.

So perhaps she did have cause to resent Patrick for his attitude toward Thomas: there may have been real rancor. Yet it seems unlikely that the final rupture came from him. His wedding announcement for Ellen (his oldest living girl) identified her as his "3d daughter," implying that he not only regarded his stepdaughters as *daughters* but still thought of Anna as the second one, meaning, *not* broken with. That was in May 1852, six months before she and Thomas left India forever. How she felt about Patrick at that point can only be surmised, but it is clear that he considered her part of his family. It would not be Patrick who disowned Anna but Anna who disowned Patrick.

A Bungalow in the Conductors' Lines

The Donohoes' life in Disa came to an end when Patrick was transferred to Aden, a British possession on the Arabian peninsula. Administered from Bombay, Aden had been developed into a coaling station for company steamers plying between India and Suez. When George Grenville Malet was traveling to Europe on furlough and his vessel pulled into port, he found it "a most wretched looking place" and didn't go ashore. An Indian newspaper termed Aden "a mere cinder, with a cantonment on top." It was "a kind of penal station," a modern historian writes; "few officers could stand long periods in Aden or Gujarat without losing their health; some also lost their lives or went berserk." Not long before Donohoe arrived, two subordinate engineers were "drunk and riotous" in the afternoon, a captain engineer refused to have anything to do with military works, and the man in charge sailed for England leaving a large debt on the books.

The officer appointed to get things back on track was Colonel Charles Waddington, the executive engineer for the Northern Provinces and thus Donohoe's top boss in Disa. A seasoned administrator, Waddington needed the best men he could get. So in late 1847 or early 1848 Anna's capable stepfather sailed to Aden to sweat it out for two or three years. He would be back in Pune, however, for her wedding on Christmas Day, 1849.

Since Anna left nothing on record about Aden, it is uncertain whether she and her mother and other family members joined Patrick. There is reason to think they were with him in March 1849, but it also seems likely, in view of the port's rugged conditions and blistering heat, that they spent most of this period in the Bombay Presidency.

However, they didn't stay in Disa. From now on, Pune, a choicer location, was the family's permanent base no matter where Patrick was sent. Mary Ann is known to have been living there in late 1849, and Anna would recall spending "a year or two" in Pune before marrying. At some point Patrick secured a house in the conductors' lines—the neat rows of houses assigned to men who had reached that relatively high grade.

Eighty miles east of Bombay, Pune had been the seat of the peshwa, the chief minister of the Maratha princes and one of the most powerful men in India. When the Maratha Confederacy was smashed in 1818, the peshwa's splendid capital was taken over by the British, for whom it became "the finest station in Western India." Travel writer James Gray found its "bracing and invigorating" climate "doubly welcome after the relaxing heat of Bombay." In monsoon season, company engineers would "flock in with their families . . . too happy to exchange their tents and jungle life, for comfortable bungalows."

The Donohoe bungalow was in the large British camp a few miles outside the city walls. This settlement included the regimental and civil lines, laid out in graded rows, and a number of private homes belonging to English residents. According to Gray, most of the houses were "thatched bungalows . . . enclosed by hedges formed of the prickly pear." It is a mark of Patrick's success that by the time he died on 30 October 1864, he had title to at least one additional bungalow. His final rank, deputy commissary and subengineer first class, was about as high as a man not born a gentleman could rise.

In his laborious thirty-six-year march through India and Aden, Anna's stepfather achieved something else few enlisted men could match: he accumulated enough property to justify a last will and testament. This document, signed five days before his death, lists the usual insignia of middle-class life: "Household furniture, linen and wearing apparel, Books, plate, Pictures, China, Horses and Carts." All these possessions together with his "houses . . . in the Conductors lines" (houses in the plural) were left to his "dear wife for her own use and benefit absolutely." She was also designated sole executor and was thus granted powers a tyrannical spouse might have withheld. The burial was conducted by the Roman Catholic military chaplain at Pune. Patrick ended, as he began, in the Church.

Against all odds, we have written (if indirect) evidence of Anna's reaction to his death, which occurred while she was working at the royal palace in Bangkok. Since all relations with her family had terminated, it took three months for the news to reach her. When it finally arrived, she had her eight-year-old son write a short letter to her daughter in England—a letter whose politeness and polish reveal his mother's close supervision: "Dearest Avis[,] Many thanks for your kind letter. I am very well but Mama has been sad because her Uncle is dead but Mama says he did not think of us." Mama's one uncle, William Vaudrey Glasscott II, had died nine years earlier. The death referred to can only have been Patrick's. On the evidence of this letter, Anna was already rescripting her past for her children. The only father she had known was rubbed out and nameless, turned into an uncle who wasn't concerned for her welfare and left her nothing.

And yet we have her son's report that she was saddened by his death. Was that because he did not "think of us"—bequeath a legacy? No doubt, yet more was involved than a forfeited inheritance. The deepest currents of Anna's ardent young life had been mixed up in her stepfather trouble, and now all that turmoil was back on the surface.

A review of her history since leaving home would have shown ten years as the wife of a talented but unsuccessful office worker followed by six hard years as a self-supporting widow. Thomas had been a bold, strenuous, straight-talking man and a loved companion, but he had also been arrogant and quarrelsome, with a truculence that harmed his employability. From the point of view of the engineer who opposed the marriage, he was an unreliable provider who left his widow in distress—as might have been predicted.

Unlike Patrick, a practical engineer who built a successful life within the rigid colonial structure, Anna was an aspiring dreamer who defied the whole massive system by daring to wed an independent-minded idealist. After fifteen years of struggle it would have been hard not to wonder if her choice had been a mistake. Yet how could the loyal widow admit that her plodding stepparent had been right?

Like so many others who have had to make a fateful choice under extremely hard conditions, Anna ended up creating a fictional version of her life based on a scapegoat. Transforming Thomas into a noble officer, she cast Patrick as the tyrant whose rancorous disposition lay at the bottom of her troubles. This story, or something like it, was all but inevitable. She *had* to become a fantasist. Where Patrick built a life using metal, stone, and mortar, along with exact measurement and prudent calculation, Anna built a life out of storytelling. This was the fruit of the tree that produced her.

The tree would bear a second crop in Bangkok, where she transformed an old and polygamous king into the ultimate example of vicious domestic tyranny. The wicked king and the rancid stepfather: these were Anna's very own imaginary Siamese twins.

4

Travel and Study
with the Badgers

WHEN ANNA LOOKED BACK to the time preceding her wedding, the
shining feature was a journey to the Middle East in the company of the
Reverend George Percy Badger and his wife. Badger had been a chaplain
in the East India Company with close ties to the Byculla girls' school and a
special interest in the Arabic world. His wife, Maria, had been an adventurous missionary schoolteacher with experience in Kurdistan, Malta, and some
Greek islands. In Anna's mellow retrospect, traveling with this unusual couple had been a genuine intellectual birth. She would speak of them to her
grandchildren "with the happiest appreciation, saying that Mr. Badger taught
her how to observe and opened her mind to perceive surfaces & to analyze
below them, & to enjoy study."

As always, the challenge is to discern what happened. The biographical
sketch Anna gave her lecture agent had this to say about the trip's occasion
and scope: "Unable to endure the domestic tyranny of her stepfather, and
having an ample, independent fortune of her own, Miss Crawford [that
is, Miss Edwards] set out to travel with her friends, Rev. Mr. Badger and
wife, with whom she visited Damascus, Jerusalem, sailed down the Nile,
ascended the cataracts, and explored every city, monument, and ruin of
historic interest in all that region." Much of this must be discounted, the
stepfather's tyranny most obviously, but also the claim that the travelers
visited every historic site "in all that region"—a boast in which Anna was
playing up her role as intrepid Victorian explorer. But the story should not
be tossed out. As we shall see, it contains an authentic shard jutting up from
her storied past—that double destination, Egypt and Syria.

Anna's grandchildren had the impression that the trip lasted three years and formed a kind of traveling tutorial in geography, history, and the Arabic and Persian languages. They also believed that their grandmother had an entourage, a pair of married servants named Miriam Beebe and Moonshee. These were the same attendants, originally from India, whom she claimed to have had in Siam and whose names were generic: *Beebe* was a way of spelling *bibi*, and a *munshi* was a Muslim teacher of Persian and other tongues.

When Margaret Landon worked on *Anna and the King of Siam* in the 1940s, she realized that the trip could not have lasted three years. Shortening it to less than a year, she explained it as a tactical arrangement by which Anna's parents tried to temper her headstrong romance with Thomas Leonowens. The surmise was a shrewd one, as was Landon's insight into the trip's value: "It was a rich education for an impressionable girl, better than any the schools of her day had to offer."

Three decades later, when William S. Bristowe came out with his exposé of Anna, the journey was given a very different and highly suggestive spin: "Anna met the thirty-year-old Mr. Badger in 1845 when she was fourteen. He had arrived in India as an Assistant Chaplain and she accompanied him to the Middle East when he was transferred there in the following year. He was not married (as her account claimed) and when he did eventually find a wife she was three years younger than Anna." Bristowe was certain that Badger "paid for" his young female companion's expenses but refrained from spelling out the obvious implication. He also refrained from documenting his intriguing claims about the chaplain's matrimonial history. Still, the erotic insinuations were too good not to be true, and later scholars happily amplified them.

The most delightful version of the nymphet's Oriental travels with her clerical master appeared in 1999 in *The Story of Anna and the King*, an attractive coffee-table book accompanying the motion picture of that name. According to the professional writer who was retained by Twentieth Century-Fox to compile the volume, after fourteen-year-old Anna refused to marry the man selected by her stepfather, she "ran away to Malaysia with a missionary . . . [who] taught her Persian and Arabic and history while they spread the Word of God among the Malay. After four years Anna returned to India."

A recent biography of Anna assumes that the trip never happened, all versions being equally bogus. But there are two reasons to believe in it. The first is that explicit mention of Egypt and Syria. The second is that there simply had to be someone to push the girl beyond the narrow limits of her schooling—someone to exemplify the dignity, the *possibility*, of learning, language study, travel writing, and literary effort. Unlike the Bombay Education Society's lady patroness, who scoffed at the notion that charity girls with complexions of bister or ocher should be taught the modern *"ologies,"* George and Maria Badger inspired Anna with a dream of rising above the destiny assigned to her in India.

The Badgers merit a close look. Without them, there's an inexplicable gap in the life we are following. With them, we catch our first glimpse of a powerful aspiration.

Much Actuated by Ambition

Anna's Indian destiny had been made clear in April 1845, when her older sister Eliza, barely fifteen, married a trooper two and a half times her age. The wedding took place in Disa, where thirteen-year-old Anna left her name on the marriage register as a precocious legal witness—*A. Edwards*. Chances are, everyone assumed that *A. Edwards* would also enter an arranged marriage to a safe older man in the Honorable Company.

What the Badgers offered the girl was the thrill of alternative models. Like Maria, Anna could be a teacher and find worthwhile employment anywhere in the world. Like George, she could study and write books about the peoples of the East. She might even take a more intellectual, companionable, and gentlemanly husband than the older army men her female relatives accepted. In the end, Anna chose to be and do all three.

A basic reason Badger proved such an influence was that he, too, was a blend. Having grown up on Malta as an English Christian who spoke Arabic, he had a uniquely hyphenated identity. A girl anxious about her own mixed inheritance would naturally want to watch this older and most unusual linguistic and cultural hybrid.

He was born in Chelmsford in 1815, the son of a quartermaster sergeant in His Majesty's Eightieth (Staffordshire Volunteers) Regiment of Foot. Five years later, when the outfit was shipped to the Mediterranean, the sergeant's wife and children accompanied him. By the summer of 1821 they were in barracks on Malta, where, on 26 July 1823, the boy's father died. A year and a half later his widow, Ann, married a private in her late husband's regiment.

Growing up on Malta, young George became fluent in the island's Arabic dialect. In his teens he spent two years in Beirut, deepening his immersion in Arab culture and mastering classical Arabic while working for missionaries. A sister went even further, so to speak, marrying a Chaldean Christian and settling in Mosul in present-day Iraq. That was where their mother, Ann Badger, spent her last years, very far indeed from her native land.

Like Anna, George did not have the advantage of a good education, yet he succeeded in becoming a respected Arabist, known for his English-Arabic lexicon. Much of his early learning was scratched together while working for religious presses on Malta and in Beirut. In his twenties he wrote a well-informed guidebook to Malta, which stayed in print for decades. Often speaking up for non-English points of view, he was a century ahead of his time in preferring *Islam* to *Mohammedanism*. He could be cuttingly sarcastic about the speed with which the British resorted to violence overseas, yet there was no question but that his ultimate loyalty was to the West.

His wife, Maria Christiana Wilcox, daughter of an English clergyman, had come to the Mediterranean as a missionary schoolteacher. Far from being a budding teenager, she was three years older than George. Following their marriage on Malta in 1840, they sailed to England so that he could attend the Church Missionary Society's college in Islington. He planned to return to the Mediterranean as a missionary for the society and was duly ordained in 1842, but then, owing to his familiarity with the Middle East, his career took an abrupt and fateful turn.

It happened that, before leaving Malta, he had drafted a brief report that caused an excited stir in London's upper ecclesiastical circles. It concerned the Druse of Lebanon, a Shiite sect going back to the eleventh century. Secretive, self-contained, and concentrated in Lebanon's mountain villages, the Druse had their own reasons for seeking a strategic alliance with England. During his time in Beirut, Badger had gotten to know them, not well, but enough to claim that they were ripe for Anglican conversion. Impressed, the bishop of London asked the young man to undertake a mission to the Druse. But then Lebanon's endemic sectarian violence broke out, the mission was canceled, and Badger got an even more delicate assignment: make contact with the Nestorian Christians of Kurdistan.

This isolated sect, more properly known as the Old East Syrian Church or Church of the East, was a remnant of the ancient Persian church of pre-Islamic times. Because of its links to Christianity's earliest period, Anglicans were eager to make contact, hoping to unearth ancient manuscripts and negotiate an official union. Those were the two chief objects of Badger's mission.

So from 1842 to 1844, enduring serious hardships, he and his wife traveled by mule in what is now eastern Turkey and northern Syria and Iraq. Once, having been on the move for thirteen hours, Maria "fainted as soon as she left the saddle." In Mosul the pair contracted a fever that kept them bedridden for months. After Maria was back on her feet, she started a school for girls orphaned in a Kurdish massacre of Christians. One of her charges was a small bereft child named Rendi, who was taken into the Badgers' home and "treated as one of the family."

This strenuous mission convinced George that the Church of England was well positioned to reform the Church of the East and bring it into the Anglican fold. The plan became a fixed idea, as did his suspicion of both Catholic and evangelical missions. By now he had become a very high Anglican, with vehement opinions on ritual and apostolic authority, and he was so intemperate in defending and promoting his dream that other missionaries were alienated. "If Mr. B. were not so violent, & did not go to extremes," one of them confided, "his knowledge . . . of the habits, manners, customs . . . of those parts would make him a powerful instrument for that very reform wh. he desires so ardently. . . . I think he is much actuated by ambition."

This judgment was close to the truth. Badger was a keen observer of the Middle East, but he was also the kind of strategist who gets obsessed with big-picture visions and schemes. In later life, he would serve British interests in Oman, Egypt, and Zanzibar, not as missionary, however, but as mediator, diplomat, and double agent. His last years would be devoted to scholarship.

Following the collapse of his grand design for the Church of the East, Badger secured an appointment as assistant chaplain in the Honorable Company's Bombay Presidency, his first and last stable institutional base. It was this job that brought the frustrated international operator into Anna's world.

A Fortnight with Total Want of Sleep

He landed in Bombay in May 1845, accompanied by Maria and one of her sisters. His first assignment was to an upland city well to the south of Bombay, Kolhapur, where for the next sixteen months he performed the usual duties of a company chaplain. In late 1846 he was transferred to a more permanent post, one where his knowledge of Arabic and the Middle East would not be wasted—Aden. His wife came with him, but her precarious health compelled her to return to England several years later.

Since Patrick Donohoe would also be posted to Aden in late 1847, it is thought that his stepdaughter made contact with the chaplain and his wife there. Perhaps, yet it isn't clear that the engineer brought his family with him, and in addition the basic idea of Anna's travels in the Middle East with the Badgers has always been cloudy. Margaret Landon may have intuited the situation correctly—a strong-willed young woman in love with a man her stepfather can't stand, and a mother who arranges a cooling-off trip with a respected married couple—but that still leaves many questions. Like Bristowe, we must wonder who paid for Anna's travels. And what did it mean, socially, for a young single woman to join a respectable married couple on such an extensive trip?

On the money question, a surviving fragment of a letter of Maria's shows that in the 1840s the Badgers were financially strapped. Just to cover their "necessary expenses on going to India," they had to borrow £200. Making matters worse, the sister who was with them proved a serious financial drain. The implications: they needed extra income; Anna's trip wasn't charity. Her reference years later to an "independent fortune" shows that she knew some sort of accounting was necessary. In all likelihood, her travel expenses were paid by her mother and/or stepfather. Not only that, but, since it was customary for clergymen to supplement their income by taking live-in pupils, it may well be that the agreement included paid tutoring.

In an earlier chapter, we saw how a company chaplain in Disa helped an army officer place his Anglo-Indian children with an English cleric, an arrangement we know about thanks to a private journal. For Anna there are no such sources, yet we do have a fortuitous report of Badger's behind-the-scenes operations shortly before his travels with Anna. When the Bombay Education Society's Byculla girls' school was thrown into crisis by its headmistress's illness, he wrote from Aden to advise the bishop of Bombay that he knew of an able teacher on Malta, one Isabella Thorn, who would soon be available and, further, that "he had reason to believe that the Bishop of Gibraltar would give her a very strong recommendation." And it all worked as planned. Thorn's papers proved to be in good order, and in July 1848 she landed in Bombay and took charge of the school. Badger looks to have been an inside player in the world of colonial educational benevolence.[1]

Yet at this very time Badger himself was struggling with his own medical crisis. Dating from the summer of 1847, it was diagnosed as "Congestion of the Brain" by the senior physician posted to Aden. The medical report makes curious reading. "Intense pain in the Temples and Eyes" was the initial symptom. This grew worse, "till Delirium supervened with Symptoms of Coma. . . . The Delirium continued for a fortnight with total want of sleep. . . . Subsequently he lay for a Month, in a most precarious state, the lower part of the body being completely paralyzed nor did he regain the use of his limbs till put on board the Steamer proceeding to Bombay."

Also on this steamer (the *Acbar*, a company ship) were Maria and two servants. Badger had been given a three-month sick leave. Arriving in Bombay on 5 August 1847, he convalesced there and in Pune, recovered faster than was expected, and returned to Aden a few weeks before his leave expired. For a time his health remained "tolerably good."

But his illness—"an inveterate nervous affection," he later termed it—had not gone away. The next summer the headache came back, particularly, his doctors noted, "at the new and full Moon."[2] By 1849 it was so severe that "any mental exertion . . . brings on paroxysms of continued pain in the temples and eyes which deprive him of sleep for nights in succession and reduce him to a state verging on Delirium." He was prescribed mercury plaster, calomel, Blue Pill, compound Rhubarb Pill, large amounts of quinine, and (interestingly) occasional morphine. Nothing helped, and when his face began to swell his doctors concluded that "a change of Climate is

1. As another sign of Badger's close involvement with the Byculla school, he once preached a series of sermons at Christ Church, which served as its chapel.

2. Travelers to the hot countries often blamed the moon for their many complaints. The patroness of the Bombay Education Society had no doubt that the moon in India "has more power and influence [than in Europe], especially in fevers—the invalid generally suffering more at certain of the moon's phases."

absolutely necessary" and recommended that he "proceed to Egypt and Syria" on two years' sick leave.

On 29 March 1849 George and Maria Badger left Aden on the Peninsular and Oriental Line's largest ship, the *Bentinck*. Six days later they disembarked at Suez and the recuperative tour began. This was the trip Anna remembered.

A MIND OPENED

Badger's only known account of the tour is in his book about the Nestorians. There, in a transitional paragraph between his narratives of his two expeditions to Kurdistan, he briefly surveys his appointment as chaplain, his nervous malady, and the prescription for a change of climate and then states that he and "Mrs. Badger, the untiring partner of my wanderings, spent a short time in Egypt, and passed a summer in one of the villages on mount Lebanon." Mount Lebanon was not a political entity but a region, a part of Syria. The reality behind Anna's grandiose exploratory journey was a spring in Egypt and a summer in the refreshing Lebanese mountains.

The ship the travelers boarded for the first leg of this trip, the *Bentinck*, was the regular packet between Calcutta and Suez. The fact that it hadn't called at Bombay after rounding Ceylon (Sri Lanka) means that Anna must have arrived in Aden on some other vessel. There is no definitive documentary proof that she left with the Badgers, yet the circumstantial evidence is abundant and compelling.

The couple were used to taking single women under their wing while traveling. In Kurdistan there was the orphaned Rendi, and in Kolhapur there was Maria's younger sister, Helena (who, like Anna, was not mentioned in print). Maria was always on the lookout for benevolent projects to organize—a school for needy girls, a philanthropic sewing circle. On Malta, where events prevented her from opening an infant school, she was "not happy to remain idle" and looked forward to starting a girls' boarding school in Syria. As for George, he had recently rescued the Byculla girls' school through his artful long-distance arrangements, and in Kurdistan he had encouraged the Christian hierarchy to establish parochial schools. George knew what it was like to be young and ambitious and to be held back for lack of a proper education. He and Maria were just the sort to take a bright, energetic, rebellious girl in hand and give her the tutoring she needed.

After Egypt came Mount Lebanon. A part of Syria, which in turn belonged to the Ottoman Empire, this largely upland area was inhabited by ethnic and religious groups that had a feudal organization and a view of the world that mandated powerful patrons. The Druse relied on the British for protection; the Maronite Christians looked to France and the Roman Catholic Church. Unfortunately, these alliances seemed to foster an increase in tension and feuding, culminating in serious violence in 1845. However, the end of the decade saw a fragile détente supervised by the Turks. The summer of 1849 was peaceful.

To encourage British support, the Druse welcomed Protestant school-teachers and missionaries, who, like many others, came to regard certain villages as healthy, pleasant refuges from the heat of summer.[3] As an Arabist who was already acquainted with the Druse, Badger would have known where to go—that is, which village to select as his headquarters.[4] Anna may not have seen Damascus and Jerusalem in his company, as she later claimed, since what he chiefly needed was rest, mountain air, and the leisure in which to block out his first big literary effort: his book about his mission to Kurdistan.

Thus, it seems to have been in a quiet village retreat in the Lebanese mountains that Anna's higher education was launched: a program of study and self-improvement overseen by George and Maria Badger. That she tackled Arabic makes sense. She heard it spoken around her, and her teacher had mastered it. Perhaps he had her translate from the Koran, whose diction he regarded as "faultless," with passages of "exquisite sublimity." Its literary beauties, however, had been equaled "by more than one Arabian poet."

As for Persian, the traditional medium of diplomacy and high culture on the Indian subcontinent, Badger was no expert, but he knew the language

3. Englishmen living in Lebanon vastly preferred the Druse to the Maronites. The usual point of view was expressed by Charles Henry Churchill: "In social intercourse, in the repose and dignity of their manners, in the forms of politeness and the charms of address, the Druse Sheiks are greatly superior to the Christian aristocracy of the Lebanon."

4. In June 1849 American missionary Eli Smith, writing from Beirut, warned his mission board that the Church Missionary Society had an "agent in Syria"—Badger, it seems—whose eye was "particularly on Mosul." Fifteen years earlier Badger had been the American's employee, protégé, and friend; now they were acrimonious enemies. The Smiths spent that summer in a mountain village called Bhamdoun.

well enough to serve as field translator some years later. Persian was precisely what a young, ambitious, high-toned Anglo-Indian would want to study. That Anna acquired any fluency in speech is doubtful, as the usual method of instruction was translation from classic authors, not oral drill. Three decades later she sold a clumsy rendering of a famous poem by Saadi to an American children's magazine.

In 1847 Badger had thrown off his malaise and cut short his medical leave. Now, with his health returning, he apparently got to work on his book about his mission to Kurdistan, *The Nestorians and Their Rituals*. As he reviewed his journals from 1842 to 1844 (which the book extensively cites), he would have given Anna a practical demonstration of the program a serious literary traveler follows: scrupulous observation, regular note taking, the habit of composition. No doubt she studied Arabic and Persian, but the real lesson was the insight into what it means to be a perceptive intellectual traveler. As she fondly recalled for her grandchildren, the chaplain "taught her how to observe and opened her mind to perceive surfaces & to analyze below them."

In 1851, when the tour was a receding memory and she was married and living in Bombay, a city newspaper reported that Badger's book was finished. "As he is really a clever fellow," wrote a correspondent from Aden, "I expect it will be interesting." Parts of it were, particularly Maria's well-written report of a visit to a Yezidi village near Mosul. The Yezidis were a remnant people with a very different religion from the three surrounding monotheisms. Often seen as devil worshipers, they preserved themselves by strictly limiting external contacts. In spite of this secretiveness, they let Maria observe a sacred ritual in which a small brass statuette of a sacred fowl, the Senjaq, was brought out and displayed. Her sketch of the object was reproduced in her husband's book, which likened the stylized bird with its "flat and fluted" tail to an Assyrian bas-relief that had recently been dug up. From this and other evidences, Badger concluded that the Yezidi religion was a living relict of ancient Zoroastrianism.[5]

That, too—the skill to see things hidden for ages—was what Anna seems to have meant when she spoke of looking at "surfaces" and analyzing "below

5. Those who have not forgotten the catastrophes incident to the recent Anglo-American invasion of Iraq will recall the suicide bombings of 14 August 2007, when two Yezidi villages were flattened and hundreds of inhabitants murdered.

them." In later years she would go in for this herself, often quite recklessly, as when she theorized about "the early Aryan" priesthood or described a woman as "the purest Indo-European type."

Traveling with the Badgers was a thrilling initiation. The profound impression it made on the young woman can be seen in the advice she sent her daughter years later. Anna was in Bangkok at the time, and Avis was boarding at a genteel school in London. It was there that the nine-year-old girl attempted to make sense of this maternal counsel: "Note everything you see—try to understand the shape, form size, general appearance, inner beauties, peculiar proportions and outward aspects of everything." That wasn't the half of it. Anna also announced that Avis would be expected to follow an exacting linguistic and literary program: "When we meet again I hope your mind will be sufficiently cultivated to make you like Arabic, Persian, Hindoostani and Siamese—and then we shall have the delight of reading together some . . . fanciful but really beautiful Oriental works which I have been selecting." The mother who wrote that passage, having never been to England, sincerely imagined that she could induce a child brought up in a suburban girls' school to tackle all those languages and literatures. Anna's education had been seriously defective, and her critical judgment, historical perspective, and notion of "cultivation" would always be as vagrant as they were absolute. And yet, unlike educated Europeans, she had lived in the East and known the thrill of reading classic Asian texts in the original languages. It was only natural that she would want to pass that on to her daughter.

What Anna took from Badger was the recognition that Asia was a rich field for study and that its languages, customs, surfaces, everything merited close attention. The great irony is that, in writing and lecturing on Asian topics, she concealed her personal Asian past. Unlike her mentor, who was definitely English in spite of his inner divisions, she wasn't, quite. Uneasily aware of her vulnerability on that point, she predicated her books about Asia on a denial of the divided and fractured East that lay within—an act of suppression that allowed an unreal and at times vindictive element to enter her work, especially when it came to Siam.

Something else Anna took from Badger, the most dangerous thing of all perhaps, was a certain messianic quality—a conviction that one is specially called to bring about some grand reform. When a young person comes under the influence of an adult who knows his way around the world and also has far-reaching designs on entire peoples, nations, and religions, the experience can make a deep impression. That was the real act of seduction.[6] Just as George believed he could effect a union between the ancient Church of the East and the Church of England, Anna came to see her work at the Siamese court as having cleansed the land of slavery. One of the terms for this is megalomania, a disease she may have caught from the ambitious but frustrated chaplain.

At summer's end, Anna parted ways with George and Maria. With his two-year sick leave still mostly before him, the chaplain and his wife returned to Mesopotamia. By early December they were back in his sister's house in Mosul, and before long he was hard at work on his Nestorian book. By then Anna had returned home, no doubt by way of Suez, where travelers caught the East India Company steamers that shuttled between that port and Bombay. With a stop in Aden, the passage took two and a half weeks. Her tour had lasted half a year. Seeing Bombay from the water would have been a vivid eye-opening treat. Decades later she described the moment in *Life and Travel in India*, claiming, however, that she was a schoolgirl fresh from England seeing the city for the first time.

By late October she was in the English camp at Pune. Mary Ann was established there now, no doubt with some of her younger children. Anna's sister Eliza and her husband and first two children were living nearby.

A letter came from the clerk Anna had fallen in love with. The question it asked was one to which they both knew the answer, namely, that nothing had changed. "Do you, Annie, love me, continue to love me as of yore? But why ask you! knowing as I do, how constant and true the heart is that has blessed me with its pure and true affections!" At the end the writer asked her to "remember me most kindly to Mamma and all." Nothing was said of her stepfather, probably in Aden. The signature: "your own Leon."

6. In his last years, as his biographer reveals, Badger "had an intense *amitié amoureuse*" with a woman over forty years his junior. Inevitably, this disclosure prompts questions about the chaplain's feelings for teenage girls and his interest in the Byculla girls' school in the 1840s and 1850s. One also wonders if Bristowe's insinuations of a traveling affair with Anna were inspired by a lingering trace of this late sentimental romance.

5

Beloved Wife of
Thomas Leonowens

And darling remember that to be a wife is the sweetest boon God has
given to woman.

—Anna to daughter Avis on her honeymoon

MORE THAN THE USUAL British marriage in nineteenth-century India,
Anna's union with Thomas Leonowens was loving, companionable, and rich
in shared interests. The couple had four children to whom they were deeply
attached (two died in infancy), and they led a venturesome life in Bombay, Western Australia, Singapore, and Penang. Following Thomas's death
in 1859, Anna had good offers and could have remarried, but she chose to
remain Mrs. Leonowens for the rest of her long and active life.

When she died in 1915, fifty-five years after her husband, the gravestone
her grandchildren ordered in Montreal said nothing about her teaching in
Siam or her career as author, lecturer, and reformer. Instead, the memorial
proclaimed her the "Beloved Wife of / Major Thomas Lorne Leonowens."
Except for *Lorne*, which may have been the stone chiseler's blunder for *Louis*,
the inscription perfectly caught Anna's proud and defiant sense of her marriage. *Major*, so much more impressive than *Paymaster Sergeant*, was the
posthumous rank she awarded her husband, and *Beloved Wife*, the salient
phrase, touched on the inner truth of their match—that each had judged
the world well lost for the other.

Yet something in their married life had gone wrong. Forty years after
Thomas's death, John Thomas Pratt, one of her Anglo-Indian relatives, sent
a delicately phrased letter hinting at the problem. Writing from Beijing,

where he was starting out in the Foreign Service career that would lead to a knighthood, the youthful diplomat was nervously aware that Anna had broken with her people in India, his own line included, and thus he directed the letter not to Anna but to her daughter Avis.[1] In it he stated that he had recently learned from his mother of Anna's "unhappiness and trouble," and then he added (apparently reaching for common ground) that his mother's "married life has been almost as unhappy as that of Mrs. Leonowens."

Pratt's mother, a daughter of Anna's sister, had in fact been so badly abused by her spouse that she had secured a judicial separation on grounds of cruelty. What did her son have in mind when he likened her ordeal to Anna's? Was he privy to something about his great-aunt that never got put down on paper? Was he misinformed?

The nature of Anna's marital "unhappiness and trouble" can still be glimpsed, though the picture, as we shall see, is frustratingly grainy. But before we look at it, we should pause before one of Rudyard Kipling's wry, knowing, and openly racist depictions of life in British India.

"Kidnapped," a story about the folly of love matches in the empire, tells how a young English civil servant is abducted by friends in order to keep him from marrying a sweet young thing with lovely violet eyes—a beauty whose "opal-tinted onyx at the base of her finger-nails" gives away her Portuguese-Indian ancestry. Convinced that the man would be mad to go through with the wedding, Kipling assures us that he "came to his right mind again" and will eventually marry a "pink-and-white maiden, on the Government House List, with a little money and some influential connections." She won't be a stunner, but she will have the right skin tones, and his career will henceforth stay on track.

More than an exercise in cynicism, Kipling's story was based on the realities of Indian colonial life. The English formed a tiny fraction of the population, their role as rulers entailed a rigid separation, and their lives were hedged with constraints.[2] Young officers and civil servants could not afford

1. Pratt was not the only member of his family who proved successful. His youngest brother, William Henry Pratt, the ne'er-do-well among his siblings, became the actor known as Boris Karloff.
2. The East India Company's directors considered it imperative "to preserve the ascendancy which our National Character has acquired over the minds of the Natives of India." To that end, writes C. J. Hawes, they insisted on maintaining "a wide behavioural and social distance from all things and peoples Eastern."

to marry until their careers were well under way, and then a man had to select his wife with care, as she would be his responsible associate—his imperial helpmate, as historian Mary A. Procida puts it. From any point of view that recognized the challenges Thomas faced in India, his union with Anna was premature and imprudent. That he took the risk anyway, marrying not for success but for love, beauty, and brains, helps explain her lifelong attitude toward him. "Kidnapped" tells us why she is the *Beloved Wife* of Major Leonowens on her tombstone.

What the story doesn't reveal is that the marriage was even riskier for her, for the simple reason that Thomas was *not* on track for a decent career. He was isolated and had no money or prospects, and there was a blot on his record. Anna's stepfather had reasons to frown on the match. If a young woman in her position married a reliable subordinate, as her mother, aunt, and sister had done, she would make out reasonably well, but if she tied herself to a man on the loose, she might end up (as Kipling put it with characteristic bluntness) in "forsaken guts and creeks / No decent soul would think of visiting." Which is pretty much what happened to Anna when Thomas took her to Western Australia and she spent fifteen months in a desolate convict hiring depot. Worse yet was what happened after she joined him in Penang.

The government, Kipling joked, "should establish a Matrimonial Department, efficiently officered, with a Jury of Matrons, a Judge of the Chief Court, a Senior Chaplain, and an Awful Warning, in the shape of a love-match that has gone wrong, chained to the trees in the courtyard." Anna and Thomas were one of those Awful Warnings. Aiming at something higher than the usual partnership, they took a huge and honorable gamble. That the results were painfully mixed helps explain why Anna always spoke with pride of her wifehood . . . and never let on what it was actually like.

PAYMASTER SERGEANT

When Thomas was baptized in early 1824 in Enniscorthy, Ireland, the rector recorded his name as Thomas Lane Owens. The middle name came from his mother, born Mary Lean of Templeshanbo Parish. *Lean* was the preferred spelling.

Enniscorthy was a market town of 4,600 souls living in thatched houses on streets so steep, narrow, and irregular that the place struck a visitor as "half-oriental." Thomas's father, John Owens, a boot- and shoemaker, had a house and shop in Barrack Street near the center of town. As an artisan-tradesman, he did well enough that he let out dwelling houses and got his sons schooled. The older, Gunnis Lean Owens, became a draper (dealer in cloth) in Wexford, the county town. In 1851, soon after the Famine, this son took cabin passage to New York City on a vessel whose steerage was packed with poor Irish emigrants. Only four other men, a doctor and three "gentlemen," paid for cabins. Gunnis, it seems, had clawed his way into the gentry. But as usual the picture is murky: before crossing the ocean he went bankrupt, and he can't be traced in America.

In all likelihood, younger brother Thomas was also brought up to be a tradesman or clerk. But one can only guess, there being no extant records for him prior to 28 June 1842, the day the seventeen- or eighteen-year-old youth enlisted in the army. He did that in Liverpool, the booming port and manufacturing center that had become a magnet for job-seekers (there were weekly steam packets between Liverpool and Wexford). A recruit was paid a shilling a day. The bounty for enlisting was sixty times as much, three pounds in "cash and necessaries"—a strong inducement. For the next five years Thomas would lead a soldier's life in Her Majesty's Twenty-Eighth (North Gloucestershire) Regiment of Foot.

Unlike Anna's father and stepfather, who both joined the East India Company's "commercial" army, as it was styled, Thomas entered the more prestigious Royal Army. He did so a year after county Wexford held a hard-fought election, with the Conservative incumbent voted out of office and the local Catholic peasantry said to be "in a state of actual rebellion." That British troops were often called in to keep the peace and enforce the collection of Ireland's unpopular poor rates suggests a possible motive for the young man's enlistment: a desire to stand with the forces of (Protestant) law and order. But this is conjecture, and in any case he was deployed to England. It was there, at army depots in Chatham and Canterbury, that *Lean* turned into *Leon* and began serving as a first name, just as in his letters to Anna a few years later.[3]

3. It is often said that Anna created her last name after Thomas's death in 1859. In fact, he minted it himself. When he married her in 1849 he wrote LeonOwens as his surname. The odd capital O seems to have thrown others off, and by 1853 he was simply Leonowens.

Private Owens's military career took a dramatic turn on 7 July 1843, when he and sixty-two other recruits in the Twenty-Eighth Regiment glided down the Thames, bound for Bombay on the *Coromandel*. Sailing around the Cape of Good Hope, the vessel took nearly five months to complete its voyage. The young man would never see Ireland again.

A few days after disembarking in Bombay, he advanced from private to corporal. A month later, on New Year's Day 1844, after his outfit marched to Pune, he was again promoted, this time to paymaster sergeant, also known as paymaster's clerk. From now on, Thomas was the man who did the tedious regimental paperwork. His daily pay, one shilling ten pence, was nearly twice what he had been getting. This quick rise is a sign of the talents that made it easy for him to find clerical work in later years in Singapore and Western Australia. State records in the latter colony leave no doubt that Anna's husband was a quick study, made a good first impression, wrote a clear and elegant hand, and had an easy mastery of the protocols of bookkeeping and bureaucratic letter writing.

In November 1845 the Twenty-Eighth left Pune for the cantonment at Disa. The march took forty days, and the resulting illnesses and injuries, according to the official report, were "rather numerous." During the 1846 monsoon, there were "fevers & bowel Complaints" owing to the "humid state of the atmosphere, & the increase of vegitation," and when the rains came in 1847 more than one hundred "weakly men" had to be sent to Mount Abu to recuperate. According to a patient there, "By far the most prevalent complaint amongst our troops . . . in Guzerat [Gujarat] . . . is fever, generally intermittent."

Thomas was stationed in Disa for all of 1846 and most of 1847. Conceivably, he could have met Anna in Pune during the previous two years if her stepfather did as other engineers and took his family there for the rainy season. But the couple are more likely to have met in the cantonment at Disa, where the Donohoes had their home. One can't help but wonder how and where romance managed to bloom—at church, in the soldiers' library, during social hour in the mess room? Was Anna home on holiday from the Byculla girls' school? But the record is blank, and all we really know is that the courtship faced serious opposition from Anna's stepfather.

In 1846 Anna turned fifteen, an age when girls like her were expected to settle down with a suitable older man. Was it time for the headmistress at

Byculla to scan the secure and stable bachelors and find the one for Anna? Her older sister had been only fourteen when she accepted a man with excellent credentials, a sergeant major in the Horse Artillery who had served for twenty years and would soon be pensioned.[4]

Years later Anna claimed that her stepfather had wanted to match her with "a rich Indian merchant, an older man and in every way very objectionable." Arranged marriages were still fairly common, yet the details of this story are suspect for the simple reason that no Glascott woman ever married a merchant, whether Indian or British. They all married into the Corps of Engineers or some other well-regarded branch of the army or civil service, and the transaction brought status and security. Anna's story was a red herring, invoking the widespread disapproval of racially mixed unions in order to draw attention from the fact that her romance with a paymaster's clerk had not been prudent.

The many differences between Anna's stepfather and suitor—the former a Roman Catholic civil engineer slowly climbing the ranks, the latter a talented Protestant clerk with a mind of his own—made it all the harder for her to recognize Thomas's deficits. If she married him and he stayed in the Twenty-Eighth Regiment, her future could be both humiliating and insecure. As Myna Trustram has shown in her study of domestic life in the Victorian army, a sergeant's wife might find employment in the regimental school, but more than likely she would have to "do for" the officers—do their humble housekeeping chores for pay. For lodging, she could look forward to "a curtained off corner of the barrack hut." She would have to follow her husband's outfit when it left India, and if it returned to England, she would be made to feel her place, a fairly low one, in society. There were solid objections to Anna's young romance.

On top of all that, while Thomas was stationed in Disa he was given a disciplinary punishment. On 9 April 1846, as muster rolls disclose, he was reduced from paymaster sergeant all the way back to private. He may not have been flogged, but there is no doubt he underwent a significant loss in

---

4. After taking his pension in 1850, Eliza's husband, James Millard, found an outlet for his versatile administrative talents. Moving to Bombay, he served as inspector of roads and then as superintendent of the David Sassoon Industrial and Reformatory Institution. The founder of this establishment, a wealthy Jewish merchant originally from Baghdad, was a great-grandfather of the English poet and pacifist Siegfried Sassoon.

status and pay.[5] Whether he was punished by command of his colonel or by a court-martial is uncertain. The Donohoes would have known.

Also unrecorded was the nature of his offense. The more common ones were drunkenness, absence from duty, and insolence. Insolence would be a plausible guess in Thomas's case, given his official rebuke some years later for his "improper" tone toward a superior. Once, after leaving India, he declared that the British officers there were often "inferior in mind to the Native troops they command."

Thomas said that in Australia, where, as the record makes clear, he chafed under authority, took fierce and downright views, and was apt to get his Irish up. He definitely had a quick temper. His military punishment may well be linked to the volatile personal qualities that partly explain his disappointing career. If Anna's stepfather was the slow and steady tortoise, her husband was the perfect hare—fast, smart, gifted, and always losing in the end, a true heartbreaker.

In 1856, when Thomas was asked for his "Rank or Profession" while working as a commissariat storekeeper, he rose above his bureaucratic station with a proud one-word answer: *gentleman*. When his widow promoted him from sergeant to major, she was awarding him the elevated social status they both felt he merited. Her little fraud tells us how much her husband's low position, humiliations, and failures must have rankled.

But talent and energy are always in short supply in any army. During the period of Thomas's demotion, a phrase scribbled next to his name in the muster rolls, "on duty," shows he continued performing his work as clerk and wasn't incarcerated. After eleven months of that he was restored to his former rank, paymaster sergeant.

In late 1847, about the time Donohoe was sent to Aden, the Twenty-Eighth Regiment was ordered to leave Disa, proceed to Bombay, and embark for England. With that, Sergeant Owens faced the toughest and most momentous choice of his life. If he chose to remain in western India for the sake of the intelligent dark-eyed girl he now loved, he would forfeit his free passage home and have to find his own means of support. But what if he wasn't able to overcome her stepfather's objections: would he end up a solitary wanderer unable to return to Ireland or England?

5. Opinion was building against flogging, which was abolished in the British army twenty years later. Some commanding officers already disallowed it in their regiments.

In early 1848 three vessels sailed out of Bombay harbor carrying the men of the Twenty-Eighth back to Britain. Taking the chance of a lifetime, Thomas stayed behind. He would no longer be subject to the military's structured rules, and if Anna married him, she would not have to put up with the deprivations and humiliations of a sergeant's wife. But if the army hemmed you in, it also looked after you. From now on, as Thomas faced the battle of life, he would have to depend solely on his wits. As would Anna.

Bombay and the Color Line

Bombay (today Mumbai) was already one of the world's great metropolises, with more than half a million inhabitants. India's most culturally diverse city, it was home to a huge variety of peoples, languages, religions. Typically, even its Chamber of Commerce was "a joint Indian and European creation."

The British were in charge, yet it was the wealthy and cosmopolitan Parsis—descendants of the Zoroastrians who had fled Islamic Persia centuries before—who ran the economy. Bombay had only 1,600 nonofficial Europeans (Thomas's category), but there were 115,000 Parsis. The mercantile language was the Parsi tongue, Gujarati.

Some years later Thomas stated that while living in Bombay he had been "personally acquainted with a Gentleman Parsee, a Shipbuilder whose work in that branch of Science was Superb." He could have been referring to Cursetjee Rustomjee Wadia, the master builder who oversaw construction of the mighty eighty-gun *Meanee*, a British ship of the line whose November 1848 launch, the year's most dramatic event, was said to be watched by one hundred thousand spectators—a fifth of Bombay's population. The *Minden*, the British battleship on which Francis Scott Key composed "The Star-Spangled Banner" while being detained overnight, had been built in the Bombay dockyards by an earlier Parsi master builder, Jamsetjee Bomanjee.

Heretofore, what the young man had learned about India was picked up from within the British military, with its clean lines of authority and good-humored disdain for "blacks" (meaning anyone not white). Now he was thrown into a far more complicated world, modern in some ways, ancient in others, and full of ambiguities.

With his experience as paymaster sergeant, he soon found bureaucratic work, first at the Commissary General's Office and then in the Military Pay Office, where his position seems to have been "Assistant Military Pay officer." His workplace would have been in the part of Bombay known as the Fort. For a time he shared living quarters with two of Anna's relatives, her half-brother John Donohoe and uncle William Vaudry Glasscott. The former, called Johnny, became a clerk in his late teens and spent his life laboring in various branches of government in Bombay, Karachi, and elsewhere. Glasscott, the last child of Anna's English grandfather, was a couple of years older than Thomas. He too was a clerk, employed at the Military Board Office. He had been there since 1844 and would stay on, unpromoted, till 1852. He, Johnny, and Thomas were all fellow cogs in the colonial entity that Karl Marx derided as an "immense writing machine." If one were limited to a single encompassing image of Britain's Indian Empire, one could do worse than picture a hot and humid room full of clerks filling out forms and ledgers.

Thomas's roommates had opposite temperaments and reacted differently to the tight conditions of Anglo-Indian life. Johnny seems to have been rather wild, whereas Glasscott, accustomed to being in harness, was the epitome of steady respectability. The conflict between them is nicely evoked in a letter Thomas sent his fiancée: "I should like to know exactly what Glascott has written about Johnny, from various circumstances, and particularly from a conversation I had with him some time ago when he attempted to persuade me that Johnny was irreclaimable. . . . Before Glascott left me he took no notice of nor did he speak to Johnny because the boy had some time before offended him about some trifling matter, and after that when Johnny went near him he was ordered to 'go away from there.' That is by no means the way to treat a boy."

Glasscott and Johnny had a connection with and perhaps attended Trinity Chapel. Located in the Sonapur district, the chapel was part of the Indo-British Institution, whose mission was to serve Bombay's Eurasian population. Anna's uncle could pass as white or nonwhite. When he served on a jury for the Supreme Court's Criminal Sessions, a newspaper twice grouped him with the European jurors before shifting him to the other column: the "non-Europeans."

To be racially indeterminate in nineteenth-century British India was trying in the extreme. Nearly everyone, Indians no less than Britons, took for granted that Eurasians were products of illicit unions and had no real place in society. The English tended to picture them (quoting Kenneth

Ballhatchet) as "poor weakly-looking persons, very sallow and unhealthy in their appearance, and very small in stature." The usual modern term, *Anglo-Indian*, was then applied to Britons residing in India and rarely designated those of mixed race. The respectable eighteenth-century term, *country born*, was obsolescent. Taking its place were *Eurasian, East Indian*, and *Indo-Briton*, all polite. But none of these displaced the derogatory *half-caste* as the popular standard. Most offensive of all was *chee-chee*, a slurring term based on a notion of Eurasians' spoken English. There was even "a contemptuous nickname for a Eurasian clerk"—*cranny*.

The first Indian autobiography written in English shows what it was like to live with these categories. The author, Lutfullah, recalled how his English friends in Surat "often jestingly interrogated me whether both of my parents were natives of India, or one of them English, for my complexion and accent, said they, were different from the natives." To "such rude questions" Lutfullah always gave a gracious reply. His choked feelings came out only after he sailed for England. Happening to break his voyage in Alexandria, he was deeply moved by the ordinary good manners of the Greek consul, who treated him "with such real courtesy and politeness as never can be met with from the Christians in India." The racist denigration must have been constant and unrelenting. Even in Bombay, diverse as it was, the vulgar British term for many districts outside the Fort and Esplanade was, simply, "Black Town."

For Eurasians caught in the middle, the situation was so acute that it prompted strange and desperate remedies. About 1847 Glasscott decided to change his middle name from Frederick to Vaudry. His purpose was surely to highlight his connection with his late father, Lieutenant William Vaudrey Glascott, and thus advance his claims to the respect due to Europeans. Like most Anglo-Indians, he no doubt wished to be identified with the English side of his ancestry. But did the change make any difference? His own signature hints at the answer. Well after taking his father's full name, he would revert to the old one and sign himself *W. F. Glasscott*.

The reason Anglo-Indians identified with the whites who scorned them was that there was no better alternative. The most a Eurasian girl could hope for was to marry into the army, preferably the engineers, as Anna's sister and Glasscott's two older sisters had done. The best a boy could do was to land steady work in the colonial bureaucracy. That was the place for the

Eurasian sons of officers and senior officials, and thus a clerkship became (in the words of historian C. J. Hawes) "the apex of Eurasian aspiration."

Apex means *so high and no higher.* The better-paying and more responsible jobs were always out of reach. There is a simple explanation why Glascott never advanced beyond the grade of clerk during his eight years at the Military Board: half-castes never did, no matter how well qualified. Anna's uncle was decertified by birth and skin color.

It is at this point that we can start to understand the man Anna married and why their union meant so much to her. Instead of adopting the common view of half-castes as cringers and Hindus as blacks, Thomas came to sympathize with their points of view and grievances. He did not go native, whatever that means, but he liberated himself from the usual prejudices. We know that not from Anna's writings (for all her widowed devotion, they never bring him to life) but from the man's own arguments in a discussion class whose proceedings were recorded by an unusually diligent secretary.

This class was gathered in Perth, Australia, in 1854. Among the issues it agreed to debate was this one: "Is the alledged essential intellectual inferiority of the colored races correct?" A clearer and blunter way to say that would be: "Is it true that we whites are more intelligent than darker-skinned people?" Thomas's stated opinions on this question offer an incomparable insight into his mind, character, social attitudes, and marriage.

According to the secretary's minutes, one of Thomas's chief points was that Bombay's colonial government could not function without Hindu and Parsi clerks and accountants. Another was that the "East Indian"—Glasscott's category—had not been treated fairly, being "debarred from the advantages of education." Yet another was that Indians were as "ingenious in works of art, literature, and science" as Europeans. Thomas allowed that dark skin "makes an unfavorable impression" and that, "physically speaking, the English Officers and Soldiers are superior—for there is nothing like that British Bayonet directed with a British hand." But the British were too arrogant to be well informed. Neglecting native languages, they failed to realize that Indians "possess a fund of sound knowledge," being "excellent Mathematicians, Astronomers, and particularly well versed in the history of their own Country." Thomas was categorical: what he had learned in India was that "there is no inferiority of intellect in the Colored races."

These are not the views we associate with British colonials in south Asia. Thomas had little in common with those officers who remained oblivious of everything but billiards and pig sticking. Indeed, he came to see such types as mentally inferior to the natives they commanded, and he realized that the possession of superior military weapons and training had induced a false sense of superiority. Not only did the young man who had belonged to the dominant Protestant population in Catholic Ireland become a racial egalitarian at a time when the imperial British were growing more exclusive and isolated in India, but he worked out a general critique of Western imperial arrogance.

The reason for getting this right is that it helps explain why Thomas and Anna fell in love. As is frequently the case in mixed romances, the barriers the pair had to surmount made their union all the more precious. For Thomas of Enniscorthy, Anna offered an exit from India's enclaves of stultified Englishness. For Anna of Ahmadnagar, bright and aspiring, Thomas offered an entry into the white world and an acceptance free of condescension. Each presented the other with a rare opportunity.

My Own Dearest Annie

What little survives of Thomas and Anna's correspondence dates from after their engagement and her tour with the Badgers. There are only six letters, all by Thomas. They are mostly incomplete, and what we have are not the original documents but typed copies made in the twentieth century. It is a very small trove, it leaves many questions unanswered, and it is immensely revealing.

The first thing one notices is how often money got mentioned. Once, sending Anna a draft for fifty rupees (five pounds), Thomas explained how to cash it at the office of a *shroff* (banker). That she did so seems likely from her description, published years later, of a traditional native bank in Pune. Perhaps, like Badger, she took careful notes.

In another letter, written just before the wedding, Thomas was desperate to confirm that a financial obligation had been successfully discharged: "Did Mr. D. get the Bill on England and was he satisfied with it? You have not said a word on the subject and he has not acknowledged its receipt, so that for all I know it has miscarried, and heaven knows what may be the consequences, to poor me and Johnny." This agitated statement is the sole passage in Anna's surviving papers that names her stepfather, if only by an initial. Though the nature of the transaction remains obscure, it appears that Thomas and Johnny were in debt to Patrick Donohoe, or at least depending on his good offices.

In planning the wedding, Thomas decided to have it legalized by banns instead of a license. In a marriage by banns the chaplain's fee was seventeen rupees. In a marriage by license it was three times as much, a charge Thomas considered "heavy." That was the sort of narrow calculation that would shape the couple's wedded life. Right from the start Anna would have realized she wasn't marrying someone with a comfortable income.

But the most significant revelations in these letters are emotional, not financial. Like other men far from home, Thomas felt lonely and disconnected in Bombay and dreamed of finding solace in the woman he loved. The letters he sent Anna before and after their wedding leave no doubt as to the vigor of his desire for her. "As I peruse your dear letter of Sunday night how full of happiness I feel. Yes darling the days are long and the times hang heavy to us, loving ardently and passionately as we do, and longing to fly to each other's arms, oh my beloved, my own sweet wife, . . . how I long to hold you to my heart, to drink the bliss the highest bliss from your dear lips and to realize the highest the most exalted and most passionate delight in your arms." Drinking the highest bliss from her dear lips: the words with which the isolated wanderer expressed his ardor are strikingly Victorian *and* sensual. And it seems the passion went both ways. "You say truly my beloved," he wrote after their first child was born, "we must never part again."

But the partings continued, and a year later, when Anna and the baby were once again in Pune, Thomas sent one of his most revealing letters. A friend of hers, Elizabeth Howell, had just gotten married in Bombay's Anglican cathedral. Thomas attended the wedding breakfast and then, back in his apartment, opened his mind to his wife. He wanted her to know how remote he felt from everyone in their colonial world:

> During the breakfast altho I talked and made the most fun at table I was very anxious to get away to read your expected and wished for letter—How little did all there think as pun and story rolled from me making all laugh—that I had not a thought or feeling in Common with any one of them, that my

thoughts were far away, with you beloved of my heart, and of you. The more
I know of these people of Bombay the greater my contempt for them, they are
a dull, stupid, inert race, . . . unable as higher and purer minds are, to extract
a higher and holier feeling out of these mere daily occurrences. . . . I never
contrast you with others my beloved, because it would be absurd. . . . I often
feel . . . that had I not known you, I *never would have married*.

Thomas had left the Military Pay Office by the time he wrote this. He
was now a clerk working for Robert Frith and Company, one of the city's
leading importers, auctioneers, and mess agents.[6] His new position was on
a par with that of the bridegroom, a clerk with the merchant firm of Peel,
Cassels and Company. Both men held lower-level office jobs in the world of
business, where, as Hawes observes, "rank and station mattered less" than
in the army. But instead of feeling a common bond, Thomas placed himself
well above "these people of Bombay" even as he entertained them with his
superior wit.

Although there is no mistaking the sweeping disdain of this letter, the
arrogance is not that of someone who belongs to an entitled elite. Thomas's
mentality was resentful and beleaguered—the pride of a talented but powerless man trying to make his way in a stuffy colonial society. Feeling choked
by this society's mediocrity, he clung to a woman who offered a "higher and
purer" alternative in the privacy of marriage.

There had always been enlightened Europeans in India, men like John
Sutherland, with his vast knowledge of India's native states, and Mountstuart Elphinstone, a governor of Bombay who pushed the expansion of
native education. But by and large the colonial social order was dull and
narrow and becoming more so. What Thomas found in Anna, and she in
him, was an escape from all that.

But how do you manage that on a clerk's income? Of all the annoyances
that Thomas complained of in his letters, none proved quite so intractable
as the problem of finding an affordable home. At the time Bombay's "principal dwelling-houses," as an observer noted, were "owned by Parsee land-
lords, and . . . either inhabited by themselves, or let out at high rents to the

6. In his advertisements, Frith offered everything from bonnets and jewelry, cricket
bats and "a first rate slate billiard table," to fine clarets, brandies, and cigars. He sold
"every description of Mess Stores, of the very best quality."

English residents." Clearly, that was a market Thomas could not enter. He was able to meet the minimal property qualification for jurors—his rental quarters cost more than three hundred rupees, or thirty pounds, a year—but respectable married life required much more. For that reason alone, the three years the couple spent in Bombay would be a tale of temporary arrangements, lengthy separations, and frequent relocations.

After the wedding, Anna recalled, they lived for "a few weeks" in Parel. Her report is confirmed by a jurors' list, which names this upscale section of Bombay as Thomas's place of abode. Six miles north of the Fort (where he was employed), Parel was the site of the governor's residence and some highly desirable homes. "To Be Let," runs an advertisement, "a fine, airy bungalow, situated at Parell, recently occupied by Lieut *Goodwin*. For further particulars, apply to . . . Jeejeebhoy Dadabhoy"—a Parsi name. Probably the only way the Leonowenses could have afforded the neighborhood was as short-term house sitters.

Their next home, on Malabar Point, Bombay's westernmost extremity, adjoined the government summerhouse, which a traveler had described as "a very pretty cottage, in a beautiful situation on a rocky and woody promontory." This was where Governor and Lady Falkland moved each year during the hot season. The reason the Leonowenses could afford the adjacent house (found through another Parsi agent) was that it had been abandoned for years and was in disrepair. For an unconventional couple, however, the place was perfect, except that Thomas would have an even longer commute, eight miles.

"I have taken a large airy house in an excellent healthy situation near Government," he informed Anna before the wedding. "It is a long way from the fort, but that is of no consequence compared to the advantage of a splendid house on reasonable terms and a good situation with pure air." Air there would be in abundance: when Johnny Donohoe arrived from his "dirty hole" in the city, he had "wind enough to blow him out of bed." Without disclosing the full truth about the house, Thomas had reason to feel that Anna would be pleased with it, especially its "very extensive grounds and gardens."

And pleased she was. Her delight shines through the pages of *Life and Travel in India*, published thirty-five years later, which characterizes her first real married home as "completely isolated from the rest of the world." The house had been unoccupied for ten years, she recalled, until "by a happy accident" it was found by her husband, "who had it at once repaired, furnished, and fitted up for our use." Its original owner was an eccentric Englishman who "returned to England with broken fortunes and failing health." It was called Morgan's Folly.

Again, the story pretty much holds up. Edmund Cobb Morgan had been the East India Company's head solicitor in Bombay, a shareholder in the Bank of Bombay, and a member of the Royal Asiatic Society: one of the better sort, in other words, prominent and esteemed. Then his life fell apart. A son died, followed by two successive wives, and the solicitor took a series of medical leaves "for the benefit of his health," as the official formula went. His decline continued, and in 1840—exactly ten years before Thomas came upon Morgan's empty house, just as Anna said—he left Bombay on a two-year medical leave for the "recovery" of his health. However, instead of sailing to England, as she believed, he disembarked at the Cape of Good Hope, the usual destination for company invalids. He died there in 1847, owning properties in Bombay, South Africa, and England. His affairs were a mess, and his executors got embroiled in a South African lawsuit. The result: his fine Malabar Point country house was left vacant and untended.

According to Anna, Morgan's Folly had been built "to serve the double purpose of human and bird habitation." The ground floor, enclosed by wire screens but open to the weather, formed a cage for "rare and beautiful birds." Select trees, including a baobab, were incorporated in the structure. Over the years the hall's floor became littered with weeds and brush, and the birds mostly vanished, the few that remained being fed by a "pious Hindoo." The Aviary was Thomas and Anna's name for this romantic ruin, which became such a cherished memory that, half a century later, when she resided in Montreal and her daughter's family acquired a summerhouse on the Saint Lawrence River, it, too, was called the Aviary.

Morgan's house had a spacious upper floor with a wraparound balcony, but the rooms were more or less empty, with no curtains or carpets. The chamber favored by the newlyweds was one floor higher, a kind of tower with grand views. Furnished with "a table, a few chairs, mostly of cane, a couple of sofas and a Persian carpet" (Anna's inventory), this was the couple's refuge from Bombay's stifling heat and society.

What Anna didn't disclose was that the house was unsuitable for most of the year. During the hot months—March, April, May, October—it was a charming, refreshing retreat, but during the Southwest Monsoon, June through September, Malabar Point was "exposed to the full fury of the wind and waves" and became "almost uninhabitable." Morgan's main residence had been nearer the city's center. The Leonowenses can't have stayed in his choice country house for more than a few months. For all its delights, the Aviary was not the answer to their housing problem.

Where else they lived during their three years in India is by and large a mystery. After giving birth in Pune in December 1850, Anna was back in Bombay by 20 April, the date of her daughter's baptism. However, the next year's jurors' list had Thomas living in the crowded Girgaum district, whose "foul mirky atmosphere" (his phrase) may explain his wife's return to Pune: "I have not yet got a house," he lamented. Anna and Selina appear to have rejoined him after he found quarters on Girgaum Road, which, facing the ocean, may have seemed healthier. But then Selina died. Her burial in Colaba, the city's long southern peninsula, suggests the Leonowenses had moved yet again in their quest for a permanent home.

So the real answer to the mystery of how the couple managed to live in Bombay is that they didn't. When Anna was pregnant or needed medical attention, she had to retreat to the Donohoes' home. That is where she must have been in November 1851 when her anxious husband asked if she felt "any soreness, or weakness in your limbs." Had there been an accident? Whatever the answer, it seems that Thomas couldn't assure the level of safety and comfort her family expected and perhaps demanded. Right from the outset, the Leonowenses' unconventional married life proved too precarious to sustain. For a young aspiring couple without money, the dream of a bold new life outside the rules of colonial society would be an impossibly tall order.

HOPEFUL ORIENTALISTS

At first glance, Anna's later account of her and her husband's learned pursuits in Bombay looks as inflated as her claim that Malabar Point was their settled home. Saying nothing about Thomas's working life or strained means, she conveyed the impression that their early married life was devoted to linguistic and ethnic studies and an extended tour of India. Yet, once again, the tale proves partly true: she *did* go on with the intellectual endeavors the Badgers had encouraged.

Twice a day, according to her story, a Hindu teacher of languages—a *pundit*, to use the English form of *pandit*, a Hindu learned man—came to Malabar Point for lessons. An exacting and impoverished Brahman named Govind, he insisted they sit on opposite sides of the table and that she use her own pencil and paper so as not to pollute him. The languages he taught were Hindustani and Sanskrit.

The scene is plausible, though its usual setting may have been one of the couple's less imposing and more centrally located addresses. But did she really get adult tutoring in Hindustani? This language, spoken at home by 15 percent of Bombay's residents, was the usual medium of communication between the British and their servants and other subordinates. Also known as Camp Urdu, "the language of the camp," it originated with the Mughal incursions into India. The syntax was Hindi; the vocabulary, Urdu. When the British became the new masters, Camp Urdu continued to be the obvious choice, and the East India Company encouraged officers to learn it. That it was a language of conquest, "fit only to be spoken to a slave, being full of authority and command, brief and uncourteous," was understood by few. During Anna's time at the Byculla school and the cantonment at Disa, Hindustani would have been in constant use with the various domestic staffs. But how could she admit having picked it up in girlhood? To disclose that awkward fact would be to expose her origins. Hence her claim to have studied it with a pundit.

Sanskrit was another story entirely. This ancient and difficult language—the Latin of south Asia—was emphatically not the thing for a clerk's wife to study. It had long been taught by Hindu *pandits* and was said to be "spoken freely in the households of educated Brahmans," but Europeans didn't get to it till the late eighteenth century, when it was British policy to foster India's traditional learning. Western savants who worked at Sanskrit were the first "Orientalists." Then policy changed, and a hard-edged "Anglicist" program was adopted. Starting in the 1830s, the plan was to modernize India by making English the medium and science the subject of study. By the time Anna took a seat across from Govind, a gulf had opened between Indians and the English, now more engrossed in the rituals of club life than some tough and useless native lingo. That Anna made herself peg away at Sanskrit is one of the most intriguing things we know about her. It was a signature act, a characteristically strenuous way of going against the mainstream.

Because Sanskrit was the language of ancient Hindu and Buddhist scriptures, some European scholars considered it the key to the history of religion and beyond that to the cultural origins of Europe itself. That was part of its appeal for Anna, who, in later years, liked to picture the ancient "Aryans" and their Sanskrit-speaking priests living close to nature in some high Caucasian valley at the dawn of history.

The Aryan business exemplifies the mystical authority that Asia has had for many kinds of Westerners over the last few centuries. One of Thomas's reasons for insisting that there is no "inferiority of intellect in the Colored races" was his belief that "Solomon the wisest of all Men was a Colored Man—and from the East, and God himself spoke from the East." As this impassioned argument suggests, the Leonowenses had a devout religious motive for their interest in Eastern languages and cultures. Like many others, they were pursuing divine origins—a widespread and seductive dream.

In other words, long before Anna went to Siam she was an aspiring Orientalist. It is striking that a young woman subjected to the Bombay Education Society's narrow curriculum should go in for Sanskrit and high Indian culture, and it makes a remarkable picture: the newly married teenage bride, without money, social support, or training in critical thought, endeavoring, like mentor George Percy Badger, to break into the ranks of learned Orientalists. And she never gave up.

A quarter century later, in 1878, she taught a six-week beginning Sanskrit course at a summer school of languages in Amherst, Massachusetts.[7] But she wasn't satisfied with her level of mastery, and in her late sixties she resumed study at the University of Leipzig. Germany led the world in linguistics, and her professor, Ernst Windisch, was an eminent "Indologist." To gauge her knowledge, he had her read a passage of Sanskrit. "Meine Dame, meine Dame!" he said. "Wo haben Sie das gelernt?" (My lady, my lady! Where did you learn that?) Her reply, "von einem Pundit [from a pundit], Herr Doktor," vastly pleased him. Since the university did not admit women at that time, she would have been a *Gasthörer*, sitting in on lectures without being enrolled. She was given "the freedom to all the Oriental Classes," and she studied the Rig Veda and Mahabharata.

7. Amherst College announced, no doubt on her authority, that she had "studied Sanskrit, Persian, and Hindostanee for twelve years under Brahman 'Pundits,' or Professors in India."

In Bombay, too, doors were opened, thanks to her Sanskrit lessons. Once, she and Thomas were invited by a rich, young Brahman householder to an evening of traditional entertainments. They included a martial exhibit by Rajput wrestlers, an enactment of the story of Nala from the Mahabharata, and performances by a troupe of nautchnees, or nautch girls—professional dancers trained from childhood. The detailed description of the varied dances that Anna published many years later must have been based on notes taken at the time. In it she made much of the girls' athletic prowess and physical beauty, noting how a gauzy costume revealed "the whole outline of a very lovely form."

Anna's attention was riveted by one particular nautch girl whose face "was of the purest oval," with large, "almond-shaped" eyes and a mouth "half pouting and almost infantile in its round curves, but with an expression of dejection and sorrow." As she watched the fascinating dancer, she tried "to picture her strange life, wondering who she was and how her parents could ever have had the heart to doom her to such a profession." It was hard, she wrote, "to remove my eyes from that pensive and beautiful face."

After the show, Anna was invited to meet the lady of the house, Kesinèh, who lived in purdah. Far from regarding the secluded wife as backward or oppressed—the usual attitude of Western ladies—Anna found that "the narrow distinctions of races and creeds seemed to fade away: I only felt here was another woman like myself, and she a mother." Kesinèh, it appeared, was equally fascinated by the lovely dancer and eager to know who her "owner" was. "If you hear anything about her you will let me know," said Anna, "for I have fallen in love with her." She spoke "half in jest and half in earnest."

To say good-bye, she repeated the formula her pundit had taught her: "Ram, Ram, devâ Ram!" (May Rama bless you!) Then, lifting her hands to her forehead, she "lightly kissed" Kesinèh's sleeping baby. With that, the young wife sprang up, embraced her visitor's neck, touched foreheads, and uttered a "tender Hindoo farewell."

Whether this encounter went exactly as Anna claimed three decades after the fact is an open question. As she undoubtedly knew, the official visits made by English ladies to upper-class Indian matrons were stiff and obligatory rituals, token efforts at crossing a racial, cultural, and linguistic divide. By contrast, Anna presented herself as that rarest of English matrons—one with the warmth and savvy to make effective contact with Eastern women. That would be her central message in her books and lectures about her life and work in royal Siam. No matter where she had gone, she had always found herself in rapport with attractive darker-skinned women. Of course, nothing was said of her own mixed-race past. In her many satisfying exchanges, the white mask was never removed.

With Muslims Anna seemed to feel a special bond. Her description of a Friday service at the great mosque in Aurangabad (which she may not, in fact, have seen) is marked by an appreciation so insistent as to be preachy: "The earnest voice of the *moolah* [mullah], the deep responses of the assembled congregation, their expressions of devotion and self-abasement, were sufficient to bring Christian and pagan into sympathy." When she was invited to the wedding of the daughter of another mullah, she found the chief attraction to be "the gentle loveliness of the bride and the beauty of her dress." In Anna's detailed and caressing description, published long afterward (drawn perhaps from notes taken at the time), the bride's expensive outfit completely covers her, veiling even "her eyes and nose, leaving only her mouth and chin visible." The young woman is clearly not a Westerner, yet we are not asked to regard her as oppressed or "other." The writing aims to bring Christian and pagan into sympathy.

After she left Asia and carved out a new life in North America, Anna made an adventurous trip to Russia that took her as far south as Kazan. Invited into the household of a friendly Muslim merchant, she "could not keep [her] eyes from following" one of his five wives, a young Georgian "with such a lovely face . . . her hands, feet, form, all so perfect and symmetrical." Her host's eleven children struck her as "extraordinarily fine looking," not at all like "the dirty Russians." The local mosque, simple as it was, also impressed her. Unlike Orthodox churches, which were "bursting with pictures of Gods, Christs, saints, angels, hells & devils flaring and glaring with lights & candles, golden robes, censors and gold and precious stones," the mosque's simplicity spoke to Anna of "the power of Mohammedanism in Russia!! It was a noble protest, a puritanism, and a unitarianism . . . a living voice for the worship of the 'One God in spirit and in truth.'"

This synthesizing openness forms a striking contrast with the usual Western distancing from Islam. Particularly surprising is the identification of the religion with Puritanism and American Unitarianism. In Anna's mature opinion, Islam was not much different from these stripped-down forms of Christian faith. Did this view commend itself to her because it reconciled her three spiritual lineages—evangelicalism, the liberal Unitarianism she took to in New York City, and the possible Muslim faith of Lieutenant Glascott's *bibi*? Perhaps . . . but it must be stressed that the grandmother's Muslim affiliation is conjectural.

Anna saw Kazan in 1881. Three years later, when she brought out her memoir of India, the pervading idea was that she and her husband had gone everywhere and taken in everything and recognized no barrier or color line. But there were two telltale omissions. Unlike the books by well-credentialed Britons, hers had nothing to say about receptions at Government House, or the commander in chief's annual ball in Pune, or the social rituals at Mahabaleshwar hill station, those pukka sahib ceremonies from which Anna and her sort were excluded. Nor was anything said about the clubs where everyone was always popping in between tea and dinner. Instead, we find an occasional remark about English aloofness and then, at the end, this sudden, sweeping, unexpected complaint: "The viceroy and the great English grandees are separated from the natives . . . by law and custom which nothing can overcome, and the officials around whom the whole Indian empire revolves are often ignorant of the Indian languages, races, religious and social prejudices, and mode of life. . . . I have often heard gentlemen of great intelligence in other respects speak of the people of India with profound contempt, classing in one indistinguishable mass . . . Hindoos, Parsees, Mohammedans, Arabians, Persians."

In this aggrieved statement, Anna was summing up her fundamental criticism of the unknowing exclusiveness of the ruling British. Her point resembled her husband's critique of imperial arrogance, but with a key difference. Thomas wagered everything to make common cause with Eurasians—living with William Vaudrey Glasscott and Johnny Donohoe, falling in love with Anna and marrying her—whereas she, already one of them, did the reverse: she denied her mixed-race origins. With nothing more to lose, Thomas let fly with all his angry vehemence. His wife's position was too threatened for that. Her anger had to be choked, moderated, redirected. This was the hidden fracture line in their union. Who would guess from the passage quoted above that the writer *was one of* that "mass" the powerful English so often regarded with "profound contempt"?

And that is the other thing missing from Anna's mature "recollections" of India: her real history. Because she suppressed both her mixed-race past and her brilliant escape from the future it entailed, her writing was incomplete and false, and knew itself to be false, and became intricately corrupted. The need to conceal turned into a habit of lying. Fact and fantasy got entangled, and a haughty pedantry infected her tone.

Yet her writing was also enriched. Again and again, as she described the young nonwhite women she encountered in Bombay, Pune, Kazan, and Bangkok, she could not take her eyes off them. These young and graceful non-Europeans, living a version of the life she had put behind her—the life of her lost Indian grandmother—were the secret sharers who gave meaning to her life. It was her hidden identity with them that gave power to her writing.

6

Selina's Death and Keesah's Last Long Look

WHEN ANNA AND THOMAS'S first child died, the couple's married life turned the corner that was probably inevitable: from hardship to irreparable trouble.

The baby had come into the world under trying circumstances. While the expectant mother was with her parents in Pune, the father remained in Bombay, working away at his grind and anxiously awaiting news. When it came, he gave full expression to his relief: "I have just received Dr. Nohoe's letter informing me of your safe delivery of a little girl. . . . Oh, my darling my beloved Annie what feelings of delight and deep gratitude to God did I experience when I learned that our long and ardently expected baby had come home, and that you were both doing well. . . . I trust my love you did not suffer much, and that you are now all right; be careful of yourself and our darling baby." Like any new parent, he took for granted that the worst lay behind.

Four months later, when the child was baptized in Bombay's Anglican cathedral, she was given a name loaded with family history. On Anna's side there had been Selina, Countess of Huntingdon, whose name was given to Cradock Glascott's one daughter. But the immediate source was surely on Thomas's side. Not only was his younger sister named Selina, but there had been a previous sister of that name who died before he was born.

With her own Selina Anna grew extremely close. As she later wrote, "The strong instinct of the mother out-weighs and overrules every other sentiment of my life, and this is not mere talk—but . . . a deep law of my nature." Unfortunately, the record is so thin that we have only a single report of her as a young mother. It dates from a period in late 1851 or early 1852 soon after her sister Eliza Millard moved to Bombay from Pune. From time to time the sister's daughter, three-year-old Eliza Sarah, was left with Anna. Some fifty years later, when Eliza Sarah had become a lonely middle-aged woman living in London and was overcome by a "flood of old recollections," she wrote that "I was a great pet of hers (Mrs. Leonowens) and often went over and spent a week at a time with her and my little cousin Selina. . . . I wonder if she has as vivid a recollection of her little niece Lizzie as I have of my kind and beautiful Aunt Annie who then was an accomplished pianiste." These tender words, set down long after "Aunt Annie" had broken off relations with her birth family, the unoffending niece included, have the stark and isolated quality typical of early memories. One wonders about that piano playing, mentioned nowhere else. Who owned the expensive instrument, Leonowenses or Millards?

Nothing is known about the circumstances of Selina's death in May 1852 except that it happened during the hot season and the child was interred in a part of Bombay new to her parents: Colaba, the long narrow sickle curving southward into the Indian Ocean. Like Malabar Point, this little peninsula is cooled by sea breezes and would have been healthier than crowded Girgaum. Had Selina been taken there as a precaution? The burial register notes her age with touching exactness: seventeen months.

Two decades later Anna authorized a statement about her life-threatening grief for distribution in a lecture agency's advertising circular: "When Mrs. Leonowens was only eighteen, the death of her mother, and at the same time of her first baby, came upon her with such terrible force of pain that her life was for some time in danger. Accompanied by her husband, she sailed for England." That she reduced her age by two years is not surprising: she would always be loose with ages and dates, and in addition she may have wished to stress her young vulnerability. The voyage to England was a bigger stretch, but that, too, is understandable: it was part of a program of self-whitening and decolonizing. The same is true for the equally imaginary death of her mother: like so many others who have been driven to cover up a dark-skinned ancestry, Anna needed a rock-solid excuse for never having to produce her parent for her children. But there is one very odd and seemingly gratuitous misrepresentation: that her mother died at the same time as her daughter. Did Anna come up with this in order to present herself as uniquely bereaved and desolate—not simply a childless mother but a motherless child?

Whatever her idea, for the remainder of her life there could be no pain for Anna that was remotely comparable to the pain of bereavement. After the death of her second child she seems to have fallen into despair, and when her husband died five years later her agony was so intense that she became "a little deranged." That Grandmama succumbed from time to time to a kind of absolute grief was notorious with her family in Canada, who blamed this susceptibility on "the terrible lesson" she had learned in the East, that "all loved persons must be snatched from her."

In 1889 a good friend of Anna's suddenly died. Writing about her anguish to a mutual acquaintance, she described herself as being "purposeless and exhausted." Her usual energy was gone, and she fell into a collapse so complete that she couldn't get out. And yet, as the letter containing this admission makes clear, she was absolutely relentless in describing her condition. Unable to stop, she circled around and around her anguish, consumed by feelings that simultaneously excited and depleted her.

Another time, while living in Siam and experiencing serious stress, she reportedly sent her sister Eliza a letter threatening to kill herself. Because of that, there is a question to be asked about Anna's grief for Selina. Was the young first-time mother suicidal? Was her life "in danger" or "despaired of" because, quite simply, she wanted to die?

We can't know, but it does appear that bereavement was Anna's personal black hole, a state so deadly and energetic that it threatened to consume all impulses and desires.

The Story of Kisa Gotami

However, Anna was a person of remarkable resources, and over time she found an oblique and powerful way to articulate her grief. Her vehicle was an ancient Buddhist parable recorded by the prolific Buddhist scholar Buddhaghosa in the fifth century A.D. It concerns a young mother who cannot accept the death of her infant son. Anna heard it from the royal concubine who became her best friend at the Siamese Court, Son Klin, who, not incidentally, as we will see, was of Mons (Burmese) ancestry.

Learning one day that Anna "had recently lost a very dear relative," Son Klin told her the story in order to offer consolation and teach the way of enlightenment; she spoke "in a voice full of the tenderest sympathy and affection." A decade later, when Anna was a public figure in New York, she would often recite this tale both from the lectern and in private. Her second book, *The Romance of the Harem*, published in 1873, gave the full text. The dear relative was very likely sister Eliza, who had died in Bombay in June 1864, a year or so after Anna refused to be reconciled with her.

Son Klin may indeed have told the story to Anna, but inspection of her text shows that its source was not a private oral performance but a recently published translation. In 1870, three years before her version saw print, a certain Captain T. Rogers translated a Burmese version of Buddhaghosa's parables. The book came with an imprimatur by Max Müller, the eminent linguist and historian of religions whose introduction singled out the story that so impressed Anna: "If it were only to give to the world that one apologue of Kisâgotamî, this small collection of Buddhist parables deserve[s] to be published." A footnote in *The Romance of the Harem* referring to Müller announces (rather brazenly) that "the Birmese text is slightly different from that of the Siamese." In fact, the so-called Siamese text was a rewriting of the translated Burmese one. As Anna so often did, she was offering something she had read as if it came straight out of her life. At the same time, like the honest actress she was, she projected herself so deeply into the parable that she made it her own. Her version goes as follows:

> In the village of Sârvâthi there lived a young wife named Keesah, who at the age of fourteen gave birth to a son; and she loved him with all the love and joy of the possessor of a newly found treasure. . . . But when the boy was able to walk, and could run about the house, there came a day when he suddenly fell sick and died. And Keesah, not understanding what had happened to her fair lotus-eyed boy, clasped him to her bosom,[1] and went about the village from house to house, praying and weeping, and beseeching the good people to give her some medicine to cure her baby.
>
> But the villagers and neighbors, on seeing her, said: "Is the girl mad, that she still bears about on her breast the dead body of her child?"[2]

1. This is one of the passages that reveals Anna's reliance on Rogers. In his text the mother carries the corpse "on her hip" (a detail a footnote calls attention to). Only at this one point does his version, like Anna's after him, have the body "clasped to her bosom."
2. In Rogers's version the neighbors exclaim, "Is the young girl mad that she carries about on her breast the dead body of her son!"

At length a holy man, pitying the girl's sorrow, said to himself: "Alas! this Keesah does not understand the law of death; I will try to comfort her."

This kindly man tells Keesah that he knows of a physician who can heal her boy and advises her to seek his help; he is called the Buddha. Taking this advice, the bereft mother searches for and eventually finds him and asks for his medicine. He says he can help her, but first she must bring him a few mustard seeds.

As she was about to set out, the pitiful Buddha, recalling her, said: "My sister, the mustard-seed that I require must be taken from a house where no child, parent, husband, wife, relative, or slave has ever died."

The young mother replied, "Very good, my lord," and went her way, taking her boy with her, and setting him astride on her hip, with his lifeless head resting on her bosom.

Thus she went from house to house, from palace to hut, begging for some grains of mustard-seed.

Wherever she goes, she is offered mustard seeds, but when she declares that the house from which they come must be one in which no one has died, she is repeatedly told that no such house exists. At last, worn out, she sits down and reflects:

"Alas! this is a heavy task I have undertaken. I am not the only one who has lost her baby. Everywhere children are dying, parents are dying, loved ones are dying, and everywhere they tell me that the dead are more numerous than the living. Shall I then think only of my own sorrow?"

Thinking thus, she suddenly summoned courage to put away her sorrow for her dead baby, and she carried him to the forest and laid him down to rest under a tree; and having covered him over with tender leaves, and taking her last look of his loved face, she betook herself once more to the Buddha . . .

"Sister, hast thou found the mustard-seed?"

"I have not, my lord . . . for the people in the village tell me there is no house in which some one has not died; for the living are few, but the dead are many."

"And where is your baby?"

"I have laid him under a tree in the forest, my lord," said Keesah, gently.[3]

"Then," said the Buddha to her, "You have found the grains of mustard-seed; you thought that you alone had lost a son, but now you have learned that the law of death and of suffering is among all living creatures, and that here there is no permanence."

On hearing this Keesah was comforted, and established in the path of virtue, and was thenceforth called Keesah Godami, the disciple of the Buddha.

The excellence of this story is not the only reason Anna was fond of telling it. She, too, had been Kisa, devastated by the death of an only child. And because it was partly her story, she changed it. In Rogers's translation, the young mother, "putting away her affection for her child," gathers her "resolution" and leaves him in the forest without further ado. In Anna's version, she summons "courage to put away her sorrow," but then comes a tender scene in which she takes a last lingering look at the baby's face. Unlike Buddhaghosa's mother, who resolutely frees herself from grief, Anna's mother clutches all the tighter in the act of surrendering. Fervent Victorian feeling is spliced into Buddhist doctrine and discipline.

Remarkably, we have a firsthand report of how Anna acted out the story's climax for her audiences. In 1875 she gave a lecture titled "Buddha and the Buddhists of Siam" in Chicago, where, thanks to the success of her books and her reputation as a public speaker, she packed the city's Grand Opera House. Reviewing her performance, the *Chicago Daily Tribune* praised her "rich, harmonious, and sympathetic" voice and gave two long columns to a summary of her talk, which included a retelling of the story of Kisa. It wasn't a new one for the reporter. He had heard it before. "Almost every one who knows of Mrs. Leonowens," he wrote, "knows the tale, but no mother in that audience, could have listened to it as she told it without the tears starting to her eyes."

Is it a surprise that the Chicago of 1875 would take such interest in a lecture on Buddha? Part of the explanation is that Anna made Buddhism easy, turning an ancient moral tale into the scaffolding for a modern stage

3. In 1894, when Anna spoke at the first meeting of the Halifax Local Council of Women, she gave the story an improving benevolent spin by having Kisa say at this point that "her heart was sick for all those who had suffered as she had."

performance. After Buddhaghosa's mother grasps the universality of death, she simply places the corpse in the forest and walks away. But after Anna's mother achieves understanding and buries her dead baby, she stays, as the *Tribune* noted—and here we see Anna's vivid reenactment—to "press her cheek over and over again to the sod."

The dramatic performance at the Grand Opera House was not one of peace but torment. Rather than teach a lesson in Buddhist serenity, Anna caused her listeners' tears to start. She gave her paying audience her own maternal anguish and in that way attained one of the ends of Victorian sentimental art: a powerful emotional release.

TRAVEL FOR HEALTH

The Leonowenses' second child, a boy, was born eight months to the day after Selina's 24 May 1852 burial. It may have been too soon for Anna to have realized it, but even as she sank into depression she was probably already pregnant again.

In all likelihood, the care she received involved a reprieve from humid Bombay. May was a sweltering time of year, the rains were imminent, and invalids would soon be seeking refuge in Pune. Four months later, when the monsoon ended, the hill station of Mahabaleshwar would become the favored resort. Since a restorative trip was the usual prescription for "nervous" complaints, Anna may have been taken to one or both of these places. In Pune there was the familiar Donohoe bungalow in the conductors' lines, and if her despondency persisted, she could try the cool refreshing air of Mahabaleshwar.

Three decades later Anna published a book about a lengthy, unexplained tour, *Life and Travel in India: Being Recollections of a Journey before the Days of Railroads.* In it she claimed to have explored much of the Deccan plateau by bullock cart, accompanied by Thomas and a pundit (there is no mention of Selina). After a brief sail from Daman to Surat, she investigated the province of Gujarat and then capped her travels with a voyage around the subcontinent to Calcutta.

An ambitious excursion of that sort might have been prescribed for a memsahib with months at her disposal, yet it was obviously out of the question for Anna and her husband, especially in the summer of 1852. Thomas could not have afforded an extended leave from Robert Frith, and the monsoon rains that followed Selina's death would have made travel by bullock a nightmare. Once again, Anna was representing her married life as a grand and leisurely affair, freed from mundane necessity. This was not her first piece of fictitious travel writing. Fourteen years earlier, she had concluded *The English Governess at the Siamese Court* with a fraudulent account of a journey to Angkor Wat.

However, behind the outsized claims of *Life and Travel*, we catch a glimpse now and then of the author's actual experience. A case in point is her admiring description of Mahabaleshwar: "There are now a little Protestant church, reading-room, library, hotel, barracks, handsome European villas and bungalows, with bridle-paths all along the most picturesque points. There is no more beautiful and healthful sanitarium to be found anywhere in the East. We spent two delightful months, November and December, at the travellers' bungalow. The weather was perfect."

Since she and Thomas embarked for Singapore in mid-November, the last half of that month and all of December can be ruled out. Yet nowhere else does her book get so specific about chronology, and in no other location (apart from Bombay and Pune) do we read of such a lengthy stay— a stay that gets mentioned immediately after Mahabaleshwar is described as a "beautiful and healthful sanitarium." If this was the associative leap it appears, it may well be that Anna went there for therapeutic reasons.

However, her stay could not have begun before October, when Mahabaleshwar is transformed from one of the wettest spots on earth to one of the most invigorating and pleasant. This was where the proprietor of Morgan's Folly had come thirteen years earlier to repair his shattered health. "In the morning, when you wake," wrote Lady Falkland, who loved the place, "you think you have received a new set of bones." Which was what Anna was literally building now that her unborn child was in its sixth or seventh month. Her pregnancy would have been an additional reason to go there . . . if she really did.

TRAVEL FOR WORK

About the fact of her next journey, to Singapore and Australia, no conjecture is needed. This would be one of the best-documented, most dangerous, and least therapeutic voyages she would undertake.

Gold had been discovered in South Australia, and Bombay's newspapers were full of reports of easy wealth and plentiful employment in the southern continent. After it was misleadingly announced that two vessels would sail directly to Australia in October 1852, ninety-three soldiers in the Royal Army applied for a discharge, and several families from Pune and elsewhere sold out and came to Bombay, camping at the Colaba depot. There were also "a few in civil life . . . who, having missed their way here, are waiting anxiously for an opportunity to get away to Australia."

Anna's uncle William Vaudrey Glasscott belonged to the latter group. During his eight years as an able but unpromoted employee of the Military Board, mixed-race clerks grew increasingly dissatisfied. Excluded from the better positions, they found their monopoly of government clerical work undermined as English education spread among Hindus. As the job market tightened, a widely read essay predicted that "the educated native community of India, whether Eurasians, Hindoos, Parsees, or Mahomedans," would have to look "for other fields of employment." Worried Eurasians complained to Parliament that they "continue to be superseded by Europeans quite inefficient." But now, thanks to gold, Australia became a land of opportunity for those with darker skins. There was even official encouragement, especially in Madras, for those who were young, literate, and able to emigrate. When Glasscott chose to uproot himself, he was part of a demographic movement.

Thomas, too, had strong incentives for trying his luck elsewhere. His inability to afford a suitable home in crowded and expensive Bombay or to properly support a wife in distress was surely a prime consideration. Given his experience in the army, the government bureaucracy, and the private sector, he could reasonably expect to find work elsewhere in the empire, especially in a booming place like Melbourne. Happily, he was on good-enough terms with his employers that when he reached the southern continent his letters of recommendation were judged to be "very respectable testimonials."

So Glasscott, Thomas, and Anna resolved to leave Bombay. When direct passage to Australia failed to materialize, they decided that their next best route would be by way of Singapore, and they booked passage on the *Ganges*, a steamer operated by the Peninsular and Oriental Line, the giant company that dominated eastern shipping. The vessel was scheduled to clear Bombay harbor on 16 November 1852.

But what did these plans mean for Anna, who was ten weeks from delivering her next child? What did they mean for her parents, who had provided care and a physician for her first childbirth? There is every reason to suppose that Mary Ann and Patrick were anxious about her well-being. Were they free with advice? Were they pressing? Family ties were very strong. No Glascott, man or woman, had ever left India. Even Uncle Glasscott would return.

We know nothing about the discussions that preceded the voyage, but it is hard to imagine Mary Ann and Patrick *not* objecting to their son-in-law's decision to embark on a risky voyage to a remote colony at such a time. What if Anna went into labor at sea? Why did her rash, improvident husband have to leave *now*?

Which brings us to a key question about the life we are trying to follow: was this the moment when Anna, siding with her husband in a high-stakes wager, broke with her parents? That would explain many things, including the shocking claim that the mother who lived till 1873 died in 1852—the year that Mary Ann died, so to speak, for Anna.

A terminal quarrel between mother and daughter would not be as agonizing as Selina's death or the last long look of Anna's Kisa, but the bitter emotional residue could easily last a lifetime. If that is how it was with Mrs. Leonowens, there would have been one more painful secret, a guilty one, that she could tell no one.

7

An Accidental Life in Perth, Western Australia

THE VESSEL FROM WHICH Anna, Thomas, and Glasscott disembarked in Singapore on 4 December 1852 was a reliable modern steamship that plied between Bombay and Hong Kong on an announced monthly schedule. The one on which they set out for Australia was different in every respect, starting with its dubious name.

The *Alibi* was a barque, a sailing ship with three square-rigged masts. Worked by a crew of south Asians (lascars, as they were called), the vessel hauled freight and passengers from one eastern port to another: Calcutta, Penang, Singapore, Amoy (today Xiamen). That it wasn't listed in Lloyd's exhaustive *Register of British and Foreign Shipping* suggests it may have skirted some of the usual rules.

In November 1852, after the *Alibi* returned to Singapore from China, a shipping agency advised travelers to Australia that cabins were available:

FOR PORT PHILLIP [MELBOURNE]

The A.1 fast sailing barque "Alibi" of 318 Tons, Capt. Bell, will sail for the above Port positively on the 24th Instant [i.e., the current month, November]; for passage, having superior accommodation, apply to, Jose D'Almeida & Sons.

In fact, the barque did not sail until 10 December—six days after the voyagers from Bombay stepped off the *Ganges*.

Did it feel as if luck was with them? Cabins were still available, no other ship would leave for Australia that month, and the *Alibi* must have been cheaper than the Peninsular and Oriental's fast new Australian Line, which charged 160 Straits dollars for a second-class berth to Melbourne. What the travelers didn't know was that the barque was in poor repair and that its captain would be entering Australian waters with only "an outline chart" of the continent's reef-lined coasts. Trusting their lives to his care were twenty deck and steerage passengers and the trio from India. Heavily pregnant, Anna would not have been able to dine at the captain's table. For her the trip would mean confinement in her and Thomas's cabin.

The first leg of the voyage ended 21 December, when the *Alibi* was "obliged to put into Batavia [Jakarta] leaky" and was "detained" for repairs that took three weeks. Anna was then in her ninth month.[1]

Finally setting sail again, the barque reached Anyar in the Strait of Sunda on 14 January 1853. Ten days later, on the 24th, somewhere south of Java in the Indian Ocean, Anna went into labor with her second child, a boy. Three months later the date was noted in a baptism register in Perth, the sole surviving clue that the baby was born at sea.

We can only guess why Anna never revealed the circumstances of his birth. Was the scene—a close and poorly lit cabin, a pitching ship, a descent into pain and fear—too squalid to be revisited? There is no indication of other female passengers and no reason to think a surgeon was on board. Did her husband cut the cord? Did a ship's officer do it? Did it all feel desperate, improvised, sordid? Was there guilt and recrimination? In earlier medical episodes Thomas had been all anxiety and solicitude ("I trust my love you did not suffer much," "Are you getting strength now dearest?"), and now his hurry to get to Melbourne had resulted in *this*.

Six weeks later the *Alibi* was off the coast of Western Australia. These were extremely dangerous waters, especially during the first three or four

1. "The Stolen Trunk" (1878), one of Anna's autobiographical stories, takes place on a passage from Ceylon (Sri Lanka) to Java on a steamship called the *Batavia*. Consulting the daily indexes to *Lloyd's List* at the Guildhall Library, one finds that no ship of that name left Ceylon or Bombay. The *Ganges*, however, had put in at Galle, Ceylon, on its way from Bombay to Singapore. It must have been this passage, together with the *Alibi's* lengthy call in Jakarta, that furnished the nautical framework for Anna's tale, which, tellingly, with no explanation given, has her dining alone in a Jakarta hotel room and not joining her husband on his sightseeing. Once again, in the midst of dignified claims, she was flashing back to one of her ordeals.

months of the year, the period of greatest tropical cyclone activity; wrecks littered the reef-lined shore. It was the captain's plan to take on water and provisions at Fremantle, the port at the mouth of the Swan River a short distance downstream from Perth, the administrative center of colonial Western Australia. On 8 March, retiring to his cabin, he left orders to be called the instant land was sighted or danger threatened. At 4:30 in the morning he was given a warning. Fifteen minutes later the second mate went below a second time and found him still in bed, and just about then the ship struck a reef. Scraping over it, the vessel was brought to anchor in the hallows between reef and shore. She floated, but there was no safe channel back to open water and no sign of human life on land, nothing but sand, low hills, and treeless bush.

For eight days the *Alibi*'s captain, crew, and deck passengers tried to find a way out of this trap. Groups of volunteers rowed out to search for water and find help, but all they brought back was "a frightful description of the country." A boat was wrecked in the surf, men were scattered on shore without water, and shipboard rations were reduced to "half a pint of water and a little rice each day." The captain decided to abandon ship but at the last minute was persuaded to lighten the vessel by throwing cargo overboard and seek safe passage through the reef. Bringing up planks, furniture, and granite slabs, the desperate passengers and crew pitched them into the water along with cases of cigars, shoes, tapioca, and tea and even two casks of rum. Then a deck passenger climbed a "foreyard-arm" and, peering down, guided the ship to open water.

It was later determined that they had been stranded in the vicinity of Moore River, sixty miles north of Fremantle, which they reached in two days' sailing.[2] The voyage had taken more than three months, far longer than it should have.

Perth's newspapers ran lengthy stories about the near disaster. One, contributed by a regular Fremantle correspondent, was a neutral report of testimony at a judicial proceeding initiated by the captain. The other, appearing

2. The part of the jettisoned cargo that floated was bought by a speculative auctioneer and salvaged from a beach. Conceivably, the slabs and other heavy durable goods still rest beneath sand and water. A place to look would be the vicinity of Seabird, a newly developed village and an anchorage for lobster fishing boats.

in the *Perth Gazette*, was an eyewitness report by a passenger who stayed on board during the eight-day ordeal and didn't join the deck passengers (who were "mostly . . . seamen") in their quest for help and fresh water. The report was highly critical of the captain.

One week after this anonymous firsthand account appeared, the *Gazette* printed an angry riposte from a certain H.A.E. defending the captain. Aware of the identity of the passenger-reporter, whom he termed "officious," H.A.E. insinuated that the passenger had been of little help and sneered at him for having more "soldiership" than seamanship.

The target of this bitter reply and thus the author of the *Gazette's* account must have been Anna's husband. As an ex-soldier with little seafaring experience, he would quite reasonably have chosen to stay with his wife and infant son instead of risking the surf with other men. The critical view of Captain Bell's performance is in line with the tart, censorious tone of Thomas's expressed opinions in Western Australia. Evidently, one of his first acts after finally reaching Australia was to get embroiled in controversy.

Anna's own account of the near tragedy, composed long afterward, forms part of the brief autobiography she gave her grandchildren. According to this (most implausible) segment of her narrative, she and Thomas were sailing from India to England when "the ship 'Alibi' went on some rocks, through the carelessness of the captain, I believe, and we were rescued by another sailing vessel and taken to New South Wales. Here I buried my second baby, an infant son, and still dreadfully ill, we took a steamer for England and finally settled down in St. James's Square, London for nearly three years." In fact, there had been no rescue by another ship, the travelers never reached their destination in New South Wales, and the contrast between raw Western Australia and the splendid address she claimed could not have been greater. This was the second time she planted herself in the neighborhood of royalty (the first being her supposed birth in Caernarfon). No doubt the continent's reputation as a dumping ground for Britain's human refuse partly explains her lie. Still, her tale had its genuine elements: her child's death, her unstable health, and, ironically, the *Alibi's* true name. Also, she blamed the accident on the incompetence of the captain, just as Thomas had done. That she said nothing about their companion with the giveaway name, William Vaudrey Glasscott, was of course inevitable.

Finding Work

The travelers were lucky in arriving when they did. Western Australia, founded in 1829 as a "free" colony, had grown so slowly in its first two decades that it had been far outstripped in wealth and population by the more prosperous eastern colonies. Then, long after penal stations had been created in New South Wales and elsewhere, the colony reversed policy in 1850 and began accepting shipments of British convicts. The results were dramatic. Between 1849 and 1852 the total imperial revenue allocated to Western Australia almost quadrupled from £9,600 to £37,000. This ballooning administrative budget brought numerous opportunities for free immigrants and forever changed the face of Perth. Originally a place of "swamps, sand-heaps and lakes," in the words of a settler, the capital began to look like a raw boomtown. "Within the last few months," the *Gazette* reported in October 1853, "a marked change has taken place in the appearance of the town . . . from the many fresh buildings which have sprung up in all directions. Not only in our principal streets is this change noticeable, but at the back of the town, innumerable small dwelling houses have been erected." A year later the population rose to 2,755.[3]

Five days after the travelers arrived, Governor Charles FitzGerald received a formal announcement from William F. Mends, head of the commissariat: "I beg to submit for the sanction of His Excellency the Governor the employment of Mr. T. Leon Owens, recently arrived from India, and who bears very respectable testimonials: as a Temporary Clerk in this Department, at five shillings per diem, from the 23rd instant." On 1 June the new employee's "ability and anxiety to make himself useful" (Mends's words in a later communication) brought a raise of a shilling a day.

By then Glascott had also become a writer in the commissariat. Provisionally appointed at the beginning of May, within three weeks he was deemed acceptable—"tolerably conversant with office work, and his services being much required." The language of his appointment, measurably cooler than for Thomas, probably reflects his relative inexperience in commissariat

3. Immigration to Western Australia peaked the year the Leonowenses arrived. In 1849 there had been only eleven newcomers. The number jumped to 316 in 1850, dropped a little in 1851, surged to 739 in 1852, and reached a high of 965 in 1853. It fell to 480 in 1854 and plummeted to 96 in 1855. The boom had ended.

procedures. If so, the lack of preparation didn't matter. Mends's office was so busy that he had to have additional staff. So by month's end, when the *Alibi* was repaired, stocked with new cargo, and cleared at last for Melbourne, the travelers from Bombay remained on shore. Tiny Perth was their new home.

The commissariat was the arm of the imperial government that bought, stored, and distributed food, tools, machinery, building materials, weapons, and other goods. Though its traditional role was to supply the army, in Western Australia it also provided for newly arrived convicts and the pensioned soldiers who guarded them. Every November the central office in Perth solicited sealed bids for everything from beef, mutton, and potatoes to hay and fuel wood. These goods were kept in storehouses managed by duly appointed storekeepers, who answered to Mends, the deputy commissary general, not to the local magistrates. The commissariat's partial independence of the colonial government was to play a critical role in Thomas's stormy tenure as storekeeper in 1855–56.

Meanwhile, his work in India had prepared him well for his duties in the central office. Not only was he familiar with military and Treasury protocols, but his private-sector employer in Bombay had been a mess agent as well as an importer. Still, the new job was hardly something a man of ability could regard as permanent, especially if he had a wife and child to support. After five months Thomas resigned in favor of a more secure and apparently better-paying post in the central post office.

Here, too, the press of work had been building. The postmaster general, Anton Helmich, an old colonial hand who ran the post office in his home, made it known in July that he badly needed clerical help. He and the Leonowenses attended the same church, and when a new position was announced Thomas had the inside track. His application, submitted on 1 September, spoke of his "regularity and attention to business" at the commissariat. Helmich warmly supported him, stating that the "gentleman has from the assistance he has already afforded, proved to me his fitness in every way." Nine days later Thomas had the job, at one hundred pounds a year.

But the new position quickly soured. There were no holidays, the workday ran to twelve hours, and the duties were out of proportion to the remuneration. Two years later, after a series of clerks had taken the job only to resign, a newspaper editorialist was not surprised that "it is impossible to retain them, and that they secure the first vacant situation which offers either more pay or requires less work." It was Thomas who set this pattern. On 15 December, three months after going to work for the post office, he quit.

He went back to the Perth office of the deputy commissary general and stayed there until October 1855, when he agreed to take a far more challenging post—commissariat storekeeper at an isolated convict hiring depot. The quasi-military commissariat was Anna's husband's true employment home, the imperial sector in which his office skills brought in the best salary he could hope for in Western Australia.

SUPERINTENDED BY MRS. LEONOWENS

Thomas's unsettled employment during the Leonowenses' first year in Australia had a dramatic result: at the end of 1853 Anna advertised a school for young ladies. This is the earliest known sign of her interest in teaching, the work with which she would support herself in Singapore, Bangkok, and the United States and that led to her self-invention as "the English governess."

Parents in Perth who wanted to educate their daughters had two choices: the free public Perth Colonial Girls' School and the Academy for Young Ladies conducted by the Sisters of Mercy. The latter institution was much the better one, well established and with a trained staff and many courses and options. Aiming to instill "a sincere and practical love of all the Christian and social virtues," the Sisters of Mercy received broad support; today the school flourishes as Mercedes College. By contrast, the government institution, seen as a free school for the poor, was not well funded or staffed. A letter to a newspaper signed "A Parent" complained that one of its teachers couldn't even spell *grammar*. "If matters go on much longer as they do at present," this writer grumbled, "the parents of the pupils will transfer them to another school, where they will obtain an education, although at the risk of changing their faith." An editorialist considered the government's female schools "thoroughly inefficient, as is fully evidenced by the number of Protestant children of all classes who are instructed by the Sisters of Mercy."

The advertisement Anna placed in the *Western Australian Almanack* for 1854 listed the standard subjects to be taught but named no references who could attest to her competence. Instead, there was an appeal to sectarian Protestant loyalty—in her words, "the principles of the Reformed Religion." Clearly, she was hoping to fill a niche.

PERTH YOUNG LADIES' SCHOOL.
SUPERINTENDED BY MRS. LEONOWENS.

THE course of Instruction pursued at this Seminary embraces the
following:—

English Grammar	History
" Composition	Music
Arithmetic	Drawing
Writing	Plain Needlework
Geography	Ornamental do. [i.e., ditto]
The use of the Globes	

TERMS—6 guineas per annum. Music and drawing extra.

The utmost care is devoted to the improvement of the Pupils at
this school, and whilst their minds and manners are studiously cultivated, the principles of the Reformed Religion are carefully instilled.

If Anna was superintendent, one would assume a staff of more than one.
Or did she plan to run the school in her home while looking after baby
and household? One can only guess, as there is no evidence apart from this
notice that the "Seminary" so much as opened. A search through Perth's
two newspapers turns up no references of any kind. The probable explanation is that the school existed only as an inflated public prospectus and that
the sectarian patronage Anna hoped to attract never materialized.

Promotional imposture is not unknown in rapidly growing economies,
and Anna was hardly averse to stretching the truth, especially when floating
an enterprise to bring in needed income. The deadline for getting an advertisement into the *Western Australian Almanack* was 20 or 24 December.
These were the dates Perth's newspapers announced on the 14th and 16th
of that month. Given that Thomas quit his post office job on the 15th, one
wonders if his wife drafted her notice for a new school at the last minute
and in a state of pressing financial anxiety.

Perhaps, but remembering that she eventually became both schoolmistress and author, we must allow for other motives: a desire for independent
work, the stirrings of ambition. Harriet Beecher Stowe's *Uncle Tom's Cabin*
became a phenomenal worldwide best seller in 1852 and 1853, turning its
author into a new kind of global celebrity. This novel captured public interest

in Bombay before Anna's departure and in Perth after her arrival, and it would play a role in her life in Siam and America, becoming a kind of model.[4] It would have been difficult and unusual for a married woman with a baby to start a school of her own in the 1850s, but Anna wasn't cut from the usual mold. If she took her cues from Stowe's well-publicized career, she may have concluded that a determined and high-minded woman could do anything. That is what her advertisement for a seminary fundamentally represents: a first bid for public attention.

A Second Beloved Child, and a Third

Six weeks after landing in Australia, Anna and Thomas had the Reverend William Lowe, minister of Perth's Wesley Church, baptize their infant son. The congregation's register of baptisms, cited earlier, is triply significant: it tells us that the couple had left the Church of England and joined the Methodists, it shows that the baby had been born on 24 January and thus at sea, and it stands as the only known record of his name: Thomas.

In March one year later a local newspaper announced his death: "On Thursday the 16th instant, the beloved and only child of T. Leonowens, Esq., aged 13 months." Death notices were composed, submitted, and paid for by the family of the deceased. Why did T. Leonowens, Esq., the presumed author, speak of himself but not the mother? Perhaps to shield her in her terrible devastation.

"Beloved and only child": the words are as dignified as they are bleeding. Twice, now, the Leonowenses had lost an only child, the first at a year and a half, the second at an age when he would have begun walking. One thinks of Kisa Gotami, whose boy also died when he "was able to walk, and could run about the house." Anna's later phrase for herself following her son's burial—"still dreadfully ill"—suggests that the burial buried nothing. The words look like a decent verbal dressing for an unspeakable injury that just would not heal. Unlike Kisa, who left her tiny corpse in the forest and grew calm and wise, Anna buried hers in the sands of Perth and was sick . . . with what—grief? despair?

4. On 11 October 1852 the *Bombay Gazette* noted that the novel "has lately been imported into this country, and has created quite a sensation. . . . It gives a decided blow to the domestic institution of the Southern states. . . . [E]very lover of freedom will wish it success. . . . Every one interested in the subject of American Slavery should read this book."

But once again she was already pregnant. On 25 October 1854, seven months after her son's death, she gave birth to a daughter, Avis Annie, whose name, like Selina's, came from the father's family in Ireland.

As Avis grew up, either she was led to believe that she was born in London or she consented to the pretense. One way or another, her true birth country had to be concealed if her mother was to maintain that she had spent her early twenties in a fashionable part of the metropolis rather than a remote colony where unmentionable things happened.

The Swan River Mechanics' Institute

About Anna's social life in Western Australia we know exactly nothing. Her husband is another story, as we can not only trace his career as an expert government employee but virtually overhear him talking and arguing with his peers.

Two years before the couple arrived in Perth, an organization had been formed for men who wished to improve their minds and develop their powers of argument. Drawing a mostly middle-class membership of clerks, businessmen, teachers, ex-army men, and bureaucrats, the Swan River Mechanics' Institute assembled the best library in the colony and sponsored debates on topics "of a literary, scientific or other useful character." In 1854 Thomas emerged as one of the institute's most active members: he was elected auditor, served on the executive committee, often spoke up in a discussion class, and even gave a lecture. Thanks to a secretary's detailed minutes of the discussion class's arguments, we have an incomparable record of his strongly defended views on several controversial issues. These minutes show that he must have been very well matched with his opinionated and outspoken wife.

On 27 January 1854, six weeks after Thomas left the post office for his old job at the commissariat, the Swan River Mechanics' Institute held its annual business meeting in its new headquarters. There were upbeat reports and rousing speeches and a resolution to thank the governor, which "carried with acclamation—three times three, and one cheer more." When an ex-sergeant stood up to move that "what has been done is but a beginning; and this meeting pledges itself to increased zeal and energy for the current year," the motion was seconded by "Mr. Leonowens"—the first time his name appears in institute records. The infectious enthusiasm had evidently swept him up.

The next month the Monday night discussion class considered the question "Was the execution of Charles 1st justifiable?" Opinion ran mostly against the king, and when a man named Gray argued that "the people delegate to the Sovereign the power to rule but [only] according to Law," the previously silent "Leon Owens" presented his downright opinions on the issue. The secretary recorded them as follows: "Charles was a traitor he acted despotically. Approves of Grays remarks. The people justly maintained their rights. These are facts. Charles was guilty of High Treason. He was therefore a traitor because he made War upon his own subjects. The Puritans of that day were the Holiest & best men of the time. Charles 2nd was an abandoned Wretch. Denounced Charles 1st as a traitor and doesn't approve of capital punishment. Charles was an arbitrary king."

These very rough notes make it clear that Thomas was a stalwart Protestant whose views on political liberty and English constitutional history were heavily influenced by the seventeenth century's religious wars. Particularly striking is his judgment that the Puritans were "the Holiest & best men of the time," an opinion that nicely harmonized with his wife's scheme for a school inculcating "the Reformed Religion." One wonders: Did his contempt for the "abandoned" King Charles II work its way into her denigration years later of Siam's polygamous King Mongkut?

It was hardly unusual for an Irish Protestant to sound like a republican firebrand at a time when anti-Catholic sentiment was on the rise in the English-speaking world. The great surprise is the force and conviction with which Thomas opposed English attitudes toward people of color. When the discussion class took up the question "Is the alledged essential intellectual inferiority of the colored races correct?" he was in his element. In two consecutive sessions in June 1854 he vigorously argued that people of color had the same mental capacities as whites. Educated Indians, he insisted, had a history of distinguished achievement in mathematics, shipbuilding, and other fields, and in the army the rank-and-file natives had often proved superior "in mind" to European officers. As for "East Indians" (Eurasians), the fact that they had been denied the same "means of education" as the English sufficiently explained "the absence of . . . high acquirements."

Thomas's arguments, obviously based on his personal experience in India, made an impression on his fellow discussants. When debate ended, the original proposition was amended to read: "That the alledged inferiority discernable in the colour[ed] races is not an inherent attribute of their nature but the effects of a steril [sic] mind for want of cultivation." Put to a vote, it carried with "only two dissentients."

Unlike most officers and men, Paymaster Sergeant Leonowens had thought about an issue whites preferred to ignore—the social disabilities inflicted on Anglo-Indians. In the 1920s and 1930s the mixed-race writer and activist Herbert Alick Stark (grandson of John Sutherland) would bitterly complain that even though Eurasians had been the key "intermediaries . . . the important wheels . . . cranks and pivots in the machinery of the [East India] Company's operations," they were denied recognition and promotion. Not until the last half of the twentieth century did historians look at this discriminatory treatment and try to grasp its meaning. So how did a young self-educated man from county Wexford wake up to the problem by the 1850s? The answer surely lies in his union with a biracial woman—a bond that prompted some searching thought about imperial power. Behind Anna's husband's vehement defense of the intellectual capacity of the "colour[ed] races" lay an intimate eye-opening personal engagement.

Soon after the vote with "two dissentients" he got a flattering invitation from the institute: "to deliver a lecture, at a time most convenient to himself, and on any subject, he may deem necessary." His announced topic, "Study of History," was a fitting choice for someone who admired Indians "versed in the history of their own Country" and who had read *The History of the Popes*—a Protestant exposé of secret papal strategy during the Counter-Reformation. For Thomas, the study of history meant throwing the light of day on sectarian conflict, the abuse of power, the struggle for liberty, and the long war against ignorance and superstition. Studying history was a liberal and liberating endeavor.

On 11 September 1854 twenty-eight listeners came out for his lecture. Anna may not have been one of them, as this was six weeks before Avis's birth. The minutes tell us that the talk "was listened to with marked attention, and at intervals during its delivery elicited rapturous applause from the Members present at its conclusion Mr. Johnston passed a very high and well merited Compliment to Mr. Leonowens for the ability and talent displayed, throughout the delivery of his very interesting lecture—After which a vote of thanks to the lecturer was passed by acclamation."

Frustratingly, the recording secretary said nothing about the substance of the talk, and neither did Perth's newspapers. In spite of this silence, which seems odd, there is still a way to follow the speaker's remarks, the aggressive pungency of which nicely explains those bursts of applause: the lecture had evidently been as topical as it was caustic.

During the preceding months the discussion class had been mired in a question that was agitating the entire English-speaking world: "Are Mesmerism, Table Turning, and Spirit Rapping true Phenomena of Nature?" Some members saw "spirit phenomena" as authentic; others saw them as patently fraudulent. The issue absorbed the class, and debate went on and on. Thomas attended but said nothing. Finally, taking a vote, the talkers decided that "Mesmerism and Table Turning are established facts [but] . . . there is not sufficient evidence before us to establish spirit rappings." Two weeks later came Thomas's lecture.

Two decades later his widow's second book about Siam incorporated a largely irrelevant chapter on the history and persistence of the English belief in witchcraft. From the opening paragraphs the tone was polished and sarcastic, not quite her usual style:

> It might be difficult, at the present time, anywhere in any enlightened Christian community, to find persons of the most ordinary intelligence who entertain the smallest faith in witchcraft.
>
> But yet there are thousands upon thousands who implicitly believe in spirit-rapping and in table-turning, in mesmerism and animal magnetism, and in Mr. Joseph Smith and Brigham Young, his successor, who exhibits such extraordinary powers in prophecy and sensualism at Utah.

Evidently, Anna kept her husband's lecture manuscript and then, years later, inserted part of the talk—his one public triumph—into *The Romance of the Harem*. This quiet revival of his attack on modern credulity and Mormon "sensualism" tells us how much she must have respected his opinions. It also reveals the commitments she herself carried to Siam, a land known for its rich spirit lore and institutionalized polygamy. Behind her often hostile and unreliable account of King Mongkut and his harem stood her late husband's hot disdain for Brigham Young and his houseful of wives.

In Thomas's final contribution to the discussion class, he went on at length about the tyrannical nature of Czar Nicholas and the degraded character of the Russian people.[5] Sarcastically dismissing another member's "panegyric" of the czar, he read a long and intemperate passage from a current publication and ended by "flatter[ing him]self" that everyone would find his "proofs" impregnable and persuasive. The next speaker began with the tart observation that, while "a good deal has been advanced," he did not feel "edified thereby."

Men who are as independent, aggressive, and abrasive as Thomas, and as certain of their correctness, are not to everyone's taste. He was a proud and unusual self-taught man who was admired by many and idolized by his wife. Like him, she too would prove a "difficult woman," as the king of Siam found to his chagrin. Husband and wife were both dedicated to fighting the good fight, and they both punched well above their weight.

5. Again, there is a similarity between his censorious opinions and those of his wife, who in 1881 disparaged "the dirty Russians" and their "false and idolatrous form of worship."

The Convict Hiring Depot at Lynton

IN OCTOBER 1855 THE LEONOWENSES left Perth and sailed three hundred miles north to a desolate anchorage called Port Gregory. Traveling six more miles by land, they reached their arid, rocky, treeless destination: the convict hiring depot in Lynton, to which Thomas had been sent as commissariat storekeeper. For the next fifteen months this formidably isolated place—the northernmost outpost of white settlement in Western Australia—would be Anna's home. Beyond, for thousands of miles, lay a coast scarcely touched by Europeans.

A convict hiring depot was a government station where ticket-of-leave men were hired out to farmers and other free settlers. Ticket-of-leave men were convicts whose good behavior had earned them a conditional release. By planting hiring depots in remote localities, Governor FitzGerald hoped to promote agricultural settlement and economic development. In particular, it was thought that if convicts built a road from Port Gregory to the Geraldine lead mine thirty miles distant, pig lead could be shipped at competitive rates to Singapore. Like many another dream of development, it seemed a good idea.

Construction of the depot had begun two years earlier using limestone blocks quarried at the site and thatch from rushes on the tiny Hutt River. By the time Thomas and Anna arrived, the commissariat had probably been "weather-boarded and shingled," but living arrangements were still very primitive. Since there was no local timber, rafters and planks had to be shipped all the way from Fremantle and were thus quite costly.

From the start, the governor had been warned by London that if expenses were not reduced, "the proper remedy will be to break up the outlying convict depots." By 1857 it was obvious that the depot was a losing proposition. Thomas was its last storekeeper, and when he and Anna returned to Perth the station was abandoned. Today, with the jail and a few other buildings partly restored, the site is a moderately intact, accessible, and highly evocative remnant of Western Australia's convict history. However, the building in which the Leonowenses lived and worked, the commissariat, has fallen. As you stand and stare helplessly at the rubble, you begin to grasp what it meant to make a home here. For the rest of her life, Anna maintained an absolute silence about the place.[1]

But to follow this, the grimmest and most obscure phase of her wedded life, we must return to the man who preceded her husband in his arduous post—Uncle Glasscott.

A Faithful Imperial Servant

It was in August 1853, after five months as clerk in Perth's central commissariat office, that Glasscott was appointed the first full-time storekeeper in Lynton. The depot was then only a few months old, the storehouse had not been built, and huge challenges lay ahead. Like the first convicts and pensioner guards, he would have lived under canvas. By the following April a few buildings had been finished, but the jail and hospital had not been started, and the commissariat storehouse had no rafters.

Something in addition to the lack of timber held back progress—the tangles of bureaucracy. Because of the division of powers in imperial administration, there had to be two storehouses, the commissariat store and the depot store, each with its own jealous keeper. Nominally independent of colonial government, the commissariat storekeeper issued "supplies . . . sufficient to last six months" to the superintendent, and the latter officer then moved them to the depot store and saw to the "detail issues." Only after the Lynton hiring depot proved too costly to sustain did the colonial secretary, the newly appointed Frederick Barlee (who opposed the station's continuance), complain about "the absurdity and unnecessary expense of

1. On GoogleEarth, S 28°12′36.71″ and E 114°18′39.23″, one can see the outline of the commissariat. It's the L-shaped building that resembles a slightly flattened Utah.

the double system of issue: the two stores . . . divided only by a nine inch wall." For as long as Glasscott and Thomas were in Lynton, however, that nine-inch wall was the basis of their professional existence and dignity.

Another feature of their working life was the colonial British hierarchy, for this was not a place of frontier equality. The chief local landowner, Captain Henry Ayshford Sanford, was a recent arrival who had named Lynton after his north Devon village. Still finding his feet, he pushed forward a number of speculative enterprises, mainly whaling and raising grain, sheep, and horses. Commanding and impulsive, he arranged matters as he saw fit. Once, when a barque went aground in Port Gregory, he was seen on shore rapidly stripping his clothes off. "Good God, he will never attempt it," the ship's master was heard to say, but Sanford plunged in and actually swam to the mariners' rescue.

Soon after Glasscott went to work, he had a run-in with this forceful and volatile man. Someone suspected that government timber had been used in Sanford's new house, and the storekeeper was asked to investigate. Doing so was not without risk. Once, when another man accused the captain of being "a chisel trying to cheat Govt out of some planks," the accuser had a hatchet thrown at him that "cut his wrist severely." After Anna's uncle submitted the results of his investigation, the captain sent a letter to his brother expressing confidence that "Glasscott's complaints" would be dismissed. And they were: the brother, William A. Sanford, colonial secretary from 1852 to 1855, was the second most powerful man in the colony.

The case illustrates the intrinsic weakness of a storekeeper's position. Because the British Treasury directly controlled the commissariat's purse strings, the department was nominally independent of colonial administration. But because the local elite—the large landowners and the magistrates—stood so much higher than mere storekeepers, this independence was apt to be precarious.

The magistrates were local administrators vested with the powers of government. The one that Glasscott worked with was William Burges, a prosperous Irish settler who had come to Australia twenty-three years earlier with servants and a shipload of supplies and was thus deemed worthy of an enormous land allotment. In 1850 he was appointed resident magistrate of the large Champion Bay district. When the convict depot was opened in Lynton, he got another appointment, visiting magistrate for Port Gregory.

Privately, he ran a large sheep station near the mouth of a river. Influential and well-to-do, Burges was in all respects the epitome of Western Australia's conservative gentry.

The big challenge a storekeeper faced was how to hold his supplies against a magistrate's requisitions. Soon after Glasscott took hold of his new job, Burges sent the colonial secretary a request: "The Commissariat officer at Port Gregory makes a demur about supplying the Colonial Government with . . . flour, which he says he cannot spare. . . . I hope instructions may be sent to him by the first opportunity to supply stores for the use of the Gaol here [in Champion Bay]." In fact, Glasscott had been following protocol, and Burges, who was supposed to rely on local suppliers, not the commissariat, had not. Hence Governor FitzGerald's answer: "The settlers must be prepared to supply flour to the Govt at a fair rate." What the governor didn't know was that his plan for stimulating the local economy ignored local conditions. Grain did poorly in Lynton's climate and soil, and the pensioners settled there were losing their crops.

So policy had to evolve, and before long Burges was authorized to requisition whatever was "absolutely necessary for the maintenance of prisoners." Glasscott got new orders, which he followed, and the two men developed a smooth working relationship, "pull[ing] well together," as Burges noted later. In addition, Glasscott served as Burges's clerk, took over his customs work, and acted as postmaster. In performing these varied functions, he followed regulations to the letter. When the *Mary Queen of Scots* was driven ashore (this was the vessel Sanford plunged in to save), Glasscott arranged "for a guard to protect the wrecked property." But when the master wanted his crew fed from commissariat stores, Glasscott demanded a written pledge of full repayment. Among the salvaged goods were five gallons of gin. According to Burges's approving report, "Mr. Glasscott made no attempt to charge duty on the gin, so long as he saw it used only for the shipwrecked seamen and others who were assisting in saving property . . . but when he saw it put into a cart, and . . . sent away up the country," he seized and held the import till the duty was paid. Clearly, Glasscott was a punctilious servant of the imperial command.

What is not clear, owing to the absence of personal documents, is how the man stayed sane at his isolated post or what his attitudes were toward the area's suppressed indigenes, the Nanda people. In May 1855 a new storekeeper arrived. Two months later Glasscott sailed to Fremantle. By mid-October he was once again in Bombay, this time as master of the Indo-British School for Eurasian boys.[2] Since schoolmasters were mostly imported from Britain, the appointment tells us that Anna's uncle's abilities had at last been recognized: he now held a position commensurate with his talents. But the new life came to an abrupt end on 5 February 1856, when he died of "dysentery and fever" in the city's European hospital. His age was thirty-three or thirty-four.

How did Anna feel about the death of this man with the telltale name pointing to her mixed-race lineage? Was there a degree of relief? All we can say is that her lifelong silence about him was in marked contrast to the way his name was memorialized in India. When her mother gave birth two years later, in 1858, the baby was called Vaudry Glasscott Donohoe. When the next generation's males were born, their middle names were Vaudry and Glascott. These evidences of family origin were valued and kept in circulation by Anna's Anglo-Indian relatives. She, on the other hand, informed her children that her first male British ancestor in India had been a Crawford.

As C. J. Hawes has shrewdly observed, "British credentials were vital to the self perception of educated Eurasians. These necessarily required a repudiation of their Indian maternal ancestry." That was one point on which Anna saw eye to eye with her people in India. It was the British founder, Glascott or Crawford, real or fictive, who counted and whose surname was brought out and exhibited. His *bibi* could be, and was, forgotten.

TWELVE BY THIRTEEN FEET

Between Glasscott's and Thomas's tenures as commissariat storekeeper, another man, Archibald Edgar, had a go at the job but quickly proved that he lacked the suppleness to manage its contradictions. When faced with Burges's demands, he stubbornly maintained that Mends had "*told* him not to make any issues whatever on the requisition of the Resident Magistrate." In retaliation, Burges had Edgar removed on grounds that he failed to respect

2. Because Anna had severed relations with her family in India, Glasscott's return meant that they at last got a firsthand report on her fortunes in Australia. At that point, however, the news would have been that she and her husband had just been transferred to a remote outpost. This grim disclosure gave sister Eliza an additional motive to try to contact her possibly distressed sister in Bangkok—an overture Anna repulsed. See chapter 13.

his superiors and engaged in private retail sales. The government sided with the magistrate, but commissariat headquarters backed the storekeeper and even produced a copy of the instructions given him. The employee who signed this document, warranting it a "true copy," was none other than *Thos Leonowens.*" His signature tells us something very interesting: he must have known he was headed for trouble when he himself agreed to go up north.

It was on 4 October 1855, five weeks after Edgar was sacked, that Thomas, Anna, and one-year-old Avis boarded the schooner *Perseverance* for their new home. Like Edgar and his family, they apparently lived in a room designed to be the commissariat office.[3] Its dimensions, according to an engineer's report, were twelve by thirteen feet (3.7 × 4 meters). For fifteen months this tight, undomestic space was Anna's home . . . and prison. Outside, the wind rarely let up, the terrain was desert-like, the vegetation scrubby. In summer the valley enclosing the depot became a cauldron. The winter of 1856 brought "one continued heavy down-pour accompanied with tempests of winds." The well was caved-in and useless. When a new colonial secretary toured the northern districts, he was shocked at how "very rough" everything was. "The morals of the Inhabitants are at a somewhat low ebb," he reported, "and the want of females is very apparent."

These were the conditions (except that winter had turned to spring) in which Anna gave birth to her fourth and last child on 22 October 1856. The government didn't pay for the obstetric expenses of employees' wives, but at least there was a station doctor handy, and she wasn't on the *Alibi.* The baby was called Louis Gunnis Leonowens, the middle name coming from Thomas's brother. Louis was destined to accompany his mother to Siam in 1862 and play a role in her first book, *The English Governess at the Siamese Court;* he figures in all three movies based on her life in Bangkok. Despite her claim that he was born in London, he may have known better: in his teens he sailed to Australia to seek his fortune. He eventually found it in Siam, thanks to lucrative timber concessions awarded him by his old pal, King Chulalongkorn. His last place of abode was Albert Hall Mansions in London. At his death in 1919 his estate was worth £66,904. Louis died rich.

3. Before Edgar's arrival, Burges noted that, "as he is a married man, I can no longer have the use of the Commissariat Office," the implication being that this room would have to serve as the couple's home. The only known alternative, a boardinghouse where workers came to drink, would not have been suitable for the respectable Leonowenses.

There was no way the boy's luckless father would find his fortune in Lynton. By mid-1855 the Western Australian economy had begun to contract, and the government was forced to recognize that its obligations exceeded its income. The budget came under close scrutiny after a new governor arrived, Arthur Edward Kennedy, who not only proved more autocratic than FitzGerald but was more disposed to criticize, pry into details, and make a point of official dignity. When the Geraldine lead mine ceased operations and went up for sale in London, the whole rationale for the convict hiring depot in Lynton vanished.

Meanwhile, Thomas's work necessitated a sixty-mile ride to Champion Bay each month, a duty that obliged him to keep a horse. Recognizing his abilities and diligence, Burges asked him to serve as magistrate's clerk, as Glasscott had done. When the letter of appointment was submitted to Mends, Thomas's boss in Perth, he gave his consent with some reluctance: "*As there is no suitable person . . . for the duty of Magistrate's Clerk,* I have no objection to Mr. Leonowens holding this temporary post, with the understanding that it is not allowed to interfere, in any way, with his Commissariat duties." That storekeepers and magistrates had conflicting interests was an old story.

Thomas's resignation of his clerkship on 4 August 1856 may be a sign that the interfering had begun. Or perhaps he was just too busy: that same month he complained that there was too little time between the overland mail's arrival and departure for him to answer communications from headquarters. Colonial Secretary Barlee's smooth reply—"it is assumed" that the two and a half days currently allowed are "ample"—can't have soothed the storekeeper's temper. His wife was then in her eighth month of pregnancy.

For his part, Governor Kennedy was provoked by the gap between the sums spent on Lynton and Port Gregory and the slender returns. A fact-finding mission in September 1856 resulted in some sobering conclusions about the northern economy. Two months later, when a farmer offered his potatoes to the Lynton depot at twenty pounds a ton, an unheard-of price, the governor hit the ceiling and had his secretary send Burges a stern warning. "I am directed to invite any remarks from yourself and other settlers in the District as to the reason of these prevailing high prices, and further . . . to request you will make it known generally among the settlers in your district . . . that H.E. [His Excellency] has doubts if prices range as at present, as to the advisability of closing the Depot altogether." Governor Kennedy, Magistrate Burges, and Commissariat Storekeeper Leonowens, all born in Ireland, would now find themselves fighting over potatoes.

Several barrels of the precious tubers sent to Port Gregory got "wet and heated" and started to rot. Thomas stored them in an empty jail cell. On the afternoon of 18 November Burges found them there and at once objected, calling them a danger to health and ordering "their immediate removal." In response (Burges reported), "Mr Leonowens stated in very strong terms that they should not be removed, that the Gaol was an Imperial Building, and that he would make what use he thought proper of it. I took no notice of his remarks but ordered Mr Snowdon the Gaoler to have them removed which was accordingly done." Burges covered himself by having two medical officers affirm in writing that storing potatoes in the jail's close quarters could produce "disease" and "contagion" among the prisoners.[4] At the time there were no prisoners.

The next day, feeling more conciliatory, the magistrate offered the use of his own office for temporary storage. Thomas's reply, correct in form and icy in content, reveals the hand of a skilled bureaucratic writer. Scribbling at top speed without quite lifting pen from paper (a faint ligature joining his angry words is visible), he wrote:

> I have to thank you for the offer conveyed in your letter (2nd) of this date, viz to give up your office to store the potatoes in; at the same time it is my duty to observe that as you vacated the Building and it has been unoccupied for some months, the charge of the same rests with me, and according to the Regulations of the Service it can only be allotted for the purposes of the service by me . . .
>
> Under any Circumstances, your offer is very much too late, the Potatoes having been sent to the Port for shipment this morning.
>
> > I have the honor to be
> > Your obedient Servant
> > Thos Leonowens

4. These fears were based on a widespread misunderstanding of Ireland's recent famine (which Burges and Thomas had missed). As Cecil Woodham-Smith notes in *The Great Hunger: Ireland 1845–9*, the fungus that caused stored potatoes to rot was thought to be a "result of the heat and fermentation which accompany the processes of decomposition." Thus, wet and heated potatoes could be seen as dangerous in themselves.

Then, instead of writing "Commissariat Storekeeper," Thomas penned a grander phrase: "in Charge of Imperial Buildings at Port Gregory." The imposing title was consistent with the claim recorded on his son's birth certificate one week earlier, namely, that the father's "Rank or Profession" was, quite simply, "gentleman"—still a powerful word.

There was another confrontation that day between Burges and Thomas. The magistrate had been trying to secure a hand mill with which prisoners sentenced to hard labor could grind grain. When a mill finally reached Port Gregory, arriving with the bad potatoes, the storekeeper refused for unknown reasons to turn it over. The magistrate's response was summary and humiliating. In Thomas's version of events, "you [Burges] stated yesterday in my store and before some Ticket of Leave men that if I wanted Labor to work the Mill I must employ it myself, and turning to Mr Snowdon [the jailer] you ordered him not to supply me with Labor."

Evidently, the air was thoroughly poisoned, and not by potatoes, with Burges maintaining that he would be the one to put prisoners to work and Thomas insisting on the independence of the commissariat. His long, starchy, defiant reply rang four changes on the key word, "interfere": "Nor do I recognise your authority to interfere in the matter of the Mill received by this Department. . . . I am compelled however reluctantly, to state that your interference in this matter is quite unprecedented. . . . It is impossible that such undue and improper interference with the public service in matters where according to my instructions you have no right whatever to interfere—can be submitted to."

The acrimonious correspondence was sent to the higher-ups in Perth for comment. Backing Thomas's contention and echoing his language, Mends, his boss, "submitted that Mr Burges's interference in regard to the potatoes was altogether unnecessary, because the Commissariat Storekeeper is entirely and solely responsible for their proper keeping." That the jail was empty "should . . . have prevented any interference on Mr Burges's part." But Mends could not approve of Thomas's tone. Regretting that he had "reason to animadvert upon Mr Leonowens style of correspondence," he assured the governor that he would "remind the Storekeeper of what is always due to the office of Resident."

Kennedy agreed, but with a difference. The letter he had his secretary send Burges mildly informed him that the governor "considers it advisable that you should not interfere" and then assured him that Thomas would receive a sterner rebuke: "The correspondence of Mr Leonowens has been submitted to the Head of his Department [Mends] with a view to prevent a recurrence of communications, which His Excellency considers to be improper in tone & substance." The difference is that Mr. Burges got discreet advice on how to conduct official business in future, whereas Mr. Leonowens was treated as an inferior in the hearing of his antagonist and bluntly ordered to mend his manners.

The quarrel reflected more than the inherent conflict between magistrates and storekeepers or the fact that Lynton's convict depot was in its last days and tempers were fraying. Underneath was a sharp colonial-British class division. Commanding a large private estate unrelated to his government job, Burges was an undisputed member of Western Australia's conservative elite. Thomas thought of himself as a "gentleman" who had an informed liberal outlook and wielded an able pen, but, economically, he was a beset functionary whose working identity depended on the department that paid his salary. When the two men squared off against each other, Burges was backed by the full weight of the government whose rules he had fudged, whereas Thomas, a stickler for protocol, sustained a wound to his professional independence and personal dignity.

Anna, busy as she was with her three-year-old daughter and newborn infant, could not have escaped the unfolding drama. Sharing the confinement of a twelve-by-thirteen-foot room in the commissariat, she had to be aware of her husband's ordeal: his furious scribbling in defense of his hopeless job, his inevitable and humiliating personal defeat. She could not help getting an earful of the petty, ongoing tragedy of bureaucratic life.

MOVING ON

And then it was only history, the kind that doesn't matter and soon gets forgotten. Governor Kennedy decided the depot was too much of a drain and must be shut down. Thomas's "Imperial Buildings" were abandoned and began their slow decay. He and Anna returned to Perth, where he was taken on as Mends's assistant, a step up from clerk; evidently, he was far too useful for the quarrel with Burges to count against him. In March the commissariat storekeeper in Perth proposed him for renewed membership in the Swan River Mechanics' Institute, but the nomination never came up for a vote. On 3 April 1857, four years after accidentally landing in Western Australia, the Leonowenses took passage on the *Lady Amherst*, a thirty-year-old vessel that had been refitted for the transport of horses and was now bound for Singapore, where it docked on the last day of the month.

The trip took less than a third as long as the eventful outbound ordeal on the *Alibi*. That voyage and its horrors, along with so much else that had happened in Perth and Lynton—the death of Anna's first son, the collapse of her plan for a young ladies' seminary, the association with convicts at that raw northern outpost, the pain of seeing her husband beaten down in his difficult and unrewarding job—would have been reason enough to draw a veil over her life in Australia. From now on, one guesses, she had an absolute benchmark for failure and futility, and with it one more standing motive for doing *whatever* it took to succeed.

9

Widowed in the
Straits Settlements

Singapore, already an entrepôt of global trade, was another universe from tiny Perth and forsaken Lynton. A bustling multiethnic city administered by Britons and populated largely by Asians, it numbered 50,000 Chinese, 13,000 Indians, 11,000 Malays, and 2,500 Europeans and Eurasians. When an American naval surgeon sailed into the crowded harbor, he marveled at the number and variety of seafaring vessels, from the "great lumbering, red-painted, goggle-eyed Chinese junks, to the fine, large and elegant clipper-ship of the States." Scanning the ships' flags of many nations, his eye was caught by one he had never seen: "the white elephant banner of Siam."

Only four decades had passed since Stamford Raffles realized that a harbor at the relatively narrow southern opening of the Strait of Malacca—the bottleneck for Europe's trade with China—would have incalculable commercial and military advantages. Raffles got the East India Company to acquire Singapore at a time when the island was mostly equatorial forest. Now it was one of the strategic island ports—Malta, Helena, Bombay, Penang, Hong Kong—that anchored the immense arch of Britain's maritime empire.

When the Leonowenses arrived in 1857, the business district was lined with two-story whitewashed godowns full of rubber and pepper bound for Europe and opium, rice, tin, and cotton goods heading to China.[1] A free port that imposed no duties, Singapore was a natural base for international

1. "Godown" is from the Malay *godong*, meaning "warehouse" or "storehouse."

trading companies. Most were British and European, but there were also Chinese, Parsi, Arab, and Armenian firms. One was American. For a man like Anna's husband, who got on well with Asians and had worked for the commissariat and a Bombay importer, Singapore was an excellent place to look for employment.

But civil service was out. The Indian "Mutiny," erupting just as the Leonowenses arrived, would straiten the administrative budget in Singapore (which was still governed from Calcutta). And thanks to the quarrel in Lynton, Thomas would not have been given the necessary testimonials by Western Australia's governor or colonial secretary. But he surely carried good strong letters from both the central commissariat office in Perth and Bombay's Robert Frith and Company.

So, returning to the private sector, Thomas became a clerk once again, this time for the Singapore branch of the Borneo Company Ltd. His new office was in Commercial Square, and his home was on Brass Bassa Road, near the city center. For the next fifteen months, he and Anna would be living in one of the world's most energized marketplaces.

Of all the contingencies that shaped her fate, few were as consequential as her spouse's employment by the Borneo Company. Organized in London the previous year, the firm was run by Glasgow merchants who had traded in the South China Sea and were now looking at Sarawak and Siam. Thomas's boss was William Adamson, an assistant who would soon be manager of the Singapore branch. Clearly marked for success, Adamson impressed others as both "entirely unassuming" and "a very keen, able man of business." In time he became so closely tied to the port's commercial and civic growth that a local historian was tempted to equate "the history of Mr. Adamson" with "that of Singapore." That was the kind of man, famous for his diverse interests and connections, who would eventually put Anna forward for the most important job of her life.

Like many businessmen in Southeast Asia, Adamson came from dissenting stock in northern England and lowland Scotland—people with the same zeal and enterprise as Thomas's admired Puritans. Adamson worshiped with the Presbyterians, Singapore's largest Protestant society after the Church of England, yet he was anything but parochial. He partnered with Chinese businessmen, and he even excelled in amateur theatricals as a light comedian. It was never forgotten how he once played "a woman's part."

According to Adamson's minister, the Reverend Thomas McKenzie Fraser, the local Presbyterian Church attracted "two fifths of the European inhabitants," including "a considerable number of young men, clerks in the various mercantile houses." This seems to have been the church Thomas and Anna joined. Two years later it would be one more vital link, providing Anna with some desperately needed support from Reverend Fraser.

We have one more fact about the Leonowenses' life in Singapore. In April 1858, a year after settling in, Thomas was voted foreman of a jury that exonerated a Chinese man accused of stealing jewelry. This tells us he played a role in civic affairs and was known and respected, just as in Perth. He and his wife were part of the life of the city. They must have had friends. The point is simple, but it serves to expose the unreality of a widely circulated story about Anna's supposed turning point: the claim that she settled in Singapore *after* being widowed and that in order to start a school there she "reinvented" herself, devising an undiluted English past. In fact, though she would indeed return to Singapore and open a school, it seems obvious that she could not have taken on a new identity and history in a place where she was already known. In all likelihood, she was seen as Anglo-Indian as long as she lived in the Straits.

Meanwhile, trying to support his family on a clerk's salary, Thomas had his own future to invent. In May or June 1858, his jury duty finished, he apparently found it: a promising opening at the managerial level. Leaving Anna, Avis, and Louis on Brass Bassa Road for the time being, he left for Penang, three or four days distant by steamer. The plan, one guesses, was for the family to join him if the new position worked out.

The Pinang Family Hotel

Penang (also spelled Pinang) was to the northwest of Singapore at the opposite and much wider end of the Strait of Malacca. Located on Prince of Wales Island, it impressed early Western travelers as one of earth's most Eden-like places. Its two distinctive features were the steep forested hill that rose to a height of 2,700 feet and the lowland plain that held the growing city and a scattering of country homes shaded by nutmeg trees and areca palms. Within the city proper were the shops and houses of the 71,000 Malay and 29,000 Chinese, who greatly outnumbered the 2,200 Europeans.

Two years before Thomas's arrival, an American diplomat on his way to Siam was surprised to find that Penang had no hotel. Someone else noticed the opportunity, and in 1858 a respectable establishment, the Pinang Family Hotel, opened for business. It was probably to manage this new enterprise that Thomas left Singapore.

On 9 September, a few months after his move, an advertisement began running in the *Singapore Free Press*:

THE PINANG FAMILY HOTEL.
Corner Penang Street.

These Premises are situated close to the Beach, and command a clear and extensive view of the Straits and the opposite Coast. The apartments are large and airy.

Ladies and Gentlemen visiting or calling at Penang, will find every attention paid to their comfort and convenience at this Establishment, during their stay.

When Anna left Singapore to join her husband, her departure was recorded in a newspaper passenger list, though rather oddly: "July 17 per *Viscount Canning* to Pinang, Mrs. Marcus and two children, and Mrs. Leonowens." The oddity is that Anna apparently traveled alone, while the other woman had two children, perhaps in her cabin. Could these have been Avis and Louis? They surely wouldn't have been left behind.

Subsequent passenger lists help clear up the mystery. In September Mrs. Marcus's husband went up to Penang on the same steamer his wife had taken and then returned to Singapore on 1 October—with her but with no children. Evidently, Avis and Louis *had* been consigned to Mrs. Marcus's care.

But why? A plausible explanation is that, with all the headaches of moving and two small children to tend, Anna needed support, privacy, rest. Since Mr. Marcus was chief engineer in the firm that owned the *Viscount Canning*, his wife would have been able to accompany and assist the young mother at little or no cost. That Mrs. Marcus stayed on in Penang for more than two months is a hint that Anna may have needed serious assistance. Was she "dreadfully ill" again? Had there been another physical or emotional collapse?

In Bombay Thomas had not been able to find a permanent, healthy, affordable rental outside the crowded city center. If he and his family resided in the Pinang Family Hotel and their rooms approximated the advertisement's promise, they would at last have had a home as "large and airy" as their Malabar Point Aviary. But we can only surmise: except for a veiled allusion in *The English Governess* to a "happy home . . . in Malacca" (a common way of referring to the Straits Settlements), Anna never let on that she had lived in Penang, let alone that "Major" Leonowens had operated a hotel there.

All we have from her is a curious anecdote. At the time there was a shortage of young, single, good-looking European women in the Straits. Although it was customary for mothers to have an ayah, or nurse, give their children a daily outing, Anna seems to have performed the chore herself, whether from preference or economy. One day, when out with Louis and Avis, she had an encounter she liked to recall for her grandchildren. She set it in London during her fictitious residence in St. James's Square, but it must have occurred in Penang or Singapore. In a granddaughter's version, "a gay young man-about-town was attracted, and managed to open a conversation with her, in which she met him with equal gaiety and frankness. Finally, when she was preparing to go home, he asked when he might see her again, to which she mischievously and demurely replied, 'My mistress does not allow gentleman callers.' 'Then when will you walk with me again?' 'Neither will my mistress permit me to walk with you again.' And womanlike she enjoyed disposing thus of that poor young man."

In her first book about her life in Siam, Anna portrayed herself as something of a tease. When King Mongkut asked her age, she "demurely" replied that she was 150 years old, stopping him in his tracks. *Demure* was her word for the coy, flirty, mischievous manner that threw men off balance and momentarily checked their power. *Demure* was one of the ways Mrs. Leonowens coped with poverty and powerlessness, not to mention the humiliation of being taken for a servant.

Thomas's Death

On 8 May 1859, near the end of her first year in Penang, Anna's world went down in ruins. Thomas died, quite without warning, and she found herself with no supporting family, no source of income, no home, and two small children to bring up. The husband she had placed at the center of her life was gone, and nothing was left standing.

A chaplain's entry in the register of burials at St. George's Church gives the cause of death as "Apoplexy" and says that Thomas had been a "Hotel Master." This is the only evidence of his livelihood and social position in Penang.

His age was put down as thirty-two, three years too young. After his interment in Northam Road Cemetery, the simple and dignified epitaph made him even younger:

Sacred
To The Memory Of
Thomas Leonowens
Who Departed This Life On The
7th Of May 1859
Aged 31 Years & 5 Days
Lord Have Mercy

The misleading ages probably came from the widow. Was he actually born on 2 May, as the very specific "5 Days" implies? We cannot say, as Anna was notoriously inaccurate about such matters, and the natal date recorded in Ireland (25 January 1824) was for baptism, not birth. Tellingly, the gravestone doesn't make Thomas a major—a promotion in rank dating from Anna's years in America, where no one knew better.

Exactly how he died may never be known for certain. In the story Anna told her grandchildren, Major Leonowens was determined to join "his brother officers" on a tiger hunt in Province Wellesley (the English name for the mainland opposite Penang). Anna begged him not to, but he insisted, promising to be back by the following evening. It was the hot season, and by the time the tiger was tracked and killed, the tropical sun, directly overhead, was blazing: "The other men begged him to wait for the cool of the evening, but he was not to be dissuaded. He reached home at the appointed hour, only to drop from his horse unconscious at his wife's feet. The sun had done its worst."

Did it happen? The "brother officers" and the melodrama prompt a degree of skepticism. If the tale had been cooked up for *Youth's Companion*, it could have been titled "The Faithful Husband; or, A Promise Kept in the Tropics" and given a pen-and-ink sketch of a wife kneeling at a death-bed. One is struck by Anna's apparent calculation that North Americans would accept the impossible, namely, that Thomas could leave Singapore for a hunt in Province Wellesley, three or four days distant by steamer, and ride home the next afternoon. She knew no one wanted the truth about Southeast Asia.

Yet her story, however doctored, was based on fact. The geography comes right as soon as one realizes that the Leonowenses were living in Penang, not Singapore. Tigers were still a menace, and there was a policy of eradication: on Prince of Wales Island the bounty was one hundred Straits dollars, and in Province Wellesley, where the big cats remained abundant, the so-called Kling people were said to be "active in Tiger trapping." May was the hottest month, and everyone knew that a Westerner who exposed himself ran the risk of sunstroke or apoplexy. "Heat-apoplexy" was what Kipling called it. "Heatstroke" is the modern term.

In Western Australia Thomas had been used to riding sixty miles from Lynton to Champion Bay, but now he was a city man in the tropics. He may have overestimated his endurance, dying of exhaustion and dehydration if not exactly heatstroke.[2] "Exposure," Anna's word for the cause of death, is a good one, as it would have been in character for her husband to keep his vow by taking a deadly chance. In India he not only had been solicitous of her well-being but had risked his future for her. Was his death a last succinct expression of his love? Whatever the answer, for the rest of her life she wore a brooch of curved tiger claws, the emblem of her loss. Presented to her by the hunting party, the claws are at her neck in the two photos of her repro-duced in this book (see pages 182 and 197).

Of the three bereavements Anna suffered in her ten years of marriage, Thomas's death was by far the worst. It was a terrible calamity, and the immediate result was what she later termed a "long and serious illness."

2. As Anna very likely knew, Lieutenant Colonel John Sutherland had famously suffered a "sunstroke while out riding" with the maharaja of Bharatpur in June 1848; he died in the maharaja's palace. According to Philip D. Curtin, it was "believed that water, like wine, should be drunk in moderation, especially in hot weather. Warm water was also said to be dangerous." For a dehydrated person in the tropics, these were dan-gerous beliefs.

The best account we have of this breakdown comes from someone who got the story straight from Anna—Laura Winthrop Johnson, the American friend who helped her start a private kindergarten on Staten Island. The first time they met, Anna related the history of her life in the East Indies. When she came to her husband's death, she spoke freely of the extremity of her grief. Impressed, Johnson sent a friend a verbatim report of what Mrs. Leonowens admitted: "'I had a fever & was a little deranged,' she said simply, 'and was nursed by a good lady Abbess there, or I should have died.'"

Anna's disclosure of her derangement is consistent with her hints about her other prostrating illnesses, especially in Bangkok, where stress and fever led to dire "fancies," as she termed them. Another reason to trust Johnson's report is its surprising mention of a Roman Catholic savior, the "good lady Abbess." It is the unexpected detail that counts, especially if it fits what is on record elsewhere. Modern histories of the first convents in the Straits Settlements show that a Sister Joseph, originally Miss Spooner, arrived in Penang in 1858 to take charge of a convent school. The next May—the month Thomas died—this establishment moved into the former Government House on Light Street, not far from the Pinang Family Hotel. It would have been quite in order for the nuns of the Light Street Convent to care for the young widow and her children after her collapse. A sister institution in Singapore, the Convent of the Holy Infant Jesus, had as one of its specific missions the care of destitute widows.

Anna also got aid and comfort from a Protestant cleric. When she and her children departed Penang, the man who had evidently been her Presbyterian minister in Singapore was with her on the steamer. His name adjoins hers in a newspaper's list of passengers disembarking in Singapore: "June 25 per *Hooghly*, from Pinang . . . Revd. T. M. Fraser, Mrs. Leonowens and (2) children."

It was a month and a half since Thomas's death. If Anna had required help on her trip to Penang the previous year, her need was now twenty times greater. Badly damaged, she was not yet able to stand on her own. To whom could she turn? Having broken with her family, she couldn't go back to India. Reverend Fraser may not have traveled to Penang for the express purpose of taking charge of her, but he was surely an immense comfort on her return to Singapore and an indispensable resource as she took up her life once again.

A Struggling Schoolmistress

Singapore had been the right place for Thomas to land an office job, but how could an Anglo-Indian widow with a warm manner, a dignified presence, considerable learning, and large, unrealized ambitions contrive to support herself? Short of marriage—and Anna seems to have had enough of that—there was only one answer.

By year's end she had opened her school. Its initial location in Armenian Street, home to only two of Singapore's "principal inhabitants," may not have been suitable, and it soon moved to Beach Road, where city directories for 1861 and 1862 show her as the proprietor of a private school. A livelier part of town, Beach Road had several "well kept European hotels." Perhaps Anna conducted her school in one of these, in her rooms.

In Perth her ambitious plan for a seminary for girls from evangelical homes had fallen through. By contrast, on Staten Island, where her private kindergarten succeeded, there was both a need for the school and an energetic contact able to mobilize the local elite. For Singapore the questions are: Who backed her? What sorts of pupils did she seek and attract? The story she put out in North America—that she taught the children of the "*other* resident officers' wives"—isn't credible for the obvious reason: Anna didn't belong to that club, and she had no hold on its patronage or charity.

The reason for lingering over the question of her client base is that a mixed-race teacher would have had a mixed reception in Singapore. Shortly before Anna returned to the city, an editor at the *Straits Times* derided the prejudice against Anglo-Indians with force and verve: "Time was, when narrow minded bigots, and upstart boys, and beardless ensigns, and prejudiced Colonels, and hoodwinked commanders-in-chief ran down the Eurasians. The half castes, quarter castes, East Indians, Indo-Britons, Anglo Indians . . . were sneered at, frowned upon, hedged round, despised, dishonoured, and disgraced. . . . Is this not similar to the sin of the American Planters, who sell their own children to slavery?" *Uncle Tom's Cabin* was by "a noble woman," and "invidious distinctions of race" are "unworthy of men who glory in British ascendancy." But a later editor merely shrugged at the "over-sensitive objection taken to all who are descended in any way from the people of India, no matter how remote the descent." By the mid-1860s, observes a historian of colonial Singapore, white society had grown "staid, respectable, narrow-minded," "Eurasians were held in contempt," and "old-timers regretted the passing of the early, informal days when wealth, race and colour were of little account."

Given the variety of attitudes and the overall trend, one guesses that Anna served the small Eurasian middle class and the floating population of Westerners who came to Singapore to try their luck. Within the latter group were a photographer and his wife, the Thomas Heritages, who resided on Queen Street for a couple of years. Their daughter Susan was a friend of Avis's and very likely a pupil of Anna's. Other pupils may have been found through Reverend Fraser and the Presbyterian connection.

Anna would give her Staten Island backer the impression that the school had "got on tolerably," but the picture that emerges from contemporary directories is bleaker. In 1861 the *Straits Calendar* listed eight schools and seminaries in Singapore. For five of these the entries included page numbers to which those who sought further information could turn. Anna's entry has her name and address—"Leonowens, Mrs; Beach Road"—and that's it: no page number or details. The listing left her at a disadvantage, making her school look small, marginal, out of the running. It was the same in 1862, except that now there were nine schools, and she was cut from the directory's list of principal inhabitants.

More than two years had passed since her husband's death. Anna was back on her feet, a self-supporting woman with capacities that hadn't been tested and two growing children aged seven and five. But her school was barely surviving. If a better opportunity came along, no matter how out of the way, she might have to risk it.

An Opening

Little is known of Anna's relationships outside marriage during her ten years with Thomas. It is only after her widowed return to Singapore that a few friends emerge from the shadows. Foremost among them are William and Margaret Adamson, who approved her for Siam, and Francis Davis Cobb, who encouraged her to move to New York. All three evidently saw her as someone who merited special support.

Cobb may have been Anna's first American, one of the few in Singapore. Only twenty-four, he and his partner in business had recently left Boston on a ship loaded with "merchandise bought on borrowed capital."[3] They reached Singapore in early 1861, well after Anna had come to terms with Thomas's death. When word came that the South had seceded and hostilities had begun, the partner sailed back to the States to enlist. Staying on, Cobb found a home on Beach Road—Anna's street—and the two got acquainted. He knew her as a hard-pressed working widow with two small children, an unusual and attractive woman. Husbandless, she was no longer obliged to rebuff interested men.

For Anna, Cobb was a new type: a liberal New England Unitarian with some money, a willingness to experiment, and a feel for what was possible. He may have seemed direct and effervescent, but for all that she soon realized that he was solid through and through, a kind, tactful, trustworthy ally. Once, when she sent him something from Bangkok, he dashed off a witty complaint about "your costly gift which I do not forgive you. How can I cure your bravery? Are you unconquerable? We are beyond that condition which requires gifts for remembrance sake, so please do not send me any more." Less on guard than the feisty and expert Anglo-Irish clerk she had wed, the young merchant was fond of play and paradox, especially in language. Years later she described him as "one of the most charming men I have ever met . . . so fine and noble."

William Adamson, a more astute businessman than Cobb, had greatly extended his range since the year Thomas worked for him. In 1859, two days after his former clerk died in Penang, he married Margaret Hamilton, daughter of a Glasgow factory owner and East India merchant. Like her spouse, Margaret had been raised as a religious Independent and was willing to pitch her tent at the far ends of the earth. Three years later one of her sisters married Dr. James Campbell, the Scots surgeon attached to the British consulate in Bangkok, where he would be Anna's doctor and his

3. In 1945, when Cobb's long-lived daughter read Margaret Landon's unlikely claim that Cobb had gone to Singapore for his health after losing a lung to tuberculosis, she wrote the author that his motive was business. Contemporary newspapers back up the daughter. On 28 September 1860 a notice appeared in the *Boston Daily Advertiser*: "Wanted, a Ship, to load for Batavia and Singapore, out and home. Apply to Thayer & Peabody, 134 State street." Two months later and six days after the notice ceased running, the paper announced two departures: "In the *Hollander*, for East Indies, George H. Dana, Francis D. Cobb."

wife—her name was Ailison—one of her friends.[4] These were vital points of contact, and they all went back to Adamson and his knack for connecting people.

But his most important connection as far as Anna was concerned was with Siam's hereditary monarch. On 4 June 1859, while she was in deep grief in Penang, the newly wedded Adamsons left Singapore for Bangkok, where William spent the next two years expanding the Borneo Company's operations. Perhaps his chief accomplishment there was to gain the trust and friendship of King Mongkut, who had opened his country to Western commerce and would often rely on William's counsel and good offices.

In April 1861 the Adamsons moved back to Singapore. Nearly two years had passed since Anna's own return, and it looked like her little school was failing. At year's end Adamson learned something interesting. It came from Tan Kim Ching, another of Singapore's spectacularly successful businessmen. Chen Jinzhong, as his name would be spelled today, owned concessions and rice mills in Siam and Saigon, joined Westerners in many civic enterprises, gave generously to a hospital founded by his father, registered marriages for Fujian dialect speakers, settled quarrels, and, not incidentally, served the king of Siam as his consul general and special agent in the Straits Settlements. The news this savvy operator had for Adamson was that the king was looking for a qualified English teacher for his children in Bangkok.

Everything fell into place. Adamson was familiar with the king's oddities and could imagine what it would be like working for him. A governess fresh from Britain would not be up to that, but there was a woman in Singapore who might be—his late clerk's struggling widow. On the instant, Mrs. Leonowens's vague origins, wanderings, travails, and odd authority were converted from liabilities to assets. She had experience teaching; she was as tough, correct, and high-toned as she was warm and motherly; she had to have something more remunerative than her sad little school; and she was English enough for the Siamese, who weren't anxious about racial or ethnic purity.

Before informing Anna of this surprising opening, Adamson undoubtedly talked it over with his wife. One of the few Western women who had

4. Ailison arrived in Siam as a bride in late 1862. In 1870 she was one of the two Bangkok friends to whom Anna sent the first magazine installment of *The English Governess*.

lived in Bangkok, she would have had an opinion on the teacher's ability to handle the stresses a lone woman would experience there. Neither Margaret nor William had observed Anna's derangement in Penang or her depressive episodes in Australia. They may have had no cause to question her emotional sturdiness.

So the couple broke the news to Anna, who was glad to hear of the opening. Her terms, she decided, would be 150 Straits dollars a month and permission to live with or near the Protestant missionaries, most likely the Presbyterians. Then the Adamsons introduced her to Tan Kim Ching.[5]

After hearing about Anna from his agent, the king replied that her terms were not acceptable. Proud of his linguistic abilities, he wrote by hand in his inimitable English. He made things clear. Anna's salary would be one hundred dollars, and she wouldn't be living with the missionaries. She would reside in or near the palace. She was to teach the English language and useful school subjects and not convert his children to the Christian religion. If she accepted these terms and arrived in Bangkok with a "husband or manservant," he would provide "a brick house in nearest vicinity of this palace."

Once everything seemed settled, the king wrote directly to Anna and invited her with courteous formality "to our royal palace to do your best endeavorment upon us and our children." He repeated that she was to provide "knowledge of English language, science, and literature, and not for conversion to Christianity; as the followers of Buddha are mostly aware of the powerfulness of truth and virtue, as well as the followers of Christ." Evidently, he liked to explain his decisions, not just announce them. He didn't sound like the usual sort of king. Had he forgotten to mention the brick house?

Anna would always describe herself as *governess* at the Siamese court, but in fact the word never appears in the correspondence about her terms of employment. *Governess* meant supervisory companionship, the teaching of manners as well as the standard school subjects. She, however, was employed for the standard subjects. She was to be the royal schoolmistress, or rather, as the king put it in his letter to Adamson, the "School Mastress."

5. In America Anna named Orfeur Cavenagh, governor of Singapore, as the intermediary, thus distancing herself from the Chinese and linking herself to an Englishman at the top.

FEARFUL TO CONTEMPLATE

Of all the decisions that Anna had to make before embarking for Siam, the most trying was what to do with Avis. Although the child was barely seven, her mother quickly resolved to send her halfway around the world for the pukka English schooling Anna herself had never received. It was a wrenching break but one that Western parents far from Europe accepted as the unavoidable downside of foreign residency. Louis, however, was too young for boarding school and would have to go to Bangkok.

Because the king seemed to want Anna to enter into her duties at once, she felt compelled to leave Singapore before completing arrangements for her daughter. She had sent an inquiry to an eminently proper school near London, but the questions of ship passage and traveling companions were not yet settled by the time her steamer left the harbor. In this latest emergency, she was once again helped by others. Francis Davis Cobb, her American friend, booked Avis's passage on the *Ranée*, a sailing ship he judged to be slow but safe. British photographer Thomas Heritage and his wife opened their home to the child and then took charge of her on their return voyage to London. After seeing the group on board, the kindly Cobb wrote Anna to assure her that Avis had been "talkative and merry" and in constant motion as she explored the ship.

The boarding school to which the child was sailing was run by four aging sisters. Located in Fulham, at the time a quiet suburb full of market gardens, the Misses King's School occupied a dignified, three-story, early Georgian mansion on Bridge Street. Avis was the youngest girl by far.[6] Was an exception made for her? Whatever the answer, the unmarried King sisters loved her dearly and became closely attached, and the result was that, in spite of unsettled beginnings, Avis turned into a domesticated English girl quite unlike her mother.

The child's genteel and orderly world was the antipodes of her mother's new home. Previously, no matter where Anna lived, she had been under the Union Jack and its promises of law and liberty. Now, in spite of the extraterritorial rights the English had negotiated for themselves in Siam, she felt

6. In the 1861 census, taken the year before Anna went to Siam, none of the Misses King's thirteen scholars was younger than eleven. By the time Avis showed up she was eight.

she was entering a realm of great danger as she steamed up the wide tropical Chao Phya River.

Every nineteenth-century travel writer from the West was thrilled by the magical spectacle that Bangkok offered newly arrived steamer passengers: the flamboyant tapered spires of Buddhist wats, the flaring palace rooflines, the floating wooden houses lining the broad river. Anna appears to be the one visitor on record whose heart was lifted by a passing glimpse of the American Presbyterian Mission. To her anxious eyes, the white chapel, "pleasant dwellings," and gently swaying tall trees "imparted a promise of safety and peace"—a promise the king had not permitted her to accept. The steamer throbbed on, and as she found herself floating into the heart of the city, "the gloom and mystery of the pagan land . . . filled [her] with an indefinable dread."

Mary Mattoon, who was to become one of her good friends in Bangkok, belonged to that Presbyterian mission. Fifteen years earlier, as she prepared to leave her home in New York State, an alarmed acquaintance had broken out, "Oh Mary if you were only going to India or China where there is English rule . . . but to go to that heathen out of the way country where a heathen king has absolute power—oh it is fearful to contemplate."

Mary had laughed off these silly fears. But Mary had a husband, an unusually able one, and she hadn't been traumatized. That Anna embarked for Siam in spite of her very real terrors and without the support of a Mrs. Marcus or a Reverend Fraser shows us as nothing else how brave and resolute she was, and how desperate.

BANGKOK

1862–1867

10

King Mongkut of Siam

BANGKOK WAS NOT THE TIMELESS, unchanging place you might have thought as you stepped off the boat. It had been the administrative center of Siam for less than a century following the destruction of the old capital, Ayutthaya, by Burma. Since that event, a series of able leaders—a general named Taksin, the Chakri dynasty of kings, the Bunnak family of king-makers and royal ministers—had guided the nation back from catastrophe. Thanks to them and others, Bangkok had grown into one of the world's most remarkable cities.

When Anna arrived in 1862, King Mongkut, the fourth Chakri monarch, had sat on the throne for eleven years.[1] That *mongkut* means "crown" suggests that he may have been the designated successor of his father, Rama II. But the succession had been anything but straightforward, and Mongkut's royal character had proven to be quite different from that of his predecessors.

Born in 1804, he was the eldest son of his father's one royal wife and would thus have been the leading candidate for the throne. But his half brothers, the sons of lesser wives, included some able older men. Of these, the most eminent and powerful, Prince Chetsadabodin, was seventeen years his senior. By 1824, when Rama II became mortally ill, Chetsadabodin had

1. Thais identify King Mongkut not by this name but by his coronation title, Phra-chomklao. Because their way of designating kings is a challenge for outsiders, a twentieth-century monarch renamed the Chakri kings Rama I, Rama II, and so forth. I follow this simplified usage except in the case of Rama IV and Rama V, whom I refer to by the names that have become standard in the West, Mongkut and Chulalongkorn.

been trusted with weighty responsibilities, whereas Mongkut, only nineteen, was still untested. He had the obvious dynastic credentials, but his older half brother was the seasoned administrator. Who should run the country? In the delicate back-room negotiations that frequently determined the succession in old Siam, the experienced son of a minor wife was given the preference.

Tacitly yielding his claim, Mongkut underwent a Buddhist ordination a few weeks before his father's death and for the next twenty-seven years lived as a monk. Although it was customary for highborn Siamese men to enter the monkhood for a brief period, few made a career of it. Westerners took for granted that the royal prince did so to preserve his life as the rightful heir and regarded Chetsadabodin (Rama III) as a usurper. Mongkut himself would promote this view during the tense interval preceding his ascent to the throne in 1851, when he gave an American missionary and journalist a private account of his history in order to "get a correct statement in the Singapore papers." This version of events, double-checked by Mongkut and published with his approval in the *Straits Times*, claimed that Rama III, "taking advantage of circumstances[, had] usurped the throne." That was the understanding that Anna would promulgate in *The English Governess at the Siamese Court* with her usual high drama and careless dating: "In 1825 [actually, 1824] a royal prince of Siam (his birthright wrested from him, and his life imperilled) took refuge in a Buddhist monastery and assumed the yellow garb of a priest."

In fact, for Mongkut the yellow robe seems to have been a calling as much as a refuge—a particularly attractive alternative to the secular order. Even today, Thai monks form a distinct and honored class, deferred to, treated with signal politeness, allowed to go first when boarding a water-taxi or an airplane. The monkhood gave the young high prince a sphere in which to act and maintain his dignity without presenting a challenge to Rama III. It also gave him an opportunity to enlarge his intellectual horizons far beyond anything his forebears had dreamed of. Thanks to his quarter century in the monkhood, Mongkut turned out to be a kind of philosopher-king, with all that this term implies of good and bad: principled and far-sighted but also, at times, impractical and high-handed.

His first religious home, Wat Samorai, was a small but well-regarded forest wat on the northern outskirts of Bangkok. Quickly realizing that he wanted more than a quiet rural retreat with huge trees could offer, he moved to Wat

Mahathat, a large, centrally located temple with facilities for learned textual study. Here, demonstrating his aptitude for linguistic and erudite pursuits, the young man excelled as a student of Pali, the Sanskrit-like classical Indian language of Buddhist scripture. As he pored over ancient texts, he came to see Siamese Buddhism as contaminated by inauthentic accretions. Growing more and more uneasy about the foundations of established religious practice, he fell under the influence of a respected Burmese monk who expounded what seemed to be the true and original ordinances.

Returning now to the isolation and relative freedom of Wat Samorai, Mongkut devoted himself to purifying Thai Buddhism, a goal he hoped to achieve by instituting a more rigorous asceticism and reforming the rites for consecrating wats and ordaining monks. His young followers formed the nucleus of a new order, the Dhammayutika, meaning those who adhere to the true law. He also made pilgrimages to distant wats and shrines, traveling as far north as Sukhothai, the ancient capital, where he brought to light a royal stone inscription preserving the earliest known Thai (or Lao) script.

In addition, Mongkut reached out to Christian missionaries. His first contact was Bishop Pallegoix, a man of broad and humane learning who headed the French Catholic mission. The two clerics taught Latin and Pali to each other and had discussions about astronomy, geography, and history. By 1830 Mongkut realized that the earth must be round and that the Buddhist cosmos was a fable, an encumbrance to be discarded. From now on he would regard Western science as a fount of wisdom and power.

Unlike Pallegoix and other Catholics, the American Protestants who had come to Bangkok as missionaries did not strike the Siamese as proper priests: they had no ancient sacred language, wore no robes, weren't celibate, and seemed to pursue secular lives. But they were up-to-date Westerners and men of candor and learning, and Mongkut was bent on picking their minds. The first Protestant he got to know well was Dan Beach Bradley of rural New York State. Pugnacious and opinionated, Bradley was nevertheless a keen observer who did not shrink from contact with Thais and whose detailed private journals remain a priceless record of old Siam. It was he who relayed Mongkut's succession story to a Singapore newspaper.

Bradley had not gone to college, but he did have a year of medical school. In 1836, advised that Mongkut required his professional skill, he was rowed upriver to Wat Samorai, where, sitting across a table from the royal monk, the American discovered that he was suffering from an ear infection, "a simple Otitis for which I prescribed."

Two weeks later, hearing that a second consultation was required, the missionary-doctor found that the patient's condition had worsened:

> He had had a complaint in his head & Right ear a long time which had come to be a paralysis of the nerve which proceeds out of the scull just behind the ear & supplies the muscles of the face, consequently the right side of the face was much relaxed and the mouth drawn round to the left side. To talk he was obliged to take hold of the right side of his mouth & support it. The right eye was much congested with blood and the lids a little relaxed and there was also some tumefaction under the right ear.

By the time the infection subsided, the nerve was dead. For the rest of his life the right side of Mongkut's mouth had an unsightly droop, a feature imitated, needless to say, by none of the actors—Rex Harrison, Yul Brynner, Chow Yun-Fat—who have portrayed him on Broadway and in Hollywood.

At the end of 1836 Mongkut left his forest wat for the second time and returned to Bangkok, this time to the newly rebuilt and endowed Wat Bowonniwet.[2] The move had the approval of his reigning half brother, who appointed him abbot, in this way enlarging the young monk's authority and scope of action. Empowered to proceed with his program of reform and innovation, he dispatched a delegation of monks to Sri Lanka to make contact with Singhalese Buddhists and bring back authentic and undefiled texts of Pali scriptures. He decreed that the Singhalese pronunciation of Pali, however difficult for Thai speakers, was the true and original sound and must be adopted. He insisted on a minor change in how the robe should be worn. As Mongkut put these reforms through within the Dhammayutika order, he gave signs of a trait that became more pronounced after he was crowned: an insistence on literal detail, a dogmatic absolutism.

But he was a modernizer as well as a restorer of ancient practice. It was under his direction at Wat Bowonniwet that the first Thai printing press

2. Located a mile northeast of the Grand Palace on the corner of Thanon Bowonniwet and Thanon Phra Sumen, this wat remains a center of Buddhist study. Its grounds are built up with classrooms and dormitories for students from Sri Lanka, India, and Nepal. It is still associated with the royal family.

went into operation. Like many of his innovations, this one represented a robust expansion of the limits of Siamese culture. Determined to break out of those limits, Mongkut approached Bradley in 1839 with some unusual requests: Could he have daily English lessons at a wat near Bradley's home? And could one of his young monks move in with the missionary in order to study and prepare himself "for a visit to England or America for information"? The lessons at the wat do not seem to have materialized, but the thirty-five-year-old prince had made clear his desire to internationalize himself.

According to Prince Damrong Rajanubhab, a son of Mongkut who became a leading historian, "the most important event that influenced Siamese thought about Western Culture" was England's humbling of China in the Opium War of 1839–42. One lesson for China's traditional clients, such as Siam, was that it was time to start studying English. But the event that finally pushed Mongkut to arrange for lessons was the arrival of letters from Sri Lankan monks composed in this difficult Western tongue—conclusive evidence that there was a new "language of intercommunication among all the nations."

This time he turned to Jesse Caswell, an American missionary whose religious faith went hand in hand with a passion for spreading useful and theoretical scientific knowledge. Along with proclaiming the Gospel, Caswell distributed modern maps of Asia and gave lectures on the earth's spherical shape, the lunar cycle, the cause of eclipses, and so forth.[3] Although some of his science-based disclosures conflicted with the traditional Buddhist cosmology, they dovetailed very nicely with the royal abbot's program of reform. When Caswell brought an electrical apparatus to Wat Bowonniwet, Mongkut "took great delight in forming a large circle of priests and administering the shock."

So Mongkut came up with a proposal: if Caswell would give English lessons to him and his followers, the missionary would be allowed to preach the Gospel within the Buddhist wat in a specially prepared room. It was a clever offer, one in which the devout American "clearly saw the finger of God."

---

3. The chemistry lectures Caswell composed for his Thai servants are preserved in his commonplace book. Lecture 1 states that air is made up "of two simple substances, called Oxygen & Nitrogen," and that water "consists of two elements called Oxygen & Hydrogen." Committed to paper in the 1840s, these lecture notes may represent the first time the names of these gases were spelled in the Thai alphabet.

In his original application for missionary work, Caswell had stated that he not only was "never melancholy" but had "more uniformity of feeling . . . than is common"—a useful temperament in the lonely and often discouraging profession he had chosen. Now he would have an opportunity to show just how equable he could be.

English instruction began on 1 July 1845. The plan was to teach four days a week, allotting forty-five minutes to a class of monks followed by a few minutes with Mongkut alone to clear up "any difficulties which he may have met with." By the end of the month the class was often half empty, but Mongkut was proving "much more persevering" than expected. According to Caswell, he "never misses a lesson, and plies me with so many questions, that I am commonly obliged to tear myself away from him." Three months later he was so "indefatigable" that he was getting a full hour of daily private instruction. When another missionary wanted the Lord's Prayer rendered into Pali, Mongkut did the work in no time. He began translating a religious tract into Thai. The missionaries were thrilled. Did they have a key convert in the making? Caswell was finding Mongkut to be "in an inquiring state of mind on religious subjects, and frank and gentlemanly in all his discussions. He appears to despise much, if not all of his own religion. . . . Should it please the great Head of the church to bow the heart of this man to his own blessed will, it is impossible to predict the influence he might exert in favor of the truth."

But Mongkut had made clear from the outset that his aim was to "communicate with English and American friends for knowledge of sciences & arts not for any least admiration or astonishment of vulgar religion." What Caswell and the other evangelicals could not grasp was that the royal monk had a more free-ranging mind than they. More loosely tethered to the supernatural, he approached Jewish and Christian myths with the same secular openness he brought to Buddhist legends, and the missionaries were utterly shocked. Regarding his freedom as "rank infidelity" or "horrid blasphemy," they would always remember and shudder at his frank admission to Caswell, "*I hate the Bible mostly.*" For his part, Mongkut could not understand why these scientific Americans insisted on the truth of ancient scriptures that repeatedly broke the laws of nature.

After a year and a half of exhausting pedagogy, Caswell realized that the prince would never be converted. The lessons, seen now as a waste of time, were terminated, and the missionary went back to his regular work.⁴ There too, however, he was stymied, for no matter how much he prayed and preached and translated, he won no converts. In his grim annual report for 1847, he concluded that "*the fundamental doctrines of Buddhism* and of *Christianity are antagonists*." The gulf between the two religions was unbridgeable. It was as Rama III (reportedly) said when advised to restrain the missionaries: "Do not be troubled about them; none will join them but Chinamen."

But if the lessons were called off, the friendship was not. Mongkut continued to drop in on Caswell "for translations," and the American remained patient and helpful. That he felt no bitterness in spite of his frustrated proselytizing points to a difference between him and Anna, who was touched to the quick by Mongkut's freedom of mind. There would be genuine rancor in her aspersions on his "extreme scepticism."

A couple of years after the English lessons ended, Caswell died of "erysipelatous inflammation of the lungs," and his widow sailed back to America. Some years later, after Mongkut was crowned king, he sent her generous cash gifts in memory of her husband: one thousand dollars in 1855 and five hundred dollars in 1864. For the time these were substantial sums.

When Mrs. Caswell sent a daguerreotype of her husband to Siam, the king was deeply moved, telling Bradley "with much emotion" that the missionary "had, as it were, come to life again." A few years later Mongkut decided that the grave of "his reverend teacher" needed a monument. As he explained to Bradley, Caswell had "taught him the English language which has made him what he is, highly respected by the great western powers." In nineteenth-century Siam, the king's English had immense strategic value.

Anna, too, was a widow and an English teacher, but when the time came for her to leave Siam after five and a half years of royal duties, she was given no valuable gifts, and a requested loan of two hundred pounds was denied. The difference is telling. Something had gone wrong. Instead of the generous warmth that marked the king's relations with Caswell, there would be suspicion and acrimony.

---

4. Arriving years later, Anna had an inflated idea of the lessons' extent and influence. Her claim that Mongkut "placed himself under the permanent tutorship" of Caswell seriously overstated the role of Western pedagogy in forming the king.

THE REIGN OF RAMA III

Westerners living in Siam during the reign of Rama III were universally unhappy with his rule. He set high duties on imports, allowed no resident diplomats other than the Portuguese consul, and in other ways kept European influence to a minimum.

According to a surgeon who accompanied the American diplomatic mission of 1833, there had been a time when Chetsadabodin was more open. The surgeon gathered as much from private conversations in Bangkok with the Portuguese consul, Don Carlos Manuel de Silveira, who had lived there for thirteen years and was fluent in the language. Don Carlos confided that prior to 1824, the year Chetsadabodin became Rama III, he had been "very anxious" for information about European law and custom, so much so that the two men would "spend the whole night" talking. Once on the throne, however, the new king spurned his former companion and informant. In the consul's opinion, this coldness reflected the government's determination to insulate Siam from the West.

As Don Carlos foresaw, the American mission failed. When its leader met with the *phrakhlang*, he was informed that the United States would not be allowed to open a consulate in Bangkok, as this "would only create disturbance in the country, by giving information to foreigners as the Portuguese Consul had done." The *phrakhlang* was the minister in charge of foreign relations and various other departments. At the time the office was held by Dit Bunnak, the most powerful man in Siam after the king.

Rama III proved as inaccessible to his own people as to Westerners. According to a Thai historian, he followed the ancient rule that "no common eyes may be cast upon his divine body. Consequently before the King proceeded along the streets, the King's policemen went ahead telling everybody to close his doors and windows and not to look at the king. The King's archers would be on the close look-out to see whether anybody had disobeyed and peered among the holes, then they would at once be shot at." Which is to say, shot in the eyes. Fortunately, it was permitted to look at the king as he sat in state at court. What impressed Bradley the first time he beheld him was his corpulence and how "light of complexion [he was] for a Siamese."

A leading American scholar has characterized Rama III as "first and last a strong man, a man of action. He was thoroughly conservative, adverse to change and new ideas, not an intellectual like his father Rama II or his half-brother and successor Rama IV." What this assessment leaves out is the king's positive achievements. During his reign the traditional religious arts of sculpture, mural painting, and architecture flourished, and at least one innovation was encouraged: the building of Western-style square-rigged ships instead of slower and less maneuverable Chinese junks. Most importantly, according to historian Barend Jan Terwiel, Rama III succeeded in holding the aggressive Western powers at bay without provoking "direct clashes."

Still, Siam remained a closed society under this king. When people spoke his name, according to a resident foreigner, they "did so in a timid whisper" as if "a spy might be at hand." The year after Caswell's English lessons ended, Mongkut reportedly said that he "wished to flee from his country and take refuge . . . in the British dominions." The outburst vividly conveys the royal monk's frustration. It also shows two traits that would work against him as king: his initial innocence about British power and his "frank and ingenuous state of mind, even to a fault" (Bradley's penetrating judgment).

As Rama III's reign drew to a close, there was an upward spike in official secrecy and suspicion. When a Thai named Khun Mote tried to print the first Siamese-language edition of the nation's laws, Rama III ordered all copies and unbound sheets destroyed. In 1850 another American envoy was sent to Siam to try once again to negotiate a consular treaty and trading concessions. Arriving in Bangkok by himself, without ceremony or a dignified escort, he was not taken seriously, and the royal audience he sought was denied. Soon afterward Sir James Brooke, the so-called rajah of Sarawak, arrived on a similar mission for the British. Although he showed up with a more impressive entourage, not to mention a reputation for the brutal use of force, he too got nowhere.

Such was the state of affairs in early 1851 as King Rama III became terminally ill: official intransigence, great suspicion of the West, great anxiety regarding the succession.

A NEW DAY

It was Dit Bunnak, the *phrakhlang*, who broke the stalemate. Aging, calculating, and with splendid rolls of belly fat, Dit presided in the old way: barechested and from a position of strength. Two weeks before the king's death, at a time when all claimants to the throne were guarding their intentions, a meeting was held at which Dit announced that no one had a better claim to the monarchy than Prince Mongkut and that his younger brother, Jutamani, should be *uparat,* or "second king."⁵ Anyone who contested their succession would have Dit to contend with. Bringing armed units into Bangkok, he installed a guard at Mongkut's wat, and the transition proceeded quietly.

Prior to his coronation, Mongkut gave a private interview to Bradley and another missionary about his plans: "He seemed to make us his confidential friends. . . . He told us that he would be glad to have Siamese young men learn the English language & thought favorably of having a college established in Bangkok for this purpose. He also said that . . . he would rule after the plan of a limited monarchy." To the two Americans it felt like a benign top-down revolution.

During the cremation of Rama III, a ceremony of great pomp, the newly crowned king spotted Bradley in the crowd and "came down from the funeral pile a long way & gave me his hand." No Siamese ruler had ever done such a thing. The attendant courtiers had to scramble on all fours in order to remain lower than the revered monarch. Afterward, when Mongkut was back in his high seat, Bradley eavesdropped on an exchange between two officials: "When has Siam ever had a king who was pleased to show so much respect to Foreigners?" The reply: "He would not do this to sailors. He will do it only to Foreigners of respectability like the Doctors."

One of King Mongkut's first decrees was that his subjects need not hide during his processions and would not be shot by archers if they looked at him: "All householders shall, on such an occasion, be permitted to appear before the sight of His Majesty, so that He may graciously take the opportunity to speak to those of His acquaintances among them some such words of greeting as to gladden their hearts." The detailed explanation of his reasoning would be a characteristic feature of his decrees.

Twice a year there was a royal ceremony called Drinking of the Water of Allegiance. In previous reigns the members of the royal family drank the

5. Jutamani was four years younger than Mongkut, spoke and wrote better English, and interested himself in watch repairing, shipbuilding, and Western military practices. He was also a connoisseur of Siamese and Laotian music and dance. The usual Western translation of his title, *uparat,* as "second king" is misleading, as he exercised few administrative functions and had no real power under his older brother.

water in the presence of the king. In Mongkut's opinion, "such a one-sided pledge would only bind those who took the water to be loyal, whilst the sovereign, who did not take the water, would not be bound to keep any promise or be loyal on his own part." Only if the king also took the pledge "would the water of allegiance become truly sacred."

In 1949, appalled by Margaret Landon's portrayal of Mongkut as a cruel tyrant, a Thai author and statesman, Seni Pramoj, termed him "the first and foremost democrat of our country." That was an exaggeration, yet it is true that Mongkut set out to demystify the monarchy and limit the nobility's privileges. A decree of 1861 criticized "the practice of past kings in recruiting young children by force for *lakhon* training in the royal court." Children meant girls, and the girls in *lakhon*—the traditional dance and drama troupes—generally slept with their powerful patrons.

Still, Mongkut's original hope of distributing power more equally was largely unrealized. Court etiquette continued to require everyone except Westerners to prostrate themselves, lying prone in a way that left elbows and forearms calloused. Nothing was done about the *sakdina* system, in which the lower orders were tattooed with the mark of the superiors to whom they owed annual service. Like slavery, marking didn't become illegal until after Mongkut's death. And his decree that the minor gentry were ineligible for high positions in the leading ministries actually reduced social mobility.

His major achievement for good or ill was to open the nation to the West. In 1855 first the British and then the Americans and others sent diplomatic missions to Bangkok to negotiate treaties. The king and his leading ministers, the *kalahom* in particular,[6] were at a disadvantage in the negotiations, not least because they already favored the West, and in the end they conceded virtually everything: the abolition of trading monopolies, the establishment of consuls, and extraterritoriality. The latter ensured that Europeans who broke Siamese laws would not be tried in Siamese courts. The treaties effectively eroded national sovereignty, precisely as Rama III had feared.

During the yearlong interval between negotiations and the signing of the treaty with England, Mongkut realized he had made more concessions than the Japanese in their recent American treaty. But the momentum was

6. Sisuriyawong, the *kalahom*, was in charge of the southern provinces and other areas of government. Because of his forwardness in dealing with Westerners he was seen by many, including Anna, as the "prime minister."

unstoppable. Papers were signed and stamped, consuls were appointed, trade exploded. By the time Anna showed up, Western capital and hardware were pouring into Bangkok. Steam rice mills and a steam-driven sawmill, operated by Westerners, were up and running. The police were under the control of a European appointed by the king, and so was the harbor traffic. In emergencies the English schoolmistress would have the right to call in the British consul. It was a threat she would make use of. She would not be as vulnerable as she imagined.

The First English Teachers in the Palace

When Mongkut was crowned, his twenty-seven years of celibacy ended, and he was presented with a large number of concubines selected from the eligible daughters of leading families. The custom served both to honor the monarch and to install a family member near the seat of power. It is thought that the young women regarded their life at court as one of signal privilege and prestige.

The king's wives, concubines, and younger children lived in an extensive walled enclosure, the Inner Palace, along with scores of aunts, half-sisters, and previous kings' widows. All these aristocratic women had their own retinues and servants, and in addition there were the market women, the armed guards or police ("Amazons"), and a number of officials, including female judges. The size of this city of women during the Fourth Reign is generally put at three thousand. King Mongkut was the one man who entered at will.

During his monkhood Mongkut had met the American missionary wives, most of whom were well educated. Sarah Blachly Bradley had graduated from Oberlin College, and others had worked as schoolteachers before marrying and sailing to Siam. Impressed with their learning and professional experience, the new king asked an unusual favor of them: that they make regular visits to the Inner Palace and teach the English language to his young brides. No previous Siamese monarch seems to have dreamed of such a thing.

English class began in August 1851. Sarah Bradley, Sara Sleeper Jones, and Mary Lowrie Mattoon taught in rotation, each going to the palace two days a week and entering at the river gate. After some eight months of this, they requested what the king termed "the large place of teaching English language." From then on, it seems, the class met in the home of the concubines' "chief governess," a member of the Bunnak family. As the dignified but nonnoble woman followed the lessons, she picked up a smattering of English. Ten years later she would respectfully address Anna as "sir."

Along with initiating the concubines into the mysteries of English, the missionary wives taught astronomy, geography, and Bible history, conducting these supplementary lessons in the homes of the king's unmarried sisters and nieces. Unlike Anna, these first palace teachers were not warned against religious proselytizing. Also unlike her, they taught in the Thai language. Her own mastery never reached that level.

Although Mattoon's husband suspected that English would do the king's wives "about as much good as French does many boarding school misses at home," he saw the extra classes as a means "to get religious books & Christian instruction" into the palace. Writing home, his wife boasted that she had covered "Bible history through Joseph—& am now on the history of Moses." The religious motive was very strong. But something was developing that proved more vital and enduring than religious indoctrination: warm cross-cultural friendship. Mattoon in particular grew so attached to her students that she visited them daily in spite of her severe asthma, a hemorrhaging lung, and weight loss.

In September 1854, three years on, the lessons ended. Abruptly, the Americans found the palace gate closed to them, with no explanation given. No doubt there had been too much Christian talk—the thing Anna was warned against a decade later. But the chief problem lay elsewhere, in an unsigned letter to a Singapore newspaper that was harshly critical of King Mongkut. Convinced that Bangkok's Protestant missionaries were behind the attack, the king not only broke all contact but limited their travel in order "to prevent their meddling with politics." This, the low point in relations, lasted till 1855, when Sir John Bowring, having come to Siam to negotiate the treaty with England, made peace between the king and the American Protestants. But the palace teaching never resumed.

Of the three teachers, Mattoon left the fullest account, in letters and an essay. The latter, composed after Anna's sensational books were out, was meant to be "just a plain account" suitable for a Presbyterian readership that included children. It glances at typical scenes within the walls, such as a group of women sitting on a platform in a courtyard making something with paste and artificial flowers, but it rarely lingers. Not much is made of the word "harem." We learn that most of Mattoon's students lost interest except for "a few young wives" who wanted to be able to converse with the king in English. Once "a sweet-faced young girl" pilfered the royal spectacles and was placed in confinement. At the time Anna was living in India or Australia. Two decades later she gave the anecdote a lavish fictional treatment in which she made herself a participant. She sold the tale to an American children's magazine that specialized in "true stories."

Over time, the teachers' "visits to the houses of the different ladies of the palace became more and more extended." But their dwellings, Mattoon confided, did not at all resemble "the clean, sweet, pleasant homes of an intelligent Christianity. Only a few of them had much that was attractive about them." The one thing this vague picture shows with any clarity is how a casual Siamese interior struck a neat Yankee housekeeper.

When the American took her family daguerreotypes to the palace, the princesses made "a great ado" over the portrait of a sister-in-law, who was pronounced "extremely beautiful." Years later, after Mattoon made a return visit, her former pupils agreed that she, too, had been "*very beautiful* but sickness had taken it all away." The product of a homely, rural, egalitarian culture that was less concerned with refined female beauty than the Siamese court, she seems to have been amused by the unflattering report.

Mattoon returned for another visit in 1863, by which time Anna had been at her job for over a year. The brief account that Mattoon sent her family reads, "Mrs. L, the English lady, is still teaching in the King's palace. I went with her again one day taking my little girls Mary & Emma with me. My two old pupils Ladies Talap & Klin met me with delight and made us partake of some tiffin they had prepared for us." One of Mattoon's American pupils described her manner as "ever gentle and kind, no words of anger or of harshness ever escaped her lips." It looks as if this particular missionary wife brought a natural sympathy for Siamese ideals of feminine delicacy and social exchange.

Certainly, her friendship with Lady Talap was no ordinary one. As it happened, Mattoon not only suffered the same agony Anna had gone through, a first child's death in infancy, but the baby died just as the palace lessons were getting started in September 1851. Although the stricken mother felt his death "most keenly" (her words), she forced herself to go to the palace when her turn came around. "O how precious is the memory of the sweet boy," she wrote her sister, "& how often in imagination do I press his cherished body to my heart." Her grief was only too obvious to Talap, who was profoundly moved by the anguish of this strange modern educated working woman.

There was a consequence ten years later when Anna arrived at the Inner Palace and had a mysterious encounter with Talap. At this point everything was still fresh and strange for the schoolmistress, including the Thai practice of lounging sociably on a spotless marble or tile floor, always so much cleaner than Western floors (as Mattoon might have remembered before lifting her eyebrows at Thai housekeeping). The concubine, a small, refined woman whom Anna saw as a "child-wife" (another mistake), "lay down on the cool floor, and, using her betel-box for a pillow, beckoned to me. As I approached, and seated myself beside her, she said: 'I am very glad to see you. It is long time I not see. Why you come so late?'"

At this point Anna knew no Thai, and the "baby-talk" with which she replied was useless. Helpless and embarrassed, she sat holding five-year-old Louis on her lap. Talap lay beside them and, using her limited English to entertain her guest, sang "a scrap of the Sunday-school hymn, 'There is a Happy Land, far, far away.'" As the concubine's rusty English phrases came back, she added, "I think of you very often. In the beginning, God created the heavens and the earth." Seven years had passed since the missionaries' last class, and the memorized Bible verses and rote phrases seemed to be all that remained.

But then Talap gracefully "half rose, and, looking around, cautiously whispered, 'Dear Mam Mattoon! I love you. I think of you. Your boy dead, you come to palace; you cry—I love you'; and laying her finger on her lips, and her head on the betel-box again, again she sang, 'There is a Happy Land, far, far away!'"

Nothing else written by Anna quite equals the magic of this uncanny scene, with its delicate blend of sympathy and foreignness. Talap had not seen Mattoon since palace lessons ceased, and as she thought about her teacher and friend, those long-ago days of heartache and English flushed to life, and she brought up what she had learned: how to express feeling in this funny Western tongue. Was Talap seeing Anna as a sort of proxy for Mem Mattoon? Was she under the impression that this *was* Mem Mattoon, altered by age? To a Thai eye, especially one confined to the palace, European faces would look much more alike than Asian faces.

Whatever the answer, Anna's dignified comment on Talap's speech—"So spontaneous and ingenuous a tribute of reverence and affection from a pagan to a Christian lady was inexpressibly charming to me"—anticipates a central theme of her writing: her pleasure in communing with Asian women across the barriers of language, culture, religion, ethnicity.

Jumping ahead to 1944 to see how Margaret Landon would handle this powerful liminal scene, we find a new and ominous line of thought. Instead of savoring the charm of an affection uniting East and West, this mid-twentieth-century Anna loses herself in a conspiratorial daydream involving the West's great mission in the East. Thinking about Talap's whispered speech, she wonders what the woman can be getting at? Surely, there is a meaning behind the furtiveness, but *what*? Then Anna *gets it*:

> This childlike woman locked away behind the high walls of the Forbidden City was trying to send a message to the outside world. She wanted to tell Mrs. Mattoon of her sympathy for the other woman's sorrow in the loss of a child. . . . She had devised this unique way of sending love and comfort. . . . Anna looked at Lady Talap with renewed interest. There she lay, imprisoned by walls and customs, which made her hardly more than the plaything of a king, but for all that she bore the marks of Mrs. Mattoon's character. Anna fell to dreaming. How many minds enchained by age-old fetters would she set free?

Overlooking or obscuring the fact that Mattoon's child had died a decade earlier, Landon sees Talap as trying to send a covert message of sympathy. As Landon's Anna figures this out, she disengages from the personal encounter and gives herself to fantasy, "dreaming" about her coming crusade in Siam. The dream turns the refined concubine into a king's "plaything," a "childlike" victim whose "age-old fetters" may fall away thanks to the aggressively benevolent Western Christian who has come to Bangkok.[7] The dream is presented as absolutely noble and good, yet the statement that Talap "bore the marks of Mrs. Mattoon's character" has a grim and sinister association.

7. *Dream*, a very important word for Landon (not to mention American culture in general), reappears in the title of her second and last book, a novel: *Never Dies the Dream*.

As Landon knew, "marking"—a tattoo that records who owns you—was done to underlings in old Siam. Landon's "marks" hints at a type of spiritual ownership that Mem Mattoon, "ever gentle and kind," may well have found repellent.

At the time Landon composed her version of the episode, America was fighting the Japanese and looking forward to an expanded role in the Far East. Thus, instead of a touching moment of contact between East and West, we are given an imperial daydream of well-meaning intervention. Something is about to be done to Talap for her own good.

And there we have it in another form: the basic dilemma of nineteenth-century Siam as it faced the growing power and aggression of the West. If the country ended its isolation and allowed Westerners in, they would inevitably misunderstand, meddle, and seek to dominate. How is a small, agrarian, thinly populated nation to meet that threat? Rama III tried to preserve Siamese independence by keeping the door shut. Reversing policy, Mongkut gave Western diplomats and merchants a relatively free hand. He had second thoughts, but he believed in progress and enlightenment, and he still admired the powerful English.

And so he invited into the Inner Palace a schoolteacher whose fractured history and character he could never have imagined: a woman who had resolved to rise above the limits imposed on Anglo-Indians; who had insisted on a risky love match over a prudent arranged union; who regarded her marriage as the thing that ennobled her; who intended to be as principled and uncompromising as her late husband; and who would now find in the royal Siamese harem the antithesis of everything she stood for.

The king of Siam was about to meet one of the most formidable and unstable products of the British Empire.

1 1

The English School Mastress
Comes to Bangkok

THE ENGLISH GOVERNESS AT THE SIAMESE COURT opens with the dramatic events of the author's arrival in Bangkok—her unnerving encounter with the *kalahom*, her weird audiences with King Mongkut, her setbacks in securing a decent house. Although the treatment of these matters is generally too sensational to be trusted, it leaves no room for doubt on one point. Anna's foray outside the empire got off to a very shaky start.

In Singapore her position as an independent, self-supporting schoolmistress would have marked her as sufficiently unusual, but when she went to work at the court of Siam she was undertaking a venture not advised for single white women: crossing the gulf between herself and the "natives." More challenging yet, as critic Chu-Chueh Cheng has noted in an acute analysis of Anna's situation at court, she was seen at one and the same time as a "social inferior and racial superior." Her status was ambiguous, it wasn't clear how much respect was due her, and she felt a strong compulsion to assert her dignity.

For these and other reasons, moving to Bangkok resulted in an emotional ordeal she found hard to parse. Years later, attempting to explain why she was "very uncomfortable there at first," she told a new friend that "they did not know how to treat Europeans, and I had not even a room to myself." As a husbandless woman going to work outside the relative safety of the empire, Anna was convinced that she had to make a point of her superior Western immunities. But how could she establish that kind of understanding if her new boss did not know how to treat Europeans?

In *The King and I* the heroine whistles a happy tune and meets each challenge with courage and aplomb. Although the real Anna was more troubled and driven, she too followed the strategy of maintaining a high and correct tone. Always extremely careful about presentation, she seems to have dressed well in spite of the terrible heat and to have pointedly snubbed those who did not. If she was treated with disrespect, her dignity would stiffen into haughty contempt. Homely Dan Beach Bradley of rural New York State, vastly impressed, looked up to her as "well versed in European court etiquette."

The trouble with all that magnificence was that it had to be paid for. One symptom of its emotional cost was Anna's persistent exhaustion, often resulting in tears or collapses. Another was that she took offense where none was intended. Yet another was that, in relating her experiences after the fact, she tended to be accusatory and even delusional, settling for simple outside explanations for her discomfort and anxiety.

The truth was, the king of Siam required no lessons in how to treat Europeans. Another truth: if you were not the high European lady you allowed him to think you were, your performances were apt to go wildly out of control.

SNUBS

The letter of appointment King Mongkut sent Anna on 26 February 1862 said that he would "expect to see you here on return of Siamese steamer Chow Phya." Taking him at his word, she quickly wrapped up her affairs in Singapore, said good-bye to Avis, whom she wouldn't see for almost six years, and embarked for Siam with her son, Louis.

The steamer *Chow Phya*, named for the river flowing through Bangkok, hauled passengers and freight between that city and Singapore. Built in Hartlepool, as an early Singapore annalist recalled, it had a hull of "very good half-inch iron plates, and there has been no vessel in the Straits like her." The skipper, George Orton, was English, but the owner was Siamese, and so were the onboard arrangements. The bridge was stacked with boxes and bales, and at mealtime the passengers were served informally. "There is not even a dining table!" a French count exclaimed. The instant you boarded the *Chow Phya* for the Gulf of Siam, you knew you were leaving the European order of things.

In *The English Governess* Anna is accompanied by "Moonshee, my Persian teacher, and Beebe, my gay Hindostanee nurse." If a female servant was in fact taken along, as seems likely, she would have been an all-purpose domestic rather than a nurse for Louis (who was never left behind when Anna had business at the palace). As for the Persian-speaking *munshi*, or language teacher, he seems to have been created for the occasion. The tales of his misadventures serve as ethnic comic relief, and the speeches he makes— "Peace be with thee, O Vizier of a wise king!"—sound bookish and unreal. The telling fact is that no Westerner in Bangkok ever mentioned this bizarre and unnecessary encumbrance. Anna was portraying herself as a dignified memsahib traveling with the regulation entourage. Her second book would bring on another imaginary male retainer, "my Hindostanee syce, or groom."

When the steamer reached the mouth of the Chao Phya River, Anna went ashore to inspect her first Siamese wat. The impressions she gathered there for later literary use—rotting garbage, "a rabble of priests," "packs of mangy pariah-dogs"—form a dramatic contrast to her picture of the pristine American Presbyterian mission, seen in passing as she entered Bangkok. Viewing the Christian chapel as an island of order and safety in a scene of sinister degradation, Anna approached the city in a state of mind very different from that of European visitors, who were universally struck with wonder. The same Parisian who objected to the *Chow Phya*'s dining arrangements doubted that the "world has a greater or more striking spectacle" than Bangkok as seen from the river.

After the steamer reached its moorings, a dragon-prowed boat rowed up, and a man Anna characterized as a "native chief" mounted the deck "with an absolute air." It was Chuang Bunnak, the *kalahom*. At once the deckhands prostrated themselves, as did his attendants (whose crouching reminded Anna of "huge toads"). All Westerners who had dealings with this minister saw him as strikingly advanced and civilized. For Sir John Bowring he was "a most sagacious man, towering far above every other person whom we have met—of graceful, gentlemanly manners, and appropriate language." By contrast, vulnerable-feeling Anna had eyes only for his air of command and "audacious" bare chest. Failing to grasp what it meant to be greeted by such an eminent personage, she took offense at the "almost indecent attire" of the "semi-nude barbarian."

In Margaret Landon's *Anna and the King of Siam*, the bare chest would be taken as a sign of menace: "Some sixth sense acquired from long years in the Orient suggested that the absence of a jacket indicated an absence of respect for her and for the position that she was to fill." If that was Anna's thinking, she would have been misreading the signals. In the Fourth Reign, Siamese men were required to clothe the upper body at royal audiences, but bare chests were acceptable elsewhere, especially in the hot season, and March can be very hot. Several years earlier, when Prince Wongsathirat Sanit called on an American diplomatic delegation in April, he was "so annoyed by the heat that he threw off his grass-cloth jacket, leaving his broad person entirely naked down to the loins. He had scarcely more than taken his seat, when the [*kalahom*] came in without any other dress than the sarong." The man who recorded this scene in his journal rightly assumed that there was nothing immodest or insulting in the attire of these two powerful men.

By contrast, Anna's reaction to the *kalahom*'s dress and manner was so haughty that he was provoked to wash his hands of her for the time being. As recounted in *The English Governess*, his polite inquiries terminated as follows:

> "What will you do? Where will you sleep tonight?"
>
> "Indeed I cannot tell," I said. "I am a stranger here. But I understood from his Majesty's letter that a residence would be provided for us on our arrival; and he has been duly informed that we were to arrive at this time."
>
> "His Majesty cannot remember everything," said his Excellency; the interpreter added, "You can go where you like." And away went master and slaves.

Surprised and not knowing where to turn, Anna shed indignant tears at this "heartless arbitrary insolence on the part of my employers."

In fact, as her narration reveals but somehow fails to recognize, it was she who had been insolent, resentfully insisting that the king was "duly informed" and in other ways failing to acknowledge the *kalahom*'s courtesy. Her touchy dignity was proving counterproductive, inviting insults rather than warding them off.

Later that evening Anna was introduced in the half-darkness to one of the king's brothers, corpulent Prince Sanit (the man who removed his jacket in front of diplomats). By all accounts, Sanit was jolly and easygoing, helpful to Westerners, and universally liked. Anna's view, so far as one can tell from her arch report of their meeting, was rather less friendly: "Was it a bear? No, a prince! For the clumsy mass of reddish-brown flesh unrolled and uplifted itself, and held out a human arm, with a fat hand at the end of it." Although one assumes that she did the polite thing and took the extended hand, her narrative invites the reader to disregard it and focus instead on physical features seen as undignified and disgusting.

That first night she was rescued and given a bed by the English harbormaster and his wife, John and Margaret Bush. The next morning the hostess made her appearance "*en déshabillé,*" inspiring the strange remark in *The English Governess* that she looked "scarcely so pretty as at our first meeting." The cattiness seems gratuitous, a poor return for hospitality. But Anna was reinforcing the lesson that was implicit in her lofty manner, namely, that Westerners are obliged to be on guard against the comfortable undress and lack of dignity they encounter in Bangkok. They must stand up straight and dress well and never yield an inch to native ways. There is a line they must not cross, and when they do, a smart slap on the wrist will be in order.

Indeed, that is the very punishment Anna has just administered to the *kalahom* and Prince Sanit. Instead of acknowledging favors received, she has taken it upon herself to deliver proper snubs. Putting people in their place: that is the responsibility the new teacher has shouldered in spite of her anomalous and unstable position.

Although we do not know to what extent Anna actually carried out this program, it seems she had not forgotten the lessons taught by her mixed-race mother. Protect your Englishness morning noon and night. Rewrite the letter till it's perfect. Sit your pony. Never give in, as the harbormaster's wife has given in, to the soft, invasive, demoralizing Orient.

FIRST AUDIENCE

Unlike Rama III, King Mongkut struck Westerners as a strangely approachable monarch. Some could not help staring at his frequent spitting and few remaining teeth, blackened from the betel he chewed, but most visitors realized that the habit was universal in Siam and chose to focus on his character traits: his candor, curiosity, generosity. They noted his thinness, liveliness, and abrupt manner and invariably commented on his odd spoken English, which he liked to exhibit. An early German anthropologist complained of his *polternden Aussprache*—blustering foreign accent. The French count had difficulty following him and regarded his volubility as absurd. Bowring found his talk "highly intelligent, but . . . carried on in the language of books rather than of ordinary colloquy." A hurried American diplomat who wanted to get down to business found him "pedantic beyond belief." Among those who recognized his humor was John Thomson, a Scottish photographer who called him "a decided wag." All visitors had something to say about Mongkut's eccentricities, but no one left anything on record remotely like the weird madness of Anna's first audience.

It took place in early April, two and a half weeks after her arrival. Assuming she would go to work at once, she had grown restless and irritated. What she didn't know was that the king had been tied down by his many ceremonial duties.

When the helpful harbormaster escorted her and Louis to the royal audience hall, she found it full of courtiers crouching on the floor as custom required, resting on their elbows with their bent legs drawn up beneath them. To approach the throne by stepping over their heads, Anna wrote in *The English Governess*, "was a temptation as drolly natural as it was dangerous." The impulse reflected her impatience with time-wasting rituals, as did the remarkable act she next took credit for. With the excuse that five-year-old Louis was "tired and hungry" (or so we read in her book), she pushed forward into the audience hall without being announced. Seeing her enter in this unceremonious manner—a breach of protocol no other outsider is known to have attempted—the king "advanced abruptly, petulantly screaming 'Who? who? who?'"

Although Anna was the only one who described Mongkut as screaming like this, his physical movements did attract comment, being impulsive and perhaps ungainly. In the eyes of Bradley, a longtime observer, they were "quick and nervous." In the opinion of the French count, who wrote quite colorfully about his one brief week in Bangkok, the king of Siam was "perfectly ugly, and takes after the monkey."

After Anna was introduced by the harbormaster, Mongkut proceeded "to march up and down in quick step" as if meditating what to do. Abruptly stopping, he pointed at the new teacher and demanded, "How old shall you be?" In *The English Governess* the question is made to seem precipitous and rude. In fact, it was neither: asking the age of a new acquaintance is customary and polite in traditional Thai culture.

For the new teacher, who would always conceal her year of birth and other vital details, the question was anything but routine. It was expected, however, thanks to the preparatory coaching of Captain Bush (who whispers "Forewarned, forearmed!" at the scene's opening). So Anna had her answer ready: "Scarcely able to repress a smile at a proceeding so absurd, and with my sex's distaste for so serious a question, I demurely replied, 'One hundred and fifty years old.'"

The writing here deserves the closest attention. That scarcely repressed smile is not so much the puckish look that prepares for a joke as the coy smirk with which one dissembles a sense of superiority. We are to understand that Anna was not about to allow for differences in custom and that she regarded the proceedings with a good-natured contempt. There is such a strong claim of cultural authority here and such a keen sense of "demure" womanliness that one can't help wondering if that offhand remark about "my sex's distaste" for serious questions partly explains the writer's chronic inaccuracy about dates, ages, facts. Did Anna feel it was unwomanly or unladylike to care for these?

The king, surprised by her answer, begins "to perceive the jest" and chooses to play along: "In what year were you borned?" Her answer, wildly off—1788—calls up an expression on his face that is "indescribably comical." But he is not to be outdone:

> "How many years shall you be married?"
> "For several years, your Majesty."
> He fell into a brown study; then, laughing, rushed at me, and demanded triumphantly:—
> "Ha! How many grandchildren shall you now have? Ha, ha! How many? How many? Ha, ha, ha!"
> Of course we all laughed with him; but the general hilarity admitted of a variety of constructions.

Appearing in the first magazine installment of *The English Governess*, this was one of Anna's signature stories. In it, she represented herself as seizing the initiative and breaking the rules in a suitably feminine way and the king as caught off guard and following her lead.

Did anything like this scene take place?

The historian Barend Jan Terwiel has plausibly surmised that Anna's evasion of the age-question "may well come close to something that actually happened." But did she thrust herself forward in the audience hall? That she got away with this bold challenge to protocol looks suspiciously self-flattering, and in addition the act appears oddly isolated and without consequences. Afterward it is never referred to.

Her account of her work assignment also seems to go off the rails. "I have sixty-seven children," the king supposedly declared. "You shall educate them, and as many of my wives, likewise, as may wish to learn English." He also announced that she must help him with his foreign correspondence—a duty that hadn't been mentioned in negotiations with William Adamson and Tan Kim Ching (and that would not have been assigned to an untested employee). The fact is, most of the royal children were too young for school, and the secretarial work would not be imposed for another year or two. Anna's narrative of her first audience greatly exaggerates Mongkut's peremptory unreasonableness.

What her employer actually said can be inferred from Bradley's summary of the "Noticeable Events" of 1862, published in the next year's *Bangkok Calendar*. His entry for Anna gives us the date of her first audience and much more besides: "April 3rd—Mrs. Leonowens, an English lady, commences services as governess of the children of his Majesty. . . . She will probably have thirty or more pupils of little princes and princesses, all brothers and sisters, who have attained to sufficient age to be taught the rudiments of an English education." Employing the future tense, the entry records what Anna had just conveyed to Bradley about her assigned duties. There were to be half as many pupils as in her published narrative, nothing was said about additional chores, and she came away with the impression that her labors were about to commence.

There is one other piece of evidence, found in Anna's first letter to seven-year-old Avis. Here she drew a much more positive picture than in her later account: "We went to the King's Palace which is even more beautiful. The King was so kind to Louis; he took Mamma's hand and led her to the Queen who put her[self] down on the ground [i.e., prostrated herself] as soon as the King came to her." Even though this sketchy report was aimed at a child too young to be a skilled reader, it seems more trustworthy than the polished account in *The English Governess*, composed years after the fact. As the letter indicates, Mongkut did take a special interest in Louis, and the bit about Lady Talap (who was a wife or concubine, not the queen) is consistent with what we learn elsewhere.

In sum, Anna may have given a teasing number for her age, but so far she felt no animus against Mongkut and no desire to challenge him by striding into court. She was eager to succeed at her new job, and the last thing she wanted was to provoke a royal explosion. The petulant screaming and much of the rest were invented later, after her feelings against the king had hardened and she decided it would be good to show the American public how masterful she had been in confronting a willful tyrant.

SECOND AUDIENCE

While waiting for her school to open, Anna was given a temporary apartment in the *kalahom's* palace, where she began her study of the Thai language. This was the one time she may be said to have lived in a harem.

Impressed with her resolve and energy, Chuang Bunnak said to her, "Siamese lady no like work; love play, love sleep. Why you no love play?" The next day, eleven Siamese children, offspring of his relatives and dependents, appeared in Anna's room. Teaching them would be her interim job before the real work started in the Grand Palace.

This story finds confirmation in two contemporary notes she sent to Bradley. The first, dated 21 April and surviving with his papers, says that the *kalahom* "thinks the writing books too good for beginners—I therefore beg to return you twelve of them—We would feel greatly obliged if you could kindly procure some less expensive With 12 slates and pencils and Pens— Ink." The second message, written the next day, says she has "got starte[d]" with the lessons. Her reason for troubling Bradley with her requests, she writes, is that she has "no messenger to send" for schoolroom supplies. Simple and down-to-earth, the dashed-off notes give us a feel for her practical difficulties.

Her next meeting with Mongkut, far more contentious than the first, concerned the question of her residence. In his letter to Adamson, the king had stipulated that she was to live in or near the palace to save him the bother of having her conveyed "to & fro almost every day." Not knowing her marital status, he said that if she had a "husband or manservant," she would be given "a brick house in nearest vicinity of this palace."

Although the great majority of Bangkok's dwellings were built of wood, "some of the better houses," according to a traveler, were of brick and sat in enclosures. Providing a home of that sort for the schoolmistress would entail a substantial outlay. But a widow with no male servant could live in the palace at no extra expense.

Instead of going into this question, the letter of appointment the king sent Anna ended with a brief and courteous statement, "We beg to invite you to our royal palace." Simple words, yet they harbored a critical ambiguity: she could assume that they referred to her work, whereas he may have had her living arrangements in mind.

For this second audience, Anna was escorted by the *kalahom*'s older, unmarried sister. An authority on palace custom and etiquette, she had been in charge of Mongkut's many young brides following his accession and, like some of them, had studied English under the missionary wives a decade earlier. As the pair traveled by boat to the palace landing on the left bank, the elderly woman opened a schoolbook of Anna's. "With a look of pleased surprise," she saw the English alphabet she used to know and "began repeating the letters. I helped her, and for a while she seemed amused and gratified; but presently, growing weary of it, she abruptly closed the book, and, offering me her hand, said, 'Good morning, sir!'" Making a joke of the woman's limited English, Anna neglected to explain that *khun*, the Thai word corresponding to "Mr." or "Sir," also means "Mrs." or "Madam" and is thus used for men and women alike. Thinking in her own language, the woman naturally assumed that "Sir" also meant "Madam."

On this visit Anna met the king in the women's quarters, not the audience hall. When he announced that she would be living in the palace, she replied ("with a secret shudder at the idea of sleeping within those walls") that that was unacceptable: with no privacy or freedom to come and go, she would feel like a prisoner. Recalling what she thought had been agreed, she added, "In your gracious letter you promised me 'a residence adjoining the royal palace,' not within it." With that, his face turned purple and he exploded: "'I do not know I have promised. I do not know former condition. I do not know anything but you are our servant; and it is our pleasure

that you must live in this palace, and—*you shall obey.*' Those last three words
he fairly screamed."

The buried ambiguity in the prior correspondence may indeed have
given rise to an argument over living quarters. But the clash laid out in *The
English Governess* (with a second instance of royal screaming) is so violent
and at odds with the rest of the narrative that it is hard to know what to
believe. A moment's reflection shows that if Anna had the male servant she
claimed, Mongkut could not have asked her to reside in the palace; that is
clear from his letter to Adamson. Even more striking, the "gracious letter"
she herself received from the king—a document reproduced from date-line
to signature at the start of her book—does not contain the words she quotes.

Perhaps she had seen the Adamson letter in Singapore and was now recalling the offer of a house while forgetting the bit about a manservant. What
is certain is that her written account of the confrontation was designed to
draw out the dramatic possibilities of the scene: there she was in the harem,
a defenseless white woman with her small boy at her side, face to face with
an absolute Oriental despot who goes back on his word and tries to cow her
into submission.

However, Mongkut *was* known for his fits of anger. In Anna's story, after
she advised him that she would perform her duties but could not promise
total obedience, "he roared,—'you *shall* live in palace'" and began issuing
frantic commands to his docile women. Frightened and indignant and feeling the tears start, Anna turned on her heel and headed for the door. When
she heard "voices behind us crying, 'Mam! Mam!' I turned again, and saw
the king beckoning and calling to me. I bowed to him profoundly, but
passed on through the brass door. The prime minister's sister bounced after
us in a distraction of excitement, tugging at my cloak, shaking her finger
in my face, and crying, '*My dee! my dee!*' [not good] All the way back, in
the boat, and on the street, to the very door of my apartments, instead of
her jocund 'Good morning, sir,' I had nothing but *my dee.*"

In effect, Anna had laid down an ultimatum. Forced to yield, His Majesty
"repented" and agreed to separate lodgings. She would seem to have won a
major victory, but when she was taken to the house selected for her within
walking distance of the palace, it amounted to little more than two win-
dowless rooms. The neighborhood smelled like a fish market, there was no
"bath-closet or kitchen," the furniture was broken, the matting "filthy." "And
this was the residence sumptuously appointed for the English governess

to the royal family of Siam!" In outrage, Anna turned on her heel a second time and retreated to her temporary apartment across the river.

In the end she was given the suitable private dwelling she demanded. That it was situated on the right bank near the *kalahom*'s palace meant that the king had quietly dropped his requirement that she reside near his court. He was now committed to providing a boat and rowers to carry her across the broad Chao Phya River on her working days, the "to & fro" business he had hoped to avoid.[1]

How closely did Anna's story of her quest for a home match actual events? It happens that an English traveler by the name of E. B. Lewis learned of her house problem and wrote about it in a travel essay. The interest of the piece lies in the fact that it was published in 1867, three years before Anna's highly embellished story saw print in *The English Governess*. Here, then, is what seems to be her protostory:

> On the first arrival of the governess for the royal children, the accommo- dation fitted to an English lady had been but very shabbily provided. After repeated applications through the first minister [the *kalahom*] for the redress of these grievances without effect, she took the opportunity of remonstrating (on the occasion of an interview) with his majesty in person, declaring her determination not to remain in the royal service unless his majesty could more fittingly discharge the duty of a host to a lady. The king, whose subjects of every degree tremble and prostrate themselves before him, was so much astounded at the independence of spirit displayed towards his august person by a simple individual and a lady, that he sent for his minister in all haste, and ordered that whatever she demanded should be given her immediately, but that on no consideration could her services be dispensed with, or could she be allowed to depart.

If Lewis's account seems to express Anna's triumphant point of view, there is a simple explanation: she was the informant. As a Singapore passenger list reveals, "Mr. and Mrs. Lewis" visited Bangkok in February 1863 near the

1. After a couple of years Anna moved to another and better house, a brick one. In the neighborhood of the eastern wall of the Grand Palace, this second home put her close to her daily work, as her employer originally wanted. Strangely, nothing she wrote about her life in Bangkok has anything to say about this important move across the river. It was Margaret Landon's careful detective work that brought it to light.

end of the teacher's first year of work. Two months later, passengers leaving on the *Chow Phya* included "Mrs. Leonowens" as well as the Lewises. Anna had obtained her first badly needed leave of absence and was sailing to Singapore for a month's recuperation. During the five-day voyage, she evidently recounted her search for a house to her fellow travelers, one of whom would incorporate the tale in "Recollections of a Visit to Bangkok," published four years later in London in *Bentley's Miscellany*.

What the Lewis essay gives us is the story Anna was telling in 1863, years before she began writing for publication. On balance, it seems likely that she threatened to leave if she wasn't given a decent house and that Mongkut, impressed with her stately demands, required the *kalahom* to find something suitable (which explains why her home adjoined the minister's palace across the river). The embellishments—the king's spectacular rage, Anna's impulsive exit—were created later, after relations had soured.

She also exaggerated the time it took for her to settle in. Taking her at her word, Landon's novelized account has her languishing into July—four months—before a house is found and her teaching begins. During this interval she struggles with depression and apathy and very nearly gives up. For Landon's Anna, this is the psychological crisis, the test she has to pass before she is fit for her heroic work of freeing a nation.

In fact, as the Thai edition of Mongkut's correspondence makes clear, he and the schoolmistress had come to a satisfactory understanding by 21 May. On that day, in a letter to Adamson, the king assured the man who had gone out on a limb in recommending Anna that "the Lady Leonowens our School mistress is now well happy [*sic*]. I beg to enclose the testimonial note written for information to you from her herewith."

Two months had passed, negotiations were over, the new teacher had shown she must be treated as a European, and she was hard at work introducing His Majesty's older children to their ABCs. Who would have guessed that the Lady Leonowens had been schooled at a Bombay charity institution for mixed-race children?

THE MOST HIDEOUS WORD
SHE EVER WROTE OR UTTERED

Eight years later Anna came out with her account of her first audiences with King Mongkut and her fight for suitable accommodations. The dramatic narrative formed part of an essay in the *Atlantic Monthly* titled "The English Governess at the Siamese Court," the first of four installments preceding the publication of the book that made her famous. The focus was on the king's history and personality: his petulance, bad English, crazed learning, general outlandishness, and deep-dyed hypocrisy. Anna included a confidential passage from a letter of his and in other ways laid bare what she believed to be his secret motives. All told, it was a devastating portrait of a monarch who had many good qualities but was also vicious, deceptive, overbearing, and absurd. The article gave the impression that the author had been an insider at court and that her information was highly privileged.

The *Atlantic* was America's most distinguished magazine. Justly proud of having broken into it at the start of her new career, Anna posted copies to two old friends in Bangkok: Ailison Campbell, wife of the British consular surgeon and sister-in-law of Adamson, and George Orton, captain of the *Chow Phya*. What she wrote to them is lost, but we do have her exactly contemporaneous letter to Bradley, to whom she boasted that her article was "creating quite a sensation here if one may judge from the papers." Near the end, elated by her success and writing rapidly, she asked after friends in Bangkok and then added, seemingly on the spur of the moment, "Bangkok is the most hedious word I have ever written or uttered" (the end of the letter is reproduced in the illustration gallery). She apparently meant *hideous*, accidentally reversing the first two vowels.

Nothing in the letter leads up to or explains or in any way connects with this stark statement. It is just suddenly *there*, an oddly misspelled expression of settled aversion. In the sentences that precede it, Anna politely asks after various friends. In the sentence that follows—"And with kind wishes for yourself and family I am yours truly"—she reverts to genial formulas. It is as if the outburst had never been. You have to go back and look again to make sure you got it right. *Bangkok is the most hedious word I have ever written or uttered*: an eruption of loathing in the midst of standard courtesies. The disconnect between surface and depth is glaring and absolute, an extreme example of a prose style that tends to be patchy, not well integrated, and marked by abrupt changes in tone or level of diction.

When Anna's friends in Bangkok received their copies of the *Atlantic*, they were so struck that they each showed it to the country's leading journalist, Samuel Jones Smith. Formerly a missionary, Smith was now publisher, editor, and writer in chief of the *Siam Weekly Advertiser*, the English-language paper in which he put on record his reaction to the exposé of Mongkut.

A few weeks earlier, Smith had printed a respectful sketch of Anna as "an English woman, who served the King faithfully in the double capacity of teacher . . . and private amanuensis." Now, confronted by her article, he reminded readers that she had been a famous storyteller who left "deep impressions in the memory of many in Bangkok," and then he studiously avoided anything like a straightforward summary or appraisal. Professing himself unable to decide when the author's language was "to be taken in its simple, and when in its ironical sense," he treated the piece as if it were a dangerous joke. Perhaps, he suggested, it should be given to "dyspeptic, and otherwise ailing people."

Smith was walking on tiptoe. In spite of the freedom Western journalists enjoyed in Bangkok (and they were by and large freer then than now), certain royal matters could not be aired in print. It was simply not possible to discuss Anna's representations of the king's character and conduct. Yet how could an author with many local friends be called a liar? The closest the journalist came to speaking his mind was in his summary statement that her "pithy little article is susceptible of severe criticism, and baffles any attempt to pronounce which to admire most in its overrought [*sic*] artistic colourings, studiously blending vanity, burlesque, caricature, humor, satire and irony." Too cautious and hamstrung to spell out the "severe criticism" he had in mind, Smith could only intimate that Anna's literary debut was a vain and overcooked literary performance.

This poorly articulated review merits attention for two reasons. The first is that it offers the one assessment of her writing by a resident of Bangkok familiar with local conditions. The second is that Smith, too, was Eurasian, with a history as globalized as Anna's. He had been born south of Bombay in an area colonized by the Portuguese. His father, James Smith, was a private in the Royal Army's Sixty-Ninth Regiment; his mother, Mary, whose surname wasn't recorded, seems to have been Portuguese-Indian. About four years old when his father's regiment was ordered to return to England, the boy somehow ended up in Burma, where a Baptist missionary couple, the Reverend John Taylor Jones and his first wife, adopted him. Brought by them to Bangkok in 1833, Samuel Jones Smith, as he was henceforth known, became a bright, bilingual, energetic Christian. He went to the States for his education, returned to Siam as a missionary in 1849, and ended by marrying Sara Sleeper Jones, one of the first three teachers in the palace. Since Sara was also his adoptive father's second wife, Smith may be said to have married his mother, replacing, perhaps, the one left behind in India.

Maw Smit, as he was called in Thai, meaning Doctor Smith, went on to publish a number of important Siamese legal and literary texts and to became a well-known figure in Bangkok. Treated with reserve by other missionaries, he was the one Eurasian among them, the one missionary Anna knew but never named in her writings, and the one Anglophone resident who publicly criticized her work. What was his private opinion of his fellow Anglo-Indian? One notes that, unlike Bradley, he was clear about her role at court: not governess but teacher and amanuensis.

Following the publication of Anna's second book, *The Romance of the Harem*, Smith's newspaper pointedly noted that the volume had been "very severely criticized" in the latest *London and China Express*. This was a weekly newspaper produced in London for distribution in East and Southeast Asia, where each issue, as an old Singapore hand remembered, was eagerly awaited. Smith's reference was to a withering review that announced that Anna's new book had surpassed "its predecessor in sensationalism and incredibility." Nothing could be believed, not even those parts "for which the authoress vouches on her own experience." Such were the judgments that Maw Smit wanted Bangkok's Westerners to notice.

And not just Westerners: if the *Advertiser* had a readership similar to that of the *Bangkok Recorder*, an earlier newspaper for which there survives a partial subscription list, Smith's remarks would have been seen by a number of highly placed Siamese.

Top left: Anna's mother's father's father, Reverend Cradock Glascott. From *Evangelical Register; or Magazine for the Connexion of the Late Countess of Huntingdon* 2 (April 1827): facing p. 161. Engraving removed and clipped to "Reminiscences of the late Rev. C. Glascott," MS bound in *Two Sermons on Occasion of the Death of the Revd. C. Glascott, A.M. Late Vicar of Hatherleigh, Devon* (London: Longman, 1831). Image reproduced by permission of Devon Heritage Centre, Exeter.

Top right: Anna's nephew, Reverend Thomas Arthur Savage, principal of Cathedral High School, Bombay. From *Times of India*, 19 June 1918, 8. © The British Library Board. All Rights Reserved.

Bottom right: Eliza Sara Millard Pratt, Anna's niece and the mother of Boris Karloff. Courtesy of Sara Karloff.

Anna Leonowens. Studio portrait by Napoleon Sarony of New York, ca. 1870.
Courtesy of Wheaton College Special Collections, Wheaton, Illinois.

Anna's son, Louis T. Leonowens. From *The Leonowens Story* (Bangkok: Louis T. Leonowens, Ltd., 1975). Courtesy of Wheaton College Special Collections, Wheaton, Illinois.

Anna's daughter, Avis Leonowens Fyshe. From her *carte de visite*. Courtesy of Wheaton College Special Collections, Wheaton, Illinois.

Thomas Leonowens's signature on a petition in Western Australia strengthens the impression, gathered elsewhere, that he was a man to reckon with among his peers and his betters. From Petition to Governor and Legislative Council by Members of the Swan River Mechanics' Institute, 10 April 1855, Consignment 136, item 061, State Records Office of Western Australia. Courtesy of the State Records Office of Western Australia.

Earliest known photo of the jail (*center left*) and other structures at the convict hiring depot at Lynton. The depot was abandoned in 1856–57. The photo dates from ca. 1930. Courtesy of the State Library of Western Australia. All rights reserved.

Tan Kim Ching (Chen Jinzhong), Singapore businessman and agent of King Mongkut. From Song Ong Siang, *One Hundred Years' History of the Chinese in Singapore* (1902; reprint, Kuala Lumpur: University of Malaya Press, 1967), facing p. 92.

TAN KIM CHING

Mongkut, king of Siam. The photograph was taken in 1865 by John Thomson, who described the king's outfit as "a sort of French Field Marshal's uniform." Courtesy of Wheaton College Special Collections, Wheaton, Illinois.

"Please come & ride on our Eliphunt": King Mongkut to David Olyphant King of Salem, Massachusetts, 28 December [1855]. King Family Papers. From the Collections of the Newport Historical Society.

". . . it is said that you wish to ride on Eliphunt if it be so, please come & ride on our Eliphunt here & travell in this city & visit every[?] beautiful our Churches & monasteries of Boodhist priests you will be interesting in seeing of some Siamese manufactures in curiousity. I beg to remain your welwisher[?] S P P M Mongkut, Rex Siamensium." The initials stand for Somdet Phra Paramendr Maha, royal honorifics.

Mary Mattoon. *"No words of anger or of harshness ever escaped her lips. . . . Her power was in her kind and gentle deportment"* (posthumous tribute by a former pupil [II F 1 folder33, MKL Papers]). Image from Mattoon Family collection (RG275-2-9), courtesy of Presbyterian Historical Society, Presbyterian Church (U.S.A.), Philadelphia, Pennsylvania.

Reverend Stephen Mattoon. *"One of the greatest men I have ever known"* (Anna to Avis, Bangkok, 4 December 1865 [VI C 4:2 folder 29, p. 102, MKL Papers]). Image from Mattoon Family collection (RG275-2-9), courtesy of Presbyterian Historical Society, Presbyterian Church (U.S.A.), Philadelphia, Pennsylvania.

TWO MISSIONARIES WHO BECAME PIONEERING
BANGKOK JOURNALISTS AND PUBLISHERS.

Reverend Dan Beach Bradley.
Of the missionaries Anna
knew in Siam, Bradley
stood out for his energy and
outspokenness. His command
of Thai was said to be
"uncommonly fluent and
exact" (Samuel Jones Smith,
"The Late Rev. D. B. Bradley,
M.D.," *Siam Repository* 5
[July 1873]: 394). Courtesy of
Oberlin College Archives,
Oberlin, Ohio.

Reverend Samuel Jones Smith.
From a *carte de visite*. Smith was
the one Bangkok missionary who
publicly criticized Anna's books.
Reproduced with the kind
permission of Anake Nawigamune,
author of *Farang nay muang sayaam*
[Westerners in Siam].

Sisuriyawong, the *kalahom* (minister of the south and the military), also known as Chuang Bunnak. "A most sagacious man, towering far above every other person whom we have met" (Bowring, *Kingdom and People*, 2:282). Courtesy of Wellcome Library, London.

Gabriel Aubaret, French naval officer and consul. "Our consul . . . is working with all his might for the grandeur of his country. . . . I do not believe the Siamese love him" (Beauvoir, *Java, Siam*, 343). From *Gabriel Aubaret* (Poitiers: Librairie H. Oudin, [1897]), frontispiece.

Louis Leonowens, Prince Chulalongkorn, and others, ca. 1865. The large Western-type palace on the right, the Ananta Samakhom Hall, was built by King Mongkut on inadequate foundations and demolished by his son King Chulalongkorn. Courtesy of the National Archives of Thailand.

Prince Chulalongkorn and his two full brothers, born in 1860 and 1857. The brothers' one full sister, Fa Ying (as Anna called her), had died by the time this photo was taken. Courtesy of Wheaton College Special Collections, Wheaton, Illinois.

Prince Chulalongkorn. Courtesy of Wheaton College Special Collections, Wheaton, Illinois.

A royal child and his crouching attendant, who holds his fan still and is careful not to let the soles of his feet face the child or touch the woven mat. John Thomson, photographer. Courtesy of Wheaton College Special Collections, Wheaton, Illinois.

Conclusion of Anna's letter to Dan Beach Bradley, 17 May 1870. After mentioning young King Chulalongkorn, Anna wrote, "If you have time will you not write and tell me all you know about him? How are all at Bangkok. Bangkok is the most hedious word I have ever written or uttered. And with kind wishes for yourself and family I am yours truly A H Leonowens." Dan Beach Bradley Family Papers (I/1/335), courtesy of Oberlin College Archives, Oberlin, Ohio.

Anna Leonowens in old age. Courtesy of Wheaton College Special Collections,
Wheaton, Illinois.

Kenneth and Margaret Landon. Margaret and Kenneth Landon Papers, courtesy of Wheaton College Special Collections, Wheaton, Illinois.

12

Anna and the Siamese
Understanding of Human Sexuality

MUCH OF WHAT ANNA would have to say about hideous Bangkok was shaped by a visceral distaste for Siamese sexual attitudes and practices. Deeply repulsed, she seems to have experienced the kind of reaction that Samuel Jones Smith characterized as a "shock to the moral sensibilities . . . on first observing the habits of polygamists." The word to notice there is *habits*—a signal that Smith had something in mind more fundamental and systemic than polygamy per se.

The gulf between the Siamese and Western understandings of human sexuality was very likely unbridgeable. For the Thais, as critic Sutham Thammarongwit notes, sex had long been regarded "as something ordinary," a point of view that Anna and many Westerners saw as low and repellent. For them, the joys of sex (married, of course) had the specialness that Thomas Leonowens had invoked in a passionate letter to her: "How I long to hold you to my heart, to drink the bliss the highest bliss from your dear lips and to realize the highest the most exalted and most passionate delight in your arms." Sex thought of in terms like that, terms touching on the sacred, was never something ordinary.

Given that marriage for love had been Anna's great pivot—the choice that saved her from everything her mother, aunt, and sister had accepted in India—it is no surprise that she detested Siamese sexual codes. What is startling is the intensity of her hatred and the turn to violence in her stories about sex and the palace. To grasp the distinctive nature of her recoil, we need to begin with a brief survey of the reactions of other foreigners.

A Black, Black Record

When missionary Dan Beach Bradley and his first wife, Emelie Royce, arrived in Siam in 1835, they took for granted, like all Americans and Europeans of the time, that the two sexes do not wear the same attire and that a modest woman will both conceal her breasts and present their shape beneath a tailored bodice. In Bangkok, as Emelie quickly discovered, another set of rules was in play. "The dress of the females differs in nothing from that of the males," she wrote in dismay; "the former generally have a cloth thrown over the shoulders, but it is worn with little regard to modesty." Before long, she was overcome by a chronic and involuntary disgust: "The heathen are a constant cause of irritation. . . . [Y]ou cannot hide your eyes from their shameful nakedness, nor close your ears against their vulgar and awfully obscene conversation."

Emelie's husband's reaction to Siamese sexual customs was equally grim. After sacking a native employee for having sex with a single woman, he complained that "there is nothing in the customs of this people nor in their religion to prevent the males having improper intercourse with unmarried females." He was learning what historian Anthony Reid has observed about Southeast Asia generally: "Pre-marital sexual relations were regarded indulgently, and virginity at marriage was not expected of either party."

Missionaries were not the only outsiders who believed that the Thais lacked a sense of restraint or decency. Townsend Harris was the man who negotiated the 1856 Siamese-American treaty and then became the first American minister to Japan. When he spotted a lingam in a Bangkok shrine, he noted in his journal that "its accurate form makes its exhibition a filthy one." A bachelor, Townsend was as shocked as Mrs. Bradley by the women's "scanty clothing," which, he noticed, hid their breasts only "when the wind does not blow it about." Both observers, it should be said, were well educated. Emelie had been a teacher at a girls' school, and Townsend had been president of the Board of Education in New York City and had years of experience trading in East Asia.

During Anna's tenure at the palace, a Mrs. Eastlake and her five-year-old son survived a shipwreck and were rescued by a Chinese junk on its way to Bangkok, where they arrived without proper attire. A doctor's wife who had lived in China, Eastlake was an adaptable and good-humored traveler.

Preparing for a royal audience, she borrowed a gown that proved ludi-crously short and then asked about her son: Should he wear the usual native costume? The consul "smiled and said, 'If you will go to the window, you will see the style of dress worn by the small boys and youths of Siam.' I did so, and on a grassy sward, half-a-dozen lads were playing, entirely nude, with only a cord and small metal shield, about the size of the palm of the hand, dangling below the waist. Involuntarily turning toward my friend, I found he had modestly withdrawn from the room." The interesting detail here is the consul's modesty—his reluctance to meet the eyes of this West-ern woman after she had seen all those poorly concealed penises.

For English speakers, the easiest way to deal with such matters was silence. Thais were less constrained, partly because their language lacked a class of words considered obscene. Among the many Thai pronouns, each suitable for defined social situations in a highly stratified society, there is one for boys and men that simply means "penis." Unlike our English "prick," which is always spoken with attitude, the Thai word does not carry a feeling of contemptuous indecency. *Hey, penis, what's new?* a woman in the north-eastern section of the country may casually say to a village boy. The usage can be as unconscious as the nakedness of the boys observed by Eastlake.

Was that the sort of thing Emelie Bradley had in mind when she shud-dered at the natives' "vulgar and awfully obscene conversation"? We don't know, and the reason we don't is that her assumptions about the correct use of language mandated silence and an averted glance. What could be seen and spoken in one linguistic culture with little or no self-consciousness was so obscene in the other that it could not be named: naming was filth. And yet it is not the case that anything goes with Thais. Patting a friend on the head, an innocent act in the West, has always been deeply offensive in Thai-land, whose customs have a weave of frankness and prohibition that can't be intuited by Westerners.

Accompanying all those hooded American glances and silent headshakes were the most lurid suspicions of Asian depravity. In 1886 a female mission-ary who had recently returned from Siam had this to say about the coun-try's monkhood: "The actual sins of the so-called holy Buddhist priests would make a black, black record. If God, to-day, visited His wrath upon existing Sodomites as He did upon the ancient city, many of the wats of Siam would be appropriate sites for Dead Seas!" This horrified certainty that monks were buggering one another was in all likelihood deluded. As noted by Peter Jackson, who has investigated sexual attitudes and practices in old Siam, Thai Buddhism may not have condemned "same-sex eroticism between laymen or laywomen as a sin," but it has always strictly regulated the sexual behavior of monks.

One of the things that proved especially hard for Westerners to grasp was the position of women in old Siam. That they were freer than in many Asian societies was obvious: they were not required to veil themselves or live in purdah, and they often ran a business. But they were assumed to be inferior and subservient to men and in certain transactions seemed to be treated as property. "In the poorer classes the greater number of daughters are sold in marriage," Bishop Pallegoix reported and then immediately added, "Yet they are not regarded as slaves but as properly wedded spouses." This nuanced account got at a cultural ambiguity outsiders often missed. In spite of the exchange of money, it wasn't the case that wives were literally owned.

Given the frequency with which Western businessmen took mistresses they later abandoned, it seems clear that many foreigners thought of Siamese women as available sex goods. But the true predators were those who sailed to the tropics for girls. Shortly before Anna came to Bangkok, a case was heard at the British consulate "of a young girl who was injured during sexual congress with a Continental European." James Campbell, the consular surgeon (and before long Anna's doctor), was asked to state his opinion on the age of puberty in Siam. His answer, that "15 years was about the rule," went against the widespread assumption that the menses commenced "earlier in hot climates than in cold." His opinion was challenged by the defendant, whereupon Campbell conferred with the ex–royal physician and an old nobleman, drew up some (quite opaque) tables, read a paper to the Obstetrical Society of Edinburgh when he sailed back to Scotland to get married, and had it published in the *Edinburgh Medical Journal*. The point of his short anonymous paper was to present the mixed results of a fact-based, nonsensational inquiry into an aspect of human sexuality in Siam, along with various speculations.

Most readers wanted something different: if not a black, black record, at least a highly colored account full of strategic silences, pursed lips, and moral horror. These were the expectations Anna would satisfy in *The English Governess at the Siamese Court*.

THE SIAMESE HAREM

When Townsend Harris's small diplomatic delegation reached Bangkok in 1856, one of the king's ministers was "disappointed that a larger number of officers had not come, and immediately inquired the reason." Like all Siamese, the minister assumed that people with real power had an entourage. The same rule held in premodern Europe, as we see in *King Lear* when the self-deposed monarch is deprived of his attendants.

When it came to female retinues, this widely accepted rule was applied differently in the East. As Bradley blandly put it (after thirty years in Bangkok had rubbed away his rough edges), "the customs of the Siamese, from time immemorial, have ascribed honor and glory to their princes and lords, somewhat in proportion to the wives they have and maintain." He quoted a Siamese writer of the Third Reign who had asked, "Can he be a king, or even a noble, or lord, and not have a multitude of concubines?" The question was rhetorical. Everyone knew the answer. Men of stature have a harem, period.

"Harem" was defined in Noah Webster's dictionary as "a seraglio; a place where Eastern princes confine their women, who are prohibited from the society of others." In the Arabic source for our English word, the root meaning is "prohibit." Similarly, in old Siam the standard term for concubines was *naang haam*, literally, "ladies forbidden." As in other Eastern nations, the royal Siamese harem was characterized by seclusion, forbidden access, and familiar intercourse with one adult male only. One result: no channels existed by which accurate information about the institution could reach Western eyes and ears.

The author knows of no memoirs by royal nineteenth-century Thai concubines. Apart from Anna, whose great claim was that she alone had access to the king's women and could speak for them, what little is known about life in the Siamese harem derives from kings and nobles and the occasional visitor.

In 1863, Anna's second year, Mongkut read in Bradley's *Bangkok Calendar* that he was believed to have more wives than his younger brother, Jutamani. The king had a shrewd idea what Westerners suspected about him and his women, and here was a chance to address their misconceptions. His correction, excerpted in the next year's *Calendar*, pointed out that in 1851 Jutamani had forty-eight wives, and "since that time his wives increased every year. He endeavor alway to obtain wives especially from the

Laos. Now he has one hundred and twenty wives at least." Mongkut himself had "only a little above thirty wives." Exact or not, by making these numbers public the king was breaking with the traditional assumption that a man's harem was proportional to his power and dignity.

A more momentous break took place six years before Anna's arrival when Mongkut decreed that concubines, chaperones, maids-in-waiting, and dancers were free to resign their positions and return to the outside world. Although this new freedom was denied those concubines who were mothers (the *chaochom maandaa*), it was a major reform, and as such it made an impression on Bradley and Smith, who both commented on it. Anna never mentioned it. Instead, she would represent her employer's harem as an archaic sex prison, with dire punishments reserved for anyone who tried to escape.

Another of Mongkut's reforms involved the schooling of girl concubines, a process that went as follows, according to information gathered by Bradley:

> The daughters of the nobles and lords, which are presented to the king, are always given while quite young; and are then taken to the royal palace, and placed under matrons and governesses . . . whose most sacred duty is to see, that they are preserved in perfect chastity, and schooled and trained . . . until they shall pass their puberty. In all previous reigns, very few of this large school of girls have failed to become royal concubines. But in the present reign, it would appear, that the king has seen fit to give but a small minority of them such preferment. The remainder are retained as maids of honor, with the privilege of asking and obtaining permission to retire from the royal palace whenever they wish to do so.

Did Mongkut truly refrain from having sex with reluctant new partners, as Bradley seems to imply? With his drooping lip and abrupt manner, the thin old man may well have been an unattractive mate in the eyes of young women. But then again, three of his last four children were born to first-time mothers. Unlike Rama III, who apparently fathered no children during his last two decades, Mongkut continued to take new bed partners up to his death. Yet he liberalized the harem as an institution.

Although he was definitely lord and master of his women, they still found ways to manage and even defy him. Chaochom Maandaa Thiang, the so-called head wife, had great skill, according to Anna, in deflecting his rash impulses. The same was true of Chaochom Maandaa Piam, who, according to Anna, appeared humble and compliant while ably securing appointments for her relatives. In one particular matter, the tradition of "lying near the fire," his wives openly disobeyed him. According to this custom, which was also observed in Vietnam, a newly delivered mother was exposed to a fire's smoke and heat for days or weeks. Lying near the fire was thought to ward off certain threats, and Mongkut's women refused to give it up in spite of the disapproval of the king and Western physicians. A note from Mongkut to Bradley complains of this conservative resistance: "The Mother of the little child too is yet well according to the Siamese custom of lying near of fire but I don't pleasing [i.e., am not pleased] believing your knowledge of the same curing [your way of treating a woman after childbirth] is indeed better . . . but I am sorry I can not introduce your custom to even my wives herein."

Mongkut had other woman troubles. Decades earlier, before becoming a monk, he had married a granddaughter of King Taksin named Noi. They lived apart during his long monkhood and then resumed married life after his coronation. But now he had dozens of young consorts with whom the aging Noi could not compete, and she found herself on the shelf. One day, as he traveled to Ayutthaya by royal barge, a boat with some unidentified women sped forward past his own, violating protocol. No one knew who was in charge. Uneasiness grew. In Mongkut's account of the episode (sent to a concubine he tenderly addressed as Turtle), the offenders "laughed merrily and with the utmost abandon." When guards gave chase, they discovered that Noi was the instigator, with the purpose, the king believed, of ridiculing him "in front of my new young wives." For this breach of security and decorum, he had her sent back to the Inner Palace, where she remained unrepentant.

It was an honor to become the concubine of a king or nobleman, yet life as a *naang haam* could be a letdown. John Thomson, the photographer who visited Bangkok in 1865, published a vivid report of the depressed state of feeling in the harem of Krommamuen Alongkot, a junior half brother of the king. Alongkot was an astronomer and astrologer whose workshop was cluttered with broken instruments. His appearance was "haggard," and he looked older than his age, fifty-three. His twelve or sixteen wives passed the time embroidering, smoking cigarettes, and chewing betel nut, looking timid and unhappy. To Thomson their lord confided that it was "a difficult task to keep [them] cheerful." Two years later he died of tuberculosis. Clearly, it could be a very dull life belonging to the harem of a man of little prestige who was in declining health.

One gets a more detailed and positive picture in *Four Reigns* by Kukrit Pramoj. Written in the early 1950s, this classic Thai novel follows the life of a young woman named Phloi who enters the Inner Palace as an attendant of a refined single lady. Although she hates leaving her family compound and her mother, she quickly adjusts to her new home. The reigning monarch is Chulalongkorn, son of Mongkut; the year is 1892. As Phloi masters the deferential and exacting code of speech and manners in the palace, she makes friends with a girl her age and comes to appreciate her aristocratic mistress's humor and sympathy. The word *sanuk*, Thai for "fun," appears frequently in *Four Reigns*. As portrayed by Pramoj (a man), the harem is a rich and satisfying female society, a city of women sufficiently large and diversified to give scope to all types—leaders, performers, tomboys, born rebels. The encircling wall whose gates are locked at night becomes a source of comfort. That the wall may someday "cease to be" is a terrifying prospect. When the time comes for Phloi to leave the Inner Court and marry the man who has been selected for her, she does so with great reluctance.

There is little question but that *Four Reigns* gives an idealized representation of daily life in the Inner Palace. Provoked by the distortions of Landon's *Anna and the King of Siam*, Pramoj wanted to create a sympathetic account of his country's aristocratic past. He was not a reactionary, however—quite the reverse: he was a liberal and cultivated man whose novel does seem to catch at the royal harem's complex actualities.

Anna's Representations of
the Siamese Harem

The photographer's account of Alongkot's bored wives backs up the chief point that Anna's two books would make about harem concubines: that their days were spent in trivial and listless pursuits. "They are nearly all young women," she reported, "but they have the appearance of being slightly blighted. Nobody is too much in earnest, or too much alive, or too happy. The general atmosphere is that of depression." This was the atmosphere in all harems. Each was marked by "apathy" and "deadness" and showed signs of "barbarous cruelty." If a *naang haam* seemed cheerful and contented, that was a sign she was "unconscious of the terrible defacement" she had undergone. Harems were prisons, and concubines led empty, infantile lives.

These stark judgments were related to Anna's view that motherhood was a sacred calling that must be fulfilled within a monogamous union. Wedded to this ideal as firmly as anyone in Victorian England or America, she brought a principled and fully formed detestation of harems to her work in Bangkok. During her first weeks in the *kalahom's* palace, his wives teasingly asked whom she would rather marry, him or the king. Her lofty answer (or so she later wrote) was that "an English, that is a Christian, woman would rather be put to the torture, chained and dungeoned for life, or suffer a death the slowest and most painful you Siamese know, than be the wife of either."[1] To become a *naang haam* was to suffer an ultimate defilement, a kind of soul murder.

How was redemption possible for these degraded women? The answer: "Always when a woman becomes a mother her life changes; she passes from the ignoble to the noble; then she becomes pure, worthy, honorable." Like a number of Anna's statements about harem life, this one looks like it was based on a prescriptive moral outlook rather than scrupulous observation.

In spite of her success as a self-supporting teacher and author, she devoutly believed that women could best fulfill themselves in a Western-type marriage. A woman *should* be dependent, intimately, on a male breadwinner. Yet a case could be made that dependency was the sore point in her own insecure married life, particularly at the hiring depot in Lynton, where her situation was comparable to that of the convicts her husband provided for. Behind Anna's fervent denunciations of harems lay an unasked question about her own life: how free had *she* been?

One of her most ambitious stories tells how a beautiful young woman, born in India, avoids involuntary concubinage in Bangkok. In the happy ending, the heroine weds a Siamese "duke," who willingly gives up status and privilege in order to live with her. Their small home far from the capital is said to be "a lovely little cottage, where the ex-duke, his mother, and his

---

1. Anna's answer suggests that she arrived with a preconceived idea of Siamese sadism. In fact, though Mongkut was responsible for a lethal flogging in 1856, his reign saw few executions and proved remarkably mild.

sweet wife" reside amicably together, and where "the grand old trees are dressed in tender green, and the bright sun touches with its golden-yellow light every nook and corner of the lovely scene around." We are asked to believe that the former aristocrat and his mother find the trees, sunshine, and sweet wife a satisfactory compensation for the privileged life they have relinquished. In this over-the-top idyll of domestic bliss, we see the obverse of Anna's great horror of the harem.

Many others attacked polygamy but rarely with her solemnity and vehemence. Mary Mattoon, the Presbyterian missionary wife who had taught in the Inner Palace in the early 1850s, was more temperate in her judgments. Mrs. Eastlake, photographer Thomson, and consular surgeon Campbell were also more restrained, as was Bishop Pallegoix. Townsend Harris was disgusted with Siamese sexual practices, but even he was milder than Anna. For most visitors, the customs of the country were so unlike anything in the West that, inevitably, judgment was softened. No one matched her ferocity.

At times her horror became so extreme and visionary that it attained a kind of rapture, as when she drew the contrast between Bangkok's lower classes and palace concubines: "The children of the poor—naked, rude, neglected though they be—are rich in the freedom of the fair blue sky, rich in the freedom of the limpid ocean of air above and around them. But within the close and gloomy lanes of this city within a city, through which many lovely women are wont to come and go, many little feet to patter, and many baby citizens to be borne in the arms of their dodging slaves, there is but cloud and chill, and famishing and stinting, and beating of wings against golden bars." This is powerfully said and seriously unreal. It is doubtful that many Siamese women of the time would have chosen a life of poverty outside the palace over an aristocratic life within and even more unlikely that the poor (who had masters they were compelled to serve in specified ways) would have considered "the freedom of the fair blue sky" a fair compensation for the hardness of their lives.

Paying no attention to Mongkut's decree granting most palace women the right to a formal release, Anna's books describe them as confined for life against their will: "How I have pitied those ill-fated sisters of mine, imprisoned without a crime! If they could but have rejoiced once more in the freedom of the fields and woods, what new births of gladness might have been theirs,—they who with a gasp of despair and moral death first entered these royal dungeons, never again to come forth alive! And yet I have known more than one among them who accepted her fate with a repose of manner and a sweetness of smile that told how dead must be the heart under that still exterior." As was often the case with Anna's reports on Siamese harem life, this eloquent passage was more sermon than report. In fact, it was a jeremiad, one that not only reflected strong prior commitments but discounted what the writer had seen for herself: the concubines' "repose of manner." Her best friend in the harem, Chaochom Maandaa Son Klin, recalled being glad to enter the Inner Palace; there had been no "gasp of despair." Although she became disillusioned and would have preferred living outside, she would never have exchanged her refined and protected life for "the freedom of the fields and woods"—that is, for rice paddies and tropical forests.

Anna's hatred of the harem was inspired in part by the militant evangelicalism that sees itself as the source of republican liberty. This fighting spirit was something she shared with her late Anglo-Irish husband, who had extolled the Puritans responsible for beheading Charles I as "the Holiest & best men of the time." Anna's own testimony was that she "had never looked upon the sickening hideousness of slavery till I encountered its features here; nor, above all, had I comprehended the perfection of the life, light, blessedness and beauty, the all-sufficing fulness of the love of God as it is in Jesus, until I felt the contrast here,—pain, deformity, darkness, death, and eternal emptiness."

This fierce statement made such an impression on Margaret Landon that, instead of paraphrasing it (her usual procedure in *Anna and the King of Siam*), she reproduced it entire and verbatim. To do so, she claimed that it formed part of a letter to Francis Cobb, the American friend in Singapore. When Landon was advised to cut the passage for the British edition, perhaps because of the cloying religious language, she refused on the grounds that it captured Anna's essential point of view. In this, she was probably right.

What Landon missed were the hidden wrinkles in Anna's hatred of polygamy. In her early teens, she had been expected to follow custom and marry an older man, as her sister had done. Her refusal had been the formative choice that opened a path closed to other Eurasian girls. However, marrying for love had also resulted in a terribly insecure wifehood and a lifelong defensiveness about that. Now, working in Mongkut's harem, she found herself in a securely enclosed domain where *all* the wives had been given as teenage brides to *one* older man. It was a grotesque version of what she had rejected, and she was overcome with disgust and a sense of entrapment.

Unlike the first palace teachers, who had husbands and ongoing domestic lives, Anna brought to her work in the harem an intense nostalgia for what she and Thomas had at the Aviary, their refuge on Bombay's Malabar Point. After his death the troubles that ensued upon those brief months receded. No longer a clerk or hotelkeeper, he became the gallant officer whose untimely death delivered her to a life of anxious labor. The cottage of her fictional Indian heroine, bathed in golden light, was the idealization of everything she had lost.

Ironically, her widowed isolation was made all the keener by the closeness of the women of the Inner Palace. Members of an ancient and complex institution, they shared a world she wasn't part of: a language she studied without mastering; a vast accumulation of jokes, pastimes, festivals, and seasonal rituals; a palette of tastes and smells infinitely richer than a beef, mutton, and potato cuisine afforded; clothing that was better adjusted to a tropical climate than Britain's colonial wardrobe; and a dense social web of duties, pleasures, and graduated aspirations. Aware of her secret Asian identity, Anna defended herself against this overwhelming female world by drawing on her Western superiority: the pity she could feel for "sisters" in subjection.

Unlike them, she had no native land. There was no home to which she could dream of returning. There was only the free and powerful West— the future market for the fictions that would emerge from her solitude, deracination, and problematic identity.

A CHARNEL HOUSE OF QUICK CORRUPTION

When Mongkut sent Dan Beach Bradley the statistics on his harem, he wanted to put to rest the scandalized idea Westerners had of his sexual profligacy. As it turned out, he was wasting his time. That was the very idea Anna would seize and exploit.

The king's daily schedule—his prescribed activity for each hour of the day and night—formed an item in most Western books about Siam. The one book that struck an insinuating note at nine o'clock in the evening was

The English Governess. At that hour, Anna wrote, he retired "to his private apartments, whence issued immediately peculiar domestic bulletins, in which were named the women whose presence he particularly desired, in addition to those whose turn it was to 'wait' that night." The wink-wink quotation marks were dropped when the passage was revised for a youth magazine.

The next day, when it was time for the king's midmorning nap, he was tended "by a fresh detail of women,—those who had waited the night before being dismissed, not to be recalled for a month, or at least a fortnight, save as a peculiar mark of preference or favor to some one who had had the good fortune to please or amuse him."

Anna was not alone in believing that Mongkut's fickle choice shifted from one female to another. In fact, as shown by the birth records of his eighty-two offspring, he had stable, long-term preferences. Thiang gave birth to ten children, Piam (the supposedly clever wife) to six, and three other concubines had five children each. One could argue that, all things considered, Mongkut was not an inconstant husband.

In another titillating passage, Anna claimed that he pursued a vigorous worldwide search for fresh playthings: "Beside many choice Chinese and Indian girls, purchased annually for the royal harem by agents stationed at Peking, Foo-chou, and different points in Bengal, enormous sums were offered, year after year, through 'solicitors' at Bangkok and Singapore, for an English woman of beauty and good parentage to crown the sensational collection; but when I took my leave of Bangkok in 1868, the coveted specimen had not yet appeared in the market." The date of Anna's departure was 1867, and the rest of the passage is equally fictitious. Mongkut's letters to two of his agents, David Olyphant King in Shanghai and William Adamson in Hong Kong, are extant, and, needless to say, they never mention choice Chinese girls.[2] Nor does the subject arise in his extensive correspondence with other foreigners. There is not a shred of evidence for the massive, expensive, ongoing enterprise Anna described. Her only source, if any, would have been gossip. Townsend Harris was not the only Westerner who liked

2. Adamson broke his residence in Singapore to spend a year or two in Hong Kong. King came from a wealthy mercantile family of Salem, Massachusetts. Thanks to the fact that the Kings had a summer place in Newport, Rhode Island, Mongkut's letters to his agent in Shanghai now rest in the vaults of the Newport Historical Society.

to whisper that the king was "much given to women." As for her motive in telling the tale, her word "sensational"—added between serial and book publication—is all the hint one needs.

During her last full year in Bangkok, a Singapore newspaper insinuated that the king tried to procure a certain princess for his harem. Hoping, it seems, that Anna would speak up for him and squash the imputation, he sent her a "very private post script" with an agitated denial: "There is no least intention occurred to me even once or in my dream indeed! I think if I do so, I will die soon perhaps!" His trust was misplaced: Anna not only published the postscript but presented it as a case of nasty royal hypocrisy.

Her most flamboyant and arresting accusation was that Mongkut's harem was a refuge for vicious cross-dressing sexual deviants.

> Within these walls lurked lately fugitives of every class, profligates from all quarters of the city, to whom discovery was death; but here their "sanctuary" was impenetrable. Here were women disguised as men, and men in the attire of women, hiding vice of every vileness and crime of every enormity,—at once the most disgusting, the most appalling, and the most unnatural that the heart of man has conceived. It was death in life, a charnel-house of quick corruption; a place of gloom and solitude indeed, wherefrom happiness, hope, courage, liberty, truth, were forever excluded, and only mother's love was left.

A footnote explains that all this sexual corruption had been cleaned up by Mongkut's "successor (and my pupil), the present king."

What does one make of this? To begin with, the accusation of transvestism seems odd when speaking of a culture in which men's and women's ordinary attire was so similar that Western visitors had trouble telling the sexes apart. More important, the Siamese and Lao have traditionally found cultural roles for gays and various cross-gender preferences. The mid-twentieth-century aristocrat Seni Pramoj (brother of Kukrit) thought of the royal harem police of his early childhood as women who had renounced the rules of female decorum: "Heavy and coarse in appearance," they "swore vilely on all occasions." As a small boy he hated "to be taken past their quarters because they smelled dreadfully."

Still, it simply can't be true that fugitives "of every class" were made welcome in the harem. This was a highly guarded precinct from which men were excluded, no matter what their attire. Not one of the doctors, mission-aries, missionary wives, or others who were granted access to the Inner Palace ever so much as hinted that it was a sanctuary for sexual "profligates from all quarters of the city." Instead, the thing that struck virtually all visitors was that the king's youngest children wore no clothing other than hats and gold jewelry. That Mongkut would have exposed these cherished and privileged innocents to an urban underclass, pedophiles included, is inconceivable.

Was Anna's "sanctuary" passage intended to further denigrate the king, adding to hideous Bangkok's black, black record? Probably, but as Peter Jack-son suggests, there is another interpretation: the passage may be an inflamed reaction to the same-sex theatrical performances of the time. Anna's "men in the attire of women," he writes, "do not seem to have been male cross-dressers but rather actors performing in one of the all-male troupes in which, as in Elizabethan England, men played both male and female roles on the stage. What Leonowens saw as the 'unnatural,' 'vile' 'vice' of trans-vestism was in fact a misperception of what Siamese of the time regarded as normative gender performances by . . . male actors." The male troupes that used to perform the classical Thai repertory are no more, but the comic ensembles that remain popular in some rural areas, if only on DVDs, often feature one or two slender and elegant "lady boys."

One of the very rare nineteenth-century accounts of a Siamese man's imitation of a graceful woman dates from 1863, when Orfeur Cavenagh, governor of Singapore, paid a state visit to a nearby rajah. The entertain-ment put on by the host included a number by three Siamese men. The governor's memoirs have a brief, nonjudgmental description: "There were three dancers, two dressed as men, and one, of very effeminate appearance, as a woman; the last, after dancing for some time, bent back her head until it touched the mat on the floor, from which she picked up with her mouth one or two dollars, evidently intended to be the reward of the feat of remov-ing them." Cavenagh was much impressed by her/his elaborate and expen-sive costume.

The next year, when missionary Sarah Bradley got a visit from her old Oberlin College roommate, Anna escorted the traveler along with Sarah and her husband to a performance of a traditional play in the Grand Palace. Since Anna wrote nothing about the outing, all we know is what we find in

Dan Bradley's journal. The idea, it seems, was to "show Miss [Mary Atkins] the heathenism of Siam and she there had such views of it as quite horrified her and made her feel that it is almost a hopeless work to preach the gospel to such a people—Mrs Leonowens gave Miss A an introduction to His Majesty the king who had the generalship of all parts of the performance being on his feet nearly all the time moving about from place to place guiding and directing by word of mouth and by the pointing of his cane."

It is quite wonderful to learn from this entry that Mongkut acted as choreographer and prompter, and it is utterly frustrating to be told so little about the performance that we can't even guess what horrified Mary Atkins (who happened to be the teacher at Mills College in California who was chiefly responsible for the school's early growth). What was ordinary for the Siamese was so shocking for the trailblazing Americans, not to mention the trailblazing Anglo-Indian, that it didn't get put down on paper for posterity.

13

A Teacher Strained
at Every Point

IN SINGAPORE ANNA HAD BARELY been able to maintain herself, and before that, in her ten itinerant years as a wife, her husband's expert office skills had failed to bring in a secure and comfortable income. It was only by going to work in an institution she saw as oppressive and degrading that she found the key to independence and success.

A promising early sign was the flow of courteous letters from her royal employer. They showed that he saw her as a person of stature and was willing to make the effort to communicate in English. Even after she caught on to Thai, it was the king and not the teacher who jumped the linguistic divide. He was pleased to have her services and determined to ensure her continued satisfaction. At the start of her second year, Louis summed up the royal attitude by writing his sister in London, "They all love us well."

The schoolroom provided by the king was inside the walled and guarded precinct that was home for his wives and children and hundreds of relatives and dependents. This was the Inner Palace, the southern half of which was a warren of workshops, markets, and kitchens staffed by women, many of whom, like Anna, returned to their outside homes at night. Her own place of work would have been in the more aristocratic northern half, probably not too far from the buildings that visitors today know as the Grand Palace.

The English Governess makes the schoolroom out to be quite imposing, with an inlaid marble floor, gilded pillars, and vaulted roof. Built for a use other than teaching, it is variously referred to in Anna's writings as a "wat" and a "pavilion." If "wat" was right, the building would have been a consecrated temple. If it was a pavilion, which seems more likely, it would have been a roofed, open-air structure of a kind the Thais call a *saalaa*. According to her, its name was Watt Khoon Choom Manda Thai, which she translated as "Temple of the Mothers of the Free" (the word *thai* also means "free"). As for the three middle words, *khoon* was and is the polite term of address that is now rendered as *khun*, and *chom maandaa* was the title for minor concubines who had given birth (*chaochom maandaa* was reserved for the more prestigious mothers). There seems to be no written record of the building. If Anna's name for it was not made up, one surmises that it had served the lesser concubines in some way before being assigned to her. During her tenure the main piece of furniture was the large table at which her pupils did their lessons.

All the evidence suggests that she was an effective teacher: authoritative, enthusiastic, affectionate, and remembered by pupils with real warmth. For Anna, guiding the young was not just a livelihood or path to fortune, it was an identity. All the same, she was careful to present herself in her first book as a lady and not as someone defined by the daily grind. As a few reviewers noted, one of the oddities of *The English Governess* is that it has very little to say about her classroom work, the title notwithstanding.

It was only in her second book, *The Romance of the Harem*, in a chapter wittily titled "Stray Leaves from the Royal School-Room Table," that she printed a few good stories about her work: how a brightly colored snake dropped onto the table and slithered auspiciously toward Prince Chulalong-korn, the future king; how disappointed her pupils were when she revealed that the moon was uninhabited; and how they refused to believe there could be such a thing as snow.

While it makes sense that Siamese children would have had their doubts about snow, many of Anna's schoolroom stories are not credible. In one of them, told partly to show how ignorant her "simple pupils" were, she gave a detailed description of "the only map—and a very ancient one it was—which they had ever seen." This "map" consisted of two rectangles. The larger, stand-ing for Siam, was filled with the ample silver figure of a king. The smal-ler, standing for Burma and placed to the north (i.e., on top), held a black, impish, weak-looking creature. According to Anna, this highly schematic

SIAMESE MAP.

Fred Arthur Neale's "Native Map of Siam." From *Narrative of a Residence at the Capital of the Kingdom of Siam* (1852), 55.

design was understood by the court of Siam to be a representation of the physical world.

In fact, the only place she had seen this symbolic depiction of Siam's superior power relative to Burma was in Fred Arthur Neale's *Narrative of a Residence at the Capital of the Kingdom of Siam*, from which she took her description almost word for word.[1] Neale had been shown the "map" during an audience with Mongkut's predecessor (who "indulged in a confidential chuckle" afterward). Anna's silent theft illustrates what may be her worst practice as a travel writer: claiming an I-was-there authority for stories gathered from others. Often, as with her map fraud, she took a questionable report from the reign of Rama III and pinned it to his very different, reform-minded successor.

What she and Neale both failed to realize was that the image was a cartoon, comic in intent and based on standard iconology. The court knew what maps were. Not only had Western examples been brought to Ayutthaya in the seventeenth century, but several finely detailed early nineteenth-century maps produced in Bangkok have recently come to light in the Grand Palace. Products of the first three reigns, they exemplify a Siamese tradition of pictorial geography that did not equate north with up. Rama III's jeu d'esprit would not have been seen as cartographic in *any* Chakri reign, least of all Mongkut's.

About her textbooks Anna had little to say. The only ones named in *The English Governess* were "Webster's far-famed spelling-books." That she also assigned a child's history of England is evident from a letter by an older, advanced student. And thanks to a book order relayed to the Presbyterians' head office by a missionary, we know she wanted twenty-four copies of McGuffey's *First Reader* and twelve of Peter Parley's *Universal History*, two American standards. The same order included thirty-six copies of Richard G. Parker's *Juvenile Philosophy*, a clever introduction to scientific thinking. The titles may have been suggested by Mary Mattoon, the Presbyterian friend who had taught in the States. Since Anna's textbooks were designed for American or English children, her pupils must have been baffled by

1. For parallel passages, see appendix 3, "Anna as Plagiarist." That Neale's image adheres to the Western practice of putting north at the top is one of many reasons for doubting the accuracy of his illustrator, who would not have seen the original. Thongchai Winichakul discusses the image in *Siam Mapped* (34–35).

the weird and alien assumptions—the references to four seasons, for example, and the practices associated with them. In the Thai climate and culture there are three seasons, hot, wet, and cool.

Of all her texts, the most unusual was *Juvenile Philosophy*. Intended to promote careful attention to the phenomena of daily life, the book consists of a series of Socratic mother-daughter conversations. Look in my eyes, Mother says, and tell me what you see. The child sees a large white part, a smaller blue circular part, and in the center "a little round place, which looks very black." Taking the girl to a dark corner, Mother asks if the black place looks any different. "It looks a little larger." There are more questions and answers, followed by the aha moments. The iris has a color because it reflects light. The center is black because it *doesn't* reflect light! Light bouncing off objects and entering the eye: that's *seeing*! Other chapters consider color and light, evaporation and condensation, fire, heat, and wind. The book was a physics text without the math, prodding children to think in an abstract way about the physical processes they take for granted. Given the king's scientific curiosity and the tradition of science teaching going back to Bishop Pallegoix and Jesse Caswell, *Juvenile Philosophy* was an excellent choice for Anna's pupils. Regrettably, it isn't known what use she made of her thirty-six copies.

But her most important subject by far was English. Today the standard method for teaching foreign languages is oral drill, with repetition and variation. In Anna's time the preference was for reading, writing, and translating, often from the Bible. That this was her approach is evident from a passing reference to "our simple exercises of translating English into Siamese and Siamese into English."

In her third year she had her two oldest and most expert girls write polite notes to nine-year-old Avis in London. Princess Ying Yualacks wished that she could "see all the beautiful places I read of in My History of England." Princess Somawati said that before she was allowed to begin composing, "your Mamma our kind Governess wished me to improve in my hand writing." Produced under close supervision, the two letters (still extant) must have gone through draft after draft. Handwriting, spelling, grammar, and general layout are all copybook perfect, quite unlike the king's sloping lines and clumsy scrawl and imperfect command of grammar and idiom. Clearly, Anna gave more stress to correctness than to facility or self-expression. This was the teacher who would one day boast that *her* mother made her copy a letter thirteen times to get it right.

How much of a taskmaster was she? Decades later she was so bent on making prodigies of her six Canadian grandchildren that she insisted on drilling them in Sanskrit. When eight-year-old Max failed the high-school entrance examination he was forced to take much too early, the "frightened little culprit was severely chastised and condemned to study eight hours each day during the long summer holidays," as a pitying older sister never forgot. That sort of discipline was out of the question in Bangkok, where classroom routine was interrupted by Anna's illnesses and the frequent excursions, ceremonies, and festivals her pupils were required to observe or join. Of these, the Songkhran festival in April was the most exciting, with everyone getting drenched from the flinging of water. When water-tossing monks came near the schoolroom, the children made "a frantic rush, often in the midst of their recitations, to prostrate themselves on the pavement within reach of these purifying showers." For Anna, the festival was a "great annoyance."

After she left Siam, Bradley wrote that, because of "the almost daily breaks which the regal customs . . . occasioned in every plan and system of teaching she adopted, it was impossible for her to make really good scholars of any of her pupils." This statement gives us the teacher's first depressed postmortem on what she had achieved. A year later, however, an English-man happened to hear "a considerable number . . . of the Princesses speaking English." After encouraging rumors of the young king's reforms reached Anna herself, she settled on what would be her permanent summing-up: by forming the crown prince's mind and character, she had been a profound force for good in Siam.

The truth lies between her two opposed and extreme assessments. In March 1865 Mongkut had advised her that Chulalongkorn had "much desire to going on with English. On him is my greatest affection, I hope you will do your uttermost for him." The prince's private lessons seem to have begun soon after his tonsure ceremony (which marked his departure from the harem). The tutoring ceased in July 1866 when he began his Buddhist novitiate, but it resumed after he moved into his own residence in the palace complex.

As Mongkut hoped, his son did profit from Anna's special attentions. The letter he sent her in 1869, one year into his reign, shows a decent if labored command of English. But it was most likely a later tutor, Francis George Patterson (whose father ran a school on Jersey), who gave Chulalongkorn his mastery of the language. And of course the young man had Siamese teachers for Pali and other subjects. It can't be said that Anna formed the future king. Still, historian David K. Wyatt is undoubtedly correct in his wry conjecture that daily "contact with another culture in the person of a stubborn and opinionated, Western, Christian woman" left a deep and indelible mark.

A MOTHER-TEACHER WITH POWERS AND ENERGIES

Secular readers may not realize how compromising it was for an evangelical like Anna to promise not to Christianize her pupils. "The King's agreement with the English lady[2] speaks well for the faithfulness of the [three] Missionary ladies, in the past," wrote a scandalized American missionary agent, "but what a responsibility does a woman assume who covenants to be silent . . . oh it is fearful."

Criticism of this kind touched a nerve and had to be countered. Anna did so in three ways: by presenting herself as a woman of high, unbending, absolute principle; by claiming to have saved a nation from the curse of slavery; and by engaging in a degree of proselytizing on the sly. When the king objected to the religious indoctrination, she maintained (in Bradley's words) that "it was as impossible for her to give his children lessons from English books utterly stripped of all reference to the Christian's God and Redeemer, as it would be for him to teach them from Siamese books without the least reference to Buddh. . . . The king, it was said, saw the force of the defense and yielded to it." Once again, it seems, Mongkut had to back down before the determined woman. And yet she *was* instilling Christian ideas: that 1869 letter of Chulalongkorn's, written two years after her teaching ceased, piously invokes "divine Providence" not once but twice. Anna published a facsimile of the handwritten document in *The English Governess*.

2. For Americans, Anna was "English" on several accounts, such as her speech, manners, and (supposed) parentage. But the basic reason was that, like other colonials, she was an English subject. In this respect she resembled Samuel Jones Smith, who, while clearly Eurasian, was invariably classed as English by Bangkok's Americans. By contrast, in Britain, with its history of excluding mixed-race Anglo-Indians from certain privileges, Englishness was apt to be more slippery and contested. There, you could be English in one way (a subject of the queen) but not in another (having pigmented skin). This problem was one that Anna would not have to worry about in the States.

To begin with, the Bangkok job had not been a noble mission but an extreme expedient for earning a living. There is a hint of this point of view in Anna's second book, where she remembers having felt "a kind of despair" as she waited for her pupils in the empty schoolroom. The place was a "delicious retreat," but it gave her a sensation she "could never analyze . . . as if I were removed to some awful distance from the world I had known, and . . . excluded from any participation in its real life."

The passage shows how well Anna wrote when she allowed herself to expose her malaise. The feelings that surfaced in the empty school were disturbing, persistent, and fundamental. A moment of peace, a calm and quiet interval, and there would be a familiar undertow of melancholy alienation. She missed the world she "had known," but where *was* that world? It couldn't be Bombay or Disa or Pune or Perth or Lynton, none of which she would ever truly acknowledge. Was it Penang? Singapore? Could it be England, still unseen? One of the things that makes Anna so intriguing is that, by inventing an alternate history, she turned herself into the ultimate exile: cut off at the roots from what she was.

One way to resolve this trouble was to be the complete schoolmistress, with a high manner and a polished skill in holding others' attention. Anna had views on correct enunciation, the use of the voice, and the impression a teacher should strive to make, and all of this merged with her sense of being a loving nurturer. As we have seen, she felt that "the strong instinct of the mother out-weighs and over-rules every other sentiment of my life." Just as Harriet Beecher Stowe believed that *Uncle Tom's Cabin* was inspired by her maternal grief,[3] Anna considered herself a true mother-teacher, one who rose above personal tragedy, was faithful to her calling, and redeemed Siam. Casting herself in this role did more than confer a rewarding public identity, it settled a private torment.

But the role was extremely demanding. Years later, while living in Halifax, Nova Scotia, Anna gave a lecture on education that set forth her ideal of the dedicated teacher. The language here is extraordinarily revealing:

3. On 2 November 1855, when Anna was living in Western Australia, the *Perth Gazette* quoted Stowe's already famous statement, "It was at [my son's] dying bed, and at his grave, that I learnt what a poor slave-mother may feel when her child is torn from her."

The child is a bundle of potentialities, plastic as clay in the potter's hand, ready to be moulded into whatever shape or form the parent, the teacher, the school and its environment may determine. . . . From the moment a boy or girl begins to attend School the powers, energies, and influence of the teacher will be strained at every point in order first to win the respect and confidence of the child and then to develop it in the right direction. . . . Every act every movement of the teacher is an object-lesson, the voice the manner, the pronounciation [*sic*] the accent the smile the nod of the head the wave of the hand all these are distinct object lessons which stamp themselves indelibly on the mental perceptions of the child.

The two chief elements here are the amorphousness of the child, who is mere clay, and the totality of the effort made by the teacher, who is "strained at every point." Just as a properly educated child is wholly the product of nurture, the successful teacher is an utterly self-conscious performer, with every tone and gesture minutely calculated. It is not the child who brings "powers" and "energies" into the classroom. It is the omnipotent and alarmingly unnatural teacher.

Keeping that in mind, if one rereads the passage, it suddenly turns inside out and becomes a strange, sad confession. *Now* it explains how little Anna Harriet Edwards had been reconstructed by her schoolmistress at the Bombay Education Society's Byculla School and placed before the world as a noble product of English training. And yes, the lecturer had it right: that refashioning *had* made it possible for her to go to the court of Siam and be the influential English Governess.

But how does a lone woman in a remote non-Western land fulfill these exhausting maternal and pedagogical requirements while strained at every point?

Let Us Pause When We Speak of a Weaker Sex

About the strain there is no doubt whatever. Anna was making a heroic effort to earn her livelihood in a place that had no independent Western women. Every working day she had to cross one of the world's major rivers with her son (and once she fell in and nearly drowned, or so she said). Severed from her family and Anglo-Indian past, she was forging (in both senses) a new identity. There were strange customs, a hard language to learn, and a far-away daughter to worry about: seven-year-old Avis, bound for England in an old sailing vessel beating its way around the southern cape of Africa. More than five months passed before the *Ranée* finally reached London on 3 October 1862, and then it took another month or two for Anna to hear of her daughter's safe arrival. By then, she had spent the better part of a year in a state of intense effort and anxiety.[4]

Near the end of that first year, the inevitable happened: a traveler who had known her in Bombay spotted her by the river as she and Louis made their way to the palace. He drafted a report of the encounter and gave it to a Singapore newspaper, which published it. As will be seen, the facts about Anna's origins in Bombay are garbled or deliberately altered, perhaps to shield her privacy. No matter: this hitherto unknown sketch puts her physical and psychic exhaustion before us as nothing else.

AN INCIDENT AT SIAM

The Kingdom of the White Elephant
To the Editor of the Daily Times

Dear Sir,—As my friend and I were on the return after a fatiguing morning's ramble round and about the town of Bangkok, we spied a pretty boat rowed by four oars, the men standing to their work, coming towards our direction; curiosity arrested our steps as we watched the Gondola approach the very spot where we had stationed ourselves, the rowers attached the boat to the landing and knelt down,—while out of it came a sturdy English boy and a Lady whom the boy handed out with an air of protection very unusual in one so young. To my intense surprise, in the Lady, faded and care-worn, I recognized one whom I had met years ago in the most brilliant circles in Bombay—and I fancied by the manner in which she clutched the boy and hurried out of our sight that she recognized me as well. My friend being an adept in

4. The *Ranée* cleared Singapore on 15 April 1862, a month after Anna left for Siam. Reaching the Strait of Sunda on 13 May, the ship sailed west across the Indian Ocean. Except for a vessel that spoke with her on 10 June, nothing was reported of her until she docked in Gravesend. How Avis looked back on this tremendous childhood transit isn't known.

Siamese, we discovered from the boat men that she came there every day. My interest was fully awakened—while I doubted if this woman so pale and faded was the same lovely girl that drew so many around her; nor could I understand by what fate she was here in this dangerous place,—the niece of one of our gallant Major Generals of India by the mother's side, and connected with England's aristocracy by the Father's.

I determined to renew our acquaintance if possible, and gratify my curiosity, and I betook myself alone the next morning to the same spot, but had to wait a longer time than I had expected—at length, the boat came in sight; the boy was paddling out of one of the windows with a long oar. He handed the lady out in the same manner, they passed, the Lady looking at me as if I was only one of the posts that supported the jetty or landing, with a dignity in her step, and courage in her eye—that completely baffled all attempt at recognition and filled me with respect and admiration for one thus leading a life of labour and such labour—as it must be trying to one of affluence and ease in the home of her gallant old uncle. Let us pause when we speak of a weaker sex.

From Yours truly

A PASSER BY.

Bangkok, 10th March, 1863.

It *has* to be Anna, the only unmarried self-supporting "English Lady" known to be living in Bangkok in the 1860s. That there was some other respectable woman working there—from Bombay—with a son—crossing the river every day—her name nowhere appearing in print—just isn't supposable. This is *Anna* with six-year-old Louis, seen at the palace landing after being rowed across the Chao Phya River by the king's boatmen.

But a correction is in order. It isn't the likable twentieth-century hoop-skirted icon we see here but the real Mrs. Leonowens: extremely dignified, hard to approach, hard at work, and tougher than we dreamed. This is exactly how she would treat a sympathetic face from her past, cutting the man dead. That she looked "faded and care-worn," under enormous pressure yet stiffly holding up, seems absolutely right. We will never get a clearer view of the formidable woman pursuing her daily routine in Bangkok.

Still, the unlikely verbal snapshot leaves us eager for more, especially regarding motives. Why did "Passer By" choose to publish his quasi exposé? Why did Anna refuse to acknowledge a face from her Bombay past?

The answers lie somewhere in the letter written a third of a century later by John Thomas Pratt. This appeal (we looked at it in chapter 5) was sent to Avis in 1899 in an effort to mend relations. In it Pratt wrote that he had asked his mother about her famous aunt and been told something surprising: that his mother's mother (Anna's sister Eliza) had once "met a certain Captain Baldwin who had met [Anna] in Siam." Pratt had the impression that these successive meetings occurred a decade after she and Thomas had left India. November 1852 being the date they set off for Australia, a decade would just about bring us to March 1863, the month "Passer By" visited Bangkok.

According to Pratt, after his mother talked to the captain in Bombay, she wrote Anna and presently "received a very strange reply evidently written under the influence of strong emotion and showing what great sufferings Mrs. Leonowens had endured. She said that in consequence of these sufferings she had determined to cut off all communication with her relations with whom her sad past was bound up, that it was enough for them to know that she and her children were well, happy and rich, that she would answer no further communications from her relations and she even went so far as to say that if anyone came to Siam to find her she would commit suicide."

Were "Passer By" and Captain Baldwin one and the same? Not only would Singapore be the first port of call for a vessel leaving the mouth of the Chao Phya River for Bombay, but, according to Pratt's mother, Eliza died "soon after" she received Anna's letter permanently severing relations. More exactly, the date of death was 13 June 1864, fifteen months after "Passer By" saw Anna: time enough for all the events to unfold in sequence.

So it appears that a ship captain or captain in the army caught sight of Anna in Bangkok and was rebuffed. He wrote the encounter up and gave it to a Singapore paper on his way to India, and when he reached Bombay, where Eliza resided, he told her about his strange experience at the palace landing, no doubt mentioning the "care-worn" look. Concerned, Eliza wrote Anna and was in turn rebuffed in language that was never forgotten, as this was the sisters' last exchange of letters.

Pratt's mother was Eliza's firstborn daughter, Eliza Sarah. In 1863 she was still single, in her early teens, and presumably living at home. The informant from whom Pratt got the story, in other words, was a plausible and well-positioned witness, not only old enough to understand and be confided in but present at the scene of action.

No record of Captain Baldwin has been found, but except for this name, possibly misremembered, the reported suicide threat is credible and should be taken seriously.[5] It exposes the wound that Anna had to mask in *The English Governess*: her extreme strain, unease, and alienation. The most she could say in print was that "no friend of mine knew at that time how hard it was for me to bear up, in the utter loneliness and forlornness of my life, under the load of cares and provocations and fears that gradually accumulated upon me." She could write about the pressure of work, the illnesses, accidents, threats, and hostile attacks (often exaggerated), but her true "forlornness" could not be revealed.

Thanks to an unsigned sketch in a Singapore newspaper and a letter written a third of a century later by a great-nephew Anna never knew, we can sense her raw emotional state after teaching for a year in Bangkok, where she felt so hard-pressed and anxious that suicide seemed like an option if someone from India "came to Siam to find her."

The fear was not simply that her cover would be blown. It was that the massive Anglo-Indian social order from which she had escaped at great personal cost was lying in wait and eager to snatch her back. There was only one way to treat that face at the landing. Show nothing, don't stop, keep moving.

5. Stephen Jacobs, the biographer of Boris Karloff, has unearthed evidence that his mother, Eliza Sara/Sarah Pratt (see photo on page 181), who suffered years of spousal abuse, became so suicidal that, as a servant reported, "razors were never left about the house."

14

The Death of Fa Ying

AT THE TIME ANNA'S "CARE-WORN" FACE was exposed in a thinly
disguised newspaper sketch, she was so exhausted that she was on the verge
of breaking down; as she put it, "my health began to fail." Given a month's
sick leave, she and Louis boarded the *Chow Phya* on 30 March 1863 and
departed for Singapore. This was the voyage on which she told a British
travel writer her indignant story of the squalid house initially assigned to
her in Bangkok.

In Singapore she put up at the Hotel d'Europe at 10 Beach Road, the
same street she had previously lived on. Beach Road being Francis Davis
Cobb's address as well, we can assume he saw his hardworking friend and
got an earful about Siam. Did friendship deepen to the point that she had
to think about appearances? Possibly: her account of the month-long rest
moves it to a later period when Cobb was gone from Singapore.

In this version of events, Mongkut grants the recuperative leave quite
grudgingly, declaring that "if I must be idle for a month, he certainly should
not pay me for the time; and he kept his word. Nevertheless," she at once
added, "he wrote to me most kindly, assuring me that his wives and children were anxious for my return."

Happily, a typed copy of this letter has recently come to light. Showing no trace of ill will, it reveals that concubines Talab and Son Klin were
already recognized as the teacher's particular friends. Even more interesting is the attention the letter gives to money matters. Reminding Anna that
Tan Kim Ching will be her banker in Singapore, the king urges her to get in

touch with him at once to facilitate her business. He cancels an earlier request that she bring back a large number of "guineas or golden coins," with the explanation that a certain Prussian has agreed to supply him with "£300 Sterlings from Calyphania or Austral. land [California or Australia]." However, he still wants her to get some four hundred ten-shilling coins for him. If it seems odd that he would impose such errands on a teacher and detail his fiscal operations to her, one can only recall what Bradley observed in his obituary: that Mongkut could be "frank and ingenuous . . . to a fault."

Signing off, the king reminded Anna where her chief duty lay: "My children and ladies who are your pupils are expecting your return on next opportunity of next Steamer, and required me to transmit to You their respect and sincere regard." All her friends were well, he assured her, even though "cholera and fever are prevailing among our people."

The letter is dated 16 April 1863. Carried on the *Chow Phya*, it reached Singapore a week later. Assuming that Anna followed her employer's wishes, she and Louis would have been on board when the steamer left for Bangkok on the 28th. By early May they were home. Two weeks more and it would be definite: the cholera had prevailed.

Entirely Overcome and Wept like a Child

King Mongkut's queen left four children at her death in 1861. Chulalongkorn was the eldest. The second, her only daughter, born during Sir John Bowring's mission of 1855, was the darling of the court. Following her golden nameplate ceremony her name became Chanthonmonthon, but she continued to be called Chao Fa Ying, the term of address for a princess whose mother and father were both royal.[1] *Chao* means "ruler" or "lord," as in Chao Phya, the name of the river and also the steamer named after it. *Fa* means "sky" and, like English "heaven," has a glowing cloud of meanings. *Ying* is the ordinary word for "girl." Fa Ying, Anna's shortened name for her, might be rendered as Celestial Daughter.

From infancy Fa Ying received special treatment. Well before she was weaned, King Mongkut recalled, "whatever could be done in the way of

1. At a certain point in this ceremony Mongkut performed the same special symbolic act for Fa Ying that he had done for Chulalongkorn: "came out to take the princess's hand in stepping on and off the palanquin." This was a signal of her august standing.

nursing His Majesty has done himself, by feeding her with milk obtained from her nurse, and sometimes with the milk of the cow, goat &c. poured in a teacup from which His Majesty fed her by means of a spoon, so this Royal daughter was as familiar with her father in her infancy as with her nurses." After she grew up a little, he liked to hold her on his lap, take her hand while walking, and have her sit beside him. There is a mildewed daguerreotype or photograph showing him with the girl seated on his lap. She may be about two years old. She looks a little dazed.

By Anna's time, Fa Ying had become a winsome, intelligent, tenderly loved child. One day, as we read in the chapter devoted to her in *The English Governess*, she walked into the schoolroom, settled herself on the teacher's lap, and asked to be taught to draw. She told Anna she liked her better than her Sanskrit teacher, who "bends my hands back when I make mistakes. I don't like Sanskrit, I like English. There are so many pretty pictures in your books."

According to Anna, the king allowed this special child to drop Sanskrit. From that point, whenever Fa Ying's brothers and sisters were at their exacting language drills, she would be with Anna, drawing or watching her teacher draw, but "oftener listening, her large questioning eyes fixed upon my face, as step by step I led her out of the shadow-land of myth into the realm of the truth as it is in Christ Jesus." It is a model Victorian moment, a devoted Christian mother-teacher kneading and molding her precious charge. A decade later, reworking the scene for *Youth's Companion*, Anna had the child "nestling close into my arms" and begging for stories "about your beautiful Jesus!" By then, 1881, the aggressive evangelicalism had pretty much evaporated, so instead of a strident "truth as it is in Christ Jesus," we read of a nonsectarian "realm of purity and truth."

Did such scenes take place? The king's account of Fa Ying's education does not mention drawing or Sanskrit, or, rather, Pali, the closely related language of Buddhist scripture. Instead, he recalled the child's precocity in studying modern languages: "She was well educated in the vernacular Siamese literature which she commenced to study when she was 3 years old, and in last year [1862] she commenced to study in the English School where the schoolmistress, Lady L—— has observed that she was more skillful than the other royal Children, she pronounced & spoke English in articulate & clever manner which pleased the schoolmistress exceedingly." Unlike princes, who memorized Pali chants and prayers during their Buddhist novitiate, princesses studied classic Thai literature. In all likelihood, Fa Ying's Sanskrit/Pali lessons were imaginary.

On 13 May 1863, a week and a half after Anna's return from Singapore, Fa Ying joined other members of the royal family in final preparations for the ritual cremation of an older half brother. The next day, a royal messenger found Dan Beach Bradley and delivered an urgent request from the king: would he come at once to the palace to see the daughter of his late queen consort? The girl had been "seized with the cholera at 10 o'clock" the previous night.

Cholera, as everyone knew, could kill with terrifying rapidity. When the medical missionary reached the audience hall, the king took his hand "with a nervous grip" and led him to a room where some wives and children were sitting on the floor. From there two young sons led him "through a long series of rooms & aisles, & porches and open courts" to a group of attendants and Siamese doctors gathered outside a closed door. After a hurried conference, Bradley entered the sickroom, where the girl "was lying on a mattress on a carpet under a square canopy" (for the mosquito netting). "Her pulse was nearly imperceptible—skin quite cold & breathing labored. She was perfectly conscious wakeful & restless." She had been medicated with chlorodyne, a sedative composed of chloroform, morphine, and other ingredients that was widely used as a treatment for cholera.

Dr. James Campbell arrived. Bangkok's leading physician, he had final authority in prescribing for the patient, to whom he administered more chlorodyne and also chloric ether. Bradley had nothing to do now but remained anyway, "as His Majesty wished to have me present." Forced to attend the cremation ceremony elsewhere, the king sent messengers at frequent intervals; he was desperate for good news. By late afternoon the child was in "a deep sleep." To Bradley's eyes she "looked beautifully." His heart "yearned for her." She was obviously dying. At four or five that afternoon he left. As he walked out of the labyrinthine palace, he saw people "weeping in secret places for her."

Bradley's account of the girl's last illness was written in the same matter-of-fact style as his other journal entries. He mentioned his sorrow but didn't make much of it, assuming, no doubt, that it counted for little when weighed against the grief others felt; he was only the doctor, after all. He made no pious reflections except to regret that the stricken father could not "appreciate the consolations of the gospel."

Anna's narrative of Fa Ying's death is very different. Composed after she left Bangkok, it quotes two documents by the king but doesn't seem to draw on diaries or memoranda of her own. Instead, it is full of dramatic and picturesque touches, it gives lavish attention to her feelings, it foregrounds her Christian faith, it is occasionally at variance with Bradley's sober journal entry, and there are internal inconsistencies.

It begins with a colorful genre picture of the Oriental scene observed by Anna and her son as they sat on their waterside balcony on the morning of 14 May: processions of yellow-robed monks carrying their bowls, "myriads of fan-shaped bells scatter[ing] aeolian melodies on the passing breeze," market boats gilded by the early sunlight.

The spell is broken by a royal boat skimming across the river. "There is cholera in the palace!" the king's slaves cry. "Her Highness, the young Somdetch Chow Fâ-ying, was seized this morning. She sends for you. O, come to her, quickly!" Anna is handed a note that reads, "Our well-beloved daughter, your favorite pupil, is attacked with cholera, and has earnest desire to see you, and is heard much to make frequent repetition of your name. . . . I fear her illness is mortal, as there has been three deaths since morning." Like all of the king's written messages Anna quotes, this one sounds authentic. Among other things, it tells us that the boat found her in the afternoon rather than the gilded morning.

"In a moment" she took a seat. Desperate to reach the palace in time, she "entreated," "flattered," "scolded" the rowers, but their progress was so slow that she grew "fierce with impatience." When at last she reached Fa Ying's chamber—"my Fâ-ying," she would write—she was so out of breath and overcome with emotion that she "stood panting." But she was "too late! even Dr. Campbell . . . had come too late."

There is no mention of Bradley, who had evidently left. Although the attendants were still chanting *P'hra-Arahang* in order to concentrate Fa Ying's mind on the Buddha, Anna could see that there "was no need to prolong that anxious wail," as the child had already "soared into the eternal, tender arms" of Jesus. When the teacher stooped "to imprint a parting kiss on the little face" (an act not in keeping with Siamese custom), the mourners produced "a sudden burst of heart-rending cries."

Just as in her performance of the story of Kisa Gotami in a Chicago opera house, Anna was inserting the ties of affection into Buddhist discipline and detachment. In fact, she was giving North American readers a Southeast Asian version of an iconic Victorian scene—the untimely death of a preternaturally sweet young girl. Her public would not have forgotten the deaths of Little Nell in *The Old Curiosity Shop* and Little Eva in *Uncle Tom's Cabin* and, just two years earlier, in 1868, Beth in *Little Women*.

Unfortunately, a key element in the scene, the tender deathbed parting, had been missing. Repairing this deficiency, Anna added a touching passage to the version of the story she sold *Youth's Companion*: "With breaking heart and eyes overflowing with tears, I crept near to the little dying princess' bed; she opened her eyes, put out her arms. I clasped her close to my breast; she nestled closer, then became very still. When I looked again my darling was dead."

Because of her elevated position and closeness to Fa Ying, Anna was given the unenviable task of breaking the news to the king. But as it turned out, no words were needed. The instant he saw her expression he "covered his face with his hands and wept passionately." The next day, after Anna gave a report of this to Bradley, he noted in his journal that the king "was entirely overcome . . . and wept like a child."

Although nothing would seem more understandable and deserving of respect than this open parental agony, when Anna narrated the scene in *The English Governess*, she described the king's tears as "strange and terrible," welling up as they did "from a heart from which all natural affections had seemed to be expelled, to make room for his own exacting, engrossing conceit of self." This judgment, so harsh and estranging, gives one pause, especially as coming from a parent who had lost her first two children. Virtually all outsiders who observed Mongkut playing with his children were charmed by the frank pleasure he took in them. Anna is the only one who called such scenes "delusive."

Why so suspicious of his paternal feelings? The question seems all the more pressing in light of what she did within a year of Fa Ying's death: she wrote her sister Eliza that things were at an end between them. Is it possible that Anna got matters reversed—that it was she who expelled natural affections? When she excoriated Mongkut for egotism and a lack of family feeling, was she writing about herself without knowing it?

The great paradox is that, while no one had better survival skills or a tougher shell than Mrs. Leonowens, her path in life required her to be the ideal, loving mother-teacher. The contradiction was as absolute as the difference between her fancy account of Fa Ying's death and Dr. Bradley's flat, on-the-spot record.

LIKE THE FLAME OF A CANDLE
LIGHTED IN OPEN AIR

Two days later a lengthy memorial of Fa Ying, written in English, was issued by the king. Printed copies went out to official representatives, including Singapore's Tan Kim Ching, who saw that it was published in the *Straits Times*. This is the document that explains how Mongkut nursed the child with human, cow, and goat milk. Anna would take a copy to North America and quote from it at length in *The English Governess*, including the statement that the "schoolmistress on the loss of this her beloved pupil, was in great sorrow and wept much."

The memorial concludes with somber philosophical reflections on the fragility of life: "But it is known that the nature of human lives is like the flames of candles lighted in open air without any protection above & every side, so it is certain that this path ought to be followed by every one of human beings in a short or long while which cannot be ascertained by prediction, Alas!" Nothing is said about reincarnation, nor are there any consolatory sentiments, last embraces or kisses, or tales about flying up to the arms of a loving deity. Still, like others ravaged by loss, the enlightened monarch could not entirely escape the pull of magical thinking. As reported by the minister who chronicled his reign, he was so shaken that he "wondered if this misfortune had struck because he had failed to have the ashes of the royal ancestors taken out to be honored by celebrations as had formerly been done."

There were no remedies, but there was the balm of open, heartfelt sympathy. The tears Anna shed when Mongkut broke down showed him how much this Western woman cared for his children and how generously she interpreted her remit. Her painfully honest tears made this the moment that solidified her position at court. Suspicion relaxed for the time being, she became a valued confidante, and her influence grew. The king decided to formalize her new status, and it wasn't long before Anna was a member of the minor nobility, with the title *chao khun khruu yai*—most noble high teacher.

15

The Slave Chained
to the Ground

ANNA'S FIRST USE OF HER new status at court was to present a petition on behalf of a slave owned by one of the previous king's concubines. Her intervention succeeded, and when she became a writer and lecturer in the United States her dramatic account of the episode helped make her reputation. In 1872, giving a "Free Lecture for the People" at Cooper Union, she impressed a reporter for the *New York Times* with her "pathetic story of a female slave whose release she procured from the King." That autumn the story was published in the *Atlantic Monthly* under the title "L'Ore, the Slave of a Siamese Queen." A fuller version was incorporated into *The Romance of the Harem.*

The tale of La-aw, the most substantial of Anna's Bangkok stories, goes to the heart of what she was all about.[1] It shows how benevolent and effective she could be, it has a rising tension and a gripping trial scene, it is grounded in the social order, and it deals with a type of criminality that shows up in Siamese records, the sadistic punishment of a runaway slave. There is even a contemporary letter authenticating some key facts. All the same, whole episodes seem to have been invented, the embellishments are stereotyped and sensational, and the orientalizing is so insistent that the human business is badly compromised. Instead of presenting a candid report, Anna treated her role in La-aw's manumission the same way she handled her prior history

---

1. Anna rendered the slave's name as L'ore. Since this gives a false idea of pronunciation, I spell it La-aw. It means "fine," "fair," "beautiful." The accent is on the second syllable.

in India, Australia, and the Straits Settlements: she *fixed* it, laying on the fanciful gloss she believed was required. Discerning what actually happened is a real challenge.

THE BOUND SLAVE'S STORY

As reconstructed by Margaret Landon, the train of events began in early May 1863, immediately after Anna's month-long rest in Singapore. Going to work as usual during the three-day celebration of the birth, enlightenment, and death of Buddha, she found her schoolroom empty and was told she should join her pupils at a ceremony in the Dusit Maha Prasat Throne Hall. Built in the reign of Rama I (and open to tourists at the present day), this was one of the Grand Palace's most spectacular and important ceremonial halls. Anna would have known exactly how to reach it starting from her school. Instead, implausibly, she claimed she got lost walking there.

So, confused by the maze of Inner Palace pathways and buildings, she finds herself in "one of those gloomy walled streets, into which no sunlight ever penetrated, and which are to be found only in Bangkok, the farther end of which seemed lost in mist and darkness." The ground is covered with "pale night-grass," the stone benches are "black with moss and fungi." Ending up in a cul-de-sac of high brick walls, she sees a massive brass door whose shadow falls on the "deserted street, like an immense black pall," and realizes she is quite lost. Seasoned readers, on the other hand, know exactly where she is: the well-known land of Oriental noir, rife with emblems of ancient wrong.

Her tone and setting in place, she opens the door and finds a deserted courtyard. Along the walls are dwarfed trees overgrown with tall grass. The windows are shuttered, and the shutters resemble "those used in prisons." In the center on the bare ground sits a woman nursing a four-year-old boy. Naked above the waist, she stares at the intruder with stony, defiant eyes.

When Anna steps inside to ask for directions (the door swinging shut behind her with an "ominous thud"), she sees that the woman's hair is matted and filthy and that her leg is chained to a stake driven into the ground. Her skin is sunburned. There are broken umbrellas nearby. Suddenly, it is no longer misty and gloomy but blazing hot. Horrified, Anna realizes as never before "the apathy, the deadness, and the barbarous cruelty of the palace life."

After some coaxing, the woman tells her story. Her name is La-aw, she is Muslim, and she was born into servitude, her mistress being Chaochom Maandaa Ung, a former royal concubine. Intelligent and reliable, La-aw served Ung well and eventually became "chief attendant" to her daughter, Princess Butri.

Ung has a more central role in Anna's story than Butri, but, historically, it was the daughter, born in 1828—Rama III's last child—who held an exalted post at court. Butri had been *phuu upakaan*, patron or supporter, of Mongkut's late queen. She had taught young Chulalongkorn his letters and was in other ways a powerful and cultivated figure in the Inner Palace hierarchy. Anyone who was her chief attendant, whether slave or free, would have been in a high and honored position.

One day La-aw was given a small bag of money and sent outside the harem "to purchase some Bombay silk of the Naikodah Ibrahim." The merchant, too, was Muslim, and when their eyes met something flashed between them. Dazzled, she drew her "scarf more tightly around [her] chest, and sat down silent and wondering."

As more errands followed, the attraction grew. One day a female slave owned by the *naikodah* whispered to La-aw that he would like to give her enough money to buy her freedom. Soon after, making good on this hint, he said to her in private that "thou hast awakened all my love and pity" and handed her twice the sum needed, asking only that she "forget not thy deliverer."

The archaic language was meant to correspond to the refined and often florid diction that was mandatory at court and differed from ordinary Thai speech. Anna, too, was fond of gorgeous rhetoric, complaining on one occasion of the "difficulty of finding a fit clothing for the fervid Eastern imagery in our colder and more precise English." By making the court slave's narrative an ornate literary performance, she was able to satisfy her own taste for purple prose. Here is how she had La-aw describe her feelings while waiting for the right moment to purchase her freedom: "I waited my time like a lover lying in wait for his mistress, like a mother watching the return of an only child, and I waited long and anxiously, praying to God, calling him Allah! calling him Buddha! Father! Goodness! Compassion! praying for liberty only, praying only for freedom." From the paired opening similes (lover, mother) to the multiple terms for God and the two matched phrases at the end, the artificial elaboration is quite striking. There is no way that Anna could have grasped and retained all this after only a year or so in Siam. "Translating" gave her the necessary excuse for the high, fine writing she loved.

When La-aw eventually tried to buy her freedom, Ung refused, merely saying, "If thou wishest to be married . . . I will find thee a good and able husband, and thou shalt bear me children, even as thy mother did before thee; but I will not let thee go free."[2]

Realizing that her mistress would never relent, La-aw escaped by diving into the Chao Phya River and swimming to freedom. This part of the story, almost certainly invented by Anna, has some remarkably unreal moments, as when the swimmer says, "Finding my strength failing me, I made for the opposite bank"—a claim impossible to accept once one has seen the river's width and rapid flow through Bangkok. But Anna had to get La-aw to the west bank, where the city's Muslim merchants were located. It was there that the fugitive slave was married to the *naikodah* by Islamic rites.

Always a fervent defender of marriage, Anna had La-aw describe her wedded bliss in language that loses touch with Thai realities: "I moved about as one drunk with strong wine. . . . I thanked God for the sun, the beautiful summer days, the radiant yellow sky, the fresh dawn, and the dewy eve. Light, pure light, shone upon me." In fact, Thais hate and avoid sunlight. In their culture, shade is a customary metaphor for comfort and peace, and a tiered umbrella is the symbol for royalty. Would sunburned La-aw have waxed ecstatic over "light, pure light"? Anna was imagining a bride for the northern latitudes, where clear summer days are appreciated much more than in the tropics.

The bride's joy ended abruptly. Sitting on the steps of her new home, she was seized, bound, gagged, and carried back to Ung, who had her chained in the courtyard. There was a brief reprieve when her son was born, but ever since, for four years apparently, she has been confined without shade in her mistress's secret prison.

La-aw's tale is governed by the same dualism as the other narratives comprising *The Romance of the Harem*: the horror of slavery versus the fulfillment

---

2. In Landon's version of this scene, Ung's dignity and calm power are not in evidence. "'Never!' she screamed in a terrible voice. 'Be still at once! I'll never set you free!'"

of marriage. Will the abused wife be able to leave the oppressive harem and resume wedded life? Only if Anna, herself once happily married, intervenes.

THE REDEEMABLE SLAVE IN SIAMESE LAW

The Thai word for "slave" sounds roughly like *thaat*, with the first *t* aspirated and the *h* silent. Semantically, the word is even harder to get. Because there was nothing in feudal Europe or the American South that corresponds to the old Siamese *thaat*, the standard and inevitable English translation—slave—is seriously misleading.

In the opinion of missionary-journalist Samuel Jones Smith, "no phase of Siamese slavery has in it anything so horrible and revolting as those systems that prevailed on the American continent, which treated the slave as a chattel, with no rights white men were bound to respect." What Anna's first readers brought to her books was a living memory and hatred of the Slave Power, as it was called, in the defeated Confederacy. When that revulsion was transferred to slavery in nineteenth-century Siam, it lost part of its point.

There were three types of *thaat*: captives or prisoners of war, those born or sold into servitude for life, and redeemable slaves like La-aw. In Bishop Pallegoix's estimate, at least one-third of the Siamese population consisted of *thaat*, most of them redeemable.

Redeemable slaves may be thought of as having mortgaged themselves to borrow money or as having been mortgaged by a parent or spouse. In principle, they had a right to pay off the debt at any time or to arrange for another to pay it off or buy them. Their children had the same right, namely, to purchase or transfer their ownership. This type of *thaat* might be translated as "debt slave." An alternative term would be "bondwoman," in the special sense of one who has sold a bond on herself with no terminal date. By contrast, a Western indentured servant bonded herself for a stated period and wasn't seen as a slave.

Unlike American slaves, redeemable *thaat* were not bought and sold in markets, did not belong to a race captured elsewhere, and were not imagined as less than human. Masters were legally obligated to provide them with rice and fish, and if the obligation wasn't met, the *thaat* had legal remedies. If treated in such a way that their ability to work was impaired, they could in theory redeem themselves at a reduced price. These rights did not insure humane treatment, but they formed an incentive for masters not to brutalize their *thaat*. In the opinion of Pallegoix, who knew Siam as well as any European, the Thais often treated slaves much better than domestic servants were treated in France.

A Thai authority on the sociology of old Siam, Akin Rabibhadana, has flatly said that "to carry over the idea of Western slavery and apply it to *thaat* is to misunderstand *thaat* completely. The only way to understand *thaat* is in the context of Thai social organization," which was (and is) based on "client and patron relationships." As in feudal Europe, nearly everyone owed fealty or service to a superior. Commoners were tattooed with their masters' marks, the nobility had duties toward the king, and so forth. Except for Chinese immigrants and Western residents, no one was a free agent in the sense of being empowered at all times to act in his or her own best interests. Like others, the *thaat* had defined functions, duties, and even rights, since masters had reverse obligations.

Rabibhadana's reading of Siamese social class is richly informed by the extant documentation, yet because the *thaat* point of view did not get recorded, it is hard to know how they regarded their status and treatment by masters. As Hong Lysa observes, Rabibhadana's stress on client-patron relationships leaves out the fact that clients had little choice: if they didn't submit to registration by tattooing, they would be considered squatters, with no legal title to the land they occupied and worked. Anthropologist Katherine A. Bowie doubts that slavery was as benign as Pallegoix, Rabibhadana, and others supposed. In her view, half the population of Chiang Mai were *thaat*, and most of these were harshly treated captives rather than debt slaves. Her analysis applies chiefly to the formerly Laotian region of northern Thailand.

Since few outside observers were in a better position than Anna to describe the workings of Thai slavery, it is extremely unfortunate that she chose to fictionalize and in other ways distort matters. Her summary of the slave laws misrepresented tattooing as branding, and elsewhere she painted with a very broad brush. "Slave" was her word for all dependents, from the rowers who brought the news of Fa Ying's illness to the retinues who followed and crouched before important men like the *kalahom*. Whenever she saw an act of prostration she saw slavery. When messengers or attendants did their assigned work, she saw slavery. Her hot moral fervor blunted her powers of discernment and description.

There is no doubt that Siamese society was far from being open and democratic. Class divisions were hard and fast, and there was actually less upward mobility under Mongkut than under his grandfather Rama I. Because the judiciary was not independent, lower classes faced daunting obstacles in stating grievances and seeking judicial relief. I know of no recorded narratives by runaway slaves, such as the one Anna says she heard from La-aw, and there are few judicial records of masters prosecuted for cruelty toward their *thaat*.

During Anna's last year in Bangkok a case of this kind occurred. According to the *Dynastic Chronicles*, a "commoner-wife" of Mongkut's "was greatly displeased because one of her slaves . . . had run away. When the slave was found and brought back, [the concubine] had the slave punished. With her hands tied, the slave was whipped, until she died. . . . The death occurred within the Inside Quarter of the Grand palace. The King therefore requested [the concubine] to organize and give propitiatory plays to insure the protection of the spirit, the *kwăn* of the Grand Palace. These plays were to be offered at all the palace gates."

Decades later there was a similar case during the Fifth Reign. A former concubine of Mongkut's named Wad, a woman of proven toughness, was in charge of Inner Palace discipline. When a runaway servant was recaptured, Wad (in the words of the scholar who brought the episode to light) "had her chained and whipped for over six months, until the woman died. . . . The servant, Noei, was pregnant, but was made to do heavy work like fetching water and firewood, despite her wounds and bruises, and suffered a miscarriage. Witnesses who saw her just before her death testified that she was bruised on her face, body, and limbs; her body bore both old and fresh cane marks and open wounds that were septic." After Noei was buried, the police unearthed her body, and Wad was sentenced to two years' imprisonment. But then, "on account of her high rank," she was pardoned by King Chulalongkorn.

As is the case in many human societies, Siam's upper crust had so much power that the welfare and rights of dependents were easily ignored. La-aw's story, in which a royal concubine tramples on a *thaat*'s right of redemption, shows how hard it could be to claim this right without an influential patron's support. A year or two later Anna would urge Mongkut to scrap the entire system of slavery. Now, however, working within the system, she made herself a patron in order to free one of its brutalized victims.

THE TRIAL

After listening to La-aw, Anna went to Naikodah Ibrahim and informed him of his wife's secret imprisonment. Together with several other Muslim merchants and a mullah, she drew up a petition to the king. When the time came to present it, she attached a little book nicely suited to his tastes: *Curiosities of Science.*

Anna's account of her intervention is backed by some strong supporting evidence. The view of one scholarly commentator that her "books on Siam were largely plagiarisms or inventions" may be true, but there are still authentic patches.

The ephemeral volume she named existed. A British popularizer of science named John Timbs had inaugurated an ongoing publication titled *Things Not Generally Known, Familiarly Explained: Curiosities of Science.* By 1860 it had reached its second series and third thousand. As Anna knew, this was just the sort of thing Mongkut relished.

Equally exact is her term for La-aw's husband. *Naikodah* or *nakohda* comes from a Persian word for the master of a seagoing Indian vessel. When a *naikodah* took charge of commercial goods on a voyage, he operated as a merchant trader, just as Francis Davis Cobb did in sailing from Boston to Singapore. In 1833 two Arab *naikodahs* came to Siam in the hope of "reopening the trade between Bombay and Bangkok." Two decades later, John Bowring noticed the presence of "a few Anglo-Indians from Bombay and Surat." By Anna's time, there were thirty or so Muslim merchants doing business on Bangkok's southwest bank at Mussulman Square and Mussulman Row. They sold "sundry European articles," yet much of their trade, according to a British consular officer, consisted of "the rich materials composing the Court-dresses, and the sumptuous costumes of their theatrical establishments." Throughout Southeast Asia, in fact, brilliantly dyed fine silk cloth from Gujarat had been the major luxury import for centuries. That La-aw was commissioned to buy "some Bombay silk" fits the historical context to perfection.

The man who headed this merchant community, Naikodah Esmail Soolamanjee, enjoyed Mongkut's special patronage. Classed by Bangkok's Westerners as a "British Indian," he and his Bombay associates had much in common with Anna in spite of the difference in religion. From their point of view, she would have been the ideal person to submit a petition. Were they the ones who alerted her to the unlawful detention, thus prompting her search? Whatever the answer, Anna had to dissociate herself from any and all British Indians in telling the story in the West. Her improbable tale about getting lost and finding the slave by accident was probably a cover-up for the actual train of events.

Her name for La-aw's husband was Naikodah Ibrahim. Scrolling to the page for Muslim merchants in Bangkok directories for the 1860s, one finds a Năcoda Ebhrahim in chamber 6 of a new building in Mussulman Row. A member of the Siam Company of Mussulman Merchants, he looks to be the very man in question.

But the best evidence by far for her story's factual basis is a short, undated letter from the king himself. It was sent to Anna, who published half of it in *The Romance of the Harem*. What is given here is not her excerpt but the greater part of a typed copy recently found in Thailand. The original letter seems to be missing.

Grand Royal Palace.

Bangkok.

To Lady Leonowens,

My dear Maam!

I have liberty to do enquiry for the matter you complained to hear, for the princess Pra-Ong Brittry [i.e., Butri], the daughter of Prince Chow Chan [i.e., Chaochom] Manda Ung who is now absent hence. The princess said that she knows nothing about the wife Nai Kunda but certain children were sent her from her grandfather, maternal, that they are off springs of his maid-servant and these children shall be in her employment. So I ought to see the Chow Chan himself [i.e., herself, Ung] and enquire of the truth of the matter. . . . I shall give favourable attention to your complaint, if it can be done without doing violence to the property of the princess' grandfather, maternal

I beg to remain

Your true and well wishing friend

S.P.P. Maha Mongkut R.S.

This copy of a document dating from the period when Anna's influence was at its peak clearly reveals how well disposed the king was toward her. Even though her request ran counter to the interests of a family of powerful aristocrats, he stated that he would "give favourable attention" to it. No less striking is that, in publishing the letter, she left this promise out. It was one of two key omissions.

Nai being the Thai word for "master," "Nai Kunda" may be a stab at the unfamiliar "naikodah." That and other mistakes would have been the transcriber's, not the king's.

Since Ung was an older woman beyond childbearing years, she was no longer required to reside in the Inner Palace. Her absence explains the state of the courtyard in which La-aw was held. Notwithstanding Anna's comparison of the shutters to "those used in prisons," the simple fact is that the place was unused and neglected.

After Ung returned to the palace (in Anna's story), the king ordered Khun Thao App, a high official, to investigate and resolve matters. App was the woman's name; *khun thao* was her title. Since the king knew of the friendship that had already developed between her and Anna, the appointment is significant.

In two other stories in *The Romance of the Harem*, App calmly presides over the judicial torture of an innocent person. In Anna's mind she was the chief woman judge in the palace, but that may have been a mistake: a letter of Mongkut's speaks of her as "Lady Abb, Bearer of Royal Command." But whatever her actual official function and character may have been, in determining La-aw's fate she is said to be "scrupulously just." As is so often the case in Anna's portraits, there are no shades of good and bad. *This* App has a "supreme" fitness for her high office, never decides a case in private, has freed most of her slaves, lives a pure and simple life, and has beautiful arms and hands.

However, her power to rule in favor of the redeemable *thaat* does not come from her standing or the dignity of the law but from the king's written mandate. Lacking that, App would be powerless to proceed against "great ladies" like Ung and Butri. If Anna had failed to enlist the king's sympathetic interest, La-aw's legal position would be hopeless, that is, correct but unenforceable.

The climax of Anna's story is the dramatic judicial confrontation between the judge and the powerful former concubine. Summoned as a witness, Ung takes a good two hours before appearing with her daughter Butri and

"an immense retinue of female slaves, bearing a host of luxurious append-
ages for their royal mistresses' comfort during the trial." When asked about
La-aw's whereabouts, Ung throws a "malicious glance" at App and remains
silent, the epitome of aristocratic disdain.

The proceedings take place in an open-air *saalaa* filled with a "rabble
of slave women and children, crouching . . . with eyes fixed on the chief
judge." Revealing the onlookers' thoughts and feelings, Anna assures us that
"not one of those slave-women, lowly, untaught, and half clad as they were,
but felt that in the heart of that dark, stern woman before them [Judge App]
there was as great a respect for the rights of the meanest among them as for
those of the queen dowager herself." In fact, there was probably no one who
didn't assume that App was there to enact the royal mandate.

The case is open-and-shut. The critical transaction occurs at the beginning, when the judge reads the letter the king has sent her. This document,
which is tantamount to the royal writer's presence, declares App's authority
to act, and Ung and Butri duly prostrate themselves, signaling their submission. When questioned, Ung cannot explain or justify her refusal to release
La-aw. Instead, she asks, "What if every slave in my service should bring me
the price of her freedom?" App replies,

"Then, lady, thou wouldst be bound to free every one of them."
"And serve myself?"
"Even so, my august mistress," said the judge, bowing low.
The dowager turned very pale and trembled slightly as the judge declared
that L'ore was no longer the slave of the Chow Chom Manda Ung, but the
property of the Crue Yai.

The *crue* or *khruu yai* is of course Anna herself, her title following Fa Ying's
death. As soon as she puts down forty ticals, the slave will belong to her. As
to whether Ung should be punished, the question doesn't arise.

The next day, when Anna returns to the brass door and pushes it open,
intending to take possession, the deserted courtyard has a very different
look, with the great ladies sitting in state surrounded by their retinues. No
one deigns to notice the burly female blacksmith who frees La-aw from her
chains or seems surprised when the freed woman remains prostrate, refusing to move. Anna is mystified until someone whispers, "They have taken

away the child." Unless the boy is produced, the redeemed *thaat* will not join her new owner.

So Anna goes back to App, who removes "a dark roll" from a box and carries it to the courtyard. "There sat the august ladies, holding small jewelled hand-mirrors, and creaming their lips with the most sublime air of indifference. Lore still lay prostrate before them, her face hidden on the pavement. The crowd of women pressed anxiously in, and all eyes were strained towards the judge. She bowed before the ladies, opened the dark roll, and read the law: 'If any woman have children during her bondage, they shall be slaves also, and she is bound to pay for their freedom as well as her own. The price of an infant in arms is one tical, and for every year of his or her life shall be paid one tical.'" At once four ticals are pressed on Anna by sympathetic bystanders.

When the boy is brought to La-aw, she turns "up to heaven a face that was joy itself." Rising to her feet for the first time in years, she is unable to walk without the help of her well-wishers. At the palace gates the growing crowd is joined by "hosts of Malays, Mohammedans, and Siamese, with some few Chinese," all waving colorful pieces of clothing converted to banners. By the time the redeemed mother and son reach the boat that will float them to Mussulman Square, the procession has become something new to Siam: a spontaneous public celebration of the triumph of justice over hereditary privilege. Thanks to Anna, Bangkok has had a new and thrilling taste of liberty.

WE ARE MUCH PLEASED THAT
YOU HAVE SO MUCH INTEREST

Mongkut's sympathetic letter tells us that La-aw must have been released, just as Anna claimed. Thanks to her, a redeemable *thaat* was freed from an aristocrat's private and illegal detention. But why has everything from the brass door's "ominous thud" to the final march of triumph been calculated for maximum theatrical dramatic effect? Why did Anna have to tart up her admirable accomplishment?

It is helpful to think about aspects of the case she was silent about. Among them is the idyllic nature of La-aw's union with the *naikodah*, which we are asked to take on faith. Fred Arthur Neale, the Englishman who was in Bangkok during the Third Reign, felt sorry for "the unhappy girls who oftentimes fall to the lot of Arab merchants from Bombay and the Red Sea, who are residing for commercial purposes at Siam." Clearly, suspicions of that sort would have been out of place in Anna's deliriously happy ending.

Her narrative is also silent about the woman La-aw served as "chief attendant," Ung's daughter. A photograph of Princess Butri in her later years eloquently conveys her austere and authoritative presence. Having taught Chulalongkorn to read and write in Thai, she may be thought of as Anna's predecessor. So how was Butri's status at court affected when another teacher, an apparent Westerner, showed up and rapidly gained the king's favor? How did she feel when La-aw was transferred from her and her mother to the newcomer? What does it mean that in the trial's climactic moment Anna, the victor, is identified for the first and last time as the *khruu yai*—the big teacher? Behind a story of liberation we glimpse a struggle for power and precedence between rivals.

Then there is Anna's most crucial omission. As the newly found transcript of the king's letter shows, he not only welcomed her involvement in the case but encouraged her to take an interest in the welfare of the lower classes. The second passage deleted from her published excerpt reads as follows: "We are much pleased to observe that you have so much interest in the condition (bodily) of the life of our common people, whereas the foreign missionaries are chiefly regarding the souls of our common people, and disregardful of their well doing and well living on this life, which was to our thinking to be of more importance to our people at present." In effect, Mongkut was authorizing Anna to become more active in aiding slaves and prisoners, which she presently did with a persistence he had not foreseen. As for his purpose, maybe he hoped her activism would help him curb the powers of an aristocracy he was too weak to challenge. Or maybe he was merely expressing his feelings of the moment.

Anna's motives for concealing his endorsement are easier to deduce. Again and again, in books, articles, and lectures, she would present her employer as the embodiment of willful Asian despotism and herself as the independent reformer who boldly defied him. The problem with his benevolent encouragement was that it undercut this message and along with it the gendered politics and claims of sisterhood in *The Romance of the Harem*. In spite of the fact that a despotic woman was the evil force in La-aw's life and

Mongkut the benign and powerful enabler of her emancipation, Anna's story subtly inculpates the king and awards top honors to App and herself. The title of the first of two chapters, "Slavery in the Grand Royal Palace of the 'Invincible and Beautiful Archangel,'" draws attention to the ironic discrepancy between the palace's beautiful name and inner rot.[3] The second chapter, on the other hand, "Khoon Thow App, the Chief of the Female Judges," points to the story's force for good. In this way the patriarchal monarch comes to stand for the vile system that App and Anna, working together, successfully undermine.

The trial that freed La-aw would have been an unusual event for nineteenth-century Bangkok. However it went, it is to Anna's great credit that she helped instigate it. But her breathless treatment was naive and misleading. In a system governed not by law but by patronage, justice is predetermined, and all trials are show trials. Without a nod and a written authorization from the king, nothing could have been done. If Anna was in fact present, she may have been the sole observer who failed to realize she was watching a ritual public enactment of a decision made in private.

Finally, one can only wonder about the striking resemblance between the harsh treatment of La-aw and an exactly contemporaneous incident in the American Civil War involving abolitionist Abby Hopper Gibbons, one of Anna's most helpful backers in New York. In May 1863, while serving as a supervisory nurse in Maryland, Gibbons found an African American man "tied to a tree in front of the Guard-House" as punishment for insolence and disobedience. He was held there for four hours. Her indignant intervention aroused the wrath of a regimental colonel, who submitted a complaint about this "Protectress-General of all who get themselves into trouble." In the colonel's view (which Gibbons sturdily put on record), the annoying female had gone "beyond her proper sphere, and might be disposed of." Though not a fabulist like Anna, Gibbons was an aggressive, freedom-loving woman after Anna's own heart.

It is clear that Anna played a vital role in redeeming a wrongly and cruelly held *thaat* and that this was a splendid thing to have done. But was the *thaat* chained to the ground, not for four hours but for four years, out in the

3. A footnote explains the quoted words as a translation of "the official title of the royal palace at Bangkok." In fact, they are the first words of the long official name of Bangkok itself.

open, unable to stand, with her child present and no one else in evidence, or was this extreme treatment modeled on a fellow crusader's story, with the horror stepped up a hundredfold?

Because of Anna's proven exaggerations, deceptions, and frauds, the question has to be raised. Can it be settled? If not, La-aw may walk free, but her rescuer may be stuck, doomed to remain the nonredeemable debt slave of her own storytelling.

16

A Troubled Crusader

NOT LONG AFTER THE DEATH of Fa Ying and the release of La-aw, Anna was asked to accompany the king and some concubines and pupils on an excursion to Ayutthaya, the ruined capital of the previous dynasty. The trip, by river and canal on a steam-powered boat, was the first of several royal excursions she was invited to join. She was now a recognized member of the court, with a distinct role to play in its ceremonial activities.

She was away from home for eight days. On her return, she learned what was likely to happen if you did not employ a watchman. As Dan Beach Bradley recorded in his journal, "Mrs Leonowens called at our house having returned from the old city yesterday and found to her great grief that her house had been broken open during her absence & plundered of all its valuable contents which she estimates at more than $800." In Straits dollars, she had lost the equivalent of eight months' salary.

The crime epitomized the contradictions of her position. On the one hand, she was doing amazingly well: she had found better work than anything her talented husband could have hoped for, she had a king's confidence and good wishes, she had made friends in the palace, and she could justly applaud herself for having freed a wrongly held *thaat*. Her daring venture outside the empire appeared to be a brilliant success.

Yet she had a constant sense of being an alien in a dangerous place, exposed and vulnerable. One evening, after she threatened to go to the British consul with a complaint that the *kalahom* refused to take seriously, she was knocked unconscious (she later claimed) by a stone thrown at her head as she sat on her porch. She blamed the attack on her bête noire, a certain half brother of the *kalahom*. Another time (and again, we have only her word for it), a minor official who claimed to speak for the *kalahom* strongly advised her to resign as schoolmistress. The longer she stayed in Bangkok, the more she believed that she was the target of persecution and that her life was in peril. Her impressionable boy would look back at Siam as "such a dangerous place." Yet Louis was favored by the king and treated like an adopted son, and Bradley, who often took note of Anna's troubles, never mentioned the stone-throwing incident, which may not have happened.

Still, she must have had enemies in high places. She could be very superior, she put people in their places, and she was disposed to challenge the status quo in a society she scarcely understood. Her defeat of La-aw's powerful mistress would surely have had repercussions. For the elite, Anna was becoming a dangerous busybody; for others, a kind of public defender. In *The English Governess* she would cast herself as the reluctant champion of the oppressed:

> [When] the women and children of the palace . . . saw that I was not afraid to oppose the king in his more outrageous caprices of tyranny . . . [they] secretly came to me with their grievances, in full assurance that sooner or later I would see them redressed. And so . . . I suffered myself to be set up between the oppressor and the oppressed. From that time I had no peace. Day after day I was called upon to resist the wanton cruelty of judges and magistrates. . . . In cases of torture, imprisonment, extortion, I tried again and again to excuse myself from interfering, but still the mothers or sisters prevailed, and I had no choice left but to try to help them.

Anna did speak for victims, yet the passage is highly problematic. Beyond the fact that La-aw was tortured by one of "the mothers" and not the king, there are always questions to be asked about someone who demonizes another while assuming the role of a redeeming savior, "suffer[ing her]self to be set up between the oppressor and the oppressed."

Anna's second book, *The Romance of the Harem*, gave further emphasis to the king's despotic mischief and her humanitarian resistance. Dedicated to "the noble and devoted women whom I learned to know, to esteem, and to love in the city of the Nang Harm," the volume was a "record of some of the events connected with their lives and sufferings." It largely consists of six separate narratives about oppressed women. In four of these stories—about La-aw, Lady Rungeâh, the princess of Chiang Mai, and Tuptim—Anna acts as a benevolent outside agent. In two of them Mongkut is a sexually voracious despot whose pursuit of women results in acts of revolting cruelty and inhumanity.

Was he guilty as charged? Nothing from Anna's pen gives a more deadly picture of him than the tales of Tuptim and the princess of Chiang Mai. Chapters 18 and 19 will consider them in detail. Here, as we try to discern her actual life at court, we turn from what she wrote after the fact for her American public to a recently discovered letter involving one of her generous interventions. Written by Mongkut to Anna, the document makes clear that she continued to urge justice for the enslaved, just as she said, and that the king did in fact become less sympathetic and more annoyed with her petitions. But this window on their dealings also reveals something very different from anything we get in her books.

Not Induced to Hurried and Rash Steps

The letter is dated 12 May 1864, a year or so after the La-aw incident. Anna isn't known to have mentioned it, and the original handwritten pages seem to be lost. What we have is an old typed copy, reproduced in facsimile in a book lately published in Thailand, *Saaylap wang luang* (Palace spy), by Graireuk Naanaa and Pramint Kruathong.

The letter responds to Anna's petition to free Cheng and Dang, two slave girls owned by Lady Peeah. As with La-aw, the king has inquired into their legal status, and he now advises Anna that they were born on the estate of Peeah's father and that he cannot annul their "obligation to serve their lawful mastress." Unlike La-aw, a redeemable *thaat* whose owner had no permanent legal title, Cheng and Dang can't be released by judicial fiat. If Mongkut told Peeah to sell them—to Anna, say—it would be "greatest violation of Siamese law and custom." Unable to act, he suggests that she go directly to their owner and by "wise and persuading discourse" acquire the slaves for one hundred ticals. That will be the only way for her to "appease [her] strong desire" to free them.

So much for the business part of the letter. Then comes a much longer "very private postscript," prompted, it seems, by Anna's having said to the king some three months earlier that slavery was "a great blot on the Siamese nation." His answer at the time was that Thai servitude was much less onerous than Western wage slavery, with its mines, factories, and child labor, to which she replied that no nation "can ever be great" if it permits the selling of human beings. Stung by her directness and her placing Siam with backward and lesser states, the king now lays out the answer he has been meditating.

With few exceptions, he says, Thai masters allow *thaat* "all which is requisite for good living," namely, rice, clothing, bamboo huts, a basic education by monks, and freedom to enjoy "games and sports." In London, Manchester, and Glasgow, by contrast, free-market laborers work for low wages, reside in crowded and unhealthy rooms, have a wretched diet, and turn to alcohol for "relief from present misery and difficulty." He also observed that the West's wealth was partly derived from past exploitation of slave labor.

Mongkut was making the case for a paternalistic social system organized on different principles from Anglo-American free-market individualism. His idea, a very old one, was that of a benevolent autocracy in which the few rule the many for their own good and the good of the whole. He noted that the Buddhist Dharmapada regulated slavery, unlike the Western scriptures, which accepted the institution as it was, neither ameliorating nor outlawing it.

But Mongkut's basic point was that he was not at liberty to act as Anna urged. In a surprisingly candid passage, he admitted—"very privily"—that the Thai people "are not pleased on me . . . but have more pleasure on another amiable family." His reference was to his younger brother, Jutamani, the so-called second king, whose sophistication and suavity appealed to Westerners. Convinced that the Siamese, too, preferred his brother to himself, Mongkut believed it would be too risky for him to emancipate the *thaat*—a step the nobility would regard as a "violation of . . . common law and ancient custom."

These fears were not unrealistic. Taksin, the king who restored order after the fall of Ayutthaya, became vulnerable partly because of his harsh methods of reform. Forced to abdicate, he was beheaded. Similarly, in the early years of the Fifth Reign, the then *uparat* ("second king") opposed Chulalongkorn's reforms and orchestrated a palace revolt that, while suppressed, had a chilling effect for years. In spite of the conspicuous deference and ceremony of the Siamese court, there was a latent threat of violent revolt. Indeed, the deference might be seen as a grand and fragile illusion—how a state is propped up in the absence of a stable constitutional system. Hence Mongkut's conclusion that it "shall be good course for me to go circumspectly . . . and not be induced to hurried and rash steps by strong advise of philanthropic individual however well dispositioned." Reform would have to be prudent and gradual.

At the time Mongkut put these reflections on paper, only three years had passed since the emancipation of Russian serfs, and scarcely a year since Abraham Lincoln's Emancipation Proclamation (which excluded Border States and was ineffective in much of the South). Britain had abolished slavery in its colonies in 1833, yet it sided with the Confederacy. It was in Liverpool that the *Alabama*, the fast and lethal Southern cruiser, was built, and when the ship put into Singapore in 1863 it was supplied with the coal it needed to continue its attacks on the Yankee merchant fleet. The slavery question was more snarled than Anna allowed. It was not a matter of Despotic East versus Free West.

Like the intellectual he was, Mongkut concluded by seeking Anna's reply. Although it isn't known whether she took up the challenge, it is clear that the pair had a remarkably frank debate on a social issue that Siam would sooner or later have to resolve. That this "very private postscript" was written by a hereditary Asian ruler, that he was doing his utmost to persuade a teacher in his employ of the wisdom of his policy, and that she never breathed one word about it afterward in her self-aggrandizing books goes against all standard ideas. Kings and commoners are not thought to argue like this, with no hedging, flattery, or abrupt dismissals. Anna's role in the debate could have been one of her proudest boasts, if only she had been willing to cease demonizing her employer.

The mental agility Mongkut exhibited in his letter is in striking contrast with the intellectual fecklessness of Yul Brynner's king in *The King and I*. Brynner played a well-meaning tyrant who knows no history, operates on instinct, and is fatally perplexed by the transition from tradition to modernity. Such was the unreal monster that theatergoers took to their heart in 1950s New York and London.

Polite and respectful as he was, Mongkut could not help venting his growing irritation with Anna's absoluteness and repeated petitions. "I shall doubtless without hesitation," he wrote near the end of his postscript, "abolish slavery in our kingdom of Siam in accordance with your expressed desire for the distinguishing of my reign." At first glance, this looks like a statement of intent for the future. In fact, the king was being sarcastic, mocking the teacher's arrogance and righteous conviction. It's a nice example of his curt and caustic wit, something Western visitors occasionally commented on.

Irony at her expense was something Anna couldn't tolerate. She may or may not have replied at the time, but after the king's death she settled the argument by informing the West that King Mongkut had been wrong in the worst way, wrong morally, wrong in his heart. Instead of reporting her great debate with him or reflecting on the problems he brought up, she won the argument by pronouncing him a wicked Asiatic despot. He had the potential to be a great leader, but he denied his better impulses and made himself into a cruel and duplicitous fiend: that, in essence, would be her claim.

Thomas Leonowens had maintained with hot conviction that the Puritans had done well in beheading King Charles I. In time the Irish Protestant's antiroyalism found new life in his widow's fierce moral condemnation of King Mongkut of Siam. Husband and wife were each absolute in their hatred of absolute monarchs.

Whether Anna bought Cheng and Dang for one hundred ticals and set them free, as Mongkut proposed, isn't known. Perhaps not; otherwise, we would have heard about it.

Long and Dangerous Illnesses

Anna's literary treatment of her life in Siam was informed by her revulsion with sexual practices there, her resentment of the king, the specter of financial insecurity, and her determination to create a readership. But there was something else that kept her from reporting events fairly: the illnesses that afflicted her in Bangkok. Some of these must have had an infectious or parasitical source. Others involved heat and "nerves." "A nervous illness," as she confessed decades later, "is more trying than anything else." The result: from time to time her judgment and sense of reality underwent something like an eclipse.

In early 1864, about the time she told the king that slavery was "a great blot" on Siam, she contracted a gastrointestinal sickness that nearly killed her. Her brief account in *The Romance of the Harem* says that she was confined to her room for "a month or more" and that she was lucky to have survived "an illness so fatal as cholera." Cholera was thought to be sporadically endemic in Bangkok. In her case it may or may not have been the correct diagnosis. On 8 February Bradley scribbled a memorandum in his personal copy of the *Bangkok Calendar*: "Mrs Leonowens very sick." That same day he noted in his journal that she was reported to be "at the point of death with a wasting diarrhea said to be the dregs[?] of the measles from which she had been recovering." Diarrhea was what had killed Uncle Glasscott eight years earlier in Bombay.

When she eventually returned to work, Anna found that her best friend among the concubines was taking credit for her survival. Chaochom Maan-daa Son Klin had vowed to "save seven thousand lives" if Teacher was preserved. Now, as good as her word, she had a servant purchase seven thousand live fish in a market and release them in the river "with great pomp and ceremony."

In June of that year Anna came down with another illness, this one so grave that she had to be cared for in the large two-story home of Mary and Stephen Mattoon. At night, when her illness was at its "crisis," the mission-ary couple sat up with her. Since their house was squeezed between Taksin's old palace and the huge and magnificent Wat Arun, the fevered patient would have heard the constant tinkling of the "sweet toned bells" (Stephen's phrase) suspended from the temple's projections.

Since Bangkok had no hospital or even hotels, the Mattoons were used to putting up guests, apparently seeing this as part of their mission. At the time they nursed Anna, Mary was so emaciated from asthma and other complaints that she was preparing to leave Siam; early the next month she embarked for New York. That she and her husband took Anna in on the eve of this major upheaval shows how sick and needy the teacher must have been. Three years later, when the couple were living in upstate New York, they would once again open their home to her during her first North American winter.

Since Mary had also been a palace teacher, she and Anna had a lot to talk about. One of the stories she seems to have told concerned a girl who, in the early 1850s, long before Anna came to Bangkok, stole Mongkut's eyeglasses. Decades later Mary recalled the incident in an essay composed for a book about Siam and Laos. Her account was brief and unembellished:

One of our pupils, a sweet-faced young girl, stole the king's spectacles, and sold them—to increase her spending-money, I suppose. I asked to be led to her quarters, thinking I might be of some service to her. I went, and upon arriving at the place, a sort of enclosed court with open rooms, I inquired for her, and her pleasant face peeped out from behind a screen, where she was confined, and returned my salutations. She seemed totally untroubled by her situation; its commonness made the disgrace unfelt, I suppose. Presently a female officer passed and turned a stern eye upon me, and I quietly left, seeing that I could be of no service there.

The story is told very simply. Facial expressions are "sweet," "pleasant," or "stern," motives aren't plumbed, there is no suspense, and nothing is resolved. There isn't even a moral lesson. The phrase "I suppose," used twice to differentiate what Mary saw from what she surmised, shows how careful she was to make her modest narrative as veracious as possible. Because of that, her rudimentary description of the Inner Palace prison—"a sort of enclosed court with open rooms"—has an unexpected authority. We can feel confident, as we can't with Anna's prison stories (one of which we will meet in the next chapter), that this was what an incarceration center looked like in the early 1850s.

Eight years before Mary recorded the incident, Anna appropriated it, developed the main character, inserted herself as a wise older mentor, and sold the tale to *Youth's Companion*. Naming the girl Mai Prang, Anna made her an attractive, intelligent, light-hearted maid of honor, aged fifteen. The first time she entered the schoolroom, it seemed to Anna "as if an electric stream went through me, thrilling me into the most delightful expectation." The girl was "so quick, so responsive, so full of intelligent appreciation" that Anna decided to train her as a classroom assistant. But then she turned moody, unpredictable, and defiant. Once she disrupted class by bringing a pet monkey. Ordered to take it away, she "dashed her books on the floor" and left "in a towering passion." The 1946 motion picture, *Anna and the King of Siam*, does this scene well, with Linda Darnell adding a sultry undercurrent to the girl's sullen rebelliousness.

The next time Anna saw Mai Prang she was one of fifteen young women being whipped for stealing the king's gold spectacles. Visiting her in prison (not described), the teacher asked the unrepentant girl—"chief of the gang"— why she stole them. The answer backed up Anna's leading point about the harem, that its inhabitants led stultifying lives: "I did it for a change, because it would be something new, you know. We were all so tired of the dulness and stupidity of our lives here." Anyway, being whipped and jailed was nothing compared to the fun of seeing the ridiculous spectacle the king made when enraged: "He roared, and threw things about, and stamped and thundered like a wild beast. . . . [W]e all rushed to our rooms, and shrieked with delight. . . . I never enjoyed anything so much in my life."

In the end the mischievous girl burst into tears, embraced her teacher, and from that moment became an "earnest and diligent" classroom assistant. Anna's wise patience had paid off, redeeming a gifted troublemaker and giving her a purpose in life.

This purloined story, published the same year as *The Adventures of Tom Sawyer*, had everything the juvenile American reader was thought to require: a stupid exemplar of the stuffy adult order, a young authority-tweaking protagonist, a risky practical joke, and an edifying last-minute turnaround. A raw product of Southeast Asia had been refined into the plated wares of America's Gilded Age.[1]

After Anna was well and in her own home again, Louis sent Avis a photo of the "house where we went to stay when dear Mamma was so ill." The next year, when Stephen Mattoon left Siam to join his wife in New York, Anna reminded her daughter of his and Mary's generosity: "One of my best friends here is about to leave for America. Do you not remember the name of the lady who nursed me in my long and dangerous illness . . . ? She is in America now and her husband, the Rev. Mr. Mattoon is one of the greatest men I have ever known." Anna was recording her debt to the Mattoons. Because of that, one wonders in what light she regarded her theft many years later of Mary's story. One also wonders whether Mary read Anna's version of the tale and, if she did, what the plain and honest woman thought of her friend's splendid literary abilities.

MY HEALTH SUDDENLY BROKE DOWN

As time passed, Anna grew more reluctant to join the king on his excursions. In March 1865 he wanted her to travel up the Chao Phya River to Sawankhalok, two-thirds of the way to Chiang Mai, with some of her pupils.

1. Several months later, forgetting what she had invented, Anna published an account of a "young woman, named Mai Prang." Missing her, she questioned a pupil, who answered by drawing a finger across her throat. Mai Prang "had been secretly made away with."

Instead, she insisted on staying home, to the royal party's "universal regret," as Mongkut graciously wrote afterward.

In October, when cooler weather set in, Louis wrote Avis that "Mama is not well and the Doctor says she will have to leave Siam if the winter . . . does not improve her health." The boy also reported that his mother had consented to join the next royal expedition, which would be heading "up the river . . . to visit a beautiful Watt temple far away in the country call[ed] Phra Pa Thom" (i.e., Nakhon Pathom). Louis looked forward to the adventure with his fellow pupils, but his mother was full of the grim suspicions she put on record in *The English Governess*. The *kalahom* having been ordered "to prepare a cabin for me and my boy on his steamer, the Volant," she wrote, "one of my anxious friends made me promise her that I would partake of no food nor taste a drop of wine on board." Someone, the *kalahom*'s evil brother perhaps, supposedly wanted to poison her. "I cite this incident," she added, reasoning rather strangely, "to show the state of mind which led me to prolong my stay, hateful as it had become."

Anna had been under a strain from the night she arrived in Bangkok, but her fear of poison was a sign of an increasingly inflamed state of mind. Chances are there was no cause for alarm. According to the crime statistics the (British) police commissioner gave Bradley's newspaper, during the first twelve days of 1865 Bangkok had two burglaries and three cases of assault and battery—this in a city whose population was thought to be 400,000. Central Siam was safe for Europeans. The last thing the government wanted was for a prominent British subject like Anna to die under suspicious circumstances.

Late in the year, according to Louis (who wasn't a witness), a thief entered his mother's room at night. This may have been the same encounter Anna liked to recall for her grandchildren. Waking up, she saw "a well greased arm" and "sinuous brown body also well greased" emerging from under her bed with her red lacquer trunk, whereupon she flung her lighted lamp at the intruder and fainted. She blamed the attempted burglary on the *kalahom*'s brother, her embodiment of persistent, devious, cowardly malice.[2]

2. To judge from Anna's stories, the burglars of Asia always lubricated themselves before slithering into the rooms of sleeping Western women. In India the Thug who entered her mother's room in a tent "was smeared with some kind of grease, so as to enable him to slip away easily from an enemy's grasp." In Jakarta the Chinese thieves

But it was Mongkut himself who became her enemy in chief during her last year and a half. Once, after she repeatedly offended him by refusing to be anything less than principled and upright, she and Louis were mobbed at a palace gate by "a party of rude fellows and soldiers, who thrust us back with threats, and even took up stones to throw at us." She believed that she and Louis might have been killed if not for a group of "poorest slaves" who rallied to their defense. "It was, indeed, a time of terror for us. I felt that my life was in great danger. . . . I became nervous and excited as I had never been before."

After Anna's death a friend of her old age printed an odd story about her last year in Siam. One day when the king was "in a fit of uncontrollable rage" he "roared: 'Will none of my people rid me of this woman?'" It was the same question King Henry II had famously asked in a fit of anger at Thomas à Becket: "Of the cowards who eat my bread, is there not one who will free me from this turbulent priest?" Anna wasn't present when Mongkut invited his attendants to do away with her, but she was certain he had done so and that the attack at the gate was the consequence.

Siam was a land in which talented outsiders could attain great influence, provided they kept their wits about them. The notorious case in point is Constantine Phaulkon, the Greek adventurer who became a trusted advisor at the court of King Narai in the 1680s. After becoming head of the important Mahatthai Ministry, at that time in charge of the civil bureaucracy, Phaulkon overplayed his hand, was suspected of being in league with French and Jesuit interests, and was killed. His strange and tragic career was of particular interest to Anna, whose lengthy account in *The English Governess* emphasized his singular abilities, his intrigues and accomplishments, and the torture he endured before death. Curiously, she began her sketch by noting that he came from "respectable parents" and was thus no lowlife adventurer. Phaulkon's story had elements suggestive of her own extraordinary career and helps explain her fear of assassination.

In March 1866 she wrote her daughter that "hot weather has set in and I find I am fast losing my strength." Bangkok's great heat, a focus of dread,

---

who tried to steal Anna's red trunk had "the upper parts of their bodies smeared with oil." They, too, were dispatched by means of a thrown lamp. On that occasion, however, instead of fainting, Anna "sank exhausted on [her] pillow, not caring what happened."

seems to have been her excuse for not accompanying the next royal excursion, which left for Phetburi on the 25th. A letter she got from the king spoke of the hot ground and "burning sun," showing, it seems, that he understood how much the heat bothered her. As considerate as ever, he reminded her that "our royal family are very regardful of you and your son Louis."

A few months later, according to *The English Governess*, she suffered her worst collapse yet. "In the summer of 1866 my health suddenly broke down, and for a time, it was thought that I must die. When good Dr. Campbell gave me the solemn warning all my trouble seemed to cease, and but for one sharp pang for my children . . . I should have derived pure and perfect pleasure from the prospect of eternal rest." The passage is as striking for its silence about her symptoms as for its insistence on her eagerness to die. Was this the feeling that overcame her after the deaths of her first two children, or was it another kind of emotional breakdown? In the absence of solid information, one surmises that many factors—the heat, the pressure of work, the threat of illness, the loathing of Bangkok, the anxiety about her uncertain future—had rendered intolerable the strain of "keeping up," that is, of maintaining her dignified and authoritative self-possession. A complicated exhaustion could easily produce an intense desire for the "pure and perfect pleasure . . . of eternal rest." It may have been the old suicidal urge.

What restored her to life, or so she told a friend in old age, was a message from the king offering to bring Louis up if she died. The kind offer had the opposite effect of what was intended: it aroused Anna's immense powers of resistance. As her friend put it, "rather than commit her boy to the king, whatever it cost her, she would live! She pulled herself together with a desperate rally."

This story of triumph through sheer will nicely sums up Anna's sense of her life. A heroic survivor, she believed in the maxim that "great misfortunes as well as great affections develop the intelligence." This rule, a commonplace with strenuous Victorians, fits her case well. And so does the contrary rule, namely, that trauma can deform the mind and leave the imagination vulnerable to toxic fantasies. The question is, do we take her reports on "the peculiar desolation of my life in the palace" as basically objective, or do we take them as distorted imaginative products? There are impenetrable obscurities here, yet it does seem that some of her experiences were self-created, the projections of a troubled mind.

Soon after reaching Bangkok in 1862 (according to her later account), she had this reaction: "My head throbbed with pain, my pulse bounded, my throat burned. I staggered to my rooms, exhausted and despairing, there to lie, for almost a week, prostrated with fever, and tortured day and night with frightful fancies and dreams." The fundamental change in her state of mind during five and a half years at court was that she stopped thinking of these terrors as figments. They became real . . . for her.

Of all the Americans who reviewed *The English Governess* in 1870, the single best informed, George B. Bacon, believed that Mrs. Leonowens "was at no time in peril of her life or liberty, as she imagines herself to have been." Another independent-minded reader, Thomas Sergeant Perry, didn't care for the way the author dwelled on her "mental anguish." In fact, that anguish, however insistent and off-putting, was a vital element of Anna's emotional life in Siam. She was doing hard labor, lifting herself to a new level, and she was much more stressed than readers, particularly Margaret Landon, realized. Not only did Anna's physical and mental health deteriorate, but her point of view was clouded whenever she looked back at this phase of her life. In spite of her success in reclaiming her sanity after settling in North America, it appears that some of her Bangkok memories were and always would be essentially delusional.

17

Getting in Deeper

Son Klin in the Dungeon

AS ANNA'S RESPONSIBILITIES EXPANDED in her last two or three years, she became King Mongkut's private secretary in his dealings with the West. Some of his diplomatic correspondence is in her hand, including the letter of condolence he sent the American vice consul after President Lincoln's assassination.

She also acted as confidante, informal advisor, and go-between in some delicate matters, functions *The English Governess* would emphasize over her classroom work. "What with translating, correcting, copying, dictating, reading," she would write, "I had hardly a moment I could call my own." By her account, there were times when the press of events kept her busy till ten at night. In the process she gained a better understanding of Siam's weak position relative to the European powers. She also learned pretty directly what the quick-tempered king was like in his various moods.

When she asked for the raise that had originally been held out as a possibility, her royal employer grumbled about her many petitions:

Why you should be poor? You come into my presence every day with some petition, some case of hardship and injustice, and you demand "your Majesty shall most kindly investigate, and cause redress to be made"; and I have granted to you because you are important to me for translations, and so forth. And now you declare you must have increase of salary! Must you have everything in this world? Why you do not make *them* pay you? If I grant you all your petition for the poor, you ought to be rich, or you have no wisdom.

Although the speech must have been a reconstruction from memory, it catches the flavor of Mongkut's English along with the centrality of quid-pro-quo exchanges in the life of the court. Since official business was often greased by gifts and bribes, everyone assumed that Anna must be making a good thing out of her submissions. The king himself openly acknowledged that royal appointments were "keys to open the doors to wealth," and he was not embarrassed to let her know that he granted her petitions partly because she was "important to me for translations, and so forth."

What that meant, however, was that each new petition brought fresh obligations and entanglements. Her employer's "and so forth" was more than a manner of speaking. Anna was getting in deeper.

In early 1865, as another hot season came on, she found herself entangled in a new case of hardship and injustice. Klin, the concubine to whom she was closest, had committed an offense and was punished, apparently by imprisonment. Anna intervened, procured a royal pardon, and five years later offered a dramatic account of the episode in her first book.

Chaochom Maandaa Son Klin, to use her full title and name, had acquired the rudiments of English in the early 1850s from Mary Mattoon and the two other missionary wives.[1] Years later, when Mary came to the Inner Palace for a visit, it was Klin and also Talap who welcomed and entertained her. Klin would be Anna's special friend at court, helping her learn the Thai language and sending her some two dozen effortful English-language messages. She read and reread the novel Anna brought into the palace, *Uncle Tom's Cabin*, and even took to signing herself "Harriet Beecher Stowe." Among all the women the teacher got to know in the harem, Klin stood out for her eager interest in the larger world and her independence of mind.

Whereas most of the king's wives came from high-born Thai families, Klin had Burmese roots, being of Mons descent. During the reign of Rama I a forebear had come to Siam and been put in charge of a military corps. An uncle, Phya Khien, held an important post in Nakhon Khuenkhan, a city under the jurisdiction of the Ministry of Military Affairs. The family had done well in Siam, yet Mongkut seems to have felt a residual distrust,

1. Like many older Thai women's names, the name Son Klin may have reference to flowers. Its literal meaning is "hide scent" or "hidden smell." Since *klin* can refer to stinky as well as fragrant odors, Anna's translation, Hidden Perfume, is somewhat exalted.

perhaps because Burma was the ancestral enemy. There are indications that Klin was marginalized in the palace. She had one child by the king, a boy born in 1855, and that was it. Like Anna, though not to the same degree, she remained something of an outsider, not fully assimilated and seriously dissatisfied with her life as a *naang haam*.

Her son, Kritaphinihaan—Krita for short—was one of Anna's foremost pupils. He was favored by Mongkut and promoted to high office by Chulalongkorn, but his mother harbored a lifelong sense of grievance. When she learned that Burma had been colonized by England, she urged Anna to write Queen Victoria, advise her that Klin was "a British subject, and could read and write English," and plead her case. Anna declined to do so.

Like other wives, Klin had her own dwelling. One of its walls was decorated with a painted landscape, which the out-of-favor concubine interpreted as an allegory of her life: "That big green tree there," she said, "is like unto me when I was young and ignorant, rejoicing in earthly distinctions and affections; and then I am brought as a gift to a great king, and only think how grand and how rich I may become; and there you see that I am drooping and my leaves are withering and begin to fall."

A photograph of Klin taken decades later shows her standing at the edge of a simple roofed platform with a tiled floor, no walls, and two naked lightbulbs. Although the furnishings are indistinct, one can just make out a triangular Thai pillow. The lightbulbs are shining; it must be night. As in all of her known photos, she holds herself erect and has an extremely dignified composure. Dressed very plainly, she looks as if she has just stood up, barefoot, for her picture.

What Anna tells us about this woman is not always consistent with other sources. Disregarding the concubine's earlier lessons with the missionary wives, Anna gives the impression that it was she who introduced Klin to the English language, starting with the alphabet. When Klin first showed up in the schoolroom, she would fearfully avoid the teacher and keep "her eyes riveted" on the pages of Webster's spelling book. Instead of looking dignified, she seemed "so dejected and forlorn, so hopeless and timid," that "she crouched almost under the table." When Anna offered her private lessons in English, she "dropped on the marble floor, took hold of my feet, and embraced them in a transport of delight." The picture is of a beaten-down subordinate rescued by her kind teacher.

In fact, Klin had a mind of her own and was quite capable of taking a strong line. The one thing Talap says of her, in whispers, is that "she is not prudent, you know,—like you and me." An apology Anna received from Klin conveys a sense of her impulsive, outspoken, and even reckless side:

> My dearest Teacher
> many many milloins [millions] thanks for your very kind note and I am very most sorry . . . because I am very badly [i.e., was very bad] and made you angry for a little thing and I made my face very ugly because I thinking for I love you and your child more than any one and more than my elder Sister indeed and I love you like my Mother too my dear Teacher I beg your thousand pardon with kindest regards I am
>
> > yours love ownly
> > very most affectionately
> > Klin Harriett Beecher Stowe
>
> . . . please forgive I writing very dirty. K.

That the cursive script is less neat than in Klin's other surviving letters explains what she meant in her postscript, "writing very dirty." The writer was well aware that Teacher expected careful penmanship.

This hasty and effusive apology shows that Klin valued family connections, was quite conscious of the impression she made, and was able to misbehave and give offense. That side of her character—proud, imposing, aristocratic—is largely undeveloped in Anna's narrative. Anna's Klin, meek and inoffensive, is the opposite of Ung, the arrogant noblewoman who chains La-aw to the ground. Thus, when Klin is confined in conditions as harsh and unfair as La-aw's, readers can't help but see the punishment as arbitrary and sadistic. Reacting to the story, the feminist *Englishwoman's Review* called Anna's friend "a sad and gentle woman, pale with sorrow," while terming Mongkut a "royal madman" given to "sentencing delicate and tender women to the dungeon and the lash."

Anna gets her first intimation of the concubine's punishment after going to her home one afternoon for a Thai lesson. Klin's son, Krita, is there, anxiously gazing in the direction of the royal palace, from which his mother has not returned following a royal summons. The next morning the worried boy is in the same place, waiting and looking. He doesn't speak his fears, and it is Talap who informs Anna that Klin is in prison. Talap has no idea why, but she does know how to get to her: by bribing the female guards.

Anna's visit to Klin's underground cell is one of the unforgettable set pieces in *The English Governess* and even more so in Landon's *Anna and the King of Siam*. The sketch artist who illustrated the latter, Margaret Ayer, drew Anna in a bonnet and hoop skirt, positioned beside an opened trap door and gazing down the stairs she is about to descend. "Lady Son Klin in the Dungeon," as Landon's chapter is called, offers a grim vision of the horrors of despotic incarceration. Only the most hardened reader could fail to loathe a tyrant responsible for such cruelties.

When Anna reaches the bottom of the steps, she finds herself standing on rotten planks resting on mud oozing up between them. The cell is furnished with a makeshift bed formed by rough boards placed on trestles. On it lies the concubine, "her face turned to the clammy wall." The amenities are a silk mantle covering her feet, a vase of flowers, two lighted candles in gold candlesticks, and a small Buddha. The air is stifling.

When Anna speaks, the concubine has difficulty turning and sitting up, her feet being chained. She is here, she explains, because she petitioned that the appointment held by her late uncle be given to her brother. What she didn't know was that the position had been conferred on another and that the king assumed this was public knowledge. Reacting in fury, he accused her of plotting against the crown and had her imprisoned, interrogated, and beaten on the mouth with her slipper. "I am degraded forever," she says.

Klin gets our sympathy, of course, yet as usual there are problems with the story, starting with the description of the dismal subterranean cell. The one Westerner who left an eyewitness account of an Inner Palace prison was Mary Mattoon, who found the girl who stole the king's spectacles in "a sort of enclosed court with open rooms," with the culprit's "pleasant face peep[ing] out from behind a screen." This sketch of a detention area by a writer who tried to be accurate bears no resemblance to Anna's stereotyped picture. (Mattoon was, however, "credibly informed that [Mongkut] ordered one of his wives to be put in chains and in prison for forgetting to wear a certain ring.")

The best Western account of a Siamese prison *outside* the palace comes from Bishop Pallegoix, who quoted a man jailed for twenty days as saying, "Father! I don't believe that hell itself is more horrible than that prison." The bishop's word for such hells was *cachot*, meaning "dungeon." His account of penal practices under Rama III is entirely convincing, and one of the reasons for that is that he was careful to distinguish between firsthand and secondhand knowledge, a distinction Anna consistently blurred. Her picture of Klin's cell could very well be based on something she read. Since Pallegoix's book was a major source for her, one can't help wondering: did Klin's dank cell come into existence as a vivid imagining of *cachot*?

One of Anna's pieces for *Youth's Companion* speaks of "a great pillared hall" in which the women of the Inner Palace were tried for petty offenses. The hall's floor is said to consist of "trapdoors, which open to subterranean cells," but as the sketch continues, the word "cells" yields to a colorful substitute: "dungeons." Cells beneath an elevated first floor would have been feasible, but, as has often been pointed out, especially by Thais, dungeons could not have been excavated in the Grand Palace's waterlogged subsoil. Anna's elegant variation illustrates her fondness for the sensational over the exact in her choice of words.

Another problem involves Krita, who, we are told, physically handed his mother's petition to the king. About ten years old, the boy is said by Anna to have "the same air of timidity and restraint" as Klin.[2] She being out of favor, he, too, seems targeted for slights and insults. When the moment arrives for the "trembling lad" to reach the petition up, the king "dash[es] it back into the child's face."

This brutal rebuff (which Anna didn't observe) is in line with her overall account of Mongkut's paternal callousness. According to her, not only did the king's children live in terror of "that fatal enemy, their father," but their mothers taught them from infancy how to outwit him. This picture is at variance with the many travel writers who described the king's open and obvious pleasure in his children. Bradley went out of his way to say that he "never apparently abated his affection for any one of them."

The truth is, Krita was well treated. In February 1865, not long before his mother was punished, he was taken on a royal excursion to Kanchanaburi, where he added his signature to a letter Anna got from the king. The next year he and three half sisters were given full honors in the topknot-cutting

---

2. In Landon's paraphrase, Krita "had the same diffident air of being unwanted as his mother. For the shadows of the harem fell even across the hearts of children." The misleading "unwanted," not used by Anna or at first by Landon, appears in a later draft.

ceremony. When Louis eventually returned to Siam during King Chulalong-korn's reign, he found that Klin's son had become "a bit of a swell." In 1883 the twenty-eight-year-old prince got a coveted diplomatic assignment: envoy extraordinary and minister plenipotentiary to Great Britain and the United States. The following year, making his first official trip to the West, he met his former teacher in the Siamese diplomatic suite in New York City's Fifth Avenue Hotel. Anna's report of this improbable reunion says that Krita hugged her "just as he used to do when a little boy" and doesn't so much as hint at ill treatment in childhood.

Some of Anna's most shocking stories rest on an absolute trust in the testimony of one person only. "It was horrible," she says after hearing Klin's story, "to witness such an abuse of power at the hands of one who was the only source of justice in the land." But of course Anna wasn't a witness: all she knew of the transaction between monarch and concubine was what the concubine had disclosed. Was there more to it? This was a person with a mind and a temper, the nobility to which she belonged was not a collection of innocents, and court life was full of intrigue. Ignoring these complicat-ing factors, Anna presents a Manichaean drama in which a rash, unfeeling, arbitrary overlord mistreats a completely truthful and innocent person. "Here, truly," Anna reflects as she stares at Klin on her trestle, "was a perfect work of misery, meekness, and patience."

Still, the story *did* have a basis in fact. It is on record that Klin was pun-ished and that Anna was instrumental in her pardon. Confirmation comes in the newly found letter (glanced at in the last chapter) in which Mongkut expressed regret that she had not joined the excursion to Sawankhalok. Dated 18 March 1865, a few weeks after the royal trip to Kanchanaburi that included Krita, the letter concludes with this terse postscript: "I beg to inform you I have pardoned Lady Klin your scholar at his Excellency's request."

His Excellency was the *kalahom*. That this influential minister had appealed to the king fits very nicely with Anna's report, namely, that after talking to the prisoner she asked the *kalahom* to plead her case. At first, he refused to intervene, but when she told him that Klin could not have known that the wished-for appointment had been given to another, the *kalahom* sent for his secretary, verified that the announcement of the promotion had been delayed, and promised to act. "That very night," Anna writes in *The

English Governess, "he repaired to the Grand Palace, and explained the delay to the king, without appearing to be aware of the concubine's punishment." The ruse worked, and when she went to school on Monday, she learned to her joy that Klin had been released.

This sequence is consistent with Mongkut's known itinerary. On 2 March he returned to Bangkok with Krita and others and then, only a couple of days later, left for the north. The story's events—Klin's offense, imprisonment, and interview with Anna, followed by Anna's appeal to the *kalahom*— apparently took place in the brief period between the two expeditions. Indeed, the shortness of this interval explains two oddities: that the *kalahom* crossed the river to speak to the king "that very night" (to catch him before he left for Sawankhalok), and that the king wrote from up north to advise Anna of the pardon (there hadn't been time to do so before his departure).[3]

So the tale *was* founded on events—events that were later embellished with an oozing underground dungeon and other features that would appeal to readers. Chief among them was Anna's adroitness as a behind-the-scenes operator, effectively pulling the wool over Mongkut's eyes. In fact, as the postscript from Sawankhalok makes clear, he was well aware of her interest in the case. Rightly assuming that she would be pleased by the pardon, he called Klin "your scholar," a hint that he regarded the pardon as a favor to Anna.

Hence the inevitable request: that she confer with him—"secretly"— about a new British plan for a telegraph line through Siam. The quid pro quo could not be clearer. You have your Klin back, the letter says, and now you must place your judgment and discretion at my service so that I can deal wisely with this latest British scheme.

Klin, too, paid her dues, presenting her friend and benefactor with an emerald ring and some Siamese coins in a purse with gold thread. Anna's benevolent and principled intervention had paid off in hard cash. Without intending it, she had done what the king advised when she asked for a raise. Ready or not, the teacher was becoming more deeply enmeshed in the intricate patron-and-client transactions that defined palace life.

3. In his letter from Sawankhalok of 18 March, Mongkut spoke of "our stay here 13 days up to tomorrow." Since he had traveled nearly three hundred miles upriver on the Chow Phya steamer (which "did good voyage"), he would have departed Bangkok on the 3rd or 4th at the latest. That left no more than a couple of days for the Klin incident to run its course. Whatever happened happened fast, just as in Anna's version of events.

18

Anna and Tuptim

NOTHING ANNA WROTE ABOUT HER LIFE in Bangkok was more horrifying than the story of Tuptim, a shocking first-person exposé of the sadism of the Siamese monarchy.

After dropping a hint of events in *The English Governess*, Anna spelled them out in *The Romance of the Harem*, which opens with the harrowing account of a humble young woman who is given to the king as an "offering." Revolted by her forced sexual service, Tuptim runs away and enjoys a few months of innocent happiness with the man she loves. In outline, the story follows the same sequence as that of La-aw: compulsory servitude, ingenious escape, bliss with a loved man, recapture. This time, however, instead of seeing that the captive is freed, King Mongkut turns his back on justice and humanity and has her tortured directly in front of Anna's house and then burned alive.

When Margaret Landon composed her inspirational best seller in the 1940s, she assumed that the narrative was based on fact. Devoting two chapters to it, she placed them near the end, at a point where Anna's relations with the king have become embittered and intolerable. Landon's powerful retelling caught the eye of that special group of readers whose business is not with the truth of history but with what plays well—the scriptwriters for stage and screen. The result: Tuptim became a compelling dramatic victim for the American entertainment industry, with her precise fate depending on the needs of the script: in the 1946 Rex Harrison–Irene Dunne film she was burned at the stake, in *The King and I* of 1951 and 1956 she got an ambiguous reprieve, and in *Anna and the King* of 1999 she had her head lopped off (but only after attaining a satisfactory inner Buddhist peace). In other respects, the adaptations took the same line: they raised her social level from humble to aristocratic, used her unfair treatment to bring Anna's conflicted life at court to a thrilling climax, and implied that the concubine's terrible doom caught at the truth about old Siam. This, viewers were led to believe, was what could and did happen to attractive women during the reign of King Mongkut.

ANNA'S STORY

One reason the story seemed plausible to nineteenth-century readers is that it had an exact historical context: the moment when Napoleon III, seeking to expand the French colonial sphere in Southeast Asia, staked a claim to a client state of Siam: Cambodia. The challenge facing Mongkut was an extremely delicate one: how to preserve his nation's regional prestige and power without giving France a pretext for further territorial claims or an actual military incursion. Painfully aware of his relative weakness, he was struck by the irony that in Europe, the source of the threat, he was seen as an absolute monarch.

One day (according to Anna's story), while the harassed king was presiding at the founding of a wat, he suddenly burst out, "*I* an absolute monarch! For I have no power over French. Siam is like a mouse before an elephant! Am I an absolute monarch? What shall *you* consider me?" By this time Anna had decided that he *was* a classic despot, but she didn't wish to provoke him any further, so she remained silent.

As the king voiced his complaint, he absentmindedly "flung gold and silver coins among the work-women" who were breaking up the pots that were being thrown into the site to form the wat's foundation. Then he noticed one of the workers, a girl "of fresh and striking beauty, and delightful piquancy of ways and expression." She made a vivid impression on Anna too: "Very artless and happy she seemed, and free as she was lovely; but the instant she perceived she had attracted the notice of the king, she sank down and hid her face in the earth, forgetting or disregarding the falling vessels that threatened to crush or wound her. But the king merely diverted himself with inquiring her name and parentage; and some one answering for her, he turned away." The scene is designed to show Mongkut exercising his absolute authority while claiming to be powerless. It also shows something Anna would make a point of: his readiness for novel sexual diversions.

So much, a few short paragraphs, appeared in Anna's first book. Her hook set, she didn't enlarge on the king's interest in the free and lovely girl until the publication of *The Romance of the Harem*, which informed readers that, one week after the scene at the wat, Anna caught sight of her in a corridor where bribes and gifts were left for the king. There, among precious spices and objects of gold and bales of silk, lay Tuptim, prostrate and waiting, her eyelashes darkened with kohl and her fingers "made pink with henna." Beside her crouched the two women who intended to present her to the king.[1]

A few months later Anna happened to see Tuptim showing off an exquisite gift, a gold casket shaped like a pomegranate with an interior lined with rubies. It was her new betel box, given by the king. It symbolized her name, which meant both "pomegranate" and "rubies," and it further implied that she was now the one he expected to "wait" on him in his private upstairs chamber. Tuptim was the new "favorite."

But the girl was young, innocent, impulsive, and unused to harem life. Instead of following orders, she hid herself, forcing the other women to search for her while the impatient king grew angry. Once, Anna found her "crying bitterly" as a senior wife scolded her for her disobedience. She was "utterly sick at heart," she protested through tears, and "could not go up stairs any more." The sexual service she was expected to render the elderly monarch evidently revolted her.

One day Tuptim asked Anna to write down the name of the young monk, Khun P'hra Bâlât, who occasionally preached in the palace. As eventually came out, Bâlât and Tuptim had known one another as children and were "tenderly attached" at the time she was snatched up for the harem. It was this event that led her fiancé to become a monk, and it was because she still loved him that she loathed "waiting on" the king.

A year or so later, Anna learned that the unhappy concubine had gone missing and that a large reward had been offered for information on her

1. Anna may have been the one contemporary writer who claimed that women were given to King Mongkut in this way. Dan Beach Bradley, a persistent critic of royal polygamy, mentioned no such custom in his essay "How the Kings of Siam Obtain Their Wives."

whereabouts. When she was finally discovered outside the palace, her head and eyebrows were shaved, and she was dressed in the costume of a novice. She had been sharing a monk's cell with Bâlât, who, we are asked to believe, had no idea the novice was female and his former fiancée.

As everyone knew, monks were not to have any contact with women, not to touch, not even to gaze at them. That Tuptim was a royal concubine made Bâlât's unintended offense all the more serious: a capital crime against the king.

The trial, like the judicial hearing in the story of La-aw, is one of Anna's most thoroughly orchestrated scenes. The setting is a dilapidated hall whose floorboards were "worm-eaten" and whose walls and ceilings were the home of "monstrous" spiders. The presiding judges included Khun Thao App, who had ordered the release of La-aw. Although App appeared to sympathize with the accused, she was subordinate to the chief judge, who was cruel, leering, and implacable: "'Go on,' said the dreadful man, with a scornful smile at the childish form before him; 'we shall find a way to make you speak.'" Like the other men, he "grinned maliciously" when Tuptim insisted that even though she shared Bâlât's cell, he never recognized her, and the two remained innocent.

Observing the trial, Anna was mesmerized by the dignity of the accused. Until now an unformed juvenile, she seemed transformed or, more precisely, "transfigured into a proud, heroic woman." Sitting there, "she seemed so calm and pure, that one might think she had already crystallized into a lovely statue." The effect was enhanced by a shaft of sunlight, which, "streaming across the hall, fell just behind her, revealing the exquisite transparency of her olive-colored skin."

Tuptim did not give her testimony as a commoner might, hesitantly and in awe of her high-born and hostile judges, but with an unstudied eloquence:

"P'hra Bâlât, whom you have condemned to torture and to death, has not sinned. He is innocent. The sin is mine, and mine only. I knew that I was a woman, but he did not. If I had known all that he has taught me since I became his disciple . . . I would have tried to endure my life in the palace, and would not have run away. . . . I grew quiet and happy because I was near him, and he taught me every day. . . . You can ask his other disciples who were with me, and they will tell you that I was always modest and humble, and we all lay at his feet by night. . . . I did not so much want to be his wife after he became a p'hra (priest), but only to be near him."

The presiding judge replied that no one believed her, and he ordered her to name the confederate who shaved her head and provided the monk's robe that enabled her to leave the palace. Refusing to betray her servant, Tuptim "folded her chained hands across her bosom, as if to still its tumultuous heaving, and replied, 'I will not!'"

Incensed, the judge commanded that she be given thirty lashes on the spot and that her lover, already incapacitated from torture, be carried in as an object lesson. The girl's garment was ripped from her back and the first blow had been struck when Anna stepped forward and ordered the female police to cease their flogging "as they valued their lives." Since she was known to have influence with the king, the head judge declared proceedings suspended until she returned with an official royal pardon.

The king was at breakfast. Anna approached without ceremony (so she said) and made her breathless appeal: "If you had known from the beginning that she was betrothed to another man, you would never have taken her to be your wife. She is not guilty; and the priest, too, is innocent. Oh! do be gracious to them and forgive . . ." Unable to go on, she dropped to the floor. "'You are mad,' said the monarch; and, fixing a cold stare upon me, he burst out laughing in my face. I started to my feet as if I had received a blow. Staggering to a pillar, and leaning against it, I stood looking at him. I saw that there was something indescribably revolting about him, something fiendish in his character which had never struck me before, and I was seized with an inexpressible horror of the man."

This sudden unmasking is the story's second transfiguration. Earlier, in the dismal courtroom, Tuptim had quietly revealed her statuesque majesty. Now, in the palace, the all-powerful king has shown himself to be a laughing fiend. The drama has brought out the opposed spiritual essences of the two central actors.

However, as Anna turned to leave, he impulsively relented and, calling her back, granted her petition. But now she felt so "utterly sick and prostrated" that, instead of going to her schoolroom and starting the day's lessons, as her employer advised, she returned home, taking for granted that he would do as he said.

By now, Anna no longer lived on the river's right bank but in a brick house near the Grand Palace. Located just outside the palace wall, her house was near an open area to the east that she would term a "common." As she tried to restore her shaken nerves, she became aware that this place was the scene of excited activity. Stakes were being driven, pillories erected, and strange large machines dragged into place in front of her windows.

The king had changed his mind. A transcript of the trial had been placed before him, and when he read it, "he repented of his promised mercy, flew into a violent rage against Tuptim and me, and, not knowing how to punish me except by showing me his absolute power of life and death over his subjects, ordered the scaffolds to be set up before my windows." This was not the first time that the king had lost his temper. But now his rage was so extreme that he was bent on punishing Anna as painfully as possible. She would have no choice but to witness a display of his power in its most dreaded form: Tuptim and Bâlât were to be "exposed and tortured" in front of her eyes.

The ensuing scene is more drawn out and excruciating than its counterpart in any twentieth-century adaptation by Broadway or Hollywood. Tortured and interrogated on a pillory, Tuptim continued to maintain her innocence in a clear, bell-like voice: "I have not sinned, nor has the priest my lord Bâlât sinned. The sacred Buddh in heaven knows all." Although we are not told in so many words what exactly was done to her, it seems her fingers were broken or pulled, one after another. Over and over she was "convulsed" with agony. The crowd went wild. Trumpets blared. Above it all, gazing from the palace windows high above Anna's house, the king, concubines, princes, and princesses took in the edifying spectacle on the common. Finally, unable to stand the horror any longer, Anna fainted.

She was unconscious for hours. When she revived, it was evening, the scaffolding and the mob were gone, and there was nothing to be seen but "a thick mist loaded with sepulchral vapors." In the fading light a solitary walker crossed the common: Phim, Tuptim's loyal servant, who told the teacher with "wild, glistening eyes, and her whole soul in her face," that her mistress had been burned alive. As she spoke, Phim seemed to be gazing at a vision of the martyr "holding up her mutilated hands" in the rising flames, still maintaining her truth and honor: "See, these fingers have not made my lips to lie."

For the next month Anna had nothing to do with the king. When she was finally summoned to his breakfast room, he let her know that he had changed his mind one last time: "'I have much sorrow for Tuptim,' he said; 'I shall now believe she is innocent. I have had a dream, and I had clear observation in my vision of Tuptim and Bâlât floating together in a great wide space, and she has bent down and touched me on the shoulder. . . . I have much sorrow, mam, much sorrow, and respect for your judgment.'"

On the site near Wat Sah Katè where the couple had been killed, the remorseful king erected two memorial *chedis* with the inscription: "Suns may set and rise again, but the pure and brave Bâlât and Tuptim will never more return to this earth."

DID ANYTHING LIKE THIS HAPPEN?

The question seems crucial. If this painful story was a report (more or less) of an episode from Anna's life at court, it reveals something very damaging about the historic King Mongkut. If not, it reveals something about its author that we must confront and try to make sense of.

Supposing the story to be a report, a moment's reflection shows that the dialogue could not be an exact translation of what was said. Anna could not have jotted down everyone's remarks or recalled them exactly. The story's spoken words *must* have been devised by the author, no matter whether they are judged to be history or fiction.

But it is not just the words: *everything* in the story is presented as if captured for readers by a magical recording device. Whatever we are asked to visualize—the worm-eaten floor in the courtroom, the shaft of sunlight that haloes Tuptim, her look of being "crystallized into a lovely statue"—comes with a high-gloss definition and a powerful emotional charge. The same is true for the remarkably vivid people, from the coarse and leering judge to the passionately devoted servant (one of Anna's recurring types): they all have an essence that is grasped as easily as if they were stock types, most notably when the heroic victim and the fiendish but waffling king show their inner nature. Every last narrative bit has been perfectly remembered, and sharply etched, and artfully elaborated, and endowed with an obvious meaning. Nothing is vague, doubtful, or left hanging. We even get a final vision of Tuptim in Buddhist "heaven." The story is perfectly rounded: crystalline, dramatic, spellbinding, amazing. It doesn't look like a narrative based on an imperfect memory of an experience. What it looks like is polished fiction.

Supposing that to be the case, the intended readership would have to be Western, given the many developments that are wrong for Siam. That Bâlât becomes a monk after being disappointed in love, or that Anna bursts into the king's breakfast room without ceremony, or that the torture scene takes place in the open air: such actions and events are as unlikely as the basic premise that a concubine could disguise her gender and live undetected with the man who loves her. Only a foreigner who thought that Siamese men and women looked alike would find that plausible.[2]

The story's improbability becomes clearer if one considers Tuptim's social class. The first time we see her, she is one of the "work-women" at a construction site smashing pots. Used to outdoor labor in a tropical climate, she would seem to be a lower-class person who hasn't led a refined or protected life. But she is lovely and artless, and as the story unfolds she undergoes a transformation so thorough that she is given a new and nobler past. Thus, we learn at the end that she has the same respectable origins as Bâlât (who becomes a preacher in the Grand Palace after spending no more than a year in the monkhood). In the torture scene, Tuptim pronounces the Thai word for Buddha not like "the common people" but like "the more educated." Anna went to the trouble of pointing this out in a footnote.

All this social blurring and upward bounding, a sign of the story's fancifulness, would have been most unlikely in Siam's structured society. It is just what one looks for, however, in popular fiction, where the heroes so often prove to be aristocrats in disguise. The blurring is also a sign of the extent to which the author poured her own life story into that of her heroine. Having begun in a charity school for Eurasian children, Anna had acquired the speech and manners of "the more educated," and she would go on to win a full entrée into the ruling white world. When she and Tuptim entered the court of Siam, both made a dramatic upward bound; naturally, both required new pasts. When Anna drew attention to "the exquisite transparency of [Tuptim's] olive-colored skin," she was endowing her heroine with

2. In *The English Governess* two of the captions for engravings mistake the gender of the people shown. The "Siamese Actor and Actress" (p. 176) were in fact two women. Even more oddly, "The Presentation of a Princess" (p. 102), based on a photograph of Prince Chulalongkorn's topknot-cutting ceremony, gives him blond Western curls.

her final piece of equipment, an upper-class complexion. This was never someone who had to work out in the sun.

By speaking truth to power and standing up to the worst the social order can inflict, she does what Anna and Thomas did in Bombay when they launched their bold marital adventure in defiance of colonial society. It was because Tuptim was the creation of an ambitious fantasist that the tale made hash of social reality and appealed to readers.

But not all readers. Henry George Kennedy, the dismissive British reviewer who knew Siam, was struck that after Anna obtained the king's "verbal promise that the woman's life should be spared," she "coolly went home, without taking a single step to see that the pardon . . . ever reached the judge's hands!" With La-aw, Anna remained fully involved until the slave was redeemed. With Tuptim, she suddenly found herself "utterly sick and prostrated," unable to carry on.

This psychic collapse at the key moment announces that something chronic and morbid has entered the narrative, something closely related to the author's protracted breakdowns in India, Australia, and Penang and her early reaction to Bangkok, when she "staggered to [her] rooms, exhausted and despairing, there to lie, for almost a week, prostrated with fever, and tortured day and night with frightful fancies and dreams."

Anna's fullest description of one of her collapses is found in another story in *The Romance of the Harem*: "Nervous, and undecided what to do, I returned home, where I remained prostrated with a sense of approaching danger. From time to time I had had similar conflicts with the king, which very greatly disturbed my already too much impaired health. All manner of fears which the mind so prodigally produces on such occasions came crowding upon me that evening, and I felt, as I had never before, weighed down by the peculiar sadness and isolation of my life in Siam." To judge from this and other such passages, Anna's collapses involved a lacerated sense of exposure, of unprotected isolation. The man she had loved and relied on was dead, she was alone in the world, the king was her enemy, and could she stand it? Which is to say, the public torture and execution of Tuptim was an enactment of a dreadful secret fantasy.

The reason Anna faints during Tuptim's ordeal and doesn't resume consciousness until it is over, a period of several hours, is that the concubine is herself. The scene *has* to take place in front of her house. The king *has* "to punish" the bad sleeping woman. She *must* not wake until her lovely other self and Asian scapegoat, her pomegranate, her special ruby, has been murdered. This is Anna's punishing dream of suffering and suicide, presented as the historic truth about a nation's actual monarch.

But the story also represents the merging of a private psyche with contemporary literary trends. The period in which she wrote the story, probably the late 1860s, saw a tremendous vogue in the English-speaking world for "the sensation novel," a type of fiction that featured bold heroines and ingenious disguises and desperate expedients and dire forms of revenge. Sensation novels were mostly about women in extreme situations and were mostly written by women. In America there was Louisa May Alcott, who, like Jo March in *Little Women*, loved blood-and-thunder fantasy fiction, and in England there was Mary Elizabeth Braddon, whose novel *Lady Audley's Secret*, a compelling read, scandalized sober reviewers and captured the market. When Anna composed the story of Tuptim, she was not only exorcising private demons but putting those demons to work in order to reach a big new readership. At one and the same time the tale was an expression of psychic depths and a shrewd commercial product.

I Tell the Tale as It Was Told to Me

Two decades after Anna left Bangkok, an Englishwoman named Florence Caddy brought out a memoir of a voyage to Siam on a private yacht. In it she briefly described two *chedis* near Wat Sahkèt (her spelling of Anna's Wat Sah Katè) that were dedicated to the "memory of the pure lovers, Bâlât, the priest, and Tuptim, 'the pomegranate,'—who suffered death and torture in the last [i.e., Fourth] reign for their faith to each other. The inscription on the obelisks runs thus; 'Suns may set and rise again, but the pure and brave Bâlât and Tuptim will never more return to this earth.'"[3] Although this would seem to authenticate the story, caution is in order, as we see in

3. If Anna invented the two penitential *chedis*, as seems likely, she may have been inspired by a notorious event preceding her arrival in Bangkok. In 1856 a man named Seng, a Siamese employee of the new British consulate, witnessed a lease of land to Europeans. Mongkut reacted with one of his occasional rages and had Seng given ninety-nine lashes, of which, thanks to a prescribed opium plaster, he died. The British lodged a vigorous protest, and Mongkut was criticized by his own council. In response, he humbly proposed (in Dan Beach Bradley's words) "a perpetual monument stating his offence." Anna would have heard about this from Bradley and the Mattoons.

the next sentence: "Mrs. Leonowens, the governess at the Court, says she knew the girl." Caddy was taking the story on faith, along with its "translation" of the inscription. The giveaway is that her English version of the inscription is identical with that in *The Romance of the Harem*.

Aside from this derivative report, no historical source from the nineteenth century mentions the torture and burning of Tuptim and the monk. The pair were supposedly punished in front of a large crowd in a public area outside the palace walls, yet the event is not so much as alluded to in the voluminous records of foreign missionaries, the files of the English and American consulates, the English-language press of Bangkok and Singapore, or the *Bangkok Calendar*'s annual summaries of noteworthy events. To date, no record of the execution has been found in the archives of the Fourth Reign.

Nor was it mentioned in the *Dynastic Chronicles*, which did, however, record a similar execution: that of a nobleman who used his wife as go-between to pursue a royal concubine named Choi. Choi was spared when the intrigue came to light, but the man and his wife were put to death. That was in 1859. In 1866, near the end of Anna's time in Siam, Dan Beach Bradley drew attention to the execution by listing it in "Notable Days," a feature of his annual *Bangkok Calendar*. For whatever reason, he had decided to keep its memory alive. This event gave Anna the outline of a story she titled "The Favorite of the Harem," and this in turn inspired a versified account by Helen Hunt (later Jackson), "The Story of Boon."[4] In later years, Hunt Jackson wrote *Ramona*, the widely read novel about Indian removal in southern California.

The palace code of law and custom (*kot monthienbaan*) prescribed death for adulterous royal wives. In Bishop Pallegoix's summary, "amorous intrigues with the queen, royal concubines, or princesses" were acts of lèse-majesté and were therefore capital offenses. The guilty man would have his neck broken with a club; the guilty woman was "sewn into a leather sack containing a large stone and thrown alive into the middle of the river." Since she drowned without being touched by ordinary hands, her royal presence

---

4. When Choi dances for the king in Hunt's lurid poem, his "bleared and lustful eyes / . . . marked her for his next new prize." When he decides on the death sentence, "Fierce his red wrath gleamed." Inevitably, readers would have judged Mongkut to be a cruel, degenerate tyrant.

suffered no disrespect or indignity. Such were the traditional forms of punishment. Public torture and burning were not the Siamese way.

Pallegoix's book, published in 1854, reflected the practices of Mongkut's reign less closely than those of the Third and earlier reigns. The book also predated the 1856 reform that authorized childless concubines to leave the palace and take a husband. If Tuptim had existed, she could have applied for a dismissal and married Bâlât.

In her preface to *The Romance of the Harem*, which includes the story of Choi as well as that of Tuptim, Anna defended her credibility in a curious way. Tacitly conceding that she drew on material other than firsthand experience or observation, she declared that "most of the stories, incidents, and characters are known to me personally to be real, while of such narratives as I received from others I can say that 'I tell the tale as it was told to me.'" In this way, refusing to vouch for the truth of her tales, Anna shielded herself from charges of inaccuracy or misrepresentation. As to which of her stories were "received from others," she was silent.

It would be one thing if she got her tales from eyewitnesses but a very different thing if she trusted the rumors circulating within Bangkok's foreign community or the travelers' tales that made it into print. On balance, it appears that the story of Tuptim was based on hearsay that was fleshed out by the author's memory and imagination and the drama's intrinsic demands. That is what it meant for Anna to tell "the tale as it was told to me": to take a number of fugitive hints and expertly stitch them together.

Essentially, she had three sources: a credible rumor that attractive Bangkok girls had formerly been snatched up by nobles; the execution of a royal concubine and her admirer during the Third Reign; and a bad translation of a purported Thai song about a philandering monk burned at the stake. These were the chief materials Anna "received." Tellingly, all three dated from the Third Reign. None had anything to do with Mongkut.

In Samuel Jones Smith's view, conditions for Siamese women were far better in Mongkut's reign than under Rama III, when "a pretty girl of the common people could not be trusted alone even in the vicinity of her own door. They were stolen frequently, when found in the streets to present to the nobility to become play actresses in their theatres." And to sleep with their patrons, Smith could have added. That was the bad old practice that inspired the scene that sets Tuptim's story in motion—Mongkut's accidental notice of an attractive young commoner. That Anna actually observed this is far less likely than that it was "received from others."

In 1838, when Mongkut was still an abbot, a loving but chaste affair between a royal concubine and a young official was discovered. According to Walter F. Vella's history of the Third Reign, "the couple had never met or spoken face to face, but they had, through go-betweens, exchanged gifts, poems, and professions of love." They planned to seek the concubine's release, but before they could act they were informed on. A jury found that the pair had broken the law and condemned them and eight others to death. This punishment was consistent with the penal code and a traditional idea of royal sanctity; there is no reason to think sentence was passed in anger. When Bangkok's few Western residents learned of the executions, they made sense of them as best they could. The account published in the United States by a former missionary stated that the couple had been (like Tuptim and Bâlât) "tenderly attached" but were "ruthlessly torn asunder only a few days before the expected consummation of their nuptials, that the ambition of the lady's parents might be gratified in the elevation of their daughter to the royal harem." True or false, some such version of the tragic event would have been part of the lore that Bangkok's Westerners handed down to newcomers.

As for Tuptim's death at the stake, that came from the same traveler's book that gave Anna her "map" of Siam and Burma, Fred Arthur Neale's *Narrative of a Residence at the Capital of the Kingdom of Siam*. Neale was a quick and graceful writer, and when his book about Syria proved a modest success, he dashed off a lively little volume about Siam, where he had spent some time during the reign of Rama III. One of the things he included was what he called a native song—a lament by a monk who has broken his vow of celibacy and is now suffering the penalty together with his paramour:

> Behold the faggots blaze up high
> 　The smoke is black and dense;
> The sinews burst, and crack, and fly:
> 　Oh suffering intense!

This sensationalistic "translation" by a traveler with limited experience in Siam and an imperfect command of the language appears to be the basis for Tuptim's painful doom.

In fact, not only was no one burned at the stake in Siam, but executions were infrequent. Missionary Frances Davenport had the impression that there were fewer than twenty during the twenty-seven years of Rama III's reign. Siamese monarchs, she wrote, ruled with "mildness, clemency, and a humane regard for the welfare of their subjects." Indeed, "the archives of few countries exhibit less of regal cruelty, despotism, and the ruthless exercise of power."

Anna's account of Mongkut's irritation at how he was seen by the aggressive European powers, which forms the frame of her story, is plausible and commands belief. But what she put inside the frame, beginning with the king's sexual interest in a pretty commoner and ending with her death at the stake, came from facts and rumors, mainly rumors, involving the previous reign. Speaking with an eyewitness's authority, she pinned what she had heard about Rama III to the quite different monarch she had known. I was there (she was saying), I saw this unfold from beginning to end, I did what I could to save the noble and innocent girl, but the impulsive sadism of the king I worked for and knew so well defeated my efforts. Her narrative was a shocking—and shockingly fraudulent—exposé.

She told her tale well and was universally believed, at least in America. Thomas Sergeant Perry, a sophisticated New Englander and early friend of Henry James, wrote in his warmly favorable review that nothing "could be imagined more truly tragic" than Tuptim's true-life story. At the same time, he was struck that "the incidents have a completeness; they concern the whole lives of the actors in a way that is not so often seen in our lives, with their manifold, varying, interwoven conditions." That this seasoned reader failed to ask the obvious next question—aren't characters likely to be fictive if they are seen and rendered so completely?—says something about the credulousness that Anna induced in her American public.

The English reception was more mixed. Florence Caddy may have left Bangkok believing that she had seen the *chedis* for Tuptim and her lover, but others were skeptical. The *London and China Express*, a weekly newspaper that represented the interests and point of view of Britons living and working in the Far East, found "evidence of so much exaggeration—if not sheer invention—about these hearsay narratives" that it roundly condemned the volume containing the story of Tuptim. That "an Englishwoman could . . . endure for any length of time the horrors of such a pandemonium as [Mrs.

Leonowens] describes" was "altogether inconceivable." Had the reviewer caught a whiff of mixed-race origins, and was he insinuating (I guess at his gender) that *that* might explain the author's defective taste? Whatever the answer, the reviewer clearly approached the book as someone who knew Southeast Asia.

A more polite, detailed, and damaging evaluation appeared in the English weekly with the best title to be the forerunner of the *Times Literary Supplement*—the *Athenæum*. Filling six columns at the head of the literature section, this review of *The Romance of Siamese Harem Life* (the British title of *The Romance of the Harem*) took direct aim at Anna's inaccuracies and misrepresentations. One-sided as it is, this is easily the most informed contemporary assessment of the book. Instead of retelling Tuptim's story, as Perry did, the anonymous reviewer brought his knowledge of Siamese history and society to his task, and thus he asked the necessary question, "whether burning people to death is a practice ever known in Siam." Openly doubting that the story had "any grain of fact," he put it directly to the author, asking her to "state to us, if she can, the precise month and year" that Tuptim was executed.

The man who wrote this review, Henry George Kennedy, had lived in Siam as long as Anna and had a better command of the language. A graduate of Cambridge University with honors in classics, he had taken a civil service exam and been appointed student interpreter at the British consulate in Bangkok. During his five or six years there—years that overlapped Anna's stay and Tuptim's supposed burning—he rose to be second assistant. He was back in London by 1870, in time to review Anna's first two books in the *Athenæum*. Ownership of this journal had recently passed into the hands of Charles Wentworth, Lord Dilke, who hoped to make it the premier organ of critical reviewing in Britain. Kennedy became Dilke's private secretary.[5]

We can be categorical: no one was better qualified to assess Anna's books than Kennedy, and no one challenged their truthfulness with equal directness and knowledge. Her response was silence. She never put on record the

5. By etymology and tradition, as Alan Bray points out in *The Friend*, a "'secretary' was a man who could keep a *secret*." Hence Kennedy's reflections on "the propriety of [Anna's] conduct in spending years in the service of the Siamese King, taking his pay, accepting his kindnesses, and afterwards publishing" her exposé.

date of Tuptim's execution, nor did she ever retract anything she had written. As private and steely as they come, she left behind nothing remotely resembling a confession or apologia. She had offered the public a falsified eyewitness account of her life in Siam, and when it was exposed she fell back, successfully, on her formidable dignity.

What drove her to concoct the story? The answer partly goes back to India, where, unlike her sister and other Eurasian girls, Anna may have turned down the older suitor selected for her. Tuptim's preference for Bâlât over King Mongkut repeated her creator's early life-changing choice of Thomas Leon Owens. Anna and Tuptim both gambled on a high-risk life with the young man they loved. They both won and they both lost. They were two ardent girls who wouldn't compromise, and they both went the distance.

But India is only part of the answer. To better understand why Anna wanted to vilify her former employer and set him before the world as a monster, we must follow her final stressful months in Bangkok and her first anxious year in New York.

19

Leaving Bangkok

DURING HER LAST TWO YEARS AT COURT, as Anna's feelings about her work grew more conflicted, she began to object to certain secretarial assignments, her quarrels with King Mongkut took on a nasty edge, and a new anxiety came to the fore: her children's future. Avis was on the verge of womanhood, and Louis, a great favorite of the king—"an adopted son," in Bradley's eyes—was assimilating to Siamese ways. Their mother's hope of steering them toward a regular Western life made her all the more desperate to get out of Bangkok. But then what? If she settled in England, she would have to work, and what English school would take a mixed-race teacher with obscure family connections? Wouldn't she be seen as a dubious sort regardless of her correct and dignified manner?

Her Singapore friend, Francis Cobb, seems to have understood her worries. In 1865, as the time approached for his return to America, he sent a warm declaration of support. Insisting that she would *not* be abandoned, he had three points to make. First, she must be sure to inform him of her plans for leaving Bangkok.

Secondly. Will you ask my aid and assistance of me to come "home" when you are ready?

Thirdly—any anxiety, apprehension regarding Avis or Louis will you confer with me and seek my counsel? And will you be always so great, pure and brave, loyal, and fearless, yourself always and no other?—Do not doubt God. He has pleasure in store for you—Put your foot upon me dear and step upwards.

This generous statement made a profound impression, especially after Anna heard that Cobb had broken his voyage in England and visited Avis at her boarding school. Did the bachelor-merchant hope to marry Avis's attractive mother? Perhaps, but he also had a more indefinite prospect in mind. An admirer of Ralph Waldo Emerson, Cobb had a New England Unitarian's trust in God's benevolence and America's future. What he wanted was for Anna to feel that a glorious new life was on the horizon and that he would help her reach it. His message (was *this* the way Americans talked?) could not have been more different from what she had been hearing in Siam or the British Empire.

Cobb's promise became a kind of talisman, something for Anna to clutch and hold in reserve as Bangkok's shadows, real and imaginary, deepened around her.

THE PRINCESS OF CHIANG MAI

On 7 January 1866 Mongkut's younger brother, the *uparat*, or "second king," died, apparently of tuberculosis. A man of many talents, Jutamani had mastered English along with watch repairing, shipbuilding, and military drill, and in addition he was devoted to the arts of comedy, dance, and music that were indigenous to Laos and northern Siam. With no major administrative duties, he more or less withdrew to private life, passing the time in Saraburi (as the official chronicler noted) in a "Laos-style pavilion"; he particularly "enjoyed playing the Laotian reed mouth-organ known as *khaen*." His accomplishments and suave demeanor appealed to Western visitors, as did the fact that he didn't chew betel and was thus one of the few Siamese whose teeth weren't stained. He named his firstborn son George Washington.

Like most outsiders, Anna was struck by the contrasts between Jutamani and Mongkut: the one, a master of elegant leisure; the other, an impulsive, eccentric ruler with a sagging lip. Unlike other foreigners, she knew from the king's own confidential letters how uneasy he was about his brother's popularity.

For Anna, who had one full sibling—a sister slightly older and apparently quite different in character—this brotherly contrast was a key to Mongkut's personality. She had no doubt that the two were rivals and that the king was driven by covert resentments and jealousies. In her view, the admiring memorial he wrote and circulated after the *uparat*'s death was blatantly hypocritical, a cover for sinister designs.

Two months after Jutamani died, someone in Bangkok sent a lengthy report on current events in Siam to a Singapore newspaper. Apropos the late *uparat*'s children, the unknown correspondent made a highly insinuating claim: "Phraong Tui, the eldest Princess, was a great favorate [*sic*] of her father, and had he consented, would probably have been at the head of the harem of the First King." In plain English, Mongkut had wanted one of his brother's daughters to be his queen, but Jutamani had frustrated him.

It wasn't long before this juicy gossip reached the king's eyes. Shocked, he sent an immediate and emphatic denial to Anna: "What was said therein for a princess considered by the speaker or writer as proper or suitable to be head of my harem . . . there is no least intention occurred to me even once, or in my dream indeed! I think if I do I will die soon perhaps!" Then he cautioned, "This my handwriting or content hereof shall be kept secretly." After signing his name he added a second reminder: "The writer hereof beg to place his confidence on you always." Chances are, he wanted his amanuensis to act discreetly to quash the rumor within the foreign community.

Four years later, after Anna had found a home in America, she not only published the confidential segments of this letter but dismissed the king's denial as the disgusting equivocation of a goatish and insincere man. She interpreted his denial of any desire for his niece as nothing but a cover for his real purpose—to make a personal prize of his late brother's choicest wife, the high-ranking princess of Chiang Mai. She had been the one he had his eye on. His indignant protest was a "sham."

Today the city of Chiang Mai is the cultural center of northern Thailand and a popular tourist destination, but in the 1860s it was a remote vassal state of Siam that few Westerners had seen. It took eighty-nine days for the first Protestant missionaries to get there from Bangkok. The language was Lao, which, though closely related to Thai, has a distinct script and six tones instead of five. When Chiang Mai's aging king came down to Bangkok in 1866, he was an object of intense curiosity to the resident foreigners, who typed him as a colorful barbaric chieftain. Their opinion was confirmed three years later when he apparently connived at the murder of Christians.

The age-old way to guarantee a vassal king's good behavior is to hold his children as honored hostages. Since Chiang Mai formed a buffer between

Siam and its old enemy, Burma (controlled now by Britain), it was in Bang-kok's interest to keep the king of Chiang Mai from reaching any inconve-nient agreements with either nation. Mongkut would have had a powerful incentive to detain one or more members of the royal family.

Anna's thrilling account of the escape of the princess of Chiang Mai appeared in her second book, *The Romance of the Harem*. Her part in events dated from the evening of 10 August 1866, several months after Mongkut's agitated denial, when she was sitting in her house thinking about her trou-bles with the king and listening to distant thunder. Suddenly she realized that two eyes were staring at her from just outside her house.

It was a woman, and when Anna agreed to hear her tale she "sprang" through the window and identified herself as Mae Pia, loyal personal slave of the princess of Chiang Mai. Tall and graceful, the servant wasn't wearing a Thai *phanung* but rather the long tight northern skirt called a *pasin*. She said she had rowed up the Chao Phya River to request a favor: Would Anna carry a private letter to the princess? "Alas! dear lady," Mae Pia said, "she is now, and has been ever since the death of her husband, the second king, a prisoner in the palace of the supreme king, and neither does her brother nor any one else know whether she is alive or dead." The letter was in a small red cloth sack. On the outside was some writing in a script new to Anna. Mae Pia assured her that the message was merely a greeting from the princess's brother, who was visiting the governor of Paklat, a river town nine miles south of Bangkok.

Her errand completed, the loyal slave "sprang" through the window a second time, and as she vanished in the direction of the river, the gather-ing thunderstorm broke in all its fury. Anna could scarcely imagine the "solitary woman" rowing back to Paklat and "battling with the tremendous currents" in the dark.

Mae Pia is the hero of the story, with Anna playing the role of clandestine go-between and message runner. First, she had to learn where the princess was held, and then she had to get access to her palace prison cell with-out arousing suspicion. After finally succeeding, Anna found the woman's "wasted form" lying on a plank, with two women attending her; it seemed she had given up all hope. But she came to life the instant she received Mae Pia's communication. Judging from her excited discussion with her atten-dants, Anna surmised that the message proposed something she was loath to accept. Finally, she was persuaded, and the result was a second note in the strange unreadable script. It was intended for the brother at Paklat. Anna was asked to deliver it.

Finding an excuse to visit the river town, she performed this errand and then talked to Mae Pia for what proved to be the last time. The faithful slave was so elated that her handsome face grew "more expressive" than ever as she spoke: "I do not know what I am going to do, but something shall be done to save her, even if I die for it."

Back in the Grand Palace, Anna contrived another interview with the princess. Realizing now that this helpful Westerner could be trusted, the prisoner related the story of her life, the key to which was that she and Mae Pia had both been nursed by Mae Pia's mother and had thus become "sisters in the flesh, as we are indeed in spirit." As for Jutamani, the first time the princess saw him she was smitten. "God forbid that I should disparage the supreme king of Siam," she told Anna (who of course agreed), "but every one who knows them will admit the superiority of the younger brother."

Mae Pia wooed him for the princess. Dispatched to his pavilion in Saraburi, she pleased him so much with her singing that she was kept "almost always by his side." Presently, deeply moved by one of her songs, he confessed his love for her mistress.

Soon after their union—and here the princess's story was interrupted by "a burst of passionate tears"—Jutamani went into a decline. Dying, he urged his bride to return to Chiang Mai lest she "fall into the power of his elder brother." Her love, however, was so strong and true that she refused to leave her husband even though she shared him with 120 other wives (a detail that somehow fails to get mentioned). After he died, she was installed in royal quarters in Mongkut's palace, and before long the king, "ignoring my deep sorrow and deeper love for my late husband, offered me his royal hand in marriage. Openly and proudly I rejected the cruel offer, for which reason I am here again a prisoner, and perchance will remain forever."

The interview in which the princess recounted her life was the last time Anna saw her. Soon after, it was discovered that she had been spirited away from the prison and a "deaf and dumb changeling" substituted for her. The two attendants remained behind.

What had happened? The investigating authorities decided that the "changeling" must undergo an exorcism to release her from the spell binding her tongue and that the ceremony should be conducted in a certain ancient Hindu temple known as Brahmanee Wade in the northeastern quarter of Bangkok.[1]

Eager to have the mystery explained, Anna rode there on horseback accompanied by her "Hindostanee syce, or groom"—a servant mentioned nowhere outside this story. Brahmanee Wade proved to be a complex of "temples and monasteries" in a spectacular natural setting. Unlike the rest of Bangkok, which sits on flat ground just above sea level, the sacred compound had "a deep, narrow valley" with "sloping sides of grass and furze-clad steeps." In the bottom a "little mad stream roared and fled darkly on."

The "changeling" was Mae Pia, of course. There were dark stains on her clothing, her mouth was tightly closed, and her unnaturally pale face had a look of crazed agony. Three blasts from a conch shell summoned a shaggy hermit who dwelt in a cave on the far side of the valley. At his direction, an exorcism was performed to free the changeling from the spell that kept her from speaking. After the rite proved ineffective, her mouth was opened to receive the "magic water," at which point it was at last discovered that "an evil fiend [had] torn out her tongue."

At the end of these foolish and pointless ceremonies, Mae Pia was released, and the princess's two attendants told Anna all about her amazing exploit. Having somehow acquired the keys to the prison, the clever and capable slave surmounted the ten-foot-high palace walls with two notched planks, opened the royal prisoner's cell, and saw her safely over the walls to freedom. On the river was her brother with a boat that would carry her to Burma. They begged Mae Pia to join them, but, refusing to desert the two attendants, she threw away the keys, cut out her own tongue, and returned to the cell. Now, no matter how much she was tortured, she could never betray her cherished foster sister.

Such was the hidden train of events by which the proud and beautiful princess of Chiang Mai eluded the lust of King Mongkut, an escape made

1. At this point Anna interrupted the story of Mae Pia and the princess of Chiang Mai to insert an irrelevant and surprisingly detailed essay on the history of the belief in witches in England. Filling an entire chapter, the essay rapidly surveys such episodes as the 1716 witchcraft trial that sentenced a woman and her child to death, noting that even such men as John Wesley and Richard Baxter credited the evil powers of witches. In my opinion, the bulk of this chapter was taken from the manuscript of Thomas Leonowens's 1854 lecture in Western Australia, "Study of History."

possible by Anna's service as intermediary and the heroic self-sacrifice of Mae Pia, the sweet singer of Laos whose voice was now forever stilled.

It was a fabulous scoop. Anna was there, she talked to the women, she had the story straight from them, and there was no one else in the world who could have gotten it.

But Did She Get It Straight?

When Margaret Landon wrote *Anna and the King of Siam* in the 1940s, she took for granted that this cloak-and-dagger tale was a record of events, and so did reviewers. According to *Time*, what made the book as a whole "quietly engrossing reading is that its fantastic story is true." Fantastic and engrossing, yes. Quiet and true, no. The story of the Lao princess was sensational fiction in the guise of eyewitness reporting—that is, fiction meant to be taken as fact. Its chief source was Anna's inflamed state of mind during her last two years in Siam and her first anxious years in America.

The narrative does have accurate details, such as the *pasin* worn by Mae Pia, Jutamani's interest in Lao women, and the musical culture of northern Thailand. An early Western traveler to Chiang Mai found that "the princesses have female vocalists among their retainers, some of whom have splendid voices and are quite charming in their wild way." Many details are wrong, however, particularly the business at the wat, and the core of the story has nothing to do with historical events. As Chantasingh has noted, a modern biography of Jutamani mentions a "favorite Laotian wife" from Vientiane (today the capital of Laos) but is silent about any connection with Chiang Mai's royal house. There is no reason to think that the *uparat* was survived by a princess of that line or that Mongkut tried to force any of his widows into his own harem.

When the story was published Henry George Kennedy raised a few of the obvious objections:

> The first remark we should make is, that if any such princess were in custody in the palace, and her brother residing with the governor of a town hard by [Paklat], they were being detained as hostages. . . . Had the brother wished to write to his sister, what need to employ a well-known English lady as his go-between, when a small sum given to the gaoler would have effected the object in view? Is it possible for the slave girl to have twice scaled those lofty

double walls, and escaped without discovery? Where did she get keys to fit the prison-doors?

Having recently returned from Bangkok after years as a British consular officer, Kennedy was better informed about Siamese conditions than all other reviewers in the West. No one was in a better position to spot the improbabilities in Anna's story or to notice her implicit trust in the claims of interested parties: "Is it a fact that [Mae Pia] cut out her own tongue? That the wealthy princess may have corrupted her gaoler, and so managed to run away, is quite possible; and those semi-savages from the Laos States may also have cut the tongue of a substituted slave, and then effected their escape. . . . But, as the mutilated changeling could no longer speak, and the principals to the transaction had fled, there seems to be very little evidence to support the version supplied by the author."

A detail Kennedy didn't take up was the site of the exorcism, Brahmanee Wade in northeast Bangkok. According to Anna, this temple was an ancient center of Hindu worship, with a centuries-old hall whose roof was "crumbling away." As she waited for the exorcism to start, she passed the time making "sketches and memoranda" of the various statues, "Vishnu lying comfortably on the thousand-headed snake" and so forth.

All this was as bogus as the Hindustani groom. Wat Brahmanee Wade was none other than Wat Bowonniwet, the temple where Mongkut had spent years as an abbot before becoming king. The establishment Anna identified as a Hindu center happened to be the headquarters of the modern Dhammayutika sect, which Mongkut had founded—a sect that sought to *purify* Thai Buddhism of Hindu elements. Rather than being a place of archaic and quite spurious rituals, this was where the first Siamese printing press had gone into operation and where Jesse Caswell had taught English to the future king and given the monks a shock with an electrical apparatus.[2]

2. Wat Bowonniwet, founded ten years before Mongkut was appointed abbot in 1837, became the "busiest centre" of nineteenth-century Thai Buddhism under his leadership. In developing it, he built a nearby monastic retreat whose Sanskrit/Pali name was Wat Paramanivāsa. The Thai equivalent may be anglicized as Wat Bramaniwet, which Anna spelled Watt Brahmanee Wade. Her passage about "the Brahmin ascetics, from which the place is named," shows that she saw "Brahman" in the word. On that basis, it seems, she posited an entire and quite specious Hindu history.

Just to the north ran a canal, which, in Anna's time, would have been much busier than now. Present-day visitors to the complex of shrines, dormitories, and administrative offices will find not a wild canyon with a rushing mad stream at the bottom but a quiet, elongated pool. The setting is as flat as any other part of Bangkok.

Although the story of the princess of Chiang Mai was aimed at readers who knew too little about Siam to perceive its fancifulness, it would be a mistake to write it off as wholly fraudulent. There was some genuine local color, and, more to the point, for all her distortions and inventions and sensationalizing, Anna was expressing her convictions. Apparently not realizing that the princess would have been a hostage, Anna genuinely believed that Mongkut meant to add her to his harem. Anna was certain of this, and certain as well that whatever the princess said was entirely veracious and to be taken at face value. Even more than the story of Tuptim, this one rests on the premise that some people are absolutely truthful, while others, namely, the king, are so profoundly duplicitous that they can never be trusted.

It is fascinating how much Anna insisted on this premise in narratives that appear to be first-person historical reportage but prove to be fiction. The longer she worked for Mongkut, the more she made him the carrier of the shiftiness within herself that she could never acknowledge. As critic Chu-Chueh Cheng suggests, she *had* to insist on the king's dubiousness in order to cancel her own "marginality." If she was to be the noble English Governess, he must represent the Asiatic identity she had discarded.

Hence the steady trend in her narrative treatments of Mongkut and his women. In the early (1863) story of La-aw, Anna and the king acted in concert to free a female *thaat* from an oppressive mistress. Two years later, in the story of Son Klin, the king was the oppressor and Anna the shrewd rescuer who manipulated him into freeing a victim of his intemperate rage. Finally, with the princess of Chiang Mai, the king became fully defined as an evil male tyrant and Anna as the special secret agent who, acting in solidarity with other women, most notably Mae Pia, foiled his purposes.

Such was the emerging pattern in the stories Anna would tell about her employer. As he became more wicked, she became more pure, heroic, truthful, and devoted to her sisters in subjection . . . in stories that became less and less trustworthy.

The Aubaret Libel Suit

Twice during her last year at court Anna intervened in Siam's struggle to preserve its independence and territorial integrity against the aggressions of imperial France. Her modest and well-documented role in this historic conflict forms a striking contrast to her dramatic claims about the freeing of the princess of Chiang Mai.

It was in 1851, the same year Mongkut was crowned, that Napoleon III seized power in a coup d'état and set in motion his plans for the restoration of French glory. Determined to rebuild the colonial empire that had been shredded by the British, he fixed on Southeast Asia as a region of vital interest. Since Britain already had possession of Burma, the Straits Settlements, and the south China ports, there appeared to be only one route to south-central China and its enormous markets: the Mekong River, which, rising in Yunnan, flowed south through the Lao states and Cambodia before debouching in Vietnam. Thanks to the accidents of geography and history, Siam's long-standing vassal kingdoms were now in the sights of a great Western power.

During Anna's time in Bangkok, Napoleon III's chief emissary in Southeast Asia was a naval officer named Gabriel Aubaret (see page 191). Bold and energetic, a whiz at languages, and a devotee of the Catholic Church and Gallic honor, Aubaret was a ruthless practitioner of gunboat diplomacy. In 1863 he compelled Norodom, king of Cambodia, to enter treaty relations with France that effectively made that nation a French protectorate.

Previously, Cambodia had been a client of its two stronger neighbors, Siam and Vietnam. When a Singapore paper revealed that its powerless king had signed a secret pact with Siam reaffirming the old relationship, Aubaret was outraged. Interpreting the secret second treaty as a flagrant instance of Oriental duplicity, he made it a pretext for demanding further concessions from both countries.

For a time Aubaret and Mongkut remained on correct and even cordial terms. The consul visited wats, took a conspicuous interest in Siamese ceremonies, and was charmed by the king's children, especially Chulalongkorn. In letters home the Frenchman expressed admiration for the king's "profound erudition" and command of English. "No one is more original than the Siamese king; he has for me a very particular friendship."

But no one believed, Mongkut least of all, that Aubaret was in Bangkok to make friends. He was a man of force, and when a quarrel broke out between a French Catholic priest and a Thai parishioner, the consul allegedly attacked the official who tried to make peace. This man, Mom Raachoday, judge of the International Court, was used to dealing with fractious Europeans, but when he called on Aubaret the Frenchman grabbed his betel box, threw it out of the house, and "taking *Mom* himself by his *top-knot* . . . sent him after the betel box." As was justly said by Dan Beach Bradley, who reported the story in his newspaper, "no greater insult in the eyes of Siamese could have been offered."

Speaking for France, Aubaret demanded that Siam enter a new treaty ceding all authority over Cambodia. When negotiations became stalemated, owing in part to the *kalahom*'s refusal to make any more compromises, Aubaret lost patience and committed another impropriety. This time Anna was caught up in the consequences.

On 14 December 1866, just outside the Grand Palace, at an eastern gate that stood "within 10 rods" (165 feet ór 50 meters) of her house, the king and various dignitaries gathered for a royal procession. Also present was E. Lamache, the French officer who commanded the palace guard, and as he drilled the corps, putting them through their paces, Aubaret walked up to Mongkut and gave him a note concerning the Cambodian question. According to Bradley's *Bangkok Observer*, the consul spoke "disparagingly of . . . [the *kalahom*], saying in substance that the French and Siamese Nations could never hope to enjoy any peace so long as His Excellency was allowed to hold the place he does, and he must be humbled or the most serious consequences would result." As the whole world knew, Napoleon III considered the coup d'état a proper tool of modern statecraft. The previous year the French had rattled nerves by sending a modern gunboat upriver to Bangkok. Whatever the consul's exact intentions, he was acting like a provocateur, and official Siam was deeply alarmed.

A few days after Bradley ran his story about the incident, Aubaret charged him with defamation at the American consulate. He demanded fifteen hundred Straits dollars in damages, a sum that would have broken the missionary-publisher. Realizing that his account was partly in error, Bradley offered an apology and partial retraction: the consul had merely sought to have the *kalahom* removed from the treaty commission, not from office.

But Aubaret wouldn't bend. Instead, he presented Bradley with a fresh non-negotiable demand—the names of his Siamese sources.

It was about this time that the count de Beauvoir made his flying visit to Siam. A strong believer in the Second Empire's expansionism, he saw Aubaret as a heroically "audacious and firm" champion of French civilization. "The most animated, virile, and striking figure" in Bangkok, he was also isolated and exposed—in the count's eyes, as lonely as Robinson Crusoe.

Matters came to a boil in January. On the 11th Aubaret gave an ultimatum to a Siamese minister, stating that if he didn't receive a definitive answer by the next day, he would "consider the discussion entirely closed, leaving the government of Siam to take sole responsibility." That same day Mongkut wrote a letter to Napoleon III complaining of the consul's offensive conduct. In addition, having lost faith in his waffling British allies, he resolved to send his own Siamese delegation directly to Paris.

As a royal secretary, Anna was privy to the developing crisis. When she saw Bradley on the 18th, she not only disclosed the latest developments but let it be known that her son had heard the consul's threatening words in December and would be able to testify in his defense at the trial. However, the boy was the only witness the defense could produce. The king and his ministers all had reasons of their own for being unhappy with Bradley, and no one cared to provoke French anger by seeing that an irritating foreign publisher received full justice.[3]

When Anna informed Mongkut that her son might appear "as a witness," the king (in Bradley's private record of what he was told by her) "was struck with alarm . . . and said in much anger that [Louis] should do no such thing—Mrs. L. left him in a rage and became more fully determined than ever to render me all the help she could by the testimony of her son— She determined that she would take counsel of Mr K[nox] the Eng[lish] Consul and would inform me in the evening." But even as she met with

---

3. The Fourth Reign's official annals preserve a fascinating trace of the government's nervousness about the aggressive American press. In the year of the Rat a drought sent the price of rice soaring, and a belief spread that a royal decision to move certain statues of the Buddha had caused the misfortune. Mongkut's ministers feared that "people might sneak such complaints to the American printing office" so that "we will not be able then to detect the ones who complain, but the matter will bring dishonor to the royal name."

Knox, a royal messenger showed up with an intimidating order: "She must by no means allow her son to testify." If she did, she would incur "a heavy fine." Aubaret was a very real danger and must not be given a pretext for representing the Siamese government as anti-French. Anna was blocked.

The presiding judge was the new American consul, James Madison Hood, formerly a ship captain and member of the Massachusetts and Illinois legislatures. His initial ruling was not what one might expect, that Aubaret must prove malice, but rather that Bradley must prove that his published article was based on fact. Since none of his sources was able or willing to testify, the result was a foregone conclusion, and he was found guilty of libel.

In determining damages, Hood appointed two American missionaries to serve as assessors. It was at this point, with the public part of the trial ended, that Mongkut finally gave his frustrated secretary permission to act. The statement she promptly drafted and sent the assessors exemplifies her style at its loftiest:

Having been informed that the final decision on Dr. Bradley's case just heard, now rests with you, and believing . . . not only in your deep interest in the welfare of Siam and her present sovereign, but also your honor as gentlemen of no ordinary merit, I have, feeling it my duty as a friend, solicited and obtained the permission of [His Majesty] to lay before you, though strictly for your own *private* information, such particulars as will neither compromise the Siamese government nor involve the peculiar trust which devolves upon me in my present position; which are briefly the following.

That the unprecedented demand made by the French Imperial Consul did create a consternation in the minds of all orders of the Siamese, that I heard the natives, to the very guards stationed under my chamber window, both agitate and discuss the matter of the Prime Minister's removal with a nervous apprehension of what might come next—and that both myself and my son were very much alarmed.

In the earnest hope that in committing this slight testimony to your confidence, I may render some small service to a friend,

I have the honor to remain,

Dear and Rev. Gentlemen,

Yours faithfully,

A. H. Leonowens.

The keen partisanship and high dignity are reminiscent of the tone her husband had taken at the convict hiring depot in Western Australia. But Thomas's office letters were more expert than Anna's, which reflect her naïveté about the procedures by which facts get established, whether in courts of law or in the stories she would soon be writing. That she heard the guards anxiously talking about Aubaret shows that a sense of alarm had quickly spread among the Siamese. But as evidence of his actual words, this testimony was useless. Further, a court of law is debarred from considering "*private* information," that is, testimony that cannot be aired and challenged.

Disregarding Anna's letter, the missionaries fined their colleague one hundred Straits dollars. For Bradley, whose paper had in the meantime folded, the judgment was a painful defeat. To support and indemnify him, his friends in Bangkok took a collection, which Aubaret, his honor vindicated, refused to accept.

The effect on Anna was to intensify her resentment of the king. Not only had he suppressed the evidence that might have exonerated Bradley, but in her view he had been too fearful of the French and too prone to act ignobly. She would have nothing to do with the hard reality of the case, namely, that this was a public crisis in which reasons of state took precedence over justice for individuals.

What seems most revealing is the contrast between her two interventions—the one that was fantasized and the one that was real. In the princess of Chiang Mai story, there was nothing, not even high palace walls, that could not be overcome by female self-sacrifice and derring-do. In the Bradley lawsuit, on the other hand, the complications were such that Anna's resolute efforts came to nothing. How to replace the frustrations of mundane life with a gorgeous alternative: that, it seems, is what she was all about, from her hard life in India to her brilliant American career as Oriental fantasist.

Putting This with That, and That with This, and Getting Bolder

When Mongkut sent a team of trusted Siamese negotiators to Paris to resolve the Cambodian impasse, he did so because he had come to suspect (as he wrote one of the envoys) that the English no less than the French "think of

us as animals for them to gnaw on." But now a new problem arose. Because
an Englishman, Sir John Bowring, was Siam's official agent in European
commercial treaties, someone would have to inform him that he would
not be needed in this French matter. For this, the king turned to Anna,
asking her to explain matters tactfully. She would be free to say "anything
[she] liked."

For the last twelve years Bowring had taken a strong interest in Siam.
Of all the king's European contacts, he was easily the most influential. Any
diplomatic secretary would have seen the necessity of the task Anna was
given. But her principles, Western loyalties, and self-importance rose in
protest. Just as she believed Jutamani would have been a better king than
Mongkut, she was convinced that Bowring should be the negotiator rather
than a native Siamese. Also, she bristled at the implicit slight to an Englishman who had been "promised" the job. So instead of drafting the letter,
she put her foot down, "emphatically declining to do 'anything of the kind.'"
If we can trust her account of the face-off, and perhaps we can, the king
exploded, and there was a rupture lasting several weeks. Anna stopped going
to the palace and added bars and locks to her house.

But the king needed her for his foreign correspondence, so, backing
down once again, he finally sent for her. It was 12 May 1867, two months
before she would leave Siam. "As I sat at my familiar table, copying, his
Majesty approached, and addressed me in these words:—'Mam! you are
one great difficulty. I have much pleasure and favor on you, but you are
too obstinate. You are not wise. Wherefore are you so difficult? You are only
a woman. It is very bad you can be so strongheaded. Will you now have any
objection to write to Sir John, and tell him I am his very good friend?'" She
had no objection. Her conscientious firmness had been vindicated.

Anna's initial refusal to send a diplomatic excuse to Bowring is consistent
with the view of herself she put across in her books: brave, undefended,
always standing up for the right. Far from interfering in Thai diplomacy,
she had simply spoken up for truth and square dealing. But that was not
how official Bangkok saw her. The chief royal scribe, a man she called P'hra
Alâck, was critical of her role in the Bowring affair. A letter of his preserves the only known confidential reaction to Anna by one of her Thai
contemporaries:

Ma'm Leonowens, who is the royal children's teacher, is getting more naughty, putting this with that, and that with this, and getting bolder. A few days ago while we were having an audience in the evening, she sent her son into the throne hall, requesting an audience, saying that she had an urgent business. The king told her to come in, but she might have been intimidated by the fact that there were several ministers and nobles in the congregation. The king suspected that she might have been sent by the British consul, to discourage the king from sending our envoy to London, and then encourage the idea of sending Sir John Bowring instead, [in which case] she might be able to collect some thousands.

Mongkut's crass guess at her motives may not have been so far off. Bowring could be a very useful backer, and Anna had every incentive for seeking his good offices at a time when she was anticipating her departure for the West.

After finally writing Bowring for the king, Anna received a reply that eventually reached her in Ireland. Voicing a mild regret at the king's preference for Siamese negotiators, Bowring allowed that he could have been a more effective agent and also hinted that he had pulled strings and gotten Aubaret reined in (and in fact the consul perceptibly lowered his crest). A calm, courteous, veiled statement from a consummate insider, the letter seemed to imply that Anna, too, was an accredited power behind the scenes; she reproduced it in full in *The English Governess*. What she didn't know was that an earlier letter from Bowring to Mongkut had gone into matters in much more detail and touched on his real feelings at being sidelined in Paris.

Anna was not the first outsider to get a taste of power in the Siamese court. The parallel between her life and that of Constantine Phaulkon, the seventeenth-century Greek who became a confidential advisor to King Narai and was assassinated, was surely on her mind. But there was a closer parallel: the last months of her late husband's service at the Lynton convict hiring depot in Western Australia. There, with his loyal wife at his side, the bootmaker's son who termed himself a "gentleman" had become so righteous and obstinate that he got an official reprimand. Now, during her last months in Bangkok, it was his widow's turn to be punctilious and stiff-necked, growing bolder, standing on her dignity, defying her employer, and proving "one great difficulty."

FRIENDS TO GRAPPLE

On 24 June 1867 Bradley wrote in his journal, "Mrs Leonowens has determined to return to ~~Europ~~ England and has this day had all her goods sold
at auction." She had been given a leave of absence of six months or a year
to recover her health and find a suitable English school for Louis. The
assumption at court was that she would return and resume her work, but
the auction tells us that she had another idea in reserve.

Her Siamese friends loaded her with gifts of food so that she wouldn't
starve in the cold and unfruitful North. Chulalongkorn sent her thirty
Straits dollars, and the king gave Louis a silver buckle and one hundred
dollars for "sweetmeats on the way." In his sententious farewell to Anna, he
told her that she was "much beloved by our common people, and all inhabitants of palace and royal children," and that even P'hra Alâck, the scribe
who had called her naughty, was sorry to see her go, and then he said, "I am
often angry on you, and lose my temper, though I have large respect for
you. But nevertheless you ought to know you are difficult woman, and more
difficult than generality. But you will forget, and come back to my service,
for I have more confidence on you every day. Good by!" Anna's last good-
bye to her pupils and to her friends among the king's wives was protracted
and painful, and in the end she had to tear herself away.

Sorriest of all to see her go was her fellow outsider, the Thai-Mons concubine Son Klin, who sent Anna a mournful plea to "come back to us. I
am like one blind—I cannot see clear Oh! Come and lead me on the right
way. . . . I am praying to your Jesus and to my teacher the Buddha to be very
tenderly with you and make you well."

The steamer that took Anna and Louis down the Chao Phya River on
5 July 1867 was the same one that had brought them upstream in 1862, but
everything else was changing: Bangkok had a telegraph, some gaslights, and
a few of its first streets, and Anna, in spite of her troubles, had become a person of standing and achievement. Five years earlier she had felt alone and
exposed. Now, as Bradley noted in his journal, she was "escorted some distance down the river by a large company of her European and American
friends."

In Singapore she caught the overland mail steamer to Suez, from which
she no doubt made the usual transit to Cairo and Port Said, followed by

another steamship passage, this time for London, arriving in September Perhaps one reason nothing is known of her first impressions of England (a strange and arresting blank) is that she immediately left for Enniscorthy, Ireland, home of her late husband. There, she was welcomed by his brother-in-law, Thomas Wilkinson, who, with his many daughters, occupied a modest house on a steep street called Castle Hill. Since this had become Avis's second home during school holidays, she may have been there already, waiting for her mother.

Wilkinson, a solicitor, acted as Anna's agent and advisor. For her son's education, he apparently steered her to the Kingstown School, a respected establishment near Dublin that Louis promptly and passionately hated from the bottom of his half-Siamese heart. Only yesterday he had been petted by a real king, and now it was canings and Latin and cold, damp weather. However, he got on well with the other boys, and he liked the sports.

Anna's grandchildren never forgot the "force and conviction" with which she quoted the advice Polonius gave Laertes: "Those friends thou hast, and their adoption tried, / Grapple them to thy soul with hoops of steel." If she didn't return to Siam, she would have to find employment in England or America. Which she would risk would have to depend on the friends to be grappled.

Would it be Sir John Bowring in England? A friendly note arrived in Enniscorthy from him, saying that he "should have been happy to have seen you in London,—to have offered you any services, and to have talked with you about Siamese affairs." This was promising, especially from a man who was "a sincere friend . . . of women's progress." But Bowring's adoption had not been tried. He and Anna hadn't met. He was elderly and upper class. What could she reasonably expect of him? What would he think of her harsh reports about his friend King Mongkut? How safe would she feel in a country where her mixed-race past could resurface at any time?

No, the only Western friends whose adoption she had tried were American: Mary and Stephen Mattoon, who had nursed her in Bangkok, and Francis Davis Cobb, who had pledged his undying support. Mary was a generous, capable angel, and the two men were absolutely solid. Both had served as acting American consuls, Mattoon in Bangkok and Cobb in Singapore. Both knew the East, were well acquainted with Anna, and were now reestablished in the States. They were the ones to grapple.

Since Cobb was no longer a bachelor, there would be no awkwardness if Anna and Avis stayed with him and his wife in New York City. As for the Mattoons, they had a home now in upstate New York in pleasant Ballston Spa, where Stephen was minister of the First Presbyterian Church. They, too, would welcome her.

If it turned out she had no future in America, could she still go back to Bangkok? Could she stand going back? Uncertainties like these can be extremely wearing. Since she had not yet got her health back, she consulted an Irish doctor, one who seems to have had great skill in reading anxious minds, for what he found upon examining her was that she "required a more bracing climate"—in other words, *not* Bangkok.

So, hedging her bet, she decided on a return to Siam . . . by way of the States. She booked a cabin on the *Denmark*, which she could board at Queenstown on its passage from Liverpool to New York City (Queenstown is Cobh, the deepwater port in Cork Harbor), and then she dashed off a brisk note to Fulham announcing that Avis would not be able to take leave of her teachers, and would they please forward her box and key?

In reply, one of the elderly Misses King wrote to say how hurt they all felt. For five years they had been the girl's surrogate mothers. They had brought her up and loved her as a daughter, and now there was this "sudden wrenching asunder." They could well understand that Anna felt pressed and that "her thoughts must always be preoccupied" with the need to earn a living, but, still, they wanted her to know how "distressed" they were by her letter, which had not offered "one word of regret." In fact, they were offended by "the manner as well as the tenor of your announcement."

This sharp rap on the knuckles shows how unprepared Anna was for the complex array of ceremonial decencies that were part of English life. Unlike the King sisters, with their genteel manners and insular mentality, she was a product of the far side of the empire. She was a stranger, a woman compelled to forge her own path, keep her armor bright, maintain a firm, high tone, and from now on (one imagines) be more careful in dealing with those who had no idea what it meant to be without a home and a native land.

AFTER BANGKOK

1867–1915

20

The English Governess
Comes to America

ANNA AND AVIS LANDED IN New York City on 14 November 1867. They were supposed to be met by Francis Davis Cobb, but at the last minute he was called away by an uncle's death. Regardless, Anna's first steps in North America went far more smoothly than her nerve-racking introductions to Western Australia and Siam, for there at the dock, ready to take charge, was Cobb's good friend James Sloan Gibbons.

A banker, radical Quaker activist, and author of a rousing Civil War enlistment song—"We are coming, Father Abraham, three hundred thousand more"—James was the first of many philanthropists who would help Anna. His wife, Abby Hopper Gibbons, had been a volunteer nurse in the war and was now a full-time worker on behalf of the needy and oppressed. With her gray Quaker dress and her many blue-ribbon contacts in the world of organized benevolence, Abby was to be the one who put Anna in touch with an elite circle of New Englanders. From the moment the anxious wanderer reached New York, in other words, she was in the hands of a well-to-do humanitarian support group.

On his return from Singapore, Cobb had gone into business as a broker or banker with an office near Wall Street. His home was on Manhattan's west side, where he lived with his newly wedded wife, Katherine, daughter of a leading Unitarian minister. When James Gibbons delivered Anna and Avis to the Cobbs' front door, Katherine was there to greet them, backed by a typically warm and sly note from Francis: "You must be as happy as you can till I come back then you must be a little happier."

During the weeks that Anna spent with the Cobbs, she was taken to see the city's attractions, among them Central Park, then newly landscaped. But her first reaction to the New World seems to have been disapproving. For someone brought up in the strict class system of the British Empire and bent on presenting herself as a true English lady, the American scene could be disconcertingly incorrect and vulgar. But Francis and Katherine were wonderful, and Anna never forgot how they "did everything that could possibly be done to help her over her first hard days in a land of strangers."

From New York City she and Avis traveled up the Hudson Valley to spend some weeks with Stephen and Mary Mattoon in their new home in Ballston Spa. In Bangkok Anna had come to regard Stephen as "one of the greatest men [she] had ever known," and she was not alone: a Siamese official held him in highest esteem for his sober good sense, for learning the language and customs, and for never telling lies or getting angry. Now, as a Presbyterian minister, Stephen was in a good position to help Anna find work teaching. Mary, too, had a global competence, having taught in an American academy before going to Siam, where she had been one of the first palace teachers. The Mattoons knew what it was like to earn one's bread in a land of strangers, they had already borne with Anna in sickness and in health, and they were kindly, altruistic, steadfast, and discreet.[1]

Were there any other Americans as well qualified to ease Anna's entry as the Cobbs and the Mattoons? In addition to being literate, idealistic, and generous, three of them had lived in Bangkok or Singapore and could understand the visitor's problems of adjustment. Katherine Cobb was the only one who hadn't known the stresses of living abroad, and yet she proved especially welcoming and reassuring. *The English Governess* would be dedicated to her in "grateful appreciation of the kindness that led you to urge me to try the resources of your country instead of returning to Siam."

Or so Anna wrote. In fact, returning to Siam had not been an option.

---

1. After three years at Ballston Spa, the Mattoons left for North Carolina to take charge of a struggling freedmen's school, Biddle Institute. The school might not have survived, let alone have grown into Johnson C. Smith University, one of the historic black colleges, if they hadn't taken hold. Mary spent the rest of her life working there. A letter expresses her surprise at how little interest Northern white Presbyterians took in the welfare of Southern ex-slaves. Norman Thomas, the perennial candidate for president on the Socialist Party ticket in the mid-twentieth century, was a grandson of the Mattoons.

A First Anxious Winter

On 2 November 1867, just before leaving Ireland for the States, Anna had sent a desperate last-minute offer to King Mongkut: if he would allow an advance on her salary, she would sail back to Bangkok and resume her work. The return address she gave was the only one she had: care of her brother-in-law in Enniscorthy, Thomas Wilkinson.

For more than half a year, as she and Avis stayed with the Cobbs and Mattoons and then found a temporary berth in Catskill, Anna waited in suspense for the king's decision. If security alone had been her goal, she could have gotten a job as a teacher or married George Orton, the *Chow Phya*'s trusty skipper, who sent kisses from the Gulf of Siam; he was emphatically available. Instead, finding herself beached in an unfamiliar society and climate, and with her future apparently resting in the hands of an Asian monarch, she began a book that would introduce the American readers she scarcely knew to a land that meant nothing to them except as the home of the "Siamese" twins (and *they* were seven-eighths Chinese). Such were the unlikely conditions in which *The English Governess at the Siamese Court* took shape and color.

The letters Anna wrote during this interim are not extant, but those she got from Ireland give a rough idea of her anxious state of mind. "You must be very tired writing," wrote Selina Wilkinson; "I hope you are not doing too much for your health's sake." Thomas Wilkinson had doubts about her book's prospects. Eleven-year-old Louis, on the other hand—he was a dreamer like his mother—hoped it would "sell well in New York." He also hoped she would not "go back to Siam because you will be in such a dangerous place and I will . . . feel so unhappy thinking of you being among all those French peapel who hate you or praps a robber might come and may be do some thing to you or if you were walking up that green and one of those priests comeing up to you and saying something to you rudely." The boy had his mother's inflamed sense of Bangkok hostility.

Driving her pen as hard as she could, Anna set out to tell the story of her life in Siam while also explaining the country's history and customs. No Westerner had been given an entrée to king and harem equal to hers. No one could report so fully from inside palace walls or had better materials for a gripping exposé of slavery and sexual bondage. Her book could be simultaneously dignified and salacious, an unbeatable combination in an era when Mormon polygamy was the object of worldwide curiosity and loathing.[2]

However, Anna's nephew, Thomas Lean Wilkinson, a young London barrister just starting his career, was dubious. Realizing how bent she was on airing her resentment of Mongkut, he feared that "publication might break between you and the King of Siam." He, too, assumed that she might have to go back to work for the king.

Finally, in May, the long-expected royal letter arrived in Enniscorthy. Opening it, Anna's brother-in-law made a copy as a precaution against its loss at sea, then forwarded the original to New York. An accompanying note was full of concern: "I am very anxious about you just now as I know you must be in great suspense expecting to hear from His Majesty and greatly upset in your plans. I only hope the letter may be satisfactory to you, for it is not even intelligible to me. . . . I hardly know whether to continue to write, as you may embark for Ireland immediately."

To Anna's eyes the letter was clear enough. Stating that he was too busy to go into detail and would instead communicate through his English agent, Mongkut failed to show the personal regard that had been conspicuous in all previous letters. At times his tone even became curt and noncommittal, as when he said, "I can allow the Loan of £200 to you freely but it may be not." Particularly striking was his claim that, if he accepted her terms and she failed to return, foreigners might conclude that he was "a shallow minded man and rich of money etc. etc." His reference was to a complaint he had published three days before Anna left Bangkok to the effect that he was falsely reputed to be rich, "shallow minded," and easily fleeced by foreign adventurers. He added a postscript—"and Son Klin of course is awaiting her teacher's return"—followed by one of the concubine's characteristic exclamations: "My dear Teacher Oh my Goodness Gracious." In sum, the letter was an ambiguous brush-off, showing Mongkut as feeling indifferent about Anna's return and openly suspecting her candor and honesty.

2. In 1855, when Anna and Thomas were living in Western Australia, the *Perth Gazette* ran a lurid account of Brigham Young's "fifty to sixty wives and concubines" headlined "Horrible Mormon Revelations." Fifteen years later Anna's first book would characterize the *kalahom*'s harem as his "private Utah." The risqué and witty metaphor substituted for the magazine version's simpler and more respectful "ladies."

To read this message through her eyes, situated as she was in the spring of 1868 with no home, no country, no certain means of support, and two children to educate, is to sense her dismay, resentment, and anger. Instead of treating her proposal with respect, the king had given her the back of his hand and left her to cope as best she could. It was the old story, the pattern that had become her life's myth. *Always* she was abandoned in her dire need by those she depended on: her rancorous stepfather, her dear husband, and now her arbitrary and ungracious employer.

But this time there was something she could do. The thing that Mongkut regarded with extreme sensitivity—his reputation in Western eyes—was in her pen-wielding hand.

Returning to New York City, apparently to the Cobbs', Anna slaved away on her manuscript, working so rapidly that by year's end she was ready to start a second book about her life in Siam. But well before the first one was done, a dramatic event on the far side of the globe removed the last of her inhibitions and restraints.

On 18 August 1868 a total solar eclipse was expected over a part of the Malay peninsula ruled by Siam. Mongkut had done the calculations and determined that a beach at Hua Wan would be the ideal location from which to view the celestial event. Eager to show the world, the French especially, that his nation was as up-to-date as Europe, he set in motion a huge expedition complete with elephants and royal wives and foreign scientists and a full complement of dignitaries, including his son Chulalongkorn and the *kalahom*. The latter hoped to convince his tradition-minded concubines that eclipses were not caused by some great beast swallowing the sun and that it wasn't necessary to make a loud banging noise to ensure that the heavenly body would be safely disgorged.

The sky was so overcast that the experiment nearly fizzled, but at the last minute the clouds parted and the eclipse became visible. To the dismay of the court's astrologers, the king's calculations were impeccable. It was a tremendous vindication, a triumph over the superstition and intellectual laziness he had been battling since his days as a monk. But there was a price to pay. Back in Bangkok, it was found that he had contracted a disease in the peninsular jungle. Whatever its exact nature may have been, it gradually weakened him until, on 1 October 1868, he died. A month and a half later a brief report of his death appeared in the *New York Times*. That may be how Anna learned of it.

There must be other nineteenth-century novels besides H. Rider Haggard's *King Solomon's Mines* and Mark Twain's *A Connecticut Yankee in King Arthur's Court* in which a modern man astounds a backward people by predicting a solar eclipse. It was a feat that summed up the arrogance of the West, then at the height of its technological advantage. But an Eastern monarch had already pulled off the trick and by paying with his life had also shown that scientific enlightenment has a cost.[3] As a Thai historian puts it, "Mongkut won the struggle against the orthodox court astrologers and indigenous cosmology. But it was a tragic victory. He sacrificed himself for his cause."

The account of the expedition that Anna inserted in *The English Governess* betrays an unmistakable disposition to belittle it. Rather than recognize the king's serious scientific and foreign policy concerns, she stressed his flamboyant and "indiscriminate hospitality." In the source she relied on, the *kalahom* was said to be "quite ecstatic with joy, and . . . on the alert taking all the observations he could with his long telescope." In her rewriting of this, he was so "boisterous" that he went "skipping from point to point to squint through his long telescope." Although she handled the king's death with respect, she treated the expedition itself as a grand royal farce, neither a triumph nor a tragedy.

Behind this treatment lay a desire to deny Mongkut's progressive side—to make him a showy imitator rather than a true supporter of scientific progress. This reluctance to award proper honors would culminate in Yul Brynner's 1951 Broadway portrayal of a monkey-like barbarian who preens himself on being scientific but understands nothing.

Anna had another motive for downplaying the tragedy of the expedition. Not only did the king's death free her to disclose various confidential matters, such as his "Very Private Post Script" of April 1866, but she now knew she would never be embarrassed by one of the attention-getting, English-language rebuttals he liked to publish.

To be blunt, Mongkut's death was a godsend. She had enjoyed special access to a one-of-a-kind Oriental despot and his harem, she was free to write her adventure up in a way that would catch the eye of readers, she

3. How did he do it? Perhaps the answer is in the book he asked William Adamson to get for him in 1862, *The Simple and New Method of Computation of Solar and Lunar Eclipses for Every Place on the Surface of the Earth.*

could adopt a lofty tone while taking private revenge, and she could feel confident that she would not be corrected or contradicted.

STATEN ISLAND

On 19 July 1868, while Anna and Avis were living with the Cobbs in New York City, Katherine gave birth to her first child, and the house instantly grew smaller. It was time for the long-term guests to leave—time for Anna to make another try at supporting herself with a private school as in Singapore and, before that, in Perth.

It was at this moment that she or the Cobbs turned to the resourceful Abby Hopper Gibbons. Knowing exactly what to do, Gibbons sent a question to a friend living in West New Brighton, the select part of Staten Island's North Shore. The friend was Laura Winthrop Johnson, a benevolent and cultivated New Englander. The question was: Do you have "an opening for a school in [your] neighborhood, in case a Mrs Leonowens, an accomplished woman, of experience in teaching, should come [t]here"? As Gibbons must have known, Johnson had a young daughter, and so did her well-to-do neighbor and friend Elizabeth Gay, and before long an answer came back: yes, we have an opening.

Originally from Massachusetts, Johnson, like many of her neighbors, belonged to the class that Oliver Wendell Holmes called New England Brahmins: a confident and well-educated elite, conscious of pedigree but frank, upright, unassuming, and civic-minded. She was a descendant of John Winthrop, the first governor of Massachusetts Bay Colony. Elizabeth Gay was married to Sydney Howard Gay, an early abolitionist who, more recently, had been managing editor of the *New York Tribune*.[4] Another West New Brighton Brahmin was George William Curtis, well-known travel writer, magazine editor, and reformer, and yet another was Francis George Shaw, whose son, Colonel Robert Gould Shaw, had been shot and killed while leading a charge on a rebel fort in South Carolina. Johnson herself had lost a brother, Theodore Winthrop, in the war.

These were the fighting abolitionists who, by joining in Anna's assistance, would subtly influence her to cast her life in Bangkok as a phase of the war

4. In 1846, when Harriet Jacobs, the escaped slave who became an autobiographer, was pursued by her old Southern master, it was Sydney Howard Gay to whom her brother appealed.

on slavery. The help she got from Curtis is alluded to in her preface to *The English Governess*, and when the time came to bring out her second book, *The Romance of the Harem*, with its stories of harem women she had tried to rescue, she acknowledged her debt to Shaw "for valuable advice and aid in the preparation of this work for the press."

Anna knew what Brahmins were from Bombay, and Johnson had what it takes to recognize an extraordinary person. The day the two women met in her spacious house on Bement Avenue, a stone's throw from the Gays, Curtises, and Shaws, would always be a red-letter day for both of them. Decades later Anna claimed to remember the encounter "as clearly as if it happened yesterday." Johnson did better, leaving us a detailed record about a month after hearing from Gibbons. Writing on 16 August, just two days before the moon's shadow fell on a scientific king on the other side of the globe, she said:

> The word Indian takes me to Mrs Leonowens, and I think I must tell you all about her though it is a long story, for it is one that interests me much. Mrs Gibbons, of whom you must know . . . spoke so highly of her that I wrote that we were hungry for a good school, and I thought we ought by all means not to let such an opportunity slip, to send Mrs L. to see me and I would do all I could &c. In fact I was inspired with the idea that this was just the thing we wanted. On seeing her I was convinced of it, and told her she *should* have a school, and should have a room in our house to begin it if she could not do better. You know in these things if somebody doesnt do something nothing is done. . . . Mrs L seemed so modest so capable so agreeable, so uncommon a person in fact, that I could not help wanting to help her and ourselves too.

Summarizing Mrs. L.'s account of her life, Johnson wrote that after the death of her husband, "a British officer," she "kept a boarding school" in Singapore:

> Then she had an offer from the King of Siam to come to his Palace and educate his children, which she did for six years, soon also becoming his private secretary, learning half a dozen oriental languages for the purpose. Her accounts of it all are very amusing. She makes you laugh and cry. "I was very uncomfortable there at first, said she, they did not know how to treat

Europeans, and I had not even a room to myself, but after awhile I did better." Imagine her possessing her soul in peace among those Asiatics, in such a Babel as the hundreds of wives & concubines and slaves and children of that worthy monarch must have made, & studying languages, and actually succeeding in teaching those people something. She showed me a letter from the King and one from the Heir Apparent, written in very fair English.

She had to separate herself from her children and send them to England to be educated, and as they grew up she felt that she must leave Siam and make a home for them somewhere, and she preferred the independence she should have in this country.

She has great energy, and Mrs Gay and I are doing our best, and I think she will succeed here. . . . You must see by and by some sketches about Siam she is to print in Harper's Mag. She has a very sweet daughter of fourteen with her. Her son is at Dublin University. You would be interested in her,—she is a lady of refinement.

Inevitably, Johnson garbled some details. She thought the husband had died in Siam, and she either forgot or wasn't told that Louis had accompanied Anna there. But in all likelihood the listener wasn't responsible for all the distortions. Her belief that Thomas had been an officer and that his widow picked up six Asian languages in Siam instead of two (Thai and Pali, neither of them mastered) was partly a product of Anna's self-promotion. It had taken her two months to secure a house of her own in Bangkok, but the picture she left in Johnson's mind was of living and working in a harem packed with "Asiatics." The report that her travel sketches were to appear in *Harper's Monthly* may have reflected an early phase of negotiations with the magazine.

But the main thing we get from Johnson's letter is her overriding conviction that she had met the most capable, energetic, amazing woman ever. That was the impression Anna made on America's Brahmin class, and later impressions were even better. When she was asked to tea, she proved "a most agreeable woman, and talks with a fervor and fire you seldom meet with, making you see and feel the East."

A small, affordable house was found about a mile from Johnson on the edge of an industrial area known as Factoryville, home of the New York Dyeing & Print Works. Here, for the next four years, on the corner of Richmond

Terrace and Tompkins Court, Anna and her daughter operated their kin-dergarten. A notice in the local newspaper set forth its attractions: "A first-class Boarding and Day School for young girls, West New Brighton, Staten Island, N.Y. Apply to Mrs. LEONOWENS, Principal." But the advertisement came later. To begin with, Anna depended on her backers, Johnson and Gay, who in addition to sending their own girls canvassed the neighborhood for pupils.

The school was a clear success. A dictated letter from Johnson's five-year-old daughter tells us she was learning "to sing and spell and draw and write and sew and geography and play and have fun"—so much fun that when it was time to go home the girl would beg "to stay a little longer." Mrs. Leonowens, her mother wrote, "has the true gift for teaching, and every one thanks me for securing her to the neighborhood." She taught "with enthu-siasm, which is the only way."

In fact, fourteen-year-old Avis may have been the effective teaching staff. Decades later it dawned on a former pupil that she had been "the real teacher, though I remember Mrs. Leonowens sitting at a big table in the school-room. Here Mrs. Leonowens wrote her books." Could Anna have managed her literary work without a well-trained child others saw as dependent if not intimidated? A few years after the school closed, Johnson thought the young woman was "improved . . . in her manners—talks more and better." Once, as Anna prepared for a lecture trip, she described her daughter, now married, as "feeling a little nervous at my leaving her." One of Avis's own daughters saw her as "a bit oppressed . . . entirely governed by Grandmama's wishes." Avis was beautiful, yet no one remembered her as they remem-bered Anna, "a brunette with waving hair, parted above a pair of brilliant, eager, searching eyes, rather a tanned skin, and a warm-hearted, affection-ate manner which endeared her to all who met her."

Rather a tanned skin . . . In Britain the dark complexion might have been seen as the Anglo-Indian stigma, but in America it merely drew wondering comment: Was this the result of exposure to the tropical sun? In 1945 an eighty-year-old named Louisa Loring Dresel would read Margaret Landon's *Anna and the King of Siam* and then write to the author about her first sight of Anna. Dresel had grown up on Boston's Beacon Hill next door to James T. and Annie Fields, whom Anna often visited following the publica-tion of *The English Governess*. Introduced to the heroic traveler in 1884 in

Annie Fields's parlor, nineteen-year-old Dresel got a lasting impression of "a very vivid personality, with very intense dark eyes, and a dark complexion, which I somehow connected with Siam!"

In spite of the support Anna got from the North Shore's Brahmins, her years on Staten Island were far from easy. Johnson in her initial enthusiasm thought of the home-and-school as "a snug little house," but eventually, opening her eyes, she realized it was near "such a dreadful neighborhood." For Anna it was just an "old cottage" with a "tangle of a garden." The print and dye works were too close, and so was Factory Lake, a mosquito-rich source, in all likelihood, of the malaria that afflicted her. By 1873 she was able to afford a house that was so much better it merited a name: Hawthorne. The next year, with two books out and her reputation made, she felt she "really must leave the island at the earliest opportunity," and before long she was living in Manhattan.

Several years later, having joined her married daughter in Canada, Anna revisited Staten Island. Stopping to look at the old cottage, she saw that it had been repaired and "looked quite decent." Suddenly, "the old feeling of pain came across me, which seems to be associated with our life on the island, and I could have wept passionately." A granddaughter blamed such feelings on "the strain & care of her early years in the States," and that was surely the case, but a more searching explanation, one involving Anna's long history of schoolroom toil, is also in order. To have a last look at the small home-and-school in shabby Factoryville was to call up a train of memories going back to her hard labors in Bangkok, and before that to Singapore, where her school had done only "tolerably," and before that to remote Perth, where she had tried and failed to open her first school, and before that to the primal site of educational strain and care: the Bombay Education Society's enormous orphanage for Eurasian girls—a place of confinement, strict training, and eventual liberation that she could speak of to absolutely no one.

Serialization

The friend to whom Johnson described her dramatic first meeting with Anna was not just anyone. America's most important literary hostess, Annie Fields was on easy terms with any number of writers, most of them from New England but a few from abroad, including Charles Dickens. Her husband, James T. Fields, owned the *Atlantic Monthly* and was senior partner in Fields and Osgood, Boston's blue-chip publishing firm. The Fieldses' back parlor on Charles Street was a shrine to literature, famous for its lavish display of books and letters. Chances are, one of Laura's motives in writing about the marvelous storyteller—"she makes you laugh and cry"—was to catch the interest of Annie's influential husband.

Founded four years before the start of the Civil War, the *Atlantic* was conceived as a high-quality monthly that would publish the best current writing. Closely associated with the antislavery movement and the newly invented Republican Party, it stood for what Ellery Sedgwick, the magazine's historian, terms "Yankee Humanism." Its first cover bore a portrait of John Winthrop, first governor of Massachusetts and first American ancestor of Laura Winthrop Johnson. The magazine had a lock on the New England eminences—Emerson, Hawthorne, Holmes—but it also sought travel sketches and fresh material by women, which was where Annie Fields came in. As Sedgwick puts it, she helped "form a network of personal relationships, to encourage [women's] literary production, and to ensure their publication, generally in the *Atlantic*." For Anna, it all worked as smoothly as the famous Underground Railway: from obscurity she was passed to the Cobbs, from the Cobbs to Abby, from Abby to Laura, from Laura to Annie, and from Annie to James T. Fields and the most exclusive type case in North America.

By February 1870 arrangements were mostly settled. As Mary Mattoon headed south to her and Stephen's impoverished freedmen's school in Charlotte, North Carolina, she took a side trip to Staten Island to see her old friend from Bangkok. She found her "very busy with school" and some exciting literary engagements: a series of forthcoming essays in the *Atlantic* followed by book publication in autumn. In spite of tight quarters and the press of schoolwork, Anna appeared to be on the high road to success.

But if she was starting at the top, she was still more of a teacher than a writer, and in addition she was unfamiliar with the demands of American publishing. As a reviewer would justly complain, *The English Governess* was full of "padding not very skilfully inserted, and very disorderly in its arrangement." After encountering Anna in cold print, Johnson herself would confide to Annie Fields that she "does not write like a practised and experienced writer." Nor was that surprising: a brilliant raconteur with a dramatic manner is all too likely to flatten on the page.

Fields was the kind of editor who shaped manuscripts. As Sedgwick notes, he liked to "negotiate topics and treatments before a piece was written." In Anna's case, presented with a manuscript in need of expert tuning, he apparently turned to John Williamson Palmer.

Forgotten today, Palmer had a solid connection with the *Atlantic*, being its chief Southern contributor before Mark Twain. He was friends with the man who dreamed the magazine up, Francis Henry Underwood, and with its first editor, James Russell Lowell, who extravagantly admired Palmer's work and regularly accepted it. But there was a further reason he was asked to knead Anna's manuscript into shape: he too was a one-of-a-kind exotic, a Marylander who had traveled off the map in Southeast Asia.

As a boy in Baltimore, Palmer had somehow gotten to know the Siamese twins, who were so glamorous in his eyes that he decided to run away to Bangkok equipped with a letter of introduction to their mother. Although he never realized this fine boyish dream, he traveled to San Francisco, Honolulu, Hong Kong, and Calcutta after taking his medical degree. His best adventure was in Burma, where he served as naval surgeon in England's invasion up the Irrawaddy River in 1852. Palmer's two books about his life in Asia were expertly done: breezy, full of knowing winks, certifiably moral in the end. In Lowell's eyes, he united "the eye of a poet" with "the polished coolness of the man of the world, and the *brownness* of the man of the nineteenth-century" (Lowell's intriguing italics). During the Civil War he sent reports from Rebel territory to a Northern newspaper. He gathered folk songs and wrote dramatic performance poems, such as the much-loved "Stonewall Jackson's Way." A heavy drinker, he had the moxie to write about his stay in an inebriate asylum and then get it published in the *Atlantic*.

Such was the seasoned traveler, wordsmith, and grandstander who guided Anna into print. Of her part in this collaborative effort all that survives is a letter sent to Palmer on 8 July 1870, a month and a half after the *Atlantic* had published the third number of *The English Governess*. Among other things, the letter assured him that she had "no intention now of entering into negotiations with any other publisher." From the sound of this, there had been problems between her and Fields and Osgood, problems that were now ironed out.

This letter offers glimpses of Anna's literary operations that we get nowhere else. It shows that she expected to be "busy for a year at least" on a project she called "the Pali translation." Whatever this was, it would have been unlikely to find a commercial outlet in the United States, which, as Robert Irwin has observed, had yet to make "a significant contribution" to Eastern studies. Aiming at her lifelong goal of gaining recognition as a learned Orientalist, Anna did not realize how narrow American curiosity could be. A land of opportunity, America was also a land of limits much tighter than those of Britain, with its broad empire and many scholarly niches and elites.

Part of Palmer's job, then, was to help Anna see how to write about Asian matters for American readers. Chances are, the coaching did not go smoothly. As King Mongkut said, she was a "difficult woman," with a spiky moral sense and a prose style dignified to the point of grandiloquence.[5] Her advisor, on the other hand, had such a "free-and-easy manner" and was so "thoroughly American" that he was "over-indifferent to tradition and convention" (Lowell's judgments). Given these polar contrasts, Palmer was probably not expected to take the starch out of Anna and get her to sound more American. The whole idea, after all, was for her to be "the English governess."

Instead, his basic assignment was to help her select and arrange the *Atlantic's* prepublication installments. Hence the chief revelation in Anna's letter: that she would now "endeavour to go on with the new material in the order you have suggested." In other words, after balking at Palmer's editing, she was now ready to accept it.[6] This belated concession may well explain

5. However, there were a few Americanisms that Anna liked and used. In her account of the bargaining of Bangkok's Muslim traders, she wrote that a "new bidder 'sees that'" (if I may be permitted to amuse myself with the phraseology of the Mississippi bluff-player) and 'goes' a few ticals 'better.'" The *New York Times* singled out this passage as not only vulgar but "at variance" with the author's correct diction. The good gray lady couldn't imagine how much American poker and its bluffing appealed to the masked foreign lady.

6. William Dean Howells, the *Atlantic's* brilliant, antisensational, and somewhat prudish assistant editor, was given a free hand in selecting the magazine's contents, with Fields "reserving to himself the supreme right of accepting things I had not seen, and of inviting contributions." In all likelihood, Howells had nothing to do with Anna's appearance in the magazine. The long list of respected *Atlantic* contributors that he compiled late in life included many minor writers, Palmer among them, but omitted Anna. One wonders: Had he been against publishing her? Was Palmer asked to edit her because Howells wouldn't?

the anomalous gap that followed the third installment of *The English Governess*. It seems there had been a serious disagreement.

"The new material" was the fourth installment, scheduled for August. Like the preceding numbers, this was not an intact segment of the book but a composite: most of chapter 11 followed by all of chapter 9 and parts of chapters 12 and 2. It was a cut-and-paste job designed by Palmer and executed by Anna, who wrote out the printer's copy in longhand, a task one imagines her performing at her Staten Island schoolroom table while her daughter, now fifteen, carried on with the teaching.

All along, the installments had shown signs of a master's hand in the art of image making. The opening number had casually revealed that King Mongkut thought of Anna as "the Lady L——," a title proper to baronesses and the like. The second number had as its climax the text of Sir John Bowring's letter to her, a confidential document that appeared to treat her as a fellow high-level insider. A powerful image was being created for American readers who had a residual colonial mentality (which may have been most of them): the highborn British lady, correct, a little insolent, at ease wherever.

The basic idea of the fourth number as shaped by Palmer is that the governess's authority is so complete and perfect that her startling disclosures are utterly trustworthy—and there's more to come in the book. From the opening sentence, which speaks of her "free access" to royal archives, she seems to have been privy to all the goings-on in the Grand Palace, including how Mongkut was tended by his women during his midday naps. This exciting glimpse of plural connubiality is followed by a boring survey of Siamese literature, but then we return to the harem and the intimate views we have been waiting for: Anna's ceremonial introduction to her many pupils in order of age (just as in *The King and I*); her first sight of Son Klin, who enters the schoolroom in fear and trembling; and the sad tale of little Wanne, daughter of an out-of-favor wife. In the climax we are taken into the *kalahom*'s harem for a direct look at what polygamy does to women. We see how the concubines conduct themselves, like vapid and giddy girls with no depth of feeling or dignity. Whose harem would you rather join, they ask Anna, the *kalahom*'s or the king's? Drawing herself up for the reply that concludes the installment, she declares with crushing solemnity that since both men are pagans, "an English, that is, a Christian, woman would rather be put to the torture, chained and dungeoned for life, or suffer a death the slowest and most painful you Siamese know, than be the wife of either." Stunned, the young wives stare at her as if she is someone "they could neither convince nor comfort nor understand." They leave in silence, but then she hears them "laughing and shouting in the halls," heedless as ever.

The reason so much sensational material was packed into the August number was that it offered the last chance to catch the public's eye before the book went on sale. The tactic did not go unnoticed. That December the review in the *New York Times* began by recalling how the installment of "four months ago . . . excited much curiosity."

Who wouldn't be curious? It was the August number that assembled Anna's most inflamed and questionable inventions. There were the vicious "women disguised as men, and men in the attire of women" who found sanctuary in the palace. There was the king's lustful worldwide hunt for Chinese, Indian, and English beauties, and there were the clever overseas agents who tantalized him with photos of the latest British specimen, "freshly caught, and duly shipped, in good order for the harem." There were the midnight sessions of the king's secret council, which kept the populace under "terrifying" surveillance: "Spies in the employ of the San Luang penetrate into every family of wealth and influence. Every citizen suspects and fears always his neighbor, sometimes his wife." The message of the fourth installment was that Mrs. Leonowens was a one-of-a-kind insider whose strong humanitarian motives were untainted by personal bias and that her book would expose one of the most tyrannical and lubricious regimes known to history.

What the reading public could not know was that the author was an embittered outsider and that the presentation played to distinctly American concerns. Anna was now *America's* English Governess, a product shaped on one side by the powerful group of high-minded antislavery New England Brahmins to whom she owed so much and on the other by an adventurer and canny spinner of tales who showed her how to package her goods. These were the makers of taste and opinion who helped shape her writing and, without intending it, perfected the vehicle for a vengeful denigration of a progressive king and his poorly known agrarian nation.

When *The English Governess* came off the press in late 1870, with a gorgeous gold-embossed cover showing a ceremonial Siamese yacht, Palmer was singled out for thanks: "And finally, I would acknowledge the deep obligation I am under to Dr. J. W. Palmer, whose literary experience and skill have been of so great service to me in revising and preparing my manuscript for the press." The first reviews were so good that Anna sent them to her collaborator, now on the staff of a Baltimore newspaper. With his usual informality he replied that he "always thought the book would be a positive success. Feel more than ever confident now." He would be "happy to take hold of the sequel in the spring," he added. But Palmer's editorial ghosting was finished. When *The Romance of the Harem* came out a couple of years later, there was no mention of him.

JOURNEY TO ANGKOR WAT

The penultimate chapter of *The English Governess*, "The Ruins of Cambodia.—an Excursion to the Naghkon Watt," tells of the author's overland journey to the temple complex now known as Angkor Wat, a trip covering some 250 miles. This chapter is at once the oddest in the book and the most characteristic.

Among its surprises, given the dread of hot tropical excursions that had grown on Anna while living in Bangkok, is how fast, easy, safe, and charming the journey proved: "The rainbow mists of morning still lay low on the plain, as yet unlifted by the breeze that, laden with odor and song, gently rocked the higher branches in the forest, as our elephants pressed on, heavily but almost noiselessly, over a parti-colored carpet of wild-flowers. Strange birds darted from bough to bough among the wild myrtles and limes, and great green and golden lizards gleamed through the shrubbery as we approached Siemrâp." Gliding through the jungle like a fabulously well-accoutered memsahib, the excursionist savored the comfort and delights of the "romance of Eastern travel."

Anna's account appeared ten years after Angkor Wat had been inspected and described by the French explorer Henri Mouhot. Taken to the complex by a missionary in January 1860, Mouhot grasped its importance and took extensive notes. Continuing his travels, he ended up in what is now northern Laos, an area seen by few Europeans, and it was there, on 29 October 1861, in the vicinity of Luang Prabang, that he made his last journal entry: "Have pity on me, oh my God . . ." He died twelve days later.

Mouhot's journals, with their detailed descriptions and drawings of Angkor Wat, were given to his destitute British wife, who turned them over to the Royal Geographical Society. At the time, as has been said, this organization was the "undisputed directorate" of global scientific exploration. Translated into English, the manuscripts saw print in 1864. The Western public was electrified. A new wonder of the ancient world had been found in the jungles of Asia!

As of July 1867, when Anna and Louis left Siam, very few Europeans had visited Angkor Wat. Two who managed to do so were the Scottish photographer John Thomson and Henry George Kennedy, the consular interpreter who would review Anna's books about Siam. Taking the overland route, as she purportedly did, the pair set out on 27 January 1866. Unlike her, they had to travel by foot and by boat, as the elephants they had been promised were unavailable.[7] Instead of enjoying the romance of Eastern travel, they were troubled by bureaucratic delays, swarms of mosquitoes, sleepless nights, a storm that ruined some of their supplies, "extensive desert plains," and of course a burning tropical sun. Thomson contracted "jungle fever," which might have been fatal if not for "the unremitting attention of Kennedy, who administered strong doses of quinine every four hours." The photographer grew so weak that the travelers considered turning back. The excursion took nearly three months.

Back in Bangkok, Kennedy drew up a report for the Royal Geographical Society, which published it in 1867. One can imagine his feelings three years later as he read Anna's account of her pleasant touristic jaunt. Choosing not to expose her, he carefully surmised in his review of *The English Governess* that "the author, though speaking as an eye-witness, paid but a flying visit." He called attention to an error no actual visitor could have made and mocked her descriptive phrase—"moderately colossal"—for a statue little more than life size, but it was not till 1873, when reviewing *The Romance of the Harem*, that he asked her in print "to state the month and year" of her trip. This was tantamount to accusing her of fraud.

The challenge went unanswered. Two years later, however, Anna had no choice but to defend herself when Kennedy's traveling companion accused her of plagiarism and fraud in his widely reviewed book, *The Straits of Malacca, Indo-China and China; or, Ten Years' Travels, Adventures and*

7. Even with elephants, the trip would have been slow. When Archibald Ross Colquhoun led an expedition through Burma and northern Siam he found that "ten or twelve miles" was an elephant's "usual daily distance when on a protracted march."

Residence Abroad. Thomson could not "make out," he wrote, "how her elephants could have 'pressed on heavily, but almost noiselessly, over a parti-coloured carpet of flowers.'" With the same air of innocence, he observed that certain passages in "Mouhot's posthumous narrative . . . read like extracts from Mrs. Leonowens' own valuable work." He cited chapter and verse:

> For example, we find, on p. 305 of "The English Governess at the Court of Siam":—
> "The Wat stands like a petrified dream of some Michael Angelo [what is a petrified dream?], more impressive in its loneliness, more elegant and animated in its grace, than aught Greece and Rome have left us."
> In M. Mouhot's work, vol. i., p. 279, the same Wat is thus described:—
> "One of these temples—a rival to that of Solomon, and erected by some ancient Michael Angelo—might take an honourable place beside our most beautiful buildings. It is grander than anything left to us by Greece or Rome."

Thomson's point was obvious. Not only had Anna never seen Angkor Wat, but she had stolen her account from the published journals of the late Henri Mouhot.

Among those who reacted was young Henry James. Writing for the *Nation*, he noted noncommittally that "in Siam Mr. Thomson made sundry interesting observations—though his statements are occasionally at variance with those of Mrs. Leonowens." The reviewer for the *New York Times* went further, advising readers that Thomson "intimates very broadly that a lady who has recently written upon this region . . . has drawn too freely upon Mouhot's narrative, while she has fallen into errors of fact which one who had actually visited the country could hardly have committed."

The day after this saw print, Anna sent a defiant reply to the *Times* asserting that Thomson's doubts about her visit were entirely

> without foundation, for it is as much a fact as that he visited Cambodia, and what is more, that I used all my influence with the late King, and with the Minister of Foreign Affairs, to procure him *passports* to enable him to do so.
> My own passports, which took me to Cambodia and back, from both the Kings of Siam and Cambodia, are still in my possession, with several hundred

pages of manuscript, notes and translations, made during the journey. Yours truly,

A. H. LEONOWENS.

It was a magnificent bluff. Ignoring the charge of plagiarism, she did not give the date of her excursion to Cambodia or offer to make her passports or manuscripts available. And it worked. A. H. LEONOWENS was not to be stared down. Instead, it was the *New York Times* that blinked, heading her letter with a contrite "AN INJUSTICE CORRECTED."

It isn't known whether Anna owed this victory to George William Curtis, political editor at *Harper's Weekly*, or Sydney Howard Gay, who had left Chicago and was now on the editorial staff of the *New York Evening Post*: such men, like William Cullen Bryant, the *Post's* editor, would have quietly defended an antislavery fighter who had been smeared. But about her audacity there is no question. Repeating the claim she had made in *The English Governess* (and again getting John Thomson's first name and nationality wrong), she wrote: "Those of my readers who may find themselves interested in the wonderful ruins recently discovered in Cambodia are indebted to the earlier travelers, M. Henri Mouhot, Dr. A. Bastian, and the able English photographer, James Thomson, F.R.G.S.L. [Fellow of the Royal Geographical Society of London], almost as much as to myself."

In the annals of brazen claims and sheer effrontery, those last six words surely call out for lasting recognition. They show that Anna's cool authority was much more than a strategy for selling books and earning a living. Ultimately, it was a way of meeting a hostile world and matching and raising its contempt—"seeing" the bet and "going it one better," to use the gambling lingo she fondly adopted. What had begun as a fight for dignity in the Bombay Presidency had turned into a high-stakes international contest.

Ultimately, the contest was for celebrity status. Anna came to New York at a time when there was tremendous interest in trailblazing explorers. In the words of Robert A. Stafford, a historian of British colonialism, "the old model of the explorer as self-effacing, duty-driven national servant" had been succeeded by the "larger-than-life celebrity whose sensational exploits acted out both personal obsessions and public fantasies." This summation identifies with precision the arena in which Mrs. Leonowens was vying for preeminence and stardom—vying *as a woman* in a male-dominated game.

In three years of hard work Anna succeeded in becoming America's expert on Siam and the abuses of Eastern despotism and polygamy. But she wanted more: to be seen as the bold exploring woman who had outdone the whole lot of European men pushing their way into the virgin Asian jungle. Without revealing her true history, she wanted it understood that she had already been there. There was a reason known to her and her only why Western readers were in debt to Mouhot and other men *almost* as much as to herself.

Which leaves us with a tantalizing question: Was it because the mythic jungle was Anna's secret place of origin that her fancied return by elephant was so smooth and swift and magical? Was that the sweet fantasy behind the pretended journey to Angkor Wat?

2 1

Success and Decline

THE ELEVEN YEARS THAT Anna spent in the States, from age thirty-six to forty-seven, were the most successful and liberating she had known. Steadily distancing herself from the "peculiar sadness and desolation" into which she had fallen in Siam, she found a career as writer and lecturer, the support of friends, reformers, and publicists, and the gratifying validation of fame. Out of her traumatic past she created a brilliant new life.

Avis, too, prospered. While still in her teens, she found work as a teacher at Miss Comstock's School on West 40th Street. Then, thanks to the manners and accent she had picked up from the King sisters in London, she was taken on at Miss Haines's select school in Gramercy Park. And then she started a kindergarten of her own on Sixth Avenue across from Reservoir Park.[1] That was in 1876, twenty-three years after her mother had tried to open a school in Western Australia's tiny capital. One year after that inconspicuous failure Avis had been born. Was it a kind of vindication to see the girl doing so well in the New World metropolis, and with its best people—Frederick Barnard (president of Columbia College), Mrs. Robert Minturn (daughter of the Shaws of Staten Island), William Cullen Bryant (poet, journalist)—serving as references? Avis ran the school in the Amsterdam, the apartment house that was home for her and her mother.

But they stayed at the Amsterdam for only two years. Avis thought of herself as English, not American, and she also took for granted that she was

1. Today this pleasant tree-shaded place, renamed Bryant Park, is in back of the stately building erected on the site of the former reservoir—the New York Public Library.

330

meant for wifehood, like her mother. The year she went into business for herself an energetic Scotsman began courting her: Thomas Fyshe, headed for a banking career in Canada. She married him in 1878, closed her school, and left New York City for Halifax, Nova Scotia.

Mother and daughter had grown very close during their decade on Staten Island and Manhattan. Anna approved of Avis's marital choice but missed her so acutely that she began to unravel, for the first time in years. Adding to her distress, she found that, except for juvenile readers, the public was losing interest in her stories. At loose ends, she joined her daughter and son-in-law in Halifax, only to feel stifled by the long cold season and provincial stuffiness and isolation. In 1880 she returned to New York and became a teacher again, entering a five-year contract with the newly founded Berkeley School. The next year, lonely and exhausted, she broke her contract and went back to Nova Scotia and the Fyshes. From now on she would say that her mission in life was to educate her grandchildren. Demanding that they rise above the common lot, she would take them abroad for years at a stretch, mainly to schools in Germany.

And there were countless other projects into which she poured her energy, among them a brave journalistic trip to Russia and a school of art and design she helped found in Halifax. She worked for female suffrage and decent conditions for women prisoners, read widely on mythology and religion, lost her faith in Christianity, and became a fierce anti-imperialist. After reading Henry George's *Progress and Poverty* she decided, like many North American progressives, that rent was the root cause of social ills. "Reduce rents," she explained to Annie Fields (who was not a convert), "and give the poor more space to live in and on, and at once a betterment social & moral will appear among them." When Fields and Osgood dropped her she turned to minor houses for her last two books on Asia. Neither made much of an impression.

Although she was still passionately interested in the East, her last years produced no final burst, no vivifying exploratory return to her shadowy beginnings. Unlike George Percy Badger, her mentor, she was not to have a fertile old age as scholar and writer. The past was frozen: she was the English Governess once and for all, the Englishwoman whose noble pedagogy inspired a king in the making to abolish slavery. That was the formula, and while it made her famous, it locked her in a cage, leaving her raw experience out of reach. The book that could have been her best, a memoir titled *Life and Travel in India: Being Recollections of a Journey before the Days of Railroads*, proved an evasive travelogue, its few honest memories buried under a mass of generic travel-writing detail.

In all, Anna had six years of success, from 1870 to 1876. One reason she faded is that her billing—female raconteur of dramatic inside tales from Siam and India—was too specialized for an extended run. Another is that her devotion to her grandchildren and her many philanthropic projects kept her from growing as a writer. Another is that the doubts about her veracity and good faith appear to have gained traction. And there is one more: the likelihood that a memoirist who severs her roots will find her future writing stunted. Call it nemesis or retribution, that was the fate of Mrs. Leonowens.

American Celebrity

But first came the taste of glory. At teas, dinners, and other gatherings Anna told her stories from the far side of the world with such panache and drama that she made an unforgettable spectacle. Three decades after her death, the Cobbs' daughter could still "see her deep set eyes and hear her moving voice as I write."

If this indelible impression was the natural effect of a vivid and commanding personality, it was also the product of calculation. Granddaughter Avis put it this way: "She was the life of every party, and she put her mind on being it. . . . She would have a bite before going to a luncheon or dinner, explaining that she could not eat and entertain at the same time, therefore she would eat first." When the grandchildren noticed that she "never seemed to tell anything the same way twice" and pointed out her inconsistencies, she refused to be corrected. Instead, she "put us in our places, telling us that she must tell her stories according to the mood she was in or she couldn't tell them at all, and we gradually realized what she meant."

What she meant was that her stories were not just history but entertainment and that performance had its own exacting demands. Anna was an oral storyteller who gave herself to the power of the moment—a spellbinder who needed an audience to mobilize her resources. But spontaneity was not equivalent to artlessness. She would always insist that "language is meant to be spoken even more than to be written" and that speech must be correct, unhurried, and clearly enunciated, with timbre and emphasis skillfully controlled. Behind Anna's success as lecturer was a trained and deliberate presentation. With her attractive face and figure, her authoritative manner, and what Americans heard as "English intonation," she made a fascinating exhibition as a free-spirited, world-exploring woman. Stepping up to the lectern, she became the modern Scheherazade, a mysterious female with a unique past and an endless supply of colorful Oriental tales.

The leap from private storytelling to paid speaking seems to have been an easy one in spite of the fact that men dominated the lecturing field. Following the success of *The English Governess at the Siamese Court*, Anna's friends on Staten Island rented a hall, sold tickets, and cleared a handsome $145 for her. A few months later she read from her book at a church benefit held in the large parlor of the John C. Henderson mansion. A local newspaper reported that the room had been got up "in the most superb and tasteful manner" and that the performance had "the most delightful character."

Lectures, a popular form of diversion and self-education, were a rich and varied world of their own. There were agencies that set up tours for a fee, discussion clubs that listened to their members' formal speeches, and benevolent organizations that sponsored improving talks for the great unwashed. In 1872 Anne Lynch Botta, a famous New York literary hostess, arranged for Anna to give one of the Cooper Union's Free Lectures for the People. Leading citizens like Gordon and Emily Ford (he owned the *Brooklyn Eagle*, she was a granddaughter of Noah Webster) were invited to sit on the platform, and Anna held forth on the "Courts and Customs" of Siam in the building's cavernous hall. Reporters were present, and the next day the *New York Times* ran a long and respectful summary of her speech. Among other things, she dwelt on "the malignant superstitions of the natives, and the barbarous practice of immolating human victims on the dedication of public structures" (a long-disused custom she hadn't witnessed), and then she announced that her pupil King Chulalongkorn had just "emancipated 15,000,000 slaves." The evening, as uplifting as it was riveting, concluded with "the pathetic story of a female slave whose release she procured from the King"—the tale of La-aw.

Two months later the *Times* had an editorial on Chulalongkorn's tour of India and Singapore and the splendid progress Asia was making, thanks to the West. The next day a prominent reformer named Robert Dale Owen was inspired to send a letter to the editor. A strong advocate for abolition,

Owen was thought to have hastened President Lincoln's Emancipation Proclamation. He was also an advocate for mediums and table tippers, including a spectacular English fraud, Nelson Holmes. The point of his letter to the *Times* was to extol the woman who had brought freedom to Southeast Asia:

> Siam is remote and little known, and thus this act of emancipation, though it manumitted the bondsmen throughout a nation of fifteen or twenty millions of people, has attracted but little attention here. There is probably not one person in a hundred among us who realizes the fact that such an event—one of the landmarks of civilization—was brought about by the quiet teachings of an English lady within the walls of a Siamese harem. There are hundreds less worthy of the title than Mrs. *Leon Owens* who have taken rank among the benefactors of mankind.

The letter was headed "Honor to Whom Honor Is Due."

This powerful endorsement slowly made its way around the globe and into the hands of Bangkok's Samuel Jones Smith, who printed it in his newspaper along with a dry prediction: "It will doubtless create a smile upon the countenances of foreigners and natives who were personally acquainted with the Lady." He, too, favored the immediate abolition of debt servitude and for that reason put on record what was obvious in Bangkok: "To disabuse the minds of those who have not the means of knowing better, we have only to add that neither slavery, nor the system of marking the people in Siam have ceased to exist."

The truth was, Chulalongkorn was a minor whose powers were limited during the first five years of his reign. A regent administered the kingdom, old arrangements were in force, and emancipation would not arrive for decades. But there was a moment when national salvation seemed at hand. After the young king effected a minor reform in the conditions of debt servitude, a rumor started that slavery would terminate on the Siamese New Year in April 1872, a date coinciding with Anna's Cooper Union talk. This thrilling mirage—it was reported as fact in the *New York Times*, which substituted the Western New Year—may have been the basis for her announcement. In presenting herself as one who had carried light to the heart of darkness, she was probably acting in good faith.

Was there really and truly a faraway kingdom where lasting social progress could be consummated without the compromises and bloodshed that had stained America? As you sat and listened to Mrs. Leonowens's stirring words, you knew the answer was *yes*.[2]

TRAVELING LECTURER

Summer was the season for writing lectures and winter the time for going on the road and delivering them. Popular speakers found it advantageous to leave the business side to a manager, and Anna was no exception. From about 1873 to 1875 she had James Redpath, head of the nation's chief lecture agency, the Boston Lyceum Bureau, schedule her engagements. Now, if an outfit like the Free Religious Association of Boston wanted her for its cutting-edge series on world religions, she could answer as befitted a professional: "My agent Mr J. Redpath of Boston will arrange the Sunday on which it would be most convenient for me to speak, and inform you of his decision."

Redpath ran a large and attractive stable of lecturers. To advertise his wares, he issued *Redpath's Lyceum*, an enticing catalog aimed at the local committees that selected their town's winter speakers. With most lecturers, the promotional material amounted to a bouquet of good reviews, but for "*MRS A. H. LEONOWENS*" he wisely began with a biographical sketch. He said it came from a letter she sent a friend.

This promotional material marks the first appearance of the fictive life story that Anna would later give to her grandchildren (and that Margaret Landon would deliver to the world). Nearly everything is here: Anna's birth in Wales to a respectable couple, her placement with Mrs. Wallpole when her parents sailed to India, her own arrival there at age fifteen. America's lyceum committees learned about her tyrannical stepfather, her star-crossed marriage to a British officer, the *Alibi's* near disaster, the loss of her fortune in the failure of the Acra Bank, and her husband's unexpected death. The story made much of her hard luck and suffering, but only to show how bravely she met all challenges, especially in Bangkok. There, disregarding her "pain and torture," she "went earnestly to work, not to proselyte my

2. Which may explain why, in late 1873, Smith once again stated in his Bangkok newspaper that "the announcements that some have made that slavery . . . had been abolished in Siam are, to this day, false."

pupil (now king of Siam), but to inculcate such principles as would help, in time, to ameliorate the condition of his own country."

It was the classic tale of hardship overcome and ending in triumph—not only a woman's personal triumph but a nation's collective victory over slavery. That the story first showed up in a lecture agency's advertising circular is a sign of its double function: both a cover story for Anna's mixed-race origins and a shrewd commercial pitch in the competitive world of popular entertainment.

Adding to the image of incorruptibility, the circular stated that Mongkut left Anna a legacy that "the Siamese government threatened to withhold . . . if she should publish her book,—which she did, and which they did." Owen's letter to the *Times* was printed along with glowing reviews from the feminist *Woman's Journal* and newspapers in Boston and Washington. At the end was a description of the rich womanly spectacle the speaker made as she stood at the rostrum dressed in "silk of the oriental hue, yellow, which contrasted admirably with her dark and abundant hair." Did these last words make the sale? A small-town audience could hardly ask for better entertainment in the depth of winter than a handsome, inspiring, exotic female speaker.

As Anna prepared for her first lecture tour in 1872–73, some sound advice came in the mail from Owen. A veteran traveler and speaker, he had a satchel full of rules for the lecture circuit. Sit in the center of the railroad car in case there's an accident. Carry a pint of good sherry in case the train is "detained by snow." If there is a serious delay, ask the conductor to telegraph ahead to your next engagement. On arrival, be sure to insist on peace and quiet "*for at least one hour*" before your lecture. And never give more than seventy-five of them in a season.

Sometimes the quiet hour proved elusive. A letter Anna wrote in the warmth and safety of a Boston hotel vividly describes her latest ordeal: heavy snows in northeastern Vermont, stalled trains and bad connections, anxious telegraphing, a mad dash from depot to lecture hall, and in the end (characteristically) "a most enthusiastic reception." The next day, "utterly prostrated and sick," she paid the price.

One reason Owen sent Anna his road advice was that she had already approached him with a question about the management of her career. It seems that Fields's successor, James Osgood, had been pressing her to let him bring out her next book, *The Romance of the Harem.*[3] Osgood felt certain the book would "materially aid" her success as lecturer, but Anna feared the demand for her readings would fall off if listeners could get her stories in printed form. Her concern shows how lucrative she found the lecture circuit as compared to the book trade. Pleading for Owen's "council and sympathy," she entrusted him with her file of Osgood correspondence. At the close she was "most cordially yours." After signing her name she asked, "When do you return to New York?"

How does an old and influential man respond to an attractive younger woman who leans on him in this way? The answer—always—is that he tries to help her in any way he can. Owen apparently advised Anna to let Osgood have her book, and in addition, as we have just seen, he praised her as a great unsung emancipator in a letter to the *New York Times*. His statement appeared a month after her appeal for advice.

Unlike the female lecturers who wore the modified trousers known as bloomers, Anna (in granddaughter Avis's opinion) was "not one whit mannish." She dressed well, wearing lavish outfits that evoked her life in the East. In her best-known photo, a portrait from the New York studio of Napoleon Sarony, she is wrapped in a shawl and leaning forward in an informal but dignified pose.[4] Her face is composed, her eyes are somber and shadowed, and her hair shows its tight natural curl, with a ropy ringlet dangling next to a bit of exposed neck. It's an image of a strong but "spiritualized" Victorian woman, her emphatic sensuousness offset by the outsized white cross on her bosom. The photo puts on record the strikingly mixed signals Anna sent her listeners.

With experience came a masterly public ease, a composure that had none of the strained posturing typical of male oratory of the time. Annie Fields had reservations about women taking to the rostrum, fearing they would

3. Anna's letter to Owen reveals that her original title was *The Romance of Temple and Harem*. This suggests that she regarded the fatal romance between concubine Tuptim and a monk as the collection's defining tale.

4. In an essay titled "Shawls, Jewelry, Curry, and Rice in Victorian Britain," Nupur Chaudhuri observes that British memsahibs invariably followed English fashion, thus drawing a line between themselves and "natives." On returning to Britain, however, they often made a display of Eastern shawls and jewels. A similar split can be seen in Anna, who made a point of pure British ancestry while exhibiting herself in "Oriental" attire.

violate their private female nature, but when she heard Anna in early 1874 she was relieved: "You will be glad to hear how deeply ~~we~~ I was interested in the lecture on Buddha last Sunday. I did not know our friend could speak so well in public. She was like her own dear self in private, animated by the thought and purpose of the time, utterly self-forgetful & absorbed." When the next lecture season opened and Anna spoke in Boston, staying with the Fields couple again, Annie's doubts faded even more. Clearly, Anna was "making a place for herself in spite of our many fears. I am impressed with her growth. . . . What seriousness and intensity and uprightness she possesses!" Still a spellbinder (Annie called Anna's lectures "narrations"), she now projected a more compelling candor and authenticity.

Not only that, but she was able to meet the cut and thrust of New England's most advanced critical listeners. In February 1874, one day after the talk on Buddhism that so impressed Annie Fields, she read a "paper on 'Oriental Religion'" to Boston's famously intellectual Radical Club. She had been invited by Thomas Wentworth Higginson, the versatile crusader who wrote for the *Atlantic Monthly*, officered an African American regiment in the Civil War, and served as Emily Dickinson's private reader. Proving as radical as her audience, Anna maintained that Brahmanism was essentially monotheistic, that it was superior to Christianity insofar as it made the deity male *and* female, that the Christian doctrine of the Trinity was derived from Vedic scripture, and that "the modern tendency to give [women] their rights" was merely a return to "Vedic chivalry."

Seated before her were the nation's most learned Unitarian clergymen, some of whom were put on edge by these propositions. During the lively discussion that ensued,

> the Rev. *Samuel Longfellow* evinced a decided preference for the Christian Scriptures, and remarked that there was an immense mass of stuff in the Brahmanic sacred books which was unfit for reading; he also ventured to contradict an assertion made by Mrs. Leonowens that Christ and Krishna were identical in meaning, and said that whereas the former word signified "anointed," the latter meant "black."
>
> Mrs. *Leonowens* explained that Krishna really meant "dark blue," which was the color of the robe worn by kings at their anointing, and also the hue of the sky, which was the anointing of the earth.

Reverend Longfellow (not to be confused with the poet) was right: "black," "dark as a cloud" does seem to have been the literal meaning of Krishna. But he was still no match for the speaker. After being set straight, as we read in the published summary of the discussion, he very contritely "expressed his pleasure at learning the real meaning of the name." Mrs. Leonowens could not be refuted. Even in mandarin Boston she was not to be trifled with.

Yet she was hardly a dragon lady, especially in private, where her adaptability, quick sympathies, and entertaining stories made her a sought-after guest. When starchy Charles Eliot Norton found her on the porch of George William Curtis's summerhouse in Ashfield, Massachusetts, he came away mightily impressed with her "vitality." Another time, as she stepped up to Annie Fields's door, who but the author of Uncle Tom's Cabin, the novel Son Klin had read and reread in Bangkok, came out to greet her! Not only that, but Harriet Beecher Stowe "embraced me as if she had known me all her life." Over dinner Annie's husband told one good story after another, and the ladies "laughed so immoderately" (Anna recalled years later) that "Mrs. Stowe's cap fell off as we were rising from the table, and I stepped on it to my intense mortification."

Admired and warmly received though she was, Anna struck some Americans as an uncanny exotic. Once, when she was staying with Annie Fields and a bat turned up in her room, her hostess found it curious that the two young nephews who were also visiting seemed to think "the creature was a part of her weird life."

One of Them at Last

During her eleven years in Gilded Age America, Anna shed her evangelical faith and made common cause with the more progressive and advanced Americans of the time. Expanding on previous interests, she explored the links between Christianity and Eastern religions and advocated for the women's movement and other causes, and as her reach grew she made many friends among established writers, reformers, philanthropists.

We needn't follow all these connections in order to grasp what they meant for her: that she had at last won acceptance in an elite, earnest, organized class of thinkers and doers—acceptance that capped a strenuous lifelong pursuit. She couldn't have had this particular entrée in mind when she labored at Sanskrit in Bombay or debated the abolition of slavery with the king of Siam, yet she would have been justified in feeling she had finally reached her rightful place in the world of liberating thought and action.

The big step had been her welcome by the pedigreed New England abolitionists living on Staten Island's North Shore—Laura Johnson and the Gays, Shaws, and Curtises. Through them, she made fruitful contact with the leaders of enlightened opinion in New York City, men like William Cullen Bryant, editor of the *New York Evening Post*. In 1874 the city quite literally opened its doors when she and Avis left Staten Island and moved in for two years with the president of Columbia College and his wife.

Another key figure in her ascent was Charles Loring Brace, the socially engaged minister whose mission in life was to rescue the ragged street children who were then so plentiful in America's chaotic cities. Anna got acquainted with Brace soon after getting off the boat and before long was an occasional guest at his home in Hastings-on-Hudson and also at his summer place in the Adirondacks. His wife, Letitia, daughter of Robert Neill of Belfast, an early and passionate campaigner against American slavery, was also devoted to the cause of improving the lives of destitute urban children.

Like Anna, Brace was fixated on race, which, in his view, was defined not by physical features but by language. It wasn't the color of your skin or the shape of your skull that determined your racial category but your speech, that is, the linguistic roots of your mother tongue. Was this theory designed to neutralize the color prejudice of most white Americans? Whatever the answer, it fit very nicely with Anna's linguistic pursuits and private sensitivities. One of the surprising claims in her Cooper Union lecture was that the Siamese "belong to the same family as many of the Western nations of Europe." Though mistaken, this classification had the same benign tendency as Brace's theory: it countered the widespread belief that dark skin was the mark of a fundamental difference.[5]

---

5. All the same, Anna never gave up the idea, acquired in British India, that dark skin was a sign of a sinister mongrelization. In 1884 she described the Indo-Portuguese as "darker than the darkest of the better class of Indians, showing a mixed and degenerate race." One can only wonder what she thought of her husband's insight that pigmentation was unrelated to intelligence or character. Even more, one is curious about her sense of her *own* ethnic mixture. Did she think of this as a potentially pernicious inheritance?

Through Brace, Anna met Anne Lynch Botta, who became one of her best friends in New York. Botta was known for her heterogeneous receptions— gatherings at which, as a woman of fashion quizzically remarked, "one met such celebrated people, but also such 'queer people,' all mixed together." In Andrew Carnegie's view, no one outdid Botta in "recognizing and encouraging unknown men and women." She broke boundaries in another way when she compiled her *Handbook of Universal Literature*, an early guide to world literature. An artist as well, she is known to have sculpted a bust of lovely Avis.

Anna's first visit to Botta's home at 25 West 37th Street was an unforgettable initiation: "The slight, graceful figure of the hostess stood at the head of the staircase, on the second floor, and as I ascended the long flight of steps and approached her, she, with a sudden movement, flung her strong arms wide open, seized me, and clasped me close to her breast. . . . I was utterly overcome; every barrier had been flung aside." Botta had read the early Vedic literature and, like Anna, greatly preferred it to the later laws of Manu, which taught that women were "by nature unfit for independence." Like Laura Johnson, she strongly sympathized with the dispossessed aboriginal peoples of North America.[6] A letter of hers to Anna describes a reception at which a Ponca chief, beaded and blanketed, spoke of the wrongs done to his nation. Botta's father, Patrick, had risen with the United Irishmen in 1798 and been imprisoned.

The first time Anna and Avis visited Annie Fields in Boston, their luggage went astray. For many respectable Gilded Age ladies it would have been a nightmare to be thrust into an elite social set without the carefully fitted outfits they had prepared. But the Leonowenses took it in stride, to their hostess's admiration: "They donned odd portions of raiment belonging to me and were as self-possessed . . . as if the Queen of Sheba had made her gorgeous garments entirely their own."

The queen of Sheba . . . The reference hints at how exalted and "Oriental" Anna seemed in Boston. During her week on Charles Street she made many new friends, gave two readings, and netted $387. The visit was pronounced a "perfect success," and from then on the welcome mat was out. After 1881,

6. "Gen Custer was most unpardonably rash and vain, and deserved his fate," Johnson wrote after the Battle of the Little Bighorn. "All this proves what an utter failure Grant's Indian Policy was, and what a rotten old piece of furniture the Indian Bureau [is]."

when James died and Annie entered a domestic partnership with Sarah Orne Jewett (soon to be recognized as the best writer of New England local color stories), Anna continued to visit, though not as often.

Within the circles in which she now moved, a summer home on the seashore or in the country was thought to be a necessity. It so happened that one of her cronies in New York City, John Paine, owned a waterfront property in Newport, Rhode Island. Acquired before the quiet old port became the height of fashion, Paine's place ran from the south end of Bellevue Avenue to the ocean. Known as Sea Verge, its location was as choice as any, yet instead of consorting with the fabulously wealthy set that built the huge and famously misnamed "cottages," he joined the Town and Country Club. This was Newport's highbrow alternative, a lecture and discussion group founded by Julia Ward Howe whose members included Botta, Higginson, painters Richard M. Hunt and John La Farge . . . and Anna. Spending the summers of 1874 and 1875 at Sea Verge, she helped plan the club's summer program and worked on her winter lectures. She was still driving herself, yet life had become easier, and she seems to have been less anxious. A new talk of hers, "Play the Highest Work," suggests where her mind was for the moment.

Anna had arrived. She had two books out that were widely admired, could still command an audience, and knew the best people. There had been charges of plagiarism and misrepresentation, but there was not to be a decisive exposure in the United States or Canada, and she never lost the loyalty of her top-drawer allies. When sculptor Augustus Saint-Gaudens thought of summering near Halifax, Anna was the one he turned to for leads on possible rentals. When he completed his magnificent memorial frieze of Colonel Robert Gould Shaw, she was among those given a private viewing in New York.

Anna was in her prime: healthy, vigorous, deeply engaged with others and the thought of the time. But there were obscure counterforces at work, and before long it became clear that her writing and lecturing career had peaked.

GOING DOWN-MARKET

"Do not stay at home," Mrs. William Justice, a wealthy friend from Germantown, urged Anna in July 1876; "if the *North American Review* does not accept, I beg you to allow me to be your banker *pro tem*. I am not a *large* capitalist but a very friendly one. And what is the good of having friends if one may not use them occasionally?" Enclosed was a check for $100. An essay Anna had submitted to New England's best intellectual quarterly had apparently been turned down, and it was time to be anxious once again.

In 1876 her career went into a steep and terminal decline. Disregarding her benefactor's advice, she spent the summer in New York City chained to her desk; a friend described her as "very busy, writing against time, having promised Osgood to have something ready for him by August 1st." She was racing to finish *Life and Travel in India*. This would have been her third title with the publisher, but it never appeared on his list. Instead, a second-tier firm in Philadelphia brought the book out eight years later, with a dedication to Mr. and Mrs. William W. Justice. It looks as if Anna's friendly Germantown banker had sent another check, this one for publication costs.

Writers who run into professional trouble are not inclined to be frank and open about it. Anna's only known mention of her difficulties dates from 1884, after her India book was out and she was living in Nova Scotia with her daughter and son-in-law, her self-supporting career as author and lecturer having ended. Writing to Jewett, who was making a name for herself with her quiet, honest stories of rural New England, Anna said she had read a book on Buddhism and "jotted down some notes . . . to send to some magazine." "But I am afraid," she added in one of her most revealing admissions, "I am too much a child of the East always to please Western Editors and readers." In other words, she feared that once again her submission would be rejected as being too "Eastern"—too inventive, lavish, purple—for Anglo-American tastes. This was the formula by which she explained the collapse of her career.

As this important letter suggests, Anna was not prepared to face her problems as a writer. Not only did she persist in hammering readers with authoritative pronouncements from on high, but her sensational treatment of Asian materials was growing less and less compelling when placed next to the work of realists like William Dean Howells, Henry James, and Jewett. Compared to them, her way of transforming experience into something colorful and secondhand and strategically remote from her true history had begun to seem stagy and dubious.

One indication that her name was fading is that her third and fourth books were brought out by minor houses. Another is that the album of authors' letters that James T. Fields was assembling as a capstone to his career had nothing from the author of *The English Governess*: a striking omission. After he died, his widow lent Anna's first two books to a young woman living next door. Sixty years later the opinion of this neighbor, still fresh and emphatic, was that *The Romance of the Harem* was "very inferior." In all likelihood, this mirrored the judgment of Annie and her new companion: Jewett again.

Did the deadly charges made by a few reviewers—plagiarism, misrepresentation, and the like—hurt Anna's career? When an attractive public figure is accused of fraud, suspicion tends to go underground. Anna's friends were surely reluctant to voice grave doubts about a woman as congenial, principled, and gallant as Anna, and yet there are signs of private whispering. Annie Fields had "many fears" regarding her that were not committed to paper, and while Johnson continued to back her and send sympathetic reports of her doings, she spoke of her writing only once and never expressed approval.[7]

John Paine had been glad to have her at Sea Verge in the summer, but the shrewd old man kept his own counsel as to the truth or falsity of her tales. Or at least he did prior to 1884, when Botta asked him to a reception in honor of Prince Naret of Siam. The prince turned out to be Kritaphinihaan, Son Klin's son and Anna's pupil—Krita—now the Siamese envoy to America and Britain. There he was in the flesh, a courteous and friendly Asian diplomat "sitting on the sofa hand in hand" with Anna. When the elderly Paine was introduced to the distinguished visitor, he said, "I am very glad to see you; I always thought you a myth, but now that I hold your hand I know you are a reality."

In 1876, the year Anna's work was rejected by Osgood and the *North American Review*, she effectively stopped writing for adults and began targeting a less critical but still remunerative audience. In May the leading

---

7. Johnson had ample occasion to comment on Anna's work, mentioning her at least twenty times in letters to Annie Fields and the Fords. With other writers—Higginson, Stowe, Celia Thaxter, Elizabeth Stuart Phelps, George Eliot, George Sand—she was quick to express her strong opinions. "What a brilliant book *Roderick Hudson* is!" she wrote after reading Henry James's second novel. Her letters reveal an active, informed, discriminating literary intelligence, yet she kept her judgment of Anna's work to herself. All we have is a terse, lukewarm response to an installment of *The English Governess*: "It is interesting, but she does not write like a practised and experienced writer."

American children's weekly, *Youth's Companion*, based in Boston, brought out her tale of a Buddhist monk's clumsy courtship of an English seamstress working in Bangkok. Titled "A Siamese Romance," it was the featured story, and it came with a humorous and slightly daring illustration: the amorous Buddhist extending his furled umbrella and poking the seamstress from behind (monks are forbidden to touch women). Another Bangkok tale the magazine ran that year was "Auction of a White Child." This time the illustration showed an extremely light-skinned mixed-race baby girl lying naked in a circle of dark faces. In the story, Anna is "very sad to think of this lovely white child being brought up among all those pagans," and she outbids Lady Piem, who plans to make the child a palace dancer, thus saving the girl from "a dreadful life." In all, Anna sold the *Companion* seven first-person stories in 1876, with seven more the next year. Still a self-supporting author, she was now freelancing for a magazine that had a circulation of 140,000 and must have paid well.

In 1877 the first of her tales from India appeared, a hair-raising account of a giant boa constrictor and a terrified monkey too spellbound to flee. Typically, the encounter was presented as direct personal observation and prefaced with the kind of dry pedagogical information that tells an impressionable reader *it's all true*. Like Louisa M. Alcott, who sold the *Companion* thirty-two items, Anna had found a new vein of gold. A youngster who opened the latest issue and saw the name "Mrs. A. H. Leonowens" knew just what to expect: a thrilling tale of Eastern adventure that was guaranteed authentic along with an illustration worth poring over. In all, the magazine ran thirty-six of her submissions.

Her way of hyping stories anticipated a practice the magazine later formalized as "the true story plan of 1888." Prompted by the many letters from readers who wanted to know if a particular story really happened, the plan worked as follows: the editors would solicit and pay for brief reports of actual events, assign a writer to work them up, then publish the result as "true." Which was pretty much what Anna did in her fictionalized treatment of scraps from her past.

In 1881 she undertook an adventurous tour of Russia, a nation of particular interest following the assassination of Czar Alexander II. She reached an understanding with the *Companion* and then set off as a journalistic observer, producing a total of nine polished travel sketches. According to a letter of hers, the editors were so pleased that they proposed she "live in Boston and take some portion of their editorial work." Turning them down, she said she couldn't leave her daughter's family, being already engaged in her "future great work": her grandchildren's education.

A few years later, however, she agreed to write a series of essays on the peoples of Asia for the other and lesser youth magazine headquartered in Boston, *Wide Awake*. Starting with "The Hindoos" in December 1887 and producing an essay a month, she did the Parsis, Arabs, Jews, Phoenicians, Chinese, Tibetans, and others. Twelve essays came out, and then the publisher gathered them along with three others still in manuscript, one of which dealt with the Siamese, and issued the ensemble as *Our Asiatic Cousins*.

Anna's fourth and last book, and the only one without an I-was-there speaker, this was her most sober and nonsensationalized work. Offering a sympathetic treatment of each of the peoples she considered, she focused on what she saw as their distinctive contribution to the story of civilization. Her themes were the variety of human types in Asia, the kinship of East and West, the history of religion, and the progress of humanity. Her chapter on the Arabs had this to say about Islam and its achievements: "The religion of Mohammed is high, pure, moral and even spiritual, when compared with the gross and superstitious faiths from which it has rescued a large portion of the human race; and it was the means of a very marked progress in culture, refinement, knowledge and science throughout the mediæval world."

The volume sank without a splash. Perhaps it was too earnest, instructive, and full of lofty pronouncements to appeal to a young readership. Certainly, it is hard to imagine a child voluntarily digesting this leaden book. Worse, the learning was derivative and the performance slipshod, with telltale signs of inattention and boredom, particularly in the chapter on the Thais. Here, soon after being told that everyone who approaches the king must crawl, the reader learns that the custom has been obsolete for twenty years. The chapter was a hurried cut-and-paste job, with two contradictory messages. One, the Thais have made many original and distinctive contributions. Two, they would be nowhere if Westerners hadn't taken them in hand. Anna gave Mongkut no credit for his intellectual acquisitions during his monkhood, when, according to her, he "placed himself under the tutorship of the Rev. Mr. Caswell, an American missionary, under whom he made great progress in the study of the English language, commerce, political economy, right principles of government and religion." In fact, except for English, the king had studied none of these subjects with Caswell. Anna was recycling the same canard, virtually word for word, that she had put out two decades earlier in *The English Governess*.

Yet she herself was *not* the same, having matured into a strong critic of Western imperialism, which she now derided as "the *rob* and *steal* system." Could she not sense that her insistent point about Siam's dependency on Caswell (and herself) was the *rob* and *steal* system directed at Siamese dignity? Did it never occur to her that the book that made her famous exemplified the European arrogance she now detested? It looks as if the internal division that began with her determination to be English and nothing but English, leaving her Asian side to be expressed in covert top-down sympathies, had become more absolute and less self-aware than ever. One could say that the split within her wanted to speak out, and was straining to speak out, and couldn't speak out.

From the outset there had been a fissure in her writing: a systematic disconnect between herself as writer and herself as subject of her writing. Now, in her 1889 essay on Siam, this disconnect took a weird and ultimate form. The following passage leads up to the epochal reforms of her star pupil:

> When [Chulalongkorn] . . . was nine years of age, his far-seeing father secured an English governess in order that the prince with the rest of his royal family should enjoy the benefits of a good English education. For nearly seven years did the English governess at the Court of Siam devote her life, health and best efforts to the education, moral and spiritual elevation of her large class of royal pupils, fostering with jealous care every high quality, every noble impulse and every lofty aspiration in them all; but above all in the heir-apparent.

Except for one easily overlooked detail, the passage said nothing new. Again Anna stretched her five and a half years in Bangkok to seven, the magic number. Again she emphasized her high-minded devotion to her pupils and the redemptive effect on Siam. This had been her life's great achievement, and of course it bore repeating. Yet, strangely, nothing was said to indicate that she, the author, the one writing these words, *was that governess*. No one who didn't already know that would have realized she was talking about herself.

In this, Mrs. Leonowens's final statement of what she had accomplished in Siam, the English Governess stepped forward as a thing apart—a perfected creation with a life of her own. Free and detached, the splendid person Anna had invented for the New World's consumption attained an independent apotheosis. Anna the living writer, meanwhile, was lost in a daze of sleep writing, as un–*Wide Awake* as can be imagined.

Self-invention is a term that comes easily to most Americans. For us, it is what folks do if they leave one way of life for another, and it is generally for the best, especially for immigrants who successfully make a new life in the United States. What's lost sight of is that self-invention is also a self-discarding: a splitting, a severing. We tend not to dwell on that or to wonder how the discarded part is to be dealt with henceforth. We don't think of the old self as a kind of limb that has been amputated, and we don't reflect that, just as a severed arm persists as an insistent phantom, the cast-off self may be a chronic irritation. Just who is the real self here, it asks and asks again, and who is the phantom?

To trace Anna's New World life is to glimpse the pathology of self-invention.

Not to Be Awakened

So how exactly did the aging Mrs. Leonowens see herself? What was it like to look back at the gifted, ambitious, striving girl she had been in India? When she gazed into her most private and guarded of inner mirrors, did she ever see a woman who had been less upright and honest than she could have been? Did she see herself as masked and deceptive? Did she see a mixed-race Anglo-Indian? Were there second thoughts about the path she had taken? Would the face in the mirror have been a surprise to her—and to us?

Since her biographer must rely on paper evidence, and since questions like these could not possibly have been written down, let alone resolved, it may seem pointless to press for answers. The reason it isn't pointless is that we rightly expect someone with Anna's vital, expressive powers to find a way to hint at the thing that must remain hidden. In her case there are two types of evidence, each suggesting that when she looked back from the vantage of old age she felt the presence of a buried self and was troubled.

The first type appears in her passionate expressions of grief and mourning. After Laura Johnson died in 1889, Anna sent two brooding letters to their mutual friend, Annie Fields. In general, the flow of affection in Anna's messages was so steady and unvaried that it easily sounds perfunctory. The friends or acquaintances she mentioned would generally be "dear," especially if they were famous—dear Emerson, dear Longfellow, dear Whittier, dear "Miss Jewitt" (whose name Anna always misspelled). But there was nothing perfunctory in the two letters about dear Laura.

The earlier one shows signs of an intense effort by Anna to clarify and control her feelings. We read of "excessive emotion" and "hot scalding tears" and that she has felt too "purposeless and exhausted" to be able to write. In spite of this lassitude, she mustered her huge energies to sum up Laura's life and character: her lack of religious belief, her loyalty and devotion to others, her apparent disappointment in life, her stoic heroism. She was a tragic figure, in part because her children were "blind to her noble generosities."

Anna had more to say about this blindness, and she returned to the theme in her second and longer letter. Now she insists that it was not only Laura's family but her "most intimate friends [who] failed to understand her." Distressed by this insight, the letter writer offers a pained confession: "Oh I have seen such mute agony in those dear eyes, that I have been pierced to the heart, without daring to offer sympathy!!"

The memorial composed after Anne Lynch Botta's death is surprisingly similar. Although it was written for publication, it too proclaimed an uncontainable grief and drove toward a final summation of the deceased, but only to concede that Botta had not been understood and never would be. Again we read of scorching tears and "a flood of memories" and "a desire unspeakable, strong as life itself, to speak, to cry aloud, to waylay the careless, the indifferent, the stranger." There is an imperative need to declare the truth about the dead woman's "great soul"—to say it out at last—yet the imperative fact is that Botta's soul, like Laura's, must remain unknown, "for what man or what woman shall dare to think that he or she has fathomed the impersonal and illimitable soul of another!" Over thirty pages in length, Anna's tribute was the second longest in a volume devoted to Botta and the most passionate by far: "Let the hot burning tears flow."

What is striking about these intense remembrances is the double compulsion: the drive to express the inner being of a heroically devoted woman followed by the painful admission that no one knew her. A strong and "unspeakable" desire to reveal a woman yields to the stern truth that she must remain veiled.

Like the two letters about Johnson, the Botta memorial was composed in Kassel, Germany, where Anna was overseeing the education of her Fyshe grandchildren and perfecting her German. Years later, Avis Selina Fyshe would explain her grandmother's recurring and debilitating bouts of grief as the emotional residue of her life in the East, where she was forced to learn the hard lesson, especially during the Mutiny, that "all loved persons must be snatched from her." The explanation is a little too pat, and not merely because none of her people died in the Mutiny. Anna's trouble went deeper than obvious outward causes. For her, grief was its own fertile and generative source. Like the Laura she projected, she had a profound and hopeless melancholy, and with it a permanent need for occasions on which to express it—occasions that eased the burden of a hidden past that could be neither acknowledged nor excised.

From girlhood Anna had surmounted obstacles by making energy and enthusiasm a kind of default mode. Her sorrow, lassitude, and tragic sense of life were denied an outlet, so that mourning for others became a way to tap and release a hidden trouble. In spite of her powerful sense of sisterhood, she had not only broken with her one and only sister but claimed that her mother was dead when she was very much alive. There had to be a price to pay, even for the ironclad English Governess. Anna's way of paying it—and in the process rendering proper honors to her own buried self—was through her keening lamentations for her dear, dead, unknowable female friends.

The other evidence of her private view of herself is in Florence in a room she never saw: the New Sacristy of San Lorenzo, where a statuary group by Michelangelo presents an allegory of human life. At age seventy-three Anna read John Addington Symonds's evocative description of the ensemble and was deeply impressed. It isn't clear how much she knew about the author, a gay Victorian man who did little to hide his sexual orientation, but it appears she was thinking in a new way about the hidden things in her own life. Something obscure had been clarified for her.

The dominating statues in the New Sacristy are the seated brooding figures of Lorenzo and Giuliano de' Medici. Beneath recline four nudes, two female and two male, who embody the cycles and oppositions inherent in human life. What impressed Anna was Symonds's interpretation of the females, Dawn and Night:

Dawn starts from her couch, as though some painful summons had reached her, sunk in dreamless sleep, and called her forth to suffer. Her waking to consciousness is like that of one who has been drowned, and who finds the return to life agony. . . . Opposite lies Night, so sorrowful, so utterly absorbed in darkness and the shade of death, that to shake off that everlasting lethargy seems impossible. Yet she is not dead. If we raise our voices, she too will stretch her limbs, and, like her sister, shudder into sensibility with sighs. Only we must not wake her.

According to Symonds and his chief source for the episode, Giorgio Vasari, when Night was first exhibited a minor poet wrote a flattering quatrain that urged viewers to wake the lifelike sleeper and listen to her speak. Spurning the glib compliment, the sculptor replied with a sullen quatrain that was truer to his conception:

Dear is my sleep, but more to be mere stone,
So long as ruin and dishonour reign:
To hear naught, to feel naught, is my great gain;
Then wake me not; speak in an undertone.

Anna's response is found in a letter to Annie Fields. Praising Symonds's life of Michelangelo as "a wonderful revelation of the man," she singled out for comment the critic's dramatic interpretation of the female statues: "I never took in the full meaning of his great bits of Sculpture before, especially that one of 'Night and Dawn.' I am sure you know those wonderful lines, but I cannot refrain from quoting them." Which she then did, copying word for word the metrically clumsy translation of Michelangelo's quatrain.

Why was she so moved? Avis's death three years earlier must have contributed, yet that shattering loss involved nothing like ruin or dishonor. Mrs. Leonowens was receiving a direct personal message in Night's hopeless statement that nothing is so dear as to be mere stone. Anna was spoken to, and what she heard caught at the meaning of her life.

That life had been founded on the substitution of British ancestry for shameful "half-caste" origins. That was the lie that had made possible Anna's brilliant Dawn—her dignity and learning, her crusading spirit, her chronic fakery. Much had been done, but now there arose an uneasy sense that to pass that life in review, to be absolutely Wide Awake, would be a torment. Symonds's Michelangelo had handed her a mirror in which she could see that she was stone now and that stone was better than the alternative.

In 1910, ending a reign of more than forty years, King Chulalongkorn died. Soon after, in a moving last letter to Annie Fields, Anna found a way to articulate her sense of standing apart from herself. "The great sorrow of a long life," she wrote, "is to feel as I do stranded and alone on this side of it."

In 1912 she suffered a severe disabling stroke. She died in 1915, the second year of the Great War. She was eighty-three.

MEM LEONOWENS'S SHADOW IN SIAM

In Bangkok, meanwhile, her distortions and fabrications had become a standing source of outrage, resentment, embarrassment, and denial. The relative freedom of the press that foreign residents enjoyed under Mongkut was curtailed by his successors, and nuanced historical judgment was inhibited by the reverence due the throne. As a result, it became impossible for anyone in Siam (Thailand after 1939) to sift Anna's truths from her lies and offer an authoritative rebuttal. Until recently, critiques remained superficial, often amounting to a stiff official insistence that she played a negligible role at court.

In 1873, soon after Henry George Kennedy's critical review of *The Romance of the Harem* appeared in the *Athenæum*, King Chulalongkorn's secretary sent an official complaint to the London-based journal about "the untrustworthiness" of Anna's books. He mentioned her deadliest libels—the burning of Tuptim, the sacrifice of living humans under gateposts—but he failed to make an effective case. His hapless statement was prefaced with an editorial note that it was "printed verbatim."

Chulalongkorn himself was mortified by Anna's treatment of his father and his wives. He too had concubines, and among his wives were three half sisters. In 1892, when a school for daughters of the upper nobility was planned, he pointed out that "slanderous rumors" spread by his old teacher were still circulating and warned that "care should be taken to prevent palace gossip from reaching the English teachers." Westerners actually think we worship white elephants, he complained, "and the matter of women is the worst of all." Soon after, when a school for his own daughters was afoot, he again emphasized the need to "prevent any European teacher from spreading

palace gossip as Mrs. Leonowens had done." According to historian David
K. Wyatt, "the 'Anna Leonowens theme' [was] a constant feature of all such
discussions of palace education in this period."

A few years later, in a final dramatic clash of a kind one looks for in fiction
more than in history, King Chulalongkorn challenged Anna face to face on
her portrayal of his father. He was in the midst of his first trip to Europe,
and she was passing through London as she accompanied a granddaughter
to Leipzig (for musical training), and so she asked for and was granted an
audience. It took place on 19 August 1897 at the Siamese legation in South
Kensington. Since no one seems to have been present other than the king,
Anna, and granddaughter Anna Fyshe, these three must be the ultimate
sources for the strikingly contradictory accounts of what happened.

The least informative account is the one found in Margaret Landon's
Anna and the King of Siam, where the king grandly declares that "it was
through the principles laid down in [Anna's] teaching that he had formed
the plans by which he had transformed his kingdom." This version of events
came down to Landon by way of Avis Selina Fyshe, the granddaughter who
hadn't been there. Highly flattering to Anna, it echoed her repeated and
long-standing claims and did not so much as hint at royal displeasure.

The least flattering account, published in 1922, was by an English traveler who had access to several high-level Siamese and a Western agent of
the court of Siam. This version, which must go back to Chulalongkorn
(who had died in 1910), was very likely altered in transmission so as to give
a more humiliating picture of Anna.

> "Mem," he said, in a course of conversation, "how could you write such
> unkind things about my father? He was always very good to you."
>
> "That is true, Majesty," the former governess admitted in some confusion,
> "but the publishers wouldn't take the book unless I made it sensational. And
> I had to do it because I was in financial difficulties."
>
> When she had departed the King turned to one of his equerries. "Send the
> poor old lady a hundred pounds," he directed. "She meant no harm and she
> needs the money."

Surviving letters show that, while Anna was indeed given the money, it was
offered with respect and not because of need (she was comfortably supported

by her Canadian son-in-law). But the grossly improbable element here is her embarrassed admission. Not only is it suspiciously close to the official Thai explanation of her motives as author, but one simply cannot imagine this bold, proud, self-respecting woman behaving so abjectly.

When granddaughter Anna Fyshe belatedly learned of this version of events, she heatedly denied its accuracy. By then nearly fifty years had passed since the encounter in London. Ordinarily, one distrusts memories as old as that from an interested person who was only sixteen at the time, but this second Anna had been a keen and rebellious girl who chafed under her domineering grandmother and had no desire to glorify her. What's more, she produced her first brief account of the meeting *before* learning of the insulting version. Here, then, is how Anna Fyshe recalled the scene in 1962 for readers of *Chatelaine: The Canadian Home Journal*:

> The prospect of meeting a real king, and an exotic one at that, was indeed exciting. . . . But what was my utter astonishment when a dapper, elegant, olive-skinned young man in European clothes entered the hotel room, rushed with outstretched arms toward Grandmama and embraced her with every sign of great affection. . . .
>
> Regarding Grandmama intently, he exclaimed, "Oh, *Mem*, what have you done with your beautiful curls?"
>
> "Well, Your Majesty, I just screwed them up on top of my head. Nowadays it is no longer the fashion to wear curls," was her reply.
>
> Then I was presented and made my curtsy, and the two of them had a long talk about her life in America, her work, her health, everything about her seemed of great interest to him.
>
> After a while he fell silent, and then said, sadly and in evident distress, "*Mem*, why did you write such a wicked book about my father King Mongkut? You know that you have made him utterly ridiculous and now the whole world laughs at your descriptions of him and at his memory. Oh, why, how could you do it?"
>
> With bated breath I waited to see how Grandmama would stand up to so grave a rebuke from a real king. But, without a moment's hesitation she replied, "Your Majesty must surely understand that if I wrote a book at all about my life at the Court of Siam, I had to write the whole truth. And the truth is that your royal father King Mongkut was a ridiculous and a cruel, wicked man."

Chulalongkorn would not accept this, and an "excited discussion . . . ensued," an argument one cannot imagine a Siamese monarch having with one of his own subjects.

Regrettably, the adolescent onlooker seems to have had her fill of hearing about King Mongkut, and she ceased paying attention. Sixty-five years later, writing her article for *Chatelaine*, she was not able to say how the quarrel was patched up—though patched it was, judging by the one-hundred-pound note Anna received afterward and the long, humble thank-you letter she returned to "Your Most Gracious Majesty."

This account of the confrontation does not give us everything we want, and in addition it is not without inaccuracies; among other things, it places the scene in a hotel rather than at the Siamese legation. Still, biographical testimony doesn't get much better than this. At every point where it counts— the king's slender elegance, his remark about Anna's ringlets, his polite interest in her North American life, his voicing the painful question that has been weighing on him for decades—granddaughter Anna Fyshe's report seems spot-on. It is absolutely *right* that Anna, confronted by King Chulalongkorn himself in a final direct encounter, refused to cave. *Everything* she had written about his father was true. *Nothing* had been distorted or exaggerated or extenuated. He had been a cruel, ridiculous tyrant, and she had been the soul of honor and veracity and absolute conscientiousness, a bold and dignified voice speaking truth to power.

Young Anna Fyshe was not in a position to doubt this, but her private reflections were shrewd and penetrating: "Just like Grandmama, I thought, nothing ever stumps her."

Which is where we will have to leave Mrs. Leonowens: eternally unstumped.

AFTERLIFE

1944

TO THE PRESENT

2 2

Raised from the Dead
by Margaret Landon

WHEN MRS. LEONOWENS DIED in Montreal on 19 January 1915, aged eighty-three, she was forgotten by the world at large. Her books had been out of print for years, and there would be no obituary in the *New York Times*, formerly her champion. The death notice in the *Times* of London identified her as the "mother of Louis T. Leonowens."

Three decades later, thanks to the dedication of an aspiring writer and an unlikely chain of events, she came to life again. In this reincarnation she was not Mrs. Leonowens, the steely product of British India with a hidden past and roiled emotions, but Anna, the slight, earnest, indomitable heroine of *Anna and the King of Siam*. Its author's first book, it told the inspiring story of the "governess's" victory over barbarism and became a huge best seller.

Born, raised, and educated in the upper Midwest, Margaret Landon had spent ten years in Siam as a missionary and teacher before writing *Anna*. A respecter of facts and a conscientious worker, she was the kind of sober Nordic evangelical who did her best to be perfect in an imperfect world. The idealistic protagonist of her second book, a novel, would remind herself at a difficult moment that "the Christian life was in essence a daily truing up of every thought and action against a standard that was absolute." For Landon, that "truing up" was what Anna was all about. Confronted with a supreme challenge at the court of Siam, she had maintained an absolute and unbending integrity. She had lived up to the standard that Landon herself followed, and in due course she emancipated a nation of slaves. To question the veracity of such a woman was unthinkable.

So it became Landon's high purpose to tell Anna's story as faithfully as possible, with its moral lessons made clear. This project transformed a biographer who saw herself as a person of integrity into a spokesperson for someone unimaginably tougher and trickier. Landon channeled Leonowens—the public, ostensible Leonowens—and did so with such skill and conviction that the old lies were given a new, worldwide currency. A writer who aimed at absolute purity gave herself in good conscience to a program of vengeful, self-promoting falsification.

But Landon was not a total innocent. Although she began without expectations of a large readership, she realized as she worked that there was a commercial potential. After she signed a contract with a publisher, her mind became more fixed on possible royalties, and her narrative became more novelistic. As she admitted afterward, "I was concerned about money since I had two children almost ready for college. In fact, it was the desire to buy a house and to educate the children properly that drove me those hard years during which I was writing *Anna.*" A familiar combination of motives lay behind her project: piety, dedication, a sense of external pressure, and financial opportunism.

The upshot was that the evangelical ex-missionary inadvertently turned the same trick as the patrician abolitionists who came to Anna's aid in the post–Civil War era: she helped put across a bogus story of the redemption of a despotic Asian nation. Released in the summer of 1944, *Anna and the King of Siam* revived this narrative at a time when the Allied crusade against the Fascist powers was reaching a climax and Americans were imagining a new global role in postwar Asia and Europe. Once again, as the United States defeated the forces of evil in a terrible total war, its citizens took to heart a cheering fantasy about a brave and true woman who cleaned up one of the world's darkest corners. In the 1870s the fantasy got part of its appeal from the North's defeat of the Slave Power; in the 1940s, from the end of American isolationism and a nascent sense of international responsibility. In each era, by demonstrating what an upright Westerner had done for a benighted land, Anna's story articulated a developing sense of national purpose. She was a shining symbol, a model.

A PRECIOUS PRIVATE RECORD

Six years after Anna died, a talented girl named Margaret Mortenson who dreamed of attending Vassar College was sent by her Midwest Methodist parents to a quality nondenominational evangelical school on the outskirts of Chicago: Wheaton College. There she made two good friends without whom *Anna and the King of Siam* would not have seen the light of day. One was Muriel Fuller, a junior who asked the attractive incoming freshman to be her roommate and quickly became a virtual older sister. The other was Kenneth Landon, a bright and energetic Presbyterian who in 1926, one year after Margaret graduated, married her.

Following the wedding, Kenneth announced that he felt a divine call to serve as a missionary to the Siamese. Margaret didn't share this conviction and was stricken and tearful, but, once again accommodating herself, she worked hard to learn the language and then accompanied her husband to their assigned station in the remote south, some five hundred miles from Bangkok. Her chief responsibility was superintending a girls' school. Since Kenneth was often away from home traveling and preaching, it was up to her to resolve the many practical challenges she encountered as "the only white woman" present. She and Kenneth worked in Siam from 1927 to 1937.

In August 1930 a colleague brought out from hiding a copy of *The English Governess at the Siamese Court*. By now Margaret had a feel for Siamese attitudes and customs, which alternately charmed and appalled her. At the time the reigning monarch was Prachathipok, a grandson of Mongkut's. As she was handed the book, she was told, quite misleadingly, that the Siamese government had done "everything in their power to keep it from being published" and, failing at that, had "tried to buy the whole edition to prevent its distribution." Taking for granted that this was the true and forbidden record of Siamese court life sixty-five years earlier, she waded in and for the next few hours was conscious of nothing else. When she finally laid the volume down, she was "in a daze, surprised to find myself still in the world of today."

Not only had she found a magic window into Siam's obscure past, but it was the only window there was. Anna, in Margaret's opinion, had been the sole outsider who "set down what she was told and what she saw. . . . Hers is the only private record, the only account of the private life of a Chakri king ever made. All else is a public record, the official account, or, in a few instances, the accounts of those who served a king and who considered that loyalty to him required a totally bland and complimentary picture."

After Margaret returned to the United States in 1937 she got her former roommate to look at Anna's amazing volumes. By now Muriel was living in New York City and working in the publishing industry. Aware that Margaret

wanted to write about Siam, she made a suggestion. "Why don't you combine the biographical parts of the two books to make one? Omit the long
discussions and descriptions. They only bore people who aren't students of
Siamese history. Then fit the various incidents together in sequence."

But Landon had another project in mind, a biography of Edna Cole, the
forceful missionary-teacher who had been principal of Bangkok's Wang
Lang School for decades. Founded in the 1870s by Harriet House (whom
Anna had known), Wang Lang developed under Cole's leadership into the
girls' school of choice for the Siamese aristocracy. The key figure in its
development, she had forty years of letters "written from the inside and so
human," as Landon enthused. Unfortunately, when the hopeful biographer
traveled to Saint Joseph, Missouri, in 1939 to examine the precious archive,
its eighty-four-year-old owner proved suspicious and unhelpful. Once, when
questioned about a certain incident, she "asked for the letter and destroyed
it." Since she refused to let the documents out of her home, Landon had to
abandon the project. In her words, "a dream died."

So she went back to Muriel's idea and got to work on a book about the
other teacher: Anna Leonowens. Taking for granted that Anna was an honest and reliable witness to history, Landon set about organizing her stories
chronologically and giving them an appealing narrative form; she imagined
a readership of a few thousand. Still full of regret about her preferred project,
she failed to recognize the difference in kind between Cole's archive and
Anna's "record"—the one a collection of raw documents, the other a body of
writing shaped for public consumption. Landon's premise that Anna's books
were a treasure trove of unfiltered historical materials was never questioned.

Meanwhile, her husband, with his driving energy and reputation for bril-
liance, had finished his doctorate in Southeast Asian history at the University of Chicago, where he wrapped up his coursework and dissertation in
one headlong year. In 1942 he went to work for the State Department and
moved to Washington, D.C., with Margaret following soon after. There,
thanks to her spouse's government connections and academic training, she
got access to the books and other materials that a sound historical narrative
would require. But her real breakthrough came before the couple left the
Midwest, at a time when she was vainly searching for information about
Anna's mysterious origins.

It was the spring of 1939, soon after the Cole project collapsed. Kenneth and a group of ministers were having lunch in Evanston when the Very Reverend Gerald Grattan Moore, dean of Saint Luke's Cathedral, hearing that Kenneth had been to Siam, said, "Mother would like to meet you. She had a friend—the wife of a cousin, in fact—who used to live in Siam many years ago. Mother still talks about Aunt Annie and her letters from Siam." Mother, age ninety, turned out to be the former Eliza Avice Wilkinson of Enniscorthy, whose Aunt Annie was none other than Anna Leonowens. The two had met in 1867, when Anna stayed with her Irish in-laws during her transit from Siam to New York. Thanks to Kenneth, Margaret now had a pipeline all the way back to the fabled English governess.

Although the letters from Siam had been lost, the Moores were able to put Landon in touch with Mrs. Leonowens's granddaughter in Montreal, Avis Selina Fyshe, who had papers. Far more trusting than Cole, Fyshe let Landon borrow or copy what she needed, including her own attempt at a life of Anna based on personal memories and original letters. Thanks to this generosity, *Anna and the King of Siam* became a much richer book than it would otherwise have been, and a far more misleading one. That is because lying among the precious documents that Landon now saw was Anna's brief account of her pre-Bangkok years. The thrilled biographer had no way of knowing that this had been a publicity release and was for other reasons utterly unreliable. With everything falling into place so beautifully, she never dreamed that the project to which she now gave herself with all her zeal and earnestness rested on a foundation of sand.

REACHING A MASS READERSHIP

From 1939 to 1943, as the world became engulfed in the biggest war in modern history, Landon soldiered away on her demanding book. More diligent and responsible than most popularizers, she looked for every available source of information, including official Siamese biographies of the nineteenth-century nobility. She dug up Anna's old *Youth's Companion* stories, located the papers of early missionaries to Bangkok, read the learned articles in the *Journal of the Siam Society*, and consulted with Seni Pramoj, the well-informed Thai ambassador in Washington, D.C. (who had broken ranks with his Japanese-allied Thai government). Thanks to her husband's connections in the State Department and elsewhere, she saw materials no other researcher could have gotten at.

With all these advantages, Landon had serious handicaps. She was a working wife with a husband and three children to care for, she had not been trained as a historian, and because of the war she couldn't travel to London and dig into the East India Company's baptism, marriage, and death registers. But the real handicap was internal: the sense of partisanship. From start to finish Margaret's faith in Anna's probity was so absolute that she never scrutinized the telltale silences and contradictions. Nor did she doubt that the other side—the side that rejected Anna's claims about King Mongkut, that is, the mostly Thai side—was animated by royalist loyalties and official secrecy. Like Anna, Landon let everything hang on a single, exceptional, trustworthy witness.

A polarized narrative can have great popular appeal, particularly in wartime. And if the opposing sides consist of a bold, honest, undefended woman and a social order sunk in corruption and ancient privilege, so much the better. Anna's story had terrific human interest, and Landon showed real skill in managing its dramatic tensions.

Her crucial decision as she crafted her narrative was to move from exact factual summary to appealing fictionalization. At first, she meticulously paraphrased, keeping much of Anna's nineteenth-century diction, but the more she tried to make matters real for modern readers, the more she invented. She created dialogues that Anna had merely glanced at or summarized. She imagined how Anna must have felt in various situations. She worked out Anna's sequences of thought, her debates with herself, and her inner crises and in the process steadily obscured the gaping differences between her subject and herself.

Landon conceived of the narrative she was creating as a hybrid: historical in substance but fictional in form. For the history she went to Anna and a variety of authoritative documents; for the fiction, to the stock phrases, gestures, reactions, and so forth of the American 1930s and 1940s. Thus, when Anna has a fever and is tormented by "hideous fancies," Landon dramatized her delirium by imagining the sort of obsessive dream moviegoers would have seen again and again: "standing beside her bed" was the *kalahom*, "looking at her as he had the first time they met on shipboard.

There was the same sardonic look on his face, as if he personified all the forces arrayed against her. She would scream and reach out her hands to push him away, only to encounter space." When Son Klin tells Anna how the king punished her, Anna passes "one hand over her eyes as if to banish something she seemed to see." Along with stagy poses we encounter equivalent clichés of movement and language, as when Son Klin lies "still as death" or doubts "her own eyes." Landon's version of the stolen-spectacles story is full of this type of thing. Within a page and a half we find Prang speaking "with a toss of her head," "pouring out a torrent of words," making "a flood of accusations," going "off into gales of laughter."

Colorful and somewhat vulgarized, Landon's fictionalizing mode was quite unlike her usual sober style and Anna's dignified prose. It was more remote yet from British colonial realities of the nineteenth century, and it was inconceivably distant from Prang's Fourth Reign setting. Landon was adapting older materials for a world in which action words were the one best tool for grabbing and holding the flickering attention of a mass modern readership. In a culture where readers had little use for anything beyond the familiar and the hackneyed, often regarding clichés themselves as vivid, lively, and appealing, the careful, exact description that Landon naturally preferred was now at a discount.

But of course the whole point was to take Anna's entertaining stories and string them together for the common reader. That was what Landon did, drawing on her knowledge of Siam, her gift for storytelling, and her sense of what effective writing amounted to. No one but she could have written the book, and no nation other than twentieth-century America could have given her the tools with which to write it.

KING MONGKUT DEHUMANIZED

Landon would always insist that her treatment of King Mongkut was impartial and balanced—that she portrayed his character in all its complexity. But if one compares her early and late drafts (preserved at Wheaton College) and simultaneously lines up Anna's original brush strokes with Landon's, it becomes clear that the more she thought her way into her heroine's head, the more she wanted to expose and ridicule her heroine's royal employer. Loyalty to the one meant defacement of the other, and the result was that

Landon's king was even more absurd and vicious than Anna's had been. The decision to fictionalize was insidiously transformative.

One of Landon's early drafts has Anna reflect that "in many grave considerations [the king] displayed a soundness of understanding and clearness of judgment, a genuine nobility of mind, established on ethics and philosophic reason, that were wholly admirable." Respectful to the point of pomposity, the sentence paraphrases a passage in *The English Governess* so closely that it also conveys Landon's initial desire to mirror Anna without cheapening her. By the final draft, however, paraphrase had yielded to fiction, and the stuffy language was gone, as was the respect for Mongkut's intellectual character. As published, *Anna and the King of Siam* has nothing resembling the sentence.

In its place is an exaggerated emphasis on the king's oppressive and ridiculous aspects. In the stolen-spectacles story that Anna wrote for *Youth's Companion* in 1876, Prang, the mischievous thief, says that when the king couldn't find his eyeglasses "he roared, and threw things about, and stamped and thundered like a wild beast." Landon's rewrite adds a second and more belittling comparison: "He roared and danced around *like a puppet*, and stamped his feet up and down, and thundered like a wild beast" (italics added). Later, in a passage not based on anything Anna wrote, Landon has Prang fondly recall the foolish display of rage: "If you could have seen the King bouncing around *like a shuttlecock* with his face all purple, and shrieking *like a parrot* . . ." Not only do we now have four similes—two toys and two animals—but the three contributed by Landon are conspicuously smaller and less powerful and dignified than Anna's thundering beast. The king has been diminished into a figure of juvenile slapstick humor.

Landon's handling of this episode raises some hard questions about her methods and intentions. Originally, as we have seen, it was Mary Mattoon, one of the first palace teachers, who knew Prang and remembered the theft. Her unadorned account appeared in a book of essays, *Siam and Laos, as Seen by Our American Missionaries*, issued in 1884 by the Presbyterian Board of Publication—the same denomination that commissioned the Landons to serve in Siam. An avid collector of papers and other materials belonging to the Mattoons, Margaret *must* have seen her predecessor's version of the story and realized that Anna's narrative was not the firsthand report it claimed to be (like the spectacles, it had been stolen for resale). So why did

Margaret disregard her fellow missionary's plain and honest report in favor of another's meretricious version?[1]

And why give added emphasis to Anna's boast that she expertly redeemed her wayward pupil? Wise in all matters, Landon's Anna perceives that the girl is "like a colt" and sets out to tame her, and by the end of the chapter she has prevailed: "The saddle was on. From that day forward as long as Anna stayed in Siam, Prang was her loyal assistant in the school." The edifying Sunday school psychology is fully worked out, as is the hackneyed simile. But how could Landon have settled for this in historical narration? As thorough as she was, didn't she notice the awkward fact that the "loyal assistant" isn't mentioned outside the story? Was *this* what she understood by history in fictional form?

The chapter she titled "The King's Birthday" is based on another of Anna's tales for children. Historically, Mongkut was the first Siamese monarch who celebrated his birthday on a day defined not by the lunar but by the solar—that is, the European—calendar. Every year, as 18 October came around, he invited Bangkok's Western visitors and residents to dine at the palace. When Henri Mouhot attended in 1858, he observed that, "instead of being seated, [the king] stood or walked round the table, chewing betel and addressing some pleasant observation to each of his guests in turn." By 1862, the year Anna arrived, the dinner was a well-established custom. In 1863, however, 18 October fell on a Sunday, the missionaries' mandatory day of rest, and so the king obligingly postponed the event to the 19th so that they could attend. As Dan Beach Bradley noted in his private journal, "His Majesty was particularly gracious and had his table prepared in a far more comfortable place than he has ever before had." There is no reason to think that anything went wrong.

In the account of that year's dinner that Anna wrote for *Youth's Companion* in 1877, the king makes a colossal fool of himself. The farcical train of events begins when she is summoned to the palace and finds her employer

1. Without going into the Landons' retrospective feelings about the missionary work they abandoned, it may be noted that their difficulties in Siam led Kenneth to submit a lengthy complaint about the head of the Presbyterian mission. Similarly, Margaret's *Never Dies the Dream* pays close attention to the oppressive nature of the missionary organization whose financial support is vital for the charity school the selfless heroine strives to maintain.

"in a dreadfully excited state of mind," capering here and there and shrieking, "Eighteenth of October, eighteen hundred and sixty-three!" It seems
that a Singapore newspaper had described him as "a spare man," and the
king, assuming that *spare* means "old and unneeded," is leaping about as
proof that he still retains his youthful agility. He is certain that a missionary
is to blame for the insulting word, and he has resolved that his next birthday
dinner will demonstrate his prowess and command. As if such dinners had
never been held, all the arrangements are dumped onto Anna. *Her* king
and court know nothing about banquets, not even realizing that silverware
and napkins are in use in the West. The result is a cascade of mishaps, with
Anna saving the day again and again.

Landon's version of the farcical dinner has two telling additions. One
of these involves the toast the English consul proposes at the feast's conclusion. Writing in 1877, Anna had him declare, "It would be a sad day for
Siam when her King became a spare man." This was meant for children, yet
neither Anna nor her editors thought it necessary to explain that the toast
was ironic or to make it clear that the joke went past the flattered and
fatuous monarch. In 1944, on the other hand, Landon spelled everything
out: "A look of surprise flitted across the faces of some of the guests. Had
Sir Robert, who was known as a heavy drinker, had perhaps—well, one
too many! But the King's smile was that of a pleased child. He looked triumphantly at the missionaries, still innocent of their fault and unaware of
his displeasure. Ha! He had proved his point, he had!" If one didn't know
better, one would suppose that Anna's understated irony was intended for
adults and that Landon's modern rewrite, which dotted every *i* and (to use
her idiom) snorted with disdain, was meant for readers with the taste and
comprehension of children.

Her other insertion, far more consequential, is found at the point where
Mongkut is introduced to an attractive single Englishwoman whose low
neckline calls attention to her cleavage and shoulders. The king is trans-
fixed. It is the banquet's critical moment: an international incident in the
making.[2] Anna will intervene, of course, but before she acts Landon breaks

2. Chances are, Anna got this part of her *Youth's Companion* story from a notorious
Third Reign incident in which Rama III was so taken by the looks of a teenage American
girl wearing glasses that, "rising from his seat and fixing his gaze" on her, he broke protocol during a royal levee and insistently questioned her, to her great embarrassment.

for a long digression about His Majesty's frustrated concupiscence. She folds in the passage from *The English Governess* that details his worldwide hunt for the white concubine he supposedly desires, and to this she adds the story that Anna seems to have told a friend in her old age: how the king gave her a diamond ring that signified his readiness to raise her "even to royal dignities." For many reasons, the friend's story is not credible: it came as a surprise to Anna's own grandchildren; she never published it; and as a widow with children she would not have been eligible for concubine, let alone queen. Still, Landon accepted it, in the process devising a fabulous gift for Oscar Hammerstein and Yul Brynner: a basis for the riveting sexual tensions of *The King and I.*

Mongkut turned fifty-nine in 1863. He was thin, his physical movements were abrupt and possibly awkward, and because an ear infection had killed a nerve thirty years earlier the right side of his face was unresponsive. His mouth was stained from betel, and his teeth were gone. In Landon's account of Anna's first audience, the young woman is so repulsed by his looks that she thinks of a "withered grasshopper." Glancing sideways, she "shudder[s]" at "the rigidity of his features." He, meanwhile, watches her closely "out of hard shrewd bird's eyes." This colorful, pejorative, unfeeling language (none of which is in *The English Governess*) effectively prevents readers from taking a sympathetic or even neutral interest in the man. He becomes a repellent alien, sinister and inscrutable.

When Landon narrated the Tuptim story, she invoked the bird's-eye comparison a second time. There, after Anna has begged Mongkut to pardon the runaway concubine and then dropped to the floor, unable to speak further, the king "looked at her out of the glittering narrow eyes that reminded her so often of a bird's." In fact, as far as one can judge from Anna's writings, she was never reminded of a bird's eyes. This was Landon's image, a way of signalizing Mongkut's supposedly cruel and inhuman nature.[3]

A few sentences later, in her single rawest addition to Anna's tales, Landon offered a less avian but still animalistic motive for the king's sadism: his

3. The novel Landon wrote after *Anna and the King of Siam* briefly brings on an aged Siamese woman who is said to have "the bright cold eyes of a bird of prey." A minor character who traffics in humans, chews betel, squats on the floor, and is "naked to the waist, her flaccid breasts hanging against her flanks," she functions as a racially inflected image of Southeast Asian degradation and mercenary corruption.

"bestial need to sate in blood the injured pride of the scorned male." The reason Mongkut wants Tuptim dead is that she has rejected him sexually— as has Anna by refusing to understand his intention in giving her the diamond ring.

Mongkut had fits of rage, yet there is nothing in the historical record apart from Anna's writings to justify this grim sexualized interpretation of the man. A former Buddhist abbot, he was by and large a peaceable and enlightened head of state. He was the first Chakri monarch to allow childless concubines to resign their position and leave the Inner Palace. Nothing seems less in character than the feral sexual drive that Landon pinned on him, and so the question inevitably arises: Where did she get this stuff?

An answer is suggested by her novel *Never Dies the Dream*, which runs its course in Bangkok and builds to a bizarre act of violence. The perpetrator, however, is not a man but a woman: the oddly named Mani Soderstrom, young, good-looking, very physical, and half-European, half-Thai. Her surname comes from her current husband, a Dane. From early on Mani aggressively pursues other men, particularly the handsome male lead, also a Dane. When she finally realizes that he doesn't want her, she attaches razors to her fingers, crouches in the shadows, attacks him like a raging beast, and very nearly kills him. Landon modeled the episode on an incident in which a "Siamese girl . . . used safety razor blades between her fingers to attack her lover when she was angry with him." But dramatically and psychologically, the attack emerges from three proverbial or, rather, stereotypical motives: the scorned woman's fury, the Oriental's lurking cruelty, and the "half-caste's" potential for erratic outbursts.

Mani's lethal explosion helps us make sense of Landon's reading of Mongkut. This, she was saying, is what human sexuality comes to when it isn't under the control of monogamy and certain other Western Christian institutions. Like the coltish Prang, men and women have to have the saddle on in order to function well.

Rites of Terror

Leonowens made two grave accusations against Mongkut's government. In the one she maintained that his royal council kept the populace in a state of terror through systematic surveillance. In the other she reported that randomly selected bystanders were murdered in an archaic sacrificial rite designed to create guardian spirits. Landon popularized both claims, in the process giving new life to her heroine's most defamatory libels.

Mongkut's council, consisting of six leading ministers, was known to Westerners as the Senabodi and was thought to convene at midnight. These nocturnal deliberations inspired a good deal of rumor and speculation, of which the inflamed suspicion put on record in *The English Governess* stands as a kind of ultimate. There, the advisory council is jumbled together with a judicial institution called the San Luang, and this fictitious body is said to employ the infamous tactics of the Inquisition: universal surveillance, secret informers, midnight trials, dire punishments.

The sensational accusation grew out of anti-Catholic paranoia. George Percy Badger, Anna's mentor, had been exercised about the Roman Church's "secret motives" and "designs" in the Middle East, and her husband had studied Leopold von Ranke's documentary history of secret papal strategy during the Counter-Reformation. In much of the English-speaking world, the pope was thought to be directing a global war on freedom—a sinister campaign in which the Jesuits were the well-trained advance team.

It was that kind of thinking that underlay Anna's astonishing notion of a Siamese reign of terror patterned after the Inquisition: "Twice a week," she wrote, the king "held a secret council, or court, at midnight. . . . Since the occupation of the country by the Jesuits, many foreigners have fancied that the government is becoming more and more silent, insidious, secretive; and that this midnight council is but the expression of a 'policy of stifling.' It is an inquisition,—not overt, audacious, like that of Rome, but nocturnal, invisible, subtle, ubiquitous, like that of Spain; proceeding without witnesses or warning; kidnapping a subject, not arresting him, and then incarcerating, chaining, torturing him, to extort confession or denunciation."

The passage has a typical slipperiness. Introduced as something "fancied" by foreigners, the "policy of stifling" is converted by the very next sentence into something factual and certain: "It is an inquisition." Was Anna carried away by a fevered train of thought, or was this a cleverly designed appeal to prejudice? Whatever the answer, her accusation was unjustified. Siam has never undergone a Jesuit "occupation," nor has its government had a policy of inquisitorial surveillance and control. The evils that come with feudal systems were plentiful and rampant, but there was nothing like the Inquisition.

As Henry George Kennedy noted in his *Athenæum* review, Anna was confusing the Senabodi or advisory council with the San Luang—the judicial appellate court that met (of course) in daylight. Anyone as familiar with Siamese administration as Landon was should have been clear that these were distinct entities, yet, for all her extensive research, she ended up perpetuating Anna's invention of a fictitious composite body that exercised systematic inquisitorial powers. Landon's rewrite (which wisely dropped the Jesuit angle) went as follows: "Twice a week at midnight [the king] held a secret council of the San Luang (*the Royal Inquisition*). . . . The San Luang was silent, insidious, secretive. It was an inquisition, not overt and audacious like that of Rome, but nocturnal, unseen, ubiquitous like that of Spain. It proceeded without witnesses or warning; kidnaping [*sic*] a subject, not arresting him; and then incarcerating, chaining, and torturing him to extort a confession or denunciation" (italics added).

San is the ordinary Thai word for a court of law. *Luang*, a word with many uses, may be rendered as "honorable" or "royal." Landon's surviving drafts show that her initial translation of *san luang* was the same as Anna's—"Royal Judges." In Kennedy's opinion, "King's Court" would have been preferable. Perhaps that is why the final manuscript Landon sent her publisher had "The Royal Court." But this, too, was problematic, as it suggested a monarchical rather than a judicial institution. So what we find in the book as published is "San Luang (the Royal Inquisition)"—not a translation but a shocking misrepresentation of the meaning of the Thai phrase. Thanks to her faith in Anna's veracity, Landon ended up saying what her sober judgment would have pronounced untrue.[4]

She also accepted without question Anna's startling claims regarding the custom of foundation sacrifice. Known to have been practiced in earlier periods of Siamese and Burmese history, this ancient custom was so widespread that it was mentioned in Jewish historical scripture, which condemned it. The idea was to create guardian spirits during the construction of important gates and other civic structures. This was done by crushing living people and leaving their corpses underneath the foundation.

---

4. In her copy of *The English Governess*, Landon scribbled "San Luang" in the margin beside Anna's passage, then underlined and circled the words. This was one of only three or four verbal notations in the entire book.

There are no credible reports of this cruel practice from nineteenth-century Siam. In the words of Margaret's husband, whose graduate work was in Siamese history, it was a custom of "the fifteenth, sixteenth, seventeenth centuries." But gruesome travelers' tales never die, and in 1831 Barthélemy Bruguière, a French priest who had spent two years in Siam, published an essay in the *Annals of the Association of the Propagation of the Faith* that claimed that foundation sacrifice was still being done.

In Bruguière's telling, after the king has met in secret with his council, he sends an officer to the gate that is being built. The officer calls out a name. If a passerby turns his head, he is detained. In all, three men are taken in this way. On the appointed day they are feasted, brought to the gate, and placed in a ditch with a heavy weight suspended above their heads. The king commands them to guard the gate from invaders, the rope holding the weight is cut, and the men are converted into protective ghosts.

This obscure priestly account, dating from the reign of Mongkut's predecessor, would not have come to Anna's attention if it hadn't been quoted in Bishop Pallegoix's magisterial description of the kingdom of Siam. Pallegoix, however, cautioned readers not to believe it. "As for me," he wrote, "I remember reading something like this in Siamese annals, but I would not want to affirm the truth of what is here reported." The Reverend William Dean, an early Baptist missionary who worked in Bangkok for several years beginning in 1835, was equally skeptical. When he translated Bruguière's article for the Canton-based *Chinese Repository*, he warned readers against its claims regarding foundation sacrifice: "We are not aware that any custom of this kind exists in Siam."

Ignoring Pallegoix's judicious caution, Anna accepted the report. Not only that, she silently rewrote it as something she could personally vouch for, moved it into the Fourth Reign, and folded it into her story of Gabriel Aubaret's threatening approach to Mongkut.[5] Or, rather, *stories*, for, strange to say, *The English Governess* has two wildly divergent accounts of the king's response to the aggressive French consul.

---

5. When Anna spoke at the Cooper Union in 1872 and harrowed a reporter from the *New York Times* with "the barbarous practice of immolating human victims on the dedication of public structures," she would have been recycling Bruguière without acknowledgment.

In the honest account, Anna reproduced the cool and dignified reply the king sent the Frenchman. In the other, she claimed that, after being "waylaid" by him, "the poor king, effectually intimidated, took refuge in his palace behind barred gates; and forthwith sent messengers to his astrologers, magicians, and soothsayers, to inquire what the situation prognosticated. The magi and the augurs, and all the seventh sons of seventh sons, having shrewdly [sic] pumped the officers, and made a solemn show of consulting their oracles, replied: 'The times are full of omen. Danger approaches from afar. Let his Majesty erect a third gate, on the east and on the west.'" There follows the sacrifice of innocent bystanders, cribbed from the French priest and presented as something Anna knew to have happened.

This second version of the story, an obvious fabrication, was designed to hold the Fourth Reign up to ridicule. Although there were astrologers at court, Mongkut had little faith in their prognostications and openly challenged them. The claim that he cowered behind a corps of soothsayers and magicians is contravened by everything that is known about him, especially during his long monkhood, when he welcomed Western science and tried to cleanse Thai Buddhism of its superstitious elements. As for Anna's "seventh son" business, I have found no mention of this in the literature on Thai folklore.

In *The English Governess* the two irreconcilable accounts of Mongkut's reaction to Aubaret are separated by forty pages. In *Anna and the King of Siam* Landon not only included both but, confoundingly, placed them back to back with no explanation given. Few if any readers appear to have noticed the stark contradiction. But no reader was left in doubt that people were murdered and buried beneath gates in Anna's Siam.

The more improbable Anna's claims about Thai superstition, the more Landon seems to have insisted on their veracity. When she read a scholarly article about Wat Bowonniwet, the modern Buddhist temple where Mongkut had been abbot and that Anna misrepresented as an ancient, moldering Hindu site, she had this reaction: "[Anna] tells of spending an hour or two sketching the figures in the temple at which the trial of Mae Pia took place. . . . In a long account of it that appeared in the *Siam Society Journal* there is no hint that any part of it was ever devoted to Brahmanism, and yet such must have been the case." Such must have been the case: that was Landon's default position, no matter how the evidence stacked up. Her faith was perfect and unassailable.

Five years after the publication of the British edition of her book, the Englishman who gave it an extremely favorable review in the *Times Literary Supplement*, Godfrey Eric Harvey, had second thoughts. An expert on Burmese history, Harvey had been trying to authenticate various reports of gate sacrifice. Because the latest reliable date he could come up with for Burma was 1751, he wrote Landon asking her to kindly furnish the date of Anna's event. Had Anna seen it for herself, he wondered? If not, who were her informants? At the time it wasn't known that her account had been plagiarized.

Nearly five months passed before Landon answered the Englishman's simple, obvious, embarrassing letter. Her reply, running to nine single-spaced pages, went far and wide for reports bearing on the matter but left the central questions hanging. Her answer boiled down to this: that because the Siamese were well aware that foundation sacrifice "would have appeared barbarous to the European residents of Bangkok," they "would have wished to conceal" it. It was the Thais who "would have" lied, not Anna.

Shortly before this exchange, Landon brought out her second and last book, *Never Dies the Dream*, much of which was very well done. Intriguingly, the first name of her heroine, an honest, devout, idealistic, white American woman working in Siam, is India. Like Anna, India is in charge of a Bangkok school, where she encounters one challenge after another. Unlike Anna, she is chiefly troubled by women who are the offspring of Western males and Asian females. The problems faced by these mixed-race women and the difficulties they cause are partly what the book is about, and thus we are informed that a particularly annoying teacher in the heroine's school "had all the pertinacity of the wronged and helpless combined with the deviousness of the Eurasian."

The deviousness of the Eurasian. The irony of ironies is that, in fashioning her warmly sympathetic account of Anna's heroic achievements in Bangkok, Landon was deceived by the mixed-race trickster of whom she was so suspicious.

To Market, to Market

Doubleday, Doran, the first publisher to whom Landon sent sample chapters, wasn't interested. The editorial consensus was that the manuscript was unsatisfactory whether considered as a novel or as a biography. As a novel, it was "too academically written," but as "straight biography," the subject was "too obscure."

Before Landon got the bad news her ebullient husband had already pitched the book to another publisher. Thanks to his Southeast Asian expertise, Kenneth had been asked to write for a magazine called *Asia and the Americas* and to join the East-West Association, an influential group pushing for greater American involvement in the Far East. The group's figurehead member was Pearl Buck, author of *The Good Earth*. The royalties reaped from this best seller and the Paul Muni movie based on it were ploughed into the John Day Company, a publishing firm that specialized in books about Asia and issued *Asia and the Americas* as its house monthly. The magazine was edited by the capable Elsie Weil. The company was run by Pearl Buck's husband, Richard J. Walsh.

At a dinner of the East-West Association in Washington's Mayflower Hotel, Kenneth was sitting next to Weil, with Walsh, her cigar-smoking boss, across the table. What happened next became a much-loved family story. As told by one of the Landons' sons, it went as follows:

> Kenneth had in mind Margaret and her unsold book. Nobody appeared to want to buy it. So Kenneth began telling stories out of the book, ostensibly to Elsie Weil but in such a voice that he cast it across the table to Dick Walsh. . . . [He] would hear the story to the end, then say . . . "Elsie, get Ken Landon to write that up for *Asia* magazine. That's a good one." . . . Kenneth told five or six of these stories, one after the other. Walsh said, "My gosh, Elsie! Landon's got something terrific there. . . . I'll bet it could be a book!" That was when Kenneth "jerked the line." "Well, Mr. Walsh, it *is* a book. It's a book already."

When sample chapters reached the company's editorial offices, the reaction was positive: this looked like a book that could open American eyes to Southeast Asia. But it had problems. The early chapters on Anna's life before Bangkok struck Walsh as aimed at children, and he wanted them revised and condensed. For Weil, Anna's piety (which Landon consistently heightened) "savor[ed] a little too much of juvenile Sunday school literature."[6]

6. As Chantasingh has noted, Landon's Anna is a more pious figure than the original. In *The English Governess*, after Leonowens is mobbed by smelly prisoners, she finds relief in "the study of the Siamese language." In *Anna and the King of Siam*, however, she turns to devotional exercises: "Anna opened her little prayer book and read . . . 'Wait on

Weil wanted a more sophisticated historical treatment, with greater attention paid to Mongkut's "struggle with the western powers" and more psychological depth and "mellowness." One thing that puzzled her was Moonshee, Anna's Sanskrit tutor. As the well-informed editor knew, it was Hindus who taught this language, not Muslims.

What chiefly puzzled Weil was: "How much of this is fiction and how much is true. If it is considerably fictionized then I think [the] characters should come more alive than they do in some of the dialogue." Walsh was less critical, but he grasped the importance of his editor's point. His advice to Landon, however, seems fairly waffling: "Stick as closely as possible to recorded facts. But no doubt you have to invent or reconstruct in many places. It will be desirable in the end to let the reader know just how much of this you have done, and how much is straight history and biography."

Landon didn't catch Weil's point about Moonshee, and she refused to budge on Anna's "deep religious feelings," as she called them, but she was amenable to the other suggestions. Significantly, she interpreted Walsh's and Weil's remarks on fiction as licensing a greater degree of novelization: "So far there has been little fictionizing. I can give chapter and verse on practically every detail, both of story and setting. Most of the conversations are as [Leonowens] recorded them. But it seems to me that there is no reason not to make the characters 'come more alive,' as Miss Weil says, by some judicious alterations." From now on, Landon would vigorously enhance the documentary record, yet the contract that she presently signed termed the book a "biography." So what was it, history or fiction? There was real ambiguity on this key point, yet the uneasiness voiced by Weil and Walsh seems to have faded.

It was Weil who came up with the title, *Anna Leonowens and the King of Siam*, which, on Walsh's advice—and with Landon's consent—was shortened by dropping the strange and difficult surname. Mrs. Leonowens would now be known as Anna.

Four months before Landon finished her manuscript, its most appealing chapters began coming out in *Asia* magazine. The seven installments

---

the Lord: be of good courage, and He shall strengthen thine heart." Objections were raised to this insistent religiosity when the British edition was in preparation.

included the freeing of La-aw, the jailing of Son Klin, and the king's birthday party, the last of which was so "delightful," Weil wrote, that "we just must have" it.

In one of his most important decisions, the publisher commissioned a professional sketch artist to illustrate the dust jacket and first page of each chapter. Margaret Ayer had spent ten years in Siam, where her father was a public-health advisor, and she skillfully caught the look of Buddhist architecture, genre scenes, and traditional dress, hairstyle, and posture; her accuracy and charm were such that King Prachathipok bought some of her watercolors. In the States her quick, dramatic treatment of character and scene led to a career as illustrator of children's books.

As portrayed by Ayer, Anna was not the starchy and difficult narrator of *The English Governess* but a slight, girlish, pug-nosed innocent, as vulnerable-looking as she was intrepid and principled. Unlike the unknown 1870s artist who dressed Anna in a plain, straight-falling gown for her *Youth's Companion* stories, Ayer clothed her in the patterned hoopskirts that had come to mean "Victorian" and were so blatantly out of place in the tropics that they became the signature emblem of her indomitability. Thanks to Ayer and Landon, Anna now became a classic ingénue: naive, demure, unthreatening, and impossible to intimidate—a Daisy Miller who wasn't vulgar and wouldn't die of malaria. That this frail and earnest figure should vanquish the Old World's evils had a delicious appeal.

One of Ayer's best sketches shows Anna taking dictation. Ceasing to write for the moment, she gazes up at Mongkut, who is standing and forcefully speaking, one hand lifted, the other making a fist. His face is shown in three-quarter view. He is scowling. Her face, seen in vanishing profile, is expressionless, but her posture is eloquent with tension as she stretches forward in her effort to understand, her bosom leaning above the table. We not only grasp the fraught relationship, we feel it from her point of view.

Ayer's treatment of Son Klin in the "dungeon" shows how well she understood the art of creating drama. Instead of trying to picture the emotional discovery scene, she drew the anticipatory moment: Anna staring down the open hatchway before descending in bonnet and hoopskirt. This was an image that *made* readers read, and Weil lavished a half-page on it in the *Asia and the Americas* serial, in spite of the strict wartime rationing of paper. Like Walsh, she knew a smart investment when she saw it.

Still, there had to be economies. Since each chapter was to be illustrated, Walsh asked Landon to combine the shorter chapters so that he wouldn't have to buy so many drawings. Landon made no fuss about this. From a publisher's point of view, she was an ideal author, and before long Walsh was revising, rearranging, and condensing on his own, subject to her approval, of course.

By now Landon had left Indiana and joined her spouse in Washington. Heavily pregnant, she drove herself very hard, revising, checking details, promptly answering queries, getting everything perfect. Once, having missed a deadline, she was "terribly disappointed" in herself. Her family was mobilized, with each child contributing to the housework "so that mother can finish her book." Finally, on 23 July 1943 at three in the afternoon, sitting at the dining room table, she did it. As she continued sitting there, "just somehow stunned" that she had reached the end, she felt her first labor pains. Twelve hours later her fourth child was born, a boy. At the time maternity often meant a week's hospitalization. For Margaret, the forced inactivity could not have been sweeter. On day three, as Kenneth told her editor, she was still savoring "what she calls her 'vacation.'"

But the question that bothered Weil and Walsh—is this history or fiction?—had not gone away. Hoping to settle it in the "Author's Note" that Walsh got Landon to write, she confided that "if I were asked to give the fabric content of the book I should say that it is 'seventy-five per cent fact, and twenty-five per cent fiction based on fact.'" In fact, she *had* been asked about "the fabric content," to employ her curious term, but she still put the question in the conditional mood and framed her answer as something she *might* say. This was more than a little coy, and it also implied that the question of fact versus fiction was of secondary importance. And how were the percentages arrived at? By word count? By fact count? If an author announces that a group of statements is part fact and part fiction but doesn't disclose which is which, wouldn't a reader be wise to withhold belief pending further disclosures? No doubt, but in 1944 virtually everyone, editors and reviewers included, seems to have accepted that Landon's book was a work of history. Within a few years it would be demoted to "novel," but it wasn't received as such.

The machinery of production was soon in high gear. The illustrated serial in *Asia* gave the book a solid boost, and by the spring of 1944 Walsh

had negotiated a contract with the nation's second biggest book club, the Literary Guild, which agreed to buy a minimum of 175,000 copies and hoped
to sell 250,000. It was now settled that the book was a success.

The key review was arranged in advance. Weil gave the first serial installments to an old friend from school, critic Ernestine Evans, who enjoyed
the stories and agreed to review the book. The launch date was 29 June. The
next Sunday Evans's front-page rave—"Harems, White Elephants and King
Mongkut: The Utterly Charming Stories of an English Governess in Siam"—
appeared in the *New York Herald Tribune Weekly Book Review*. "How to
describe this pearl among books?" she began. "Its very dust-jacket is to be
prized." Evans was able to "imagine no one else, unless it might be E. M.
Forster, who could have done so grateful a narrative." Accompanying the
review were three of Ayer's winsome drawings. The publisher could not have
paid for better publicity.

There were no bad reviews. The least enthusiastic were in the *Nation*
and the *New Republic*, both of which felt that Landon stuck too closely to
the facts and had too many of them. Lacking "the artist's flair," she failed to
make *Anna and the King of Siam* "the Arabian Nights tale" it should have
been. Still, the book was "90-percent" readable and "indisputably authentic." That it might not be true and attested history occurred to no one. This
is "not fiction, but skillful documented biography," wrote the reviewer for
the *Atlantic Monthly*, apparently not noticing the lack of documentation
(the bibliography had been eliminated by Walsh). The reviewer for the *New
York Times Book Review* admired the research that had gone into the "biography" and pronounced the king's cruelty "pathological." Scouring the best
magazines and newspapers, one looks in vain for signs of skepticism, prob-
ing scrutiny, seasoned historical judgment.

The most hard-edged endorsement came from *Time*, each issue of which
was scrutinized and touched up by the magazine's owner and editor, Henry
R. Luce. A Presbyterian of a very different stamp from the Mattoons, Luce
"was the most ardent and consistent interventionist of his day," according
to historian Robert E. Herzstein, with a particular "faith in America's God-
ordained global mission in Asia." The picture of the Fourth Reign's despotic
sadism that emerges from *Anna and the King of Siam* seems to have made a
big impression on him. For *Time*, the *kalahom* was "thick-necked, barbaric,
half-naked," some sort of thuggish native enforcer rather than the most

Westernized of royal ministers. To describe the king, *Time* quoted Landon's "hard shrewd bird's eyes." To describe his regime, *Time* advised readers that "twice a week, at midnight, the King held a secret council of the *San Luang*, the Royal Inquisition. This nocturnal Gestapo kept spies in all influential households, kidnapped subjects. It was dreaded."[7]

As the publisher of *Time*, *Life*, and *Fortune*, Luce commanded great influence and struck alliances with people of many political and religious persuasions. When the son of an Irish Catholic pal produced a useful senior honors thesis at Harvard, Luce wrote a preface for *Why England Slept* and helped make it a best seller, thus publicizing the then-unknown name of John Fitzgerald Kennedy. Luce understood what a book could achieve in a nation's political life, and he seems to have grasped the lessons of *Anna and the King of Siam*. On the surface Landon had told the story of a nineteenth-century Englishwoman and her struggles in a small and backward Asian nation, and, yes, the book read like a romance, but at bottom it made the case for an American crusade to bring freedom and democracy to the corrupt and authoritarian East. Now that the baton of empire was passing from England to America, this biography was the very thing that was needed.

Like revenants that cannot die, Mrs. Leonowens's delusions and deceptions had made their way into the American century and its big-time political-policy minds.

7. *Time's* use of a term lifted from Nazi political organization made a lasting impression on at least one reader. Thirty years later, in an otherwise painstaking statement, Landon casually ticked off the San Luang as "the local Gestapo of the period."

23

Anna in Hollywood
and on Broadway

ANNA AND THE KING OF SIAM was so successful, selling three-quarters of a million copies in the United States, that it was translated into twelve European languages and two Asian tongues, Hindi and Thai. Since Anna's Indian origins were unknown, the Hindi translation was unproblematic. Not so the Thai version, which raised sticky issues. The contract is dated 1948, but the book did not appear until 1962, with a nervous and cautionary preface by the translator, Adjaan Sanitwong. ("Adjaan" is a title meaning "distinguished teacher.")

The real money came from American adaptations for stage and screen. Of these the first and perhaps the best was the 1946 motion picture by Twentieth Century-Fox, *Anna and the King of Siam*, with Rex Harrison as King Mongkut and Irene Dunne as Anna. Five years later came *The King and I*, the Rodgers and Hammerstein musical starring Yul Brynner and Gertrude Lawrence. In 1956 this was turned into a movie, again by Twentieth Century-Fox, with Deborah Kerr in the role created by Lawrence (who had died of cancer during the three-year run on Broadway). As usual, it was the movie—an hour shorter but still an unusually faithful adaptation—that reached the larger audience. Sixty years later many elderly Americans vividly remember the king of Siam waltzing in triumph with Anna.

The agent who packaged these deals was the redoubtable Helen Strauss, who met Margaret Landon when the new author was in New York for her exciting weeklong book launch. Landon was steered through that week by

Muriel Fuller, her former roommate, who convinced her she needed an agent and introduced her to Strauss. To the dismay of the John Day Company, which had an understanding with a movie agent in Beverly Hills, Strauss signed the newly successful author up on the spot.

Landon's vogue was as short-lived as Anna's, but Strauss went on to a brilliant quarter-century as a literary agent, with clients like Bill Mauldin, James Michener, Robert Penn Warren, James Baldwin, and Paul Bowles; her autobiography bears the faux-modest title *A Talent for Luck*. But all that lay in the future as of June 1944, when Strauss signed Landon up. Until recently, she had been working in acquisitions in the New York office of Paramount Pictures. Impressed by the huge amount of material purchased by movie studios—"They bought everything. They gobbled up the best-seller lists and the bulk of magazine fiction"—it dawned on her how well she could do by jumping the fence and *selling* all those novels and stories. So in February 1944, five months before *Anna and the King of Siam* went on sale, she persuaded William Morris, the oldest theatrical agency in America, to expand its operations. Before Strauss, the only writers William Morris took on were those who wrote for radio and film. After Strauss, the company had a literary division headed by her, with Landon an early and major addition to the stable.

In *A Talent for Luck* the first of many people thanked by Strauss is Muriel Fuller, who, like a fairy godmother, was in on the creation of the modern Anna story from start to finish. It was she who had asked a bright and attractive high school senior to be her roommate at Wheaton College, shipped books to her in Siam, suggested she rewrite and rearrange Mrs. Leonowens's scattered tales, acted as scout during the launch, and at the end of the process delivered the newborn author to a very hot agent.

Just as Anna's career as lecturer had been run by the top American manager of the time, Landon's financial interests on stage and screen were tended by a leading twentieth-century theatrical agency. For all their differences, Anna and Landon had this in common: both were writers of real but limited gifts, and both were backed by the big-time facilitators. Neither writer had staying power, but thanks to the story the one invented and the other refined and the shrewd and aggressive operators who saw its potential, a powerful myth entered the mainstream of American life.

ANNA AND THE KING OF SIAM: THE MOVIE

Selling Landon's book to Twentieth Century-Fox was Strauss's first movie deal at William Morris. The price was $75,000, a sum she later characterized as "considerable . . . if not spectacular." There was no competitive bidding, partly because it was feared that the exotic Bangkok setting would require "lavish and expensive treatment": a daunting consideration, given the tight wartime economy.

But the war had been won by the time the film premiered in June 1946, and the sets and costumes proved so sumptuous that reviewers were impressed. The first time Anna and Louis enter the Grand Palace's walled precincts, they stand in awe as the camera does a slow pan of the elaborate set from left to right. Accompanying the shot are loud chords of ominous "oriental" music. *Hollywood is back,* the movie was saying to its postwar audience, *and here is what you've been missing.*

The story, too, was what Americans wanted to hear: how a fine, upright person brings democracy to a half-barbaric nation and saves it from an opportunistic colonizer. Drastically altering history, the film has Anna arrive at a time when Siam has no Western consulates and is in danger of being swallowed by England (France being out of the picture). The king and the *kalahom* are painfully aware that their nation won't survive if it doesn't acquire European knowledge and allies and demonstrate that it isn't sunk in barbarism. Threatened by British imperialism and made vulnerable by its own despotic customs, Siam can be saved, but only by Anna, and then only if she clears some very high hurdles: her own presumption, the king's absolutist whims, and the prevailing belief that no man, a monarch least of all, has anything to learn from a woman. Her efforts come to fruition in the final scene, when her protégé, the newly crowned King Chulalongkorn, decrees the end of prostration: "from this hour ancient national custom of obeisance on hands and knees is abolished." An era of "respect for one another" has arrived, and as the court rises to its feet, a look of satisfaction passes between Anna and Chulalongkorn's mother.[1] Thanks to the quiet influence of these

1. The scene is based on a court ceremony of 1873, when Chulalongkorn attained his majority and was given a full coronation. According to Prince Damrong, an eyewitness, when the assembly ceased crouching and rose to its feet in the audience chamber, "it was a most impressive and memorable sight." Neither woman was present: the king's mother had died twelve years earlier, and Anna was living on Staten Island.

firm, wise women, a revolution has been put through. "Miss Dunne," sniffed Bosley Crowther of the *New York Times*, "makes a regular bandbox heroine."

In fact, there must have been piles and piles of bandboxes on the set. The royal headgear and concubines' outfits were modeled on old photographs, and the coronation regalia seems close to the real thing. Actors wear *phanungs*, go barefoot, and bend and grovel. A few of them look like Southeast Asians, and now and then one hears a suitable and well-pronounced Thai phrase. Clearly, there was expert advice, some of which came from Landon herself. Giving the studio some "two months of working time," she drew a map of the palace grounds, "hunted up" rare magazine illustrations of musical instruments, and innocently "loaned to the costume department a box of Siamese garments," including a "lovely thing woven with gold thread." Her "biography" was acknowledged in the credits, but, as was customary for lowly authors, she wasn't invited to the Radio City Music Hall premiere. Remarkably, her costumes were returned.

Rex Harrison, imported from England for his first major American role, proved a surprisingly good fit for King Mongkut in spite of the actor's height, relative youth, and Western features. His thinness along with his agility, pacing, pointing, and squinting all evoke the figure described by Anna and others, and his mastery of the confident upper-class British manner adds to the royal illusion. Like the historic Mongkut, Harrison's king is reflective and inward-looking, absorbed in the world of thought. Even on his deathbed he demonstrates his love of the English language, his eyes lighting up at the word *generality*.

These touches of historical authenticity are subservient to the dramatic values, as the amusing banquet scene makes clear. Here, the percussive Balinese chimes and costumed Thai dancers reproduce the traditional arts of Southeast Asia, but the performance is like the occasional use of Thai: meaningless for American viewers (and also misleadingly pan-Asian). We're given three short shots of the dancing, some fifteen seconds in all, before we cut to the banquet table, where his Royal Majesty, desperate to prove that table manners are understood in Siam, is discovered dropping napkins on the laps of startled guests. As so often happens in mass-market costume drama, the genuine historic and foreign stuff has been upstaged by comedy.

The screenwriters—Talbot Jennings and Sally Benson, with Darryl F. Zanuck, head of Twentieth Century-Fox, constantly intervening—had a sharp eye for what could be mined from Landon. They cleverly updated Mongkut's offer of Siamese elephants to a wartime American president (Harrison to Dunne: "Take letter to Mr. Lincoln"), and they got a lot of mileage out of Anna's determination to get a house of her own. Ironically, the script often broke with history just by *keeping* Landon's wide-eyed renderings of Anna's least reliable tales, particularly those published in *Youth's Companion* and *The Romance of the Harem*. In effect, Landon was the naive go-between, enabling the modern masters of fantasy to update a tricky Victorian fantasist. Landon wasn't responsible for all the inventions, but she did make it possible for Hollywood to brand its product as history.

The writers got some of their best material from "The King's Birthday," a Landon chapter closely based on Anna. Tightening the plot, the movie turns the birthday banquet into a do-or-die test, an event that *must* show the British that Siam is civilized, and thus there is strong dramatic tension in the series of comic mix-ups, such as the napkins' last-minute arrival. Anna being in charge of arrangements, everything depends on her incomparable resourcefulness: she alone can save Siam. But after she has tutored the concubines in Western customs and dressed them in fancy hoopskirts, they compulsively prostrate themselves before the king and allow their hoops to flare open behind them, showing Dunne (we hear a ladylike "Oh dear") that lessons on underwear must now be arranged.[2] In almost the same breath, she preps the king on the utility of European consuls. From pantalettes to consulates: without this woman Siam would be absolutely lost.

In another prebanquet moment, Anna informs the king that his guests will use Western table utensils instead of chopsticks and that he must do the same to be seen as truly enlightened. Soon after, she finds him practicing in private, anxiously clutching knife and fork but too proud to get advice on how to hold them. As in the napkin scene, the king is a comically helpless child and Anna a wise, tactful, motherly onlooker, pursing her lips in a benevolent smile. Viewers could not have guessed that well before Anna went to Bangkok Mongkut was used to entertaining Western guests on their terms or that Thai cuisine required the use of fingers instead of chopsticks.

2. There's an amusing difference in the way the 1946 and 1956 movies stage this slightly risqué scene. In the forties, as the concubines drop to the floor and their hoops flare up behind them, the women's (shadowed) behinds are actually toward the camera. In the tamer 1950s they would be turned away from viewers' eyes.

The screenwriters' plot decisions guided later adapters, including Hammerstein in *The King and I*. It was Jennings and Benson who made England the chief Western threat and, more important, transformed the story of Tuptim into the dark subplot—the leading instance of the Asiatic despotism Anna is up against. In the musical, Tuptim would be a sympathetic victim, a "tribute" from Burma and thus a stranger to the Thai social order, but in the tougher 1946 movie she is a scheming member of that order. As acted by the statuesque and nicely bronzed Linda Darnell (who got top billing with Harrison and Dunne), she is a woman who works the system of royal concubinage for whatever she can extract from it. But then her honest side comes out, and she runs away and joins the monk she loves. Recaptured, she seems a different person: candid, direct, unsophisticated, and with long, thick, undressed hair—an improbable detail, given her recent life as a shaven-headed novice. Thanks to this new womanly wholesomeness and very sincere hair, she makes a touching victim as the flames rise around her and the monk and she screams that they are innocent. In assigning this savage punishment, Harrison does a kind of twisted-with-rage Richard III bit, his left hand lifted by his side and hanging like a claw. He also gives Dunne a chilling close-up of the fiendish look that Anna claimed she witnessed.

The movie's most successful deviation from historic fact may be the conception of Lady Thiang, imagined as the mother of Chulalongkorn. Played by Gale Sondergaard, whose somber interpretation earned an Oscar nomination as best supporting actress, this character is a composite of three women: the real concubine Thiang; Anna's friend Son Klin, also a concubine; and the late Queen Rampeipomaraapirom—the true mother of Chulalongkorn and also of Fa Ying. Unlike the historic Thiang, who had ten children and became a kind of matronly overseer in the Inner Palace, the movie Thiang is a discarded "favorite" whose life has gone empty. She has one child, a son, and like Son Klin feels bitterly disillusioned. Her boy is all she has, and as she anxiously follows his schooling she sees that it is not going well. The wallpaper panels that represented Klin's blighted life in images of defoliation now belong to Sondergaard's Thiang, whose great fear is that the blight will spread throughout the kingdom unless Anna succeeds in inspiring her son the crown prince. The scene in which Thiang interprets the meaning of the painted panels for Anna is quite powerful, thanks to the actress's deep voice and odd accent (adapted from immigrant Danish parents). With a twisted smile, no illusions, and one desperate hope, the stony woman exemplifies a character type more familiar in the 1940s than now: the siren whose sexiness has matured into a saturnine dignity.

But the most telling changes the movie made were to Anna herself. Unlike the historic Leonowens, who was always right—"just like Grandmama . . . nothing ever stumps her"—Dunne's Anna has to get off her high horse before she can become a nation's savior. From the opening scene, where she blithely assures the ship captain she knows all about Siam from a book she has read, she displays the presumptuous streak she must learn to control. After the *kalahom* appears on an elephant (an absurd detail, incidentally) to greet and assist her but then abruptly leaves when rebuffed, the captain heatedly explains how rude she has been and advises her to apologize. It is the first of three eye-opening lectures that show Anna how things work in Siam and what she must do to be effective. Like Mongkut, the spirited woman has a temper that must be reined in. What she must learn is how to rule . . . discreetly.

She gets her second lecture after cleverly manipulating the king into giving her a home outside the palace. Having won her point—"I said I'd get a house, and I've *got* it"—she announces that she's leaving: she wants nothing more to do with a ruler who must be tricked into keeping his word. The *kalahom* urges her to stay but can't break through her purring satisfaction until he breaks out in anger: "Mem, why you not see, *why*?" The *kalahom* is Lee J. Cobb, who now gets off his great speech. Because the king is so elevated above his people, there is no one who can speak frankly and offer sound advice. Isolated and confused, he is in effect "two men"—the one an old-style Siamese despot, the other a visionary leader capable of guiding his people into the modern world. He is a man of instinct who does not "live coldly with mind," as the cagey *kalahom* does, but "with heart," and he is lonelier than he knows. He *needs* this bold, right-thinking woman. *She* can save Siam, but only if she uses her finest tact to influence the proud and helpless monarch. Moved by this flattering appeal, Anna admits that she hasn't "been very understanding" and consents to stay and assist the king while running the palace school.

The third lecture follows Tuptim's execution. Horrified and determined now to leave, Anna pays a good-bye visit to Lady Thiang, who chooses this moment to explain the meaning of her wallpaper. Not mincing words, the unhappy concubine flatly declares that the teacher has labored to no effect.

By failing to give Chulalongkorn the maternal love he needs, she has left him in darkness, unenlightened and uninspired. As long as she lives, Thiang declares, she will hold Anna responsible for the blight destroying Siam.

This stern judgment is followed by an event that drastically alters Landon's book and historical fact alike. When Leonowens left Siam for the West in 1867, she put her son in a Dublin boarding school. Louis endured it for five years, then, crossing the Atlantic on his own, restlessly tried one line of work after another: an office job in New York, a railroad camp in Arkansas, a Philadelphia steamship company. Concluding that America was "played out," he worked his way to Ireland (leaving debts) and from there set off for the gold fields of Australia. After further vicissitudes, including a stint in the New South Wales police force and an arrest for fraud in a wool purchase, he showed up in Siam, where his boyhood friendship with King Chulalongkorn got him the timber concessions that became the foundation of the Louis Leonowens Company, Ltd. All this is nipped in the bud in the movie, which kills the boy in a riding accident just before he and Anna leave for the West.

The reason for this dire and sudden plot twist soon becomes clear. Devastated, Anna now takes Thiang's sermon to heart. Instead of sailing to the West, she hugs Chulalongkorn, makes him her surrogate son, becomes an inspiring mentor, and fills him with liberal Western values. In addition, she acts as royal secretary when school is not in session, thus giving the nation as a whole the benefit of her rare wisdom. Thanks to her, Siam now joins the civilized world, a consummation announced by three brass plaques, each of which, shown in succession, occupies the screen's full frame:

Her Britannic
Majesty's
Consulate
1865

Consulat
de
France
1867

1870
Consulate of the United States of America

In between we see vignettes of Anna teaching and advising. The message: *this is documented history, you are seeing it up there, it was all her doing.*

But of course the treaties that opened Siam to the West dated from the mid-1850s, well before Anna's advent. The movie alters history in many ways, but the plaques and dates are in a different category from the other counterfactual details. They are faked citations, and what they do is change the film's genre from fictionalized biography to something with the word *fraud* or *humbug* in it. "Good heavens, it's a movie, it's fiction, everyone knows that," some may think. But *did* everyone know that when the movie opened at Radio City Music Hall and thousands of other theaters in the summer of 1946? Isn't it more likely that viewers failed to realize that they were seeing falsified history and that they walked out with an uplifting idea of what Anna had achieved?

The movie ends with the old king's death and the new one's coronation, each event a milestone for the nation. Humbling himself in his final moments, Mongkut apologizes for his rages and confesses his "large respect": "You have spoken truth to me always." As speech fails, he struggles to repeat what Anna said in one of their arguments: "True progress shall lie in man's heart." A similar point is made in the triumphant coronation scene, where Chulalongkorn quotes another of Anna's lessons.

The message—the power of woman to redeem the world—was not the same as feminist empowerment. Dunne was known for her "ladylike" tones, looks, and gestures, and her reading of Anna features traditional feminine virtues: she is motherly, patient, and self-controlled, skillful in managing strong men and content to act behind the scenes. All this was in line with cultural attitudes of the later 1940s, when American women were asked to leave the wartime workforce, go back to their domestic lives, and enjoy their new household conveniences. Looking at the DVD some sixty-five years later, you know all that, and yet your eyelids twitch as the movie ends. Even if you know that a transcript of Mongkut's last words shows that Anna was far from his mind when he died, or that she was living on Staten Island at the time, or that Chulalongkorn's early reforms were influenced by his travels to Singapore and India, or that Landon's "biography" was mostly fiction, this movie itself being one of the results—even if you know all that, you still feel the emotions of a classic Hollywood curtain: resolution, uplift, tears.

Even the good gray lady could not hold out. When the State Department announced that an American writer of juvenile historical fiction, Mrs. Elizabeth Gray Vining, would go to Japan as the future emperor's English tutor, someone at the *New York Times* excitedly saw that this was exactly what had happened seventy-five years earlier in Siam, and the result was a major editorial on 29 August 1946:

> The comparison is inevitable between Mrs. Vining and Mrs. Anna Leonowens, whose intelligent labors at the Court of Siam in the Eighteen Sixties brought such beneficent results to the inhabitants of that small country and which were so well and skillfully recounted by Margaret Landon in her novel, "Anna and the King of Siam," and even more widely publicized in the motion picture of the same name. Anna Leonowens' main task, as will be that of Elizabeth Vining, was to instruct the young Crown Prince. Crown Prince Chulalongkorn of Siam was an apt pupil, not only of English but of burning faith in democracy and the dignity of the human being. When he became King one of his first acts was to free the Siamese slaves. Another was to abolish the age-old practice of prostration before his royal presence. . . . If Elizabeth Vining achieves half that success with Prince Tsugu she can consider her assignment a brilliant success.

To some of this no one could take exception. Chulalongkorn ended prostration at the first opportunity, "novel" is definitely a better term than "biography" for Landon's book, and Vining clearly succeeded (also, she apparently addressed the emperor-to-be as Jimmy). But it isn't the case that one of the king's first acts was to free Siam's slaves. The problem with the editorial is its disregard of the gap between fiction and history. There is real credulity here, a lapse in judgment and intelligence. If Landon's *Anna and the King of Siam* is rightly seen as a novel, how can its treatment of history have any authority? Why is the novel said to "recount" events rather than, for example, "imagine" them, and why is the film said to have (ominous word) "publicized" those events rather than "dramatized" them?

To judge from this editorial and the contemporary reviews of *Anna and the King of Siam* (book and movie both), readers and viewers were *not* able to keep in mind the line between fact and fiction. The response was simple and unsophisticated, even at the *Times*, whose editorial room seems to have

digested all those fake brass plaques. What that room decided in all innocence was that the Anna story really happened and that it formed a grand
historic precedent for what the United States (the one nation armed with
nuclear weapons) could now accomplish in the postwar world.

Making sense of these delusions and infatuations would take us far
afield—to the power of film to shape opinion; the use of publicity and propaganda in the USSR, Nazi Germany, and 1940s America; and the line of
filmmakers that includes D. W. Griffith, Emil Ganz, Sergei Eisenstein, Leni
Riefenstahl, and Frank Capra. Here, there is room for little more than the
short answer, namely, that, like many other American motion pictures, *Anna
and the King of Siam* was a piece of *democratic* propaganda, democratic in
two senses: it made you prefer equality over autocracy, and instead of orig-
inating in a government office it was fashioned by an entertainment business that prospered by appealing to the opinions and ideals of its audience.
In that sense, the movie represented a people—a poorly informed and now
extremely powerful people—talking to itself. It set forth a flattering and unreal model of what America could be and do in the world now that the Axis
was defeated and Europe's colonial empires were starting to disintegrate.

The reason the *Times* abandoned critical judgment was that *Anna and
the King of Siam* was a subtle and skillful piece of propaganda. Just as Leonowens had done some seventy years earlier in books and lectures, the film
told Americans what they wanted to believe. In authoritarian regimes, propaganda is created by secret central bureaus. In a market-based democracy,
it is created by big-time, image-based media whose inner operations are
proprietary and thus also secret. No doubt the latter is better than the former, better politically, but both forms of propaganda dull the capacity to
distinguish truth from lies.

For Americans of the mid-1940s the story of how Anna saved Southeast
Asia's one uncolonized nation was irresistible. With the United States turning from its isolationist past to an interventionist future, the Anna story
became an implicit and inspiring symbol of what a can-do people can do.
And what *did* we do? Many of our interventions, such as Vining in Japan
and the Marshall Plan in Europe, were obviously beneficial, while others—
in Iran, Guatemala, Vietnam, Iraq—are now seen as cases of stupid, malignant bungling. Power, idealism, and ignorance have been shown to be an
extremely dangerous combination.

The King and I

Sitting in the first audiences for *Anna and the King of Siam* was an odd couple who would form the bridge between past and future. The older of the two, Mary P. Aldrich, a stiffly conservative woman in her eighties who disapproved of show business, donated to missionaries, and rarely left her small-town Massachusetts home, had read *The English Governess at the Siamese Court* as a young girl and been "fascinated." Next to her sat Gertrude Lawrence, the English comedienne with a large jutting nose, radiant smile, buoyant stride, and genius for magnetic improvisation. In the words of an understudy, Lawrence possessed "an inexhaustible fund of nervous vitality. Her sole mainstays were guts and gallantry and a driving determination to succeed." Or as Harold Cohen put it in a famous quip, "Vitamins should take Gertrude Lawrence." A couple of decades earlier she had been starring opposite Noël Coward in *London Calling!* and *Private Lives* and enjoying a racy life in the West End theater world. Now, living and working in the States, she was married to Aldrich's son, a theatrical producer.

"Deeply intrigued" by the unusual movie, Lawrence realized that if it were converted into a musical play, it would make a terrific vehicle for the later, soberer phase of her career. She read Landon's book and, like her mother-in-law, was so "impressed by its values" that she got her agent, Fanny Holtzmann, to find out about the rights. Holtzmann talked to Landon's agent, Helen Strauss, who then approached Broadway's leading production team for musical plays, Richard Rodgers and Oscar Hammerstein II. Strongly averse to propositions from actors seeking vehicles, they had always insisted on having full control from the outset and were not enthusiastic. In addition, Rodgers was reluctant to compose tunes for someone with Lawrence's limited vocal range and habit of singing flat. But she had acquired the rights, and a private screening of the Harrison-Dunne film overcame all doubts and reservations.

By then, 1950, Rodgers and Hammerstein's string of successes— *Oklahoma!*, *Carousel*, *South Pacific*—had transformed musical theater from a scaffolding for tunes and patter into drama that took itself seriously, with the lyric numbers an integral part of the story. Before the two men teamed up, Rodgers had worked with the gay, alcoholic, seriously unstable, and brilliantly witty Lorenz Hart, whose writing had a sleek, modern feel. Hammerstein brought something sunnier and more hopeful and appealed to a broader demographic. Rodgers was wary of his traditionalism—his leanings toward "a romantic, florid kind of theatre, more operetta than musical comedy." But the new combination of composer and lyricist succeeded in bringing a fresh tone to musical theater—an egalitarian optimism that triumphed over crippling fears and prejudices.

Politically, both men were liberals who favored a free, open, mixed society. During the eight years in which they reinvented musical comedy— from 1943 and *Oklahoma!* to 1951 and *The King and I*—liberal Democrats held the White House, and federal policy favored progressive taxation, greater social equality, a chance for "the little guy." Rodgers was not a crusader, but he had principles: in the 1952 presidential race he let it be known that he supported the Democrat, Adlai Stevenson, after Dwight Eisenhower refused to take a stand against Joseph McCarthy.

The King and I was a very big deal, and it made Anna's story known as nothing else. Opening at the St. James Theatre on 29 March 1951, it ran for three years. In 1956 Twentieth Century-Fox turned it into a motion picture that did extremely well at the box office and garnered several Oscars, including best actor for Yul Brynner and costumes for Irene Sharaff. There were successful revivals on Broadway in 1977 and again in 1985, the latter closing only when Brynner, a heavy lifelong smoker, died of lung and bone cancer.

The great and lasting delight of *The King and I* may prove to be the ballet by Jerome Robbins, "The Small House of Uncle Thomas," with music by Trude Rittmann. Based on the novel Anna had given Son Klin (the concubine who signed letters as Harriet Beecher Stowe), this dance-drama is a ritualized depiction from a supposedly Thai point of view of Eliza's daring escape from slave catchers across the Ohio River. Presented as an after-dinner entertainment for English guests, it is the creation of Tuptim, who thereby gives voice to her sense of captivity on the very night she plans to escape with her lover. As she reads the explanatory script, the chorus chants, "Run, Eliza, run," and Eliza hops her pantomimic escape, holding her arms and one foot in a way that suggests the positions of classical Siamese and Cambodian dance. Pursuing her are King Simon of Legree and his "scientific dogs," who gather, dissolve, and re-form in a way that evokes the ensemble movements of Western ballet. It's a classic and riveting chase scene, and as the pitch rises and the tempo increases and the dogs leap and the runaway becomes desperate, Buddha intervenes from on high. Acting like the miracle-working Jewish-Christian deity, he turns the river to ice so that Eliza can hop across. He sends an "angel" to guide her. To screen her from pursuers, he makes "snow," a concept Anna had earlier introduced to her skeptical pupils. When Simon of Legree follows onto the ice, Buddha makes it melt, and Simon sinks beneath the waves. Cutaway shots of Mongkut frowning show that he grasps the implications. It is "immoral for king to drown," he will tell Anna later.

As an example of Southeast Asian dance, the ballet is utterly inauthentic, but for all that it is one of the triumphs of American musical theater, a combination of disparate elements possible only on Broadway. For its music, Rodgers didn't want what he termed "tinkling bells, high nasal strings and percussive gongs"—sounds a New York audience would not find "attractive." He was thinking of the Balinese music that accompanies the Siamese theatricals in the Harrison-Dunne movie. That sort of thing, the real thing (real in Bali at least), was not what he wanted, and he urged Robbins to take a "comic" approach to the choreography and not worry whether the movements were genuinely Thai or not. The goal was a pleasing illusion.

What Robbins and the ballet team came up with put a pan-Asian veneer on a proven American template. It was New York fusion, a synthetic global creation nicely illustrated by the ballerina who danced Eliza, Yuriko. A Californian of Japanese descent, Yuriko had spent part of her childhood with family ties in Japan. At age nine she was placed with a dancing teacher who, for three months of the year, took her disciplined troupe on tour, staging "European" dances for Japanese audiences. Rather than having an ordinary girlhood at home, Yuriko was rigorously professionalized from early on. One is reminded of the court dancers in old Bangkok or Phnom Penh and the well-trained nautch girls that Anna saw in Bombay. In an interview years later, Yuriko remembered her girlhood as a "very lonely life." She cried at night, didn't feel Japanese, wouldn't wear a kimono, and "maintained [her]self as an American." After her return to the States and the inevitable wartime hardships, including government internment, she was able to move to New York City by 1945. Her talent and training got her into the Martha Graham Company, where she performed in major dances: *American Document*, *Primitive Mysteries*, and *Appalachian Spring*. Robbins liked her work and urged her to audition for Eliza, her first job on Broadway.

But the outstanding example of New York fusion in *The King and I* is surely Yul Brynner himself, the actor whose interpretation of King Mongkut came to define the musical. Initially, when Rodgers and Hammerstein got to work, the play was thought of as starring Lawrence. Her priority is obvious in the playbill and the original jacket of the Decca cast recording, both of which gave her top billing. But billing isn't the whole story. In the fully realized musical, as one reviewer immediately saw, "Miss Lawrence is given no room for the flamboyant mannerism which is her real stock in trade, but must hold the fort for propriety while Mr. Brynner has all the fun."

When auditions opened for the male lead, Rodgers recalled,

> the first candidate who walked out from the wings was a bald, muscular fellow with a bony, Oriental face. He was dressed casually and carried a guitar. . . . He scowled in our direction, sat down on the stage and crossed his legs, tailor-fashion, then plunked one whacking chord on his guitar and began to howl in a strange language that no one could understand. He looked savage, he sounded savage, and there was no denying that he projected a feeling of controlled ferocity. When he read for us, we again were impressed by his authority and conviction. Oscar and I looked at each other and nodded.

The strange language may have been Romany, a bit of which Brynner had picked up in the thirties while living in Paris. A product of conditions few Americans could imagine, he invented fanciful versions of his history after coming to the States in 1941; like Anna, he understood the value of a mysterious past. The apparent facts, given in his son's biography, are that he was born in Vladivostok of a Russian mother and a father who was half Mongolian Russian and half German Swiss. After they escaped to Paris, their unruly son hung out with the Dimitrievitches, a family of Moscow Gypsies who ran a nightclub. These professional entertainers inspired the boy with an ethical code, a passion for performance and illusion, and a bravura masculinity. "When you play for a crowd," Ivan Dimitrievitch told him before his first performance at age fourteen, "lead with your cock"— exactly what Brynner was doing when he landed his career-making role in 1950.

The "savage" look and "controlled ferocity" sum up the differences between his interpretation of the king and Rex Harrison's. The latter had a
trained and expressive face and a touch of farce in his dignity, but Brynner
wore so much makeup that his face became a mask and his character that
of an authoritarian who dominates by instinct and force of will. He looked
cruel, his anger was explosive, he stalked, whirled, and pointed, and each
stylized movement had a sharply etched meaning you could read from the
back row. Reviewers likened him to a panther and other large predators. "It
is Brynner who gives the movie its animal spark," said the *New York Herald
Tribune*; "he is every inch an Oriental king, from the eloquent fingers that
punctuate his commands to the sinewy legs and bare feet with which he
stalks about the palace, like an impatient leopard."

This larger-than-life male potency was the beating heart of *The King
and I*. As embodied by Brynner, Oriental barbarism was less a matter of
age-old autocracy than the stark physical power of a man's body: shaven
head, glaring eyes, long cruel eyebrows, curling lips, sculpted torso, a right
arm that drives each statement home, and an upright index finger that com-
pels fear and obedience. This, the play said, this superenergized phallic
authoritarianism, *this* is the essence of the despotic East.

The irony is that Brynner's king had nothing in common with Siamese
tradition and everything to do with a new hypermasculine American type
made visible four years earlier by Marlon Brando in *A Streetcar Named
Desire*. Just as Brynner's Mongkut hates being called a barbarian, Brando's
Stanley Kowalski (as Harold Clurman shrewdly observed at the time)
"quotes Huey Long, who assure[s] him that 'every man is a king.'" Clurman's review went on to note that Kowalski's "mentality provides the soil for
fascism, viewed not as a political movement but as a state of being." The
result is a type of manhood that, hiding its inner divisions, presents itself
in tight shirts, conspicuous biceps, tough speech, and contemptuous attitudes. When we first see Brynner's Mongkut on his throne, he is wearing a
long-sleeved, form-hugging silk shirt with white-on-black polka dots, and
he is arrogance personified. This, we see at once, is the real thing, the male
beast in his Eastern lair. What we don't see is that we are lost in fantasy, that
Brynner is utterly unlike the thin, aging, intellectual monk who became the
fourth Chakri king, and that his act travesties the aristocratic Thai ideal of
quiet, courteous manners. Whenever he orders wives and slaves to do this

or that, what he is really doing is commandeering Asian materials to vivify a new American ideal type.

Looking at a DVD of the movie over half a century later, one sees with a shock that Brynner (an "avid Democrat," as his son pointed out) also commandeered images of Fascism. When the *kalahom* meets Anna's boat, his escort is a tight-formation drill team whose blue, flapping headdresses flow down the men's necks like flaring Nazi helmets. Affixed to the top is a weird golden Teutonic spike. After Tuptim has been captured by what are termed "secret police," she is brought on stage by the same guard. But the most insistent reference to Fascism is Brynner's look and manner. Consciously or not, his forceful authoritarianism revived Mussolini's close-cropped hair and pompous strut and square-jawed harangues—Mussolini turned into a preposterous Asian dictator for the American stage. *The King and I* was not a Fascist play, far from it, but it was grounded in Fascism's psychosexual appeal—the quality that Sylvia Plath was to express a few years later with her full-voiced madwoman extremism:

> Every woman adores a Fascist,
> The boot in the face, the brute
> Brute heart of a brute like you.

Early in development, it is said, Brynner convinced Lawrence that they should play their parts as "potential lovers," with a sexual tension that cannot find relief. The king *must* be a brute, and the high-toned Victorian teacher must find his brutality repellent *and* alluring.[3]

The musical's name for that allure is "Something Wonderful," the title of the song that Thiang (played by Dorothy Sarnoff) sings in praise of her liege-lord. Her purpose is to persuade Anna to stay in Siam and do what she can to guide the king, who needs and deserves her faithful service. To that degree, the song corresponds to Lee J. Cobb's vehement "Why you not see, *why?*" speech in the Harrison-Dunne film. Thiang sings:

3. According to Brynner's son, when *The King and I* was revived in 1977 and busloads of suburban women attended the Wednesday matinee, the atmosphere in the Uris Theatre was "positively lubricious." If that was the case, the author, who took in a matinee the following year, failed to notice it. But sniffling was audible in the final scene, and when the house lights came on, handkerchiefs were being tucked away.

This is a man who thinks with his heart,
His heart is not always wise.
This is a man who stumbles and falls,
But this is a man who tries.

The song assures Anna that no matter how badly he slips he always redeems himself by doing "something wonderful." The two words are archetypal Hammerstein, and the musical phrase devised by Rodgers fits them to perfection: intensely aspirational, rising a full step on the accented syllables.

Of course, something wonderful is something erotic. In the film the scene takes place in Anna's boudoir, with camera and actors positioned in such a way that her large white canopy bed is the salient background object. With her low-cut white nightgown and her long red hair combed out so that it falls on her shoulders, she is the image of a bride arrayed for her bedding. And what she is hearing is that no woman can or should resist the flawed but matchless monarch. This is seduction by a surrogate, and at scene's end, when Anna modestly nods yes, she will stay, we see that the seduction has succeeded.

From now on, each stage of her growing attraction to the king is accompanied by an orchestral setting of Thiang's song. At the end of act 1, when the king kneels in front of the assembled cast and implores Buddha to let the banquet for the haughty English turn out well, promising in return to give Anna the house she has been pleading for, her face swivels toward her employer the instant he says this, and we hear the music for "Something Wonderful." The album for the Decca cast recording has a photo of the business, showing Lawrence in open-mouthed astonishment as she throws a passionately grateful look at Brynner.

In act 2, after the banquet proves successful, we hear the same orchestral strain when the king removes a ring from his little finger and hands it to Anna, who takes it in confusion ("I don't know what to say"). A ring means an engagement and a promised sexual union, yet we know that Anna will never join the harem.

The King and I is about a battle between the sexes that the woman *must* win, no matter how conflicted her feelings. The battle reaches its crisis when the king prepares to lash Tuptim with a (ridiculously long) whip. Anna declares that this brutal act will undo everything he has achieved and prove that he is a mere barbarian after all. Brynner lifts his whip hand only to find that he can't use it—he can't defy the Englishwoman he has come to admire and love. He crumples and, clutching his stomach, staggers off-stage. Without malice and acting on principle, Anna has dealt him a humiliation from which he cannot recover. "You have destroyed *king*," the *kalahom* bitterly tells her.

Although the king's death in the last scene struck *Time* magazine as too "solemn," absolutely everything in this spectacularly effective piece of theater is required. As the dying monarch admits that Anna has prevailed, Chulalongkorn, her obedient charge, launches into an excited speech about all the reforms he has in mind. Very well schooled, the boy announces that there will be no more prostration. From now on everyone will stand upright and look others in the eye. Democracy is coming, and it is time for the tyrannical father-king to expire, a climax signaled not by a sagging head, as with Rex Harrison, but by a falling hand—the hand that has pointed and whipped and terrified, a living scepter-and-phallus. Since everyone's attention is on Chulalongkorn and the program he is enthusiastically laying out, no one sees the hand drop except Anna, the *kalahom*, and the audience. The minister bends to the floor in grief and homage, but Anna moves to the king's side and, taking the hand, lays her cheek on it in her first open expression of her will to surrender. And now the prince's words cannot be heard, for "Something Wonderful" is swelling to a climax, performed for the first time by the full chorus and not just the orchestra. The passionate crescendo drowns everything out in a last helpless heartthrob. The curtain falls.

Watching the movie DVD sixty years later is like following a sleight-of-hand trick in slow motion: you see how masterly it is, you wonder why it is taking so long, and you're not sure you should feel what you're feeling. But even in 1951 a few canny reviewers put their mixed reactions on record, most notably John Lardner in a deferential but double-voiced piece in the *New Yorker*. From his opening sentence, which praised the show as "so uniformly bright, handsome, ingratiating, and intelligent . . . that it is probably beyond the normal powers of human malevolence to dislike it," Lardner both invoked and suppressed the urge to grumble. He allowed that Rodgers and Hammerstein were artists "of a high order" and that the story was "reasonably adult and literate," and he was unreservedly enthusiastic about the ballet, "one of the most beguiling" he had seen, but for anyone who preferred Hart's cynicism to the "sunny cheerfulness" of Hammerstein, the musical was just "too unremittingly wholesome." Lardner made his most telling criticism at the end, and then only in parentheses, as if his bearish feelings could be disclosed only if they were safely behind bars: "(There is a touch of Walt Disney in the energetic, clean-living spirit of ["I Whistle a Happy Tune"]; for that matter, there has been a touch of Walt Disney in all the recent Rodgers-and-Hammerstein shows.)"

The comparison with the Disney studio and its feature-length cartoons caught the right note. Like *Bambi, The King and I* was a tour de force in a popular art of a distinctly American type. Both cartoon and musical had a "reasonably" adult story, both showed an amazing mastery of craft, and both created a hermetic simulacrum of life such that you couldn't look away. You were drawn into a magic world where you were offered something you couldn't turn down: a new kind of entertainment candy. What *The King and I* gave the open-mouthed spectator was sugared history and geography: history as a bittersweet love story, with Anna saving a darkened kingdom through her expert motherliness and inadmissible sexual response to a "wonderful" tyrant; geography as an absolute contrast between a stultified yet charming Eastern land and a great Western democracy that is the epitome of civilization, manners, and the rule of law while also being a threatening imperial power.

Like the Harrison-Dunne film, the musical smoothed history out by making England the sole European nation in Southeast Asia. In Leonowens's version of events and then in Landon's, France had been the great colonizing threat. In this respect Leonowens was closer to historical reality, and closer also to the British notion that they were the world civilizers and the French merely the usual cross-Channel suspects. By ignoring France and letting England be both civilizing agent and looming invader, Rodgers and Hammerstein offered a stripped-down drama that an audience could absorb in a couple of hours. And so it happened that on the American stage and screen Anna saved Siam by opposing her *own* nation. This was a boldly individualist and, so to speak, exceptionalist Anna. Able to outwit government as such, she was just the ticket for a newly dominant nation that thought of itself as free of history, benevolent, principled, and quite unlike all other imperial powers.

In 1953, after the British version of *The King and I* opened at Drury Lane Theatre (the usual London venue for Rodger and Hammerstein musicals), the reviewer for the *Times* noted that the story was "apparently founded on the actual adventures of an English governess in Siam" and called the king a "savage." This prompted a reader to send a letter of protest to the editor: "Far from Mrs. Leonowens having initiated these westernizing influences, her engagement in the royal household was only a symptom of the larger purpose which the King was pursuing." A second letter to the *Times*, this one by Direck Jayanama, a distinguished Thai statesman and the eventual author of *Thailand im Zweiten Weltkrieg*, endorsed and developed this critique. No such letters or statements appeared in the *New York Times* following the 1951 premiere, and none of the older Americans I have talked to about the musical seems to have realized how insulting it is and how false to history. Yet as soon as I point out that Mongkut was much better educated and more modern than *The King and I* makes out, and that his nation's social progress shouldn't be credited to one enlightened Westerner, everyone sees how much the musical humiliates Thailand and flatters the West. No one has trouble grasping this . . . once it is explained.

A few American scholars attempted to set the record straight. In 1957 Alexander B. Griswold brought out a sound exposé of the Anna story in the *Journal of the Siam Society*, but it made little difference, even when issued as a book by the Asia Society. In 1961 Abbot Low Moffat published an able monograph on King Mongkut, but it, too, had a limited reach. The State Department's 1971 *Area Handbook for Thailand* included a good chapter on the Fourth Reign, clearly indicating that the official view was not infected by the myth. But the myth remained the popular view.

The geography lesson in *The King and I* stands as a mordant commentary on this persistence. Based on a passage in *The Romance of the Harem*, the scene contrasts two very different ways of picturing the world: a fanciful representation of Asia that is supposed to be the traditional Siamese map and an up-to-date Mercator projection of the world's nations. Thiang begins by interpreting the traditional map, which pictures Siam as a graceful red space larger than India. Superimposed on Siam is an image of its king, whose tall, handheld weapon, Thiang explains, to patriotic applause, reveals his great power. She then points to Burma and its king, who is shown with no clothes, and says that this nudity reveals how poor he is, and there is laughter and more clapping. After Thiang's lesson is finished, Anna rolls down a modern map of the kind all schoolrooms used to have. Now her pupils and the concubines can see how small Siam is, and instead of clapping, they react with indignation and disbelief.

Never mind that nothing like this happened or that Leonowens's own description of a so-called Siamese map was lifted from an unreliable English travel writer who had visited Siam during the Third Reign. The real questions would seem to be these: If the stage Siamese have a conceited and uninformed notion of their place in the world, what is to be said of the Westerners in New York and London who applauded *The King and I*? Was there any real difference between those audiences and the pupils and concubines who clap for Lady Thiang? If so, whose bubble needed puncturing the most?

Anna and the King

In 1999 Twentieth Century-Fox released its third version of the Anna story, *Anna and the King*, starring Jodie Foster and Chow Yun-Fat. With its savvy female lead and romantic Hong Kong star, the film was clearly meant to be a smart, globalized remake. Filmed on location in Malaysia, it offers lots of Asian faces and dialogue that slips into Thai now and then, with English subtitles. The opening credits, translated into Thai against a background of traditional Siamese iconography, invite viewers to anticipate a sophisticated and culturally informed entertainment.

In fact, all this Eastern stuff is decor, a politically correct veneer on something spurious and stereotyped and cynical. To date, no treatment of Anna's life in Bangkok begins to approach the sheer awfulness of *Anna and the King*.

As is often the case with train wrecks, there are multiple explanations for what went wrong. The director was denied permission to film on location in Thailand and had to settle for Malaysia. As if in compensation, the credits fraudulently assure us that, far from drawing on Landon's book, the movie is "based" on Anna's own "diaries"—which don't exist. We are also treated to long and pointless shots of attractive scenery and teeming markets and streets, none of them recognizably Thai.[4] All these ersatz sights

4. Nong Khai, the movie's name for the remote, mountainous area in which the climactic action scenes are set, is a city (and province) in northeastern Thailand. Nowadays Nong Khai is on the tourist map as an entry point into Laos, lying just to the north across the Mekong River. As anyone knows who has traveled that way, the landscape is flat.

serve the same function as the Thai dialogue: without being authentic, they *stand for* authenticity. They are stand-ins and symbols for what is missing from the movie: a genuine and convincing cross-cultural immersion.

The same is true for the treatment of Thai history. We are assured that events are based on the historical record, and we are asked to absorb lots of names and details, yet all this "history" is fictional and specious, invented for the sake of story interest. Both of the plot's two main strands—the armed rebellion against King Mongkut and the growing erotic attraction between him and Anna—are bogus. The rebellion develops with one tired gimmick after another—a treacherous poisoning, a bridge mined with powder kegs, a last-minute explosion that saves the day—and as for the love between Foster's Anna and Chow Yun-Fat's king, this is so unconvincing that it has to be helped out by dim lighting, romantic backdrops, and other well-known aids to cinematic passion. It looks as if the action sequences were a desperate expedient for juicing up a wilting love story.

The idea of the love story is that, by going to Siam and falling in love with its monarch, Anna recovers her psychological health. On arrival, she is a brittle, supercompetent woman who talks extremely fast, has an answer for everything, and wears one of the busiest faces ever, with quick little head-shakes and bared teeth. All this seems to be Foster's idea of English manners along with Anna's tense defensiveness—her widowed desperation to survive and succeed. In addition, she has the arrogance of empire. When she assures Louis that India is truly English—"that's what being colonized is all about"—we see her Indian servant lift his eyebrows, the message being, *she* may be in the imperial bubble, but the movie isn't. Two things will help her break out: her shocked discovery of an evil English scheme to subvert Siamese independence, and her sexual response to the king. After he points out that she has suppressed her womanhood, her face grows calm, and she literally lets her hair down. Relax, slow down, be a woman, express your sexuality: that is what Anna learns from her wise and placid Asian employer.

Not only is there a kind of New Age silliness in this wisdom of the ages, but it is jarringly inconsistent with the movie's other message, namely, that Siam would not have escaped its barbaric past if Anna hadn't revealed a better path. Presenting her once again as the national savior, the movie would seem to be inside the bubble after all. Not only does she teach Mongkut and Chulalongkorn that slavery is bad and all people are created equal, but in the final assault by the vicious English-sponsored rebels, she thinks up the clever trick that saves the king and all his wives and children.

She teaches one other lesson. Previously, with Mongkut getting all the sex a man could want, he couldn't understand how anyone could "be satisfied with only one woman." Now he sees that physical satisfaction is not enough. Thanks to Anna, he realizes that, while a pliable Asian may afford erotic pleasure, only a European can inculcate the art of love.

The movie takes this Western imperial fantasy with deadly seriousness. When Anna first arrives in Bangkok, we hear a male voice-over with a foreign accent say, "She was the first Englishwoman I'd ever met. . . . She knew more about the world than anyone." We can't be sure who is speaking until the end, when Anna and the king are dancing and savoring a last tender moment together as Prince Chulalongkorn watches from a distance. The voice returns, and now we realize it is his, speaking from the future: "I was only a boy, but the image of my father holding the woman he loved for the last time has remained with me throughout the years. . . . Anna had shined such a light on Siam!"

Echoing this tribute, the movie concludes with a printed summation, the Judgment of History as it were: "Thanks to the vision of his father, King Mongkut, and the teachings of Anna Leonowens, King Chulalongkorn not only maintained Siam's independence, but also abolished slavery, instituted religious freedom and reformed the judicial system." This statement, one last fraud on the viewer, is about as accurate as the "map" of Siam and Burma. The truth is, the Thai monarchy had respected religious freedom more than most European nations, Siam did not owe its continued independence to Anna, and she had no influence on its judicial reforms.

Anna and the King is not without its charms. The portrayal of the crown prince by Keith Chin, so quiet, dignified, and undemonstrative, has an uncanny resemblance to photos of Chulalongkorn. The actor is a dead ringer, but this bit of inspired casting doesn't save the movie, which leaves one wondering whether the expansion of America's global reach has only enlarged the bubble rather than popped it.

DOES SHE HAVE A FUTURE IN ENTERTAINMENT?

The emotional appeal of *The King and I* came partly from the conceit that a bold and righteous woman could take down an absolute monarch and that her triumph would leave her with an absolute grief. At the heart of the musical lies a conflicted engagement with archetypal power. As Hilary Mantel says, and she should know, "In looking at royalty we are always looking at what is archaic, what is mysterious by its nature. . . . Royal persons are both gods and beasts."

For the postwar generation, the Anna story brought that god-beast to life at the cost of falsifying and cheapening the history of a non-Western people. If Leonowens still has a future in entertainment, it will not, one hopes, be on the basis of the legendary monster-king or her fancied romance with him. But if all that is discarded, can her remarkable life be dramatized in a way that is both entertaining and historically valid?

The answer lies in the form she herself exploited in the 1870s—the popular lecture. That is what she will be delivering tonight, and as we look at her onstage, seated to one side of the lectern and waiting to be introduced, we see a vigorous woman in her early forties. Her hair is in tight ringlets, she wears an Indian shawl, and there are two large claws at her neck. However, this is not our beloved Anna but steel-clad Mrs. Leonowens, and she is not speaking to us from the 1870s but from out of time. Her lecture has been announced as an exciting tour of a remote and exotic land, but the lecture will go off course, and the mask will slip as she speaks.

We will see more than she wants when she interrupts her boasts about all she did for Siam and abruptly recalls her hard early years. She wants to amaze us with her heroic achievements, but she can't help reverting to what is raw and painful. She collects herself for the tale of Kisa Gotami and how she hugged her dead baby boy, but suddenly she is talking about the death of her own first daughter and how shattering this was. Recovering, she starts to tell us what it meant to undertake a long ocean voyage, but again her account collapses, and we hear about the birth of her second child on the *Alibi* and the near shipwreck and the desolate convict hiring depot and the sight of her angry and humiliated husband. We hear about his promise, his dignity, their love for each other, and his failure in life and how he deserved so much better. Again she recovers, but only to become even more angry—angry, it seems, at *us*. "What do you know of the world?" she breaks out, verging on rage but controlling herself in time for the intermission.

When the curtain opens on act 2 of our evening with Mrs. Leonowens, she has her composure back. Again we see the imperious woman who has traveled everywhere and learned so many languages and studied so many religions, but religion makes her falter, and then it all comes out: that school in Bombay, the indoctrination and discipline, the delicate sneers about her skin color when Lady Falkland comes for an inspection, and then we get it straight: the despised *chee-chee* accent and Falkland's plummy tones, but that's not the worst, the worst is death, not just of little Selina but of Thomas Jr. and then of Thomas her husband, and now the foundations crack, and we hear about—and see—her temporary derangement and her struggle to support herself as a schoolmistress in Singapore and Bangkok. She lays it all out for us: homelessness, isolation, desperation, repeated collapses, the forged dignity and assumed identity, the fatigue, the constant sense of threat, and the incredible toughness. She mimics King Mongkut, his down-twisting mouth, his lively movements, his English.

Why did she hate him? Was it because everything was handed to him and she invented herself from scratch? Was it because he had taken all those youthful wives and she had turned down the safe older man picked out for her in India? These are questions she doesn't seem able to settle. She tells the story of Tuptim, and as she admits she concocted it we see her private angry unsettled face. But then, as she recalls how she stood up to King Chulalongkorn years later after he accused her of making his father look absurd, her composure returns. We see now that her strength is invincible and that this is a woman who will never bend, apologize, or explain.

The mask is in place again, and all we see as the bell rings (for this is class, and class is over) is the sovereign smile with which Teacher dismisses us to our small, safe, regular lives.

Acknowledgments

To thank those who contributed to this book is to relive an investigative journey that has lasted ten years, taken me to many new places, and left me with an odd sort of workingman's sense of the British Empire.

First of all, I want to express my gratitude to Washington State University at Pullman for access to the resources of Holland/Terrell Libraries.

At the British Library's Asia, Pacific, and Africa Collections, on which so much of this book rests, I thank Richard Scott Morel, Hedley Sutton, and others for their helpful and cheering advice as I made my way through the labyrinthine India Office Records.

Elsewhere in London, I am grateful to the staffs of the National Archives, the Guildhall Library, the Royal Geographical Society (with IBG), and Westminster Archives. Too often I failed to note the names of those who aided my quest, as when I was assisted by a generous archivist at Hammersmith and Fulham Archives and Local History Centre, but I take pleasure in recording my debt to Sheila Munton, Robert Paul, and Christopher Hassan at City University Library, London, who found exactly what I needed in the *Athenæum* house copy.

In the UK at large, I thank Allyson Lewis, archivist at the Essex Record Office; also Fiona Rees at the Derby Local Studies Library, Lucy McCann at the Bodleian Library of Commonwealth and African Studies at Rhodes House, the staff and archivists at Exeter Heritage Centre, and the librarian on duty at Glamorgan County Record Office, Cardiff. A particular thanks to June Wailing at the Centre for Buckinghamshire Studies.

For help in navigating the Church Missionary Society Papers at Cadbury Research Library, Birmingham University, I thank Philippa Bassett and others.

Among UK genealogists and local historians, I am especially grateful to Linda Anstey Garnett for her kind assistance in all matters relating to Hatherleigh and North Devon and to Kathleen Rhys for help with Welsh family records.

I am indebted to William Dalrymple for settling some difficult questions on research in India and to Lois K. Yorke for her frank assessment of certain problems any biographer of Anna must face.

To D. D. Malet, I would like to express my heartfelt thanks for granting access to a private archive and for hospitality, humor, and unfailing good-will. To Edward and Pauline de Broë-Ferguson I will always be grateful for the help with research and the exemplary hospitality, with a warm thank-you as well to Hugh Counsell.

In Ireland, I am grateful to Archivist Elizabeth McEvoy at the National Archives; to John Sutton and the Reverend Chris Long in Enniscorthy; and to Wexford archivist Gráinne Doran, who, after guiding us through the clippings, drove my wife and me to the bus station in the rain.

In Singapore, the expert and thorough preparations by Ong Eng Chuan of the National Library Board made our week's research visit one of the most intense and satisfying investigative experiences I have known. I thank Mr. Ong as well for quick, full, definitive answers to all queries.

I thank Margaret Edgcumbe for access to a private cache of letters.

In Western Australia, I am grateful to the friendly and helpful librarians at the State Library of Western Australia; to Jack Honniball for serving up the fruits of his fine research; to Sandra Simkin for sharing photos and tran-scripts relating to Lynton and Port Gregory; and above all, to Gerard Foley, senior archivist at the State Records Office of Western Australia. Early in my research, I realized that his interest and initiative were such that he would be an ideal collaborator, and I proposed we work together on an essay about Anna's life in Western Australia. The result was an extremely productive trip to Perth, an eye-opening excursion to the ruins of the Lynton convict hiring depot, and an excellent new friend. My Australian chapters would be much thinner and poorer if they didn't bear Mr. Foley's professional imprint on every page.

In Thailand, I wish to express my gratitude to Adjaan Krisana of the South-east Asian Studies Department, Thammasat University, for fielding ques-tions and alerting me to *Saaylap wang luang*; to Khun Anake Nawigamune for sharing photos from his private collection (thanks also to Adjaan Wanna Nawigamune); to Khun Korrapin of the Thai National Archives for kind cooperation; to publisher Trasvin Jittidecharak of Silkworm Books for expert and indispensable mediation; and to friend Wichian Sriwongsa for twice braving Bangkok traffic to secure the photo of Louis in the Grand Palace.

Here in the States, I will always be grateful to Ken Grossi and Roland M. Baumann at Oberlin College, which controls the Dan Beach Bradley Family Papers, for expert and dependable assistance; and to Keith Call, David Malone, and David Osielski at Wheaton College, where Margaret Landon's papers are deposited, for answering endless queries and pleas for help. And a special thank-you to Margaret (Peggy) Landon Schoenherr for consenting to be interviewed and offering gracious hospitality.

Thanks to Susan Halpert at the Houghton Library for finding letters I didn't have the wit to look for; to Gayle M. Richardson at the Huntington Library for entertaining endless queries; to Bertram Lippincott III at the Newport Historical Society for turning up some precious shards; to Dorothy A. D'Eletto, who scoured the Staten Island Institute of Arts & Sciences for me; also to Lynn E. Calvin, volunteer researcher for the Saratoga County Historian (New York); to Tevis Kimball, curator of special collections at the Jones Library in Amherst, Massachusetts; and to the consulting librarians on duty at the New England Historic Genealogical Society.

Among the many others who have pushed the research forward, I take pleasure in thanking Daria D'Arienzo and Carol Andrews; Dan Lombardo for trolling Cobb's Hill Cemetery for me; Albert J. Von Frank for telling me who Abby Hopper Gibbons was; Donna Campbell and David Nordloh for fielding queries involving William Dean Howells; Margaret Dakin and Christina Barber at Amherst College Archives for alerting me to something special; Edward Griffin for a last-minute rescue; and Pierre A. Walker for constant, expeditious, and high-value research help over the years.

To John C. Bliss, a robust shout-out for giving me access to a private archive I had been looking for and never would have found if not for a once-in-a-lifetime coincidence that will always amaze both him and me.

For languages, I thank Vivendra Singh for insights into Hindustani; Wang Baihua for kind assistance with Chinese; Midori Asahina for help with queries involving Japan; and Gunhild Kübler of Zürich for so dependably and resourcefully fielding a variety of inquiries involving German. For getting a bit of Thai into a sixty-four-year-old male brain, I cordially thank my teachers at the Southeast Asian Studies Summer Institute at the University of Wisconsin–Madison in 2005, namely, Adjaan Phatacharee Promsuwan, Adjaan Patcharin Peyasantiwong, and Professor Robert Bickner. It was Adjaan Patcharin who showed me a groundbreaking article about Anna in *Sinlapa wathanatham* (Art and culture magazine) and helped me read it.

Warm thanks to my son, Simon Habegger, for repeated and patient help in reading Thai materials; for his keen insights over the years into Thai culture, history, and language; and for the dismaying vigor with which he marked up some chapters I thought I had finished.

Others who have read chapters are retired Brigadier General Edward de Broë-Ferguson, who saved me from many blunders; Arabist Geoffrey J. Roper, who generously criticized my early treatment of George Percy Badger; Susan Kepner for marking up my Tuptim chapter; Peter Collister for much-needed advice on usage and idioms; and Professor Durba Ghosh for her keen reactions to early drafts of my first two chapters. I am grateful to my daughter Eliza Habegger and her husband, Thor Hanson, for their careful readings. I will add that I have made use of the quick critiques of Frankie Jones and Millicent Bennett.

At the University of Wisconsin Press I thank Raphael Kadushin, Matthew Cosby, Adam Mehring, Brontë Wieland, Sheila McMahon, copyeditor Mary M. Hill, and others for patiently resolving the many problems my manuscript presented. A particular thank-you to the press's two readers, especially the Thai historian for cogent suggestions, and to William L. Andrews for making it all come together.

My chief debt is to Nellie, my wife, who joined in the research, unearthed wonderful finds, and brought her usual good sense to bear on what I made of it all.

Quotations from the following archives are gratefully acknowledged:

American Board of Commissioners for Foreign Missions archives by permission of Houghton Library, Harvard University

Annie Fields Papers by permission of Massachusetts Historical Society

Benajah Ticknor Papers by permission of Bentley Historical Library, University of Michigan

Church Missionary Society Papers by permission of Cadbury Research Library, University of Birmingham, and Mr. Ken Osborne

Dan Beach Bradley Family Papers by permission of Oberlin College Archives, Oberlin, Ohio

George Grenville Malet Papers by permission of Mr. D. D. Malet

Jesse Caswell Papers by permission of Mr. John Bliss

John Thomson's rejected essay, "Notes of a Journey through Siam to the Ruins of Cambodia," by permission of Royal Geographical Society (with IBG)

Lewis Gannett Papers by permission of Houghton Library, Harvard University

Margaret and Kenneth Landon Papers by permission of Wheaton College Special Collections, Wheaton, Illinois, and Mr. John Schoenherr, Trustee, Margaret Landon Trust

Sarah Orne Jewett Materials by permission of Colby College Special Collections, Waterville, Maine

Thomas Bailey Aldrich Papers by permission of Houghton Library, Harvard University

Abbreviations

ABC American Board of Commissioners for Foreign Missions Archives

Acc 36 Colonial Secretary's Office, Correspondence Received

Acc 49 Colonial Secretary's Letterbook

AKS Margaret Landon, *Anna and the King of Siam* (New York: John Day Company, 1944)

Anna Anna Harriette Leonowens (1831–1915)

Avis Avis Leonowens Fyshe, Anna's daughter (1854–1902)

BGG *Bombay Government Gazette*

CMS Church Missionary Society Papers

DBB Dan Beach Bradley (1804–73)

EG Anna Harriette Leonowens, *The English Governess at the Siamese Court: Being Recollections of Six Years in the Royal Palace at Bangkok* (1870; reprint, Oxford: Oxford University Press, 1988)

IOR India Office Records

JTF James Thomas Fields

LTI Anna Harriette Leonowens, *Life and Travel in India: Being Recollections of a Journey before the Days of Railroads* (Philadelphia: Porter & Coates, 1884)

LWJ Laura Winthrop Johnson (1825–89)

MKL Margaret and Kenneth Landon

ML Margaret Landon (1903–93)

NYT *New York Times*

PWD   Public Works Department

RH   Anna Leonowens, *The Romance of the Harem* (1873; reprint, Charlottesville: University Press of Virginia, 1991)

SRMI   Swan River Mechanics' Institute

USPG   Society for the Propagation of the Gospel Papers

WO   War Office Records, National Archives, UK

Appendix 1

FAMILY CHART FOR ANNA LEONOWENS

Except where noted, baptisms were Anglican. Rank, where given, was the highest attained.

Thomas Glascott, gentleman, saddler, Cardiff [son of Thomas Glascott, Cardiff]
bapt 17 Sept. 1709
bur 16 May 1780
m 19 Oct. 1731[1]
Elizabeth Deer, Cardiff [daughter of Elizabeth and Evan Deer, ironmonger][2]
bur 11 Feb. 1772[3]

Thomas and Elizabeth had eleven children baptized at St. John, Cardiff. They included:

—William Glascott, currier
bapt 7 Sept. 1735

—Cradock Glascott
bapt 17 Aug. 1736
bur 22 Mar. 1739

—Elizabeth Glascott
bapt 21 Nov. 1738

—Thomas Glascott
bapt 15 July 1740

—Anne Glascott
bapt 3 June 1741

—Rev. Cradock Glascott, vicar of Hatherleigh, Devonshire
bapt 19 Nov. 1742
d 14 Aug. 1831, Hatherleigh[4]
m 1784?
Mary [Edmonds?]
b 1754/55
d 2 Nov. 1823[5]

—Rev. John Glascott
bapt 7 Nov. 1749

All five children of Cradock and Mary were baptized in Hatherleigh, Devonshire:

—Mary Ann Glascott
b 29 Jan. 1785[6]
d 25 Dec. 1857, Exeter[7]
m Samuel Walkey, surgeon

—Rev. Cradock John Glascott, vicar, Seaton, Devonshire
bapt 20 Nov. 1786
d 23 Apr. 1867[8]
m 1814 (date of license)[9]
Georgiana Goodin Bourke

—William Vawdrey [later Vaudrey] Glascott
bapt 26 July 1789
cadet, East India Company army, 1809[10]
embarked for Bombay, 1810
finished cadet school and joined Fourth Regiment Native Infantry, 1811
lieutenant, 1814
appointed adjutant, 1818
d 31 Oct. 1821, Qeshm, Strait of Hormuz
ca. 1814, in India, united with an intimate partner, her name not known

—Rev. Thomas Glascott, rector of Rodborough, Gloucestershire
bapt 29 Aug. 1792
d 20 Dec. 1876[11]
m 1819, Clifton[12]
Caroline Augusta Morris [daughter of William Morris, Esq.]
b 1794/95, Barbados[13]

—Selina Glascott
bapt 20 Apr. 1794
bur 1 May 1796[14]

—Mary Anne Letitia Cradock Glascott
b 1828/29
m 16 Nov. 1854, Seaton[15]
Alfred John de Haviland Harris, major, Madras army
bapt 1819, *d* 1881[16]

—Editha Mary Ann Glascott
b 1828/29
m 2 Nov. 1858, Seaton[17]
Rev. William Harris, curate[18]
b 1832/33

—Mary Ann Glascott
b 1815, Bombay Presidency
d 19 Aug. 1873, age 57, Pune[19]
m (1) 15 Mar. 1829, Thãne[20]
Thomas Edwards, sergeant, Corps of Engineers, Bombay army
b 1802/3, London(?)[21]
enlisted and embarked for Bombay, 1825[22]
d 31 July 1831[23]
m (2) 9 Jan. 1832, Ahmadnagar[24]
Patrick Donohoe, deputy commissary, PWD
b 1806–9, St. John's Parish, county Limerick, Ireland
enlisted, 1827; embarked for Bombay, 1828[25]
d 30 Oct. 1864, Pune[26]

—Eliza Glascott
b about 15 Aug. 1816
bur 7 Sept. 1839, Surat, age 23 years and 23 days[27]
m 3 July 1831, Sirur
Tobias Butler, asst. overseer, PWD;
b 1808, St. Canice's Parish, county Kilkenny, Ireland[28]

—William Frederick [later Vaudrey] Glasscott, commissariat storekeeper; master, boys' school, Indo-British Institution
b 1821/22
d 5 Feb. 1856, Bombay[29]

—Rev. Cholmeley Cradock Glascott, chaplain at Versailles; *d* 1882[30]

—Anna Maria Glascott, *b* 1831/32[31]
m 1866
Edolphe Andrewes Uthwatt[32]

416

Eliza Edwards
  b 26 Apr. 1830, Ahmadnagar
  d 13 June 1864, Bombay
  m 24 Apr. 1845, Disa[33]
James Milliard/**Millard**, sergeant
  major, Horse Artillery;
  reformatory superintendent[34]
  b 1806, Buckinghamshire[35]

Anna Harriet Edwards, known
  as **ANNA LEONOWENS**
  b 6 Nov. 1831, Ahmadnagar
  bapt Ann Hariett Emma[36]
  d 19 Jan. 1915, Montreal,
  Canada[37]
  m 25 Dec. 1849, Pune[38]
Thomas Leonowens
[see Thomas's family chart]

- **John Donohoe**, clerk
  b 1833/34, m 1859[39]
- Charlotte Donohoe b 1 Apr. 1835,
  Belgaum; d 12 Feb. 1838, Disa[40]
- **Ellen Donohoe**
  b 6 Dec. 1836, Sirur or Pune
  d 2 Jan. 1872, Karachi[41]
  m (1) 24 May 1852, Pune[42]
Samuel George Phillips, sergeant,
  Telegraph Service, d 1854[43]
  m (2) 7 Sept. 1858, Pune[44]
George Savage,
  conductor, commissariat
- William Donohoe, clerk
  b 1838/39, d 1886, Bombay[45]
- Mary Frederica Donohoe
  b 13 Oct. 1841, Disa
  living in Pune, 1858[46]
- James Donohoe, b 25 Mar. 1844
  RC bapt 8 Apr. 1844, Disa[47]
- Charles Patrick Donohoe b 15 Oct.
  1847; *RC bapt* 19 Oct., Disa[48]
- Blanche Donohoe, b 1853, Pune[49]
- **Vaudry Glasscott** Donohoe,
  railway ticket inspector, b Apr.
  1858, Pune; m 11 July 1877[50]
- Henrietta Cooper Butler
  b 25 Apr. 1833; m 15 Dec. 1846[51]
- Louisa Ellen Butler
  b 11 July 1835, Belgaum
  m 3 Aug. 1854, Sattarawunder[52]

James Edwards Milliard
  b 25 May 1846, Disa[53]

Eliza Sarah/Sara Millard
  b 25 June 1848, Pune
  m 27 Nov. 1864, Surat[54]
Edward Pratt, Indian Salt
  Revenue Service[55]

- Mary Henrietta Millard
  b 15 June 1852, Bombay[56]

- Henry Pennikett Millard
  b 17 July 1856, Girgaum[57]

- Edwin Haveloft Millard
  b 13 June 1858, Bombay[58]

- Alfred Thomas Millard, **first**
  assistant master, Bombay
  Education Society, Byculla
  boys' school[59]
  b 19 May 1864, Girgaum
  d 4 Oct. 1913, Bombay[60]

[Anna and Thomas's children
and grandchildren are on
Thomas's family chart.]

Rev. Thomas Arthur Savage,
  principal, Cathedral High
  School, Bombay
  b 27 Apr. 1853, Nasik [*bapt*
  Thomas Patrick Phillips]
  wrote Anna 8 July 1898[61]
  d 17 June 1918, Bombay[62]

Ellen and George's six children
included:

George Frederick Savage
  b 30 Jan. 1863, Pune[63]

Ruth Emily Savage, **teacher,**
  headmistress, Bombay high
  schools[64]
  b 10 Dec. 1869, Karachi
  d 14 Feb. 1913, Bombay[65]

Alfred Joseph **Glascott** Donohoe
  b 16 Nov. 1877[66]

Harold **Vaudry** Gustav Donohoe
  b 11 Nov. 1885[67]

Edward Millard Pratt, puisne judge,
  High Court, Bombay
  b 29 Aug. 1865
  d 28 June 1949[68]

George Marlow Pratt
  b 13 Apr. 1867, Bombay[69]

Charles Rary Pratt
  b 30 Aug. 1868[70]

Frederick Greville Pratt,
  commissioner, Northern
  Division, Bombay Presidency
  b 4 Dec. 1869
  d 6 Oct. 1949[71]

David Cameron Pratt
  b 3 Nov. 1871[72]

Julia Honoria Pratt
  b 5 Nov. 1874[73]
  m Rev. Arthur Donkin,
  vicar of Semer, Suffolk[74]

Sir John Thomas Pratt,
  consul general in China
  b 13 Jan. 1876[75]
  wrote Avis Leonowens Fyshe
  25 Nov. 1899[76]

Richard Septimus Pratt,
  consul in China
  b 11 Oct. 1882[77]

William Henry Pratt, known as
  BORIS KARLOFF
  b 23 Nov. 1887, London
  d 2 Feb. 1969, Midhurst,
  Sussex[78]

William Wilkinson, Monart Parish,
Enniscorthy, Ireland
bur 29 Dec. 1835, age 55[1]
m 1807[2] ────────────────────────
Sarah Norton, St. Mary's Parish, Enniscorthy

── William and Sarah had at least four sons and two
daughters,[6] including:

── **Thomas Wilkinson**, solicitor[7]
  b 13 Dec. 1812, Enniscorthy[8]
  d 5 Feb. 1904, Enniscorthy[9]
  m 6 Nov. 1836[10] ──────────────────────

── Mary Owens, St. Mary's Parish, Enniscorthy
  b 1812/13
  d 8 Dec. 1859, Enniscorthy, age 46[11]

── **Selina** Owens
  b 25 Feb. 1816, Enniscorthy
  bur 20 Jan. 1822, Enniscorthy (see note)[12]

── **Gunnis** Lean Owens
  bapt 27 Dec. 1818, Enniscorthy[13]
  became a draper in Wexford, Ireland
  took cabin passage to New York, 1851[14]

John Owens, boot and shoemaker,[3]
St. Mary's Parish, Enniscorthy
bur 1 Sept. 1851, age 66[4]
m 25 Feb. 1810[5] ─────➤
Mary Lean, Templeshanbo Parish, Enniscorthy

── **Thomas Lean Owens** (from early 1850s known as
  Thomas Leonowens)
  bapt 25 Jan. 1824, Enniscorthy[15]
  enlisted in Royal Army, June 1842, Liverpool[16]
  embarked for Bombay, July 1843[17]
  discharged(?), 1847[18]
  employed in Bombay, Western Australia,
  Singapore, Penang
  d 8 May 1859, Penang[19]
  m 25 Dec. 1849, Pune, India[20]────────────
  ANNA HARRIET EDWARDS—see family chart
  for ANNA LEONOWENS

── **Selina** Owens
  bapt 26 Oct. 1825, Enniscorthy[21]
  bur 1 Oct. 1875, Enniscorthy[22]

Thomas Lean Wilkinson, London barrister
  b 26 Nov. 1838, Enniscorthy[23]
  d 10 Feb. 1915, South Kensington, London[24]
  m 7 Aug. 1872[25] ────────────────
Jessie Hamilton Hoskins
  b about 1851,[26] daughter of Edward Hamilton
    Hoskins, Esq., Fanham's Hall, Herts[27]

— Maurice Lean Wilkinson
    b 1873
— Avis Mary Wilkinson
    b 18 Feb. 1875
— Agmond Edward Wilkinson
    b 1880/81[47]

— Mary Sarah Wilkinson
  bur 9 Apr. 1921, Enniscorthy, age 79[28]

— **Selina** Anne Wilkinson
  b 21 Feb. 1842
  bur 17 Mar. 1931, Enniscorthy[29]

— Martha Jane Wilkinson
  bur 14 Feb. 1925, Enniscorthy, age 81[30]

— Henrietta Wilkinson
  b 10 Mar. 1846, *d* 1896[31]

— **Eliza "Lizzie" Avice Wilkinson**
  b 9 June 1848
  introduced to Margaret Landon, 1939
  d 1941[32]
  m Rev. Harry Moore[33]──────────────── **Very Rev. Gerald Grattan Moore**, dean of St.
                                              Luke's, Evanston, Illinois
— John William Henry Wilkinson
  b 7 July 1850[34]

— Emily Wilkinson Moses
  b 26 June 1855, *d* 1931[35]

— James Carlisle Fyshe
    b 8 Mar. 1879, Halifax, Nova Scotia
    d 7 Dec. 1921, Edmonton, Alberta[48]
    m 7 Dec. 1908, **Bangkok**
  Julia Corisande Mattice, Montreal[49]

— **Selina Leon Owens**
  b 10 Dec. 1850, Pune
  bur 24 May 1852, Colaba, Bombay[36]

— **Anna Harriette Leonowens Fyshe**
    b 11 May 1881, Halifax
    d 1 Sept. 1967, Berlin
    m (1) Dr. Hermann Balser, Jena[50]
    m (2) Dr. Ernst Schultze, Berlin[51]

— **Thomas** Leonowens
  b 24 Jan. 1853 at sea (Indian Ocean)[37]
  d 16 Mar. 1854, Perth, Western Australia[38]

— Thomas Maxwell Fyshe
    b 7 Sept. 1883[52]

— **Avis Annie** Leonowens
  b 25 Oct. 1854, Perth[39]
  d 1902, Montreal, Canada[40]
  m 19 June 1878, New York City[41]──────
Thomas Fyshe, banker
  b Fifeshire, Scotland, *d* 1911, Montreal[42]

— **Avis Selina Fyshe**
    b 22 Apr. 1886
    d 5 Nov. 1961[53]

— Kathleen Roberta Fyshe[54]

— Francis Fyshe[55]

— **Louis Gunnis** Leonowens [later known as Louis
    Thomas Leonowens]
  b 22 Oct. 1856, Lynton/Port Gregory, Western
    Australia[43]
  d 17 Feb. 1919, Westcliff, England[44]
  m (1) Caroline Isabella Knox, *b* 1857, *d* 1893[45]──
  m (2) 1899 Reta May Maclaughlan
    b ca. 1879, *d* 28 Nov. 1936[46]

— Thomas George Leonowens
    b 30 Mar. 1888[56]

— Anna Harriette Leonowens
    b 1 Nov. 1890[57]

Appendix 3

ANNA AS PLAGIARIST

"I permit myself to speak," Anna wrote in *The English Governess*, "only of those things which were but too plain to one who lived for six years in or near the palace" (99). In fact, she regularly took others' observations and passed them off as her own. To judge from the telltale phrases she retained, she apparently took for granted that she would not be detected. She also failed to realize how gravely her silent appropriation of others' accounts—a travel writer's worst vice—damaged the value of her reports.

During the Third and Fourth Reigns it was understood that, while Asians had to prostrate themselves at court, Westerners were allowed to stand. Anna's treatment of this privilege was for the most part accurate and trustworthy. Once, however, in an article for *Youth's Companion*, she stole an amusing and quite fanciful report from a British writer:

On one of my interviews with the King, I was permitted, in deference to my European prejudices, to hop into the presence chamber like a frog on the borders of a marsh; while the nobles and courtiers crept in like reptiles, and remained prostrate during the whole interview. (Leonowens, "Life in the Grand Royal Palace of Siam," 276)	We were ushered into the presence-chamber of royalty: when I say ushered, I should rather have written, we hopped into the presence-chamber on all fours, like a company of frogs on the borders of a marsh; and this method of approaching the king was a leniency only accorded to us, for the Siamese themselves crept in on their stomachs, and remained prostrate during the whole interview. (Neale, *Narrative of a Residence*, 53)

During the reign of Rama III, Mary Frances Davenport and Fred Arthur Neale independently told the story of how the king brought out a certain jeu d'esprit depicting Siam's superiority to Burma. Taking for granted that His Majesty supposed the picture to be a map, both travel writers interpreted the object as an example of Siamese primitiveness. Neither was aware of the palace's exquisitely detailed geographical charts, which would come to light only in the late twentieth century. Neale's description of the "map," together with the purported reproduction supplied by his publisher (see page 217), made a great impression on Anna, who, with minimal revision, offered Neale's account as if it were her own eyewitness report.

In the centre was a great patch of red, and above it a small patch of green. On the part painted red—which was intended to represent Siam—was pasted a comical-looking human figure, cut out of silver paper, with a huge pitchfork in one hand and an orange in the other. There was a crown on the head and spurs on the heels, and the sun was shining over all. The legs, which were of miserably thin dimensions, met sympathetically at the knees. And this cadaverous-looking creature was meant for the king of Siam,—indicating that so vast were his strength and power they extended from one end of his dominions to the other. In the little patch of green, intended to represent Birmah, was a small Indian-ink figure, consisting of a little dot for the body, another smaller one for the head, and four scratches of the pen for the legs and arms; this was meant for the king of Birmah. A legion of little imps, in many grotesque attitudes, were seen dancing about his dominions. (Leonowens, *Romance of the Harem*, 240–41)

In the centre was a patch of red, about eighteen inches long by ten broad; above it was a patch of green, about ten inches long by three wide. On the whole space occupied by the red was pasted a singular looking figure, cut out of silver paper, with a pitch-fork in one hand and an orange in the other: there was a crown on the head, and spurs on the heels, and the legs, which were of miserably thin dimensions, met sympathetically at the knees, and this cadaverous looking creature was meant to represent the bloated piece of humanity seated before us [Rama III], indicating that so vast were his strength and power that it extended from one end of his dominions to the other. In the little patch of green, a small Indian-ink figure, consisting of a little dot for the head, a large dot for the body, and four scratches of the pen to represent the legs and arms, was intended for the wretched Tharawaddy, the then King of Burma. A legion of little imps, in very many different attitudes, were dancing about his dominions. (Neale, *Narrative of a Residence*, 54–56)

Whereas Neale and Davenport reported that the cartoon had been devised by the Third Reign's *kalahom*, Anna claimed that it was "painted about a century before, by a Siamese who was thought to possess great scientific and literary attainments" (Leonowens, *Romance of the Harem*, 240). Here, instead of copying, she was simply making it up.

Her accounts of Siamese geography also owed more to previous writers than she acknowledged. Her description of the short and winding stretch of the Chao Phya River between Bangkok and the Gulf of Siam—a section she had traveled at least four times—was a running revision of what she found in Neale. Her plagiarisms, far too extensive to be quoted in their entirety, include the following passages:

Ascending the Meinam (or Chow Phya) . . . we come next to Paklat Beeloo, or "Little Paklat," so styled to distinguish it from Paklat Boon, a considerable town higher up the river. . . . Though, strictly speaking, Paklat Beeloo is a mere cluster of huts, the humble dwellings of a colony of farmers and rice-planters, it is nevertheless a place of considerable importance as a depot for the products of the ample fields and gardens which surround it on every side. The rice and vegetables which these supply are shipped for the markets of Bangkok and Ayudia. (Leonowens, *The English Governess*, 129)

Towards morning we approached the second town, constructed on the banks of the Menam, after entering the river. This is called Paklat Belo or Little Paklat, to distinguish it from Paklat Boon, a large and more considerable town some twenty miles further up the river. Paklat Belo is, strictly speaking, nothing more than a village; in fact, not so large as many of the villages in the vicinity; but it is a place of some consideration, from the fact that the neighbouring land on either side of the river is laid out in vast paddy fields as far as the eye can reach, and the rice produced is here shipped and carried to Bangkok and Yuthia. (Neale, *Narrative of a Residence*, 20)

Often unwieldy, and piled clumsily with cargo, one might reasonably suppose their safe piloting to be a nautical impossibility; yet so perfect is the skill—the instinct, rather—of these almost amphibious river-folk, that a little child, not uncommonly a girl, shall lead them. Accidents are marvellously rare. (Leonowens, *The English Governess*, 130)

These canoes are piled up in a manner that would lead one uninitiated in the art of skulling to imagine their safe guidance through the waters to be a moral impossibility; yet such is the facility which practice gives to these almost amphibious people, that the canoes are generally entrusted to the care of a child not above ten years of age, and that child a girl. Accidents are very rare indeed. (Neale, *Narrative of a Residence*, 21)

Even when Anna recalled scenes she was familiar with, she would take something from Neale, as in her description of Bangkok's spectacular religious architecture:

These pagodas, and the *p'hra-cha-dees*, or minarets, that crown some of the temples, are in many cases true wonders of cunning workmanship and profuse adornment—displaying mosaics of fine porcelain, inlaid with ivory, gold, and silver. (Leonowens, *The English Governess*, 132)	The pagodas that tower up from these watts are of very magnificent workmanship, being a mosaic of the finest porcelain, inlaid with ivory, gold and silver. (Neale, *Narrative of a Residence*, 33)

Her narrative of King Mongkut's earlier life was silently based on missionary Dan Beach Bradley's long and verbose obituary. The modifications she introduced as she abridged and adapted his remarks (without acknowledgment) shed a good deal of light on her aims and procedures as a writer:

When the Protestants came [to Bangkok in the late 1820s] he manifested a positive preference for their methods of instruction, inviting one or another of them daily to his temple, to aid him in the study of English. Finally he placed himself under the permanent tutorship of the Rev. Mr. Caswell, an American missionary; *and, in order to encourage his preceptor to visit him frequently, he fitted up a convenient resting-place for him on the route to the temple*, where that excellent man might teach the poorer people who gathered to hear him. *Under Mr. Caswell he made extraordinary progress in advanced and liberal ideas of government, commerce, even religion.* (Leonowens, *The English Governess*, 239–40, my italics)	He sought his lessons chiefly from the Protestant missionaries by visiting them, and sending for them to come and visit him at his temple. . . . [H]e was ever intent on an increase of knowledge of the English language, geography, mathematics, astronomy, history, etc. But it was not until about 1845, when 41 years of age, that Chowfa Mongkut devoted himself to these several branches of learning with a real system, and with the most commendable diligence and perseverance under the tutorship of the late Rev. Jesse Caswell. . . . For a period of about eighteen months did this Prince receive Mr. Caswell at his temple from three to four times a week for the purpose of taking lessons from him. Much of the time he would send his boat for him three miles, and at other times Mr. C. would walk that distance to the temple, thinking that the

exercise would do him good. *And in order to encourage his teacher to come, he fitted up for him a commodious place by the wayside near his temple for him to rest in,* and spend as much time as he pleased daily in teaching the Christian religion, and distributing christian tracts to the Siamese people. . . . [T]he Prince made rapid advances in such knowledge as in the providence of God he was destined to require as supreme monarch of Siam; and it was, we think, then more than during all his preceding advances, that was planted in his mind those *liberal and expansive views with regard to government, commerce and religion,* which subsequently so much distinguished him above all the monarchs of this eastern world. (Bradley, "Reminiscences," 121–22, my italics)

Whether the indebtedness here amounts to plagiarism is open to question. What we see in these two columns is how Bradley's argument that the missionaries' frustrated efforts bore fruit after all (thus confirming the workings of divine providence) fed into Anna's claims for the beneficent influence of Western teachers (such as herself) on Siamese development. A missionary's labored piety was transformed into the quick, confident, market-oriented absoluteness of a none-too-scrupulous writer.

Notes

Epigraphs

"En verité le mentir": Michel de Montaigne, *Œuvres complètes* (Paris: Gallimard, 1962), 37; Michel de Montaigne, *The Essays*, trans. M. A. Screech (London: Allen Lane, 1991), 35.
"Only those who are sincere": Anna to Avis, [March 1880], quoted in VI C 4:2 folder 29b, p. 243, MKL Papers.

Introduction

4 "No friend of mine knew": *EG*, 282.
5 Chang and Eng: Ironically, the twins were seven-eighths Chinese. Irving Wallace and Amy Wallace, *The Two: A Biography* (New York: Simon & Schuster, 1978), 15.
— excellent and comprehensive accounts of Siam: Before Anna, the fullest American reports were by ex-missionary Frances Davenport, whose essays appeared in the *Southern Literary Messenger* in the late 1850s, and naval surgeon William Maxwell Wood, whose 1859 travelogue, *Fankwei; or, The San Jacinto in the Seas of India, China and Japan*, had a segment on Siam. In France, where interest went back to the 1680s, a magisterial two-volume work was brought out in 1854 by Jean Baptiste Pallegoix, *Description du royaume Thai ou Siam*. In England the standard work was John Bowring's two-volume *The Kingdom and People of Siam* (1857). Far slighter was Fred Arthur Neale's breezy travelogue, *Narrative of a Residence at the Capital of the Kingdom of Siam* (1852). Anna drew extensively on these three European books, particularly the latter.
— expert Quaker activist: Abby Hopper Gibbons, who was friends with Francis Davis Cobb, Anna's first American sponsor. See chapter 20.
6 tanned skin: A feature remembered by Mary Otis Gay Willcox, one of Anna's pupils on Staten Island (Hine and Davis, *Legends*, 93).

6 long and enthusiastic letter: LWJ to Annie Fields, 16 August 1868, LWJ Papers.
— "The inner life of the harem": review of *EG*, *NYT*, 10 December 1870, 2.
7 Henry George Kennedy: *Foreign Office List* (1871), 124, (1886), 130.
— "overwrought," open to "severe criticism": [Samuel Jones Smith], "Governess at the Siamese Court," *Siam Repository* 2 (October 1870): 429.
— the author's mistaken claims: According to *EG*, a leading Siamese minister, doubting his son's legitimacy, "named the lad *My Chi*, 'Not So,'" which the boy's mother then changed to "*Ny Chi*," meaning "Master So." The story, presented as fact, sounds like the sort of joke that circulates within a small tight foreign community. Kennedy reacted as follows: "Now 'Mai Chai' certainly means 'It is not so,' but we have heard of no one in Siam who was ever called by so silly a name. 'Nai,' meaning 'Master' . . . is the ordinary term used in addressing a gentleman . . . [and] 'Nai Chai' . . . is a genuine Siamese name; but the 'Chai' here used means 'the heart,' and is a totally different word, written in different characters, from the word 'chai,' signifying 'it is so.'" As this correction shows, Anna's errors in Thai could be quite elementary. *EG*, 46; [Kennedy], review of *EG*, 836.
— "Anna Harriette Leonowens . . . was born": Anna's "A Biographical Sketch" forms part of "Mrs A. H. Leonowens," *Redpath's Lyceum* [1873–75]: 42, preserved in the Anna Harriette Leonowens Papers. As printed, the sketch represents an edited and occasionally garbled version of Anna's original statement.
8 "I believe I was born": VI C 4:2 folder 28, p. 2, MKL Papers. ML was told by Avis Selina Fyshe that her "grandmother had been extremely reticent about her life prior to 1862 when she went to Siam. After much persuasion Mrs. Leonowens had written on eight small ruled pages a brief precis of her life" (VI C 4:2 folder 4, MKL Papers).
9 "taught King Mongkut's children": Advertisement, *NYT Book Review*, 9 July 1944, 19.
— Landon's original title . . . was cut: Richard J. Walsh to ML, 16 August 1943, VI C 2:2 folder 21, MKL Papers; Avis Selina Fyshe to ML, 9 April 1943, VI C 1:1 folder 2, MKL Papers.
— Sketches of Anna from her own time: Illustrations for two stories in *Youth's Companion* about her life in Siam, "A Royal Dinner Party" and "A Royal Tea-Party," clothe her in dresses hanging straight down. In two stories set elsewhere, "The Stolen Trunk" and "A Remarkable Performance," she appears to be wearing hooped skirts.
10 The book got a vigorous boost: "Romance of the Harem," *Time*, 10 July 1944, 102, 104.
— "The comparison is inevitable": "Elizabeth and the Prince," *NYT*, 29 August 1946, 26.
12 The reaction came in 1976: Bristowe, *Louis*, 23–29, 132.

12 Altering this to *Glasscock*: Bombay marriages, N/3/9/331, IOR; Bristowe, *Louis*, 26, 132.

— "This man is my enemy": Margaret (Peggy) Schoenherr, interview by Alfred Habegger, 10 August 2005.

— lowborn adventuress or imposter: Exemplifying this interpretation are Blofeld, *King Maha Mongkut*; and Smithies, "Anna Leonowens," 145.

— could admire the feminist pluck: One of the better Bristowe-influenced treatments is Susan Brown's "Alternatives to the Missionary Position."

13 "the illegitimate Eurasian daughter": Baigent and Yorke, "Leonowens," 402.

— "child of poverty and ignorance"; "was very heaven": Morgan, *Bombay Anna*, 45, 44. A few of this biography's more glaring errors and inventions will be noted in passing. Its central claim, that Anna created a new identity while traveling to Singapore after Thomas's death, cannot be true, as the couple had previously lived there for over a year—an easily discovered fact of which the author was unaware. See chapter 9.

— a certain 1841 Indian newspaper: Anonymous untitled article, *Bombay Gazette*, 22 September 1841. See chapter 2.

Chapter 1. Descent from the Gentry

17 "the old homestead": Anna, "Biographical Sketch," 42; VI C 4:2 folder 28, p. 2, MKL Papers.

— "land of elf and Merlin": *AKS*, 5.

18 John Wesley made his first visit to Cardiff: *The Works of John Wesley. Volume 19. Journal and Diaries II (1738-43)*, ed. W. Reginald Ward and Richard P. Heitzenrater (Nashville: Abingdon Press, 1990), 412; Wesley, *John Wesley in Wales*, 3-4.

— vestryman and overseer of the poor: John Hobson Matthews, *Cardiff Records*, 6 vols. (Cardiff: The Corporation, 1898-1911), 3:444, 455, 468. An acerbic local diarist had unusually good words for Glascott: "a very civil sober person" (*The Diary of William Thomas of Michaelston-super-Ely* [Cardiff: South Wales Record Society, 1995], 298).

— "one of the excellent of the earth": David Young, *The Origin and History of Methodism in Wales and the Borders* (London: Charles H. Kelly, 1893), 92; *The Journal of the Rev. Charles Wesley*, ed. Thomas Jackson, 2 vols. (London: John Mason, 1849), 1:255.

— inventoried at a very respectable £531: Will of Thomas Glascott.

— His wife, Elizabeth: Her father, Evan Deer, was interred "below the Spooks [spokes? spikes?]" in St. John, Cardiff. Similarly, her mother and sister were buried "below the Spikes." Few parishioners were so honored. See 12 May 1735, 17 November 1734, 3 December 1734, Registers of Baptisms, Marriages, Deaths, St. John, Cardiff.

18 "cut to the heart": Wesley, *John Wesley in Wales*, 60.

— "were not ashamed of the faith": Cradock Glascott to John Glascott, 29 December 1824, Cradock Glascott Will and Letters.

— Those defiant words came from Cradock: Baptism of Cradock Glascott, 19 November 1742, Registers of Baptisms, Marriages, Deaths, St. John, Cardiff; "Reminiscences of the late Rev. C. Glascott," 4–9. Cradock comes from Caradoc, a traditional Welsh name.

— Selina, Countess of Huntingdon: Edwin Welch, *Spiritual Pilgrim: A Reassessment of the Life of the Countess of Huntingdon* (Cardiff: University of Wales Press, 1995); Alan Harding, *The Countess of Huntingdon's Connexion: A Sect in Action in Eighteenth-Century England* (Oxford: Oxford University Press, 2003).

19 "rejoice[d] to find": Thomas Glascott to Cradock, 9 February 1773, quoted in "Reminiscences of the late Rev. C. Glascott," 3.

— fourteen years; pail of butcher's blood: Ibid., 23, 9–10.

— report sent to his patroness: *Extracts of the Journals of Several Ministers of the Gospel; Being an Account of their Labours in several Parts of England, during the Summer 1781. In a Series of Letters to the Countess of Huntingdon* (London: Hughes & Welsh, 1782), 75, 84.

— "Ah! this reminds me of good old times": "Reminiscences of the late Rev. C. Glascott," 22.

— Leaving the countess's employ: [Aaron Crossley Seymour], *The Life and Times of Selina, Countess of Huntingdon* (London: William Edward Painter, 1839), 2:458–63.

— resolved "to know nothing among you": "Reminiscences of the late Rev. C. Glascott," 29–30.

— "Never before in my life have I witnessed": Ibid., 40.

20 "The source of every evil is sin": Glascott, *Best Method*, 3. This was his only publication.

— "addicted to very gross and abominable iniquities": Ibid., 23.

— The first and third followed him to Oxford: Foster, *Alumni Oxonienses*, 2:528.

— "very much averse": Cradock to John, 3 February 1812, Cradock Glascott Will and Letters.

— Applying to cadet school: Cadet applications, L/MIL/9/119/249–55, IOR. In *Bombay Anna* Morgan asserts that William chose "not to settle for a poorly paid curacy" (17). In fact, his lack of a classical education disqualified him for the universities and thus the clergy.

21 footnote 2, derivation and meaning of *bibi*: Yule and Burnell, *Hobson-Jobson*, 78.

— An 1810 guidebook: Thomas Williamson's *East India Vade-Mecum* (1810), as cited in Collingham, *Imperial Bodies*, 73–74. On the official encouragement of concubinage in European colonies, see Stoler, *Carnal Knowledge*, 47–51.

21 "many partnerships of Indian women": Hawes, *Poor Relations*, 7.
— "solaced themselves by taking for their partners": Stark, *Hostages to India*, 20–21.
— so unusual that it caused "a great sensation": Collingham, *Imperial Bodies*, 76.
22 "connection with native women": Heber, *Narrative*, 3:373.
— felt to be "quite unvisitable": Quoted from Helen Mackenzie, *Life in the Mission*, in "Military Society in India, and Chapters of Indian Experience," *Calcutta Review* 22, no. 44 (1854): 435.
— As William Dalrymple has shown: *White Mughals*, 46–54. For other treatments of India's mixed-race unions, see Stark, *Hostages to India*, 56–59; and Hawes, *Poor Relations*. See also Thomas Edwards, "Eurasians and Poor Europeans in India" and "The Eurasian Movement of 1829–30," *Calcutta Review* 72, no. 143 (1881): 38–56, and 76, no. 151 (1883): 102–33; Frank Anthony, *Britain's Betrayal in India: The Story of the Anglo-Indian Community* (Bombay: Allied Publishers, 1969); Ballhatchet, *Race, Sex and Class*; Gloria Jean Moore, *The Anglo-Indian Vision* (Melbourne, Australia: AE Press, 1986); Peers, "Privates off Parade"; and Ghosh, "Colonial Companions."
— The consequences for mixed-race children: Hawes, *Poor Relations*, 4, 18, 19.
— Anna's grandfather spent his first year: "General Orders," *Bombay Courier*, 27 April, 11 May, and 25 May 1811; Bombay muster rolls, L/MIL/12/139/519 (30 April 1811), IOR; William Vaudrey Glascott to Cradock Glascott (copy), 26 June 1811, Cradock Glascott Will and Letters. Unaware that William was posted to Surat, Morgan assumes in *Bombay Anna* that he was stationed in Bombay for years, passed the time "exploring the city," and spent his evenings "talking and drinking" with regimental native soldiers (20, 22). These improbable conjectures are presented as fact.
— "insufferably dull and tedious": H. H. Dodwell, ed., *The Cambridge History of India. Volume VI. The Indian Empire* (New York: Macmillan, 1932), 161; William to Cradock, 26 June 1811. On the ennui of camp life, see Jeffrey Auerbach, "Imperial Boredom," *Common Knowledge* 11, no. 2 (2005): 283–305.
23 "assistance in forwarding me," etc.: William to Cradock, 26 June 1811. The commander in chief was General John Abercromby. The adjutant general was Lieutenant Colonel Robert Gordon, on whom see [Philippart], *East India Military Calendar*, 2:312–20.
— the great Henry Martyn: Avril A. Powell, "Martyn, Henry," *Oxford Dictionary of National Biography*, 37:36–37 (Oxford: Oxford University Press, 2004); John Sargent, *A Memoir of the Rev. Henry Martyn, B.D.* (Boston: Perkins & Marvin, 1831), 265–67. At Cambridge, Martyn had won top honors in the competitive mathematics examination. A gifted linguist, he translated parts of the Bible into Arabic, Persian, and Urdu. William heard him preach in Bombay between 19 February and 25 March 1811, when Martyn was en route to Persia and a

series of disputations with Muslim clerics. Dying abroad at age thirty-one, he was venerated by evangelicals, including Cradock (letter to John, 21 December 1819, Cradock Glascott Will and Letters).

23 To his brother John, the Reverend Cradock confided: Cradock to John, 3 February 1812, 5 December 1821, 3 April 1819, 21 December 1819, 2 April 1821, Cradock Glascott Will and Letters. When another son wed the daughter of a gentleman, Cradock boasted of the "very good connections" (21 December 1819).

24 never saw active service: Valentine Blacker, *Memoir of the Operations of the British Army in India, during the Mahratta War of 1817, 1818, & 1819* (London: Black, Kingsbury, Parbury, and Allen, 1821), appendix, does not mention William's outfit (First Battalion, Fourth Regiment, Bombay Native Infantry) in the returns of killed, wounded, and missing.

— In June 1820 William was shifted: *Asiatic Journal* 11 (January 1821): 82.

— sent to Suvarnadurga: Bombay military proceedings, P/357/59/1832, and Bombay muster rolls, L/MIL/12/144, both in IOR. The Suvarnadurga fort had been captured three years earlier (*Asiatic Journal* 5 [May 1818]: 525; [Philippart], *East India Military Calendar*, 3:135).

— "a fine breeze"; army convalescent hospital: Heber, *Narrative*, 3:124.

— As part of its campaign to suppress Arab piracy: Wilson, *History of British India*, 2:450–55; Kelly, *Britain and the Persian Gulf*, 180–92; Yule and Burnell, *Hobson-Jobson*, 485; *Asiatic Journal* 11 (April, May, June 1821): 408–9, 522, 627. Waite's appointment as adjutant is at P/357/47/3215, IOR; his assignment to the commissariat was reported in the *Asiatic Journal* 12 (August 1821): 195.

— The date of his appointment was 20 July 1821: Bombay military proceedings, P/357/64/4743, IOR. In *Bombay Anna*, Morgan has William sailing to the Gulf in "late December 1820 or early January 1821" and participating in various engagements there (27). In fact, he hadn't yet left the southern Konkan.

25 Thanks to a traveling English envoy: James B. Fraser, *Narrative of a Journey into Khorasan in the Years 1821 and 1822* (1825; reprint, Delhi: Oxford University Press, 1984), 28–35. In Fraser's account, Waite is "Captain Whaite the commissary." For what it's worth, Fraser and others attributed the deaths to an outbreak of cholera in the Gulf in July 1821 (*Asiatic Journal* 13 [January 1822]: 101).

— For a time William beat the odds: Cradock to John, 31 July 1822, Cradock Glascott Will and Letters; *Asiatic Journal* 14 (July 1822): 100. The base was evacuated in January 1823.

— It wasn't until July 1822: Cradock to John, 31 July 1822.

— "from a brother officer": Cradock to John, 13 February 1823, Cradock Glascott Will and Letters.

— "whose professional good qualities": *Bombay Courier*, 8 December 1821.

26 "a large packet from William": Cradock to John, 3 February 1812, Cradock Glascott Will and Letters.

— the bulk of his estate: Cradock signed his will on 25 May 1831 (Cradock Glascott Will and Letters). He died on 14 August 1831 (south wall memorial, Hatherleigh Church).

— The oldest, born in 1815, was Mary Ann: Aged fifty-seven at her death on 19 August 1873 (Bombay burials, N/3/47/294, IOR), she must have been born in 1815, given that her next younger sibling was born in mid-August 1816.

27 the second, Eliza: When she was buried on 7 September 1839 her age was recorded as "twenty three years and twenty three days" (Bombay burials, N/3/14/208, IOR). If the funeral took place the day she died, her birth date would have been 15 August 1816.

— The third, William: At his death on 5 February 1856, William was thirty-three or thirty-four ("Domestic Occurrences," *Telegraph and Courier* [Bombay], 8 February 1856; Bombay burials, N/3/30/69, IOR).

— siblings . . . present at family weddings: When Eliza Glascott married Tobias Butler in Sirur in July 1831, Mary Ann traveled the thirty-five miles from Ahmadnagar and signed as witness (Bombay marriages, N/3/10/191, IOR; John B. Seely, *The Road Book of India* [London: Richardson, 1825], pt. 3, route 2, p. 2). Six months later, when Mary Ann married Patrick Donohoe in Ahmadnagar, Eliza Butler made the reverse journey and left her name on the register (Bombay marriages, N/3/10/387, IOR).

— When Anna got married . . . Uncle William arrived from Bombay: According to a chaplain's quarterly summary of Pune marriages, Anna's five witnesses included "N. F. Glasscott" (N/3/23/266, IOR). No Glasscott/Glascott with those initials can be found in the Bombay Presidency's records. What happened was that, as the chaplain made his official copy of the original entry, he mistook Anna's uncle's tall, narrow *W* for an *N*. An exactly contemporary signature of his shows how easy it was to fall into this error: see "W. F. Glasscott," petition of 7 February 1850, D6a/24, USPG.

— This sharply defined middling status: There is no basis whatever for Morgan's notion that Anna's mother was "semi-literate" (*Bombay Anna*, 73). This prejudicial claim (stated as fact) is of a piece with Bristowe's supposed discovery that Anna came from debased lower-class origins.

— Mary Ann's first husband, Thomas Edwards: Register of recruits, L/MIL/9/41, *Lady Kennaway*, embarked 4 June 1825, also L/MIL/9/77 and L/MIL/9/100/37, all in IOR. Edwards enlisted in Westminster. His parish was variously recorded as "St. George Martyr," "St. George's," and "St. Georges Middx" (i.e., the obsolete county of Middlesex). St. George the Martyr, Queen Square, Camden, has no baptism record for him (London Metropolitan Archives). Baptism registers from St. George Hanover Square yield two possibilities: Thomas, son of

Thomas and Lydia Edwards, born on 28 June 1802, and Thomas Fortye, son of Thomas and Mary Ann Edwards, born on 3 July 1802 (Registers of Baptisms, St. George Hanover Square). Both birth dates are consistent with his declared age of twenty-two at his April 1825 enlistment.

27 transferred from the Infantry to the Corps of Sappers: Prior to Edwards's March 1827 transfer, his birthplace was given as Middlesex County. Afterward, in an apparent error copied from one muster roll to the next, it became Hereford County (L/MIL/12/151, pp. 276, 209, IOR).

28 Rutherford Sutherland: VI C 4:2 folder 28, p. 6, MKL Papers. Bristowe and Morgan dismiss the name as pure fiction (Bristowe, *Louis*, 26; Morgan, *Bombay Anna*, 4–5).

— The real link . . . was with her *mother's* father: Since Anna was born after her father died, everything she knew about him was secondhand. Granting that she both invented and suppressed, it seems likely that some of her story's elements were devised by a mother anxious about her own status. That would help explain the confused generations.

— musty 1822 casualty returns: Bombay muster rolls, L/MIL/12/146/431, IOR.

— two Indians being blown from guns: F/4/312/7138 (October 1809–February 1810), IOR. When transferred to the Twelfth Regiment, Waite, unlike Glascott, protested the loss of seniority (Bombay military proceedings, P/357/51/5368 [18 October 1820], IOR). His service record, at L/MIL/12/67/435, IOR, is undistinguished.

29 "one of the best Servants": Sutherland's service record, L/MIL/12/68/3ff., IOR. On his friendship with Metcalfe, see John William Kaye, *The Life and Correspondence of Charles, Lord Metcalfe* (London: Bentley, 1854), 2:126, 129, 154, 160, 179, 351.

— critical survey of British policy: See Sutherland, *Sketches*.

— Sutherland came from a farming family: Cadet applications, L/MIL/9/119/155–61, IOR; [Parkes], *Wanderings*, 2:183–84; Sutherland's service record; Gilmour, *Ruling Caste*, 184.

— married a Persian of high birth: Sutherland, *A Fighting Clan*, 184; Moorat, *Alfred and Eliza Stark*, 19–23, 26, 69–70, 183; Metelerkamp, *George Rex*, 247–54, 290; Winifred Tapson, *Timber and Tides: The Story of Knysna and Plettenberg Bay* (Cape Town, South Africa: Juta, 1961), 39–41; information from descendants in South Africa.

— both men were in the same battalion in 1815: Bombay muster rolls, L/MIL/12/141/151 (30 April 1816), IOR. There is no evidence for Morgan's supposition (presented as fact) that William's *bibi* came from Bombay and was his legal wife (*Bombay Anna*, 23–24).

30 footnote 3, "a Moslem lady's marriage": Gardner as quoted in [Parkes], *Wanderings*, 1:415; Dalrymple, *White Mughals*, passim.

30 "the Mother of my Children": Will of John Sutherland, probated in Calcutta on 4 January 1849, preserved in Cape Town. The family biographer who printed the will silently substituted "my wife" for the offending phrase (Moorat, *Alfred and Eliza Stark*, 69). Eliza was the youngest daughter of Sutherland. She married Alfred Stark in 1857 (Bengal marriages, N/1/92/563, IOR). One of their children (Bengal baptisms, N/1/108/14v, IOR) was Herbert Alick Stark (1864–1938), a prominent educator, Anglo-Indian activist, and author of *Hostages to India* and other books.

— Sutherland's job, acting through his Bombay agent: After his 1817 transfer to the Nizam's cavalry, his affairs were handled by Shotton and Malcolm (Bombay military proceedings, P/357/8/3459, IOR). This was the same agency that saw William's estate through probate.

— she would not have qualified for a widow's pension: A fund for the widows and orphans of Bombay officers had been created in 1816 (*Asiatic Journal* 2 [November, December 1816]: 511–12, 609), but a widow had to document her marriage to qualify. Some months after William died, the Bombay government queried the company's directors in London: Can "Native women Widows of European Soldiers" receive pensions from Lord Clive's fund? The answer was no, based on an earlier decision by the Court of Directors: the company would not "admit any persons resident in India as Pensioners on that Fund" (Bombay military proceedings, P/357/74/3727 and 3742, IOR). Nevertheless, Bombay's governor, Mountstuart Elphinstone, instituted a regional policy granting monthly allowances to native widows and their children (*Asiatic Journal* 14 [December 1822]: 612–14). Two years later London reversed its India-wide policy without going as far as Elphinstone. See Hawes, *Poor Relations*, 70; Ghosh, "Making and Un-making Loyal Subjects," 10; and Ghosh's comprehensive "Colonial Companions," 226–74.

— probate was granted by Bombay's Supreme Court: L/AG/34/29/345/2 (third quarter, 12 July 1824), IOR. Morgan interprets the agents' and attorneys' bond of sixteen thousand rupees to mean that William owed the company this amount (*Bombay Anna*, 28). In fact, as several other probate cases make clear, when bond was required it was invariably set at twice the value of the estate, just as in William's case. This was to insure the faithful performance of surrogates.

31 "'*Unto the third and fourth generation*'": Fyshe, "Anna and I," 63, my italics.

CHAPTER 2. A HARD SCHOOL

32 "all my people horses & dogs"; "Sent my dear little girl Mary to school": George Grenville Malet, journals. Mary was born on 22 June 1832 (Bombay baptisms, N/3/12/35, IOR). Her mother, whom Chaplain George Pigott identified only as "a native woman," was Fatima Bibi Sahib, a connection of Mir Ali Murad

Khan, who ruled an independent princedom near Khairpur in what is now southeast Pakistan.

33 When Malet was granted a two-year sick leave: Malet journals, 20 June 1847, 23–26 August 1847, 23–26 January 1849, 21 March 1849 (transcription by Edward de Broë-Ferguson), George Grenville Malet Papers. Murphy is identified in the *Bombay Calendar & Almanac* (1851), 934. For brief treatments of the kind of education British officers sought for their mixed-race offspring, see Hawes, *Poor Relations*, 11; and Dalrymple, *White Mughals*, 381–82. American missionaries wanted their children schooled in the States from "as early an age as possible" (William Ramsey, "Report of Bombay Missionaries," 25 November 1834, 16.1.1, reel 393, frame 116, ABC). On girls' education in late imperial India, see Buettner, *Empire Families*, 72–89, 97–104.

— John Sutherland . . . did even better: Moorat, *Alfred and Eliza Stark*, 19, 23; Metelerkamp, *George Rex*, 253, 290. Sons Eric and Robert entered the University of Edinburgh in 1846 (arts matriculation index to 1858, as communicated by Irene Ferguson, Special Collections, University of Edinburgh).

— "sturdiest and toughest of Anglo-Indian urchins": Palmer, "Child-Life," 629.

— The newly created Martinière Colleges in Bengal: Buettner, *Empire Families*, 75.

34 the Bombay Education Society: Originally called the Society for Promoting the Education of the Poor within the Government of Bombay, the organization was renamed when its mission expanded (Hawes, *Poor Relations*, 21–29). Annual reports from 1816 to 1849 are in the Asia, Pacific, and Africa Collections, British Library. In the late 1830s a second school for Eurasians was created in Bombay, the Indo-British Institution, with a more precarious financial base. Historians have paid less attention to these two institutions than to their counterparts in Bengal and Madras.

— Subscribers were allowed to recommend children: Rule no. 49 in "Extract from the Rules" as printed in annual reports.

— Sutherland was among the society's most generous and dependable supporters: Bombay Education Society, *Fourth Annual Report* (1819), 46; *Seventh Annual Report* (1822), 62; *Eighth Annual Report* (1823), 44; *Tenth Annual Report* (1825), 46. For later contributions, see annual reports from 1826 to 1834. Reports were for the year just prior to publication.

— "to be supported entirely": Barnes, *Sermon*, 16.

35 home visits strictly limited; "as it is generally found"; "no Girl shall be allowed": Bombay Education Society, *Second Annual Report* (1817), 12; *Ninth Annual Report* (1824), 10–11; *Fourteenth Annual Report* (1829), 7. The military orphanages in Bengal and Madras had similar rules; see Arnold, "European Orphans," 110–11.

35 After rising at five, etc.: Bombay Education Society, *Second Annual Report* (1817), 12; *Seventh Annual Report* (1822), 8; *Twenty-Second Annual Report* (1837), 34; *Twenty-Ninth Report* (1844), 10. Afternoons were spent on needle-work in regimental girls' schools as well (Trustram, *Women of the Regiment*, 101–2).

— "on the floor on carpets": Cary, *Chow-Chow*, 1:25.

— Once, when the younger boys neglected: Letter to the editor from "A Feeling Englishman," *Bombay Gazette*, 11 August 1841.

— "the total depression of spirits," etc.: Bombay Education Society, *Thirty-First Report* (1846), 16. The new master was the Reverend G. A. F. Watson.

— After 1826 the school was situated in the Byculla suburb: Bombay Education Society, *Twelfth Annual Report* (1827), 14. Over time the institution evolved into today's Christ Church School, a private coeducational prep school.

36 The practice of placing girls in domestic service ceased: Bombay Education Society, *Tenth Annual Report* (1825), 10.

— "either disposed of by marriage": Bombay Education Society, *Twenty-Sixth Report* (1841), 25.

— "dark beauties": Cary, *Chow-Chow*, 1:24.

— If you needed a wife; "who desire to enter"; "at perfect liberty": [Gray], *Life in Bombay*, 245–47. See also MacMillan, *Women of the Raj*, chap. 7. By official policy, all girls who "married out of the Central [i.e., Byculla] School of the Bombay Education Society" were ipso facto qualified for a pension if their husband died (John William Aitchison, *General Code of the Military Regulations in Force under the Presidency of Bombay* [Calcutta: Mission School Press, 1824], 236). This may have been a powerful incentive.

— "the straight-forward, business-like manner," etc.: Roberts, *Scenes and Characteristics*, 1:30, 25, 32.

37 Mary Ann Glascott was about fourteen: Bombay marriages, N/3/9/331 (15 March 1829) and N/3/10/191 (3 July 1831), IOR. Thomas Edwards was born in 1802 or 1803 (Register of recruits, L/MIL/9/41, IOR). That Butler was born in November or December 1808 can be deduced from the 4 January 1828 embarkation list for the ship *Edinburgh*, L/MIL/9/77/123, and the Bombay muster rolls, L/MIL/12/165, 166, 167, and 168, all in IOR.

— Tobias . . . seems to have been a basket maker: Trade recorded at L/MIL/9/77/123 and L/MIL/9/100/138, both in IOR.

— much-sought-after Corps of Sappers and Miners: For East India Company cadets at the Addiscombe military college in the mid-1830s, the "great prizes" were commissions in the Engineers (Cavenagh, *Reminiscences*, 2). Morgan's mistaken supposition that the Sappers and Miners were "of even lower status" than the Infantry (*Bombay Anna*, 30) contributes to a pervasive misreading of Anna's early years.

37 "grisly bombardier of forty": Postans, *Western India*, 1:165.

— Foster P. Thomas: 25 August 1830 embarkation list for the ship *Brunswick*, L/MIL/9/100/231, and Bombay muster rolls, L/MIL/12/155 (p. 201), 157, and 158, all in IOR.

— Harriet Cloudesley, also married to a sergeant engineer: Bombay muster rolls, L/MIL/12/155, p. 201, IOR. Henry Cloudesley had purchased his discharge from the Royal Artillery before enlisting in the company's army and sailing to India on the *Brunswick* (along with Foster P. Thomas). If Mary Ann and Harriet were close friends, that might explain Anna's middle name.

38 "At variance with the received notions": Roberts, *Scenes and Characteristics*, 1:33.

— "tranquil happiness repays": Mrs. Abdy, "Early Woo'd and Won," *Bombay Gazette*, 20 November 1841.

— When Anna's older sister married: Bombay marriages, N/3/19/123 (24 April 1845), IOR. Her date of birth was 26 April 1830 (Bombay baptisms, N/3/9/454, IOR).

— died of peritonitis at age thirty-four: Bombay deaths, N/3/38/125 (13 June 1864), IOR. She had given birth on 19 May 1864 (Bombay baptisms, N/3/38/91, IOR).

— "the stern English rightmindedness": Anna to Emily Fowler Ford, 28 November 1880, Anna Harriette Leonowens Papers. Ford was a granddaughter of lexicographer Noah Webster, the wife of a man of wealth and taste, and an estranged friend of Emily Dickinson.

— "join the ruling race on their own ground": Hawes, *Poor Relations*, 29.

39 "*My* mother sometimes made me rewrite": VI C 4:2 folder 28, p. 3, MKL Papers.

— "A little miss who cannot sit her pony": VI C 4:2 folder 28, pp. 2–3, MKL Papers.

— "His large dark eyes shone upon us": Anna, "Thief in the Camp," 397.

— The second version, intended for adults: *LTI*, 142–44.

40 Bhils, a tribal people of western India: *The Imperial Gazetteer of India* (Oxford: Clarendon Press, 1908), 8:101–4.

— Balmere: If the village existed and was given its real name, it may have been Bilimora, south of Surat near the Gujarat border, or possibly Barmer in southern Rajasthan.

41 "public treasure be kept only in Tumbrils": L/MIL/17/4/418/11 (22 January 1848), IOR.

— As Mary A. Procida observes: *Married to the Empire*, 47–53.

— The tongue the British worked at was Hindustani: Gilmour, *Ruling Caste*, 61.

— locket containing the admonition *Tibi seris tibi metis*: VI C 4:2 folder 29, p. 109, MKL Papers.

42 spoke an English nearly as barbarous: Roberts, *Scenes and Characteristics*, 1:31–33.

— "the steamer from Aden came to anchor": *LTI*, 7.

43 Military Asylum: Bombay Education Society, *Twenty-Third Annual Report* (1838), 22–23; *Twenty-Fifth Annual Report* (1840), 8–9, 14; *Twenty-Sixth Report* (1841), 11; *Twenty-Ninth Report* (1844), 24–25.

— When the new rules were finally published: Bombay Education Society, *Twenty-Ninth Report* (1844), 44 (Donohoe appearing as "Donabie," a name found nowhere else); *Thirtieth Report* (1845), 50; *Thirty-First Report* (1846), 52; *Thirty-Second Report* (1847), 59; *Thirty-Third Report* (1848), 71. There is no doubt that the lists' "Donohoe" and "Butler" were Anna's stepfather and uncle. "Butler's" assessment rose from four to eight annas soon after the uncle advanced from corporal to sergeant, and in 1846 he became "Assistant Overseer Butler" soon after the uncle rose to this new grade (L/MIL/12/176, p. 274, IOR). As for "Donohoe," in his last year as subscriber he was identified as "Serjeant and Overseer P. Donohoe."

— The payments . . . create a presumption that she, too, was schooled at Byculla: Unaware of this school, Morgan invents a fictive account of Anna's education in *Bombay Anna*, stating as fact that she "did well in the regimental school" in Pune and "finished . . . when she was about fourteen" (50, 52). No evidence exists for any of this or for the claim that she learned the Marathi language as a child (ibid., 52).

44 "forbid her pseudo-mother to come in"; "Secret conclaves, thrills, palpitations": VI C 4:2 folder 28, pp. 3–4, MKL Papers.

— The answers are to be found in the Byculla girls' school's escalating difficulties: Anonymous untitled article on troubles at the Byculla girls' school, *Bombay Gazette*, 22 September 1841; Bombay Education Society, *Twenty-Fifth Annual Report* (1840), 13, and *Twenty-Sixth Report . . . for the Year 1840* (1841), 7; *Bombay Gazette & Almanac* (1841), pt. 3, p. 40.

45 "abrupt resignation"; "the Ladies' Committee"; "at the shortest notice": Bombay Education Society, *Twenty-Seventh Report* (1842), 15–16. The *Bombay Gazette* darkly hinted that Hatteroth resigned "for reasons that are *currently known* and *duly appreciated*." Her next teaching job was at the Indo-British Institution (George Candy to A. M. Campbell, 28 January 1843, C BOM. 1, no. 185, USPG).

— Miss C. Yates . . . had reached Bombay on 8 May 1841: *Bombay Calendar & Almanac* (1842), appendix, 201. After leaving Byculla, she advertised the opening of her own private school (*Bombay Times*, 8, 11, and 22 September 1841).

— "every trifling thing": *Bombay Gazette*, 22 September 1841.

— The nature of these hideous rumors: Bombay Education Society, *Twenty-Seventh Report* (1842), 15–17.

46 "not knowing a word of English": Bombay Education Society, *Twenty-Third Annual Report* (1838), 8.

— "Eurasian social hierarchy": Hawes, *Poor Relations*, x.

— became paid pupil-teachers: Annual reports refer to the employment of older girls but never name them. In 1848, the year before Anna married, a rule was adopted that pupil-teachers "should be 15 years of age, and bound to the Mistress, to continue for three years at similar salaries to the boys' pupil-teachers" (Bombay Education Society, *Thirty-Fourth Report* [1849], 58). Had a promising pupil-teacher quit before her three-year term was up? If so, was she Anna?

— able alumnae . . . rose to be headmistress: The first pupil to become headmistress was Ellen Ford / Mrs. Berriman. Bombay Education Society, *Twelfth Annual Report* (1827), 7, and *Sixteenth Annual Report* (1831), 8; Bombay marriages, N/3/6/294, IOR.

— early training in elocution: VI C 4:2 folder 29a, p. 187, MKL Papers.

— footnote 1, "sing-song, almost Welsh" ring: Buettner, *Empire Families*, 72.

— "the English residents," etc.: *LTI*, 318, 36–37.

47 one of whose members was surnamed Conybeare: Bombay Education Society, *Thirty-Fifth Report* (1850), 4.

— far more impressive middle name: Birth no. 2583, Registry of Births, Deaths and Marriages in the State of Western Australia; Avis Selina Fyshe to ML, 8 February 1944, VI C 1:1 folder 2, MKL Papers. Another middle name belatedly given the girl was Crawford, Anna's fictitious maiden name. One wonders if this was inspired by the Honorable J. H. Crawford, a vice president of the Bombay Education Society from 1841 to 1845—the period Anna seems to have been at Byculla.

— In 1848 the Bombay Education Society got a new patroness: The Falklands arrived in Bombay on 29 April 1848 (*Bombay Calendar* [1849], viii). They left in 1853.

— "The girls are certainly singularly plain," etc.: Cary, *Chow-Chow*, 1:23–27. Lady Falkland's description of the Byculla girls' school, obviously composed after a first official visit, would have reflected conditions familiar to Anna.

CHAPTER 3. THE UNNAMED STEPFATHER

49 "a prominent position"; "domestic tyranny"; etc.: Anna, "Biographical Sketch," 42; VI C 4:2 folder 28, pp. 12, 13, MKL Papers; *LTI*, 39. Unaware of Donohoe's name, ethnic identity, and history, ML perpetuated Anna's misleading account of him in *AKS*, 9–11. In 1976 he was identified by W. S. Bristowe, who, however, altered "Donohoe" to "Donoughey," labeled him a "wild Irishman," and surmised that "his back probably bore the stigmata of the five hundred or more lashes which were meted out for bad conduct to three out of every four white soldiers in those days" (*Louis*, 27). This image of stepfatherly brutality misled

many scholars, among them Susan Kepner, who pronounced Donohoe "violent and abusive" and concluded that he took sexual advantage of Anna; see "Anna (and Margaret)," 11, 13. The first reliable if brief account of him was in Baigent and Yorke, "Leonowens," 402.

49 signature on the register: Bombay marriages, N/3/23/266, IOR. The other witnesses' names as transcribed by the officiating chaplain were John Donohoe (Patrick's firstborn), N. F. Glasscott (i.e., W. F. Glasscott, Mary Ann's brother), and Eliza and J[ames] Millard (her sister and brother-in-law). ML's statement that Anna and Thomas "married in 1851, very quietly" (*AKS*, 11) was twice wrong: the year was 1849, and the wedding was publicized.

50 "Payment of his Regimental debt": Bombay muster rolls, L/MIL/12/155/195, IOR.

— on 6 November 1831, Anna was born: Bombay baptisms, N/3/10/189, IOR.

— "palaces, mosques, aqueducts": Allen Graves et al. to Rufus Anderson, 27 March 1832, 16.1.1, reel 393, ABC.

— "general air of comfort": [Gray], *Life in Bombay*, 332–33.

— mixed-race widow was eligible for a pension: *Asiatic Journal* 14 (December 1822): 613.

— "serial monogamy": Ghosh, "Making and Un-making Loyal Subjects," 26.

— Their wedding took place in January 1832: Bombay marriages, N/3/10/387, IOR.

51 baptized in St. John's Parish: His obituary in the *Times of India*, 12 November 1864, implies a birth date in March 1809. The embarkation lists imply a somewhat earlier date of birth. Muster rolls L/MIL/12/165, 166, and 168, IOR, taken together imply a date of birth in November or December 1806. There are no extant baptism registers for St. John's Limerick from 1797 to 1825, so his parentage is unknown.

— it was up to the regimental colonel: All three army weddings in Ahmadnagar in the first quarter of 1832 were conducted by Colonel F. H. Pierce.

— Mary Ann's new husband had enlisted: L/MIL/9/42–43, ship *Edinburgh*, embarked 4 January 1828, and L/MIL/9/100, p. 140, ship *Edinburgh*, landed in Bombay on 2 June 1828, both in IOR. In spite of the fact that Donohoe was a smith, Morgan calls him a "farm boy," a label she also applies to cabinetmaker Thomas Edwards (*Bombay Anna*, 33, 31). This biographer's downgrading of Anna's family's social status is drastic and pervasive.

— he moved from the Infantry to the Sappers and Miners . . . Corps of Engineers: L/MIL/12/151–52, L/MIL/12/153, and L/MIL/12/154, all in IOR.

— Over the next several years he was posted: He was in Belgaum from 10 July to 1 November 1833 (L/MIL/12/157, p. 179, IOR), on 1 April and/or 10 September 1835 (Bombay baptisms, N/3/12/13, IOR), and on 31 October 1835 (L/MIL/12/159 [Town Major's List], IOR). He was in Sirur on 1 November

1834 (L/MIL/12/158, p. 197, IOR) and in December 1836 (Bombay baptisms, N/3/12/124, IOR).

51 In 1835 ... his name showed up on the Town Major's List: L/MIL/12/159, IOR.

— "no soldier from the corps of sappers": Jameson, *Code of Military Regulations*, 294.

— In 1837 or 1838: Vital records for Charlotte Donohoe's death in February 1838 and three Donohoe births in 1841, 1844, and 1847 show that the family resided in Disa (Bombay burials, N/3/13/378, and Bombay baptisms, N/13/15/475, N/3/RC1/373, N/3/RC2/565, all in IOR). In addition, from 1844 to 1847 the *Bombay Calendar* listed Donohoe as sergeant overseer "under the Ex[ecutive]-Engineer, Deesa" ([1844], pt. 4, Services Calendar, 239; [1845], Services Calendar, 164; [1846], 344; [1847], Subordinate Dept. of Public Works, 376). Disregarding these documentary materials, Morgan claims that in 1842 the Donohoes moved to Pune, where (we are further informed) "Mary Anne made a few rupees doing some laundry for officers' families" (*Bombay Anna*, 46, 49).

52 Patrick helped survey a road to the summit: Anna, "Thief in the Camp," 397. Mount Abu is about forty miles from Disa.

— managed to lay out a provisional route by late 1846: P/363/23/175,176, IOR. Unfortunately, official correspondence about the road never names engineers in the Subordinate Branch.

— "the immensity of labor": "Notes of Four Months Residence," *Saunders' Monthly Magazine* 3 (January 1854): 212. Mount Abu would be British India's only hill station in Rajasthan (Kennedy, *Magic Mountains*, 11–13; King, *Colonial Urban Development*, chap. 7).

— his name headed a list of promotions: L/MIL/17/4/417/115 (23 July 1847), IOR. See also P/363/37/4019, IOR.

— "the upper levels" of the PWD: MacMillan, *Women of the Raj*, 47.

— "an officer of engineers": Anna, "Thief in the Camp," 397.

53 John ... worshiped at an Anglican chapel: His signature is on a petition supporting the Indo-British Institution's Trinity Chapel (D6a/24, 7 February 1850, USPG). His wedding was Anglican (Bombay marriages, N/3/33/217, IOR).

— "superstitions of the Roman Church": Barnes, *Sermon*, 16.

— by the 1840s the Roman Church had greater respectability: Ballhatchet, *Caste, Class and Catholicism*, 13–18, 58–59; Wilson, *History of British India*, vol. 3. In 1834 Catholic burials in Disa were still being conducted by a missionary vicar, P. Emigdio Pereira (Bombay burials, N/3/11/200 and 381, IOR), but by 1838 there was a regular Catholic priest (Bombay burials, N/3/13/378, IOR).

— "Marulino Antao": Bombay baptisms, N/3/RC1/373, IOR. Donohoe's second son, William Arthur, born in 1839 (see Bombay marriages, N/3/36/35, IOR), probably had an Anglican baptism; his 1862 wedding was in Bombay's Anglican cathedral.

53 footnote 2: Burton, *Goa*, 97; *LTI*, 56; *RH*, 204 and passim.
— Father Ireneus from St. Theresa: Bombay baptisms, N/3/RC2/565, IOR.
54 the baptismal rites for their last two children: Bombay baptisms, N/3/28/101,
N/3/32/192, both in IOR. The son's birth was announced in the *Bombay
Almanac* (1859), 889; the daughter's wasn't.
— didn't care whether her grandchildren went to church: Fyshe, "Anna and I," 63.
— Twenty-Eighth Regiment marched into camp: WO17/587 (memorandum dated
1 January 1846).
55 local Protestants suffered terrible atrocities: Hugh Kearney, *The British Isles: A
History of Four Nations* (Cambridge: Cambridge University Press, 1989), 143.
— "very ruinous state": "Directory and Description of Enniscorthy: By an Obser-
vant Traveller—1824," in *Enniscorthy 2000*, 87. Thomas was baptized there that
year, 1824 (not 1823, pace Baigent and Yorke). He enlisted in 1842. The edifice
was rebuilt in 1844–46 (Kenneth S. Wilkinson, "St. Mary's Parish Enniscorthy,"
in *Enniscorthy 2000*, 350).
— footnote 3: Colm Tóibín, "The End of History," in *Enniscorthy 2000*, 396–98.
— "the Holiest & best men of the time": Minutes of 14 February 1854, SRMI.
— footnote 4: Minutes of 9 October 1854, SRMI; *Rules and Regulations for the
Guidance of the Swan River Mechanics' Institute. To Which Is Added a Catalogue
of the Library* (Perth: printed by Richard Pether, 1864), 61, State Library of
Western Australia, Perth.
56 wedding announcement submitted to two Bombay newspapers: "Domestic
Occurrences," *Telegraph and Courier* (Bombay), 8 January 1850, 2. The identical wording appeared in the *Bombay Times*, 9 January 1850. A notice in this
newspaper on 7 August 1841—"No charge is made for the insertion of domestic occurrences"—shows that such announcements were sent in by the public.
Anna's could not have been composed by the chaplain, as his register gives the
couple's names another form ("Thomas LeonOwens" and "Harriet Edwards").
It must have been Donohoe who drafted and submitted her announcement.
— announcement of Patrick's daughter Ellen's marriage: "At St. Mary's Church,
Poona, on Monday the 24th May, by the Revd G. O. Allen, Ellen, 3d daughter
of Mr. Conductor Donohoe, Department of Public Works, to Samuel George
Phillips, Serjeant, Sappers and Miners." *Telegraph and Courier* (Bombay), 29
May 1852. The first daughter would have been Anna's older sister, Eliza. The
reason Ellen was said to be the third and not the fourth daughter was that
Patrick's first daughter, Charlotte, had died.
57 "a most wretched looking place": George Grenville Malet, journals, 4 July 1847,
George Grenville Malet Papers.
— "a mere cinder": "The Past and Present of Aden," *Friend of India*, 21 April 1859,
as reprinted in *Straits Times* (Singapore), 21 May 1859, 4.
— "a kind of penal station": Gilmour, *Ruling Caste*, 185.

57 Not long before Donohoe arrived: P/363/40/5039–42 (16 December 1847), P/363/39/4684 (17 November 1847), and Z/P/3297/3202 (8 June 1848), all in IOR.

— Colonel Charles Waddington: L/MIL/17/4/418/77 and 168, IOR; *Bombay Calendar* (1847), 307, and (1848), 399. Waddington left Bombay for Aden on 2 November 1847 (*BGG* [1847], 874. Lieutenant W. S. Suart, whom he specifically requested, left on 16 January 1848 (*BGG* [1848], 48). Donohoe may have sailed on one of these dates.

— stepfather sailed to Aden . . . for two or three years: *Bombay Calendar* (1849), 692, (1850), 376, (1851), 450; *Bombay Almanac* (1851), 358.

— reason to think they were with him in March 1849: See chapter 4, page 67. Baigent and Yorke have Donohoe's family accompanying him to Aden ("Leonowens," 402).

— "a year or two" in Pune: *LTI*, 39. Thomas's letters to Anna (see chapter 5) imply that she and her mother were in Pune in October and November 1849. Although there is no reason to think Anna was schooled there, as Morgan claims, some of the Donohoe children may have attended the city's Indo-British Institution. Known to have been in operation from 1848 (Bombay marriages, N/3/22/242, IOR) to 1852 or 1853 (*Bombay Almanac* [1852], 579, [1853], 595), this obscure school moved its premises to the civil lines in 1849 ("Boarding Establishment," *Telegraph and Courier* (Bombay), Overland Summary, 17 September 1849, 1). The master, William McClumpha, was well known to at least one of the Donohoes: in 1859, having settled in Karachi, he would witness John Donohoe's wedding in that city (Bombay marriages, N/3/33/217, IOR).

— one of the most powerful men in India: Panikkar, *Asia and Western Dominance*, 75.

— "the finest station in Western India": Postans, *Western India*, 2:237. On the layout of cantonments and civil stations, see King, *Colonial Urban Development*, 79, 98–102.

58 "bracing"; "doubly welcome"; "flock in": [Gray], *Life in Bombay*, 160. Lady Falkland made the same point: "When 'the rains' are about to set in at Bombay, all Europeans who can . . . flock to Poona" (Cary, *Chow-Chow*, 1:214).

— "thatched bungalows": [Gray], *Life in Bombay*, 152–53; also Cary, *Chow-Chow*, 1:127. Anna's descriptive enumeration years later is strikingly detached: "wide fields, handsome barracks for the European soldiers, bungalows for their commanding officers, a hospital, a lunatic asylum, a pretty little church with reading-room and library adjoining" (*LTI*, 226). No one would guess that the church held memories for her.

— by the time he died; final rank: Obituary, *Times of India*, 12 November 1864; "Subordinate Officers Public Works Department," *Bombay Almanac* (1864).

58 last will and testament, burial was conducted: Bombay burials, N/3/38/269, and Bombay wills, L/AG/34/29/355 (second quarter, 1865), pp. 1–2, both in IOR. The will stipulated that Patrick's houses were not to be sold "without the united consent" of his two witnesses, one of whom was John Edwards, head accountant in the Collector's Office in Pune (*Bombay Almanac* [1864], 829). I have found no evidence that this man was related to Anna's father, Thomas Edwards.

— "Dearest Avis": Louis Leonowens to Avis Leonowens, 2 February 1865 (typed copy), VI C 4:2 folder 2, MKL Papers.

Chapter 4. Travel and Study with the Badgers

60 "with the happiest appreciation": VI C 4:2 folder 28, p. 12, MKL Papers.

— "Unable to endure the domestic tyranny": Anna, "Biographical Sketch," 42.

61 Anna's grandchildren had the impression: Avis Selina Fyshe to ML, 17 July 1943, VI C 1:1 folder 2, MKL Papers. Since the Badgers would have taken at least two servants on their Middle Eastern trip, Anna may not have required her own. In Bombay she and her husband would have servants, but the tutor she engaged there was a *pundit* (a Hindu teacher of Sanskrit) rather than a *munshi*. British colonials were dependent on their "bearer" and other upper servants and often retained them when relocating (Procida, *Married to the Empire*, 85, 100), but it would have been out of the question for Anna to keep the same pair from 1849 to 1862 as she moved from Bombay to Perth, to Lynton, back to Perth, to Singapore and Penang, back to Singapore, and finally to Bangkok.

— "It was a rich education": *AKS*, 10.

— "Anna met the thirty-year-old Mr. Badger": Bristowe, *Louis*, 28. The 1845 meeting is highly unlikely. Bristowe's mention of a wife three years Anna's junior refers to Badger's *second* wife, Elisabeth Ann Talbot, who, aged thirty-six at the time of their 1871 marriage, was three years younger than Anna, then thirty-nine. Yet Bristowe's statement was so ambiguous that some readers assumed (I did until corrected) that he meant that the wife was three years younger than Anna was *at age fourteen*. Badger-Talbot marriage registration, 3 October 1871, Clifton Registration District, Bristol, General Register Office, UK; 1871 census of England and Wales, London, Paddington, Saint Mary Paddington, District 6, 21 Leamington Road Villas; personal communication from Geoffrey Roper, 23 May 2007.

— later scholars happily amplified them: In 1995 Michael Smithies, an authority on Thai matters, conjectured that Anna's trip was "not entirely innocent; the Revd Badger seems to have enjoyed the company of young girls, and eventually married one aged eleven or twelve" ("Anna Leonowens," 138).

— "ran away to Malaysia": Cecelia Holland, *The Story of Anna and the King* (London: HarperCollinsEntertainment, 1999), 137, 28.

62 A recent biography of Anna assumes that the trip never happened: Morgan, *Bombay Anna*, 52, 54. Previously, Morgan had assumed, following Bristowe, that the chaplain was single and that Anna's trip with him was so "disreputable" that she suffered an "early loss of reputation" (Morgan, *Place Matters*, 242; and Morgan, introduction to *RH*, xv).

— Anna left her name on the marriage register: Bombay marriages, N/3/19/123, IOR.

— He was born in Chelmsford: Baptism of George Percy Badger. Geoffrey Roper, to whose scholarship and advice I am in debt, is the authoritative biographer: see Roper, "George Percy Badger"; and Roper, "Badger, George Percy," 201.

— quartermaster sergeant in His Majesty's Eightieth: Edward Badger's military career is documented in WO12/8462–67. I find no evidence that he was regimental schoolmaster.

— By the summer of 1821 they were in barracks on Malta: W. L. Vale, *History of the South Staffordshire Regiment* (Aldershot: Gale & Polden, 1969), 88.

63 his widow, Ann, married a private: Wade-Badger marriage registration, 11 January 1825, Eightieth Regiment, Half Yearly Return of Marriages Head Quarter Malta, 24 June 1825 (Army Register Book of Births, Deaths, and Marriages), General Register Office, UK.

— A sister went even further: Matilda Badger met Christian Rassam while he was working on Malta as Arabic translator for the Church Missionary Society. See I. Rassam to Secretaries, 22 March 1834, C M O 8/25, CMS; Coakley, *Church of the East*, 20–23; Geoffrey Roper, "Christian Rassam (1808–72): Translator, Interpreter, Diplomat and Liar," in *Travellers in the Near East*, ed. Charles Foster (London: Stacey International, 2004), 183–200; Denis Wright, "Rassam, Hormuzd," in *Oxford Dictionary of National Biography* (Oxford: Oxford University Press, 2004), 46:78.

— That was where their mother, Ann Badger, spent her last years: Badger, *Nestorians*, 1:70. Badger's *Sermons on the State of the Dead* (Bombay: Education Society Press, Byculla, 1861) were dedicated to the "Memory of my Mother."

— working for religious presses: At age twenty-one, hoping to be "wholly devoted" to missionary work ([Badger] to [Secretaries], received 2 May 1836, C M O 11/1, CMS), Badger applied to the American Board of Commissioners for Foreign Missions. He was turned down with the recommendation that he spend several years in America getting a college education, advice he rejected with some heat (Badger to Eli Smith, 15 July 1836, 60 [5], ABC). A few years later, influenced by high churchman William Palmer (Coakley, *Church of the East*, 35–36), he became a persistent critic of the missionary programs of American Protestants. In his view, "the principles of dissent" were not only "unscriptural" but uncongenial to "the oriental mind." Indeed, no "form of republicanism in religion has ever arisen in the East" (Badger, *Nestorians*, 1:10).

63 guidebook to Malta: George Percy Badger, *Description of Malta and Gozo* (Malta: M. Weiss, 1838).

— speaking up for non-English points of view: In 1835–36 Badger and his Chaldean brother-in-law got caught up in an English misadventure in what is now Iraq: Colonel Francis Rawdon Chesney's expedition to open a navigable route to the Persian Gulf. Two paddle steamers were transported in pieces from Liverpool to a northeast Mediterranean port, hauled overland to the Euphrates River, and reassembled. Somewhat unwillingly, Rassam was taken as interpreter (Chesney to Secretaries, 27 September 1835, C M O 8/27, CMS). He "complain[ed] very much" about the officers' irreligious spirit and begged Chesney "to allow him to leave, but all in vain." Hoping to get him released, Badger traveled from Beirut to Birecek, Turkey, where he learned that one of the two steamers had sunk in the river (Badger to Eli Smith, Aleppo, 7 March 1836, and Beirut, 18 June 1836, 60 [5], ABC). Surprisingly, his later account of the expedition was laudatory (Badger, *Nestorians*, 1:349). See also James Marshall-Cornwall, "Three Soldier-Geographers," *Geographical Journal* 131, no. 3 (September 1965): 357–65; Kelly, *Britain and the Persian Gulf*, 281–84.

— preferring *Islam* to *Mohammedanism*; could be cuttingly sarcastic: Roper, "George Percy Badger," 142, 149.

— His wife, Maria Christiana Wilcox: Maria Badger to D. Coates, 16 January [1840], C M O 11/2, CMS; *Register of Missionaries . . . 1804 to 1904* (Printed for Private Circulation), List II, no. 18, p. 262, CMS. At her death on 13 July 1866 her age was fifty-four (Kensington Registration District, General Register Office, UK).

— he had drafted a brief report: Badger, "Druses in Mount Lebanon," 28 December 1840, C M O 11/4B, CMS; D. Coates to W. C. Wilson, 21 January 1843, G/AC 1/4 32, CMS; W. O. B. Allen and Edmund McClure, *Two Hundred Years: The History of the Society for Promoting Christian Knowledge, 1698–1898* (London: SPCK, 1898) 305–6; C. F. Pascoe, *Two Hundred Years of the S.P.G.: An Historical Account of the Society for the Propagation of the Gospel in Foreign Parts* (London: SPG, 1901), 3:728; Coakley, *Church of the East*, 36–37.

64 Old East Syrian Church: Coakley, *Church of the East*, 4–5, 11. The Nestorians' dislike of sacred imagery led some in the West to see them as "the protestants of the East" (ibid., 14–15). This view suited Anglicans, who, as Irwin notes in *Dangerous Knowledge*, had long dreamed of establishing "links with the Eastern Christian Churches" (98, 88).

— So from 1842 to 1844: Badger, *Nestorians*, 1:35, 76, 192, 286, 340. On Rendi, see ibid., 1:224, 278, 386.

— The plan became a fixed idea: Ibid., 1:6–11, 176–77, 193–96, 284–85.

— "If Mr. B. were not so violent": Charles Sandreczki to Secretaries, 20 November 1850, C M O 63/34B, CMS.

64 mediator, diplomat, and double agent: Roper, "Badger, George Percy," 201.
— secured an appointment as assistant chaplain: L/P&J/3/1468 (5 February 1845), IOR.
65 He landed in Bombay in May 1845: *Bombay Calendar* (1846), 412. He was in Kolhapur by 22 June 1845 and as late as 28 September 1846 (Bombay burials, N/3/19/337 and N/3/20/297, both in IOR). He reached Aden by 3 December 1846 (Register of Aden burials, 1845–49, N/13/14, IOR). In England Maria made her home with her mother in Cheltenham.
— "necessary expenses on going to India," etc.: Maria Badger to Martha Ford (fragment), received at the Auckland post office on 20 October 1851, private archive, New Zealand.
— When the Bombay Education Society's Byculla girls' school was thrown into crisis: Bombay Education Society, *Thirty-Fourth Report* (1849), 18; *Bombay Calendar* (1849), shipping arrivals, xii; *Bombay Almanack* (1857), 633. The first thirty-five years of society reports show no other chaplain acting with comparable efficiency and effect.
66 footnote 1: Badger, *The State of the Dead*, 2nd ed. (London: Bell and Daldy, 1871), vii.
— "Congestion of the Brain," etc.: Surgeon [W.?] B. Barrington and Physician General John Patch, Camp Aden, 18 March 1849, P/414/19/127, IOR.
— Also on this steamer: Badger was important enough that his travel dates and companions were noted in the *Telegraph and Courier* (Bombay), 6 August, 25 September, and 2 October 1847; the *Bombay Calendar* (1848), xii, xxxi; and the *BGG* (1847), 806. While in Pune, the Badgers may not have crossed paths with the Donohoes, who resided in Disa as late as 15 October 1847 (Bombay baptisms, N/3/RC2/565, IOR).
— "an inveterate nervous affection": Badger, *Nestorians*, 1:360.
— footnote 2: Cary, *Chow-Chow*, 1:114.
— "at the new and full Moon," etc.: Barrington and Patch, Camp Aden, 18 March 1849.
67 On 29 March 1849 George and Maria Badger left Aden: Report by Captain J. B. Haines, 7 April 1849, P/41/4/19/216, 217, IOR; *Lloyd's List*, 18 April 1849, col. 6.
— "Mrs. Badger, the untiring partner of my wanderings": Badger, *Nestorians*, 1:360.
— Mount Lebanon was not a political entity: Salibi, *House of Many Mansions*, 69.
— "not happy to remain idle": Maria Badger to D. Coates, 14 March 1841, C M O 11/5, CMS.
— in Kurdistan he had encouraged the Christian hierarchy: Badger, *Nestorians*, 1:xvi.

68 After Egypt came Mount Lebanon: See Charles Henry Churchill, *The Druzes and the Maronites under the Turkish Rule from 1840 to 1860* (1862; reprint, New York: Arno, 1973), 91–94; Salibi, *House of Many Mansions*, 69, 162; Karl Baedeker, *Palestine and Syria . . . Handbook for Travellers*, 4th ed. (Leipzig: Baedeker, 1906), 282.

— footnote 3: Charles Henry Churchill, *Mount Lebanon: A Ten Years' Residence from 1842 to 1852* (1853; reprint, Reading, UK: Garnet, 1994), 2:322.

— footnote 4: Eli Smith to Rufus Anderson, 15 June 1849, and to Samuel Gobat, 12 July 1849, 60 (105), ABC.

— "faultless"; "exquisite sublimity"; etc.: Badger, "Mohammed and Mohammedanism," 95.

— As for Persian: Personal communication from Roper; Anna, "From Sadi," 206. In Edward B. Eastwick's translation, the poem begins "'Twas in the bath, a piece of perfumed clay / Came from my loved one's hands to mine, one day" (Sadi, *The Gulistan; or, Rose-Garden* [London: Trübner, 1880], 6). Morgan's claim that "Anna learned Persian in the homes and bazaars of Poona" (*Bombay Anna*, 55) is unfounded and implausible. During the few years that Anna spent in Pune she lived in a British station a few miles from the city. British stations did not have Persian-speaking homes and bazaars.

69 "taught her how to observe": VI C 4:2 folder 28, p. 12, MKL Papers.

— "As he is really a clever fellow": *Bombay Gazette*, 25 April 1851.

— Maria's well-written report of a visit to a Yezidi village: Badger, *Nestorians*, 1:119–27.

70 "the early Aryan"; "the purest Indo-European type": *LTI*, 86; *RH*, 103.

— "Note everything you see"; "When we meet again": Anna to Avis, 1 April [1865] and 20 June 1864, quoted in VI C 4:2 folder 29, pp. 99, 94, MKL Papers.

71 footnote 6, "an intense *amitié amoureuse*": Roper, "Badger, George Percy," 201.

— By early December they were back . . . in Mosul: Badger, *Nestorians*, 1:349, 360.

— Decades later she described the moment: *LTI*, 7, puts Anna's arrival in November 1851. The true year was 1849, probably in September or October.

— "Do you, Annie, love me": Thomas Leonowens to Anna, 20 October 1849, quoted in VI C 4:2 folder 28, pp. 14–15, MKL Papers.

CHAPTER 5. BELOVED WIFE OF THOMAS LEONOWENS

72 epigraph: Anna to Avis, 24 June 1878, quoted in VI C 4:2 folder 29b, p. 210, MKL Papers.

— "Beloved Wife": http://www.findagrave.com. Anna was buried in Mount Royal Cemetery. Louis was the middle name she gave Thomas after his death.

73 "unhappiness and trouble," etc.: John Thomas Pratt to Avis, 25 November 1899 (typed copy), VI C 4:2 folder 24, MKL Papers.

73 Pratt's mother . . . had secured a judicial separation on grounds of cruelty: Jacobs, *Boris Karloff*, 20–21.

— "Kidnapped": Kipling, *Plain Tales*, 118–23.

— footnote 2: Hawes, *Poor Relations*, 58.

74 his imperial helpmate: Procida, *Married to the Empire*, chap. 1.

— "forsaken guts"; "should establish a Matrimonial Department": Kipling, *Plain Tales*, 118, 119.

— the rector recorded his name: "Thos Lane Son of John & Mary Owens Bap. Jany 25th [1824]," Register of Baptisms, Marriages, Burials, 1798–1826, St. Mary's, Enniscorthy.

— his mother, born Mary Lean: Marriage of John Owens and Mary Lean, 25 February 1810, p. 19, Register of Baptisms, Marriages, Burials, 1798–1826, St. Mary's, Enniscorthy. The destruction of Irish records has obscured Thomas's mother's lineage. That her first son was named Gunnis Lean Owens (Baptisms, ibid., 27 December 1818) points to a connection with the Leans of Wales and southwest England. A John Lean who was born in Wales in 1782/83 and died in Devon in 1849 had a daughter named Margaret Gunnis Lean. In Cornwall *gunnis* was apparently a technical mining term, derived, one guesses, from a surname. 1841 census, Devon, Whitechurch, District 11, John Lean; 1851 census, Devon, Stoke Damerel, St. Aubyn, Margaret Lean; 1861 census, Devon, Plymouth, Margaret G. Lean; death of John Lean, Newton Abbot, Devon, fourth quarter, 1849, vol. 10, p. 125, Civil Registration Indexes for England and Wales; death of Margaret Gunnis Lean, aged sixty-three, Plymouth, Devon, third quarter, 1881, vol. 5b, p. 142, Civil Registration Indexes for England and Wales.

— Enniscorthy was a market town: *Enniscorthy 2000*, 87–88, 117.

75 John Owens, a boot- and shoemaker: *Pigot's Directory* (1824), 151. When Thomas married, he identified himself as a son of "John Leon Owens" (Bombay marriages, N/3/23/266, IOR), thus inserting into his father's name a version of his mother's maiden name. Evidently her lineage was seen as the superior one.

— let out dwelling houses: The midcentury Griffith's Valuation showed John Owens as the occupant of a house on Church Street valued at three pounds, ten shillings and the lessor of four houses on Guttle (now St. John's) Street worth one pound, ten shillings each. A Selina Owens, assumed to be his sister, leased a house and yard in Market Square worth twenty-two pounds.

— The older, Gunnis Lean Owens: Gunnis L. Owens, 1851, October, *Princeton*, New York Passenger Lists, 1851–91, http://www.ancestry.com; *Jurist*, 4 October 1851, 359, http://www.books.google.com.

— Thomas was also brought up to be a tradesman: His name does not appear on the lists of prize-winning pupils with which classical schools advertised themselves (see, e.g., "Classical and Commercial School, Enniscorthy," *Wexford Conservative*, 1 August 1838). Like William Vaudrey Glascott, he probably had a commercial education.

75 the day the seventeen- or eighteen-year-old youth enlisted: WO12/4450 (31 July 1842 muster roll).

— paid a shilling a day; three pounds in "cash and necessaries": Jameson, *Code of Military Regulations*, 719; *King's Regulations*, 469.

— more prestigious royal army: Peers, *Between Mars and Mammon*, 75–76.

— "in a state of actual rebellion": "The County Election," *Wexford Conservative*, 24 July 1841.

— British troops were often called in to keep the peace: Lawrence J. McCaffrey, *Daniel O'Connell and the Repeal Year* (Lexington: University of Kentucky Press, 1966), 39.

— *Lean* turned into *Leon*: WO12/4450–51.

— footnote 3: Thomas's first known use of *Leonowens* was in Western Australia on 1 May 1853 (Register of Baptisms, no. 150, Wesley Church, Perth). The date of his earliest known actual signature as *Thos Leonowens* is 20 January 1854 (Acc 36, 284/45–47).

76 bound for Bombay on the *Coromandel*: WO12/4451 (blue-bound register containing the 31 July 1843 muster roll) and WO17/560. Unaware that Thomas joined the army, Morgan states as fact in *Bombay Anna* that he sailed to Bombay as a civilian "in the second half of the 1840s, in late 1847 or possibly 1848" and entered the "flourishing job market" there (56–57).

— he advanced from private to corporal, marched to Pune, again promoted, daily pay: WO12/4451 (fourth quarter, 1843, and first quarter, 1844) and WO12/4452–53.

— In November 1845 the Twenty-Eighth left Pune: WO17/587 (memoranda for 1 January 1846 and 1 September 1846), WO17/596, and WO334/18 (Report Accompanying Returns of Sick and Wounded, Twenty-Eighth Regiment, 31 December 1847); "Notes of Four Months' Residence," *Saunders' Monthly Magazine* 3 (March 1854): 410.

— more likely to have met in the cantonment at Disa: I concur with Baigent and Yorke, "Leonowens," 402.

77 a sergeant major in the Horse Artillery: Bombay marriages, N/3/19/123, IOR.

— footnote 4: L/MIL/12/183, IOR; *Bombay Almanac* (1853–56), (1857), 663, (1859), 843, (1860–67).

— "a rich Indian merchant": VI C 4:2 folder 28, p. 13, MKL Papers.

— "do for" the officers, etc.: Trustram, *Women of the Regiment*, 109–10, 70.

— he was given a disciplinary punishment: WO12/4454 (second quarter, 1846). According to rules then in force, "Non-commissioned Officers may be reduced to the Ranks by the Sentence of a Regimental or other Court-Martial;—by the Order of the Colonel of the Regiment;—by Authority from the General Commanding-in-Chief" (*King's Regulations*, 174).

78 footnote 5: Information from Edward de Broë-Ferguson.

— official rebuke some years later for his "improper" tone: Acc 49, 40/1589 (1 December 1856).

— "inferior in mind to the Native troops": Minutes of 19 June 1854, SRMI. In 1838 English traveler Marianne Postans was quite biting about the ignorance of some company officers: "Knowing nothing of the country, but in its reputation for sport, and nothing of the natives, but in the character of servants, money-lenders, and traders, these hapless individuals speak in terms of severity of the whole population of India, of whose customs, manners, opinions, rights, and peculiarities, they are totally ignorant" (*Western India*, 2:228–29). When American diplomat Townsend Harris went ashore at Galle, Sri Lanka, in the 1850s, he got the impression that "the Indian officers are, many of them, much better informed than those of Her Majesty's service. The latter talk only of horses, dogs, billiards and cards" (*Complete Journal*, 37).

— proud one-word answer: *gentleman*: No. 3469, Birth of Louis Gunnis Leonowens, Registry of Births, Deaths and Marriages in the State of Western Australia.

— "on duty," restored to his former rank: WO12/4454. For a case study of another sergeant who was reduced to private and then restored, see Oddy, "Gone for a Soldier," 47–48.

— ordered to leave Disa, proceed to Bombay: The surgeon's report in WO334/18 details the regimental march to the Gulf of Cambay and the mishaps while boarding transports.

— forfeit his free passage home: Jameson, *Code of Military Regulations*, 236, 699–700. Having been in service five years, Thomas was eligible to purchase his discharge for eighteen pounds. Since his name vanishes from regimental lists, he must have been discharged, yet no record has been found. Desertion may be ruled out, given his later employment by the Military Pay Office.

79 In early 1848 three vessels sailed out of Bombay harbor: WO17/596 and 605.

— "a joint Indian and European creation": Renford, *Non-Official British*, 106.

— 1,600 nonofficial Europeans (Thomas's category), but there were 115,000 Parsis: Ibid., 15; "The Census of 1st May 1849," *Bombay Times*, 16 January 1850; *Gazetteer of Bombay*, 1:162; Christine Dobbin, *Urban Leadership in Western India: Politics and Communities in Bombay City 1840–1885* (London: Oxford University Press, 1972), 2–16. The city's most eminent Parsi was Sir Jamshetji Jeejeebhoy, merchant, fleet builder, philanthropist, and first Indian baronet. Anna praised him for doing more "for Western India . . . than any other single individual" but repeatedly docked his surname of a syllable (*LTI*, 125–26, 213, 226).

79 "personally acquainted with a Gentleman Parsee": Minutes of 12 June 1854, SRMI.

— Cursetjee Rustomjee Wadia; *Meanee*, a British ship of the line: Wadia, *Bombay Dockyard*, 297–306, 368; "The 'Meanee' Line-of-Battle Ship," *London Illustrated News*, 6 January 1849, 11–12. Another Parsi, Ardaseer Cursetjee, was chief engineer and inspector of machinery in the Bombay Dockyard and vice president of the Bombay Mechanics' Institute (Wadia, *Bombay Dockyard*, 330–44).

— *Minden*, the British battleship on which Francis Scott Key: Wadia, *Bombay Dockyard*, 208.

— he soon found bureaucratic work: Juror lists, *BGG* 19 (2nd supplement, 3 May 1849); *BGG* 20 (supplement, 2 May 1850); *BGG* 21 (2nd supplement, 1 May 1851).

— "Assistant Military Pay officer": This was Thomas's "Quality, Trade, or Profession" at his daughter's 1851 baptism (N/3/25/87, IOR). He was a "clerk" at his wedding in December 1849. On the meaning of these occupational categories, see King, *Colonial Urban Development*, 94.

80 half-brother John Donohoe: His checkered career can be followed in the lists of European and East Indian inhabitants in the *Bombay Almanac* from 1852 to 1865. Was the middle name he added circa 1860, *McCarthy*, the maiden name of Patrick Donohoe's mother?

— He too was a clerk, employed at the Military Board Office: No change in employment is shown from the 1845 *Bombay Almanac* (p. 73) to that of 1853 (p. 590). His inclusion in the 1853 directory is misleading, as he had left Bombay for Australia on 16 November 1852.

— "immense writing machine": Marx and Engels, *On Colonialism*, 67.

— "I should like to know exactly": VI C 4:2 folder 28, p. 17, MKL Papers. See also pp. 15, 18.

— Glasscott and Johnny had a connection with . . . Trinity Chapel: A 7 February 1850 petition in support of the chapel has their signatures (D6a/24, USPG). The Indo-British Institution was founded in 1838 by the Reverend George Candy, who resigned his commission in the Indian army to become a missionary to Bombay's Eurasians. For the IBI's history, see C/BOM. 1, nos. 16, 17, 185, 186, 189, USPG; *Bombay Almanac* (1851), 516–17; C I 3/O 4B/2, CMS.

— shifting him to the other column: the "non-Europeans": *Bombay Gazette*, 7, 14, 17 July 1851. Found by Nellie Habegger.

— To be racially indeterminate: Ballhatchet, *Race, Sex and Class*, 100; Hawes, *Poor Relations*, 89–90.

81 The first Indian autobiography: Lutfullah, *Autobiography*, 230, 396.

— Glasscott decided to change his middle name: The change is recorded in two annual compilations: the *Bombay Almanac*'s list of European and East Indian inhabitants and the *BGG*'s list of jurors. He was *Frederick* in the 1845–47 directories, *Vandry* in 1848, *Yandry* in 1849–50, and *Vaudry* thereafter. *Vandry* and *Yandry* must have been misreadings of *Vaudry*. Since directory information was gathered at the end of the year preceding the nominal date, 1847 must have been the year Glasscott made the change. However, in juror lists *Frederick* didn't become *Vaudrey* till 1850 (*BGG* 20 [supplement, 2 May 1850]).

81 sign himself *W. F. Glasscott*: signature on USPG petition of 7 February 1850, cited above; signature certifying a "true copy" made soon after 20 June 1854, Acc 36, 309/154.

82 "the apex of Eurasian aspiration": Hawes, *Poor Relations*, 42; also Richard Symonds, "Eurasians under British Rule," *Oxford University Papers on India* 1, no. 2 (1987): 28–32. The difference between male and female Eurasian destinies that John Malcolm observed in the 1820s perfectly applies to Anna's mother, aunt, and uncle: "The male part rarely marry with European women . . . while, on the other hand, the children of females of this class who have intermarried with Europeans, from being fairer, and belonging to another society, become, in one or two generations, altogether separated from that race of natives from whom they are maternally descended" (*Political History of India*, 2:261).

— "Is the alledged essential intellectual inferiority": Minutes of 22 May 1854, SRMI.

— According to the secretary's minutes: 12 and 19 June 1854, SRMI.

83 There are only six letters, all by Thomas: These survive as lengthy quotations in Avis Selina Fyshe's unfinished typed biography, VI C 4:2 folder 28, pp. 14–18, 29–34, MKL Papers. They date from three periods of separation: before the 1849 wedding (20 October, 14 November, and before Christmas); after daughter Selina's 10 December 1850 birth in Pune (undated fragment); and late 1851, when Anna and Selina were again in Pune (before 6 November and 11 November). Fyshe was not a trained scholar, knew little about India, was at times careless, and had trouble with the script. Her nonexistent "Girganno" (p. 33) must be an error for Girgaum, Thomas's section of Bombay in 1851–52. After Margaret Landon was sent a thermofax copy of the typescript containing these transcriptions, she decided that, owing to Fyshe's "difficulty in reading" Thomas's handwriting (ML's note, p. 14), *all* her transcribed dates were in error. Penciling in what she believed to be the correct dates, Landon made the documents harmonize with Anna's false chronology. Thus, smoothing the record, she shut her eyes to the surviving traces of Anna's actual history.

— office of a *shroff*: Thomas to Anna, 14 November 1849, p. 17; *LTI*, 225–26.

— "Did Mr. D. get the Bill on England": Thomas to Anna, before Christmas 1849, p. 18.

84 banns instead of a license: Ibid.; "Fees in Ecclesiastical Department," *Bombay Calendar* (1849), 992.

— "As I peruse your dear letter": Thomas to Anna, 11 November 1851, pp. 32–33.

84 "You say truly my beloved": Thomas to Anna (soon after 10 December 1850), 29. There is no evidence for Morgan's elaborate conjecture—presented as fact—that Thomas used "some vacation days" to go to Pune for the birth but had to miss the event when the baby proved overdue (*Bombay Anna*, 64).

— "During the breakfast": Thomas to Anna, 11 November 1851, p. 32. Anna's friend, born in Bombay and possibly raised there, was seventeen when she married (Bombay baptisms, N/3/11/336, and Bombay marriages, N/3/25/282, both in IOR).

85 He was now a clerk working for Robert Frith and Company: *Bombay Almanac* (1852), 581; juror list, *BGG* 22 (29 April 1852). On his daughter's 24 May 1852 burial record, N/3/26/118, IOR, he is Frith's "assistant." An important question is whether his employer was related to Dr. Robert Frith of Bengal, a Eurasian who had actively supported Eurasian interests; see Thomas Edwards, "The Eurasian Movement of 1829–30," *Calcutta Review* 76, no. 151 (1883): 131; and Hawes, *Poor Relations*, 128.

— footnote 6: *Telegraph and Courier* (Bombay), 16 January, 18, 22 October 1852.

— a clerk with the merchant firm of Peel, Cassels and Company: *Bombay Almanac* (1852), 576.

— "rank and station mattered less": Hawes, *Poor Relations*, 107.

— Bombay's "principal dwelling-houses": [Gray], *Life in Bombay*, 261.

86 lived for "a few weeks" in Parel: *LTI*, 40; juror list, *BGG* 20 (supplement, 2 May 1850); *Gazetteer of Bombay*, 3:286–93; Cary, *Chow-Chow*, 1:31.

— "To Be Let . . . a fine, airy bungalow": *Telegraph and Courier* (Bombay), 1 October 1847.

— "a very pretty cottage": Heber, *Narrative*, 3:100; Cary, *Chow-Chow*, 1:53, 59. Malabar Point is not to be confused with Malabar Hill.

— "I have taken a large airy house": Thomas to Anna, 14 November and before Christmas 1849, pp. 16–18. Fyshe's transcript of Thomas's description of the house as "near Government" may be incomplete. If a word was inadvertently dropped, perhaps it was the one concluding Anna's description in *LTI*: "To the right of the 'Aviary' was the government *summer-house*" (49, my italics).

— "completely isolated," etc.: *LTI*, 39–40.

87 Edmund Cobb Morgan: *Bombay Calendar* (1841), pt. 3, p. 67, and (1850), 934; *East India Registry* (1843), Bombay Establishment, p. 64; *BGG* 9 (1839), 858. For bereavements, see Bombay burials, N/3/12/328 and N/3/13/333, both in IOR. For sick leaves, see *BGG* 9 (4 April, 16 May, and 24 October 1839), 238, 365, 726; *BGG* 10 (2 January 1840), 18, 19. He returned to Bombay (*BGG* 11 [2 December 1841], 818), but apparently not for long: in 1844 he was dropped from the *Bombay Calendar*'s list of inhabitants. He died at the Cape in the Camp Ground District of Wynberg (Bombay wills, L/AG/34/29/350/2–7 [first quarter, 1848], IOR). The year was 1847, between 10 May and 9 November (Civil Trial Record).

87 "to serve the double purpose of human and bird habitation," etc.: *LTI*, 40–42.
— summerhouse on the Saint Lawrence River: Anna to Annie Fields, 29 August 1908, 8 July 1909, JTF Papers. The house was at Cap à L'Aigle, the point where the Malbaie River enters the Saint Lawrence.
— Morgan's house had a spacious upper floor: *LTI*, 41–43.
88 "exposed to the full fury of the wind and waves": *Gazetteer of Bombay*, 3:291–93.
— Morgan's main residence had been nearer the city's center: His ownership of a share in Christ Church (i.e., a pew) implies a residence in Byculla. Bombay Education Society, *Twenty-Fifth Annual Report* (1840), 13, and *Twenty-Eighth Report* (1843), 11.
— Anna was back in Bombay by 20 April: Bombay baptisms, N/3/25/87, IOR.
— the next year's jurors list had Thomas living in the crowded Girgaum district; "foul mirky atmosphere": *BGG* 21 (2nd supplement, 1 May 1851); Thomas to Anna, 11 November 1851, p. 33. According to Hawes, "most Eurasians lived in areas notorious for public squalor and high health risk" (*Poor Relations*, 88).
— he found quarters on Girgaum Road; Selina died: *BGG* 21 [*sic*] (supplement, 29 April 1852); Bombay burials, N/3/26/118, IOR.
— asked if she felt "any soreness": Thomas to Anna, 11 November 1851, p. 33. "Use cold water frequently," he prescribed, "but always dry yourself carefully afterwards."
89 a Hindu teacher of languages: *LTI*, 39, 49, 129–38; Anna, "My Sick Teacher," 34.
— Hindustani: Yule and Burnell, *Hobson-Jobson*, 417; Cox, *Short History*, 8; letter to the editor, *Asiatic Journal* 6 (December 1818): 596; Procida, *Married to the Empire*, 89–90. The 15 percent figure is from the 1901 census (*Gazetteer of Bombay*, 1:203–5).
— The syntax was Hindi; the vocabulary, Urdu: Interview with Dr. Virendra Singh, July 2005.
— "fit only to be spoken to a slave": Postans, *Western India*, 1:127. See also Mackenzie, *Life in the Mission*, 1:265.
— Sanskrit: Cox, *Short History*, 8. On the Orientalist-Anglicist debate, see Alexander Lyon Macfie, *Orientalism* (London: Longman, 2002), chap. 3.
— a gulf had opened between Indians and the English: Dalrymple, *White Mughals*, 485; MacMillan, *Women of the Raj*, 56, 60.
90 the ancient "Aryans" and their Sanskrit-speaking priests: *LTI*, 85–93.
— "inferiority of intellect"; "Solomon the wisest": Minutes of 12 June 1854, SRMI.
— taught a six-week beginning Sanskrit course: VI C 4:2 folder 29b, pp. 210, 212, MKL Papers; *Amherst Record*, 28 August 1878. On her last night, Anna was pressed into giving a lecture to "the ladies of Amherst."
— footnote 7: Amherst College, *Normal School*, 7.
— resumed study at the University of Leipzig: Avis Selina Fyshe to ML, 17 July 1843, VI C 1:1 folder 2, MKL Papers; Anna to Annie Fields, 11 November 1900 and 2 March 1902, JTF Papers; Valentina Stache-Rosen, *German Indologists:*

Biographies of Scholars in Indian Studies Writing in German (New Delhi: Max Mueller Bhavan, 1981), 106–8. Thanks to Gunhild Kübler for querying University of Leipzig archivist Jens Blecher.

91 invited by a rich, young Brahman: The scenes described in the next few paragraphs plus the quotations are from *LTI*, chap. 8. Anna's claim that her book about India was based on "voluminous notes of early travel" (p. 5) was surely true in part. Baboo Ram Chunder, her name for her host, may have been Ramchunder Bulivant, one of the "Leading Natives in Bombay" in a later *Bombay Almanack* (1868), 839.

— official visits made by English ladies: Procida, *Married to the Empire*, 177–78; Cary, *Chow-Chow*, 1:171–75. Antoinette M. Burton notes that most British feminists saw "women of India not as equals but as unfortunates in need of saving" ("The White Woman's Burden: British Feminists and the Indian Woman, 1865–1915," *Women's Studies International Forum* 13, no. 4 [1990]: 295).

92 With Muslims Anna seemed to feel a special bond: *LTI*, 252, 265.

— as far south as Kazan: Anna to Avis, 10 September 1881, quoted in VI C 4:2 folder 29b, pp. 230B, 231A, MKL Papers.

93 those pukka sahib ceremonies: See [Gray], *Life in Bombay*, 50–51, 181–82.

— always popping in between tea and dinner: King, *Colonial Urban Development*, 87.

— "The viceroy and the great English grandees": *LTI*, 29, 322.

CHAPTER 6. SELINA'S DEATH AND
KEESAH'S LAST LONG LOOK

95 "I have just received": Thomas to Anna (soon after 10 December 1850), quoted in VI C 4:2 folder 28, p. 29, MKL Papers. "Nohoe," found in no contemporary directory, must be Avis Selina Fyshe's inaccurate transcription of the physician's actual name.

— Four months later, when the child was baptized: Bombay baptisms, N/3/25/87, IOR.

— "The strong instinct of the mother": Anna to [Avis?], 1880, quoted in VI C 4:2 folder 29b, p. 217, MKL Papers.

96 sister Eliza Millard moved to Bombay: Eliza's husband was pensioned on 25 October 1850 and then or later received permission to reside in Bombay (L/MIL/12/183, IOR). The move probably took place well before 8 August 1852, when Eliza's third child was baptized in that city (N/3/26/134, IOR).

— "I was a great pet": Eliza Sarah Millard Pratt to John Thomas Pratt, [1899], quoted in John Thomas Pratt to Avis, 25 November 1899 (typed copy), VI C 4:2 folder 24, MKL Papers.

— seventeen months: Bombay burials, N/3/26/118, IOR.

— "When Mrs. Leonowens was only eighteen": Anna, "Biographical Sketch," 42. The version of this that Anna gave her grandchildren made her suffering even more extreme: "my life was despaired of" (VI C 4:2 folder 28, p. 35, MKL Papers).

97 "a little deranged": Anna's words as quoted in LWJ to Annie Fields, 16 August 1868, LWJ Papers.

— "the terrible lesson"; "all loved persons": VI C 4:2 folder 29b, p. 245, MKL Papers.

— "purposeless and exhausted": Anna to Annie Fields, 13 April 1889, FI 5055, and 10 December 1889, FI 5059, JTF Papers.

— sent her sister Eliza a letter threatening to kill herself: John Thomas Pratt to Avis, 25 November 1899.

— "had recently lost a very dear relative," etc.: *RH*, 250; Bombay burials, N/3/38/ 125, IOR.

98 recently published translation; "If it were only to give": Rogers, *Buddhaghosha's Parables*, viii, 100–101; *RH*, 253. For another early translation into English, see Mrs. Rhys Davids, *Psalms of the Early Buddhists. I.—Psalms of the Sisters* (1909; reprint, London: Pali Text Society, 1980), 106–7.

— "In the village of Sârvâthi," etc.: *RH*, 250–53.

— footnote 1: Rogers, *Buddhaghosha's Parables*, 100.

— footnote 2: Ibid.

100 footnote 3: Dow, *Anna Leonowens*, 104, 118.

— Remarkably, we have a firsthand report: "Buddha and Buddhism," *Chicago Daily Tribune*, 1 February 1875, 8. According to the advertisement (*Tribune*, 31 January 1875, 16), admission was ten cents, a fifth of what a comic lecture, "Dialect Humor," cost. The reporter was probably someone other than Sydney Howard Gay, who had moved back to New York.

101 born eight months to the day: Thomas Leonowens's 24 January 1853 birth was recorded at his 1 May 1853 baptism (Register of Baptisms, Wesley Church, Perth). This birth date is consistent with a reported age of "13 months" (*Inquirer* [Perth], 22 March 1854) at his 16 March death. Misreading "13" as "19," Morgan announces that he was born "in late July or early August 1852" (impossible, given Selina's birth the previous December) and that his parents' decision to leave India was "motivated almost entirely by the determination to keep . . . [him] alive" (unlikely, as he hadn't been born) (*Bombay Anna*, 77, 74–75).

102 "There are now a little Protestant church": *LTI*, 232. In Lady Falkland's eyes, the travelers' bungalows provided by government were "wretched-looking abodes. . . . Should the chairs have backs, seats, and their usual number of legs, the traveller who brings none with him may congratulate himself" (Cary, *Chow-Chow*, 1:189).

— "In the morning, when you wake": Cary, *Chow-Chow*, 1:142.

103 Gold had been discovered: "South Australia," *Bombay Gazette*, 9, 11 November 1852. On travelers seeking to leave for Australia, see *Bombay Gazette*, 14, 28 October 1852.

103 monopoly of government clerical work undermined: Hawes, *Poor Relations*, 122–23.

— "the educated native community of India": *Telegraph and Courier* (Bombay), 19 April 1849, citing the latest *Calcutta Review*.

— "continue to be superseded": "The Memorial of *East Indians* . . . residing in *London*," in *Fifth Report from the Select Committee on Indian Territories* (ordered printed 14 July 1853), British Parliamentary Papers, vol. 28, appendix 3, p. 114, IOR.

— official encouragement, especially in Madras: Cornish, *Under the Southern Cross*, 269–71.

— "very respectable testimonials": Deputy Commissary General William F. Mends to Governor Charles FitzGerald, Acc 36, 266/154.

— they booked passage on the *Ganges*: The names of Anna, Thomas, and Glasscott do not appear on passenger lists published in Bombay (*BGG* [25 November 1852], 2231; *Bombay Gazette*, 17 November 1852, 3; *Telegraph and Courier* [Bombay], 17 November 1852, 2). Fortunately, on 10 December 1852 the *Singapore Free Press* noted the trio's arrival on the *Ganges* on 4 December (thanks to Ong Eng Chuan).

Chapter 7. An Accidental Life in Perth, Western Australia

105 Chapters 7 and 8 are closely based on a paper jointly written by the author and Gerard Foley, "Anna and Thomas Leonowens in Western Australia, 1853–57." Presented by Foley in March 2008 at a meeting of the Royal Western Australia Historical Society, it was published electronically in March 2010 as Occasional Paper No. 1 by the State Records Office of Western Australia, with photos not in this book: http://www.sro.wa.gov.au/about-us/publications-historical-and -genealogical.

— The *Alibi*: "The Barque *Alibi*," *Perth Gazette*, 25 March 1853; daily indexes to *Lloyd's List*, reel 14; *Lloyd's List*, 22 July 1852, col. 8, 17 August 1852, col. 11, 19 November 1852, col. 8; *Lloyd's Register of British and Foreign Shipping* (1850, 1852, 1853 eds.).

— "For Port Phillip": *Straits Times* (Singapore), 16 November 1852, 4.

106 Peninsular & Oriental's fast new Australian Line: *Straits Times*, 14 December 1852, 3.

— "an outline chart"; twenty deck and steerage passengers and the trio from India: *Perth Gazette*, 25 March 1853. Glasscott was identified as a cabin passenger in "Fremantle," *Inquirer*, 23 March 1853.

— "obliged to put into Batavia [Djakarta] leaky": *Perth Gazette*, 25 March 1853; *Lloyd's List*, 14 February 1853, col. 10.

106 footnote 1, The *Ganges* . . . had put in at Galle, Ceylon: *Lloyd's List*, 29 December 1852, col. 10, and 18 January 1853, col. 11.

— the barque reached Anyar in the Strait of Sunda on 14 January 1853: *Lloyd's List*, 16 March 1853, col. 10.

— Three months later the date was noted: Baptism no. 150, Register of Baptisms, Wesley Church, Perth.

— "I trust my love you did not suffer much," etc.: VI C 4:2 folder 28, pp. 29, 33, MKL Papers.

— Six weeks later: *Inquirer*, 23 March 1853; *Perth Gazette*, 25 March 1853. All details of the incident come from these two newspaper reports unless otherwise noted.

107 cigars, shoes, tapioca, etc.: "To Be Sold by Auction," *Inquirer*, 6 April 1853.

— in the vicinity of Moore River: "£5 Reward," *Perth Gazette*, 22 April 1853; "Domestic Sayings and Doings," *Perth Gazette*, 29 April 1853.

108 angry riposte: H.A.E., letter to the editor, *Perth Gazette*, 1 April 1853.

— "the ship 'Alibi' went on some rocks": VI C 4:2 folder 28, p. 35, MKL Papers. Nothing was said of St. James's Square in Redpath's 1870s publicity (Anna, "Biographical Sketch," 42).

— reputation as a dumping ground: Colm Kiernan, ed., *Ireland and Australia* (North Ryde, New South Wales: Angus & Robertson, 1984), 34; Patrick O'Farrell, *The Irish in Australia: 1788 to the Present* (Notre Dame, Ind.: University of Notre Dame Press, 2000), 51.

109 Western Australia . . . had grown so slowly: Pamela Statham, "Swan River Colony 1829–1850," in Stannage, *New History*, 181–210.

— imperial revenue . . . almost quadrupled: Untitled editorial, *Perth Gazette*, 10 June 1853.

— "swamps, sand-heaps and lakes": J. B. Roe, "Some Old-Time Memories," *Journal and Proceedings of the Western Australian Historical Society* 1, no. 1 (1927): 6.

— "Within the last few months"; population rose to 2,755: *Perth Gazette*, 21 October 1853; census of September 1854 as summarized in the *Western Australian Almanack* (1855).

— footnote 3: Cornish, *Under the Southern Cross*, 459.

— Five days after the travelers arrived: Acc 36, 266/154, 265.

— Glasscott had also become a writer in the commissariat: Acc 36, 266/238.

110 *Alibi* repaired, stocked with new cargo, and cleared at last for Melbourne: "Fremantle" and "Wanted to Borrow, £600 on the Barque *Alibi's* Cargo," *Inquirer*, 6 April 1853; Acc 36, 266/194; "Shipping Intelligence," *Inquirer*, 4, 11, 18 May 1853; "For Melbourne Direct," *Perth Gazette*, 13 May 1853; "Notice to Passengers per 'Alibi,'" *Perth Gazette*, 20 May 1853; "Shipping Intelligence," *Melbourne Morning Herald*, 20 June 1853.

110 solicited sealed bids: "Commissariat Contracts for Annual Supplies," *Inquirer*, 8 November 1854. The large commissariat building, pictured in Simon Nevill, *Perth and Fremantle: Past and Present* (Fremantle, Western Australia: Simon Nevill Publications, 2007), 54–55, stood at the foot of Barrack Street near the present Supreme Court.

— Anton Helmich: Erickson, *Bicentennial Dictionary*, 2:1436; Honniball, "Dual Administrative Establishments," 32; "Domestic Sayings and Doings," *Perth Gazette*, 29 July, 16 September 1853; C. A. Jenkins, "Early Years of the Methodist Church in Western Australia," *Early Days* 2, no. 13 (1933): 10–12.

— His application: Acc 36, 271/268–70; Acc 49, 36 (9 September 1853); Acc 36, 267/148.

— "it is impossible to retain them": "Local and Domestic Intelligence," *Inquirer*, 8 August 1855.

111 On 15 December . . . he quit: Acc 36, 271/280. Since he left about the time the next year's *Western Australian Almanack* went to press, "Mr Leon Owens" would be shown, misleadingly, as postal clerk in 1854 (21).

— He went back to . . . the deputy commissary general: Although no application or appointment has been found, much of the 1854–55 office paperwork is in Thomas's hand (see Acc 36, 284/23, 24, 60, etc.). A 20 January 1854 signature guaranteeing the accuracy of a "true copy"—*Thos Leonowens*—proves he was working there (Acc 36, 284/45–47). Later "true copy" signatures are at Acc 36, 319/174–75, 188.

— "a sincere and practical love": *Western Australian Almanack* (1854), 46.

— seen as a free school for the poor: Colonial Secretary Frederick Barlee believed that "the primary object of public Schools . . . is the education of the poor" (*Inquirer*, 19 December 1855).

— "If matters go on"; "thoroughly inefficient": "To the Editor," *Perth Gazette*, 3 February 1854; editorial, *Inquirer*, 3 January 1855.

— The advertisement Anna placed: *Western Australian Almanack* (1854), 54.

112 This novel . . . in Bombay before Anna's departure and in Perth after her arrival: The *Telegraph and Courier* (Bombay) ran long excerpts on 20, 21, and 23 October 1852, as did the *Inquirer* (Perth) on 16 and 23 March 1853. No other contemporary novel got that kind of attention in India or Australia.

113 The congregation's register of baptisms: Anna's name is given as Harriet Leonowens. The Methodists were Perth's second largest Protestant sect, with 317 members as compared to 1,225 Anglicans (*Western Australian Almanack* [1855]).

— "On Thursday the 16th": *Inquirer*, 22 March 1854; "Notice," *Inquirer*, 18 March 1857.

— "was able to walk": *RH*, 250. In all translations the boy dies soon after learning to walk.

113 "still dreadfully ill": VI C 4:2 folder 28, p. 35, MKL Papers.
114 gave birth to a daughter, Avis Annie: No. 2583, Registry of Births, Deaths and Marriages in the State of Western Australia; no. 198, Register of Baptisms, Wesley Church, Perth.
— an organization had been formed: "The Perth Literary Institute," Research Note 422, State Library of Western Australia, Perth; "Domestic Sayings and Doings," *Perth Gazette*, 3 November 1854; Jan Partridge, "The Establishment of Mechanics' Institutes in Western Australia: A Case Study of the Swan River Mechanics' Institute," Sixth Annual Library History Forum, Monash University, Melbourne, 1995, 3–18 and appendix.
— elected auditor, served on the executive committee: Minutes of 3 July 1854, SRMI; "Domestic Sayings and Doings," *Perth Gazette*, 16 June 1854.
— held its annual business meeting: *Inquirer*, 1 February 1854.
115 "Was the execution of Charles 1st justifiable?": Minutes of 14 February 1854.
— In two consecutive sessions in June 1854 he vigorously argued: Minutes of 12, 19 June 1854.
— the original proposition was amended to read: Minutes of 19 June 1854.
116 "intermediaries . . . the important wheels": Stark, *Hostages to India*, 30.
— "to deliver a lecture"; "Study of History"; "versed in the history of their own Country": Minutes of 21 June, 21 August, 19 June 1854.
— "was listened to with marked attention": Minutes of 11 September 1854.
117 "Are Mesmerism, Table Turning, and Spirit Rapping true Phenomena of Nature?": Minutes of 31 July and 7, 14, 21, 28 August. Thomas attended all but the second of these meetings.
— "It might be difficult": *RH*, 184.
118 In Thomas's final contribution: Minutes of 3 July 1854.
— footnote 5: Anna to Avis, 10 September 1881, quoted in VI C 4:2 folder 29b, p. 231A, MKL Papers.
— "difficult woman": *EG*, 283.

CHAPTER 8. THE CONVICT HIRING DEPOT AT LYNTON

119 Geraldine lead mine: Helen Summerville, "Port Gregory," *Early Days* 6, no. 8 (1969): 74–88.
— Construction of the depot: Mathew Trinca, "Controlling Places: A History of Spatial Intent in Western Australian Convictism," *Historical Traces: Studies in Western Australian History* 17 (1997): 25–31; Lilley and Gibbs, *Archaeological Study*, 38–43, 51–54.
— "weather-boarded and shingled"; no local timber: Comptroller General Henderson's report, 9 December 1854, Acc 36, 297/42–43.
120 "the proper remedy": Duke of Newcastle to Governor FitzGerald, 8 May 1854, in *Australian Colonies* (1855), 205–6.

120 Glasscott was appointed the first full-time storekeeper: William F. Mends to Colonial Secretary William Ayshford Sanford, 23 August 1853, Acc 36, 267/69–70.

— By the following April: Lieutenant Crossman's report, 28 April 1854, in *Australian Colonies* (1855), Appendix G, 200–201.

— "supplies . . . sufficient to last six months"; "detail issues"; "the absurdity": Report by Colonial Secretary Frederick Palgrave Barlee, 6 October 1856, Acc 36, 358/20.

121 Captain Henry Ayshford Sanford: Sandra Simkin, "Historical Information on 'Lynton Heritage Site' Est. 1853," Northampton Historical Society, Western Australia, n.d.; "Loss of the Barque 'Mary Queen of Scots,'" *Inquirer*, 28 February 1855.

— Soon after Glasscott went to work: C. Gitsham to Charles Scholl, 30 October 1853, Acc 36, 309/103 (Sandra Simkin's transcript); Henry A. Sanford to William A. Sanford, 3 December 1853, entry 135, Sanford Family Papers.

— William Burges: Gillian O'Mara, *Burges Saga* (Cottesloe, Western Australia: Owen G. Burges, 2000), 4, 11, 17, 23, 25.

122 The big challenge a storekeeper faced: Acc 36, 256/197; Acc 49, 36 (26 October 1853).

— So policy had to evolve: Acc 49, 36 (2 February 1854); Acc 49, 38 (11 May 1854); Acc 36, 339/82; Acc 36, 309/138, 228; Acc 49, 38 (16 May, 28 December 1854); Acc 36, 339/9, 11, 29–32.

— In May 1855 a new storekeeper arrived: Archibald Edgar left Fremantle for Port Gregory with his wife and two children on 15 May ("Shipping Intelligence," *Perth Gazette*, 18 May 1855).

123 Glasscott sailed to Fremantle. By mid-October he was once again in Bombay: "Shipping Intelligence," *Inquirer*, 25 July 1855; "Shipping Intelligence," *Telegraph and Courier* (Bombay), 13 October 1855.

— master of the Indo-British School for Eurasian boys: *Bombay Almanac* (1856), 578. Having lost the support of the Society for the Propagation of the Gospel, the school may have been financially strapped at the time. Yet thirty-five years later it seems to have been doing well, and it was still in operation as late as 1909 (*Thacker's Indian Directory* [1891], pt. 2, p. 1027; *Gazetteer of Bombay*, 1:219).

— died of "dysentery and fever": "Domestic Occurrences," *Telegraph and Courier* (Bombay), 8 February 1856; Bombay burials, N/3/30/69, IOR. Just before Glasscott died, Reverend George Candy, his former pastor and the man who conducted his funeral, had a similar illness: "a severe bilious attack with fever" (Candy to Secretaries, 1 February 1856, C I 3/M 6, CMS).

— called Vaudry Glasscott Donohoe . . . the next generation's males were . . . Vaudry and Glascott: Bombay baptisms, N/3/32/192, N/3/51/277, N/3/59/290, IOR.

123 "British credentials were vital": Hawes, *Poor Relations*, 75.

— another man, Archibald Edgar, had a go at the job: Acc 36, 339/48 (11 June 1855), 53–55, 58, 82; Acc 49, 38/1952 (30 August 1855).

124 The employee who signed this document, warranting it a "true copy": Acc 36, 319/157.

— boarded the schooner *Perseverance*: "Shipping Intelligence," *Perth Gazette*, 12 October 1855. The passenger list named "Mr and Mrs Leonowens and child."

— footnote 3: Acc 36, 322/157; John Neary's testimony at the trial of James Johnson as reported in the *Perth Gazette*, 3 October 1856; Lilley and Gibbs, *Archaeological Study*, 84.

— Its dimensions . . . were twelve by thirteen feet: Lieutenant Crossman's report, p. 200; Captain Wray's survey.

— "one continued heavy down-pour": *Perth Gazette*, 29 August 1856.

— The well was caved-in: Acc 36, 322/157.

— shocked at how "very rough" everything was: Acc 36, 358/33v (6 October 1856).

— gave birth to her fourth and last child on 22 October 1856: Birth no. 3469, Registry of Births, Deaths and Marriages in the State of Western Australia. The date on the Port Gregory certificate is confirmed by a newspaper's announcement: "At Port Gregory, on the 22nd October, *Mrs Leonowens* of a *Son*" (*Inquirer*, 26 November 1856). When the family returned to Perth and had Louis baptized on 29 March 1857, the date of birth was changed to the 21st (no. 24, Register of Baptisms, Wesley Church). Eventually, Anna had it coincide with Avis's birthday. Thus, on 25 October 1866 in Bangkok an American missionary family was invited "to celebrate the 10th Birthday of [Master?] Louis Leonowens" (DBB, Journals, vol. 22, 25 October 1866, DBB Family Papers). Morgan's brisk rejection of Lynton as the birthplace—"I think it more likely that [Anna] stayed in civilized Perth for the birth" (*Bombay Anna*, 78)— nicely mimics Anna's own fondness for pleasing counterfactual narrative.

— The government didn't pay for the obstetric expenses: Acc 49, 40/223 (26 October 1855).

— in his teens he sailed to Australia: Bristowe, *Louis*, 36–37.

— Albert Hall Mansions; estate was worth £66,904: "Latest Wills," *Times*, 8 May 1919, 17.

125 There was no way the boy's luckless father would find his fortune in Lynton: Editorial, *Inquirer*, 11 July 1855; "Sir Arthur Edward Kennedy," in *The Cyclopedia of Western Australia*, ed. J. S. Battye (Perth: Cyclopedia Co., 1912), 1:293–94. On 30 January 1856 the *Inquirer* traced the history and difficulties of the Geraldine mine. The same issue advertised the sale of mine shares following the nonpayment of calls.

— sixty-mile ride to Champion Bay each month: Acc 36, 339/113–14; Acc 36, 367/42.

125 *"As there is no suitable person"*: Acc 36, 339/129, emphasis in original.

— Thomas's resignation of his clerkship: Acc 36, 367/92; Acc 49, 40/1349 (29 August 1856). Burges backed Thomas up in his complaint about too little time (Acc 36, 367/89).

— A fact-finding mission in September 1856: "Shipping Intelligence," *Inquirer*, 17 September, 8 October 1856; "Legislative Council," *Inquirer*, 15 October 1856.

— "I am directed to invite": Acc 49, 40/1520 (4 November 1856).

126 Several barrels of the precious tubers: Acc 36, 367/105–8.

— footnote 4: Cecil Woodham-Smith, *The Great Hunger: Ireland 1845–9* (London: Hamish Hamilton, 1962), 96.

— "I have to thank you": Acc 36, 367/110.

127 "gentleman": The birth certificate, cited earlier, is dated 12 November.

— "you [Burges] stated yesterday"; "Nor do I recognise": Acc 36, 367/112.

— Backing Thomas's contention and echoing his language, Mends, his boss, "submitted"; Kennedy agreed: Acc 36, 367/111–13, 106; Acc 49, 40/1589 (1 December 1856). Mends scribbled his opinion on a letter from Burges that had been annotated by Governor Kennedy. Then, returning the letter to the governor, he presumably sent a formal reprimand to Thomas.

128 Burges was an undisputed member: On Western Australia's conservative elite, see C. T. Stannage, *The People of Perth: A Social History of Western Australia's Capital City* (Perth: Perth City Council, 1979), 11–84.

— decided the depot . . . must be shut down: Acc 49, 40/1631 (18 December 1856); Governor Kennedy to H. Labouchere, 3 January 1857, in *Australian Colonies* (1857), 1–2.

— Mends's assistant: Thomas's reported grade at Louis's baptism, 29 March 1857.

— proposed him for renewed membership: Minutes of 16 March 1857, SRMI.

129 On 3 April . . . took passage on the *Lady Amherst*: Advertisements, *Inquirer*, 25 February–1 April 1857; "Shipping Intelligence," *Inquirer*, 8 April 1857; *Lloyd's Register* (1862); "Shipping in the Harbour," *Singapore Free Press*, supplement, 7 May 1857; *Lloyd's List*, 8 June 1857, col. 12.

CHAPTER 9. WIDOWED IN THE STRAITS SETTLEMENTS

130 Singapore . . . numbered 50,000 Chinese, 13,000 Indians, 11,000 Malays, and 2,500 Europeans and Eurasians: 1860 census figures from Buckley, *Anecdotal History*, 683; and Tan Tai Yong and Andrew J. Major, "India and Indians in the Making of Singapore," in *Singapore-India Relations: A Primer*, ed. Yong Mun Cheong and V. V. Bhanoji Rao (Singapore: Singapore University Press, 1995), 18.

— "great lumbering, red-painted"; "the white elephant banner": Wood, *Fankwei*, 142.

— Only four decades had passed since Stamford Raffles: Buckley, *Anecdotal History*, 1–17.

130 footnote 1: King, *Colonial Urban Development*, 90.
— Singapore was a natural base for international trading companies: Cameron, *Our Tropical Possessions*, 52, 177–89, 272; "Merchants and Agents," *Singapore Almanack* (1858), 45ff.
131 The Indian "Mutiny" . . . would straiten the administrative budget: Turnbull, *Straits Settlements*, 50.
— Thomas became a clerk; home on Brass Bassa Road: *Singapore Almanack* (1858), 46, 64.
— Organized in London the previous year: Borneo Company Ltd. Papers; Longhurst, *Borneo Story*, 17–18, 116–17.
— William Adamson: *Singapore Almanack* (1858), 59, (1859), 60; Makepeace, *One Hundred Years*, 2:181–82; "Sir William Adamson," *Times*, 13 March 1917, 9.
— Adamson came from dissenting stock: Born in 1832/33 in Hayfield, Derbyshire, Adamson was close in age to Anna. His father, Ebenezer, was inspector of the poor in Glasgow. His father's father, John, minister of Hayfield's Independent Church, wrote controversial pamphlets with such titles as *The Unlawfulness of Instrumental Music in the Worship of God* (Manchester: Silburn & Richardson, 1823). Death of Ebenezer Adamson, 3 June 1876, Glasgow City, Partick District; 1841 census, Derbyshire, Glossop, Hayfield, District 16; 1881 census, Middlesex, Hornsey, Holy Innocents, Middle Lane, "The Chestnuts"; personal communication from Fiona Rees, Derby Local Studies Library, 6 March 2007.
— Adamson worshiped with Presbyterians: Although membership records vanished under Japanese occupation, Adamson's affiliation seems clear from the fact that Reverend Fraser officiated at his wedding ("Domestic Occurrences," *Straits Times*, 14 May 1859).
— light comedian; "a woman's part": Makepeace, *One Hundred Years*, 2:384.
132 "two fifths of the European inhabitants": Fraser's words as quoted in Robert M. Greer, comp., *A History of the Presbyterian Church in Singapore* (Singapore, 1959), 34.
— the church Thomas and Anna joined: As Singapore had no Methodist society, their one real choice was the Presbyterians. Other signs of this affiliation: Reverend Fraser's accompanying Anna on the boat from Penang, her sense of relief at seeing the American Presbyterian Mission when entering Bangkok (*EG*, 7), and the fact that she took Communion at this mission (DBB, Journals, vol. 21, 7 August 1865, DBB Family Papers).
— foreman of a jury: "Criminal Court," *Straits Times*, 21, 27 April, 22 May 1858. The jury's third sitting on 10 May is the latest date Thomas is known to have been in Singapore.
— a widely circulated story about Anna's supposed turning point: The notion that she created a new history and identity for Singapore ("where no one knew

her") was first aired in *Anna and the King: The Real Story of Anna Leonowens*, a 1999 television documentary. This specious fact is the keynote of Morgan's 2008 biography, which, interestingly, claims a special insight into the motives behind the supposed fraud: "There is no doubt that she enjoyed this new Anna, not just the role itself but the very fact that she had simply made it up" (*Bombay Anna*, 79).

132 he left for Penang: Although there is no record of Thomas's departure, he must have left in advance of Anna, who sailed to Penang without him on 17 July.

— 71,000 Malay and 29,000 Chinese, who greatly outnumbered the 2,200 Europeans: "Pinang," *Singapore Free Press*, 23 February 1860. Among the few early American accounts of Penang are Wood, *Fankwei*, chap. 12; and Harris, *Complete Journal*, 47–77.

133 surprised to find that Penang had no hotel: Harris, *Complete Journal*, 56.

— "The Pinang Family Hotel": The notice ran till 11 August 1859.

— "July 17 per *Viscount Canning* to Pinang": *Straits Times*, 24 July 1858, 2.

— Subsequent passenger lists: *Straits Times*, 11 September, 2 October 1858.

— Mr. Marcus was chief engineer: *Straits Times*, 10 July 1858; *Singapore Almanack* (1858), 49, (1860), 59, (1867), 41. The 1859 *Almanack* entry for Marcus's employer (Hamilton, Gray) shows two Marcuses among the firm's eight assistants and clerks: "F. H. Marcus" and "Robert Marcus (Siam)." The latter, a clerk in Bangkok, could not have been Mrs. Marcus's spouse. The other, Florentine Henry Marcus, also has "(Siam)" after his listing in "Principal Inhabitants." However, the microfilmed copy in the Singapore National Library (NL2363) was hand-corrected by an early reader, who crossed out "Siam" and wrote in "Chief Engineer." This, then, was the husband of Anna's friend.

134 "happy home . . . in Malacca": *EG*, 67. Because of Malacca's former prominence as port and capital, its name long remained a shorthand term for the Malayan region (Richard Winstedt, *Britain and Malaya, 1786–1941* [London: Longmans, Green, 1944], 9). That this was Anna's usage is clear from *EG*, 3, 5. She never lived in the port city itself.

— "a gay young man-about-town": VI C 4:2 folder 28, p. 35, MKL Papers.

— "demurely" replied that she was 150 years old: *EG*, 57.

135 "Apoplexy"; "Hotel Master": Burials at Prince of Wales Island, N/1/95/311, IOR. This record was found by Bristowe and made known in *Louis and the King of Siam* (29). Chaplain Arthur W. Wallis made the original entry. James Mackay, succeeding Wallis one month later (*Straits Times*, 18 June 1859), made the certified copy that was sent to Calcutta and is now in the British Library with the India Office Records.

— the simple and dignified epitaph: Corfield, "Anna Leonowens," 6 (photo).

— In the story Anna told her grandchildren: VI C 4:2 folder 28, pp. 36–37, MKL Papers.

136 Tigers were still a menace: *Straits Times*, 18 June 1859; *Overland Singapore Free Press*, 30 July 1859; *Pinang Gazette*, 13 August 1859, as quoted in the *Singapore Free Press*, 1 September 1859.

— "Heat-apoplexy" was what Kipling called it: *Plain Tales*, 86.

— footnote 2: Moorat, *Alfred and Eliza Stark*, 70; Philip D. Curtin, *Death by Migration: Europe's Encounter with the Tropical World in the Nineteenth Century* (Cambridge: Cambridge University Press, 1989), 51.

— "Exposure," Anna's word for the cause of death: Anna, "Biographical Sketch," 42.

— for the rest of her life she wore a brooch of curved tiger claws: Fyshe, "Anna and I," 62.

— "long and serious illness": Anna, "Biographical Sketch," 42.

137 "'I had a fever & was a little deranged'": LWJ to Annie Fields, 16 August 1868, LWJ Papers. Avis Selina Fyshe believed that her grandmother's "reason was gone" for a time (VI C 4:2 folder 28, p. 37, MKL Papers).

— Modern histories of the first convents: Dilys Yap, *The Convent Light Street: A History of a Community, a School and a Way of Life* ([Penang]: Dilys Yap, 2001), 17, 12. On Singapore's sister convent, see Buckley, *Anecdotal History*, 265–68; and Elaine Meyers, *Convent of the Holy Infant Jesus: 150 Years in Singapore* (Penang: The Lady Superior of Convent of the Holy Infant Jesus, 2004), 30, 41, 44.

— "June 25 per *Hooghly*, from Pinang": *Straits Times*, 2 July 1859.

138 By year's end she had opened her school: *Royal Almanack* (1860), 70; *Straits Calendar* (1861), 11, 42, (1862), 73.

— "well kept European hotels": Thomson, *Straits of Malacca*, 61.

— "*other* resident officers' wives": Macnaughton, "Mrs. Leonowens," 413, my italics.

— the prejudice against Anglo-Indians: *Straits Times*, 5 March 1859; Cameron, *Our Tropical Possessions*, 287–88; Turnbull, *Straits Settlements*, 30.

139 Thomas Heritages: *Straits Calendar* (1861), 42, (1862), 10, 73. Anna's friendship with the Heritages is evidenced in VI C 4:2 folder 29, pp. 45a, 50, 54, 60, 66, 93, 98, MKL Papers.

— "got on tolerably": LWJ to Fields, 16 August 1868.

— contemporary directories: *Straits Calendar* (1861), 11, 24–25, 42, (1862), 73.

— Only twenty-four: Although Cobb's age and middle name are often distorted, there need be no mystery. His reply to a March 1887 query states that he was born on 11 February 1837 and underlines *Davis* in his signature (Manuscript 151, Caleb Benjamin Tillinghast Correspondence). In Morgan's fictionalized account, he was born in 1840 and came to Singapore before Anna did (*Bombay Anna*, 84–85).

140 "merchandise bought on borrowed capital": Louisa Farnham Cobb (Cobb's daughter) to ML, 5 January 1945, VI C 4:5 folder 6, MKL Papers.

140 footnote 3: *AKS*, 20. As George Hazen Dana had previously been to Java and Singapore, there was probably an understanding with his old partner, Thomas Hodgson (*Singapore Almanack* [1858], 61; *Royal Almanack* [1859], 63). When Dana left, Cobb partnered with Hodgson first and then with Alexander Hutchinson. Theirs being the sole American firm in Singapore (*Royal Almanac* [1864], 71), Cobb also acted as American vice consul.

— "your costly gift which I do not forgive you": Francis Davis Cobb to Anna, 6 September 1862, quoted in VI C 4:2 folder 29, p. 60, MKL Papers.

— "one of the most charming men": Anna to Kathleen Ford, 30 July 1878, Anna Harriette Leonowens Papers.

— he married Margaret Hamilton: *Straits Times*, 14 May 1859. To appreciate the global reach of Margaret's family, one need only glance at father Andrew Hamilton's estate inventory (died on 1 September 1880, SC 36/48/93, Glasgow Sheriff Court Inventories, www.scotlandspeople.gov.uk).

— one of her sisters married Dr. James Campbell: Marriage #313, 3 September 1862, Blythswood District, Glasgow, www.scotlandspeople.gov.uk.

141 footnote 4: *Bangkok Calendar* (1863), 110; Anna to DBB, 17 May 1870, I/1/335, DBB Family Papers.

— William spent the next two years: Adamson's operations in Siam had already begun, as he is listed as a resident in the *Bangkok Calendar* (1859), 60. His and his bride's move to Bangkok was reported in the *Straits Times*, 4 June 1859; their residence there is shown in the *Bangkok Calendar* (1860), 88, (1861), 57. DBB's journal for 13 October 1860 notes that "Mr & Mrs Adamson & son [newborn?] returned from Singapore." On 29 March 1861 the family left Siam for good, resettling in Singapore (*Bangkok Calendar* [1862], 108). Three years later, in a letter to Adamson, King Mongkut spoke of being "familiar with you so long for many years" (Mongkut, *Ruamphraraachaniphonnai*, 434).

— Tan Kim Ching: Song Ong Siang, *One Hundred Years' History of the Chinese in Singapore* (1902; reprint, Singapore: Oxford University Press, 1984), 92–93.

142 footnote 5: Anna, "Biographical Sketch," 42; *NYT*, 7 April 1872, 6; Anna to Avis, 16 January 1881, quoted in VI C 4:2 folder 29b, p. 220, MKL Papers.

— the king replied that her terms were not acceptable: Mongkut to Adamson, [January 1862] (photo), Borneo Company Ltd. Papers; Mongkut to Tan Kim Ching, 26 February 1862, quoted in VI C 4:2 folder 29, pp. 39a–39b, MKL Papers. A facsimile of the letter to Adamson is in Longhurst, *Borneo Story*, 48–51. As Morgan plausibly conjectures, Anna may have been the one teacher in Singapore qualified and able to go to Bangkok (*Bombay Anna*, 86).

— the king wrote directly: Mongkut to Anna, 26 February 1862, quoted in *EG*, v–vi.

143 had sent an inquiry: On 22 November 1861, according to Harriet King's 3 February 1862 reply, quoted in VI C 4:2 folder 29, pp. 57–59, MKL Papers. That was *before* the king's job offer.

143 questions of ship passage and traveling companions: VI C 4:2 folder 29, pp. 45, 50, 54, MKL Papers.

— the Misses King's School: Charles James Fèret, *Fulham Old and New: Being an Exhaustive History of the Ancient Parish of Fulham*, 3 vols. (London: Leadenhall, 1930), 1:78. An 1865 atlas shows market gardens north and east of Fulham's High Street.

— footnote 6: 1861 census, Bridge Street, Fulham House, RG 29/27, fol. 115, pp. 7–8, National Archives, UK, as seen at Hammersmith and Fulham Archives and Local History Centre.

144 white chapel; "pleasant dwellings"; etc.: *EG*, 7. From the steamer Anna could easily see the Mission, located on the river's east bank five miles south of Bangkok's center, but the scene was also an imaginative re-creation. It was two months after her arrival that the chapel, with its cheering "green windows, freshly painted" (ibid.), was completed and dedicated (McFarland, *Historical Sketch*, 48, 56).

— "Oh Mary if you were": Mary Mattoon, autobiographical narration, II F 1 folder 35, MKL Papers.

Chapter 10. King Mongkut of Siam

147 footnote 1: Thiphakorawong, *Dynastic Chronicles*, 3:13.

— the succession had been anything but straightforward: My account of the Third and Fourth Reigns is indebted chiefly to Pallegoix, *Description*; Bowring, *Kingdom and People*; DBB, "Reminiscences"; Thiphakorawong, *Dynastic Chronicles*; Feltus, *Abstract*; Vella, *Siam*; Moffat, *Mongkut*; Wyatt, "Family Politics"; Mongkut, *King of Siam Speaks*; Wyatt, *Thailand*; and Terwiel, *Thailand's Political History*.

— That *mongkut* means "crown" suggests: Chantasingh, "Americanization," 103.

148 the experienced son of a minor wife was given the preference: Flood offers a persuasive analysis of Rama III's accession in Thiphakorawong, *Dynastic Chronicles*, 3:14–15.

— "get a correct statement," etc.: DBB, Journals, vol. 15, 25 March and 10 April 1851, DBB Family Papers; DBB, "For the Singapore Straits Times, *Bangkok, March 26th*, 1851," *Straits Times*, 8 July 1851. DBB's follow-up letter of 10 April appeared in the *Straits Times* on 15 July 1851. After Mongkut's death, he revealed that the king had been "particularly apprehensive that he might be falsely published as a usurper" (DBB, "Reminiscences," 125).

— "In 1825 [actually, 1824] a royal prince of Siam": *EG*, 54.

— His first religious home: My primary sources for Mongkut's life as a monk are Lingat, "Vie religieuse"; Reynolds, "Buddhist Monkhood," chap. 3; and Jesse Caswell's missionary reports. As Reynolds notes ("Buddhist Monkhood," 75), Lingat relied on writings of three of Mongkut's sons: Chulalongkorn's *On Wat*

Samorai, Damrong Rajanubhab's *History of Wat Mahathat*, and Damrong and Prince-Patriarch Wachirayan's *History of Wat Bowonniwet*.

149 earliest known Thai (or Lao) script: Cornelius Beach Bradley, "The Oldest Known Writing in Siamese: The Inscription of Phra Ram Khamhaeng of Sukhothai 1293 A.D.," *Journal of the Siam Society* 6, no. 1 (April 1909): 1–64. Cornelius was a son of DBB.

— By 1830 Mongkut realized that the earth must be round: From an 1845 report cited in Bradley, "Prince Mongkut," 38.

150 the American discovered that he was suffering from an ear infection: DBB, Journals, vol. 5, 7 and 23 April 1836, DBB Family Papers. No other source adequately explains Mongkut's sagging lip. Mistakenly attributing it to "a stroke of paralysis" (*EG*, 246), Anna placed it on the right side, as did DBB, who later moved it to the left in his long, important, not always reliable obituary ("Reminiscences," 138).

151 approached Bradley in 1839 with some unusual requests: DBB, Journals, vol. 7, 17 December 1839, DBB Family Papers.

— "the most important event": Damrong, "Introduction," 96.

— letters from Sri Lankan monks, "language of intercommunication": Caswell, Journal, 16 June 1845, Caswell Papers. At the time Caswell taught Mongkut he was obsessed by "Perfectionist" doctrine and virtually ostracized by other missionaries, though not by DBB.

— footnote 3: Caswell, "Chemistry," commonplace book, Caswell Papers.

— "took great delight . . . administering the shock": "Siam. Letter from Mr. Caswell, Bangkok, 1st July, 1841," *Missionary Herald* 38 (April 1842): 147–48.

— So Mongkut came up with a proposal: "Siam. Letter from the Mission, July 1, 1845," *Missionary Herald* 42 (February 1846): 47–48; "Letters from Mr. Caswell," *Missionary Herald* 42 (March 1846): 93.

152 "never melancholy": Jesse Caswell to A. Bullard, 25 November 1836, 77.1, box 14, ABC.

— English instruction began on 1 July 1845: "Letters from Mr. Caswell," 93; Bradley, "Prince Mongkut," 37; "Siam," *Missionary Herald* 42 (September 1846): 321.

— But Mongkut had made clear: Mongkut, *King of Siam Speaks*, 15; Bradley, "Prince Mongkut," 38; Feltus, *Abstract*, 85, 106; DBB, "Reminiscences," 122; *EG*, 240. On the impact of science on Thai Buddhism, see Craig J. Reynolds, "Buddhist Cosmography in Thai History, with Special Reference to Nineteenth-Century Culture Change," *Journal of Asian Studies* 35 (February 1976): 203–20. Blofeld, however, makes much of Mongkut's supernaturalism (*King Maha Mongkut*, 24).

— After a year and a half: "Recent Intelligence," *Missionary Herald* 43 (July 1847): 248; Caswell, "Siam. Annual Report of the Mission," *Missionary Herald* 44 (January 1848): 15–18.

153 footnote 4: *EG*, 240.

— "Do not be troubled about them": "Siam. Letter from the Mission, November 5, 1846," *Missionary Herald* 43 (May 1847): 158.

— "for translations": Mary Mattoon to "Brother & Sister," 6–10 July 1847, II F 1 folder 3, MKL Papers.

— "extreme scepticism": *EG*, 97.

— "erysipelatous inflammation of the lungs": *Bangkok Calendar* (1859), 47, (1870), 7.

— he sent her generous cash gifts: *Bangkok Calendar* (1862), 109; Bradley, *Siam Then*, 176–77.

— When Mrs. Caswell sent a daguerreotype: Feltus, *Abstract* (1 July 1854, 31 July 1861), 170, 222.

— she was given no valuable gifts: Chantasingh, "Americanization," 117.

154 According to a surgeon: Journal II, revision, chap. 9, pp. 216–17, Benajah Ticknor Papers; Thiphakorawong, *Dynastic Chronicles*, 3:90.

— "would only create disturbance": Journal II, revision, chap. 9, p. 220, Benajah Ticknor Papers.

— Rama III proved as inaccessible: Jumsai, *King Mongkut*, 29; Pallegoix, *Description*, 1:259; Feltus, *Abstract*, 36.

— A leading American scholar: William Gedney, "Patrons and Practitioners: Chakri Monarchs and Literature," *Crossroads* 2, no. 2 (1985): 9; Vella, *Siam*, 46–50; Damrong, "Introduction," 96; Hong, *Thailand*, 65; Terwiel, *Thailand's Political History*, 132.

155 "did so in a timid whisper": [Samuel Jones Smith], "Recoronation. The Past and the Present," *Siam Repository* 6 (1874): 127.

— "wished to flee"; "frank and ingenuous": DBB, "Reminiscences," 123, 138.

— When a Thai named Khun Mote: DBB, Journals, vol. 15, 7 and 10 October 1850, DBB Family Papers; "Phya Krasab," *Siam Repository* 5, no. 4 (October 1873): 450–51. Once in power, Mongkut bestowed high honors on the printer and put him in charge of the mint.

— In 1850 another American envoy was sent to Siam; a similar mission for the British: "Somdetch P'ra Nang Klow," *Siam Repository* 2 (January 1870): 76; Terwiel, *Thailand's Political History*, 129–30.

156 "He seemed to make us his confidential friends": DBB, Journals, vol. 15, 27 March 1851, DBB Family Papers.

— During the cremation of Rama III: DBB, Journals, vol. 16, 6 May 1852, DBB Family Papers.

— "All householders shall": Pramoj, "King Mongkut," 41.

— Drinking of the Water of Allegiance: Thiphakorawong, *Dynastic Chronicles*, 2:413.

157 "the first and foremost democrat": Pramoj, "King Mongkut," 33.

157 "the practice of past kings": Rutnin, *Dance, Drama*, 78.

— minor gentry was ineligible: Rabibhadana, *Organization*, 157–58.

— abolition of trading monopolies: Hong, *Thailand*, 67–68.

— treaties effectively eroded national sovereignty: see Jumsai, *History*, 90.

— Mongkut realized he had made more concessions than the Japanese: Harry S. Parkes, *File Concerning Harry Parkes' Mission to Bangkok in 1856* (Bangkok: Khana Kammakan, 2521 [1978]), 30–31. Terwiel, *Thailand's Political History*, 146–49, sheds light on the tense transitional relations between Mongkut and the Western powers in 1856.

158 extensive walled enclosure: Bowring, *Kingdom and People*, 2:270; Pallegoix, *Description*, 1:286–88; Mattoon, "Missionary Ladies," 320. The latter is the chief source on the palace teaching of 1851–54. Another, "Am[erican] Female Teachers in the Royal Palace," *Siam Repository* 2 (January 1870): 133–34, was probably by Sara Sleeper Jones Smith, a former teacher who married the *Repository's* owner-editor. Before going to Siam, Sara had been principal of New Hampton Female Seminary in New Hampshire (Corfield, *Bangkok*, 81). In 1870 she sailed back to the States to help raise money for what would be the famous Wang Lang School, founded after her return ("Passengers," *Siam Repository* 2 [July 1870]: 326; "Ladies' Seminary: Opposite the Two Royal Palaces," *Siam Repository* 6 [1874]: 398).

— Mongkut had met the American missionary wives: Mattoon, "Missionary Ladies," 321.

— English class began in August 1851: Feltus, *Samuel Reynolds House*, 110; Mongkut to DBB, 23 May 1852 IV/2, DBB Family Papers; DBB, "Reminiscences," 127.

159 taught astronomy, geography, and Bible history: DBB, "Reminiscences," 127. Sarah Bradley, DBB's second wife, was surely the source for this essay's details on the teaching. Previously, she taught for pay in the palace of the king's half brother, Prince Wongsathirat Sanit (Feltus, *Abstract*, 207–8).

— Although Mattoon's husband suspected: Stephen Mattoon to sister, 8 September 1852, II F 1 folder 8, and Mary Mattoon to Sister E., 25 June 1853, II F 1 folder 9, both in MKL Papers; "Recent Intelligence," *Foreign Missionary* 11 (December 1852): 120; Stephen to sister, 3 February 1853, II F 1 folder 9, MKL Papers.

— unsigned letter to a Singapore newspaper: "Siam," *Straits Times*, 12 September 1854; Stephen Mattoon to sister, 22 November 1854, II F 1 folder 10, MKL Papers; Bowring, *Kingdom and People*, 2:323; Feltus, *Abstract*, 173; Feltus, *Samuel Reynolds House*, 128–30; Jumsai, *King Mongkut*, 107–8; Terwiel, *Thailand's Political History*, 143–44.

— "just a plain account": Mattoon to sister Charlotte, 16 September 1882, II F 1 folder 28, MKL Papers.

160 pilfered the royal spectacles: Anna's dramatic treatment is in "Life in a Siamese Palace."

— When the American took her family daguerreotypes: Stephen Mattoon to sister Harriet, 14 July 1853, II F 1 folder 9, MKL Papers; Mattoon to Anna M. B. Lowrie, 26 August 1862, II F 1 folder 17, MKL Papers.

— "Mrs. L, the English lady": Mattoon to Walter Lowrie, 23 September 1863 (transcript by ML), VI C 4:2 folder 17, MKL Papers.

— "ever gentle and kind": Tribute by a former pupil at Argyle Academy in New York State, where Mary Lowrie had been the preceptress before marrying Stephen Mattoon and going to Siam (II F 1 folder 33, MKL Papers).

— "most keenly"; "O how precious": Mattoon to sister E., 5 April [1852], II F 1 folder 8, MKL Papers. Lowrie died on 7 September 1851 (DBB, Journals, vol. 16, 30 August, 6 and 7 September, 1851, DBB Family Papers). When bad health forced Mattoon's return to the States, she felt she was abandoning her child's grave (to sister Annie, 18 December 1862, II F 1 folder 17, MKL Papers).

161 Anna arrived at the Inner Palace and had a mysterious encounter with Talap: EG, 62–63. Talap, too, had lost a first child, in 1853, eight days after its birth (Thiphakorawong, *Dynastic Chronicles*, 4:307).

— under the impression that this *was* Mem Mattoon?: I am in debt to a reader for the suggestion.

162 "This childlike woman": *AKS*, 73.

CHAPTER 11. THE ENGLISH SCHOOL MASTRESS COMES TO BANGKOK

164 The English School Mastress: "School Mastress" is taken from King Mongkut to William Adamson, [January 1862] (photo), Borneo Company Ltd. Papers.

— position as an independent, self-supporting schoolmistress: On the anomalous position of such women in colonial Southeast Asia, see Stoler, *Carnal Knowledge*, 55–61.

— "social inferior and racial superior": Cheng, "Frances Trollope's America," 144.

— "very uncomfortable there": Anna's spoken words as quoted in LWJ to Annie Fields, 16 August 1868, LWJ Papers.

165 "well versed in European court etiquette": DBB, "The Liberality & Courtesy of the Late King of Siam," *Bangkok Calendar* (1870), 133.

— "expect to see you here": EG, vi. Three passengers were identified in the *Straits Times* for 15 March 1862: "Mr. Davidson, Mrs. Leonowens, and Mr. Smith." The latter may have been the Reverend Samuel Jones Smith or pilot John Smith, both resident in Bangkok.

— steamer *Chow Phya*: Buckley, *Anecdotal History*, 674; Beauvoir, *Java, Siam*, 245–46.

166 "Moonshee, my Persian teacher, and Beebe, my gay Hindostanee nurse"; "my Hindostanee syce": *EG*, 3, 23; *RH*, 189.

— rotting garbage; "a rabble of priests"; etc.: *EG*, 6–7; Chantasingh, "Americanization," 79.

— doubted that the "world has a greater or more striking spectacle" than Bangkok: Beauvoir, *Java, Siam*, 255.

— After the steamer reached its moorings: *EG*, 8–9, 15; Bowring, *Kingdom and People*, 2:282–83.

167 "Some sixth sense": *AKS*, 33. The passage comes from a later scene, but the point holds.

— men were required to clothe the upper body at royal audiences: Thiphakorawong, *Dynastic Chronicles*, 1:5; DBB, "Reminiscences," 137.

— "so annoyed by the heat": Wood, *Fankwei*, 182. The costume would have been a Thai *phanung*, not a Malayan sarong.

— his polite inquiries terminated as follows: *EG*, 9–10.

168 "Was it a bear? No, a prince!": Ibid., 11–12.

— "*en déshabillé*"; "scarcely so pretty": Ibid., 14. Bristowe's remarks on the snubs seem to reflect an unquestioning allegiance to older English social gradations: "Anna naively describes how she snubbed a number of other Princes and nobles. . . . [Her] pose did not deceive the small population of English people of good family and she was never to enter their social circle" (*Louis*, 30–31). I know of no evidence that Sir Robert Schomburgk, Henry Alabaster, and Henry George Kennedy, all in the British consulate, "remained aloof," and that *Chow Phya* skipper George Orton, the Anglo-Irish Thomas George Knox (consul from 1864), and the North British Campbells and Adamsons—all friends of Anna—were not considered "people of good family."

— Unlike Rama III: Mrs. A. Vernon Rose Eastlake, "Excerpt from the Account of the Wreck of the *Hotspur*," chap. 15, VI C 4:4 folder 8, MKL Papers; Lewis, "Recollections," 628; Bastian, *Reisen*, 70; Beauvoir, *Java, Siam*, 331–32; Bowring, *Kingdom and People*, 1:441; Harris, *Complete Journal*, 145; Thomson, *Straits of Malacca*, 90.

169 Anna's first audience . . . to Mongkut's peremptory unreasonableness: *EG*, 57–59.

— "quick and nervous": DBB, "Reminiscences," 138.

— "perfectly ugly, and takes after the monkey": "*parfaitement laide, et tient beaucoup du singe*" (Beauvoir, *Java, Siam*, 304).

171 "may well come close": Terwiel, *Thailand's Political History*, 158–59.

— "April 3rd—Mrs. Leonowens, an English lady": *Bangkok Calendar* (1863), 110.

— "We went to the King's Palace": Anna to Avis, quoted in VI C 4:2 folder 29, p. 50, MKL Papers.

172 "Siamese lady no like work": *EG*, 71.

172 This story finds confirmation: Anna to DBB, Monday morning [21 April 1862] and 22 April [1862], I/1/271, DBB Family Papers. Anna claimed that she began teaching at the *kalahom*'s "more than two months" (*EG*, 71) after her mid-March arrival in Bangkok. In fact, five weeks had passed. No doubt it felt longer.

173 "to & fro"; "husband or manservant"; "a brick house": Mongkut to Adamson, [January 1862] (photo), Borneo Company Ltd. Papers.

— "some of the better houses": Wood, *Fankwei*, 170.

— "We beg to invite you to our royal palace": *EG*, vi.

— For this second audience . . . "nothing but *my dee*": Ibid., 61–66.

174 from date-line to signature: Ibid., v–vi. Anna was scrupulously and surprisingly exact in quoting Mongkut's writings. Examples: (1) his circular on the death of Fa Ying (ibid., 119–22; *Straits Times*, 6 June 1863); (2) his witticism on the pope and the keys of heaven (*EG*, 256; *Bangkok Recorder*, 28 June 1866); (3) his paragraph on transliterating Thai (*EG*, 256; I/1/326, DBB Family Papers); (4) his letter to Anna of [24] February 1865 (*EG*, 268; VI C 4:5 folder 26, MKL Papers); and (5) his "Very Private Post Script" (*EG*, 266–67; VI C 4:6 folder 14, MKL Papers; Graireuk and Pramint, *Saaylap wang luang*, [56–57]).

— "repented," etc.: *EG*, 66, 68–69. In Anna's memory, she rejected the shabby house before teaching at the *kalahom*'s. The actual sequence of events is uncertain.

175 footnote 1: ML to Avis Selina Fyshe, 14 April 1943 (carbon), VI C 1:1 folder 2, MKL Papers. Anna was still living on the right bank when Louis wrote the undated (1864?) letter transcribed in VI C 4:2 folder 29, p. 107, MKL Papers. Nearly two decades later, after joining the royal cavalry, he found himself "living next door to our old house"—the second, brick home (VI C 4:2 folder 29b, pp. 241, 239, MKL Papers). Carelessly, Morgan has Anna living "on the same side of the river as the palace" right from the start (*Bombay Anna*, 91).

— "On the first arrival of the governess": Lewis, "Recollections," 630.

— a Singapore passenger list: *Straits Times*, 7, 14 February, 4 April 1863. The title of Lewis's essay puts the Bangkok visit in 1862, an obvious error.

176 Landon's novelized account has her languishing into July: *AKS*, 86–90.

— "the Lady Leonowens our School mistress": Letter of 19 May 1862 (postscript dated 21 May), in Mongkut, *Ruamphraraachaniphonnai*, 424.

177 the first of four installments: *Atlantic Monthly* 25 (April 1870): 396–410.

— contemporaneous letter to Bradley: Anna to DBB, 17 May 1870, I/1/335, DBB Family Papers.

178 "an English woman, who served the King": "Europeans in Siamese Employ," *Siam Repository* 2 (July 1870): 403.

— "deep impressions in the memory," etc.: "Governess at the Siamese Court," *Siam Repository* 2 (October 1870): 429. The notice originally appeared in the

Advertiser's news summary for the week ending 23 June 1870. The one Western Australia paper to comment on *EG* was the *Fremantle Express* of 15 October 1870, which reproduced the description of Mongkut's death from the June *Atlantic Monthly*. Introducing the excerpt, the editor wrote, "The following interesting account is we have been given to understand from the pen of an English Lady named Leonowens who has been governess at the Siamese Court, and formerly resided in this colony" (found by Jack Honniball).

178 Smith, too, was Eurasian: Baptism of Samuel Smith, 9 August 1820, Cannanore, India, Madras baptisms, N/2/7/398, IOR; "Missionaries," *Siam Repository* 2 (July 1870): 394; McFarland, *Historical Sketch*, 24, 27, 32; Anake, *Farang nay muang sayaam*, 168–69. The date of birth (6 July 1820) given in Smith's baptism record is the same as the date shown in Anake's photo of his gravestone (181). Unfortunately, the epitaph is badly garbled in Corfield, *Bangkok*, 94.

— About four years old when his father's regiment: The 1824 *Bengal Directory and General Register* has the Sixty-Ninth Regiment "Under Embarkation Orders for Europe" (33).

179 Treated with reserve by other missionaries: Feltus, *Abstract*, 253; McFarland, *Historical Sketch*, 43. Smith's name is absent from Anna's list of missionaries "entitled to special mention" (*EG*, 242). Yet she clearly knew him: a sketch, "City of Forbidden Women," tells an anecdote about his wife (36).

— "very severely criticized": *Siam Repository* 5 (July 1873): 265.

— each issue . . . was eagerly awaited: Buckley, *Anecdotal History*, 679.

— "its predecessor," etc.: Anonymous review of *RH*, *London and China Express*, 7 February 1873, 133.

— an earlier newspaper for which there survives a partial subscription list: "List of Outstanding Accounts," [20 or 26] July 1865, I/1/321, DBB Family Papers.

CHAPTER 12. ANNA AND THE SIAMESE
UNDERSTANDING OF HUMAN SEXUALITY

199 "shock to the moral sensibilities": "Marriage," *Siam Repository* 5 (October 1873): 415.

— "as something ordinary": Sutham Thammarongwit, "'Silence' and 'Speech': The Dissimulations Concerning Sex in Thai Society" (2001), in Thai, as translated and cited in Jackson, "Performative Genders," 16, 39.

— "How I long to hold": Thomas to Anna, 11 November 1851, VI C 4:2 folder 28, p. 33, MKL Papers.

200 "The dress of the females," etc.: Royce, *Sketch*, 88, 103.

— "there is nothing in the customs": Feltus, *Abstract*, 85.

— "Pre-marital sexual relations were regarded indulgently": Reid, *Southeast Asia*, 153–54.

200 "its accurate form," etc.: Harris, *Complete Journal*, 143, 95.

201 "smiled and said": Mrs. A. Vernon Rose Eastlake, "Excerpt from the Account of the Wreck of the Hotspur," chap. 15, pp. 17–18, VI C 4:4 folder 8, MKL Papers. Eastlake reached Bangkok on 15 March 1863 (*Bangkok Calendar* [1864], 121).

— "The actual sins of the so-called": Cort, *Siam*, 151.

202 "same-sex eroticism between laymen": Jackson, "Performative Genders," 11, 2.

— That they were freer: noted by Bowring, *Kingdom and People*; Cort, *Siam*; and especially Bacon, *Siam*, 236, 238.

— "In the poorer classes": Pallegoix, *Description*, 1:228.

— "of a young girl who was injured": [Campbell], "On the Age," 233–36.

203 "disappointed that a larger number of officers": Wood, *Fankwei*, 175.

— "the customs of the Siamese": DBB, "How the Kings," 68, 70.

— "a seraglio; a place where Eastern princes": Noah Webster, *A Dictionary of the English Language*, 2 vols. (1828; reprint, Thetford, Norfolk, UK: E. H. Barker, 1832).

— standard term for concubines was *naang haam*, literally, "ladies forbidden": McFarland, *Thai-English Dictionary*, 450, 934. The modern word for royal concubine is *sanom* (Haas, *Thai-English Student's Dictionary*, 520). The most reliable Western accounts of Siamese polygamy appear to be Pallegoix, *Description*, 1:231; Wales, *Siamese State Ceremonies*, 46–50; and the writings of DBB cited in this chapter.

— "since that time his wives," etc.: DBB, "How the Kings," 68–69. Mongkut's figures for his brother's harem are round numbers and probably include childless wives. His tally of his own consorts matches that found elsewhere but may be limited to mothers. See Thiphakorawong, *Dynastic Chronicles*, 4:306–21; ML, "King Mongkut's Consorts," VI C 4:6 folder 19, MKL Papers; James Campbell, "Polygamy: Its Influence on Sex and Population," *Journal of Anthropology* 1, no. 2 (October 1870): 192–97.

204 Mongkut decreed that concubines . . . were free to resign: Moffat, *Mongkut*, 150–53, 135; Thiphakorawong, *Dynastic Chronicles*, 3:88–89. DBB thought that fifteen or twenty concubines elected to leave (Journals, vol. 17, 25 January 1856, DBB Family Papers). Smith spoke of the "laxity" of the new harem rules ("Courtship and Marriage," *Siam Repository* 5 [January 1873]: 47).

— "The daughters of the nobles": DBB, "How the Kings," 71.

— three of his last four children were born to first-time mothers: Thiphakorawong, *Dynastic Chronicles*, 4:320–21.

205 "The Mother of the little child": Mongkut to DBB, 14 July 1852, IV/2, DBB Family Papers. On "lying near the fire," see Rajadhon, *Life and Ritual*, 134–43, 146–50; and Malcolm Smith, *A Physician at the Court of Siam* (1957; reprint, Kuala Lumpur: Oxford University Press, 1982), 58.

205 "laughed merrily," etc.: Mongkut, *King of Siam Speaks*, 191–92.

— depressed state of feeling in the harem of Krommamuen Alongkot: Thomson, *Straits of Malacca*, 88–91; *Bangkok Calendar* (1868), 125.

206 That the wall may some day "cease to be": Pramoj, *Four Reigns*, 181. Notable feminist treatments of Middle Eastern harems are Leila Ahmed, "Western Ethnocentrism and Perceptions of the Harem," *Feminist Studies* 8, no. 3 (Fall 1982): 521–34; and Mervat Hatem, "Through Each Other's Eyes: The Impact on the Colonial Encounter of the Images of Egyptian, Levantine-Egyptian, and European Women, 1862–1920," in Chaudhuri and Strobel, *Western Women*, 48–55.

— He was not a reactionary: See, e.g., the obituaries in the *Independent*, 11 October 1995, and the *Times*, 16 October 1995.

— "They are nearly all young women," etc.: *RH*, 107, 44.

207 "An English, that is a Christian, woman": *EG*, 21.

— "Always when a woman becomes a mother": *RH*, 107.

— "a lovely little cottage," etc.: Ibid., 120.

208 "The children of the poor": *EG*, 103.

— "How I have pitied those ill-fated sisters": Ibid., 103–4.

209 "the Holiest & best men": Minutes of 14 February 1854, SRMI.

— "had never looked upon the sickening hideousness": *EG*, 104.

— claimed that it formed part of a letter: *AKS*, 165. A surviving revision of this page (VI A 3:1 folder 39, p. 4, MKL Papers) shows that ML pasted the "sickening hideousness" paragraph into the story of La-aw (L'Ore), an insertion she justified by pretending that the passage came from a contemporary letter to Cobb. In fact, Anna's letters to him hadn't been seen by ML. This small pious fraud is in line with her basic procedure in *AKS*: presenting Anna's later and heavily processed accounts as if they were the original and immediate experience.

— captured Anna's essential point of view: ML to A. S. White, 5 December 1944, VI C 2:2 folder 1, pp. 2–3, MKL Papers.

211 "to his private apartments, whence issued": *EG*, 99; Anna, "Siamese Royal Palace," 284.

— "by a fresh detail of women": *EG*, 97.

— Thiang gave birth to ten children, Piam (the supposedly clever wife) to six, and three other concubines had five children each: Thiphakorawong, *Dynastic Chronicles*, 4:315, 319, 320.

— "Beside many choice Chinese and Indian girls": *EG*, 94–95.

— footnote 2: That Adamson lived in China for a time is shown by the 1881 English census, which gives Hong Kong as his seventeen-year-old son's place of birth (Surrey, Croydon, Park Hill Rise), and by four royal letters to Adamson from 17 April 1863 to 1 February 1865 regarding his appointment as honorary consul at Hong Kong (Mongkut, *Ruamphraraachaniphonnai*, 431–38).

212 "much given to women": Harris, *Complete Journal*, 145.

— "sensational"—added between serial and book: *Atlantic Monthly* 26 (August 1870): 145.

— "very private post script": Mongkut to Anna, 6 April 1866, quoted in *EG*, 266–67. On the historical context and surviving transcripts of this postscript, see chapter 19, p. 289.

— "Within these walls lurked lately": *EG*, 94.

— "Heavy and coarse in appearance," etc.: Seni Pramoj's recollections as reported by ML to Richard J. Walsh, 2 September 1943, VI C 2:2 folder 21, MKL Papers.

213 Anna's "men in the attire of women": Jackson, "Performative Genders," 12. See Jackson's discerning review of Richard Totman's *The Third Sex: Kathoey— Thailand's Ladyboys*, in *Journal of the Siam Society* 93 (2005): 316–19.

— "There were three dancers": Cavenagh, *Reminiscences*, 345. For Anna's garish account of a female *lakhon* troupe with "panting bosoms," see *EG*, 44–45.

214 "show Miss [Mary Atkins] the heathenism of Siam": DBB, Journals, vol. 21, 9 June 1864, DBB Family Papers. Sadly, the extant travel diary of Mary Atkins Lynch does not cover her five and a half weeks in Bangkok.

CHAPTER 13. A TEACHER STRAINED AT EVERY POINT

215 "They all love us well": Louis to Avis, "April 22, 1863" [early May], VI C 4:2 folder 2, MKL Papers.

— returned to their outside homes at night: Anna, "City of Forbidden Women," 36.

— *The English Governess* makes the schoolroom out: *EG*, 83. In 1873 Anna claimed that the building was originally a temple dedicated to the mother of the Buddha (*RH*, 237) and in 1877 that its name, Mothers of the Free, signified "free from the superstitions of the Brahmins" ("City of Forbidden Women," 36). Cornelius Beach Bradley (1843–1936), a son of the missionary, became an authority on Thai linguistics with a position at the University of California– Berkeley. His copy of *EG* is full of scornful marginalia. Next to Anna's dignified name for the schoolroom he penciled, "absurd!—all but the first word is a person's name!" (annotated copy of *EG*, p. 83).

216 "simple pupils"; "the only map": *RH*, 240–41.

218 "indulged in a confidential chuckle": Neale, *Narrative*, 56.

— finely detailed early nineteenth-century maps: Santanee and Stott, *Royal Siamese Maps*.

— "Webster's far-famed spelling-books": *EG*, 85.

— book order relayed to the Presbyterians' head office: Stephen Mattoon to Dr. Lowrie, 25 February 1864, VI C 4:2 folder 17, MKL Papers; Strobridge and Hibler, *Elephants*, 68.

219 Look in my eyes, Mother says: Richard G. Parker, *Juvenile Philosophy: or, Philosophy in Familiar Conversations; Designed to Teach Young Children to Think* (New York: A. S. Barnes, 1850), chap. 3.

— "our simple exercises of translating English": *RH*, 18.

— "see all the beautiful places"; "your Mamma our kind Governess": Princesses Ying Yualacks and Somawati to Avis, 26 May 1864 (thermofax copies), VI C 4:7 folders 16, 17, MKL Papers.

220 "frightened little culprit was severely chastised": Fyshe, "Anna and I," 64.

— "a frantic rush"; "great annoyance": Anna, "City of Forbidden Women," 36.

— "the almost daily breaks which the regal customs": DBB, "Reminiscences," 129.

— "a considerable number": Jumsai, *History*, 86.

— "much desire to going on with English": Mongkut to Anna, 18 March 1865 (typed copy), Graireuk and Pramint, *Saaylap wang luang*, [38].

— tonsure ceremony; Buddhist novitiate: Thiphakorawong, *Dynastic Chronicles*, 2:352, 361.

— The letter he sent her in 1869: *EG*, [xiii–xvi].

221 Francis George Patterson: *Siam Repository* 4 (October 1872): 399, and 5 (January 1873): 114; Wyatt, *Politics of Reform*, 70–72. Following Anna's departure, John Hassett Chandler, an American missionary turned printer, tutored the prince for a year or so. Patterson taught from 1872 to 1875.

— "contact with another culture": Wyatt, *Politics of Reform*, 38.

— "The King's agreement": George Whipple to DBB, 14 June 1862, I/1/278, DBB Family Papers.

— "it was as impossible for her": DBB, "Reminiscences," 129.

222 "a kind of despair," etc.: *RH*, 122. The passage is reminiscent of Nathaniel Hawthorne, who voiced similar feelings in "Wakefield," the Custom-House essay, and elsewhere.

— "the strong instinct of the mother": Anna, letter of 1880, VI C 4:2 folder 29b, p. 217, MKL Papers.

223 "The child is a bundle of potentialities": Anna, "Need of Greater Public Interest in the Public Schools" (lecture manuscript), VI C folder 37, pp. 11–12, MKL Papers.

— fell in and nearly drowned: Anna, "Auction of a White Child," 397.

224 the *Ranée* finally reached London: "Ship News," *Times*, 4 October 1862, 11.

— footnote 4: *Lloyd's List*, 26 May 1862, col. 21, 15 July 1862, col. 16, 30 August 1862, col. 22.

— "An Incident at Siam": *Straits Times*, 14 March 1863, 2, microfilm NL5559, Singapore National Library. As Stoler shows in *Carnal Knowledge*, 61–67, mental breakdowns were not uncommon among European colonists in Southeast Asia.

225 It *has* to be Anna: There are no other possible candidates in the *Bangkok Calendar's* lists of European residents for 1861, p. 57; 1862, pp. 112–13; 1863, pp.

116–17; 1864, pp. 125–26; and 1865, pp. 138–39. The only other husbandless woman in the *Calendar* for 1863 was Mrs. Charlotte Dunn, widow of George A. Dunn, a partner in the American Steam Rice Mill Company before his death in 1861 (*Bangkok Calendar* [1861], 42; Bradley, *Siam Then*, 105; Strobridge and Hibler, *Elephants*, 98).

226 "met a certain Captain Baldwin," etc.: John Thomas Pratt to Avis, 25 November 1899 (typed copy), VI C 4:2 folder 24, MKL Papers. Much of John's language reappears verbatim in a 1948 letter by one of his long-lived older brothers, Charles Rary Pratt, who, confoundingly, claimed to have been the one who wrote Avis Fyshe in 1899. According to Charles, he "received a very friendly letter in reply, but got the impression that she did not want her mother's past unhappiness in Bombay raked up again." See Lindsay, *Dear Boris*, 185–86.

— More exactly, the date of death was 13 June 1864: Bombay burials, N/3/38/125, IOR.

— In 1863 she was still single, in her early teens: Eliza Sarah Millard was born in June 1848 (Bombay baptisms, N/3/22/154, IOR). In October 1864, four months after her mother's death, she married Edward Pratt (Bombay marriages, N/3/38/336, IOR). John Thomas, one of their many sons, was born in 1876 (*Foreign Office List* [1939], 390).

227 footnote 5: Jacobs, *Boris Karloff*, 20.

— "no friend of mine knew at that time how hard it was for me": *EG*, 282.

Chapter 14. The Death of Fa Ying

228 "my health began to fail"; given a month's sick leave: *EG*, 273. Anna left Bangkok on 30 March and reached Singapore on 3 April (*Straits Times*, 4 April 1863, 3).

— the Hotel d'Europe at 10 Beach Road . . . Beach Road being Francis Davis Cobb's address as well: *Straits Calendar* (1862), 73 (and p. 4 of "Principal Inhabitants"); (1863), 55, 76.

— "if I must be idle for a month": *EG*, 273.

— Happily, a typed copy: Mongkut to Anna, 16 April 1863, in Graireuk and Pramint, *Saaylap wang luang*, [35–36]. A tip of the hat to the editors for figuring out "Calyphania."

229 "frank and ingenuous . . . to a fault": DBB, "Reminiscences," 138.

— she and Louis would have been on board: *Straits Times*, 25 April 1863, 3, and 2 May 1863, 3; *Singapore Free Press*, 30 April 1863, 3.

— footnote 1: Thiphakorawong, *Dynastic Chronicles*, 2:291.

— she continued to be called Chao Fa Ying: For the meanings of the words that make up this term of address, see Chantasingh, "Americanization," 60; Haas, *Thai-English Student's Dictionary*, 123, 382–83. As Mongkut explained, the term of address would be properly used by those who were the girl's superiors or not "dependent" on her (Mongkut, *King of Siam Speaks*, 12).

229 "whatever could be done"; liked to hold her on his lap: Mongkut, circular on Fa Ying, *Straits Times*, 6 June 1863, 1; *EG*, 121.

230 mildewed daguerreotype: reproduced in Krom Sinlapakon, *Prachum phaap prawattisaat phaendin Phrabaat Somdet Phrachomklao Chaoyuhua* (Bangkok, 2547 [2005]), 35.

— One day, as we read in the chapter: Unless noted otherwise, citations are to *EG*, chap. 13.

— "nestling close"; "about your beautiful Jesus!"; "realm of purity": Anna, "The Favorite," 126.

— "She was well educated in the vernacular": Mongkut's circular; *EG*, 121.

231 "seized with the cholera at 10 o'clock," etc.: DBB, Journals, vol. 21, 14 May 1863, DBB Family Papers.

— a sedative composed of chloroform, morphine, and other ingredients: Barbara Hodgson, *In the Arms of Morpheus: The Tragic History of Morphine, Laudanum and Patent Medicines* (Buffalo, N.Y.: Firefly Books, 2001), 105.

232 *P'hra-Arahang*: On the practice of repeating this name of the Buddha, see DBB, "Siamese Customs for the Dying and Dead," *Bangkok Calendar* (1864), 53–54.

233 "With breaking heart and eyes overflowing": Anna, "The Favorite," 126.

— "was entirely overcome": DBB, Journals, vol. 21, 15 May 1863, DBB Family Papers.

— "strange and terrible," etc.: *EG*, 119. In "The Favorite" this accusation is dropped.

— "delusive": *EG*, 99. Anna repeated the "delusive" claim in "Siamese Royal Palace," 284.

234 "schoolmistress on the loss of this her beloved pupil": Mongkut's circular; *EG*, 121–22.

— "wondered if this misfortune had struck": Thiphakorawong, *Dynastic Chronicles*, 2:298.

— *chao khun khruu yai*: *EG*, 123. Both Anna and Mongkut would have known that *khruu*, the word for "teacher," comes from the same Sanskrit/Pali root as *guru*.

CHAPTER 15. THE SLAVE CHAINED TO THE GROUND

235 "pathetic story of a female slave": "Siam. Lecture by Mrs. L. Owens," *NYT*, 7 April 1872, 6.

— footnote 1, "fine," "fair," "beautiful": Sethaputra, *New Model Thai-English Dictionary*, 2:812.

236 As reconstructed by Margaret Landon: *AKS*, 163–64; *RH*, 42. Unless otherwise noted, all citations to the story of La-aw are to chapters 5 and 6 of *RH*.

— Dusit Maha Prasat Throne Hall: Smithies, *Old Bangkok*, 10.

237 Butri had been *phuu upakaan*, patron or supporter, of Mongkut's late queen: Graireuk and Pramint, *Saaylap wang luang*, 32; Thiphakorawong, *Dynastic Chronicles*, 4:305; Haas, *Thai-English Student's Dictionary*, 628. Like ML, I prefer *Butri* to Anna's less phonetic transliteration, *Brittry*. Mongkut spelled the name *Puttre* in "Near and Distant Members of the Royal Family," *Bangkok Calendar* (1868), 104–5.

— She had taught young Chulalongkorn his letters: Wyatt, *Politics of Reform*, 36.

— "difficulty of finding a fit clothing for the fervid Eastern imagery": *RH*, 144.

— "I waited my time like a lover": Ibid., 52. The *Atlantic* cut this speech. Anna's ornate style made problems for ML, who believed that her "poetic words" were meant to approximate the versified "form of the original story" La-aw had told. But ML's editor objected to the stilted diction and urged her to "tone down and shorten." Surviving drafts show she took his advice, pruning repetitions and dropping instances of inverted word order and archaic diction. In the "I waited" speech, she cut the lover waiting for his mistress and reduced the last two clauses to "Praying passionately only for freedom." See ML to Walsh, 19 November 1943, VI C 2:2 folder 21; Walsh to ML, 30 August 1943 and 7 January 1944, VI C 2:2 folder 22; and John Day manuscript, VI A 3:2 folder 20, p. 252, all in MKL Papers; *AKS*, 172.

238 footnote 2: *AKS*, 173.

239 "no phase of Siamese slavery": [Samuel Jones Smith], "Siamese Slavery," *Siam Repository* 4 (July 1872): 380.

— In Bishop Pallegoix's estimate: *Description*, 1:298. Elsewhere Pallegoix reduced the fraction to a fourth (1:235). Bowring, who got his information on Siamese slavery from "a gentleman resident at Bangkok," saw redeemable *thaat* as "the principal class" of slaves (*Kingdom and People*, 1:189, 191).

240 Thais often treated slaves much better than domestic servants were treated in France: Pallegoix, *Description*, 1:299.

— A Thai authority on the sociology of old Siam: Rabibhadana, *Organization*, 109–10; also Wales, *Ancient Siamese Government*, 58–63. In quoting Rabibhadana, I silently substitute *thaat* for his *that*, which the Anglophone mouth automatically voices as "that").

— As Hong Lysa observes: Hong, *Thailand*, 27–28.

— Katherine A. Bowie doubts: "Slavery in Nineteenth-Century Northern Thailand: Archival Anecdotes and Village Voices," in *State Power and Culture in Thailand*, ed. E. Paul Durrenberger (New Haven, Conn.: Yale University Southeast Asia Studies, 1996), 104–6.

— misrepresented tattooing as branding: *RH*, 257, 258. Elsewhere, however, Anna gave an accurate account of registration tattoos (ibid., 65).

241 less upward mobility under Mongkut: Rabibhadana, *Organization*, chap. 8.

241 "commoner-wife"; "was greatly displeased": Thiphakorawong, *Dynastic Chronicles*, 2:374–75. These events took place in the year of the Tiger, that is, between 1 April 1866 and 31 March 1867.

— "had her chained and whipped": Hong, "Of Consorts," 340.

242 After listening to La-aw, Anna went to the Naikodah Ibrahim: *RH*, 57–58.

— "books on Siam were largely plagiarisms": Michael Smithies, introduction to Blofeld, *King Maha Mongkut*, ii–iii.

— *Things Not Generally Known, Familiarly Explained: Curiosities of Science*: London: Kent & Co., 1860.

— "reopening the trade between Bombay and Bangkok": [Davenport], "Siamese Courtly Etiquette," 185.

— "a few Anglo-Indians from Bombay and Surat": Bowring, *Kingdom and People*, 1:241.

— "sundry European articles": *Bangkok Calendar* (1869), 65.

— "the rich materials composing the Court-dresses": Kennedy, "Report," 316. See also Peleggi, *Lords of Things*, 46–47.

— silk cloth from Gujarat had been the major luxury import: Reid, *Southeast Asia*, 95.

— The man who headed this merchant community: "The Late Esmail Soolamanjee," *Siam Repository* 5 (January 1873): 118–19; "Promotion," *Siam Repository* 4 (January 1872): 122; *Bangkok Calendar* (1863), 47 (nineteenth-century handwritten annotation). He did business at the mouth of the canal at Mussulman Square, a prime location.

243 Năcoda Ebhrahim: *Bangkok Calendar* (1869), 65.

— "I have liberty to do enquiry": Mongkut to Anna, [May 1863?], Graireuk and Pramint, *Saaylap wang luang*, [37]. Anna's significantly different version is at *RH*, 58.

244 the king knew of the friendship that had already developed between her and Anna: Mongkut's 16 April 1863 letter to Anna in Singapore mentions "Thuo Arb" (Graireuk and Pramint, *Saaylap wang luang*, [35]). On the meaning of App's title, see Thiphakorawong, *Dynastic Chronicles*, 4:341.

— App calmly presides over the judicial torture of an innocent person: *RH*, 32, 139.

— "Lady Abb, Bearer of Royal Command": Moffatt, *Mongkut*, 239.

— "scrupulously just"; a "supreme" fitness; beautiful arms and hands: *RH*, 59.

246 "the unhappy girls who oftentimes fall to the lot": Neale, *Narrative*, 159.

247 A photograph of Princess Butri: Graireuk and Pramint, *Saaylap wang luang*, 28. Anna carelessly described Butri as Mongkut's "favorite half-sister and queen" (*RH*, 47). In fact, she was single, the king's niece, and emphatically not his queen. ML added to the muddle by supposing that she was a former

"favorite" of the king (*AKS*, 169). Except for calling her the king's first cousin, Morgan correctly identifies her ("Textual Notes," *RH*, 280).

247 "We are much pleased": Graireuk and Pramint, *Saaylap wang luang*, [37].

248 footnote 3: *RH*, 42.

— "tied to a tree," etc.: Emerson, *Life of Abby Hopper Gibbons*, 2:22–25.

CHAPTER 16. A TROUBLED CRUSADER

250 Anna was asked to accompany: DBB, Journals, vol. 21, 11 July 1863, DBB Family Papers. She was "requested" to join, not "required," as Feltus, *Abstract*, 234, mistakenly transcribed.

— "Mrs Leonowens called at our house": DBB, Journals, vol. 21, 20 July 1863, DBB Family Papers.

— knocked unconscious: *EG*, 125–26. Anna placed the attack just before Louis's October birthday. ML supposed the year was 1863 (*AKS*, 212–17).

251 a minor official . . . strongly advised her to resign: *EG*, 272.

— "such a dangerous place": Louis to Anna, 28 April 1868, VI C 4:2 folder 29a, p. 143, MKL Papers.

— "[When] the women and children of the palace": *EG*, 270.

252 old typed copy: Graireuk and Pramint, *Saaylap wang luang*, [18–21]. The letter was first published in *Sinlapa wathanatham* [Art and culture magazine], January 2004, 82–88.

— Lady Peeah: Graireuk and Pramint, *Saaylap wang luang*, [15], interpret "Lady Khoon Peeah" as Khun Phae. The first of Mongkut's concubines to give birth, Phae produced her fifth and last child in 1861 (Thiphakorawong, *Dynastic Chronicles*, 4:306–15). ML's file on her (VI C 4:6 folder 19, MKL Papers) indicates that she died that same year. If that is correct, "Lady Khoon Peeah" must be someone else.

253 Taksin . . . became vulnerable partly because of his harsh methods of reform; the then *uparat* . . . opposed Chulalongkorn's reforms and orchestrated a palace revolt: Terwiel, *Thailand's Political History*, 58–60, 181–85.

254 the *Alabama* . . . put into Singapore: Cameron, *Our Tropical Possessions*, 271–79; Buckley, *Anecdotal History*, 706–8.

255 "A nervous illness": Anna to Annie Fields, 4 November 1902, JTF Papers.

— "a month or more"; "an illness so fatal as cholera": *RH*, 249–50.

256 "Mrs Leonowens very sick": DBB's notation for 8 February in his private copy of *Bangkok Calendar* (1864), 6. Happily, when the *Calendar's* annual issues were microfilmed, this was the copy selected for 1864. The handwriting is unmistakably DBB's.

— "at the point of death with a wasting diarrhea": DBB, Journals, vol. 21, 8 February 1864, DBB Family Papers.

— "save seven thousand lives," etc.: *RH*, 250.

256 In June of that year: Louis to Avis, 20 June [1864], VI C 4:2 folder 29, p. 107,
     Anna to Avis, 4 December 1865, VI C 4:2 folder 29, p. 102, and Stephen Mat-
     toon, lecture draft, II F 1, folder 35, all in MKL Papers. For the year of Louis's
     letter, see Anna's letter written the same day (pp. 94–95).

—   the Mattoons were used to putting up guests: In 1856 they boarded in succes-
     sion the wife of British negotiator Harry Parkes (for two months), members of
     the American diplomatic mission, and the first British consul and his family.
     Stephen Mattoon to Mrs. Alfred L. Williams, 14 June 1856, II F 1, folder 11,
     MKL Papers; Wood, *Fankwei*, 220.

—   Mary was so emaciated from asthma; embarked for New York: Stephen Mat-
     toon to "Sister Harriette," 20 April 1864, and to "Father Lowrie," 8 July 1864, II
     F 1, folder 18, both in MKL Papers.

—   "One of our pupils, a sweet-faced young girl": Mattoon, "Missionary Ladies,"
     326–27.

257 sold the tale to *Youth's Companion*: Anna, "Life in a Siamese Palace," 199.

258 footnote 1: Anna, "Life in Siam," 28.

—   "house where we went to stay"; "One of my best friends": Louis to Avis, 20 June
     [1864], and Anna to Avis, 4 December 1865, pp. 107, 102.

259 "universal regret": Graireuk and Pramint, *Saaylap wang luang*, [38].

—   In October . . . Louis wrote Avis: 22 October [1865], VI C 4:2 folder 29, p. 100,
     MKL Papers.

—   "to prepare a cabin for me and my boy on his steamer," etc.: *EG*, 272.

—   crime statistics: "Police Cases," *Bangkok Recorder*, 16 January 1865, 7.

—   population was thought to be 400,000: *Siam Repository* 3 (January 1871): 2;
     Jumsai, *King Mongkut*, 79. When Cornelius Bradley read Anna's claim that "the
     best authorities" put the population at "about one million" (*EG*, 135), he wrote
     in the margin, "400,000 is a good estimate." Her mention of "the latest census"
     raised a dry laugh: "That's a joke" (annotated copy of *EG*). As he knew, there
     had been no census.

—   Late in the year, according to Louis: VI C 4:2 folder 29, pp. 101–2, MKL
     Papers.

—   footnote 2: Anna, "Thief in the Camp," 397; Anna, "Stolen Trunk," 82.

260 "a party of rude fellows," etc.: *EG*, 279.

—   "in a fit of uncontrollable rage": Macnaughton, "Mrs. Leonowens," 423; Chan-
     tasingh, "Americanization," 93, 137.

—   Constantine Phaulkon: *EG*, 34–39. Anna took her account from Neale, *Narra-
     tive*, 212–19, and another source I have not identified.

—   In March 1866: Anna to Avis, 14 March 1866, VI C 4:2 folder 29, p. 104, MKL
     Papers; Mongkut to Anna, 29 March 1866, in Graireuk and Pramint, *Saaylap
     wang luang*, [68].

261 "In the summer of 1866 my health suddenly broke down": *EG*, 282.

261 "rather than commit her boy": Macnaughton, "Mrs. Leonowens," 424–25. Ironically, it was thanks to Siamese patronage that Louis eventually found his way in life and prospered.

— "great misfortunes"; "the peculiar desolation": *RH*, 57; *EG*, 213.

262 "My head throbbed with pain": *EG*, 70.

— Of all the Americans: [Bacon], review of *EG*, 162; [Perry], review of *EG*, 422.

Chapter 17. Getting in Deeper

263 letter of condolence: Mongkut to George W. Virgin, 3 July 1865 (typed copy), VI C 4:5 folder 27, MKL Papers.

— "What with translating": *EG*, 270.

— "Why you should be poor?": Ibid., 270, 269.

264 "keys to open the doors to wealth": Hong, *Thailand*, 12.

— Klin had Burmese roots: ML's notes on Son Klin, VI C 4:6 folder 28, MKL Papers; *AKS*, 115; R. Halliday, "Immigration of the Mons into Siam," *Journal of the Siam Society* 10, no. 3 (September 1913): 1–13.

— An uncle, Phya Khien: *EG*, 108; Graireuk and Pramint, *Saaylap wang luang*, 25.

— Mongkut seems to have felt a residual distrust: Thiphakorawong, *Dynastic Chronicles*, 1:159–60.

265 urged Anna to write Queen Victoria: Anna, "Son Klean," 147.

— "That big green tree there": *RH*, 247.

— A photograph of Klin: Graireuk and Pramint, *Saaylap wang luang*, [22].

— "her eyes riveted," etc.: Anna, "Son Klean," 147.

266 "she is not prudent, you know,—like you and me": *EG*, 106.

— "My dearest Teacher": Son Klin to Anna, n.d. (photostat), VI C 4:6 folder 22, MKL Papers.

— "a sad and gentle woman": Review of *EG*, *Englishwoman's Review* 7 (April 1871): 97.

267 drew Anna in a bonnet and hoop skirt, positioned beside an opened trap door: *AKS*, 142.

— "her face turned to the clammy wall," etc.: *EG*, 107–9.

— "a sort of enclosed court," etc.: Mattoon, "Missionary Ladies," 326–27.

— "Father! I don't believe that hell itself": Pallegoix, *Description*, 1:362.

268 *cachot*, meaning "dungeon": *Boyer's French Dictionary* (Boston: Hilliard, Gray, Little & Williams, 1830) equated the word with "dungeon." *Dictionnaire de l'Académie française*, 8th ed. (Paris: Hachette, 1932), defined it as *prison basse et obscure*.

— "great pillared hall," etc.: Anna, "Life in Siam," 27.

— "the same air of timidity and restraint," etc.: *EG*, 105, 108.

— footnote 2: *AKS*, 114; VI A 3:1 folder 27, p. 5, MKL Papers (early and middle typescripts).

268 "that fatal enemy, their father": *EG*, 155.

— "never apparently abated his affection": DBB, "Reminiscences," 138.

— added his signature: Mongkut to Anna, 24 February 1865, VI C 4:5 folder 26, MKL Papers. Part of the letter, dated "34th" February and showing Krita's name, appears in *EG*, 268. The trip's purpose and itinerary are given in Thiphakorawong, *Dynastic Chronicles*, 2:338–43.

— he and three half sisters were given full honors in the topknot-cutting ceremony: Thiphakorawong, *Dynastic Chronicles*, 2:375.

269 "a bit of a swell": Louis to Anna, 16 June 1883, VI C 4:2 folder 29b, p. 241, MKL Papers.

— the twenty-eight-year-old prince got a coveted diplomatic assignment: Thiphakorawong, *Dynastic Chronicles*, 4:308; *Foreign Office List* (1886), 314.

— "just as he used to do when a little boy": Anna to Avis, 19 May 1884 (photostat), VI C 4:7 folder 4, MKL Papers.

— "It was horrible"; "Here, truly": *EG*, 109, 108.

— "I beg to inform you I have pardoned": Graireuk and Pramint, *Saaylap wang luang*, [39].

— "That very night," etc.: *EG*, 110.

270 On 2 March he returned to Bangkok: Thiphakorawong, *Dynastic Chronicles*, 2:343.

— "secretly": Graireuk and Pramint, *Saaylap wang luang*, [38].

CHAPTER 18. ANNA AND TUPTIM

272 "'*I* an absolute monarch!,'" etc.: *EG*, 264–65.

273 So much . . . appeared in Anna's first book: This segment was also part of the *Atlantic Monthly*'s opening installment of "The English Governess."

— "made pink with henna": *RH*, 15. Further citations are to *RH*, chaps. 2–4, pp. 14–41.

279 "verbal promise that the woman's life should be spared": [Kennedy], review of *RH*, 206.

— "staggered to [her] rooms": *EG*, 70.

— "Nervous, and undecided what to do": *RH*, 145.

280 "memory of the pure lovers": Florence Caddy, *To Siam and Malaya in the Duke of Sutherland's Yacht "Sans Peur"* (1889; reprint, Singapore: Oxford University Press, 1992), 207. I am mystified by Blofeld's undocumented claim that Tuptim "is known to have lived to a good age and become a grandmother" (*King Maha Mongkut*, 94).

— footnote 3: Terwiel, *Thailand's Political History*, 147–48.

281 which did, however, record a similar execution: Thiphakorawong, *Dynastic Chronicles*, 1:210.

281 In 1866 . . . Bradley drew attention to the execution: *Bangkok Calendar* (1866),
    50. This was the first year DBB included Bangkok events in his "Notable Days"
    feature. The entry reads: "June 29, 1859: A Siamese noble executed." Dropped
    in 1867, the entry was restored from 1868 to 1872. DBB's journal is blank for
    the period of the execution.

—   This event gave Anna the outline of a story: It was Susan Kepner who first
    disclosed the historical basis for "The Favorite of the Harem" in "Anna (and
    Margaret)," 19–20.

—   footnote 4: After appearing in the *Independent*, a liberal religious weekly, "The
    Story of Boon" was published as a slender book in 1874 by Roberts Brothers, a
    respected Boston firm; quotations are from pp. 5, 25.

—   "amorous intrigues"; "sewn into a leather sack": Pallegoix, *Description*, 1:271.

282 "most of the stories, incidents, and characters": Preface to *RH*.

—   "a pretty girl of the common people": [Samuel Jones Smith], "Woman," *Siam
    Repository* 1 (April 1869): 115.

283 In 1838 . . . a loving but chaste affair: Vella, *Siam*, 10; [Davenport], "Siamese
    Courts of Justice," 223–24.

—   "Behold the faggots blaze up high": Neale, *Narrative*, 233. Griswold was the
    first to spot the connection between Neale's poem and Anna's Tuptim story
    ("King Mongkut in Perspective," 29–31).

284 Missionary Frances Davenport had the impression: "Siamese Courts of Jus-
    tice," 223, 217.

—   nothing "could be imagined more truly tragic": [Perry], review of *RH*, 237.

—   "evidence of so much exaggeration": Anonymous review of *RH*, *London and
    China Express*, 7 February 1873, 133.

285 A more polite, detailed, and damaging evaluation: [Kennedy], review of *RH*,
    206.

—   The man who wrote this review: For the attribution to Kennedy, see p. 7.
    Information on him, Dilke, and the *Athenæum* comes from Edward Hertslet,
    Foreign Office List (1886), 130; Foster, *Men-at-the-Bar*, 254; *Bangkok Calen-
    dar* (1864–70); 1881 English census, London County, Chelsea Parish, Chelsea
    Registration District, Chelsea North-East Sub-registration District, 17 Sloane
    Street; Cambridge University Alumni, 1261–1900, http://www.ancestry.com;
    Roy Jenkins, "Dilke, Sir Charles Wentworth, Second Baronet (1843–1911)," in
    Oxford Dictionary of National Biography, 16:181–86 (Oxford: Oxford Univer-
    sity Press, 2004); Stephen Gwynn and Gertrude M. Tuckwell, *The Life of the Rt.
    Hon. Sir Charles W. Dilke Bart., M.P.* (London: Murray, 1917), 1:4, 87, 359, 503,
    2:535; Leslie A. Marchand, *The Athenaeum: A Mirror of Victorian Culture*
    (1941; reprint, New York: Octagon, 1971), 89.

—   footnote 5: Alan Bray, *The Friend* (Chicago: University of Chicago Press, 2003),
    57; [Kennedy], review of *RH*, 207.

285 no one was better qualified to assess Anna's books: Unlike some of her twentieth-century assailants, Kennedy was no defender of all things Siamese. He criticized the excesses of Siamese ceremonialism, such as the mandate that remote
provinces send their best logs to Bangkok for royal cremations ("Report," 325).

Chapter 19. Leaving Bangkok

287 "an adopted son": DBB, "Audience of J. M. Hood," *Bangkok Calendar* (1866),
112.
— "*Secondly*. Will you ask my aid": Cobb to Anna, [1865], VI C 4:2 folder 29,
p. 103, MKL Papers. That Cobb left Singapore in 1865 is inferred from letters,
the *Straits Calendar and Directory* (1865), and the *Straits Almanac and Directory* (1866).
288 Cobb . . . visited Avis at her boarding school: Miss King to Anna, 2 October
[1865], VI C 4:2 folder 29, p. 99, MKL Papers.
— On 7 January 1866 Mongkut's younger brother: Thiphakorawong, *Dynastic
Chronicles*, 3:210; *Bangkok Calendar* (1868), 118. The date of death given by
Anna, 29 December 1865, was in error, as was her colorful statement that
Klieb, the concubine suspected of poisoning him, was "thrown into an open
boat, towed out on the Gulf of Siam, and there abandoned" (*EG*, 223, 233–34).
In fact, Mongkut doubted Klieb's guilt and commuted her sentence from death
to exile in the city of Sukhothai (Thiphakorawong, *Dynastic Chronicles*, 2:358).
— "Laos-style pavilion"; "enjoyed playing the Laotian reed mouth-organ": Thi-
phakorawong, *Dynastic Chronicles*, 2:355. Some typical Western reactions to
Jutamani are in Neale, *Narrative*, 87–91; Wood, *Fankwei*, 210; Bowring, *Kingdom and People*, 2:324–25; George W. [B.] Bacon, "A Morning with a King,"
Hours at Home 4 (April 1867): 531–37; and "The Late First and Second Kings,"
Siam Repository 1 (April 1869): 61–64.
289 blatantly hypocritical, a cover for sinister designs: Jutamani's accomplishments
and Mongkut's supposed envy were the subject of the second *Atlantic Monthly*
installment of *EG*. In the book this material appears in chapters 25 and 27. For
a sounder account of the brothers' personal relations, see Mongkut, *King of
Siam Speaks*, 188–89.
— "Phraong Tui, the eldest Princess": "Siam. *(From our own Correspondent.)*
Bangkok, 16th March, 1866," *Singapore Daily Times*, 26 March 1866 (reel 5215,
Singapore National Library). Writing to Anna on 6 April, Mongkut wrongly
supposed that the newspaper was the *Daily News*. On Phraong Tui, born in
1838, see Thiphakorawong, *Dynastic Chronicles*, 4:332.
— "What was said therein for a princess," etc.: Mongkut to Anna, 6 April 1866,
Graireuk and Pramint, *Saaylap wang luang*, [57]; *EG*, 266–67; VI C 4:6 folder
14, MKL Papers.
— His indignant protest was a "sham": *EG*, 267.

289 It took eighty-nine days: "Protestant Missionaries in Siam," *Bangkok Calendar* (1872), 127.

— Chiang Mai's aging king . . . was an object of intense curiosity; apparently connived at the murder of Christians: Feltus, *Abstract*, 252, 287, 290, 292.

— The age-old way . . . is to hold his children as honored hostages: For Anna's treatment of Mongkut's demand that the king of Chiang Mai "send his eldest son to Bangkok as a hostage for his father's loyalty and good conduct," see *EG*, 274.

290 Anna's thrilling account of the escape: All citations are to *RH*, chaps. 16–25, pp. 145–201. Anna first mentioned Mongkut's supposed attraction to the princess in *EG*, 274–75.

— Paklat, a river town nine miles south of Bangkok: *RH*, 165; *EG*, 131; [Kennedy], review of *RH*, 206.

293 "quietly engrossing reading": *Time*, 10 July 1944, 102.

— "the princesses have female vocalists": S. H. Poole, "Travels in the Kingdom of Cheangmai," *Bangkok Calendar* (1869), 112.

— modern biography of Jutamani: Sombat Plainoi, *The Celestial Prince Jutamani* (Bangkok: Prae Bhitthaya, 1988), cited in Chantasingh, "Americanization," 64.

— "The first remark we should make"; "Is it a fact": [Kennedy], review of *RH*, 206.

294 footnote 2: Lingat, "History," 73, 76, 86; *RH*, 189. Anna's remarks about "Watt Brahmanee Waid" in *EG*, 134, 165, 181, 195, can only refer to Wat Bowonniwet. ML rightly assumed that they were one and the same (*AKS*, [iv], 359). Anna's description of iconic Hindu statues would have been based on temples seen in India or Singapore.

295 As critic Chu-Chueh Cheng suggests: Cheng, "Frances Trollope's America," 151.

296 In 1863 he compelled Norodom . . . to enter treaty relations; Interpreting the secret second treaty: Thiphakorawong, *Dynastic Chronicles*, 2:306–7, 3:162–77, 184–86.

— For a time Aubaret and Mongkut: *Gabriel Aubaret*, 202–3. The anonymous author of this adulatory biography, published three years after Aubaret's death, had access to his letters and "*memento journalier*" (220) from Southeast Asia.

297 "taking *Mom* himself by his *top-knot*": *Bangkok Recorder*, 16 September 1865. Since DBB was hostile to Aubaret and hadn't witnessed the act, he may have overstated its offensive nature. Grabbing a man's hair was equivalent to spitting in his face, yet none of the repercussions one would expect are on record; see Lawrence Palmer Briggs, "The Aubaret versus Bradley Case at Bangkok 1866–67," *Far Eastern Quarterly* 6, no. 3 (May 1947): 268–69. In *AKS*, ML not only accepted DBB's story as factual but heightened the violence: "He grasped the prince by his hair and with all his strength swung the slight Siamese up and threw him down the stairs to the ground" (265). Kingston's recent claim that

E. Lamache committed the act is based on a misreading of DBB's journal (*James Madison Hood*, 163).

297 Speaking for France, Aubaret demanded: Pensri, *Les relations*, 49–50; Thiphakorawong, *Dynastic Chronicles*, 2:362–63, 3:216–17.

— On 14 December 1866 . . . "within 10 rods": *Bangkok Calendar* (1868), 119, 122.

— the consul spoke "disparagingly of . . . [the *kalahom*]": *Bangkok Recorder*, 22 December 1866, as quoted in *Straits Times*, 23 February 1867; Feltus, *Abstract*, 254.

— A few days after Bradley: Feltus, *Abstract*, 254–55; *Bangkok Calendar* (1868), 119.

298 "audacious and firm," etc.: Beauvoir, *Java, Siam*, 343.

— Matters came to a boil in January: Pensri, *Les relations*, 50–51.

— As a royal secretary, Anna was privy to the developing crisis: Feltus, *Abstract*, 255.

— footnote 3: Thiphakorawong, *Dynastic Chronicles*, 2:475.

— When Anna informed Mongkut: DBB, Journals, vol. 22, 19–20 January 1867, DBB Family Papers.

299 American consul, James Madison Hood: J. F. Farnsworth et al. to William H. Seward, 16 January 1864 (ML's typed copy), VI C 4:5 folder 10, MKL Papers. For an account of Hood's tenure that draws extensively on his dispatches to the State Department, see Kingston, *James Madison Hood*, chapters 10–14.

— "Having been informed": This letter of 4 February 1867 was printed with "the omission of two words" in DBB's lengthy, aggrieved account of the trial (*Bangkok Calendar* [1868], 120, 123). As William L. Bradley cleverly deduced in *Siam Then*, the two words must be "His Majesty" (134).

300 Disregarding Anna's letter: *Bangkok Calendar* (1868), 123–24; *Straits Times*, 23 February 1867; *Gabriel Aubaret*, 221.

— "think of us as animals": Thiphakorawong, *Dynastic Chronicles*, 4:230; also Moffat, *Mongkut*, 117–24.

301 "anything [she] liked"; "promised"; "emphatically declining": *EG*, 277.

— It was 12 May 1867; "As I sat at my familiar table": Ibid., 281, 280.

302 "Ma'm Leonowens, who is the royal children's teacher": Sri Suntorn-woharn to Siam's deputy consul in Singapore, as translated in Chantasingh, "Americanization," 49, from Damrong Rajanubhab, ed., *Correspondence of King Mongkut*, 4th ed. (Bangkok: Sophon-pipattanakorn, 1926), 5–6.

— After finally writing Bowring for the king: Bowring to Anna, 30 June 1867 (photostat), VI C 4:5 folder 3, MKL Papers; *EG*, 281–82; Thiphakorawong, *Dynastic Chronicles*, 4:234–36.

303 "Mrs Leonowens has determined": DBB, Journals, vol. 23, 24 June 1867, DBB Family Papers.

— leave of absence: For six months, according to *EG*, 283; "for a year or so," according to DBB, "Reminiscences," 129.

303 Her Siamese friends loaded her with gifts: *EG*, 283–84; Chulalongkorn to Anna, 1 July 1867, VI C 4:2 folder 29, p. 127, MKL Papers.

— "come back to us. I am like one blind": VI C 4:2 folder 29, p. 130, MKL Papers.

— a telegraph, some gaslights: *Bangkok Calendar* (1868), 118–19.

— "escorted some distance": DBB, Journals, vol. 23, 5 July 1867, DBB Family Papers; *EG*, 285.

— In Singapore she caught the overland mail steamer: VI C 4:2 folder 29, pp. 128, 130, MKL Papers.

304 Wilkinson, a solicitor, acted as Anna's agent and advisor: VI C 4:2 folder 29a, pp. 144, 152, MKL Papers; Bristowe, *Louis*, 35.

— "force and conviction"; "Those friends thou hast": VI C 4:2 folder 29a, p. 156, MKL Papers.

— Would it be Sir John Bowring: Bowring to Anna, 26 September 1867 (photostat), VI C 4:5 folder 3, MKL Papers; obituary, *Englishwoman's Review* 13 (January 1873): 88.

305 Since Cobb was no longer a bachelor: Francis got engaged soon after his return to the States (Dewey, *Autobiography*, 283). On 11 February 1866, his twenty-ninth birthday (Francis Davis Cobb, 8 January 1915, Town Deaths, Barnstable, Massachusetts), he wrote Anna that he was married (VI C 4:2 folder 29, p. 105, MKL Papers), no doubt surprising her. Curiously, the wedding did not come off till 4 April (1866, Sheffield, vol. 189, p. 70, Massachusetts Vital Records). He and his bride, Katherine Sedgwick Dewey, aged twenty-eight, were first cousins and must therefore have been well acquainted prior to his Singapore venture. Her mother, Louisa Farnham, and Francis's mother, Phebe Bliss Farnham, were sisters born in Newburyport. For family ties, see Dewey, *Autobiography*, 49; Cobb family gravestones, Cobb's Hill Cemetery, Barnstable, Massachusetts; 1860 census, Boston, ward 8, family 786 (Mathew Cobb); 1870 census, Boston, ward 8, family 235 (John O. Shaw); Louisa Farnham Dewey, 25 June 1884, Town Deaths, Sheffield, Massachusetts, Town Clerk; 4 September 1790 marriage intention of William Farnham of Newburyport and Hannah Bliss Emerson of Concord; and Farnham births at Newburyport, the last two items at http://www.newenglandancestors.org/research/Database/vital_records.

— "required a more bracing climate": VI C 4:2 folder 29a, p. 131, MKL Papers.

— In reply, one of the elderly Misses King: Miss King to Anna, 23 October 1867, VI C 4:2 folders 29 and 29a, pp. 130–31, MKL Papers.

CHAPTER 20. THE ENGLISH GOVERNESS COMES TO AMERICA

309 landed in New York City on 14 November: VI C 4:2 folder 29a, p. 132, MKL Papers, states that Anna arrived from Queenstown (Cobh) on 13 November. In fact, no ships arrived from Europe on that date. However, the next day the

Denmark steamed in from Liverpool via Queenstown ("Shipping Intelligence," *New York Tribune*, 14, 15 November 1867). This, then, was Anna's ship and date of arrival.

309 They were supposed to be met: VI C 4:2 folder 29a, p. 132, MKL Papers. Francis's uncle had died on 12 November on Cape Cod (Frederic Cobb, Town Deaths, p. 4, Barnstable, Massachusetts).

— Cobb's good friend James Sloan Gibbons: VI C 4:2 folder 29b, p. 214, MKL Papers. The friendship is attested in P. B. Cobb (Phebe Bliss Cobb, Francis's mother) to Sallie "Sarah" Hopper Gibbons Emerson, 11 May 1874, series 3, box 4:212, Abby Hopper Gibbons Family Papers; and Emerson, *Life of Abby Hopper Gibbons*, 2:200, 358.

— His wife, Abby Hopper Gibbons: Emerson's biography details the Gibbonses' Quaker roots, strong radical conscience, friendship with Lucretia Mott, and high standards of literacy and education. Abby's own friends included writers Caroline Kirkland and Catherine M. Sedgwick. In the 1863 Draft Riots the Gibbons house in New York City was sacked by proslavery vandals. See Emerson, *Life of Abby Hopper Gibbons*, 1:115–16, 146, 154, 246.

— Cobb had gone into business: His business address was either 68 New Street or 19 Broad Street (Trow's New York directories for 1868 and 1869). His occupation was variously identified as merchant, broker, and banker. He seems to have been well off, though not wealthy (VI C 4:2 folder 29a, p. 186, MKL Papers).

— Katherine, daughter of a leading Unitarian minister: Reverend Orville Dewey, a successful lecturer, was no crusader. His centrist positions on slavery and other issues are apparent in his *Autobiography and Letters*, 116–19, and *Moral Views of Commerce, Society and Politics in Twelve Discourses* (1838; reprint, New York: Augustus M. Kelley, 1969).

— "You must be as happy as you can": VI C 4:2 folder 29a, p. 132, MKL Papers.

310 But her first reaction to the New World: "I like America a little better than I did at first," Anna to DBB, 17 May 1870, I/1/335, DBB Family Papers.

— "did everything that could possibly be done": Macnaughton, "Mrs. Leonowens," 428.

— Stephen and Mary Mattoon in their new home in Ballston Spa: Mary Mattoon to Mrs. Morse, 21 March 1867, II B 1 folder 21, MKL Papers.

— "one of the greatest men": Anna to Avis, 4 December 1865, VI C 4:2 folder 29, p. 102, MKL Papers.

— a Siamese official held him in highest esteem: Harris, *Complete Journal*, 121.

— footnote 1: Edward F. Grose, *Centennial History of the Village of Ballston Spa* (Ballston Spa, N.Y.: Ballston Journal, 1907), 84; Mary Mattoon to Mrs. Lee, [early 1871?], and R. M. Hall, obituary of Mary (clipping), II F 1, folders 22 and 36, MKL Papers; Louisa Thomas, *Conscience: Two Soldiers, Two Pacifists, One Family* (New York: Penguin, 2011), 3–8.

310 "grateful appreciation of the kindness": *EG*, [xii].
311 On 2 November 1867: The date of her letter (not extant) is stated in Mongkut's reply.
— sent kisses from the Gulf of Siam: VI C 4:2 folder 29a, pp. 134, 136, 164, MKL Papers.
— "You must be very tired writing," etc.: letters to Anna from Selina Wilkinson [early March 1868], Thomas Wilkinson (29 January and 22 April 1868), and Louis (4 February and 28 April 1868), VI C 4:2 folder 29a, pp. 136–44, MKL Papers. As late as 10 October 1868 Louis was afraid his mother might have to return to Siam (VI C 4:2 folder 29a, p. 149, MKL Papers).
312 footnote 2: *Perth Gazette*, 3 August 1855; *EG*, 18; "English Governess," *Atlantic Monthly* 26 (August 1870): 154.
— "publication might break": quoted in Thomas Wilkinson to Anna, 29 January 1868, VI C 4:2 folder 29a, p. 136a, MKL Papers.
— "I am very anxious about you": Thomas Wilkinson to Anna, 13 May 1868, VI C 4:2 folder 29a, pp. 144–45, MKL Papers.
— "I can allow the Loan of £200," etc.: Mongkut to Anna, VI C 4:2 folder 29a, p. 145A, MKL Papers. This letter, written soon after the February 1868 cremation of Mongkut's eldest son, may partly account for the rumor recorded in Blofeld's hagiographic life of Mongkut: "There is a story that Anna . . . demanded the sum of £400 as a kind of severance pay. This being curtly refused, she then wrote to him threatening to write books that would blacken his reputation" (*King Maha Mongkut*, 69).
— His reference was to a complaint: Dated 2 July 1867; see *EG*, 260–61.
313 Returning to New York City: VI C 4:2 folder 29a, pp. 147, 149, 153, MKL Papers.
— On 18 August 1868 a total solar eclipse was expected: Thiphakorawong, *Dynastic Chronicles*, 2:532–59; [DBB], "Great Solar Eclipse," *Bangkok Calendar* (1869), 88–96. DBB's authorship is acknowledged in his journals (Feltus, *Abstract*, 278).
— a brief report of his death appeared: "The King of Siam," *NYT*, 17 November 1868, 5.
314 footnote 3: Mongkut, *Ruamphraraachaniphonnai*, 427.
— "Mongkut won the struggle": Thongchai, *Siam Mapped*, 47.
— The account of the expedition: *EG*, 248–49; [DBB], "Great Solar Eclipse," 93.
315 On 19 July 1868 . . . Katherine gave birth: See Richard Cobb in *Harvard College, Class of 1892, Report XV, Fiftieth Anniversary* (Norwood, Mass.: Plimpton Press, 1942), 57.
— "an opening for a school": LWJ to Annie Fields, 16 August 1868, LWJ Papers.
— Sydney Howard Gay: *The National Cyclopaedia of American Biography* (New York: James T. White, 1899), 2:494; W. Farrell O'Gorman, "Gay, Sydney Howard," in *American National Biography*, 8:806–8.

315 footnote 4: John S. Jacobs to Gay, 4 June 1846, Sydney Howard Gay Papers, Columbia University Libraries.

316 The help she got from Curtis . . . she acknowledged her debt to Shaw: *EG*, vii; preface to *RH*. Anna's tribute to Sarah Shaw is in Anna to Annie Fields, 10 January 1904, FI 5042, JTF Papers.

— "as clearly as if it happened yesterday": Anna to Annie Fields, 10 December 1889, FI 5059, JTF Papers.

— "The word Indian takes me to Mrs Leonowens": LWJ to Fields, 16 August 1868. There is no basis whatever for Morgan's statement that "Rev. and Laura Johnson" were "another missionary family she had known in Bangkok" (*Bombay Anna*, 173).

317 "a most agreeable woman": LWJ to Annie Fields, 11 January 1869, LWJ Papers.

— on the edge of . . . Factoryville: Location given by Mary Otis Gay Willcox in Hine and Davis, *Legends*, 92. Successive atlases by Beers (1874), Lefévre (1894), and Bromley (1917) at the Staten Island Institute of Arts & Sciences show that Tompkins Court (not Place, pace Willcox) had not yet been laid out at the time Anna lived there.

318 "A first-class Boarding and Day School": *Richmond County Gazette*, 24 August 1870, 15 November 1871, 24 January 1872.

— The school was a clear success: Laura Johnson [daughter] to Annie Fields, 15 March 1869, "misc." folder, and LWJ to Annie Fields, 18 December 1868 and [1868?—letter begins "I received your"], LWJ Papers. Laura, born on 24 May 1863 (LWJ to Emily Fowler Ford, 26 May 1881, LWJ Papers), was five years old.

— "the real teacher": Mary Otis Gay Willcox in Hine and Davis, *Legends*, 93. Born in 1861/62, Mary seems to have been Anna's pupil from the autumn of 1868 to the spring of 1869, when her mother left Staten Island to join her husband, the newly appointed editor of the *Chicago Tribune* (LWJ to Annie Fields, 18 December 1868, LWJ Papers; *National Cyclopaedia*, 2:494), and again in the 1870s after the family returned from Chicago. Mary's year of birth is inferred from the 1880 census, which gives her age as eighteen (New York, Richmond County, West New Brighton, dwelling 86).

— "improved . . . in her manners": LWJ to Annie Fields, 22 February 1876, LWJ Papers.

— "feeling a little nervous": Anna to Annie Fields, 30 March 1883, JTF Papers.

— "a bit oppressed": Fyshe, "Anna and I," 64.

— "a brunette with waving hair": Mary Otis Gay Willcox in Hine and Davis, *Legends*, 93.

319 "a very vivid personality": Louisa Loring Dresel to ML, 11 March 1945, VI C 4:2 folder 21, MKL Papers. Boston directories for 1883 and 1884 place the Dresels at 150 Charles Street, adjacent to the Fields home at no. 148. Dresel's

impression in old age that the encounter took place in 1883 or 1884 points to Anna's visit to Annie Fields in April 1884 (VI C 4:2 folder 29b, p. 243, MKL Papers). Dresel was then nineteen years old, having been born on 27 June 1864 (Massachusetts Vital Records, Births, vol. 170, p. 83).

319 "a snug little house"; "such a dreadful neighborhood": LWJ to Annie Fields, [1868?] and 4 June 1873, LWJ Papers.

— "old cottage," etc.: Anna to Avis, 2 June 1880, VI C 4:2 folder 29b, p. 218, MKL Papers.

— the malaria that afflicted her: VI C 4:2 folder 29a, p. 176, MKL Papers.

— house . . . merited a name: Hawthorne: Anna to Annie Fields, 17 August 1874, FI 5061, JTF Papers; LWJ to Annie Fields, [7 July 1873], LWJ Papers.

— "really must leave the island": Avis Selina Fyshe in VI C 4:2 folder 29a, p. 179, MKL Papers.

— "looked quite decent"; "the old feeling of pain": Anna to Avis, 2 June 1880, p. 218.

— "the strain & care": Avis Selina Fyshe in VI C 4:2 folder 29b, p. 244, MKL Papers.

— The friend to whom Johnson described: Avis Selina Fyshe claimed that it was Katherine Cobb who introduced Anna to Annie Fields (VI C 4:2 folder 29a, p. 133, MKL Papers). That Johnson was the true intermediary was first shown by Gollin, *Annie Adams Fields*, 132.

320 Founded four years before: Sedgwick, *The "Atlantic Monthly,"* 35, 62–64, 85, 93, 103–5.

— "very busy with school": Mary Mattoon to Mary Morse, 25 February 1870, II F 1, folder 22, MKL Papers.

— "padding not very skilfully inserted": [Bacon], review of *EG*, 162.

— "does not write like a practised and experienced writer": LWJ to Annie Fields, 13 May [1870], LWJ Papers.

321 "negotiate topics and treatments": Sedgwick, *The "Atlantic Monthly,"* 84.

— Palmer had a solid connection with the *Atlantic*: Underwood to Palmer, 21 February 1872, Francis Henry Underwood Papers. In all, the *Atlantic Monthly* ran seventeen pieces by Palmer.

— decided to run away to Bangkok: John Williamson Palmer, "Aunt Judy," *Atlantic Monthly* 18 (July 1866): 76–85.

— "the eye of a poet," etc.: James Russell Lowell, review of Palmer's *The New and the Old* and *Up and Down the Irawaddy*, *Atlantic Monthly* 4 (September 1859): 383.

— his stay in an inebriate asylum: [John Williamson Palmer], "Our Inebriates, Classified and Clarified" and "Our Inebriates, Harbored and Helped," each subtitled "By an Inmate of the New York State Asylum," *Atlantic Monthly* 23 (April 1869): 477–83, and 24 (July 1869): 109–19.

321 a letter sent to Palmer on 8 July 1870: John Williamson Palmer Collection.
— "busy for a year at least": The "Pali translation" may have been one of Anna's terms for the "German translation" (Anna to Fields and Osgood, 27 December 1870, Thomas Bailey Aldrich Papers) that she later submitted for publication, without success. At a time when the leading Pali/Sanskrit scholars were German, she may have produced an English version of a German translation from Pali.
322 "a significant contribution": Irwin, *Dangerous Knowledge*, 188.
— footnote 5: *EG*, 292; *NYT*, 10 December 1870, 2.
— "free-and-easy manner," etc.: Lowell, review of Palmer, 383–84. William Dean Howells judged Palmer's style to be "slangy, silly and vapid" (*Selected Letters*, ed. George Arms et al. [Boston: Twayne, 1979], 1:269) and rejected his essay about a Hindu servant in Calcutta. Fields accepted it anyway.
— footnote 6: William Dean Howells, "Recollections of an Atlantic Editorship," *Atlantic Monthly* 100 (November 1907): 594. Anna's name does not show up in Howells's voluminous correspondence, now at Indiana University (communication from David Nordloh, ca. 2005).
323 not an intact segment of the book but a composite: "The English Governess . . . IV," *Atlantic Monthly* 26 (August 1870): 144–55. Since there was too little time for Anna to read proof between her letter of 8 July and the printing of the August issue, the Siamese words the compositor mangled went uncorrected: Wanne Ratâna (a name) became Waine Ratâm, and *Ti chan* ("Beat me") became *Tu cham* (ibid., 151, 153). There was a case of lack of agreement between subject and predicate ("Neither sex wear any covering on the head" [147]; corrected in the book, [*EG*, 101]). Ordinarily, the magazine was much cleaner. The meticulous Howells may indeed have taken a hands-off approach.
— Mongkut thought of Anna as "the Lady L——": "The English Governess . . . ," *Atlantic Monthly* 25 (April 1870): 408, 410.
— "free access": "The English Governess . . . IV," *Atlantic Monthly* 26 (August 1870): 144. Following citations are to this installment (pp. 144–55). Anna's claim is dubious. Not only did she find cursive Thai script hard to read, but even a certified insider like Thiphakorawong had to get special permission from King Chulalongkorn for the free archival access that his *Dynastic Chronicles* required (3:3).
324 "four months ago . . . excited much curiosity": *NYT*, 10 December 1870, 2.
— "And finally, I would acknowledge": *EG*, viii.
325 "always thought the book," etc.: Palmer to Anna, 18 December 1870, VI C 4:2 folder 29a, p. 164, MKL Papers.
— "The rainbow mists of morning": *EG*, 300–301.
— "Have pity on me, oh my God": Mouhot, *Henri Mouhot's Diary*, 156.
326 "undisputed directorate": Stafford, "Scientific Exploration," 297.

326 Two who managed to do so were British photographer John Thomson and
    Henry George Kennedy: Details and quotations are from Thomson, "Notes of
    a Journey." DBB noted the pair's 17 April return to Bangkok (*Bangkok Calen-
    dar* [1868], 118) but left nothing on record in private journals or any published
    Calendar about Anna's supposed trip.
— footnote 7: Colquhoun, *Amongst the Shans*, 90.
— Back in Bangkok: Kennedy, "Report," 298–328; [Kennedy], review of *EG*, 836,
    and review of *RH*, 205. Given that Anna's nephew, Thomas Lean Wilkinson, a
    London barrister with literary interests, was looking out for her reputation (VI
    C 4:2 folder 29a, p. 163, MKL Papers), she was most likely advised of the
    Athenæum's damaging statements.
— Kennedy's traveling companion accused her of plagiarism and fraud: Thom-
    son, *Straits of Malacca*, 129–30.
327 Among those who reacted: Henry James, *Literary Criticism: Essays on Litera-
    ture, American Writers, English Writers* (New York: Library of America, 1984),
    1308; *NYT*, 28 February 1875, 5.
— Anna sent a defiant reply: *NYT*, 3 March 1875, 6. Morgan's statement that "as
    far as I have been able to determine, Anna made no false claims about her
    achievements (only about her background)" (*Bombay Anna*, 53) effectively
    sums up this biographer's level of attention and insight.
328 "Those of my readers": *EG*, vii.
— "the old model of the explorer": Stafford, "Scientific Exploration," 307.

CHAPTER 21. SUCCESS AND DECLINE

330 "peculiar sadness": Anna, "Biographical Sketch," 42.
— Miss Comstock's School; Miss Haines's School: VI C 4:2 folder 29a, p. 159,
    MKL Papers; New York City directories, 1869–77. Henrietta B. Haines's over-
    size entry in the directory for 1874–75 is a sign of her school's prominence.
— its best people: These and other outstanding references are named in Avis's
    advertising circular for her kindergarten (Anna Harriette Leonowens Papers).
    The premises of her former employer, Marie Louise Comstock, were nearby, at
    32 West 40th Street. Avis succeeded with her school partly because she was
    able to take over Comstock's kindergarten class (VI C 4:2 folder 29a, p. 189,
    MKL Papers).
331 five-year contract with the newly founded Berkeley School: VI C 4:2 folder
    29b, pp. 219, 222, MKL Papers; Anna to Annie Field, 27 December 1880, FI
    5052, JTF Papers.
— school of art and design: On Anna's life in Canada, see Yorke, "Edwards, Anna
    Harriette," 333–35; and Dow's somewhat fictionalized *Anna Leonowens*, 70–148.
— lost her faith in Christianity: Anna Harriet Leonowens Fyshe to ML, 21 Sep-
    tember 1945, VI C 1:1 folder 1, MKL Papers.

331 "Reduce rents": Anna to Annie Fields, 5 January 1909, JTF Papers.

332 "see her deep set eyes": Louisa Farnham Cobb to ML, 5 January 1945, VI C 4:5 folder 6, MKL Papers.

— "She was the life," etc.: Avis Selina Fyshe to ML, 9 April 1943, VI C 1:1 folder 2, MKL Papers.

— "language is meant to be spoken": Anna, "Life in Siam," 27.

333 "English intonation": VI C 4:2 folder 29a, p. 156, MKL Papers.

— friends on Staten Island rented a hall; cleared a handsome $145: VI C 4:2 folder 29a, p. 165, MKL Papers.

— "in the most superb," etc.: *Richmond County Gazette*, 28 June 1871, quoted in John B. Woodall, "Anna Leonowens' Sojourn on Staten Island," *Staten Island Historian*, n.s., 1, no. 3 (Winter 1984): 35. The benefit was for the (Episcopal) Church of the Ascension, near Anna's house.

— give one of the Cooper Union's Free Lectures for the People: VI C 4:2 folder 29a, p. 156, MKL Papers; *NYT*, 5 April 1872, 7, and 7 April 1872, 6. The Fords' printed invitation is with the Anna Harriette Leonowens Papers.

— Two months later: *NYT*, 22 June 1872, 4, and 25 June 1872, 4; Leopold, *Robert Dale Owen*, 355–56, 360–72, 400–401.

334 "It will doubtless create a smile," etc.: "Siamese Slavery," *Siam Repository* 5 (April 1873): 166–67, 170 (reprinted from the *Siam Weekly Advertiser* for 16 January).

— minor reform in the conditions of debt servitude; a rumor started that slavery would terminate: Wyatt, *Politics of Reform*, 50; "Slaves" and "Emancipation," *Siam Repository* 3 (1871): 341–42, 348 (reprinted from the *Siam Weekly Advertiser* for 25 May and 1 June); *NYT*, 8 September 1871, 4. On 15 September 1888, 9, the *Times* of London offered a sober and informed analysis of the obstacles to emancipation in Siam. The *NYT* had nothing comparable.

335 footnote 2: "Recoronation," *Siam Repository* 6 (1874): 69 (reprinted from the *Siam Weekly Advertiser* for 30 October 1873).

— From about 1873 to 1875 she had James Redpath: VI C 4:2 folder 29a, p. 173, MKL Papers; LWJ to Annie Fields, 21 December 1875, LWJ Papers. Anna's first manager was B. W. Williams of the American Literary Bureau (VI C 4:2 folder 29a, p. 168, MKL Papers).

— "My agent Mr J. Redpath of Boston": Anna to W. C. Gannett, 8 September 1873, Lewis Gannett Papers.

— but for "*MRS A. H. LEONOWENS*" he wisely began: Only pp. 42–43 are in the Anna Harriette Leonowens Papers. Although the volume and year are not shown, the fact that Owen's 1872 letter to the *NYT* is dated "last year" shows that the material must have been set in type in 1873. Since another lecturer's promotional material quotes a letter from 1875 (p. 43), we can infer that Redpath managed Anna for at least three years: 1873 to 1875.

336 sound advice came in the mail: Owen to Avis Leonowens, 15 April 1872, quoted in VI C 4:2 folder 29a, pp. 166–68, MKL Papers.

— Sometimes the quiet hour proved elusive: VI C 4:2 folder 29a, pp. 174b–c, MKL Papers.

— One reason Owen sent: Anna to Owen, 12 March 1872, box 2, folder 1, Robert Dale Owen Papers.

337 "not one whit mannish": VI C 4:2 folder 29a, p. 170, MKL Papers.

— footnote 4: Chaudhuri and Strobel, *Western Women*, 231. On colonial British views of Eurasian taste in clothes, see Hawes, *Poor Relations*, 79.

338 "You will be glad to hear"; "making a place": Annie Fields to LWJ, 15 February and 26 October 1874, addenda box 12(5), JTF Papers.

— Annie called Anna's lectures "narrations": VI C 4:2 folder 29a, p. 169, MKL Papers.

— she read a "paper on 'Oriental Religion'": Higginson, diary, 18 January and 10 February 1874, Thomas Wentworth Higginson Papers; Higginson to Anna, 4 November 1873, quoted in VI C 4:2 folder 29a, p. 177. MKL Papers; Mary Elizabeth Fiske Sargent, ed., *Sketches and Reminiscences of the Radical Club of Chestnut Street, Boston* (Boston: Osgood, 1880), 223–25; "Krishna," in *Encyclopaedia Britannica*, 15th ed. (1988), 7:7.

339 impressed with her "vitality": Charles Eliot Norton to James Russell Lowell, 4 August 1878, in *Letters of Charles Eliot Norton* (Boston: Houghton Mifflin, 1913), 2:81–83.

— "embraced me as if"; "laughed so immoderately": Anna to Avis, 29 October 1872, quoted in VI C 4:2 folder 29a, p. 169a, MKL Papers; Anna to Annie Fields, 28 July 1896, FI 5063, JTF Papers. Although it is often said that Anna and Stowe were close friends, this was their only meeting. Their one exchange of letters came six years later as Stowe prepared an historical essay on her novel (Stowe to Annie Fields, 3 October [1878], FI 3998, and Anna to Annie Fields, 15 October 1878, both in JTF Papers; *Uncle Tom's Cabin* [Boston: Houghton, Osgood, 1879], xxxv–xxxvi).

— "the creature was a part of her weird life": Annie Fields to LWJ, 26 October 1874, addenda box 12(5), JTF Papers.

340 moved in for two years with the president of Columbia College: Anna to Annie Fields, 17 August 1874, FI 5061, JTF Papers; VI C 4:2 folder 29a, p. 174, MKL Papers.

— Another key figure in her ascent was Charles Loring Brace: Emma Brace Donaldson to ML, 15 November 1945, VI C 4:3 folder 13, and Mrs. L. N. Brace to Avis, 8 March [1885], as quoted in VI C 4:2 folder 29b, p. 250, both in MKL Papers; Anna to Annie Fields, 28 July 1874, FI 5063, JTF Papers; "A Children's Friend Dead," *NYT*, 14 August 1890, 8; [Emma Brace, ed.], *The Life of Charles Loring Brace* (New York: Scribner's, 1894), 344–45; A. L. Donaldson, *A History of the Adirondacks* (New York: Century, 1921), 1:350–52; Stephen O'Connor, *Orphan Trains: The Story of Charles Loring Brace and the Children He Saved and Failed* (Chicago: University of Chicago Press, 2001), 50, 116–17.

340 Brace was fixated on race: Charles Loring Brace, *The Races of the Old World: A Manual of Ethnology* (New York: Scribner, 1871), 15–16.

— "belong to the same family as many of the Western nations": *NYT*, 7 April 1872, 6. In *Our Asiatic Cousins*, Anna urged that "the Siamese themselves claim to be of Aryan descent" (350). In fact, Thais have never claimed this. Was she misled by the many Pali/Sanskrit loan words that came into the Thai language under Indian influence?

— footnote 5: *LTI*, 56.

341 Through Brace, Anna met Anne Lynch Botta: [Botta], *Memoirs*, 99, 164–65, 25, 90.

— Anna's first visit to Botta's home: Ibid., 102, 100, 311, 1.

— footnote 6: LWJ to Annie Fields, Monday, 10 [July] 1876, LWJ Papers.

— The first time Anna and Avis visited: Annie Adams Fields journal, 1 March [1872], Annie Fields Papers, microfilm edition, 3 reels (Boston: Massachusetts Historical Society, 1981), reel 2.

342 one of her cronies in New York City, John Paine, owned a waterfront property in Newport, Rhode Island: *Newport Journal*, 17 September 1874, 2; *Newport Weekly Mercury*, 31 July 1875, 2; Virginia Galvin Covell, "A Critical Examination of the Town and Country Club of Newport, Rhode Island" (M.A. thesis, University of Rhode Island, 1964), Newport Historical Society; Anna to Annie Fields, 28 July 1874, FI 5063, and 12 July 1875, FI 5050, JTF Papers. Paine bought his Newport property in 1854 (Newport Land Evidence 32:314, supplied by Bertram Lippincott III) and began summering there (1856 *Newport City Directory*) long before the post–Civil War invasion by New York plutocrats. The location is shown on G. M. Hopkins's 1876 Newport map (Newport Historical Society). Paine's home in New York City was at 3 West 53rd Street. After his death a well-reported challenge to his will made his private life public: *NYT*, 21 December 1886, 8; 24, 25, 26, 27, 28, 31 January and 1, 3 February 1888, p. 8; 30 December 1891, 3. That Anna was friends with his second wife, Carolyn, is apparent from VI C 4:2 folder 29a, p. 189, MKL Papers; and Anna to Annie Fields, 6 February 1887, FI 5054, and 20 March 1887, FI 5058, JTF Papers.

— Augustus Saint-Gaudens: VI C 4:2 folder 29b, pp. 244, 248a, MKL Papers; Anna to Annie Fields, 9 December 1896, FI 5056, JTF Papers.

— "Do not stay at home": Mrs. William Justice to Anna, July [1876], as quoted in VI C 4:2 folder 29a, p. 158, MKL Papers.

343 "very busy, writing against time": LWJ to Annie Fields, Monday, 10 [July] 1876, LWJ Papers.

343 racing to finish *Life and Travel in India*: VI C 4:2 folder 29a, p. 193, MKL Papers.

— "jotted down some notes": Anna to Sarah Orne Jewett, 8 November 1884, Sarah Orne Jewett Materials. The book was A. P. Sinnett's *Esoteric Buddhism* (London: Trübner, 1883).

— the album of authors' letters: James Thomas Fields, autograph album, Houghton Library, http://oasis.lib.harvard.edu/oasis/deliver/~hou00689.

344 "very inferior": Louisa L. Dresel to ML, 11 March 1945, VI C 4:2 folder 21, MKL Papers.

— "many fears": Fields to LWJ, 26 October 1874.

— footnote 7: LWJ to Annie Fields, 26 January 1876, 13 May [1870], LWJ Papers. LWJ's letter to Annie of 22 February 1876 comparing George Eliot and George Sand reveals an assured and sophisticated literary taste.

— "sitting on the sofa hand in hand": Emma Brace Donaldson to ML, 15 November 1945, VI C 4:3 folder 13, MKL Papers.

— "I am very glad to see you": "Mr. Kellogg's Free Hand," *NYT*, 27 January 1888, 8; Dow, *Anna Leonowens*, 98–99. Anna reported Paine's speech while testifying in a civil suit. Her reports of seeing Prince Naret are in letters to Annie Fields, 17 May 1884, FI 5048, JTF Papers; and to Avis, 19 May 1884, VI C 4:7 folder 4, MKL Papers.

345 tale of a Buddhist monk's clumsy courtship: Anna, "Siamese Romance," 157. The story's dressmaker, Annie Elliot, may have been based on Miss Jane Elliot, whose name is among "European Residents" in the *Bangkok Calendar* (1866), 130.

— "very sad to think of this lovely white child": Anna, "Auction," 397.

— circulation of 140,000: Cutts, *Index*, 1:viii.

— account of a giant boa constrictor: Anna, "Encounter with an Ulwar Sawad," 271.

— Louisa M. Alcott, who sold the *Companion* thirty-two items; the magazine ran thirty-six of her submissions: Cutts, *Index*, 1:8–9, 2:574–75.

— "the true story plan of 1888": Ibid., 1:ix–x.

346 "live in Boston and take some portion": Anna to Avis, 4 April 1882, as quoted in VI C 4:2 folder 29b, p. 236, MKL Papers.

— a series of essays on the peoples of Asia: Anna to [Avis], 10 April 1884, quoted in VI C 4:2 folder 29b, pp. 243–44, also p. 265, MKL Papers; Anna, "Our Asiatic Cousins."

— "The religion of Mohammed is high, pure, moral": Anna, *Our Asiatic Cousins*, 119.

— everyone who approaches the king must crawl: Ibid., 352, 362. That Anna wasn't sent proof seems clear from the book's bad typos, which include a mangled honorific for Siam—"Kingdom of the Tree" rather than "Free" (ibid., 349).

346 "placed himself under the tutorship": Ibid., 359. The matching phrase in *EG*— "placed himself under the permanent tutorship" (240)—had been even more misleading, given that the English lessons lasted a year and a half.

347 "the *rob* and *steal* system": Anna to LWJ, [early 1885], quoted in VI C 4:2 folder 29b, p. 252, MKL Papers.

— "When [Chulalongkorn] . . . was nine years of age": Anna, *Our Asiatic Cousins*, 360.

349 dear "Miss Jewitt": Anna to Jewett, 8 November 1884.

— the two letters about dear Laura: Anna to Annie Fields, 13 April 1889, FI 5055, and 10 December 1889, FI 5059, JTF Papers.

— The memorial composed after Anne Lynch Botta's death: [Botta], *Memoirs*, 98.

350 "all loved persons must be snatched from her": VI C 4:2 folder 29b, p. 245, MKL Papers.

351 "Dawn starts from her couch": John Addington Symonds, *The Life of Michelangelo Buonarroti* (New York: Scribner's, 1911), 2:33.

— "Dear is my sleep": Ibid., 2:35–36.

— Anna's response is found in a letter to Annie Fields: 18 April 1905, FI 5033, JTF Papers.

352 "The great sorrow of a long life": Anna to Annie Fields, 7 January 1911, JTF Papers.

— official insistence that she played a negligible role: Damrong, "Introduction," 99.

— Chulalongkorn's secretary sent an official complaint: Rajanattianuhar, letter to the editor, *Athenæum*, 19 July 1873, 81. The statement's ineffectiveness was commented on in *Siam Repository* 5 (October 1873): 507.

— "slanderous rumors," etc.: Wyatt, *Politics of Reform*, 165, 163.

353 19 August 1897 at the Siamese legation in South Kensington: Edward Loftus to Anna, 16 August 1897 (photostat), VI C 4:3 folder 10, MKL Papers.

— "it was through the principles laid down": *AKS*, 387.

— The least flattering account: Powell, *Where the Strange Trails*, 236, xii–xiii. For ML's reaction to Powell's anecdote, see her illuminating and invincibly parti pris letter to Margaretta Wells, 9 April 1959, VI C 4:3 folder 10, MKL Papers.

— Anna was indeed given the money: Photostats of notes to Anna from Phya Srisdi, 20 August 1897, and Edward Loftus, 24 August 1897, VI C 4:3 folder 10, MKL Papers.

354 When granddaughter Anna Fyshe belatedly learned: Letters between ML and Anna Harriet Leonowens Fyshe, 2 January 1945 and 7 and 19 February 1945, VI C 1:1 folder 1, MKL Papers.

— "The prospect of meeting a real king": Fyshe, "Anna and I," 62.

355 the long, humble thank-you letter: 8 September 1897 (typed copy), VI C 4:3 folder 10, MKL Papers.

CHAPTER 22. RAISED FROM THE DEAD
BY MARGARET LANDON

359 "mother of Louis T. Leonowens": "Deaths," *Times*, 21 January 1915, 1.

— "the Christian life was in essence": ML, *Never Dies the Dream*, 138.

360 "I was concerned about money": ML, "The Sale of *Anna and the King of Siam* to Twentieth Century-Fox" (typed statement), VI C 2:1 folder 14, p. 8, MKL Papers.

361 One was Muriel Fuller: ML, "Muriel Fuller" (typed statement), VI C 1:1 folder 16, MKL Papers. ML's final retrospect on her ultimately broken relationship with Muriel is in folder 17.

— "the only white woman": "Author's Note," *AKS*, 390.

— In August 1930: Ibid., 388; ML, "Muriel Fuller," 5.

— "set down what she was told": ML, "Anna's Method of Work" (typed statement), VI C 4:2 folder 23, p. 3, MKL Papers. In the Landon Papers this concerted defense of Anna is in a folder of its own immediately after the folder holding Bonnie Davis, "Governess and Storyteller," *Bangkok Post*, 11 November 1984, 17. This somewhat slapdash exposé, relying on Bristowe but also based on original research, was the first to reveal that Anna's mother died in 1873, not 1852. "Anna's Method of Work" appears to have been ML's response.

362 "Why don't you combine the biographical parts": "Author's Note," *AKS*, 388. ML gave a slightly different account of Muriel's advice in a letter to Richard J. Walsh, 18 August 1943, VI C 2:2 folder 21, MKL Papers.

— But Landon had another project in mind: VI C 1:1 folder 3, MKL Papers.

363 "Mother would like to meet you": "Author's Note," *AKS*, 389; ML, "Kenneth's meeting with the Very Reverend Gerald Grattan Moore" (typed statement), VI C 4:2 folder 16, MKL Papers.

364 she saw materials no other researcher could have gotten at: Landon Chronicles #66, p. 423, MKL Papers.

— "hideous fancies," etc.: *AKS*, 84–85, 144–45, 200–202.

365 Landon would always insist that her treatment of Mongkut: VI C 1:1 folder 9, pp. 1–5, MKL Papers.

366 "in many grave considerations": VI A 3:1 folder 37, p. 5, MKL Papers. The passage in which the sentence would have appeared is on p. 151 of *AKS*. ML's source was *EG*, 98.

— In the stolen-spectacles story: Anna, "Life in a Siamese Palace," 199; *AKS*, 200–201.

367 footnote 1: Kenneth to Board of Foreign Missions of the Presbyterian Church in the USA, 9 October 1940 (carbon), II A 1 folder 8, MKL Papers.

— "like a colt"; "The saddle was on": *AKS*, 201–2.

— as 18 October came around: Thiphakorawong, *Dynastic Chronicles*, 3:198–99; "H.S.M's Birthday," *Siam Repository* 4 (January 1872): 7–9.

367 When Henri Mouhot attended in 1858, he observed: Mouhot, *Henri Mouhot's Diary*, 5.

— "His Majesty was particularly gracious": DBB, Journals, vol. 21, 19 October 1863, DBB Family Papers; "A Few of the Noticeable Events . . . in . . . 1863," *Bangkok Calendar for 1864*, 122.

— In the account of that year's dinner that Anna wrote: "Royal Dinner Party," 238. As Chantasingh makes clear in "Americanization," 126–27, Fourth Reign royals needed no lessons in "European etiquette and table arrangements" from Anna, who, in addition to fabricating one event after another, got both the date and the king's age wrong. It is astonishing that ML accepted her story.

368 "A look of surprise flitted across": *AKS*, 211.

— footnote 2: [Davenport], "Siamese Courtly Etiquette," 182–83.

369 raise her "even to royal dignities": Macnaughton, "Mrs. Leonowens," 420.

— a surprise to Anna's grandchildren: Avis Selina Fyshe to ML, 17 July 1943, VI C 1:1 folder 2, MKL Papers.

— "withered grasshopper," etc.: *AKS*, 60, 58.

— "looked at her out of the glittering": Ibid., 285. In the book though not in surviving manuscripts, this sentence forms its own paragraph, thus further emphasizing it.

— footnote 3: ML, *Never Dies the Dream*, 196.

370 "bestial need to sate in blood": *AKS*, 285–86.

— "Siamese girl . . . used safety razor blades": VI A 3:10 folder 19, MKL Papers; *Never Dies the Dream*, chap. 28.

371 Mongkut's council; the Senabodi; convene at midnight: [Davenport], "Siamese Courts of Justice," 218; Kennedy, "Report," 314; *Bangkok Calendar for 1865*, 127.

— "secret motives" and "designs": Badger, *Nestorians*, 1:169.

— "Twice a week," she wrote: *EG*, 99–100.

372 As Henry George Kennedy noted: [Kennedy], review of *EG*, 836.

— "Twice a week at midnight [the king] held a secret council": *AKS*, 153.

— *San* is the ordinary Thai word for a court of law: Haas, *Thai-English Student's Dictionary*, 513. For Landon's successive translations of *san luang*, see VI A 3:1 folder 37, p. 7 (earliest extant typescript) and VI A 3:2 folder 19, p. 221 ("John Day" typescript), both in MKL Papers.

— footnote 4: Porter & Coates reprint of *EG*, 100, MKL Papers.

— mentioned in Jewish historical scripture: Joshua 6:26; 1 Kings 16:34.

373 "the fifteenth, sixteenth, seventeenth centuries": Landon Chronicles #81, p. 542, MKL Papers.

— In Bruguière's telling: Bruguière, "Description of Siam," 138–39. My summary of the priest's foundation-sacrifice claims is based on his original French statement as cited by Pallegoix, *Description*, 2:50–52.

373 "As for me," he wrote, "I remember reading something like this": Pallegoix, *Description*, 2:50.

— "We are not aware that any custom of this kind exists in Siam": Attributed to Dean by Breazeale and Smithies in Bruguière, "Description of Siam," 139.

— footnote 5: *NYT*, 7 April 1872, 6.

— two wildly divergent accounts: *EG*, 259–60, 218–20. It was Alexander B. Griswold who revealed Anna's plagiarism from Bruguière, first in "King Mongkut in Perspective," 39–41, then with added discussion in *King Mongkut*, 58–59.

374 Landon not only included both but, confoundingly, placed them back to back: *AKS*, 372–73.

— "[Anna] tells of spending an hour or two sketching": ML to Avis Selina Fyshe, 13 May 1943, VI C 1:1 folder 2, MKL Papers.

375 he wrote Landon asking her to kindly furnish the date of Anna's event; Nearly five months passed before Landon answered: Harvey to ML, 15 November 1950, and ML to Harvey, 3 April 1951 (carbon), VI C 4:3 folder 2, MKL Papers. Harvey's review is at *TLS* (*Times Literary Supplement*), 5 January 1946, 3. A letter by Francis Shaw of 14 December 1962 indicates that as late as 1903 some Thais still believed in gate guardians (VI C 4:5 folder 23, MKL Papers).

— "had all the pertinacity of the wronged": ML, *Never Dies the Dream*, 3.

— "too academically written," etc.: Ken McCormick to Muriel Fuller, 4 August 1942, VI C 1:1 folder 8, MKL Papers.

376 "Kenneth had in mind Margaret and her unsold book": Kenneth Landon, Jr., synopsis of Landon Chronicles #65, p. 413; see also #77, p. 509, both in MKL Papers.

— When sample chapters reached the company's editorial offices, the reaction was positive: Richard J. Walsh to ML, 9 October 1942, VI C 2:2 folder 21, MKL Papers.

— footnote 6: Chantasingh, "Americanization," 122–23; *EG*, 60; *AKS*, 68; nine-page enclosure in ML to Richard Walsh, Jr., 27 January 1945, VI C 2:2 folder 1, MKL Papers.

377 "deep religious feelings"; "So far there has been little fictionizing": ML to Richard J. Walsh, 23 October 1942 (draft), VI C 2:2 folder 21, MKL Papers.

— the contract . . . termed the book a "biography": VI C 1:1 folder 10, MKL Papers.

— It was Weil who came up with the title: Landon Chronicles #77, p. 511, ML to Walsh, April 1943 (draft), Walsh to ML, 16 August 1943, ML to Walsh, [18 August 1943] (draft of telegram), all in VI C 2:2 folder 21, MKL Papers.

378 so "delightful . . . we just must have" it: Elsie Weil to ML, 13 March 1943, VI C 2:1 folder 1, MKL Papers.

— Margaret Ayer had spent ten years in Siam: Editorial note, *Asia and the Americas* 43 (June 1943): 360.

378 One of Ayer's best sketches: *AKS*, 123.

— Weil lavished a half-page: *Asia and the Americas* 43 (December 1943): 691; *AKS*, 142.

379 and before long Walsh was revising: Walsh to ML, 30 August and 18 November 1943, VI C 2:2 folder 21, and Richard Walsh, Jr., to ML, 14 January 1944, VI C 2:2 folder 22, both in MKL Papers.

— By now Landon had left Indiana: ML to Walsh, April 1943; ML, "The Movies to Me" (typed statement), VI C 1:1 folder 11, p. 2; Kenneth to Weil, 27 July 1943 (carbon), VI C 2:1 folder 1; Landon Chronicles #77, pp. 510–11, all in MKL Papers.

— the "Author's Note" that Walsh got Landon to write: Walsh to ML, 16 August 1943, VI C 2:2 folder 21, MKL Papers; *AKS*, 391.

380 contract with the nation's second biggest book club: Richard Walsh, Jr., to ML, 11 November 1943, VI C 2:2 folder 21, and 23 March 1944, folder 22, both in MKL Papers.

— The key review: Weil to ML, 30 June and 7 July 1944, VI C 2:1 folder 1, MKL Papers; Ernestine Evans, "Harems, White Elephants and King Mongkut: The Utterly Charming Stories of an English Governess in Siam," review of *AKS* in the *New York Herald Tribune Weekly Book Review*, 2 July 1944, 1–2.

— There were no bad reviews: "In Brief," *Nation*, 2 September 1944, 277; Ralph Bates, "Three Exotics," *New Republic*, 17 July 1944, 82; Katharine Sansom, *Atlantic Monthly* 174 (December 1944): 141; Isabelle Mallet, *NYT Book Review*, 9 July 1944, 3.

— "was the most ardent and consistent," etc.: Herzstein, *Henry R. Luce*, 1–3.

— "thick-necked, barbaric," etc.: "Romance of the Harem," *Time*, 10 July 1944, 102, 104.

381 footnote 7: ML, narrative draft prepared for C. C. Pepper, manager of the Louis T. Leonowens Company [1975], VI C 4:2 folder 6, p. 28, see also folder 14A, both in MKL Papers.

— Luce wrote a preface for *Why England Slept*: Herzstein, *Henry R. Luce*, 209; Henry R. Luce, foreword to John F. Kennedy, *Why England Slept* (New York: Funk, 1940), xiii–xxii.

CHAPTER 23. ANNA IN HOLLYWOOD AND ON BROADWAY

382 translated into twelve European languages and two Asian tongues: VI C 1:1 folders 11 and 6, MKL Papers; preface to ML, *Annaa gap phrachao grung sayaam*; ML, "Re Anna and the Thai" (typed statement), VI C 4:3 folder 13, MKL Papers.

— Margaret Landon . . . in New York for her exciting weeklong book launch: ML, "Notes from Letters to Mother, 1944," VI C 1:1 folder 3, MKL Papers.

383 "They bought everything": Strauss, *Talent for Luck*, 39–41, 45, 57. On Strauss, see Evan Brier, "Constructing the Postwar Art Novel: Paul Bowles, James Laughlin, and the Making of *The Sheltering Sky*," *PMLA* 121 (January 2006): 189–90.

— oldest theatrical agency: E. J. Kahn, Jr., "The Quiet Guy in Lindy's," *New Yorker*, 27 April 1946, 27.

— In *A Talent for Luck* the first of many people thanked: Strauss, *Talent for Luck*, 8.

384 "considerable . . . if not spectacular," etc.: Ibid., 76; ML, "The Sale of *Anna and the King of Siam* to Twentieth Century-Fox . . ." (typed statement), VI C 2:1 folder 14, p. 6, MKL Papers. The Theatre Guild owned dramatization rights to begin with but had to relinquish them after failing to sign up a theatrical producer (Richard Mealand, "Books into Films," *Publishers Weekly*, 25 November 1944, 2077).

— footnote 1, "it was a most impressive": Damrong Rajanubhab as quoted in Chakrabongse, *Lords of Life*, 226.

385 "Miss Dunne . . . makes a regular bandbox heroine": *NYT*, 21 June 1946, 20.

— "two months of working time," etc.: ML, "The Movies to Me" (typed statement), VI C 1:1 folder 11, MKL Papers.

— Zanuck . . . constantly intervening: On Zanuck's close supervision, see Chantasingh, "Americanization," 235–38.

386 Thai cuisine required the use of fingers: Ibid., 199.

388 "just like Grandmama": Fyshe, "Anna and I," 62.

389 Louis . . . tried one line of work after another; set off for the gold fields of Australia: VI C 4:2 folder 29a, pp. 174b–185, MKL Papers; Bristowe, *Louis*, 36–37; "Melbourne," *Maitland Mercury, and Hunter River General Advertiser* (Australia), 22 August 1882, 5.

391 "The comparison is inevitable": "Elizabeth and the Prince," *NYT*, 29 August 1946, 26.

— addressed the emperor-to-be as Jimmy: "Emperor's Ex-Tutor Passes Away at 97," *Yomiurishibun* [Yomiuri newspaper], 30 November 1999. Citation and translation kindly provided by Midori Asahina.

393 Sitting in the first audiences; "fascinated": Aldrich, *Gertrude Lawrence*, 334.

— "an inexhaustible fund"; "Vitamins should take": Morley, *Gertrude Lawrence*, 31, xii.

— "Deeply intrigued"; "impressed by its values": Aldrich, *Gertrude Lawrence*, 334–35.

— Holtzman talked to . . . Helen Strauss, who approached . . . Richard Rodgers and Oscar Hammerstein II: Ibid., 335–36; Strauss to ML, 19 December 1949, VI C 1:1 folder 3, MKL Papers; Rodgers, *Musical Stages*, 270; Mordden, *Rodgers and Hammerstein*, 131.

394 "a romantic, florid kind of theatre": Rodgers, *Musical Stages*, 207.

394 he let it be known that he supported the Democrat, Adlai Stevenson: Ibid., 257. On Hammerstein's liberalism, see Secrest, *Somewhere for Me*, 241.

— music by Trude Rittmann: Mordden, *Rodgers and Hammerstein*, 142.

395 "tinkling bells, high nasal strings": Rodgers, *Musical Stages*, 273.

— he urged Robbins to take a "comic" approach . . . and not worry whether the movements were genuinely Thai: Ibid., 274; and Yuriko, interview by Tobi Tobias beginning 26 April 1978, transcript, pp. 117–23, Oral History Archive, Dance Collection, New York Public Library.

— pan-Asian veneer on a proven American template: See Pamela S. DaGrossa, "*The King and I*: East and West, Men and Women," *Literary Studies East and West* 9 (1994): 90–94; and Chantasingh, "Americanization," 192–93, 201.

— the ballerina who danced Eliza, Yuriko: Yuriko, interview, 1–2, 5–8, 18, 20–27, 113–22. The playbill for the 1977 revival of *The King and I* has Yuriko as director. According to Rock Brynner's biography of his father, the latter was the force behind the production, the dancer being merely the "director of record" (Brynner, *Yul*, 204).

396 "Miss Lawrence is given no room": Walter Kerr, "The Stage: The King and I," *Commonweal*, 13 April 1951, 13.

— "the first candidate who walked out": Rodgers, *Musical Stages*, 271–72.

— A product of conditions few Americans could imagine; "When you play for a crowd": Brynner, *Yul*, 18, 20, 23–26, 92–93.

397 "It is Brynner who gives": *New York Herald Tribune* review as quoted in ibid., 88.

— "quotes Huey Long," etc.: Harold Clurman, "Tennessee Williams," in *The American Stage: Writing on Theater from Washington Irving to Tony Kushner*, ed. Laurence Senelick (New York: Library of America, 2010), 493.

398 "avid Democrat": Brynner, *Yul*, 119.

— "Every woman adores a Fascist": Sylvia Plath, *Ariel* (New York: Harper & Row, 1966), 50.

— "potential lovers": Susan L. Schulman (a press agent) as quoted in Myrna Katz Frommer and Harvey Frommer, *It Happened on Broadway: An Oral History of the Great White Way* (New York: Harcourt Brace, 1998), 108.

— footnote 3, "positively lubricious": Brynner, *Yul*, 204.

400 king's death in the last scene . . . too "solemn": "New Musical in Manhattan," *Time*, 9 April 1951, 78.

— "so uniformly bright," etc.: John Lardner, "The Surefire Boys in Siam," *New Yorker*, 7 April 1951, 70–71.

402 "apparently founded on the actual adventures"; "savage": "Drury Lane Theatre: 'The King and I,'" *Times*, 9 October 1953, 13.

— "Far from Mrs. Leonowens having initiated": Henry Maxwell, "The King and I," *Times*, 19 October 1953, 3.

402 A second letter to the *Times*: Direck Jayanama, "The King and I," *Times*, 26
October 1953, 11. *Thailand im Zweiten Weltkrieg*, published by Erdmann Ver-
lag in 1970, is available in English as *Thailand and World War II*, ed. Jane Keyes
(Chiang Mai: Silkworm Books, 2008).

— A few American scholars: Griswold, "King Mongkut in Perspective" and *King
Mongkut*; Moffat, *Mongkut*; Henderson et al., *Area Handbook*.

405 only a European can inculcate the art of love: Mervat Hatem touches on this
notion in "Through Each Other's Eyes," in Chaudhuri and Strobel, *Western
Women*, 52.

— one last fraud on the viewer: Actually, there were more frauds in a documentary produced by a Fox affiliate and shown on the A&E Network in its Biography series. Broadcast in 1999, the year *Anna and the King* was released, this is
an extra feature on the "Special Edition" DVD of the movie. It informs us that
Anna was born "in the cramped corner of an army barracks" and that in girlhood she "loved to roam the streets learning the customs" of Muslims, Sikhs,
etc. She "severed ties with her family when her young niece married a man of
mixed race." In Singapore "no one knew her," leaving her free to reinvent herself. None of this can be documented.

406 "In looking at royalty": Hilary Mantel, "Royal Bodies," *London Review of Books*,
21 February 2013, 6.

Appendix 1.
Family Chart for Anna Leonowens

1. Registers of Baptisms, Marriages, Deaths, St. John, Cardiff; will of Thomas
Glascott.

2. Will of Evan Deer.

3. Registers of Baptisms, Marriages, Deaths, St. John, Cardiff.

4. Memorial, south wall, Hatherleigh Church.

5. Cradock Glascott to John Glascott, 11 November 1823.

6. Births/baptisms of Cradock and Mary's children are from parish registers,
Hatherleigh, as relayed by Linda Anstey Garnett.

7. Civil Registration certificate of death, Exeter Registration District, vol. 5b,
p. 74.

8. Foster, *Alumni Oxonienses*, 2:528.

9. Pallot's Marriage Index 1780–1837 (ancestry.co.uk).

10. For documentation on William Vaudrey Glascott's career, see notes to chapter 1.

11. Foster, *Alumni Oxonienses*, 2:528.

12. Cradock Glascott to John Glascott, 21 December 1819.

13. 1861 English census, Gloucestershire, Rodborough, district 9, Rectory.

14. Parish registers, Hatherleigh.

15. Civil Registration certificate of marriage, Axminster Registration District, vol. 5b, p. 18.

16. Civil Registration certificate of death, vol. 3b, p. 208; List of members of Madras Military Fund, L/AG/23/10/1, IOR.

17. Civil Registration certificate of marriage, Axminster Registration District, vol. 5b, p. 21.

18. *Clergy List for 1866* (London: George Cox, 1866), benefices, p. 200.

19. Bombay deaths, N/3/47/294, IOR.

20. Bombay marriages, N/3/9/331, IOR.

21. See discussion, chapter 1 notes, pp. 431–32.

22. Register of recruits, L/MIL/9/41, *Lady Kennaway*, 4 June 1825, IOR.

23. Bombay muster rolls, L/MIL/12/155, pp. 195, 197, IOR.

24. Bombay marriages, N/3/10/387, IOR.

25. Register of Recruits, L/MIL/9/42–43, *Edinburgh*, 4 January 1828; Bombay muster rolls, L/MIL/12/153,165–68, all in IOR.

26. Bombay deaths, N/3/38/269, IOR.

27. Bombay deaths, N/3/14/208, IOR.

28. Bombay muster rolls, L/MIL/12/153,165–68, 176, IOR.

29. Bombay deaths, N/3/30/69, IOR; "Domestic Occurrences," *Telegraph and Courier* (Bombay), 8 February 1856.

30. *Clergy List for 1866*, chaplains, p. 390; Memorials, Saint Mary Magdalene, Rodborough; Foster, *Alumni Oxonienses*, 2:528.

31. 1861 English census, Gloucestershire, Rodborough, District 9, Rectory.

32. Information from June Wailling, Centre for Buckinghamshire Studies.

33. Bombay baptisms, N/3/9/454, Bombay deaths, N/3/38/125, and Bombay marriages, N/3/19/123, all in IOR.

34. Soldiers' discharges, L/MIL/10/302/225, IOR; *Bombay Almanac* (1860).

35. Buckinghamshire Parish Register 140/1/12, Centre for Buckinghamshire Studies.

36. On 27 Dec. 1831. Bombay baptisms, N/3/10/189, IOR.

37. Macnaughton, "Mrs. Leonowens," 408.

38. Bombay marriages, N/3/23/266, IOR; "Domestic Occurrences," *Bombay Times*, 9 January 1850.

39. Bombay marriages, N/3/33/217, IOR.

40. Bombay baptisms, N/3/12/13, and Bombay deaths, N/3/13/378, both in IOR.

41. Bombay baptisms, N/3/12/124, and Bombay deaths, N/3/46/89, both in IOR.

42. Bombay marriages, N/3/26/98, IOR.

43. Bombay deaths, N/3/28/159, IOR.

44. Bombay marriages, N/3/32/235, IOR.

45. Bombay marriages, N/3/36/35, IOR; *Bombay Almanac* (1863), 805; Bombay deaths, N/3/60/254, IOR.

46. Bombay baptisms, N/3/15/475, and Bombay marriages, N/3/32/235 (witness), both in IOR.

47. Bombay baptisms, N/3/RC/1/373, IOR.

48. Bombay baptisms, N/3/RC/2/565, IOR.

49. Bombay baptisms, N/3/28/101, IOR.

50. Bombay baptisms, N/3/32/192, and Bombay marriages, N/3/51/209, both in IOR.

51. Bombay baptisms, N/3/11/68, and Bombay marriages, N/3/20/381, both in IOR.

52. Bombay baptisms, N/3/12/13, and Bombay marriages, N/3/28/242, both in IOR.

53. Bombay baptisms, N/3/20/112, IOR.

54. Bombay baptisms, N/3/22/154, and Bombay marriages, N/3/38/336, both in IOR; *Times of India*, 4 November 1864, 2.

55. *Who Was Who 1941–1950* (London: Black, 1980), 4:934, entry for Pratt, Frederick Greville.

56. Bombay baptisms, N/3/26/134, IOR.

57. Bombay baptisms, N/3/30/190, IOR.

58. Bombay baptisms, N/3/32/218, IOR.

59. *Thacker's Indian Directory* (1913), Bombay education directory.

60. Bombay baptisms, N/3/38/91, and Bombay deaths, N/3/110/283, both in IOR.

61. T. Phillips Savage to "Madam," 8 July 1898 (typed copy), VI C 4:2 folder 4, MKL Papers.

62. Bombay baptisms, N/3/27/193, and Bombay deaths, N/3/119/280, both in IOR; "Thomas Arthur Savage: An Appreciation," *Times of India*, 19 June 1918, 8.

63. Bombay baptisms, N/3/37/20, IOR.

64. *Thacker's Indian Directory* (1887), 1375; *Thacker's Indian Directory* (1912), Bombay education directory.

65. Bombay baptisms, N/3/44/17 and Bombay deaths, N/3/109/148, both in IOR.

66. Bombay baptisms, N/3/51/277, IOR.

67. Bombay baptisms, N/3/59/290, IOR.

68. *Who Was Who 1941–1950*, 4:934.

69. Bombay baptisms, N/3/41/65, IOR.

70. Jacobs, *Boris Karloff*, 16.

71. *Who Was Who 1941–1950*, 4:934.

72. Jacobs, *Boris Karloff*, 16.

73. Ibid.

74. Lindsay, *Dear Boris*, 189.

75. *Foreign Office List* (1939), 390.

76. John Thomas Pratt to Avis Leonowens Fyshe, 25 November 1899 (typed copy), VI C 4:2 folder 24, MKL Papers. But see Lindsay, *Dear Boris*, 185–86.

77. *Foreign Office List* (1938), 389.

78. Obituary, *NYT*, 4 February 1969.

Appendix 2. Family Chart for Anna's Spouse, Thomas Leonowens

1. Register of Baptisms, Marriages, Burials, 1826–38, vestry safe, St. Mary's, Enniscorthy.

2. Register of Baptisms, Marriages, Burials, 1798–1826, St. Mary's, Enniscorthy, Microfilm MFCI 100/1. National Archives of Ireland.

3. Pigot's Directory (1824), 151.

4. Register of Baptisms, Marriages, Burials, 1838–, vestry safe, St. Mary's, Enniscorthy.

5. Register of Baptisms, Marriages, Burials, 1798–1826.

6. Ibid.

7. Wexford County Directory and Guide (1885).

8. Register of Baptisms, Marriages, Burials, 1798–1826, p. 77.

9. Register of Burials, 1 November 1903–, and memorial of Thomas Wilkinson and Thomas Lean Wilkinson, both at St. Mary's, Enniscorthy.

10. Register of Baptisms, Marriages, Burials, 1826–38. Since Mary Owens's baptism record hasn't turned up, it can't be proven she was the daughter of Mary Lean and John Owens. However, John witnessed her marriage, and her children addressed Anna as "aunt."

11. Register of Baptisms, Marriages, Burials, 1838–.

12. Register of Baptisms, Marriages, Burials, 1798–1826. The entry for Selina's age at death, "Mo. 14," is perplexing, as she was nearly six years old.

13. Register of Baptisms, Marriages, Burials, 1798–1826 (entry placed between Marriages and Publications of Banns).

14. "Gunnis L. Owens," 1851, October, *Princeton*, New York Passenger Lists, 1851–91, www.ancestry.com.

15. Register of Baptisms, Marriages, Burials, 1798–1826 (entry placed on blank pages following Burials).

16. Muster roll for 31 July 1842, WO 12/4450, National Archives.

17. Muster roll for 31 July 1843, WO 12/4451.

18. See discussion, chapter 5 notes, p. 450.

19. Burials at Prince of Wales Island, N/1/95/311, IOR; photo of gravestone in Corfield, "Anna Leonowens," 6.

20. Bombay marriages, N/3/23/266, IOR.

21. Register of Baptisms, Marriages, Burials, 1798–1826 (entry placed after Burials).

22. Register of Baptisms, Marriages, Burials, 1838–.

23. Ibid. Middle name spelled "Lane" in the register.

24. Memorial, St. Mary's, Enniscorthy; will of Thomas Lean Wilkinson, probated 19 March 1915, London.

25. Civil Registration certificate of marriage, Ware Registration District, Herts.

26. 1881 census, Kensington Township, Borough of Chelsea, 63 Harcourt Terrace.

27. Foster, *Men-at-the-Bar*, 506.

28. Register of burials, 1903–; will of Thomas Lean Wilkinson.

29. Register of Baptisms, Marriages, Burials, 1838–; Register of burials, 1903–.

30. Register of burials, 1903–.

31. Register of Baptisms, Marriages, Burials, 1838–; memorial of daughters of Thomas and Mary Wilkinson, St. Mary's, Enniscorthy.

32. Register of Baptisms, Marriages, Burials, 1838–; *AKS*, 389–90; memorial of daughters.

33. VI C 4:2 folder 29b, p. 243, MKL Papers.

34. Register of Baptisms, Marriages, Burials, 1838–.

35. Ibid.; memorial of daughters.

36. Bombay baptisms, N/3/25/87, and Bombay deaths, N/3/26/118, both in IOR.

37. No. 150, Register of Baptisms, Wesley Church, Perth. That Thomas was born at sea is evident from the fact that after making a port stop at Anyar on 14 January the *Alibi* did not reach Fremantle until 18 March (*Lloyd's List*, 16 March 1853, col. 10, and 28 July 1853, col. 12).

38. Death notice, *Perth Inquirer*, 22 March 1854.

39. Birth no. 2583, Registry of Births, Deaths and Marriages in the State of Western Australia.

40. Anna to Annie Fields, 21 May 1902, JTF Papers.

41. "FYSHE-LEONOWENS," *New York Sun*, 22 June 1878, clipping, Anna Harriette Leonowens Papers.

42. Yorke, "Edwards, Anna Harriette," 14:334.

43. Birth no. 3469, Registry of Births, Deaths and Marriages in the State of Western Australia.

44. Bristowe, Louis, 120.

45. VI C 4:2 folder 14A, MKL Papers.

46. Bristowe, *Louis*, 99, 129.

47. Names and birth dates of Thomas and Jessie's children are from the will of Thomas Lean Wilkinson; the decennial censuses of England and Wales; Civil Registration certificate of birth of Avis Mary, Kensington Registration District, vol. 1a, p. 197; and Civil Registration index for birth of Maurice, Kensington Registration District, Sept. quarter, 1873, vol. 1a, p. 163.

48. VI C 4:2 folder 9, MKL Papers; www.ancestry.com.

49. "Domestic Occurrences. Marriage," *Bangkok Times*, 7 December 1908, 4; Anna to Annie Fields, 5 January 1909, JTF Papers.

50. Anna to Annie Fields, 18 April 1905, 10 April 1910, JTF Papers.

51. VI C 4:2 folders 5, 9, MKL Papers.

52. VI C 4:2 folders 9, 12, MKL Papers.

53. VI C 4:2 folder 9, MKL Papers.

54. Ibid.

55. Ibid.

56. Bristowe, *Louis*, 73, 140.

57. Ibid., 140.

Selected Bibliography

PRINCIPAL MANUSCRIPT COLLECTIONS CONSULTED AND
CERTAIN INDIVIDUAL MANUSCRIPTS

Aldrich, Thomas Bailey. Papers. MS Am 1429. Houghton Library, Harvard University, Cambridge, Massachusetts.

American Board of Commissioners for Foreign Missions. Archives. Houghton Library, Harvard University, Cambridge, Massachusetts.

Athenæum (house copy identifying contributors). City University Library, London.

Borneo Company Ltd. Papers. MSS 27,174–474. Guildhall Library, London.

Bradley, Cornelius Beach. Annotated copy of *The English Governess*. Special Collections, Oberlin College, Oberlin, Ohio.

Bradley, Dan Beach. Family Papers. Oberlin College Archives, Oberlin, Ohio.

Caswell, Jesse. Papers. Private Archive, United States.

Church Missionary Society. Papers. Cadbury Research Library, Birmingham University, Birmingham, UK.

Colonial Secretary's Letterbook. Accession 49. State Records Office of Western Australia, Perth.

Colonial Secretary's Office. Correspondence Received. Accession 36. State Records Office of Western Australia, Perth.

Daily Indexes to *Lloyd's List*. Guildhall Library, London.

Fields, Annie Adams. Journal. Annie Fields Papers. Massachusetts Historical Society, Boston.

Fields, James Thomas. Papers and Addenda. Huntington Library, San Marino, California.

Gannett, Lewis. Papers. MS Am 1888–1888.4. Houghton Library, Harvard University, Cambridge, Massachusetts.

Gibbons, Abby Hopper. Family Papers. Friends Historical Library, Swarthmore College, Swarthmore, Pennsylvania.

Glascott, Cradock. Will and Letters, with a copy of a letter from William Vaudrey Glascott. Centre for Buckinghamshire Studies, County Hall, Aylesbury.

Higginson, Thomas Wentworth. Papers. MS Am 1162–1162.9. Houghton Library, Harvard University, Cambridge, Massachusetts.

India Office Records. Asia, Pacific, and Africa Collections, British Library, London.

Jewett, Sarah Orne. Materials. Colby College Special Collections, Waterville, Maine.

Johnson, Laura Winthrop. Papers. Manuscripts and Archives Division, New York Public Library, Astor, Lenox, and Tilden Foundations.

Landon, Margaret and Kenneth. Papers. SC-38. Wheaton College Special Collections, Wheaton, Illinois.

Leonowens, Anna Harriette. Papers. Manuscripts and Archives Division, New York Public Library, Astor, Lenox, and Tilden Foundations.

Malet, George Grenville. Papers. Private Archive, UK.

Owen, Robert Dale. Papers. L122. Manuscripts Section, Indiana State Library, Indianapolis.

Palmer, John Williamson. Collection. Albert and Shirley Small Special Collections Library, University of Virginia, Charlottesville.

Private Archive, New Zealand.

"Reminiscences of the late Rev. C. Glascott." MS bound in *Two Sermons on Occasion of the Death of the Revd. C. Glascott, A.M. Late Vicar of Hatherleigh, Devon.* London: Longman, 1831. Devon Heritage Centre, Exeter.

Sanford Family Papers. M386. Australian Joint Copying Project. State Library of Western Australia, Perth.

Society for the Propagation of the Gospel (now USPG). Papers. Bodleian Library of Commonwealth and African Studies at Rhodes House, Oxford.

Swan River Mechanics' Institute (later Perth Literary Institute). Records 1853–1957, Mn 326, Minutes (on microfilm). Accession 1830A. State Library of Western Australia, Perth.

Thomson, John. "Notes of a Journey through Siam to the Ruins of Cambodia." JMS 8/36 1866. Royal Geographical Society (with IBG), London.

Ticknor, Benajah. Papers. Bentley Historical Library, University of Michigan, Ann Arbor.

Tillinghast, Caleb Benjamin. Correspondence relative to legislative biography file, 1884–1909. Special Collections, State Library of Massachusetts, Boston.

Underwood, Francis Henry. Papers. Albert and Shirley Small Special Collections Library, University of Virginia, Charlottesville.

War Office. Records. Series 12, 17, 334. National Archives, UK.

Wray, Captain. Survey. Consignment 1647, no. 122, Public Works Department Plans, State Records Office of Western Australia, Perth.

SELECTED CIVIL AND VITAL RECORDS,
CENSUSES, AND VALUATIONS

Baptism of George Percy Badger. Register of Baptisms, Parish of Chelmsford, Essex, 1815. p. 47, D/P 94/1/3, Essex Record Office.

Bombay Baptisms, Marriages, Burials, India Office Records. Asia, Pacific, and Africa Collections, British Library, London.

Civil Registration Indexes for England and Wales. Family Records Centre, London.

Civil Registration Certificates of Births, Deaths and Marriages in England and Wales. General Register Office, UK.

Civil Trial Record CSC 2/1/1/60, nos. 16 and 17. Western Cape Archives and Records Service, Cape Town, South Africa.

Decennial Censuses, England and Wales.

Decennial Censuses, United States.

Griffith's Valuation.

Massachusetts Vital Records. Microfilm, New England Historic Genealogical Society.

Register of Baptisms, Marriages, Burials, 1798–1826. St. Mary's, Enniscorthy. Microfilm MFCI 100/1, National Archives of Ireland.

Register of Baptisms, Marriages, Burials, 1826–38, vestry safe. St. Mary's, Enniscorthy, Ireland.

Register of Baptisms, Marriages, Burials, 1838–, vestry safe. St. Mary's, Enniscorthy, Ireland.

Register of Baptisms, Wesley Church, Perth. Accession 1654A. State Library of Western Australia, Perth.

Register of Burials, 1 November 1903–. St. Mary's, Enniscorthy, Ireland.

Registers of Baptisms, Marriages, Deaths, St. John, Cardiff. Glamorgan County Record Office, Cardiff, Wales.

Registers of Baptisms, St. George Hanover Square. City of Westminster Archives.

Registry of Births, Deaths and Marriages in the State of Western Australia, Perth.

Town Deaths, Barnstable, Massachusetts. Barnstable Town Clerk.

Will of John Sutherland, MOOC 7/1/197, no. 28. Western Cape Archives Repository, Cape Town, South Africa.

Wills of Thomas Glascott, LL/1781/17, and Evan Deer, LL/1735/18. National Library of Wales, Aberystwyth.

Wills probated in England after 1858. First Avenue House, London.

SELECTED NEWSPAPERS

Bangkok Recorder (1865–66).

Bangkok Times (1908–9).

Bombay Courier (1811, 1821, 1837).

Bombay Gazette (1841, 1850–52, 1856).

Bombay Government Gazette (1847–52).

Bombay Times and Journal of Commerce [later *Times of India*] (1841, 1850, 1863–64).

Boston Daily Advertiser (1860).

Chicago Daily Tribune (1875).

Inquirer, a Western Australian Journal of Politics and Literature (1853–57).

Lloyd's List (1852–53, 1857, 1862).
London and China Express (1873).
New York Times.
New York Tribune (1867).
Perth Gazette and Independent Journal of Politics and News (1853–57).
Siam Repository (1869–74) [quarterly compilation reprinting material from the *Siam Weekly Advertiser* (Bangkok)].
Singapore Daily Times (1866).
Singapore Free Press and Mercantile Advertiser (1857–60).
Straits Times, and Singapore Journal of Commerce (1851, 1852, 1855–56, 1857–59, 1863).
Telegraph and Courier [Bombay] (1849, 1852, 1855, 1856).
Times (London).
Wexford Conservative [Wexford, Ireland] (1838, 1841, 1842).

Selected Almanacs, Directories, and Reports

Bangkok Calendar.
Bombay Calendar and General Directory. [In some years this annual publication bore the title *Bombay Almanac and Book of Directions*; series available at the British Library].
Bombay Education Society, Annual Reports (1816–50).
East-India Register and Army List.
The Foreign Office List and Diplomatic and Consular Year Book [London: Harrison, various years].
Lloyd's Register of British and Foreign Shipping [Guildhall Library, London].
Singapore Almanack & Directory for the Year 1858. [This annual was titled *Royal Almanack & Directory* in 1859 and 1860; *Straits Calendar and Directory* in 1861, 1862, and 1863; *Royal Almanac & Directory* in 1864; *Straits Calendar and Directory* in 1865; *Straits Almanac & Directory* in 1866; and *Straits Calendar and Directory* in 1867, 1868, and 1869. Microfilms NL2363 (1858–65) and NL2362 (1866–69). Singapore National Library].
Thacker's Indian Directory (1887–1919).
Western Australian Almanack (1854–57).

Selected Books and Articles

Aldrich, Richard Stoddard. *Gertrude Lawrence as Mrs. A: An Intimate Biography of the Great Star.* New York: Greystone Press, 1954.
Amherst College. *Normal School of Languages.* Amherst, [1878]. Box 1, folder 1, Amherst Summer School Collection, Amherst College Archives, Massachusetts.
Anake Nawigamune. *Farang nay muang sayaam* [Westerners in Siam]. Bangkok: Samnakphim Saengdao, 2006.

Arnold, David. "European Orphans and Vagrants in India in the Nineteenth Century." *Journal of Imperial and Commonwealth History* 7, no. 2 (January 1979): 104–27.

Australian Colonies. Convict Discipline and Transportation. Further Correspondence . . . (A Continuation of Papers Presented May 1854.) Presented to Both Houses of Parliament . . . London: Eyre and Spottiswoode, 1855.

Australian Colonies. Convict Discipline and Transportation. Further Correspondence . . . (In Continuation of Papers Presented 21st March 1857.) Presented to Both Houses of Parliament . . . London: Eyre and Spottiswoode, 1857.

[Bacon, George B.]. Review of *The English Governess at the Siamese Court. Nation*, 9 March 1871, 161–62. Attribution in William Frederick Poole and William I. Fletcher, *Poole's Index to Periodical Literature*, vol. 1, pt. 2, 1198. Gloucester, Mass.: Peter Smith, 1958.

———. *Siam: The Land of the White Elephant as It Was and Is.* New York: Scribner, 1893.

Badger, George Percy. "Mohammed and Mohammedanism." *Contemporary Review* 26 (June 1975): 87–102.

———. *The Nestorians and Their Rituals: With the Narrative of a Mission to Mesopotamia and Coordistan in 1842–1844, and of a Late Visit to Those Countries in 1850.* 2 vols. 1852. Reprint, Farnborough, Hants., UK: Gregg International, 1969.

Baigent, Elizabeth, and Lois K. Yorke. "Leonowens [*née* Edwards], Anna Harriette." In *Oxford Dictionary of National Biography*, 33:402–4. Oxford: Oxford University Press, 2004.

Ballhatchet, Kenneth. *Caste, Class and Catholicism in India 1789–1914.* Richmond, Surrey: Curzon Press, 1998.

———. *Race, Sex and Class under the Raj: Imperial Attitudes and Policies and Their Critics, 1793–1905.* London: Weidenfeld and Nicolson, 1980.

Barnes, George. *A Sermon Preached for the Benefit of the Society for Promoting the Education of the Poor.* Bombay: printed by Samuel Rans, 1816.

Bastian, Adolf. *Reisen in Siam im Jahre 1863.* Jena: Hermann Costenoble, 1867.

Beauvoir, Ludovic, marquis de. *Java, Siam, Canton: Voyage autour du monde.* Paris: E. Plon, 1878.

Blofeld, John. *King Maha Mongkut of Siam.* 1972. Reprint, Bangkok: Siam Society, 1987.

[Botta, Vincenzo, ed.]. *Memoirs of Anne C. L. Botta Written by Her Friends. With Selections from Her Correspondence and from Her Writings in Prose and Poetry.* New York: J. S. Tait and Sons, 1894.

Bowring, John. *The Kingdom and People of Siam; with a Narrative of the Mission to That Country in 1855.* 2 vols. 1857. Reprint, New York: AMS Press, 1975.

Bradley, Dan Beach. "How the Kings of Siam Obtain Their Wives." In *Bangkok Calendar for . . . 1864*, 68–73. Bangkok: American Missionary Association, 1864.

——. "Reminiscences of the Late Supreme Monarch of Siam [Mongkut]." In *Bangkok Calendar for . . . 1869*, 120–40. Bangkok: American Missionary Association, 1869.

Bradley, William L. "Prince Mongkut and Jesse Caswell." *Journal of the Siam Society* 54, no. 1 (January 1966): 29–41.

——. *Siam Then: The Foreign Colony in Bangkok before and after Anna*. Pasadena, Calif.: William Carey Library, 1981.

Bristowe, W. S. *Louis and the King of Siam*. New York: Thai-American Publishers, 1976.

Brown, Susan. "Alternatives to the Missionary Position: Anna Leonowens as Victorian Travel Writer." *Feminist Studies* 21 (Fall 1995): 587–614.

Bruguière, Barthélemy. "Description of Siam in 1829." Translated and edited by Kennon Breazeale and Michael Smithies. *Journal of the Siam Society* 96 (2008): 73–173.

Brynner, Rock. *Yul: The Man Who Would Be King: A Memoir of Father and Son*. New York: Simon and Schuster, 1989.

Buckley, Charles Burton. *An Anecdotal History of Old Times in Singapore*. 1902. Reprint, Kuala Lumpur: University of Malaya Press, 1965.

Buettner, Elizabeth. *Empire Families: Britons and Late Imperial India*. Oxford: Oxford University Press, 2004.

Burton, Richard F. *Goa, and the Blue Mountains; or, Six Months of Sick Leave*. 1851. Reprint, Berkeley: University of California Press, 1991.

Cameron, John. *Our Tropical Possessions in Malayan India*. 1865. Reprint, Kuala Lumpur: Oxford University Press, 1965.

[Campbell, James]. "On the Age at Which Menstruation Begins in Siam." *Edinburgh Medical Journal* 8 (1862): 233–36. Attribution from Royal College of Surgeons of England, *Medical Directory* (1881), Provincial, 418.

Cary, Amelia, Viscountess Falkland. *Chow-Chow; Being Selections from a Journal Kept in India, Egypt, and Syria*. 2 vols. London: Hurst and Blackett, 1857.

Cavenagh, Orfeur, Sir. *Reminiscences of an Indian Official*. London: W. H. Allen, 1884.

Chakrabongse, Chula, Prince. *Lords of Life: The Paternal Monarchy of Bangkok, 1782–1932*. New York: Taplinger, 1960.

Chantasingh, Chalermsri Thuriyanonda. "The Americanization of *The King and I*: The Transformation of the English Governess into an American Legend." Ph.D. diss., University of Kansas, 1999.

Chaudhuri, Nupur, and Margaret Strobel, eds. *Western Women and Imperialism: Complicity and Resistance*. Bloomington: Indiana University Press, 1992.

Cheng, Chu-Chueh. "Frances Trollope's America and Anna Leonowens's Siam: Questionable Travel and Problematic Writing." In *Gender, Genre, and Identity in Women's Travel Writing*, edited by Kristi Siegel. New York: Peter Lang, 2004.

Coakley, J. F. *The Church of the East and the Church of England: A History of the Archbishop of Canterbury's Assyrian Mission*. Oxford: Clarendon Press, 1992.

Collingham, E. M. *Imperial Bodies: The Physical Experience of the Raj, c. 1800–1947*. Cambridge, UK: Polity Press, 2001.

Colquhoun, Archibald Ross. *Amongst the Shans*. London: Field & Tuer, 1885.

Corfield, Justin. "Anna Leonowens and the Australian Connection." *Ancestor* [Victoria, Australia] 24 (Summer 1998): 6–7.

———. *Bangkok: The Protestant Cemetery*. Putney, London: BACSA, 1997.

Cornish, Henry. *Under the Southern Cross*. Madras: printed at the "Mail" Press by J. J. Craen, 1879.

Cort, Mary Lavina. *Siam; or, the Heart of Farther India*. New York: Randolph, 1886.

Cox, Edmund Charles. *A Short History of the Bombay Presidency*. Bombay: Thacker, 1887.

Cutts, Richard. *Index to "The Youth's Companion" 1871–1929*. 2 vols. Metuchen, N.J.: Scarecrow Press, 1972.

Dalrymple, William. *White Mughals: Love and Betrayal in Eighteenth-Century India*. London: HarperCollins, 2002.

Damrong Rajanubhab, Prince. "The Introduction of Western Culture in Siam." *Journal of the Siam Society* 20, no. 1 (June 1926): 90–100.

[Davenport, Frances]. "Siamese Courtly Etiquette—Titles—Forms of Ceremony—Treaties and Correspondence—King's Levees, &c. By a Traveller." *Southern Literary Messenger*, n.s., 4 (September 1857): 178–92.

[———]. "Siamese Courts of Justice. *Bribery—Trial by Ordeal—Modes of Punishment, etc.* By a Traveller." *Southern Literary Messenger*, n.s., 5 (March 1858): 216–28.

Dewey, Orville. *Autobiography and Letters of Orville Dewey, D.D.* Edited by Mary E. Dewey. Boston: Roberts, 1883.

Dow, Leslie Smith. *Anna Leonowens: A Life Beyond "The King and I."* Lawrencetown Beach, Nova Scotia: Pottersfield Press, 1991.

Emerson, Sarah Hopper. *Life of Abby Hopper Gibbons Told Chiefly through Her Correspondence*. 2 vols. New York: G. P. Putnam, 1897.

Enniscorthy 2000: Book of the Millennium. Enniscorthy: St. Senan's Parish, 2000.

Erickson, Rica, comp. *Bicentennial Dictionary of Western Australians pre-1829–1888*. 4 vols. Nedlands: University of Western Australia Press, 1988.

Feltus, George Haws, ed. *Abstract of the Journal of Rev. Dan Beach Bradley, M.D. Medical Missionary in Siam 1835–1873*. Cleveland, Ohio: Dan F. Bradley, 1936.

———. *Samuel Reynolds House of Siam: Pioneer Medical Missionary 1847–1876*. New York: Fleming H. Revell, 1924.

Foster, Joseph. *Alumni Oxonienses*. 4 vols. Oxford: Parker, 1888.

———. *Men-at-the-Bar: A Biographical Handlist of the Members of the Various Inns of Court*. London: Reeves and Turner, 1885.

Fyshe, Anna Harriet Leonowens. "Anna and I." *Chatelaine: The Canadian Home Journal* 35 (January 1962): 33, 60, 62, 63, 64.

Gabriel Aubaret. Poitiers: Librairie H. Oudin, [1897].

The Gazetteer of Bombay City and Island. 3 vols. Bombay: Times Press, 1909–10.

Ghosh, Durba. "Colonial Companions: *Bibis, Begums,* and Concubines of the British in North India, 1760–1830." Ph.D. diss., University of California, Berkeley, 2000.

———. "Making and Un-making Loyal Subjects: Pensioning Widows and Educating Orphans in Early Colonial India." *Journal of Imperial and Commonwealth History* 31 (January 2003): 1–28.

Gilmour, David. *The Ruling Caste: Imperial Lives in the Victorian Raj.* New York: Farrar, Straus and Giroux, 2006.

Glascott, Cradock. *The Best Method of Putting an End to the American War. Being the Substance of a Sermon Preached on the 13th of December, 1776; the Day of the General Fast, at Tottenham-Court Chapel (Erected by the Rev. Mr. George Whitefield).* London: J. W. Pasham, 1776.

Gollin, Rita K. *Annie Adams Fields: Woman of Letters.* Amherst: University of Massachusetts Press, 2002.

Graireuk Naanaa and Pramint Kruathong. *Saaylap wang luang ru lok maayaa khong Anna Leonowens* [Palace spy, or the illusory world of Anna Leonowens]. Bangkok: Kanyaayon, 2004.

[Gray, James]. *Life in Bombay, and the Neighbouring Out-Stations.* London: Richard Bentley, 1852.

Griswold, Alexander B. "King Mongkut in Perspective." *Journal of the Siam Society* 45, no. 1 (April 1957): 1–41.

———. *King Mongkut of Siam.* New York: Asia Society, 1961.

Haas, Mary R., comp. *Thai-English Student's Dictionary.* Stanford, Calif.: Stanford University Press, 1964.

Harris, Townsend. *The Complete Journal of Townsend Harris, First American Consul General and Minister to Japan.* Edited by Mario Emilio Cosenza. Garden City, N.Y.: published for the Japan Society by Doubleday, Doran, 1930.

Hawes, C. J. *Poor Relations: The Making of a Eurasian Community in British India 1773–1833.* Richmond, Surrey, UK: Curzon Press, 1996.

Heber, Reginald. *Narrative of a Journey through the Upper Provinces of India, from Calcutta to Bombay, 1824–1825.* 1828. 3 vols. Reprint, New Delhi: Asian Education Services, 1995.

Henderson, John S., et al. *Area Handbook for Thailand.* Washington, D.C.: U.S. Government Printing Office, 1971.

Herzstein, Robert E. *Henry R. Luce, "Time," and the American Crusade in Asia.* New York: Cambridge University Press, 2005.

Hine, Charles Gilbert, and William T. Davis. *Legends, Stories and Folklore of Old Staten Island. Part I—The North Shore*. Staten Island, N.Y.: Staten Island Historical Society, 1925.

Hong, Lysa. "Of Consorts and Harlots in Thai Popular History." *Journal of Asian Studies* 57, no. 2 (May 1998): 333–53.

———. *Thailand in the Nineteenth Century: Evolution of the Economy and Society*. Singapore: Institute of Southeast Asian Studies, 1984.

Honniball, Jack. "The Dual Administrative Establishments of the Imperial and Colonial Governments in the Convict Era." *Early Days* 12, no. 1 (2001): 27–38.

Irwin, Robert. *Dangerous Knowledge: Orientalism and Its Discontents*. Woodstock, N.Y.: Overlook Press, 2006.

Jackson, Peter. "Performative Genders, Perverse Desires: A Bio-History of Thailand's Same-Sex and Transgender Cultures." *Intersections: Gender, History and Culture in the Asian Context* 9 (2003): 1–43. http://intersections.anu.edu.au/issue9/jackson.html.

Jacobs, Stephen. *Boris Karloff: More Than a Monster*. Sheffield, UK: Tomahawk Press, 2011.

Jameson, G. I., comp. *Code of Military Regulations at Present in Force under the Presidency of Bombay*. Bombay: Government Press, 1844. India Office Records L/MIL/17/4/547.

Jumsai, Manich, M.L. *History of Anglo-Thai Relations*. Bangkok: Chalermnit, 1970.

———. *King Mongkut and Sir John Bowring (from Sir John Bowring's Personal Files, Kept at the Royal Thai Embassy in London)*. Bangkok: Chalermnit, 1970.

Kelly, J. B. *Britain and the Persian Gulf 1795–1880*. Oxford: Clarendon Press, 1968.

Kennedy, Dane. *The Magic Mountains: Hill Stations and the British Raj*. Berkeley: University of California Press, 1996.

Kennedy, Henry George. "Report of an Expedition Made into Southern Laos and Cambodia in the Early Part of the Year 1866." *Journal of the Royal Geographical Society* 37 (1867): 298–328.

[———.] Review of *The English Governess at the Siamese Court. Athenæum*, 24 December 1870, 836.

[———.] Review of *The Romance of Siamese Harem Life. Athenæum*, 15 February 1873, 205–7.

Kepner, Susan. "Anna (and Margaret) and the King of Siam." *Crossroads: An Interdisciplinary Journal of Southeast Asian Studies* 10 (1997): 1–32.

King, Anthony D. *Colonial Urban Development: Culture, Social Power and Environment*. London: Routledge & Kegan Paul, 1976.

The King's Regulations and Orders for the Army. London, 1837.

Kingston, George C. *James Madison Hood: Lincoln's Consul to the Court of Siam*. Jefferson, N.C.: McFarland, 2013.

Kipling, Rudyard. *Plain Tales from the Hills 1886–1887, Soldiers Three and Other Stories*. Garden City, N.Y.: Doubleday, Page, 1925.

Landon, Margaret. *Annaa gap phrachao grung sayaam*. Phranakhon: Prae Bhitthaya, 2505 [1962]. [Translation of *Anna and the King of Siam* into Thai by Adjaan Sanitwong.]

———. *Anna and the King of Siam*. New York: John Day Company, 1944.

———. *Never Dies the Dream*. Garden City, N.Y.: Doubleday, 1949.

Leonowens, Anna Harriette. "Auction of a White Child." *Youth's Companion*, 23 November 1876, 397–98.

———. "A Biographical Sketch." *Redpath's Lyceum* [1873–75]: 42–43. [Segment of advertising circular preserved with Anna Harriette Leonowens Papers.]

———. "The City of Forbidden Women." *Youth's Companion*, 1 February 1877, 35–36.

———. "An Encounter with an Ulwar Sawad or Boa Constrictor." *Youth's Companion*, 23 August 1877, 271.

———. "The English Governess at the Siamese Court." *Atlantic Monthly* 25 (April, May, June 1870): 396–410, 554–65, 730–43; 26 (August 1870): 144–55.

———. *The English Governess at the Siamese Court: Being Recollections of Six Years in the Royal Palace at Bangkok*. 1870. Reprint, Oxford: Oxford University Press, 1988.

———. "The Favorite." *Youth's Companion*, 7 April 1881, 126.

———. "The Favorite of the Harem." *Atlantic Monthly* 30 (September 1872): 335–45.

———. "From Sadi." *Youth's Companion*, 2 June 1881, 206.

———. *Life and Travel in India: Being Recollections of a Journey before the Days of Railroads*. Philadelphia: Porter & Coates, 1884.

———. "Life in a Siamese Palace. Who Stole the King's Gold Spectacles?" *Youth's Companion*, 22 June 1876, 199.

———. "Life in Siam. The Circuit of Forbidden Women." *Youth's Companion*, 25 January 1877, 27–28.

———. "Life in the Grand Royal Palace of Siam." *Youth's Companion*, 24 August 1876, 275–76.

———. "Lore, the Slave of a Siamese Queen." *Atlantic Monthly* 30 (October 1872): 462–70.

———. "My Sick Teacher." *Youth's Companion*, 31 January 1878, 34–35.

———. "Our Asiatic Cousins." *Wide Awake* 26 and 27 (December 1887–November 1888). [Twelve monthly essays on the Hindus, Parsis, Egyptians, Phoenicians, Hebrews, Arabs, Chinese, Tibetans, Koreans, Japanese, Malays, and Vietnamese.]

———. *Our Asiatic Cousins*. Boston: D. Lothrop, 1889. [The twelve essays from *Wide Awake* supplemented with three more on the "Khainer," the Brahmans, and the Thais.]

———. "A Remarkable Performance." *Youth's Companion*, 22 August 1878, 269–70.

———. *The Romance of the Harem.* 1873. Reprint, Charlottesville: University Press of Virginia, 1991.

———. "A Royal Dinner Party." *Youth's Companion,* 26 July 1877, 238.

———. "A Royal Tea-Party." *Youth's Companion,* 4 April 1878, 107–8.

———. "A Siamese Romance." *Youth's Companion,* 18 May 1876, 157.

———. "The Siamese Royal Palace." *Youth's Companion,* 31 August 1876, 283–84.

———. "Son Klean. The Princess of Pegu." *Youth's Companion,* 10 May 1877, 147–48.

———. "The Stolen Trunk." *Youth's Companion,* 14 March 1878, 81–82.

———. "A Thief in the Camp." *Youth's Companion,* 22 November 1877, 397–98.

Leopold, Richard William. *Robert Dale Owen: A Biography.* 1940. Reprint, New York: Octagon Books, 1969.

Lewis, E. B. "Recollections of a Visit to Bangkok, the Capital of Siam, in the Year 1862." *Bentley's Miscellany* 62 (1867): 625–34.

Lilley, Ian, and Martin Gibbs. *An Archaeological Study of the Lynton Convict Hiring Depot: Prepared for the National Trust of Australia (W.A.).* East Perth: Heritage Council of Western Australia, 1993.

Lindsay, Cynthia. *Dear Boris: The Life of William Henry Pratt a.k.a. Boris Karloff.* New York: Knopf, 1975.

Lingat, R. "History of Wat Pavaraniveça." *Journal of the Siam Society* 26, no. 1 (April 1933): 73–102.

———. "La vie religieuse du roi Mongkut." *Journal of the Siam Society* 20, no. 2 (October 1926): 129–48.

Longhurst, Henry. *The Borneo Story: The History of the First 100 Years of Trading in the Far East by the Borneo Company Limited.* London: Newman Neame, 1956.

Lutfullah. *Autobiography of Lutfullah: An Indian's Perceptions of the West.* 1857. Reprint, New Delhi: International Writers' Emporium, 1985.

Mackenzie, Helen. *Life in the Mission, the Camp, and the Zenáná; or, Six Years in India.* 3 vols. London: Richard Bentley, 1853.

MacMillan, Margaret. *Women of the Raj.* New York: Thames & Hudson, 1988.

Macnaughton, John. "Mrs. Leonowens." *University Magazine* [McGill University, Montreal] 14 (October 1915): 408–30.

Makepeace, Walter, et al. *One Hundred Years of Singapore.* 2 vols. 1921. Reprint, Singapore: Oxford University Press, 1991.

Malcolm, John. *The Political History of India, from 1784 to 1823.* 2 vols. London: Murray, 1826.

Marx, Karl, and Friedrich Engels. *On Colonialism: Articles from the "New York Tribune" and Other Writings.* New York: International Publishers, 1972.

Mattoon, Mary. "Missionary Ladies in the King's Palace." In *Siam and Laos, as Seen by Our American Missionaries,* edited by Mary Backus, 320–37. Philadelphia: Presbyterian Board of Publication, 1884.

McFarland, George Bradley, ed. *Historical Sketch of Protestant Missions in Siam 1828–1928*. Bangkok: printed at Bangkok Times Press, 1928.

——. *Thai-English Dictionary*. 1941. Reprint, Stanford, Calif.: Stanford University Press, 1944.

Metelerkamp, Sanni. *George Rex of Knysna: The Authentic Story*. Cape Town, South Africa: Howard Timmins, 1963.

Moffat, Abbot Low. *Mongkut, the King of Siam*. Ithaca, N.Y.: Cornell University Press, 1961.

Mongkut, King of Siam. *A King of Siam Speaks*. Translated and edited by Seni Pramoj and Kukrit Pramoj. Bangkok: Siam Society, 1987.

——. *Ruamphraraachaniphonnai phrabatsomdet phrachomklao chaoyuhua* [Royal writings of King Mongkut]. Bangkok, 2548 [2005].

Moorat [later Sircar], Mary A. Cunningham. *Alfred and Eliza Stark (a Romance from Life in India)*. Calcutta: Mary A. Cunningham Sircar, 1925.

Mordden, Ethan. *Rodgers and Hammerstein*. New York: Harry N. Abrams, 1992.

Morgan, Susan. *Bombay Anna: The Real Story and Remarkable Adventures of "The King and I" Governess*. Berkeley: University of California Press, 2008.

——. Introduction to *The Romance of the Harem*, by Anna Leonowens. Charlottesville: University Press of Virginia, 1991.

——. *Place Matters: Gendered Geography in Victorian Women's Travel Books about Southeast Asia*. New Brunswick, N.J.: Rutgers University Press, 1996.

Morley, Sheridan. *Gertrude Lawrence: A Biography*. New York: McGraw-Hill, 1981.

Mouhot, Henri. *Henri Mouhot's Diary: Travels in the Central Parts of Siam, Cambodia and Laos during the Years 1858–61*. Edited by Christopher Pym. Kuala Lumpur: Oxford University Press, 1966.

Neale, Fred Arthur. *Narrative of a Residence at the Capital of the Kingdom of Siam; with a Description of the Manners, Customs, and Laws of the Modern Siamese*. London: National Illustrated Library, 1852.

"Notes of Four Months' Residence on Mount Aboo, in 1851." *Saunders' Monthly Magazine* 3 (January, February, March 1854): 201–29, 297–324, 395–416.

Oddy, Derek J. "Gone for a Soldier: The Anatomy of a Nineteenth-Century Army Family." *Journal of Family History* 25 (January 2000): 39–62.

Pallegoix, Jean Baptiste. *Description du royaume Thai ou Siam*. 2 vols. Paris: Mission de Siam, 1854.

Palmer, John Williamson. "Child-Life by the Ganges." *Atlantic Monthly* 1 (March 1858): 625–33.

Panikkar, K. M. *Asia and Western Dominance*. New York: Collier Books, 1969.

[Parkes, Fanny]. *Wanderings of a Pilgrim, in Search of the Picturesque, during Four-and-Twenty Years in the East: With Revelations of Life in the Zenana*. 2 vols. London: Pelham Richardson, 1850.

Peers, Douglas M. *Between Mars and Mammon: Colonial Armies and the Garrison State in India 1819–1835.* London: Tauris, 1995.

———. "Privates off Parade: Regimenting Sexuality in the Nineteenth-Century Indian Empire." *International History Review* 20, no. 4 (December 1998): 823–54.

Peleggi, Maurizio. *Lords of Things: The Fashioning of the Siamese Monarchy's Modern Image.* Honolulu: University of Hawai'i Press, 2002.

Pensri (Suvanij), Duke. *Les relations entre la France et la Thaïlande (Siam).* Bangkok: Chalermnit, 1962.

[Perry, Thomas Sergeant]. Review of *The English Governess at the Siamese Court. North American Review* 112 (April 1871): 422–24. Attribution in Kenneth Walter Cameron, *Research Keys to the American Renaissance: Scarce Indexes,* 115. Hartford, Conn.: Transcendental Books, 1967.

[———]. Review of *The Romance of the Harem. North American Review* 117 (July 1873): 237–40. Attribution in Kenneth Walter Cameron, *Research Keys to the American Renaissance: Scarce Indexes,* 115. Hartford, Conn.: Transcendental Books, 1967.

[Philippart, John]. *The East India Military Calendar; Containing the Services of General and Field Officers of the Indian Army.* 3 vols. London: Kingsbury, Parbury and Allen, 1823–26.

Postans, Marianne. *Western India in 1838.* 2 vols. London: Saunders & Otley, 1839.

Powell, E. Alexander. *Where the Strange Trails Go Down: Sulu, Borneo, Celebes, Bali, Java, Sumatra, Straits Settlements, Malay States, Siam, Cambodia, Annam, Cochin-China.* New York: Scribner's, 1921.

Pramoj, Kukrit. *Four Reigns (Si Phaendin).* Translated by Tulachandra. Chiang Mai, Thailand: Silkworm Books, 1998.

Pramoj, Seni, M.R. "King Mongkut as a Legislator." *Journal of the Siam Society* 38, no. 1 (January 1950): 32–66.

Procida, Mary A. *Married to the Empire: Gender, Politics and Imperialism in India, 1883–1947.* Manchester, UK: Manchester University Press, 2002.

Rabibhadana, Akin. *The Organization of Thai Society in the Early Bangkok Period, 1782–1873.* Ithaca, N.Y.: Southeast Asia Program, 1969.

Rajadhon, Phya Anuman. *Life and Ritual in Old Siam: Three Studies of Thai Life and Customs.* Translated by William J. Gedney. New Haven, Conn.: HRAF Press, 1961.

Ranke, Leopold [von]. *The History of the Popes, Their Church and State, and Especially of Their Conflicts with Protestantism in the Sixteenth & Seventeenth Centuries.* 3 vols. Translated by E. Foster. London: George Bell, 1878.

Reid, Anthony. *Southeast Asia in the Age of Commerce 1450–1680.* Vol. 1, *The Lands below the Winds.* Chiang Mai: Silkworm Books, 1988.

Renford, Raymond K. *The Non-Official British in India to 1920.* Delhi: Oxford University Press, 1987.

Reynolds, Craig James. "The Buddhist Monkhood in Nineteenth Century Thailand." Ph.D. diss., Cornell University, 1972.

Roberts, Emma. *Scenes and Characteristics of Hindostan, with Sketches of Anglo-Indian Society.* 2 vols. London: W. H. Allen, 1837.

Rodgers, Richard. *Musical Stages: An Autobiography.* New York: Random House, 1975.

Rogers, T., Captain. *Buddhaghosha's Parables: Translated from Burmese.* London: Trübner, 1870.

Roper, Geoffrey. "Badger, George Percy." In *Oxford Dictionary of National Biography,* 3:201. Oxford: Oxford University Press, 2004.

———. "George Percy Badger (1815–1888)." *Bulletin (British Society for Middle Eastern Studies)* 11, no. 2 (1984): 140–55.

Royce, Nancy. *A Sketch of the Life and Character of Mrs. Emelie Royce Bradley, Ten Years a Missionary in Siam.* New York: American Tract Society, 1856.

Rutnin Mattani Mojdara. *Dance, Drama, and Theatre in Thailand: The Process of Development and Modernization.* Tokyo: Centre for East Asian Cultural Studies, 1993.

Salibi, Kamal. *A House of Many Mansions: The History of Lebanon Reconsidered.* Berkeley: University of California Press, 1988.

Santanee Phasuk and Philip Stott. *Royal Siamese Maps: War and Trade in Nineteenth Century Thailand.* Bangkok: River Books, 2004.

Secrest, Meryle. *Somewhere for Me: A Biography of Richard Rodgers.* New York: Knopf, 2001.

Sedgwick, Ellery. *The "Atlantic Monthly" 1857–1909: Yankee Humanism at High Tide and Ebb.* Amherst: University of Massachusetts Press, 1994.

Sethaputra, So. *New Model Thai-English Dictionary.* Bangkok: Thai Watana Panich, 1999.

Smithies, Michael. "Anna Leonowens: 'School Mastress' at the Court of Siam." In *Adventurous Women in South-East Asia: Six Lives,* edited by John Gullick, 94–146. Kuala Lumpur: Oxford University Press, 1995.

———. *Old Bangkok.* Singapore: Oxford University Press, 1986.

Stafford, Robert A. "Scientific Exploration and Empire." In *The Oxford History of the British Empire,* vol. 3, *The Nineteenth Century,* edited by Andrew N. Porter, 294–319. Oxford: Oxford University Press, 1999.

Stannage, C. T., ed. *A New History of Western Australia.* Nedlands: University of Western Australia Press, 1981.

Stark, Herbert Alick. *Hostages to India, or The Life-Story of the Anglo-Indian Race.* Calcutta: printed at Star Printing Works, 1936. First published 1926.

Stoler, Ann Laura. *Carnal Knowledge and Imperial Power: Race and the Intimate in Colonial Rule.* Berkeley: University of California Press, 2002.

Strauss, Helen M. *A Talent for Luck: An Autobiography.* New York: Random House, 1979.

Strobridge, William, and Anita Hibler. *Elephants for Mr. Lincoln: American Civil War-Era Diplomacy in Southeast Asia.* Lanham, Md.: Scarecrow Press, 2006.

Sutherland, John. *Sketches of the Relations Subsisting between British Government in India and Different Native States.* 1837. Reprint, Jaipur: Publication Scheme, 1988.

Sutherland, Malcolm. *A Fighting Clan: Sutherland Officers: 1250–1850.* London: Avon, 1996.

Terwiel, Barend Jan. *Thailand's Political History from the Fall of Ayutthaya in 1767 to Recent Times.* Bangkok: River Books, 2005.

Thiphakorawong, Chaophraya. *The Dynastic Chronicles. Bangkok Era, the Fourth Reign.* 6 vols. Translated by Chadin (Kanjanavanit) Flood. Tokyo: Centre for East Asian Cultural Studies, 1965–74.

Thomson, John. *The Straits of Malacca, Indo-China and China; or Ten Years' Travels, Adventures and Residence Abroad.* London: Sampson Low, Marston, Low & Searle, 1875.

Trustram, Myna. *Women of the Regiment: Marriage and the Victorian Army.* Cambridge: Cambridge University Press, 1984.

Turnbull, C. M. *The Straits Settlements 1826–67: Indian Presidency to Crown Colony.* London: Athlone Press, University of London, 1972.

Vella, Walter F. *Siam under Rama III 1824–1851.* Locust Valley, N.Y.: Association for Asian Studies, 1957.

Wadia, Ruttonjee Ardeshir. *The Bombay Dockyard and the Wadia Master Builders.* Bombay: Ruttonjee Ardeshir Wadia, 1957.

Wales, H. G. Quaritch. *Ancient Siamese Government and Administration.* New York: Paragon, 1965.

———. *Siamese State Ceremonies: Their History and Function.* London: Bernard Quaritch, 1931.

Wesley, John. *John Wesley in Wales, 1739–1790: Entries from His Journal and Diary Relating to Wales.* Edited by A. H. Williams. Cardiff: University of Wales Press, 1971.

Wilson, Horace Hayman. *The History of British India. From 1805 to 1835.* 3 vols. London: James Madden and George Willis, 1848.

Winichakul, Thongchai. *Siam Mapped: A History of the Geo-Body of a Nation.* Honolulu: University of Hawai'i Press, 1994.

Wood, William Maxwell. *Fankwei; or, The San Jacinto in the Seas of India, China and Japan.* New York: Harper, 1859.

Wyatt, David K. "Family Politics in Nineteenth Century Thailand." *Journal of Southeast Asian History* 9, no. 2 (September 1968): 208–28.

———. *The Politics of Reform in Thailand: Education in the Reign of King Chulalongkorn.* New Haven, Conn.: Yale University Press, 1969.

———. *Thailand: A Short History.* 1st ed. New Haven, Conn.: Yale University Press, 1984.

Yorke, Lois K. "Edwards, Anna Harriette." In *Dictionary of Canadian Biography*, 14:332–35. Toronto: University of Toronto Press, 1998.

Yule, Henry, and A. C. Burnell. *Hobson-Jobson: A Glossary of Colloquial Anglo-Indian Words and Phrases, and of Kindred Terms, Etymological, Historical, Geographical and Discursive*. Edited by William Crooke. Delhi: Munshiram Manoharlal, 1968.

Index

Note: *Page numbers in italics refer to illustrations.*

Abdy, Mrs., 38
abolition movement and abolition-
  ists, 5–6, 254–55, 315, 334, 340
Adamson, Margaret Hamilton, 139–
  42, 467
Adamson, William, 131–32, 139–42,
  176, 211n2, 314n3, 464, 467
Aden, 57, 65–67
Ahmadnagar, India, 26, 50
Ahmed, Leila, 477
Alâck, P'hra (Sri Suntorn-woharn),
  301–3
Alcott, Louisa May, 280, 345; *Little
  Women*, 233, 280
Aldrich, Mary Pickering Joy, 393
Alibi, 105–8, 110
Anake Nawigamune, 189, 475
Anna. *See* Leonowens, Anna Harriet
Anna and the King (motion picture),
  13, 272, 403–5
Anna and the King of Siam (motion
  picture), 3, 10, 257, 382, 384–92
App (*also* Abb), 244–46, 248
Arabic, 63, 68–70, 203
Asahina, Midori, 508
Athenæum, 7, 285
Atkins, Mary, 213–14

Aubaret, Gabriel, *191*, 296–300, 302,
  373–74
Australia: administration, 109–11,
  120–28; convicts, 109, 119–22,
  126–27; gold, 103, 229, 389. *See
  also* Perth; Swan River Mechanics'
  Institute
Ayer, Margaret, 9, 267, 378–79, 380
Ayutthaya, 147, 205, 218, 250, 253

Bacon, George B., 262, 489
Badger, George Percy, 60–71, 371
Badger, Maria Christiana Wilcox, 60,
  62–65, 67, 446; report on Yezidis,
  69
Baigent, Elizabeth, 13, 439, 442
Baldwin, Captain, 226–27
Ballhatchet, Kenneth, 80–81
Ballston Spa, New York, 305, 310
Bangkok, 144, 147, 303; crime, 241,
  250, 259; English-language press,
  178–79, 297–98, 334–35, 352
Barlee, Frederick, 120, 124, 459
Barnard, Frederick, 330, 340
Bastian, Adolf, 169, 328
Beauvoir, Ludovic, marquis de, 165,
  166, 169, 298

Beebe, Miriam, 61, 166
Benson, Sally, 385, 387
Berkeley School (New York City), 331
Blofeld, John, 427, 469, 487, 494
Bomanjee, Jamsetjee, 79
Bombay, 79–80, 84–88, 96, 103, 123, 242; Parsi community, 79, 85–86, 450, 451
Bombay Education Society, 34, 434; Central or Byculla School, 13–14, 35–36, 38, 42–48, 65–66, 223, 319
Borneo Company Ltd., 131, 141
Botta, Anne Lynch, 333, 341, 342, 349–50
Bowie, Katherine A., 240
Bowring, John, 159, 468; and Anna, 301–2, 304; on Mongkut, 169; on Sisuriyawong, 166; on *thaat*, 482
Brace, Charles Loring, 340–41
Brace, Letitia Neill, 340
Braddon, Mary Elizabeth, *Lady Audley's Secret*, 280
Bradley, Cornelius Beach, 469, 478, 485
Bradley, Dan Beach, 149, *189*, 423–24, 484; and Anna, 165, 171, 172, 220, 221, 250–51, 256, 298–300, 303; and Aubaret, 297–300; and Fa Ying, 231–32; on Mongkut, 148–50, 151, 155, 169, 268, 280n3, 367, 468, 469; on Siamese matters, 200, 203–4, 214, 273n1, 281, 476, 481
Bradley, Emelie Royce, 200, 201
Bradley, Sarah Blachly, 158, 213, 471
Bradley, William L., 491
Brando, Marlon, 11, 397
Bray, Alan, *The Friend*, 285n5
Briggs, Lawrence Palmer, 490
Bristowe, William Syer, 12, 61, 71n6, 438, 443, 465, 473

de Broë-Ferguson, Edward, 450
Brown, Susan, 427
Bruguière, Barthélemy, 373
Bryant, William Cullen, 328, 330, 340
Brynner, Rock, 509
Brynner, Yul, 3, 11, 14, 150, 254, 314, 369, 394, 396–400, 509
Buck, Pearl S., 9–10, 376
Buddhaghosa, 97–101
Buddhism, 232–33; Anna and, 97–101, 338, 343; Mongkut and, 142, 149, 234; and science, 469; and sex, 201–2; and slavery, 253
Buettner, Elizabeth, 434
Bulivant, Ramchunder, 455
Bunnak, Chuang. *See* Sisuriyawong
Bunnak, Dit, 154, 155
Burges, William, 121–22, 123, 125–28, 463
Burma, 98, 147, 149, 264–65, 321, 375
Burton, Antoinette M., 455
Bush, John, 168, 169, 170
Bush, Margaret, 168
Butler, Eliza Glascott, 27, 37, 43, 431
Butler, Tobias, 37, 43, 431, 435, 437
Butri, 237, 243, 247, 483

Caddy, Florence, 280–81, 284
Cambodia, 272, 296–97; Angkor Wat, 325–29
Campbell, Ailison Hamilton, 140–41, 177
Campbell, James, 140, 202, 231, 232, 261, 476
Candy, George, 451, 461
Cary, Amelia, Viscountess Falkland, 47, 66n2, 102, 442, 456
Caswell, Jesse, 151–53, 219, 294, 346–47, 423–24, 469
Cavenagh, Orfeur, 142n5, 213

Chandler, John Hassett, 479
Chantasingh, Chalermsri
  Thuriyanonda, 293, 376n6, 468,
  473, 480, 490, 491, 505, 508
Chaudhuri, Nupur, 337n4
Cheng, Chu-Chueh, 164, 295
Chesney, Francis Rawdon, 445
Chetsadabodin. *See* Rama III
Chiang Mai, 240, 289–91, 293;
  princess of Chiang Mai (story),
  290–93
Chin, Keith, 405
China, 105, 130, 151, 211, 296, 477
Chow Yun-Fat, 13, 150, 403–4
Chulalongkorn, 124, *192*, *193*, *194*,
  229, 241, 253, 333–34, 352–55;
  education, 220–21; how his educa-
  tion under Anna was interpreted
  in America, 10, 333–36, 347, 391;
  treatment in Hollywood and on
  Broadway, 384, 389–90, 400, 405
Churchill, Charles Henry, 68n3
Church of England, 18, 63–64
Civil War: American, 5, 6, 248, 309,
  321, 338, 360; English, 115
Cloudesley, Harriet and Henry, 37,
  436
Clurman, Harold, 397
Cobb, Francis Davis, 139–40, 143,
  228, 287–88, 304–5, 309–10, 492,
  493
Cobb, Katherine Sedgwick Dewey,
  309–10, 315, 492
Cobb, Lee J., 388, 398
Cole, Edna, 362
Colquhoun, Archibald Ross, 326n7
commissariat, 109–11, 119–28, 459
Comstock, Marie Louise, 330, 498
convict hiring depot, 119–29
Conybeare, Mrs., 47
Corfield, Justin, 475
Crawford, J. H., 438

Crawford, Thomas Maxwell, 8, 17,
  123
Crowther, Bosley, 385
Cursetjee, Ardaseer, 451
Curtin, Philip D., 136n2
Curtis, George William, 315–16, 328,
  339
Custer, George Armstrong, 341n6

Dalrymple, William, 22, 434
Damrong Rajanubhab, 12, 151,
  384n1, 469
Dana, George Hazen, 140n3, 467
dance, 91, 213, 382, 385, 394–95,
  405
Darnell, Linda, 257, 387
Davenport, Frances, 284, 425
Davis, Bonnie, 504
Dean, William, 373
Dewey, Orville, 493
Disa, India, 32, 51–54, 76–78, 440
Disney, Walt, 401
Donohoe, Ellen, 43, 52, 56, 441
Donohoe, John, 43, 53, 80, 86, 439,
  440, 442, 451
Donohoe, Mary Ann Glascott
  Edwards, 26–27, 37–42, 50–51, 57,
  96, 104, 123, 431
Donohoe, Patrick, 40, 49–59, 77–78,
  83–84, 104, 431, 439, 442; pay-
  ment of school fees, 43, 437
Donohoe, Vaudry Glasscott, 54, 123
Dow, Leslie Smith, 498
Dresel, Louisa Loring, 318–19, 344
Dunn, Charlotte, 480
Dunne, Irene, 3, 382, 386–88, 390

East India Company, 20–21, 25, 36,
  73n2, 130–31; Bombay army, 20,
  22–25, 27–29, 50–59; bureaucracy,
  27, 79–80, 81–82, 103; policy on
  widows' pensions, 50, 433, 435;

East India Company (*continued*)
Public Works Department, 49,
51–52; treatment of Eurasians, 23,
27, 32–39, 41, 46–47, 80–82, 115,
138–39
Eastlake, Mrs., 200–201
Ebhrahim, Nācoda (Naikodah
Ibrahim), 237–38, 243
Edgar, Archibald, 123–24
Edwards, Eliza. *See* Millard, Eliza
Edwards
Edwards, John, 443
Edwards, Mary Ann. *See* Donohoe,
Mary Ann Glascott Edwards
Edwards, Thomas, 17, 27, 37, 50,
431–32, 435
Elphinstone, Mountstuart, 85, 433
Emerson, Ralph Waldo, 320
Enniscorthy, Ireland, 55, 74–75, 304,
312
Evans, Ernestine, 380

Fascism, 10, 381, 397–98
Fa Ying (Chanthonmonthon), 229–34
Feltus, George Haws, 468, 484
Fields, Annie Adams, 6, 318–20,
337–39, 341–42, 344, 348, 351,
352
Fields, James T., 318–21, 322n6, 339,
344
FitzGerald, Charles, 109, 119, 122
Fletcher, William Kew, 45–46
Flood, Chadin (Kanjanavanit), 468
Foley, Gerard, 457
Ford, Emily Fowler, 38, 333, 436
Ford, Gordon, 333
Foster, Jodie, 13, 403–4
foundation sacrifice, 333, 352, 370–
71, 372–75
France, 272, 296–300, 401
Fraser, Thomas McKenzie, 132, 137,
139, 144, 464

Fremantle, Western Australia, 107;
Fremantle Express, 475
Frith, Robert, 85, 131, 453
Fuller, Muriel, 361–62, 383
Fyshe, Anna Harriet Leonowens
(granddaughter), 353–55
Fyshe, Avis Leonowens (daughter),
70, 114, 124, 143, *183*, 224, 304;
life in North America, 317, 318,
330–31, 351
Fyshe, Avis Selina (granddaughter),
363; memories of Anna, 42, 44,
350, 353, 466, 496; transcriptions
of letters, 452, 453, 455
Fyshe, Thomas, 331

Gardner, William Linnaeus, 30n3
Gay, Elizabeth, 315, 317
Gay, Sydney Howard, 315, 328
George, Henry, 8; *Progress and
Poverty*, 331
Ghosh, Durba, 50, 433
Gibbons, Abby Hopper, 5, 248, 309,
315–16, 425, 493
Gibbons, James Sloan, 309
Gilmour, David, 29
Ginger, Mrs., 44–46
Glascott, Cradock, 18–20, 23–26,
30–31, *181*
Glascott, Eliza. *See* Butler, Eliza
Glascott
Glascott, Elizabeth Deer, 18, 427
Glascott, Mary Ann. *See* Donohoe,
Mary Ann Glascott Edwards
Glascott, Thomas, 18, 19, 427
Glascott, William Vaudrey, 13, 20–31
Glasgow, Scotland, 140, 253, 464, 467
Glasscock, John, 12
Glasscott, William Frederick/
Vaudrey, 27, 80–82, 103, 109, 120–
23, 457; form of name, signature,
81, 431, 451–52

Gollin, Rita K., 496
Graireuk Naanaa, 252, 480, 484
Gray, James, 58
Griswold, Alexander B., 402, 488, 506
Gujarati (language), 40–41

Habegger, Nellie, 451
Haggard, H. Rider, *King Solomon's Mines*, 314
Haines, Henrietta B., 330, 498
Halifax, Nova Scotia, 8, 100n3, 331
Hammerstein, Oscar, II, 369, 387, 393–94, 399, 400, 509
Harris, Townsend, 169, 200, 203, 450
Harrison, Rex, 3, 150, 382, 385, 387, 397, 400
Hart, Lorenz, 393, 400
Harvey, Godfrey Eric, 375
Hatem, Mervat, 477, 510
Hatherleigh, Devonshire, 19, 20
Hatteroth, Mrs., 45, 437
Hawes, C. J., 21, 22, 38, 46, 73n2, 82, 123, 434, 454, 500
Hawthorne, Nathaniel, 319, 320, 479
Heritage, Thomas, 139, 143
Herzstein, Robert E., 380
Higginson, Thomas Wentworth, 338, 342
Hinduism, 91, 294, 338–39, 346
Hindustani (language), 89
Holmes, Oliver Wendell, 315, 320
Hong Lysa, 240
Honniball, Jack, 475
Hood, James Madison, 299
Howells, William Dean, 322n6, 343, 497
Hunt, Richard M., 342

Ibrahim, Naikodah. *See* Ebhrahim, Nācoda

incarceration, 36, 236, 238, 257, 267–68, 290
Indian "Mutiny," 8, 131
Indo-British Institution: in Bombay, 80, 123, 434, 451, 461; in Pune, 442
Irwin, Robert, 322, 445
Islam, 29–30, 63, 92–93, 237–38, 242–43, 322n5, 346

Jackson, Helen Hunt, *The Story of Boon*, 281
Jackson, Peter, 202, 213, 478
Jacobs, Harriet, 315n4
Jacobs, Stephen, 227n5
Jakarta, 106, 259–60n2
James, Henry, 327, 343; *Roderick Hudson*, 344n7
Japan, 363, 391, 395, 464
Jayanama, Direck, 402, 510
Jeejeebhoy, Jamshetji, 450
Jennings, Talbot, 385, 387
Jewett, Sarah Orne, 342, 343, 349
Johnson, Laura Winthrop, 5–6, 137, 315–20, 341n6, 344n7, 348–49, 502
Johnson C. Smith University, 310n1
Jones, John Taylor, 178
Jones, Sara Sleeper. *See* Smith, Sara Sleeper Jones
Justice, William W., Mrs., 342–43
Jutamani (*uparat*, "second king"), 156, 203–4, 253, 288–91, 293

Karloff, Boris, 73n1, 227n5
Kennedy, Arthur Edward, 125–28
Kennedy, Henry George, 7n2, 285, 293–94, 326, 372, 426
Kennedy, John Fitzgerald, *Why England Slept*, 381
Kepner, Susan, 439, 488
Kerr, Deborah, 3, 382
Key, Francis Scott, 79
Keyes, Jane, 510

King, David Olyphant, 211
The King and I, 3, 11, 165, 271–72,
    369, 393–403, 405–6
Kingston, George C., 490, 491
Kipling, Rudyard: Kim, 13;
    "Kidnapped," 73–74
Kisa Gotami (Kisâgotami, Kisa,
    Keesah), 98–101, 233
Knox, Thomas George, 298–99, 473
Krita (Kritaphinihaan, Prince Naret),
    265, 266, 268–69, 344
Kübler, Gunhild, 455

La-aw, 235–49
La Farge, John, 342
Landon, Kenneth, 198, 361–64, 373,
    376
Landon, Margaret, 8–9, 12, 198, 359–
    79, 382–83, 385, 386, 503; accep-
    tance of Anna's claims, 271, 335,
    353, 361, 372–75, 438; approach to
    documentary evidence, 366, 374,
    452; assumptions and procedures,
    209, 362, 477; fictionalization,
    364–65, 377, 379; heightening of
    effects, 167, 238n2, 268n2, 366–70,
    490; insights, 61, 65, 175n1, 490;
    interpretation of Anna, 162–63,
    176, 209, 359; interpretation of
    Mongkut, 365–70; Never Dies the
    Dream, 162n7, 367n1, 369n3, 370,
    375; prose style, 364–65, 366, 482;
    research, 362, 363, 476, 484;
    reviews of Anna and the King of
    Siam, 10, 380–81; World War II
    context, 162–63, 360, 381, 384
Lao states and Lao-speaking sections
    of Thailand, 201, 203–4, 240, 288–
    90, 293–94, 296, 325
Lardner, John, 400–401
Lawrence, Gertrude, 3, 393, 396, 399
Lebanon, 63, 67–68; Druse, 63, 68

Leonowens, Anna Harriet, 4, 14, 31,
    47–48, 118, 129, 234, 295, 330;
    accent, speech, 46, 223, 332–33;
    anxieties, 4, 112, 143–44, 164–
    65, 224, 287, 305; and Atlantic
    Monthly, 177, 319–24, 487, 489;
    attire, 336, 337, 341, 426; attitudes
    toward the English, 38–39, 46–48,
    93, 123, 221n2, 347; autobiogra-
    pher, 7–8, 31, 38–39, 42, 43–46,
    48, 96, 101–2, 108, 331–32, 426,
    432; bereavement and grief, 96–
    101, 113, 134–37, 348–50; birth of
    children, 88, 95, 104, 106, 114,
    124; bluffing, 322n5, 327–28;
    buried self, 319, 340, 347–52;
    champion of the oppressed, 235,
    242–49, 251–52, 263, 295, 333–34;
    collapses, 165, 261, 279, 336; con-
    tributor to Wide Awake, 346–48;
    contributor to Youth's Companion,
    39, 106n1, 230, 233, 257–58, 345–
    46, 367–68; dark skinned, 318–19;
    deracination, 210, 222, 305; edu-
    cation, 13–14, 34, 42–48, 60–62,
    65, 69–70, 223; embellishments
    and exaggerations, 171–72, 174,
    232–33, 235–36, 270, 314, 489;
    exactness in quoting Mongkut's
    writings, 232, 474; eyewitness
    claims for derivative material,
    216–18, 282–84, 299–300, 327–28,
    373, 420–21; fantasist, 39, 94, 207–
    9, 210, 278–80, 300, 329; fraudu-
    lent reports, 211–12, 284, 324,
    325–28, 374, 505; illness, 101–2,
    113, 133, 136–37, 228, 255–56,
    258–62; interpreted as lowborn,
    12–13, 427, 431, 435, 440; lecturer,
    7, 100–101, 235, 333, 335–39, 341,
    454; Life and Travel in India, 39–
    41, 42, 86–87, 101–2, 332, 343;

literary treatment of Mongkut, 6, 59, 169–78, 210–11, 212, 233, 247–48, 251–52, 255, 289, 295, 314; location of house in Bangkok, 172–76, 276, 474; and marriage, 36–38, 56, 59, 62, 72–74, 76–77, 82, 83–85, 87–88, 199, 207–10, 238, 286; misleading claims and stories about Siam, 207–9, 271–86, 370–73, 426, 497; ocean voyages, 67, 71, 103–8, 119, 124, 129, 133, 137, 143–44, 165, 176, 228, 229, 303–4, 305, 309; Orientalist, 88–90, 321–22, 338, 497; *Our Asiatic Cousins*, 346–47, 501; personal charisma, 46, 317, 319, 332, 338–39; prose style, 237–38, 325, 482; and race, 53n2, 70, 73, 92, 123, 340, 501; reception, 7, 100, 177–79, 235, 262, 284–85, 320, 333, 343–44; rejection of birth family and stepfather, 27, 38, 58–59, 104, 123, 226–27, 233; reliance on single sources, 269, 294–95, 364, 372; *Romance of the Harem*, 98, 179, 216, 251–52, 282, 337n3, 344; self-presentation, 165, 337; sensationalism, 39, 179, 211–12, 268, 283, 293, 323–24, 343; sense of danger in Bangkok, 144, 250–51, 259–60, 262, 311; story of the snake and the monkey, 52n1; story of the stolen spectacles, 160, 256–58, 365; story of Tuptim, 271–86, 337n3, 352, 387, 394, 398, 399; suspected of fraud and/or plagiarism, 285, 326–28, 342; sympathy with Asian women, 14, 91–92, 94, 161–62, 251–52; teacher, 70, 90, 111–13, 138–39, 141–42, 171, 172, 215–23, 230, 234, 315–19, 331; Thai language, 159, 173, 426;

tormenting fancies in Bangkok, 279–80; troubles with Mongkut, 153, 173–75, 260, 263; unanswered questions, 104, 233, 247, 248–49, 258, 261, 267–68, 285, 322n6, 329, 340, 438, 453, 484, 501
Leonowens, Louis (son), 124, *183*, *192*, 303–4, 311, 462; boyhood in Bangkok, 166, 169, 224–25, 259, 298; favored by Mongkut, 172, 251, 287; later life, 124, 389, 474, 486
Leonowens, Selina (daughter), 88, 95–96
Leonowens, Thomas (husband), 54–56, 59, 72, 74–80, 82–88, 118, 128, 132, 134–36, 199, 300, 302; civilian employment, 79–80, 85, 103, 109–11, 119–20, 124–28, 131–34, 459; form of name, signature, 75n3, *184*, 441, 449, 459; lecture "Study of History," 116–17, 292n1; letters to Anna, 71, 83–86, 452; military career, 54, 55–56, 75–79, 450; opinions, 78, 82–83, 90, 108, 115–18
Leonowens, Thomas (son), 101, 113
Lewis, E. B., 175–76
Lincoln, Abraham, 254, 263, 334, 386
Lingat, R., 468
London and China Express, 179, 284
Longfellow, Samuel, 338–39
"Lore." *See* La-aw
Lowell, James Russell, 321
Luce, Henry R., 10, 380–81
Lutfullah, 81
Lynton, Western Australia, 119–28

Mahabaleshwar, India, 101–2
Malcolm, John, 452
Malet, George Grenville, 32–33, 57
Malta, 62–63, 66
Mantel, Hilary, 406

Manuel de Silveira, Don Carlos, 154
Marcus, Florentine Henry, 465
Marcus, Mrs., 133, 144, 465
Martyn, Henry, 23, 429–30
Marx, Karl, 80
Mattoon, Mary Lowrie, 144, *188*,
    208, 256–58, 304, 310, 320, 366,
    472; palace teaching, 158–61, 471
Mattoon, Stephen, 159, *188*, 256, 258,
    304–5, 310
Maxwell, Henry, 402, 509
McClumpha, William, 442
Mends, William F., 109–10, 123,
    127–28
Metcalfe, Charles, 29
Methodist Church, 18, 54, 113, 360,
    459
Michelangelo: New Sacristy of San
    Lorenzo, 350–52
Millard, Eliza Edwards, 62, 96, 98,
    123n2, 226, 439
Millard, James, 77n4, 439
Minturn, Robert, Mrs., 330
Misses King's School, Fulham, 143,
    305
Moffat, Abbot Low, 402, 468
Mongkut, King of Siam, 11, 168–69,
    186; accession to throne, 147–48,
    156; anger, 173–74, 260, 267,
    280n3, 301; backing down before
    Anna, 174–75, 221; concubines,
    158, 203–5, 210–12, 289; and
    English language, 141–42, 151–53,
    156, 158–59, 215, 422–23; excur-
    sions, 250, 258–59, 268–70; facial
    deformity, 149–50, 369; friendship
    with William Adamson, 141,
    314n3, 467; letters to Anna, 142,
    165, 173, 174, 212, 215, 220, 243–
    44, 247, 252–55, 261, 268–70, 312;
    love of his children, 229–34, 268;
    in monkhood, 148–51, 294, 346;

outreach to the West, 149–53,
    157–58; portrayal in American
    entertainment, 11, 314, 385–86,
    388, 390, 396–400, 404–5; reforms,
    156–58, 204; science and, 149, 151,
    205, 219, 242, 313–14, 374; sensi-
    tivity to published criticism, 159,
    289, 313, 314; unusually confiding,
    152, 155, 229, 253, 289
Moonshee, 61, 166, 377, 443
Moore, Gerald Grattan, 363
Morgan, Edmund Cobb, 87–88, 102,
    453
Morgan, Susan: *Bombay Anna*, 444,
    453, 462, 466, 474, 495, 498;
    insights, 467, 484; problematic
    claims, 13, 427, 428, 429, 430, 431,
    432, 433, 435, 437, 439, 440, 442,
    447, 449, 456, 465
Mormon Church, 117, 312
Mosul, Iraq, 63, 64, 68n4, 69, 71
Mouhot, Henri, 325, 327–28, 367
Mount Abu, India, 52, 76, 440
Müller, Max, 98
Mussolini, Benito, 398

Napoleon III, 272, 296, 298
Neale, Fred Arthur, 217–18, 246,
    283, 420–23, 425, 485
Newport, Rhode Island, 211, 342
New York Times: treatment of Anna,
    7, 10, 322n5, 327–28, 333–34,
    373n5, 391–92, 402, 499
Norton, Charles Eliot, 339

Ong, Eng Chuan, 457
Orton, George, 165, 177, 311, 473
Osgood, James, 336–37, 343, 344
Owen, Robert Dale, 333–34, 336–37
Owens, Gunnis Lean, 75
Owens, John, 75, 448
Owens, Mary Lean, 74, 448

Paine, John, 342, 344, 501
Pali language, 149, 150, 221, 230, 317, 322, 481
Pallegoix, Jean Baptiste, 149, 202, 239–40, 267–68, 281, 373, 425, 468, 476
Palmer, John Williamson, 33, 321–25
Palmer, William, 444
Parker, Richard G., *Juvenile Philosophy*, 218–19
Parkes, Fanny, 29
Patterson, Francis George, 221
Penang, Malaysia, 132–37
Peninsular and Oriental Line, 103, 106
Perry, Thomas Sergeant, 262, 284
Persian language, 68–69, 70
Perth, Western Australia: growth, 109; post office, 110–11; schools, 111–12. *See also* Swan River Mechanics' Institute
Phaulkon, Constantine, 260, 302
Piam, 205, 211, 345
Plath, Sylvia, 398
polygamy, 117, 199, 203–12, 312n2, 323–24
Port Gregory, Western Australia, 119, 125–27, 462
Postans, Marianne, 450
Pramint Kruathong, 252, 480, 484
Pramoj, Kukrit, *Four Reigns*, 206
Pramoj, Seni, 157, 212, 363
Pratt, Charles Rary, 480
Pratt, Eliza Sarah/Sara Millard (niece), 73, 96, *181*, 226, 227n5
Pratt, John Thomas, 72–73, 226
Presbyterian Church, 361, 464; America, 159, 305, 310, 366, 380; Bangkok, 142, 144; Singapore, 131–32, 137, 139
Princeton Review, 7

Procida, Mary A., 41, 74
Protestant evangelicalism, 18–20, 23, 221; Anna and, 54, 111–12, 115, 209, 230; Margaret Landon and, 359–60, 376n6; Thomas Leonowens and, 115
Pune, India, 56–58, 71, 76, 84, 101, 442

Qeshm, Iran, 24–25, 28

Raachoday, Mom, 297
Rabibhadana, Akin, 240
Radical Club (Boston), 338
Raffles, Stamford, 130
Rajadhon, Phya Anuman, 476
Rama III, 147–48, 153, 154–55, 157, 163, 204; Third Reign events misleadingly ascribed to the Fourth Reign by Anna, 218, 282–84, 368n2
Ranke, Leopold von, *History of the Popes*, 55, 116, 371
Rassam, Christian, 444, 445
Redpath, James, 335, 499
Reid, Anthony, 200
Reynolds, Craig J., 468, 469
Rittmann, Trude, 394
Roberts, Emma, 36–37, 38, 42
Robbins, Jerome, 394, 395
Rodgers, Richard, 393–96, 399
Rogers, T., Captain, 98
Roman Catholic Church, 53–55, 58, 137, 371, 440
Roper, Geoffrey, 444
Royal Geographical Society, 326
Russia, 92, 118, 254, 345, 396

Saint-Gaudens, Augustus, 342
sakdina (registration tattoos, "marking"), 157, 162–63, 240
Sanford, Henry Ayshford, 121, 122

Sanford, William Ayshford, 121
Sanit, Wongsathirat, 167–68, 471
Sanskrit language, 89–90, 220, 230–
    31, 481, 501
Sarnoff, Dorothy, 398
Schomburgk, Robert, 368, 473
Sedgwick, Ellery, 320, 321
Selina, Countess of Huntingdon,
    18–19, 95
Sharaff, Irene, 394
Shaw, Francis George, 5n1, 315–16
Shaw, Robert Gould, 5n1, 315, 342
Shaw, Sarah, 495
Siam: and aggressive European
    powers, 154–55, 157–58, 162–63,
    272, 296–301; cartography, 216–
    18, 402–3; consular treaties, 154,
    155, 157–58, 384, 386, 389–90;
    patron and client relationships,
    240, 241, 248, 270; penal code and
    judiciary, 241, 244–46, 248, 274–
    75, 281–84, 370–72; reaction to
    Anna's books, 352–55
"Siamese" twins (Chang, Eng), 5,
    311, 321
Singapore, 105, 119, 129–34, 137–43,
    228–29; attitudes toward biracial
    Anglo-Indians, 138–39
Sisuriyawong (kalahom), 157n6, 190,
    297, 313; and Anna, 166–67, 172,
    175, 176, 250–51, 269–70, 314;
    portrayal in America, 364–65,
    380–81, 388
slavery: American, 113n4, 239;
    Siamese, 239–41, 252–55, 333–34,
    335n2
Smith, Eli, 68n4
Smith, Malcolm, 476
Smith, Samuel Jones, 177–79, 189,
    221n2, 472; on abduction of
    women in Third Reign, 282; on
    polygamy, 199; reaction to Anna's

books, 7, 178–79; on slavery, 239,
    334, 335n2
Smith, Sara Sleeper Jones, 158, 179,
    471, 475
Smithies, Michael, 427, 443
Somawati, 219
Sondergaard, Gale, 387
Son Klin, 97–98, 160, 209, 228, 256,
    264–70, 303, 312, 323, 387
Soolamanjee, Esmail, 242, 483
Spooner, Miss (Sister Joseph), 137
Stafford, Robert A., 328
Stark, Herbert Alick, 21, 29, 116, 433
Staten Island, New York, 5–6, 138,
    315–19, 320, 333, 384n1
Stoler, Ann Laura, 428, 472, 479
Stowe, Harriet Beecher, 113, 222,
    264, 339, 500; Uncle Tom's Cabin,
    112, 113n4, 138, 233, 394–95
Strait of Malacca, 130, 132
Strauss, Helen, 382–83, 393
Surat, India, 22, 23, 242
Sutham Thammarongwit, 199
Sutherland, John, 22, 28–31, 33–34,
    85, 136n2
Swan River Mechanics' Institute,
    55n4, 114–18, 128
Symonds, John Addington, 350–52

Taksin, 147, 205, 253, 256
Talap, 160–62, 172, 228, 266
Tan Kim Ching, 141–42, 185, 228,
    234
Terwiel, Barend Jan, 155, 171, 468,
    471
thaat. See slavery (Siamese)
Thiang, 204, 211; treatment on
    Broadway and in Hollywood, 387–
    89, 398–99, 402
Thiphakorawong, Chaophraya, 234,
    468, 476, 483, 489
Thomas, Norman, 310n1

Thomson, John, 169, 205–6, 326–28
Time, 10, 293, 380–81, 400
Tóibín, Colm, 55n3
Twain, Mark, 321; *The Adventures of Tom Sawyer*, 258; *A Connecticut Yankee in King Arthur's Court*, 314

Underwood, Francis Henry, 321
Ung, 237–38, 243–45
Unitarian Church, 140, 338
Ushrut Hussaini, 29–30

Vella, Walter F., 283, 468
Vining, Elizabeth Gray, 10, 391

Waddington, Charles, 57
Wadia, Cursetjee Rustomjee, 79
Waite, Robert, 24–25, 28, 432
Wales, 7, 17–19, 46, 335
Wales, H. G. Quaritch, 476, 482
Walpole or Wallpole, Mrs., 7, 8, 13, 42–45, 335
Walsh, Richard J., 9, 376–80, 482
Wang Lang School, 362, 471
Wat Arun, 256
Wat Bowonniwet, 150–52, 292, 294–95, 374

Wat Mahathat, 149
Wat Samorai, 148, 149
Weil, Elsie, 376–80
Wentworth, Charles, Lord Dilke, 285
Wesley, Charles, 18
Wesley, John, 18, 292n1
Wheaton College, Illinois, 361, 383
Wilkinson, Eliza Avice, 363
Wilkinson, Selina, 311
Wilkinson, Thomas, 304, 311, 312
Wilkinson, Thomas Lean, 312, 498
Willcox, Mary Otis Gay, 425, 495
Windisch, Ernst, 90
Winichakul, Thongchai, 218n1, 314
Winthrop, Theodore, 5n1, 315
Wood, William Maxwell, 425, 489
Wyatt, David K., 221, 353, 468

Yates, C., Miss, 45, 46, 437
Yates, Mrs., 13, 45–46
Yezidi religion, 69
Ying Yualacks, 219
Yorke, Lois K., 13, 439, 442, 498
Young, Brigham, 117, 312n2
Yuriko, 395

Zanuck, Darryl F., 385

WISCONSIN STUDIES IN AUTOBIOGRAPHY

William L. Andrews
General Editor

Robert F. Sayre
The Examined Self: Benjamin Franklin, Henry Adams, Henry James

Daniel B. Shea
Spiritual Autobiography in Early America

Lois Mark Stalvey
The Education of a WASP

Margaret Sams
Forbidden Family: A Wartime Memoir of the Philippines, 1941–1945
Edited with an introduction by Lynn Z. Bloom

Charlotte Perkins Gilman
The Living of Charlotte Perkins Gilman: An Autobiography
Introduction by Ann J. Lane

Mark Twain
Mark Twain's Own Autobiography:
The Chapters from the "North American Review"
Edited by Michael J. Kiskis

Journeys in New Worlds: Early American Women's Narratives
Edited by William L. Andrews, Sargent Bush, Jr., Annette Kolodny,
Amy Schrager Lang, and Daniel B. Shea

American Autobiography: Retrospect and Prospect
Edited by Paul John Eakin

Caroline Seabury
The Diary of Caroline Seabury, 1854–1863
Edited with an introduction by Suzanne L. Bunkers

Cornelia Peake McDonald
A Woman's Civil War:
A Diary with Reminiscences of the War, from March 1862
Edited with an introduction by Minrose C. Gwin

Marian Anderson
My Lord, What a Morning
Introduction by Nellie Y. McKay

American Women's Autobiography: Fea(s)ts of Memory
Edited with an introduction by Margo Culley

Frank Marshall Davis
Livin' the Blues: Memoirs of a Black Journalist and Poet
Edited with an introduction by John Edgar Tidwell

Joanne Jacobson
Authority and Alliance in the Letters of Henry Adams

Kamau Brathwaite
The Zea Mexican Diary: 7 September 1926–7 September 1986

Genaro M. Padilla
My History, Not Yours:
The Formation of Mexican American Autobiography

Frances Smith Foster
Witnessing Slavery: The Development of Ante-bellum Slave Narratives

Native American Autobiography: An Anthology
Edited by Arnold Krupat

American Lives: An Anthology of Autobiographical Writing
Edited by Robert F. Sayre

Carol Holly
Intensely Family: The Inheritance of Family Shame
and the Autobiographies of Henry James

People of the Book: Thirty Scholars Reflect on Their Jewish Identity
Edited by Jeffrey Rubin-Dorsky and Shelley Fisher Fishkin

G. Thomas Couser
Recovering Bodies: Illness, Disability, and Life Writing

John Downton Hazlett
My Generation: Collective Autobiography and Identity Politics

William Herrick
Jumping the Line:
The Adventures and Misadventures of an American Radical

Women, Autobiography, Theory: A Reader
Edited by Sidonie Smith and Julia Watson

José Angel Gutiérrez
The Making of a Chicano Militant: Lessons from Cristal

Marie Hall Ets
Rosa: The Life of an Italian Immigrant

Carson McCullers
Illumination and Night Glare:
The Unfinished Autobiography of Carson McCullers
Edited with an introduction by Carlos L. Dews

Yi-Fu Tuan
Who Am I? An Autobiography of Emotion, Mind, and Spirit

Henry Bibb
The Life and Adventures of Henry Bibb: An American Slave
Introduction by Charles J. Heglar

Diaries of Girls and Women: A Midwestern American Sampler
Edited by Suzanne L. Bunkers

Jim Lane
The Autobiographical Documentary in America

Sandra Pouchet Paquet
Caribbean Autobiography: Cultural Identity and Self-Representation

Mark O'Brien, with Gillian Kendall
How I Became a Human Being:
A Disabled Man's Quest for Independence

Elizabeth L. Banks
Campaigns of Curiosity: Journalistic Adventures
of an American Girl in Late Victorian London
Introduction by Mary Suzanne Schriber and Abbey L. Zink

Miriam Fuchs
The Text Is Myself: Women's Life Writing and Catastrophe

Jean M. Humez
Harriet Tubman: The Life and the Life Stories

Voices Made Flesh: Performing Women's Autobiography
Edited by Lynn C. Miller, Jacqueline Taylor, and M. Heather Carver

Loreta Janeta Velazquez
The Woman in Battle: The Civil War Narrative of
Loreta Janeta Velazquez, Cuban Woman and Confederate Soldier
Introduction by Jesse Alemán

Cathryn Halverson
Maverick Autobiographies:
Women Writers and the American West, 1900–1936

Jeffrey Brace
The Blind African Slave:
Or Memoirs of Boyrereau Brinch, Nicknamed Jeffrey Brace
as told to Benjamin F. Prentiss, Esq.
Edited with an introduction by Kari J. Winter

Colette Inez
The Secret of M. Dulong: A Memoir

Before They Could Vote:
American Women's Autobiographical Writing, 1819–1919
Edited by Sidonie Smith and Julia Watson

Bertram J. Cohler
Writing Desire: Sixty Years of Gay Autobiography

Philip Holden
Autobiography and Decolonization:
Modernity, Masculinity, and the Nation-State

Jing M. Wang
When "I" Was Born: Women's Autobiography in Modern China

Conjoined Twins in Black and White:
The Lives of Millie-Christine McKoy and Daisy and Violet Hilton
Edited by Linda Frost

Four Russian Serf Narratives
Translated, edited, and with an introduction by John MacKay

Mark Twain
Mark Twain's Own Autobiography:
The Chapters from the "North American Review," second edition
Edited by Michael J. Kiskis

Graphic Subjects: Critical Essays on Autobiography and Graphic Novels
Edited by Michael A. Chaney

Omar Ibn Said
A Muslim American Slave: The Life of Omar Ibn Said
Translated from the Arabic, edited,
and with an introduction by Ala Alryyes

Sister: An African American Life in Search of Justice
Sylvia Bell White and Jody LePage

Identity Technologies: Constructing the Self Online
Edited by Anna Poletti and Julie Rak

Masked: The Life of Anna Leonowens,
Schoolmistress at the Court of Siam
Alfred Habegger